Course	Introduction to Sociology
Course Number	**Soc 1**
	Sherry Miller-White
	Saddleback College

http://create.mheducation.com

ISBN-10: 1121892825   ISBN-13: 9781121892828

Contents

Credits

chapter opening excerpts

Every chapter in this textbook begins with an excerpt from one of the works listed here. These excerpts convey the excitement and relevance of sociological inquiry and draw readers into the subject matter from each chapter.

boxed features

Research Today

Sociology in the Global Community

Sociology on Campus

Taking Sociology to Work

trend spotting

social policy sections

maps

Tracking Sociological Perspectives

summing up tables

Understanding Sociology

1 Understanding Sociology

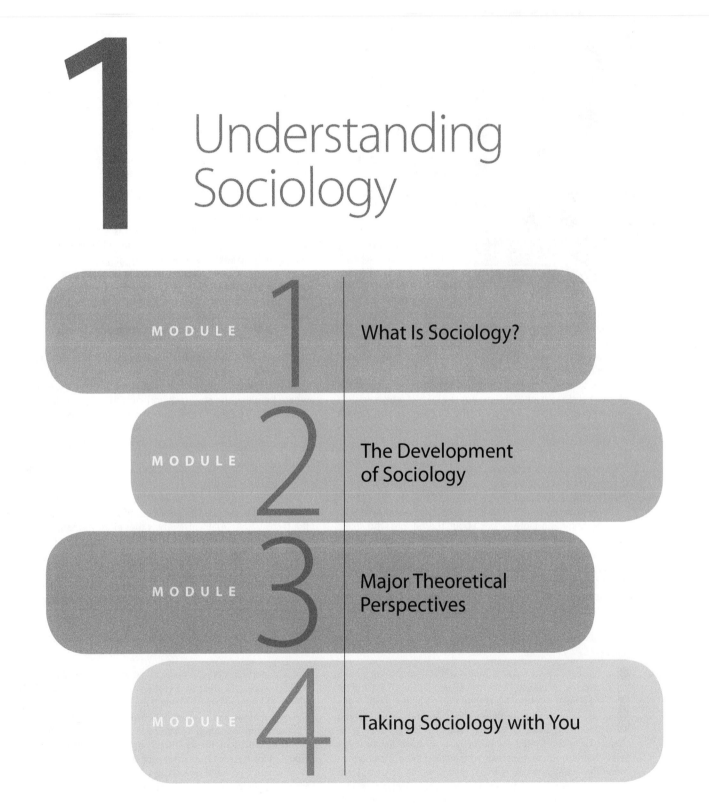

MODULE 1 What Is Sociology?

MODULE 2 The Development of Sociology

MODULE 3 Major Theoretical Perspectives

MODULE 4 Taking Sociology with You

Today you may have thought about what to wear. But did you ask yourself where those garments came from, or who made them?

Journalist Kelsey Timmerman offers some answers to these questions. His book speaks to the way we see ourselves, not only in the mirror when we're getting dressed, but in the world at large.

❝ I was made in America. My *Jingle These* Christmas boxers were made in Bangladesh.

I had an all-American childhood in rural Ohio. My all-American blue jeans were made in Cambodia.

I wore flip-flops every day for a year when I worked as a SCUBA diving instructor in Key West. They were made in China.

One day while staring at a pile of clothes on the floor, I noticed the tag of my favorite T-shirt: "Made in Honduras."

I read the tag. My mind wandered. A quest was born.

Where am I wearing? It seems like a simple question with a simple answer. It's not.

The question inspired the quest that took me around the globe. It cost me a lot of things, not the least of which was my consumer innocence. Before the quest, I could put on a piece of clothing without reading its tag and thinking about Arifa in Bangladesh or Dewan in China, about their children, their hopes and dreams, and the challenges they face.

Where am I wearing? This isn't so much a question related to geography and clothes, but about the people who make our clothes and the texture of their lives. This quest is about the way *we* live and the way *they* live; because when it comes to clothing, others make it, and we have it made. And there's a big, big difference. . . .

Workers flood the narrow alley beside the Delta Apparel Factory in San Pedro Sula, Honduras. They rush to catch one of the many waiting buses at the highway. Merchants hoping to part them from a portion of their daily earnings—$4 to $5—fight for their attention. Vehicles push through the crowd. A minivan knocks over a girl in her midtwenties and then runs over her foot. She curses, is helped to her feet, and limps onto a waiting bus.

The buildings behind the fence are shaded in Bahamian pastels and very well kept. The shrubs have been recently shaped, and the grass trimmed. In the bright Honduran sun, they seem as pleasant as a factory can get.

The lady at Delta Apparel, based in Georgia, giggled at me on the phone when I told her my plans. She was happy to tell me that their Honduran factory was located in the city of Villanueva just south of San Pedro Sula. She even wished me good luck.

Now that I'm in Honduras, the company doesn't think it's very funny.

I stand among the chaos overwhelmed. A thousand sets of eyes stare at me; perhaps they recognize my T-shirt. The irony that this is Tattoo's tropical paradise wore off long ago—somewhere between the confrontation with the big-bellied guards at the factory gate who had guns shoved down their pants like little boys playing cowboy and the conversation with the tight-lipped company representative who failed to reveal much of anything about my T-shirt or the people who assembled it. There was no way I was getting onto the factory floor. All I learned was that eight humans of indiscriminate age and sex stitched my shirt together in less than five minutes. ❞

Where am I wearing? This isn't so much a question related to geography and clothes, but about the people who make our clothes and the texture of their lives.

(Timmerman 2009:xiii–xiv, 14) Additional information about this excerpt can be found on the Online Learning Center at www.mhhe. com/schaefermod2e.

I n his book *Where Am I Wearing? A Global Tour to the Countries, Factories, and People that Make Our Clothes,* Timmerman recounts his travels to the countries where his jeans, T-shirts, and flip-flops—the uniform of today's young adult—were made. From Honduras to Bangladesh, from Cambodia to the United States, he tracked down the factories and befriended the seamstresses who labored there. Timmerman found that garment workers lived in what would be considered substandard conditions in the United States. He argues that global apparel companies should take responsibility for conditions at their suppliers' factories (Fairtrade Foundation 2010).

Timmerman's book focuses on an unequal global economy, which is a central topic in sociology. His investigative work is informed by sociological research that documents the existence and extent of inequality around the world. Social inequality has a pervasive influence on human interactions and institutions.

Although it might be interesting to know how one individual, like Kelsey Timmerman or a foreign factory worker, is affected by social inequality, sociologists consider how entire groups of people and society itself are affected. Sociologists are concerned with what people do as members of a group or in interaction with one another, and what that means for individuals and for society as a whole. For example, sociologists have considered how college students have taken sociology with them, organizing to confront the sportswear companies that underpay the overseas workers who create their team uniforms and T-shirts proclaiming their school pride (Esbenshade 2008; Silverstein 2010).

As a field of study, sociology is extremely broad. You will see throughout this book the range of topics sociologists investigate—from suicide to TV viewing habits, from Amish society to global economic patterns, from peer pressure to genetic engineering. Sociology looks at how others influence our behavior; how major social institutions like the government, religion, and the economy affect us; and how we ourselves affect other individuals, groups, and even organizations.

How did sociology develop? In what ways does it differ from other social sciences? This chapter will explore the nature of sociology as both a field of inquiry and an exercise of the "sociological imagination." We'll look at the discipline as a science and consider its relationship to other social sciences. We'll meet four pioneering thinkers—and examine the theoretical perspectives that grew out of their work. We'll note some of the practical applications for sociological theory and research. Finally, we'll see how sociology helps us to develop a sociological imagination.

What Is Sociology?

"What has sociology got to do with me or with my life?" As a student, you might well have asked this question when you signed up for your introductory sociology course. To answer it, consider these points: Are you influenced by what you see on television? Do you use the Internet? Did you vote in the last election? Are you familiar with binge drinking on campus? Do you use alternative medicine? These are just a few of the everyday life situations described in this book that sociology can shed light on. But as the opening excerpt indicates, sociology also looks at large social issues. We use sociology to investigate why thousands of jobs have moved from the United States to developing nations, what social forces promote prejudice, what leads someone to join a social movement and work for social change, how access to computer technology can reduce social inequality, and why relationships between men and women in Seattle differ from those in Singapore.

Sociology is, simply, the scientific study of social behavior and human groups. It focuses on social relationships; how those relationships influence people's behavior; and how societies, the sum total of those relationships, develop and change.

something as simple as sporting events. On college campuses in the United States, thousands of students cheer well-trained football players. In Bali, Indonesia, dozens of spectators gather around a ring to cheer on roosters trained in cockfighting. In both instances, the spectators debate the merits of their favorites and bet on the outcome of the events. Yet what is considered a normal sporting event in one part of the world is considered unusual in another part.

The sociological imagination allows us to go beyond personal experiences and observations to understand broader public issues. Divorce, for example, is unquestionably a personal hardship for a husband and wife who split apart. However, C. Wright Mills advocated using the sociological imagination to view divorce not as simply an individual's personal problem but rather as a societal concern. Using this perspective, we can see that an increase in the divorce rate actually redefines a major social institution—the family. Today's households frequently include stepparents and half-siblings whose parents have divorced and remarried. Through the complexities of the blended family, this private concern becomes a public issue that affects schools, government agencies, businesses, and religious institutions.

THE SOCIOLOGICAL IMAGINATION

In attempting to understand social behavior, sociologists rely on a particular type of critical thinking. A leading sociologist, C. Wright Mills, described such thinking as the **sociological imagination**—an awareness of the relationship between an individual and the wider society, both today and in the past (Mills [1959] 2000a). This awareness allows all of us (not just sociologists) to comprehend the links between our immediate, personal social settings and the remote, impersonal social world that surrounds and helps to shape us. Kelsey Timmerman certainly used a sociological imagination when he studied foreign garment workers.

A key element in the sociological imagination is the ability to view one's own society as an outsider would, rather than only from the perspective of personal experiences and cultural biases. Consider

Sociology is the scientific study of social behavior and human groups.

The sociological imagination is an empowering tool. It allows us to look beyond a limited understanding of human behavior to see the world and its people in a new way and through a broader lens than we might otherwise use. It may be as simple as understanding why a roommate prefers country music to hip-hop, or it may open up a whole different way of understanding other populations in the world. For example, in the aftermath of the terrorist attacks on the United States on September 11, 2001, many citizens wanted to understand how Muslims throughout the world perceived their country, and why. From time to time this textbook will offer you the chance to exercise your sociological imagination in a variety of situations.

💡 use your **sociological imagination**

You are walking down the street in your city or hometown. In looking around you, you can't help noticing that half or more of the people you see are overweight. How do you explain your observation? If you were C. Wright Mills, how do you think you would explain it?

● Sociology and the Social Sciences

Is sociology a science? The term **science** refers to the body of knowledge obtained by methods based on systematic observation. Just like other scientific disciplines, sociology involves the organized, systematic study of phenomena (in this case, human behavior) in order to enhance understanding. All scientists, whether studying mushrooms or murderers, attempt to collect precise information through methods of study that are as objective as possible. They rely on careful recording of observations and accumulation of data.

Of course, there is a great difference between sociology and physics, between psychology and astronomy. For this reason, the sciences are commonly divided into natural and social sciences. **Natural science** is the study of the physical features of nature and the ways in which they interact and change. Astronomy, biology, chemistry, geology, and physics are all natural sciences. **Social science** is the study of the social features of humans and the ways in which they interact and change. The social sciences include sociology, anthropology, economics, history, psychology, and political science.

These social science disciplines have a common focus on the social behavior of people, yet each has a particular orientation. Anthropologists usually study past cultures and preindustrial societies that continue today, as well as the origins of humans. Economists explore the ways in which people produce and exchange goods and services, along with money and other resources. Historians are concerned with the peoples and events of the past and their significance for us today. Political scientists study international relations, the workings of government, and the exercise of power and authority. Psychologists investigate personality and individual behavior. So what do *sociologists* focus on? They study the influence that society has on people's attitudes and behavior and the ways in which people interact and shape society. Because humans are social animals, sociologists

examine our social relationships scientifically. The range of the relationships they investigate is vast, as the current list of sections in the American Sociological Association suggests (Table 1-1).

Let's consider how different social scientists might study the impact of the global recession that began in 2008. Historians would stress the pattern of long-term fluctuations in world markets. Economists would discuss the roles played by government, the private sector, and the world monetary system. Psychologists would study individual cases of emotional stress among workers, investors, and business owners. And political scientists would study the degree of cooperation among nations—or lack of it—in seeking economic solutions.

What approach would sociologists take? They might note a change in marital patterns in the United States. Since the recession began, the median age of first marriage has risen to 28.7 years for men and 26.7 years for women. Sociologists might also observe that today, fewer people are making that trip to the altar than in the past. If the U.S. marriage rate had remained the same as it was in 2006, about 4 million more Americans would have married by 2010.

Similarly, sociologists might evaluate the recession's impact on education. In the United States, private school enrollment from elementary through high school declined from 13.6 percent in 2006 to 12.8 percent in 2010 as families cut back on nonessential expenditures. Sociologists might even consider the recession's effect on environmental actions, such as carpooling. In all but 1 of the 50 largest metropolitan areas in the United States (New Orleans), the percentage of working people aged 16 to 64 dropped significantly during the recession. When friends and co-workers are laid off, carpools shrink and more people end up driving to work alone (El Nasser and Overberg 2011).

Sociologists would take a similar approach to studying episodes of extreme violence. In April 2007, just as college students were beginning to focus on the impending end of the semester, tragedy struck on the campus of Virginia Tech. In a two-hour shooting spree, a mentally disturbed senior armed with semi-automatic weapons killed a total of 32 students and faculty at Virginia's largest university. Observers struggled to describe the events and place them in some social context. For sociologists in particular, the event raised numerous issues and topics for study, including the media's role in describing the attacks, the presence of violence in our educational institutions, the gun control debate, the inadequacy of the nation's mental health care system, and the stereotyping and stigmatization of people who suffer from mental illness.

Besides doing research, sociologists have a long history of advising government agencies on how to respond to disasters. Certainly the poverty of the Gulf Coast region complicated the huge challenge of evacuation in 2005. With Katrina bearing down on the Gulf Coast, thousands of poor inner-city residents had no automobiles or other available means of escaping the storm. Added to that difficulty was the high incidence of disability in the area. New Orleans ranked second among the nation's 70 largest cities in the proportion of people over age 65 who are disabled—56 percent. Moving wheelchair-bound residents to safety requires specially equipped vehicles, to say nothing of handicap-accessible accommodations in public shelters. Clearly, officials must consider these factors in developing evacuation plans (Bureau of the Census 2005b).

Table **1-1**   Sections of the American Sociological Association

Aging and the Life Course	Environment and Technology	Peace, War, and Social Conflict
Alcohol, Drugs, and Tobacco	Ethnomethodology and Conversation Analysis	Political Economy of the World-System
Altruism, Morality and Social Solidarity	Evolution, Biology, and Sociology	Political Sociology
Animals and Society	Family	Population
Asia and Asian America	Global and Transnational Sociology	Race, Gender, and Class
Body and Embodiment	History of Sociology	Racial and Ethnic Minorities
Children and Youth	Human Rights	Rationality and Society
Collective Behavior and Social Movements	International Migration	Religion
Communication and Information Technologies	Labor and Labor Movements	Science, Knowledge, and Technology
Community and Urban Sociology	Latino/a Sociology	Sex and Gender
Comparative and Historical Sociology	Law	Sexualities
Consumers and Consumption	Marxist Sociology	Social Psychology
Crime, Law, and Deviance	Mathematical Sociology	Sociological Practice and Public Sociology
Culture	Medical Sociology	Teaching and Learning
Development	Mental Health	Theory
Disability and Society	Methodology	
Economic Sociology	Organizations, Occupations, and Work	
Education		
Emotions		

The range of sociological issues is very broad. For example, sociologists who belong to the Animals and Society section of the ASA may study the animal rights movement; those who belong to the Sexualities section may study global sex workers or the gay, bisexual, and transgendered movements. Economic sociologists may investigate globalization or consumerism, among many other topics.

Source: American Sociological Association 2012.

Think about It

Which of these topics do you think would interest you the most? Why?

Sociological analysis of the disaster did not end when the floodwaters receded. Long before residents of New Orleans staged a massive anticrime rally at City Hall in 2007, researchers were analyzing resettlement patterns in the city. They noted that returning residents often faced bleak job prospects. Yet families who had stayed away for that reason often had trouble enrolling their children in schools unprepared for an influx of evacuees. Faced with a choice between the need to work and the need to return their children to school, some displaced families risked sending their older children home alone. Meanwhile, opportunists had arrived to victimize unsuspecting homeowners. And the city's overtaxed judicial and criminal justice systems, which had been understaffed before Katrina struck, had been only partially restored. All these social factors led sociologists and others to anticipate the unparalleled rise in reported crime the city experienced in 2006 and 2007 (Jervis 2008; Sarah Kaufman 2006).

Throughout this textbook, you will see how sociologists develop theories and conduct research to study and better understand

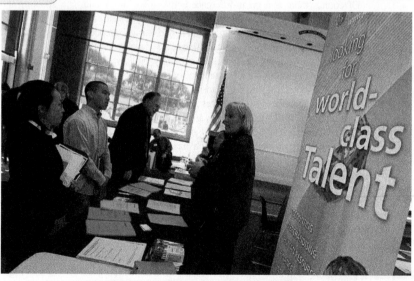

As the nation struggled to recover from a deep and lengthy recession, recently laid-off workers jostled the long-term unemployed at a crowded job fair in San Francisco. Sociologists use a variety of approaches to assess the full impact of economic change on society.

societies. And you will be encouraged to use your sociological imagination to examine the United States (and other societies) from the viewpoint of a respectful but questioning outsider.

Sociology and Common Sense

Sociology focuses on the study of human behavior. Yet we all have experience with human behavior and at least some knowledge of it. All of us might well have theories about why people become homeless, for example. Our theories and opinions typically come from common sense—that is, from our experiences and conversations, from what we read, from what we see on television, and so forth.

In our daily lives, we rely on common sense to get us through many unfamiliar situations. However, this commonsense knowledge, while sometimes accurate, is not always reliable, because it rests on commonly held beliefs rather than on systematic analysis of facts. It was once considered common sense to accept that the earth was flat—a view rightly questioned by Pythagoras and Aristotle. Incorrect commonsense notions are not just a part of the distant past; they remain with us today.

Contrary to the common notion that women tend to be chatty compared to men, for instance, researchers have found little difference between the sexes in terms of their talkativeness. Over a five-year period they placed unobtrusive microphones on 396 college students in various fields, at campuses in Mexico as well as the United States. They found that both men and women spoke about 16,000 words per day (Mehl et al. 2007).

Similarly, common sense tells us that today, violent crime holds communities on the border between the United States and Mexico in a kind of death grip, creating an atmosphere of lawlessness reminiscent of the old Wild West. Based on televised news stories and on concerns expressed by elected officials throughout the southwestern United States, this assertion may sound reasonable; however, it is not true. Although some communities in Mexico have fallen under the control of drug cartels, the story is different on the U.S. side of the border. All available crime data—including murder, extortion, robbery, and kidnapping rates, whether reported or documented in victim surveys—show that in the hundred-mile-deep border area stretching from San Diego to Brownsville, Texas, crime rates are significantly lower than in similar U.S. cities outside the area. Furthermore, the crime rate has been dropping faster near the border than in other similar-size U.S. communities for at least the last 15 years (Gillon 2011; Gomez et al. 2011).

Like other social scientists, sociologists do not accept something as a fact because "everyone knows it." Instead, each piece of information must be tested and recorded, then analyzed in relation to other data. Sociologists rely on scientific studies in order to describe and understand a social environment. At times, the findings of sociologists may seem like common sense, because they deal with familiar facets of everyday life. The difference is that such findings have been *tested* by researchers. Common sense now tells us that the earth is round, but this particular commonsense notion is based on centuries of scientific work that began with the breakthroughs made by Pythagoras and Aristotle.

What Is Sociological Theory?

Why do people commit suicide? One traditional commonsense answer is that people inherit the desire to kill themselves. Another view is that sunspots drive people to take their lives. These explanations may not seem especially convincing to contemporary researchers, but they represent beliefs widely held as recently as 1900.

Sociologists are not particularly interested in why any one individual commits suicide; they are more concerned with identifying the social forces that systematically cause some people to take their own lives. In order to undertake this research, sociologists develop a theory that offers a general explanation of suicidal behavior.

We can think of theories as attempts to explain events, forces, materials, ideas, or behavior in a comprehensive manner. In sociology, a **theory** is a set of statements that seeks to explain problems, actions, or behavior. An effective theory may have both explanatory and predictive power. That is, it can help us to see the relationships among seemingly isolated phenomena, as well as to understand how one type of change in an environment leads to other changes.

The World Health Organization (2010) estimates that almost a million people die from suicide every year. More than a hundred years ago, a sociologist tried to look at suicide data scientifically. Émile Durkheim ([1897] 1951) developed a highly original theory about the relationship between suicide and social factors. Durkheim was primarily concerned not with the personalities of individual suicide victims, but rather with suicide rates and how they varied from country to country. As a result, when he looked at the number of reported suicides in France, England, and Denmark in 1869, he also noted the total population of each country in order to determine the rate of suicide in each nation. He found that whereas England had only 67 reported suicides per million inhabitants, France had 135 per million and Denmark had 277 per million. The question then became "Why did Denmark have a comparatively high rate of reported suicide?"

Durkheim went much deeper into his investigation of suicide rates. The result was his landmark work *Suicide,* published in 1897. Durkheim refused to accept unproved explanations regarding suicide, including the beliefs that inherited tendencies or cosmic forces caused such deaths. Instead, he focused on social factors, such as the cohesiveness or lack of cohesiveness of religious, social, and occupational groups.

Durkheim's research suggested that suicide, although it is a solitary act, is related to group life. He found that people without religious affiliations had a higher suicide rate than those who were affiliated; the unmarried had much higher rates than married people; and soldiers had a higher rate than civilians. In addition, there seemed to be higher rates of suicide in times of peace than in times of war and revolution, and in times of economic instability and recession rather than in times of prosperity. Durkheim concluded that the suicide rates of a society reflected the extent to which people were or were not integrated into the group life of the society.

Émile Durkheim, like many other social scientists, developed a theory to explain how individual behavior can be understood within a social context. He pointed out the influence of groups and societal forces on what had always been viewed as a highly personal act. Clearly, Durkheim offered a more *scientific* explanation for the causes of suicide than that of inherited tendencies or sunspots. His theory has predictive power, since it suggests that suicide rates will rise or fall in conjunction with certain social and economic changes.

Of course, a theory—even the best of theories—is not a final statement about human behavior. Durkheim's theory of suicide is no exception. Sociologists continue to examine factors that contribute to differences in suicide rates around the world and to a particular society's rate of suicide. In Las Vegas, for example, sociologists have observed that the chances of dying by suicide are strikingly high—twice as high as in the United States as a whole.

Noting Durkheim's emphasis on the relationship between suicide and social isolation, researchers have suggested that Las Vegas's rapid growth and constant influx of tourists have undermined the community's sense of permanence, even among longtime residents. Although gambling—or more accurately, losing while gambling—may seem a likely precipitating factor in suicides there, careful study of the data has allowed researchers to dismiss that explanation. What happens in Vegas may stay in Vegas, but the sense of community cohesiveness that the rest of the country enjoys may be lacking (Wray et al. 2008, 2011).

MODULE 1 | Recap and Review

Summary

Sociology is the scientific study of social behavior and human groups. In this module, we examine the nature of sociological theory and the work of some of the founders of the discipline.

1. The **sociological imagination** is an awareness of the relationship between an individual and the wider society. It is based on the ability to view our own society as an outsider might, rather than from the perspective of our limited experiences and cultural biases.

2. In contrast to other **social sciences,** sociology emphasizes the influence that groups can have on people's behavior and attitudes and the ways in which people shape society.

3. Knowledge that relies on common sense is not always reliable. Sociologists must test and analyze each piece of information they use.

4. Sociologists employ **theories** to examine relationships between observations or data that may seem completely unrelated.

Thinking Critically

1. What aspects of the social and work environment in a fast-food restaurant would be of particular interest to a sociologist? How would the sociological imagination help in analyzing the topic?

2. Can you think of any explanation, other than lack of community, for the high suicide rate in Las Vegas? Does that explanation agree with Durkheim's theory?

3. Think about the sociologists profiled in this module, Mills and Durkheim. Whose work seems most relevant to today's social problems? Why did you choose that thinker, and which social problems were you thinking of?

Key Terms

Natural science
Science
Social science
Sociological imagination
Sociology
Theory

2 | The Development of Sociology

People have always been curious about sociological matters—how we get along with others, what we do for a living, whom we select as our leaders. Philosophers and religious authorities of ancient and medieval societies made countless observations about human behavior. They did not test or verify those observations scientifically; nevertheless, their observations often became the foundation for moral codes. Several of these early social philosophers correctly predicted that a systematic study of human behavior would emerge one day. Beginning in the 19th century, European theorists made pioneering contributions to the development of a science of human behavior.

Early Thinkers

Auguste Comte

The 19th century was an unsettling time in France. The French monarchy had been deposed in the revolution of 1789, and Napoleon had suffered defeat in his effort to conquer Europe. Amid this chaos, philosophers considered how society might be improved. Auguste Comte (1798–1857), credited with being the most influential of the philosophers of the early 1800s, believed that a theoretical science of society and a systematic investigation of behavior were needed to improve society. He coined the term *sociology* to apply to the science of human behavior.

Writing in the 1800s, Comte feared that the excesses of the French Revolution had permanently impaired France's stability. Yet he hoped that the systematic study of social behavior would eventually lead to more rational human interactions. In Comte's hierarchy of the sciences, sociology was at the top. He called it the "queen," and its practitioners "scientist-priests." This French theorist did not simply give sociology its name; he presented a rather ambitious challenge to the fledgling discipline.

Harriet Martineau

Scholars learned of Comte's works largely through translations by the English sociologist Harriet Martineau (1802–1876). But Martineau was a pathbreaker in her own right: she offered insightful observations of the customs and social practices of both her native Britain and the United States. Martineau's book *Society in America* ([1837] 1962) examined religion, politics, child rearing, and immigration in the young nation. It gave special attention to social class distinctions and to such factors as gender and race. Martineau ([1838] 1989) also wrote the first book on sociological methods.

Martineau's writings emphasized the impact that the economy, law, trade, health, and population could have on social problems. She spoke out in favor of the rights of women, the emancipation of slaves, and religious tolerance. Later in life, deafness did not keep her from being an activist. In Martineau's ([1837] 1962) view, intellectuals and scholars should not simply offer observations of social conditions; they should *act* on their convictions in a manner that will benefit society. That is why Martineau conducted research on the nature of female employment and pointed to the need for further investigation of the issue (Deegan 2003; Hill and Hoecker-Drysdale 2001).

Herbert Spencer

Another important early contributor to the discipline of sociology was Herbert Spencer (1820–1903). A relatively prosperous Victorian Englishman, Spencer (unlike Martineau) did not feel compelled to correct or improve society; instead, he merely hoped to understand it better. Drawing on Charles Darwin's study *On the Origin of Species,* Spencer applied the concept of evolution of the species to societies in order to explain how they change, or

Harriet Martineau, an early pioneer of sociology who studied social behavior both in her native England and in the United States, proposed some of the methods still used by sociologists.

evolve, over time. Similarly, he adapted Darwin's evolutionary view of the "survival of the fittest" by arguing that it is "natural" that some people are rich while others are poor.

Spencer's approach to societal change was extremely popular in his lifetime. Unlike Comte, Spencer suggested that since societies are bound to change eventually, one need not be highly critical of present social arrangements or work actively for social change. This viewpoint appealed to many influential people in England and the United States who had a vested interest in the status quo and were suspicious of social thinkers who endorsed change.

Émile Durkheim

Émile Durkheim made many pioneering contributions to sociology, including his important theoretical work on suicide. The son of a rabbi, Durkheim (1858–1917) was educated in both France and Germany. He established an impressive academic reputation and was appointed one of the first professors of sociology in France. Above all, Durkheim will be remembered for his insistence that behavior must be understood within a larger social context, not just in individualistic terms.

To give one example of this emphasis, Durkheim ([1912] 2001) developed a fundamental thesis to help explain all forms of society. Through intensive study of the Arunta, an Australian tribe, he focused on the functions that religion performed and underscored the role of group life in defining what we consider to be religion. Durkheim concluded that like other forms of group behavior, religion reinforces a group's solidarity.

Another of Durkheim's main interests was the consequences of work in modern societies. In his view, the growing division of labor in industrial societies, as workers became much more specialized in their tasks, led to what he called "anomie." **Anomie** refers to the loss of direction felt in a society when social control of individual behavior has become ineffective. Often, the state of anomie occurs during a time of profound social change, when people have lost their sense of purpose or direction. In a period of anomie, people are so confused and unable to cope with the new social environment that they may resort to suicide.

Durkheim was concerned about the dangers that alienation, loneliness, and isolation might pose for modern industrial societies. He shared Comte's belief that sociology should provide direction for social change. As a result, he advocated the creation of new social groups—mediators between the individual's family and the state—that would provide a sense of belonging for members of huge, impersonal societies. Unions would be an example of such groups.

Like many other sociologists, Durkheim did not limit his interests to one aspect of social behavior. Later in this book we will consider his thinking on crime and punishment, religion, and the workplace. Few sociologists have had such a dramatic impact on so many different areas within the discipline.

Max Weber

Another important early theorist was Max Weber (pronounced VAY-ber). Born in Germany, Weber (1864–1920) studied legal and economic history, but gradually developed an interest in sociology. Eventually, he became a professor at various German universities. Weber taught his students that they should employ *verstehen* (pronounced fair-SHTAY-en), the German word for "understanding" or "insight," in their intellectual work. He pointed out that we cannot analyze our social behavior by the same type of objective criteria we use to measure weight or temperature. To fully comprehend behavior, we must learn the subjective meanings people attach to their actions—how they themselves view and explain their behavior.

For example, suppose that a sociologist was studying the social ranking of individuals in a fraternity. Weber would expect the researcher to employ *verstehen* to determine the significance of the fraternity's social hierarchy for its members. The researcher might examine the effects of athleticism or grades or social skills or seniority on standing within the fraternity. He or she would seek to learn how the fraternity members relate to other members of higher or lower status. While investigating these questions, the researcher would take into account people's emotions, thoughts, beliefs, and attitudes (L. Coser 1977).

We also owe credit to Weber for a key conceptual tool: the ideal type. An **ideal type** is a construct or model for evaluating specific cases. In his works, Weber identified various characteristics of bureaucracy as an ideal type (discussed in detail in Module 19). In presenting this model of bureaucracy, Weber was not describing any particular organization, nor was he using the term *ideal* in a way that suggested a positive evaluation. Instead, his purpose was to provide a useful standard for measuring how bureaucratic an actual organization is (Gerth and Mills 1958). Later in this book, we will the concept of *ideal type* to study the family, religion, authority, and economic systems, as well as to analyze bureaucracy.

Although their professional careers coincided, Émile Durkheim and Max Weber never met and probably were unaware of each other's existence, let alone ideas. Such was not true of the work of Karl Marx. Durkheim's thinking about the impact of the division of labor in industrial societies was related to Marx's writings, while Weber's concern

FIGURE 2-1 **Contributors to Sociology**

	Émile Durkheim 1858–1917	**Max Weber 1864–1920**	**Karl Marx 1818–1883**	**W. E. B. DuBois 1868–1963**
Academic training	Philosophy	Law, economics, history, philosophy	Philosophy, law	Sociology
Key works	1893—*The Division of Labor in Society* 1897—*Suicide: A Study in Sociology* 1912—*Elementary Forms of Religious Life*	1904–1905—*The Protestant Ethic and the Spirit of Capitalism* 1921—*Economy and Society*	1848—*The Communist Manifesto* 1867—*Das Kapital*	1899—*The Philadelphia Negro* 1903—*The Negro Church* 1903—*Souls of Black Folk*

for a value-free, objective sociology was a direct response to Marx's deeply held convictions. Thus, it is not surprising that Karl Marx is viewed as a major figure in the development of sociology, as well as several other social sciences (Figure 2-1).

Karl Marx

Karl Marx (1818–1883) shared with Durkheim and Weber a dual interest in abstract philosophical issues and the concrete reality of everyday life. Unlike them, however, Marx was so critical of existing institutions that a conventional academic career was impossible. He spent most of his life in exile from his native Germany.

Marx's personal life was a difficult struggle. When a paper he had written was suppressed, he fled to France. In Paris, he met Friedrich Engels (1820–1895), with whom he formed a lifelong friendship. The two lived at a time when European and North American economic life was increasingly dominated by the factory rather than the farm.

While in London in 1847, Marx and Engels attended secret meetings of an illegal coalition of labor unions known as the Communist League. The following year they prepared a platform called *The Communist Manifesto,* in which they argued that the masses of people with no resources other than their labor (whom they referred to as the *proletariat*) should unite to fight for the overthrow of capitalist societies. In the words of Marx and Engels:

> The history of all hitherto existing society is the history of class struggles. . . . The proletarians have nothing to lose but their chains. They have a world to win. WORKING MEN OF ALL COUNTRIES, UNITE! (Tucker 1978:473, 500).

After completing *The Communist Manifesto,* Marx returned to Germany, only to be expelled. He then moved to England, where he continued to write books and essays. Marx lived there

in extreme poverty; he pawned most of his possessions, and several of his children died of malnutrition and disease. Marx clearly was an outsider in British society, a fact that may well have influenced his view of Western cultures.

In Marx's analysis, society was fundamentally divided between two classes that clashed in pursuit of their own interests. When he examined the industrial societies of his time, such as Germany, England, and the United States, he saw the factory as the center of conflict between the exploiters (the owners of the means of production) and the exploited (the workers). Marx viewed these relationships in systematic terms; that is, he believed that a system of economic, social, and political relationships maintained the power and dominance of the owners over the workers. Consequently, Marx and Engels argued that the working class should overthrow the existing class system. Marx's influence on contemporary thinking has been dramatic. His writings inspired those who would later lead communist revolutions in Russia, China, Cuba, Vietnam, and elsewhere.

Even apart from the political revolutions that his work fostered, Marx's significance is profound. Marx emphasized the *group* identifications and associations that influence an *individual's* place in society. This area of study is the major focus of contemporary sociology. Throughout this textbook, we will consider how membership in a particular gender classification, age group, racial group, or economic class affects a person's attitudes and behavior. In an important sense, we can trace this way of understanding society back to the pioneering work of Karl Marx.

W. E. B. DuBois

Marx's work encouraged sociologists to view society through the eyes of those segments of the population that rarely influence decision making. In the United States, some early Black sociologists, including W. E. B. DuBois (1868–1963), conducted research that they hoped would assist in the struggle for a racially egalitarian society. DuBois (pronounced doo-BOYSS) believed that knowledge was essential in combating prejudice and achieving tolerance and justice. Sociologists, he contended, needed to draw on scientific principles to study social problems such as those experienced by Blacks in the United States. To separate opinion from fact, he advocated basic research on the lives of Blacks. Through his in-depth studies of urban life, both White and Black, in cities such as Philadelphia and Atlanta, DuBois ([1899] 1995) made a major contribution to sociology.

Like Durkheim and Weber, DuBois saw the importance of religion to society. However, he tended to focus on religion at the community level and the role of the church in the lives of its members ([1903] 2003). DuBois had little patience with theorists such as Herbert Spencer, who seemed content with the status quo. He believed that the granting of full political rights to Blacks was essential to their social and economic progress.

Because many of his ideas challenged the status quo, DuBois did not find a receptive audience within either the government or the academic world. As a result, he became increasingly involved with organizations whose members questioned the established social order. In 1909 he helped to found the National Association for the Advancement of Colored People, better known today as the NAACP (Wortham 2008).

DuBois's insights have been lasting. In 1897 he coined the term **double consciousness** to refer to the division of an individual's identity into two or more social realities. He used the term to describe the experience of being Black in White America. Today, an African American holds the most powerful office in the nation, president of the United States. Yet for millions of African Americans, the reality of being Black in the United States typically is not one of power (DuBois [1903] 1961).

● Twentieth-Century Developments

Sociology today builds on the firm foundation developed by Émile Durkheim, Max Weber, Karl Marx, and W. E. B. DuBois. However, the field certainly has not remained stagnant over the past hundred years. While Europeans have continued to make contributions to the discipline, sociologists from throughout the world and especially the United States have advanced sociological theory and research. Their new insights have helped us to better understand the workings of society.

Charles Horton Cooley

Charles Horton Cooley (1864–1929) was typical of the sociologists who came to prominence in the early 1900s. Born in Ann Arbor, Michigan, Cooley received his graduate training in economics but later became a sociology professor at the University of Michigan. Like other early sociologists, he had become interested in this new discipline while pursuing a related area of study.

Cooley shared the desire of Durkheim, Weber, and Marx to learn more about society. But to do so effectively, he preferred to use the sociological perspective to look first at smaller units—intimate, face-to-face groups such as families, gangs, and

friendship networks. He saw these groups as the seedbeds of society, in the sense that they shape people's ideals, beliefs, values, and social nature. Cooley's work increased our understanding of groups of relatively small size.

Jane Addams

In the early 1900s, many leading sociologists in the United States saw themselves as social reformers dedicated to systematically studying and then improving a corrupt society. They were genuinely concerned about the lives of immigrants in the nation's growing cities, whether those immigrants came from Europe or from the rural American South. Early female sociologists, in particular, often took active roles in poor urban areas as leaders of community centers known as *settlement houses.* For example, Jane Addams (1860–1935), a member of the American Sociological Society, cofounded the famous Chicago settlement called Hull House.

Addams and other pioneering female sociologists commonly combined intellectual inquiry, social service work, and political activism—all with the goal of assisting the underprivileged and creating a more egalitarian society. For example, working with the Black journalist and educator Ida Wells-Barnett, Addams successfully prevented racial segregation in the Chicago public schools. Addams's efforts to establish a juvenile court

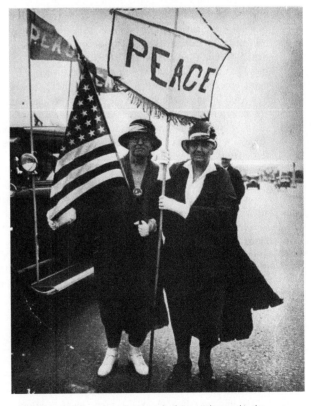

Jane Addams (right) was an early pioneer both in sociology and in the settlement house movement. She was also an activist for many causes, including the worldwide campaign for peace.

system and a women's trade union reveal the practical focus of her work (Addams 1910, 1930; Deegan 1991; Lengermann and Niebrugge-Brantley 1998).

By the middle of the 20th century, however, the focus of the discipline had shifted. Sociologists for the most part restricted themselves to theorizing and gathering information; the aim of transforming society was left to social workers and activists. This shift away from social reform was accompanied by a growing commitment to scientific methods of research and to value-free interpretation of data. Not all sociologists were happy with this emphasis. A new organization, the Society for the Study of Social Problems, was created in 1950 to deal more directly with social inequality and other social problems.

Robert Merton

Sociologist Robert Merton (1910–2003) made an important contribution to the discipline by successfully combining theory and research. Born to Slavic immigrant parents in Philadelphia, Merton won a scholarship to Temple University. He continued his studies at Harvard, where he acquired his lifelong interest in sociology. Merton's teaching career was based at Columbia University.

Merton (1968) produced a theory that is one of the most frequently cited explanations of deviant behavior. He noted different ways in which people attempt to achieve success in life. In his view, some may deviate from the socially approved goal of accumulating material goods or the socially accepted means of achieving that goal. For example, in Merton's classification scheme, *innovators* are people who accept the goal of pursuing material wealth but use illegal means to do so, including robbery, burglary, and extortion. Although Merton based his explanation of crime on individual behavior that has been influenced by society's approved goals and means, it has wider applications. His theory helps to account for the high crime rates among the nation's poor, who may see no hope of advancing themselves through traditional modes of success. Module 24 discusses Merton's theory in greater detail.

Merton also emphasized that sociology should strive to bring together the *macro-level* and *micro-level* approaches to the study of society. **Macrosociology** concentrates on large-scale phenomena or entire civilizations. Émile Durkheim's cross-cultural study of suicide is an example of macro-level research. More recently, macrosociologists have examined international crime rates (see Module 25) and the stereotype of Asian Americans as a "model minority" (see Module 33). In contrast, **microsociology** stresses the study of small groups, often through experimental means.

Sociological research on the micro level has included studies of how divorced men and women disengage from significant social roles (see Module 10) and of how a teacher's expectations can affect a student's academic performance (see Module 42).

Pierre Bourdieu

Increasingly, scholars in the United States have been drawing on the insights of sociologists in other countries. The ideas of the French sociologist Pierre Bourdieu (1930–2002) have found a broad following in North America and elsewhere. As a young man, Bourdieu did fieldwork in Algeria during its struggle for independence from France. Today, scholars study Bourdieu's research techniques as well as his conclusions.

Bourdieu wrote about how capital in its many forms sustains individuals and families from one generation to the next. To Bourdieu, *capital* included not just material goods, but cultural and social assets. **Cultural capital** refers to noneconomic goods, such as family background and education, which are reflected in a knowledge of language and the arts. Not necessarily book knowledge, cultural capital refers to the kind of education that is valued by the socially elite. Though a knowledge of Chinese cuisine is culture, for example, it is not the prestigious kind of culture that is valued by the elite. In the United States, immigrants—especially those who arrived in large numbers and settled in ethnic enclaves—have generally taken two or three generations to develop the same level of cultural capital enjoyed by more established groups. In comparison, **social capital** refers to the collective benefit of social networks, which are built on reciprocal trust. Much has been written about the importance of family and friendship networks in providing people with an opportunity to advance. In his emphasis on cultural and social capital, Bourdieu's work extends the insights of early social thinkers such as Marx and Weber (Bourdieu and Passerson 1990; Field 2008).

Today sociology reflects the diverse contributions of earlier theorists. As sociologists approach such topics as divorce, drug addiction, and religious cults, they can draw on the theoretical insights of the discipline's pioneers. A careful reader can hear Comte, Durkheim, Weber, Marx, DuBois, Cooley, Addams, and many others speaking through the pages of current research. Sociology has also broadened beyond the intellectual confines of North America and Europe. Contributions to the discipline now come from sociologists studying and researching human behavior in other parts of the world. In describing the work of these sociologists, it is helpful to examine a number of influential *theoretical perspectives,* also known as *approaches* or *views.*

MODULE 2 | Recap and Review

Summary

The thinkers who founded the discipline of sociology and developed it in the 19th and 20th centuries were reacting to the social world in which they lived.

1. Nineteenth-century thinkers who contributed sociological insights included Auguste Comte, a French philosopher; Harriet Martineau, an English sociologist; and Herbert Spencer, an English scholar.

2. Other important figures in the development of sociology were Émile Durkheim, who pioneered work on suicide; Max Weber, who taught the need for insight in intellectual work; Karl Marx, who emphasized the importance of the economy and social conflict; and W. E. B. DuBois, who advocated for the usefulness of basic research in combating prejudice and fostering racial tolerance and justice.

3. In the 20th century, the discipline of sociology was indebted to the U.S. sociologists Charles Horton Cooley and Robert Merton, as well as to the French sociologist Pierre Bourdieu.

4. **Macrosociology** concentrates on large-scale phenomena or entire civilizations; **microsociology** stresses the study of small groups.

Thinking Critically

1. Consider the work of early sociologists such as Comte and Martineau. What social problems were they reacting to? To what extent have those problems been rectified today?

2. How is 19th-century industrialization related to the development of sociological thought?

3. What are some examples of social and cultural capital that you possess?

Key Terms

Anomie

Cultural capital

Double consciousness

Ideal type

Macrosociology

Microsociology

Social capital

Verstehen

MODULE 3 | Major Theoretical Perspectives

Sociologists view society in different ways. Some see the world basically as a stable and ongoing entity. They are impressed with the endurance of the family, organized religion, and other social institutions. Other sociologists see society as composed of many groups in conflict, competing for scarce resources. To still other sociologists, the most fascinating aspects of the social world are the everyday, routine interactions among individuals that we sometimes take for granted. These three views, the ones most widely used by sociologists, are the functionalist, conflict, and interactionist perspectives. Together, these approaches will provide an introductory look at the discipline.

⬤ Functionalist Perspective

Think of society as a living organism in which each part of the organism contributes to its survival. This view is the **functionalist perspective,** which emphasizes the way in which the parts of a society are structured to maintain its stability.

Talcott Parsons (1902–1979), a Harvard University sociologist, was a key figure in the development of functionalist theory. Parsons was greatly influenced by the work of Émile Durkheim, Max Weber, and other European sociologists. For more than four decades, he dominated sociology in the United States with his advocacy of functionalism. Parsons saw any society as a vast network of connected parts, each of which helps to maintain the system as a whole. His approach, carried forward by German sociologist Niklas Luhmann (1927–1998), holds that if an aspect of social life does not contribute to a society's stability or survival—if it does not serve some identifiably useful function or promote value consensus among members of society—it will not be passed on from one generation to the next (Joas and Knöbl 2009; Knudsen 2010).

Let's examine an example of the functionalist perspective. Many Americans have difficulty understanding the Hindu prohibition against slaughtering cows (specifically, zebu). Cattle browse unhindered through Indian street markets, helping themselves to oranges and mangoes while people bargain for the little food they can afford. What explains this devotion to the cow in the face of human deprivation—a devotion that appears to be dysfunctional?

The simple explanation is that cow worship is highly functional in Indian society, according to economists, agronomists, and social scientists who have studied the matter. Cows perform two essential tasks: plowing the fields and producing milk. If eating beef were permitted, hungry families might be tempted to slaughter their cows for immediate consumption, leaving themselves without a means of cultivation. Cows also produce dung, which doubles as a fertilizer and a fuel for cooking. Finally, cow meat sustains the neediest group in society, the *Dalit,* or untouchables, who sometimes resort to eating beef in secrecy. If eating beef were socially acceptable, higher-status Indians would no doubt bid up its price, placing it beyond the reach of the hungriest.

Manifest and Latent Functions

A college catalog typically states various functions of the institution. It may inform you, for example, that the university intends to "offer each student a broad education in classical and contemporary thought, in the humanities, in the sciences, and in the arts." However, it would be quite a surprise to find a catalog that declared, "This university was founded in 1895 to assist people in finding a marriage partner." No college catalog will declare this as the purpose of the university. Yet societal institutions serve many functions, some of them quite subtle. The university, in fact, *does* facilitate mate selection.

Robert Merton (1968) made an important distinction between manifest and latent functions. **Manifest functions** of institutions are open, stated, and conscious functions. They involve the intended, recognized consequences of an aspect of society, such as the university's role in certifying academic competence and excellence. In contrast, **latent functions** are unconscious or unintended functions that may reflect hidden purposes of an institution. One latent function of universities is to hold down unemployment. Another is to serve as a meeting ground for people seeking marital partners.

Dysfunctions

Functionalists acknowledge that not all parts of a society contribute to its stability all the time. A **dysfunction** refers to an element or process of a society that may actually disrupt the social system or reduce its stability.

We view many dysfunctional behavior patterns, such as homicide, as undesirable. Yet we should not automatically interpret them in this way. The evaluation of a dysfunction depends on one's own values, or as the saying goes, on "where you sit." For example, the official view in prisons in the United States is that inmate gangs should be eradicated because they are dysfunctional to smooth operations. Yet some guards have come to view prison gangs as a functional part of their jobs. The danger posed by gangs creates a "threat to security," requiring increased surveillance and more overtime work for guards, as well as requests for special staffing to address gang problems (G. Scott 2001).

Cows (zebu), considered sacred in India, wander freely through this city, respected by all who encounter them. The sanctity of the cow is functional in India, where plowing, milking, and fertilizing are far more important to subsistence farmers than a diet that includes beef.

● Conflict Perspective

Where functionalists see stability and consensus, conflict sociologists see a social world in continual struggle. The **conflict perspective** assumes that social behavior is best understood in terms of tension between groups over power or the allocation of resources, including housing, money, access to services, and political representation. The tension between competing groups need not be violent; it can take the form of labor negotiations, party politics, competition between religious groups for new members, or disputes over the federal budget.

Throughout most of the 1900s, the functionalist perspective had the upper hand in sociology in the United States. However, the conflict approach has become increasingly pervasive since the late 1960s. The widespread social unrest resulting from battles over civil rights, bitter divisions over the war in Vietnam, the rise of the feminist and gay liberation movements, the Watergate political scandal, urban riots, confrontations at abortion clinics, and shrinking economic prospects for the middle class have offered support for the conflict approach—the view that our social world is characterized by continual struggle between competing groups. Currently, the discipline of sociology accepts conflict theory as one valid way to gain insight into a society.

The Marxist View

As we saw earlier, Karl Marx viewed struggle between social classes as inevitable, given the exploitation of workers that he perceived under capitalism. Expanding on Marx's work, sociologists and other social scientists have come to see conflict not merely as a class phenomenon but as a part of everyday life in all societies. In studying any culture, organization, or social group, sociologists want to know who benefits, who suffers, and who dominates at the expense of others. They are concerned with the conflicts between women and men, parents and children, cities and suburbs, Whites and Blacks, to name only a few. Conflict theorists are interested in how society's institutions—including the family, government, religion, education, and the media—may help to maintain the privileges of some groups and keep others in a subservient position. Their emphasis on social change and the redistribution of resources makes conflict theorists more radical and activist than functionalists (Dahrendorf 1959).

The Feminist Perspective

Sociologists began embracing the feminist perspective only in the 1970s, although it has a long tradition in many other disciplines. The **feminist perspective** sees inequity in gender as central to all behavior and organization. Because it focuses clearly on one aspect of inequality, it is often allied with the conflict perspective. Proponents of the feminist view tend to focus on

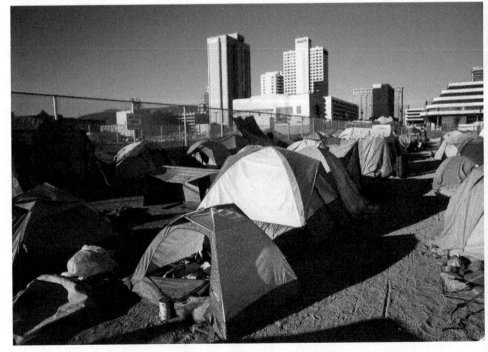

Those who take the Marxist view ask "Who benefits, who suffers, and who dominates?" How would a Marxist analyze the situation at this homeless encampment in Reno, Nevada?

MODULE 3 Major Theoretical Perspectives

Ida Wells-Barnett explored what it meant to be female and Black in the United States. Her work established her as one of the earliest feminist theorists.

the macro level, just as conflict theorists do. Drawing on the work of Marx and Engels, contemporary feminist theorists often view women's subordination as inherent in capitalist societies. Some radical feminist theorists, however, view the oppression of women as inevitable in *all* male-dominated societies, whether capitalist, socialist, or communist.

An early example of this perspective (long before the label came into use by sociologists) can be seen in the life and writings of Ida Wells-Barnett (1862–1931). Following her groundbreaking publications in the 1890s on the practice of lynching Black Americans, she became an advocate in the women's rights campaign, especially the struggle to win the vote for women.

Like feminist theorists who succeeded her, Wells-Barnett used her analysis of society as a means of resisting oppression. In her case, she researched what it meant to be Black, a woman in the United States, and a Black woman in the United States (Giddings 2008; Wells-Barnett 1970).

Feminist scholarship has broadened our understanding of social behavior by extending the analysis beyond the male point of view. Consider sports, for example. Feminist theorists consider how watching or participating in sports reinforces the roles that men and women play in the larger society:

- Although sports generally promote fitness and health, they may also have an adverse effect on participants' health. Men are more likely to resort to illegal steroid use (among bodybuilders and baseball players, for example); women, to excessive dieting (among gymnasts and figure skaters, for example).

- Gender expectations encourage female athletes to be passive and gentle, qualities that do not support the emphasis on competitiveness in sports. As a result, women find it difficult to enter sports traditionally dominated by men, such as Indy or NASCAR.

- Although professional women athletes' earnings are increasing, they typically trail those of male athletes.

use your **sociological imagination**

You are a sociologist who takes the conflict perspective. How would you interpret the practice of prostitution? How would your view of prostitution differ if you took the functionalist perspective? The feminist perspective?

Interactionist Perspective

Workers interacting on the job, encounters in public places like bus stops and parks, behavior in small groups—all these aspects of microsociology catch the attention of interactionists. Whereas functionalist and conflict theorists both analyze large-scale, society-wide patterns of behavior, theorists who take the **interactionist perspective** generalize about everyday forms of social interaction in order to explain society as a whole. Today, given rising concern over the cost and availability of gas, interactionists have begun to study a form of commuter behavior called "slugging." To avoid driving to work, commuters gather at certain preappointed places to seek rides from complete strangers. When a driver pulls into the parking area or vacant lot and announces his destination, the first slug in line who is headed for that destination jumps in. Rules of etiquette have emerged to smooth the social interaction between driver and passenger: neither the driver nor the passenger may eat or smoke; the slug may not adjust the windows or radio or talk on a cell phone. The presence of the slugs, who get a free ride, may allow the driver to use special lanes reserved for high-occupancy vehicles (Slug-Lines.com 2011).

trend spotting

The Changing Third Place

For a generation, sociologists have spoken of the "third place," a social setting between the "first place" of home and the "second place" of work. People gather routinely in the third place, typically a coffeehouse or fast-food restaurant, to see familiar faces or make new friends.

Will this social pattern persist? Sociologists have identified forces that both encourage and discourage it. The availability of free Wi-Fi definitely encourages people to seek out such establishments, but do laptops truly enhance social interactions there? And though talking among friends may be easy in the living-room settings that coffeehouses provide, proprietors don't always welcome these social gatherings. Some enforce antiloitering regulations or require patrons to make purchases at regular time intervals. Still, as the second place (the workplace) becomes less relevant to growing numbers of telecommuters, the third place may well grow in social significance.

Research Today

BOX 3-1

Looking at the Gulf Coast Oil Spill from Four Sociological Perspectives

The Gulf Coast oil spill, which began on April 20, 2010, dominated the national news in the United States for much of that year. Like other disasters, the huge spill had social effects that can be analyzed from the four major sociological perspectives.

Functionalist Perspective

In evaluating the effects of the Gulf Coast oil spill, functionalists would stress society's supportive function. For example:

- Functionalists might expect a revitalization of the environmental movement, as happened in the early 1900s after the damming of the Hetch Hetchy Valley just outside Yosemite, and later in the 1990s, after massive wildfires swept through the Everglades.

- Functionalists might note full employment in selected occupations, such as the manufacture of containment booms, even when jobs in other industries were scarce.

- Functionalists would observe that churches and other charities along the Gulf Coast provided both spiritual and material support to households affected by the spill.

- Functionalists would not be surprised that because offshore oil drilling is an integral part of the Gulf Coast economy, the governor of Louisiana strongly opposed a moratorium on deep-sea drilling, despite questions about its safety.

Conflict Perspective

Because conflict theorists see the social order in terms of conflict or tension between competing groups, they would emphasize the coercion and exploitation that underlies relations between the oil companies and Gulf Coast communities:

- The oil industry, conflict theorists would note, is a form of big business, in which profits are more important than workers' health and safety.

- Conflict theorists would emphasize the often-overlooked effect of the spill on minority groups living in inland communities, including Vietnamese Americans, Native American tribal groups, and African Americans. These groups, which were living a marginal existence before the spill, endured particularly significant economic setbacks after the spill.

- Conflict theorists would note that although news outlets tend to focus on oil spills that affect wealthy industrial countries, often the worst spills afflict communities in disadvantaged developing nations, such as Nigeria.

SWIMMING WATER QUALITY STATUS

HEALTH ADVISORY:

THE PUBLIC IS ADVISED NOT TO SWIM IN THESE WATERS DUE TO THE PRESENCE OF OIL-RELATED CHEMICALS

> Feminists would note that during times of economic upheaval and dislocation, women bear a disproportionate share of the burden in their role as caregivers.

Feminist Perspective

Feminists would note that during times of economic upheaval and dislocation, such as the Gulf Coast oil crisis, women bear a disproportionate share of the burden in their role as caregivers:

- As family wage earners leave home to seek work elsewhere, women with children or elderly dependents are left to cope as best they can.

- With time, the physical separation these families experience may turn into marital separation.

Interactionist Perspective

Interactionists would examine the Gulf Coast oil spill on the micro level, by focusing on how it shaped personal relations and day-to-day social behavior:

- Interactionists would note that difficult times often strengthen ties among neighbors and family members.

- At the same time, stressful events can contribute to social breakdowns, including divorce or even suicide—a pattern researchers observed in the aftermath of the *Exxon Valdez* oil spill in 1989.

Despite their differences, functionalists, conflict theorists, feminists, and interactionists would all agree that disasters like the Gulf Coast oil spill are a worthy subject for sociological study.

LET'S DISCUSS

1. Which of the four sociological perspectives seems most useful to you in analyzing the Gulf Coast oil crisis? Why?

2. For many people, the worldwide economic crisis that began in 2008 had disastrous personal consequences. Use the four sociological perspectives to analyze what happened to you, your family, and your community during the Great Recession.

Sources: Capriccioso 2010; Freudenburg and Gramling 2010; Greenemeier 2010; Jopling and Morse 2010; Liptak 2010; Molotch 1970; Samuels 2010; N. Wallace 2010.

Interactionism (also referred to as *symbolic interactionism*) is a sociological framework in which human beings are viewed as living in a world of meaningful objects. Those "objects" may include material things, actions, other people, relationships, and even symbols. Interactionists see symbols as an especially important part of human communication (thus the term *symbolic interactionism*). Symbols have a shared social meaning that is understood by all members of a society. In the United States, for example, a salute symbolizes respect, while a clenched fist signifies defiance. Another culture might use different gestures to convey a feeling of respect or defiance. These types of symbolic interaction are classified as forms of **nonverbal communication,** which can include many other gestures, facial expressions, and postures (Masuda et al. 2008).

Manipulation of symbols can be seen in dress codes. Schools frown on students who wear clothes displaying messages that appear to endorse violence or drug and alcohol consumption. Businesses stipulate the attire employees are allowed to wear on the job in order to impress their customers or clients. In 2005, the National Basketball Association (NBA) adopted a new dress code for the athletes who play professional basketball—one that involved not the uniforms they wear on court, but the clothes they wear off court on league business. The code requires "business casual attire" when players are representing the league. Indoor sunglasses, chains, and sleeveless shirts are specifically banned (Crowe and Herman 2005:A23).

While the functionalist and conflict approaches were initiated in Europe, interactionism developed first in the United States. George Herbert Mead (1863–1931) is widely regarded as the founder of the interactionist perspective. Mead taught at the University of Chicago from 1893 until his death. As his teachings have become better known, sociologists have expressed greater interest in the interactionist perspective. Many have moved away from what may have been an excessive preoccupation with the macro (large-scale) level of social behavior and have redirected their attention toward behavior that occurs on the micro (small-scale) level.

Erving Goffman (1922–1982) popularized a particular type of interactionist method known as the **dramaturgical approach,** in which people are seen as theatrical performers. The dramaturgist compares everyday life to the setting of the theater and stage. Just as actors project certain images, all of us seek to present particular features of our personalities while we hide other features. Thus, in a class, we may feel the need to project a serious image; at a party, we may want to look relaxed and friendly.

The Sociological Approach

Which perspective should a sociologist use in studying human behavior? Functionalist? Conflict? Interactionist? Feminist? We simply cannot squeeze all sociological thinking into three or four theoretical categories—or even ten, if we include several other productive approaches. However, by studying the three major frameworks, we can better grasp how sociologists seek to explore social behavior. Table 3-1 summarizes these three broad approaches to sociological study.

Although no one approach is correct by itself, and sociologists draw on all of them for various purposes, many sociologists tend to favor one particular perspective over others. A sociologist's theoretical orientation influences his or her approach to a research problem in important ways—including the choice of what to study, how to study it, and what questions to pose (or not to pose). Box 3-1 shows how researchers would study the 2010 Gulf Coast oil spill from different sociological perspectives.

Table **3-1**   **Major Sociological Perspectives**

Tracking Sociological Perspectives

	Functionalist	**Conflict**	**Interactionist**
View of Society	Stable, well integrated	Characterized by tension and struggle between groups	Active in influencing and affecting everyday social interaction
Level of Analysis Emphasized	Macro	Macro	Micro, as a way of understanding the larger macro phenomena
Key Concepts	Manifest functions Latent functions Dysfunctions	Inequality Capitalism Stratification	Symbols Nonverbal communication Face-to-face interaction
View of the Individual	People are socialized to perform societal functions	People are shaped by power, coercion, and authority	People manipulate symbols and create their social worlds through interaction
View of the Social Order	Maintained through cooperation and consensus	Maintained through force and coercion	Maintained by shared understanding of everyday behavior
View of Social Change	Predictable, reinforcing	Change takes place all the time and may have positive consequences	Reflected in people's social positions and their communications with others
Example	Public punishments reinforce the social order	Laws reinforce the positions of those in power	People respect laws or disobey them based on their own past experience
Proponents	Émile Durkheim Talcott Parsons Robert Merton	Karl Marx W. E. B. DuBois Ida Wells-Barnett	George Herbert Mead Charles Horton Cooley Erving Goffman

Whatever the purpose of sociologists' work, their research will always be guided by their theoretical viewpoints. For example, sociologist Elijah Anderson (1990) embraces both the interactionist perspective and the groundbreaking work of W. E. B. DuBois. For 14 years Anderson conducted fieldwork in Philadelphia, where he studied the interactions of Black and White residents who lived in adjoining neighborhoods. In particular, he was interested in their public behavior, including their eye contact—or lack of it—as they passed one another on the street. Anderson's research tells us much about the everyday social interactions of Blacks and Whites in the United States, but it does not explain the larger issues behind those interactions. Like theories, research results illuminate one part of the stage, leaving other parts in relative darkness.

MODULE 3 | Recap and Review

Summary

Sociologists make use of four major perspectives, all of which offer unique insights into the same issues.

1. The **functionalist perspective** emphasizes the way in which the parts of a society are structured to maintain its stability.

2. The **conflict perspective** assumes that social behavior is best understood in terms of conflict or tension between competing groups.

3. The **interactionist perspective** is concerned primarily with fundamental or everyday forms of interaction, including symbols and other types of **nonverbal communication**.

4. The **feminist** perspective which is often allied with the conflict perspective, sees inequity in gender as central to all behavior and organization.

Thinking Critically

1. Describe an aspect of contemporary society that you consider to be a dysfunction.

2. Describe a symbol or object that has particular meaning on your campus.

3. Relate the toys on display in your local store to issues of race, class, and gender.

Key Terms

Conflict perspective

Dramaturgical approach

Dysfunction

Feminist perspective

Functionalist perspective

Interactionist perspective

Latent function

Manifest function

Nonverbal communication

MODULE 4 | Taking Sociology with You

You've seen how sociologists employ the major sociological perspectives in their research. How does sociology relate to *you,* your own studies, and your own career? In this section you'll learn about *applied* and *clinical sociology,* two growing fields that allow sociology majors and those with advanced degrees in sociology to apply what they have learned to real-world settings. You'll also see how to develop your sociological imagination, one of the keys to thinking like a sociologist. See the appendix at the end of this chapter for more information on careers in sociology.

Applied and Clinical Sociology

Many early sociologists—notably, Jane Addams, W. E. B. DuBois, and George Herbert Mead—were strong advocates for social reform. They wanted their theories and findings to be relevant to policymakers and to people's lives in general. For instance, Mead was the treasurer of Hull House, where he applied his theory to improving the lives of those who were powerless (especially immigrants). He also served on committees dealing with Chicago's labor problems and public education. Today, **applied sociology** is the use of the discipline of sociology with the specific intent of yielding practical applications for human behavior and organizations. By extension, Michael Burawoy (2005), in his presidential address to the American Sociological Association, endorsed what he called *public sociology,* encouraging scholars to engage a broader audience in bringing about positive outcomes. In effect, the applied sociologist reaches out to others and joins them in their efforts to better society.

Often, the goal of such work is to assist in resolving a social problem. For example, in the past 50 years, eight presidents of the United States have established commissions to delve into major societal concerns facing our nation. Sociologists are often asked to apply their expertise to studying such issues as violence, pornography, crime, immigration, and population. In Europe, both academic and government research departments are offering increasing financial support for applied studies.

One example of applied sociology is the growing interest in learning more about local communities. Since its founding in 1994, the Northeast Florida Center for Community Initiatives (CCI), based at the University of North Florida in Jacksonville, has conducted several community studies, including a homeless census and survey, an analysis of the economic impact of the arts in Jacksonville, and a long-term survey of the effects of

Hurricane Katrina. Typical of applied sociology, these outreach efforts are collaborative, involving faculty, undergraduate and graduate students, volunteers, and community residents (Center for Community Initiatives 2012a).

Another of CCI's applications of sociology, the Magnolia Project, is based in a storefront clinic in an underprivileged area of Jacksonville. Part of the federal Healthy Start initiative, which aims to decrease high infant mortality rates, the project serves women of childbearing age who have little or no regular access to health care. CCI's responsibilities include (1) interviewing

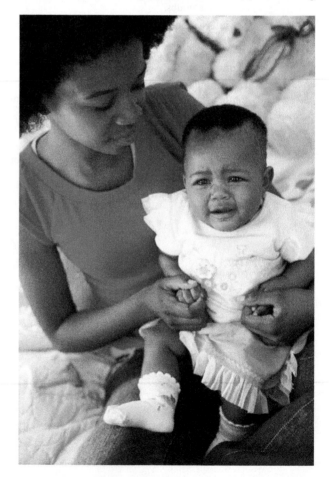

The Center for Community Initiatives' Magnolia Project, an example of applied sociology, aims to decrease high rates of infant mortality.

and surveying key community participants, (2) coordinating data collection by the project's staff, (3) analyzing data, and (4) preparing progress reports for funding agencies and community partners. Through March 2012, not a single infant death had occurred among the 293 participants in the program (Center for Community Initiatives 2012b).

Growing interest in applied sociology has led to such specializations as *medical sociology* and *environmental sociology*. The former includes research on how health care professionals and patients deal with disease. To give one example, medical sociologists have studied the social impact of the AIDS crisis on families, friends, and communities (see Module 53). Environmental sociologists examine the relationship between human societies and the physical environment. One focus of their work is the issue of "environmental justice" (see Module 55), raised when researchers and community activists found that hazardous waste dumps are especially likely to be situated in poor and minority neighborhoods (M. Martin 1996).

The growing popularity of applied sociology has led to the rise of the specialty of clinical sociology. Louis Wirth (1931) wrote about clinical sociology more than 75 years ago, but the term itself has become popular only in recent years. While applied sociology may simply evaluate social issues, **clinical sociology** is dedicated to facilitating change by altering social relationships (as in family therapy) or restructuring social institutions (as in the reorganization of a medical center).

Applied sociologists generally leave it to policymakers to act on their evaluations. In contrast, clinical sociologists take direct responsibility for implementation and view those with whom they work as their clients. This specialty has become increasingly attractive to graduate students in sociology because it offers an opportunity to apply intellectual learning in a practical way. A shrinking job market in the academic world has made such alternative career routes appealing.

Applied and clinical sociology can be contrasted with **basic sociology** (also called *pure sociology*) which seeks a more profound knowledge of the fundamental aspects of social phenomena. This type of research is not necessarily meant to generate specific applications, although such ideas may result once findings are analyzed. When Durkheim studied suicide rates, he was not primarily interested in discovering a way to eliminate suicide. In this sense, his research was an example of basic rather than applied sociology.

Developing a Sociological Imagination

In this book, we will be illustrating the sociological imagination in several different ways—by showing theory in practice and in current research; by thinking globally; by exploring the significance of social inequality; by speaking across race, gender, and religious boundaries; and by highlighting social policy throughout the world.

Theory in Practice

We will illustrate how the major sociological perspectives can be helpful in understanding today's issues, from capital punishment to abortion. Sociologists do not necessarily declare, "Here I am using functionalism," but their research and approaches do tend to draw on one or more theoretical frameworks, as will become clear in the pages to follow.

Research Today

Sociologists actively investigate a variety of issues and social behavior. We have already seen that research can shed light on the social factors that affect suicide rates. Sociological research often plays a direct role in improving people's lives, as in the case of increasing the participation of African Americans in diabetes testing. Throughout the rest of the book, the research performed by sociologists and other social scientists will shed light on group behavior of all types.

Thinking Globally

Whatever their theoretical perspective or research techniques, sociologists recognize that social behavior must be viewed in a global context. **Globalization** is the worldwide integration of government policies, cultures, social movements, and financial markets through trade and the exchange of ideas. Although public discussion of globalization is relatively recent, intellectuals have been pondering both its negative and positive social consequences for a long time. Karl Marx and Friedrich Engels warned in *The Communist Manifesto* (written in 1848) of a world market that would lead to production in distant lands, sweeping away existing working relationships.

Today, developments outside a country are as likely to influence people's lives as changes at home. For example, though much of the world was already in recession by September 2001, the terrorist attacks on New York and Washington, D.C., caused an immediate economic decline, not just in the United States, but throughout the world. One example of the massive global impact was the downturn in international tourism, which lasted for at least two years. The effects have been felt by people far removed from the United States, including African game wardens and Asian taxi drivers. Some observers see globalization and its effects as the natural result of advances in communications technology, particularly the Internet and satellite transmission of the mass media. Others view it more critically, as a process that allows multinational corporations to expand unchecked. We examine the impact of globalization on our daily lives and on societies throughout the world in Box 4-1 and throughout this book (Fiss and Hirsch 2005).

The Significance of Social Inequality

Who holds power? Who doesn't? Who has prestige? Who lacks it? Perhaps the major theme of analysis in sociology today is **social inequality,** a condition in which members of society have differing amounts of wealth, prestige, or power. For example, the disparity between what coffee bean pickers in developing nations are paid and the price you pay for a cup of coffee underscores global inequality (see Box 4-1). Kelsey Timmerman's research among foreign garment workers uncovered some other aspects of global inequality. And the impact of Hurricane Katrina on residents of the Gulf Coast drew attention to social inequality

Today, both the positive and negative aspects of globalization are receiving increased scrutiny from sociologists.

with the children; men were outside working, where they were more likely to become aware of the impending disaster. Moreover, most of the men knew how to swim, a survival skill that women in these traditional societies usually do not learn. As a result, many more men than women survived the catastrophe—about 10 men for every 1 woman. In one Indonesian village typical of the disaster area, 97 of 1,300 people survived; only 4 were women. The impact of this gender imbalance will be felt for some time, given women's primary role as caregivers for children and the elderly (BBC News 2005).

Social Policy throughout the World

One important way we can use a sociological imagination is to enhance our understanding of current social issues throughout the world. Approximately one-third of the modules in this book include a discussion of a contemporary social policy issue. In some cases, we will examine a specific issue facing national governments. For example, government funding of child care centers will be discussed in Module 15, Agents of Socialization; global immigration in Module 33, Race and Ethnicity in the United States; and religion in the schools in Module 46, Religious Organizations. These Social Policy sections will demonstrate how fundamental sociological concepts can enhance our critical thinking skills and help us to better understand current public policy debates taking place around the world.

In addition, sociology has been used to evaluate the success of programs or the impact of changes brought about by policymakers and political activists. For example, Module 28, Poverty and Social Mobility, includes a discussion of research on the effectiveness of welfare programs. Such discussions underscore the many practical applications of sociological theory and research.

Sociologists expect the next quarter of a century to be perhaps the most exciting and critical period in the history of the discipline. That is because of a growing recognition—both in the United States and around the world—that current social problems must be addressed before their magnitude overwhelms human societies. We can expect sociologists to play an increasing role in government by researching and developing public policy alternatives. It seems only natural for this textbook to focus on the connection between the work of sociologists and the difficult questions confronting policymakers and people in the United States and around the world.

in the United States. Predictably, the people who were hit the hardest by the massive storm were the poor, who had the greatest difficulty evacuating before the storm and have had the most difficulty recovering from it.

Some sociologists, in seeking to understand the effects of inequality, have made the case for social justice. W. E. B. DuBois ([1940] 1968:418) noted that the greatest power in the land is not "thought or ethics, but wealth." As we have seen, the contributions of Karl Marx, Jane Addams, and Ida Wells-Barnett also stressed this belief in the overarching significance of social inequality, and by extension, social justice. In this book, social inequality will be the central focus of Chapters 8 and 9, and sociologists' work on inequality will be highlighted throughout.

Speaking across Race, Gender, and Religious Boundaries

Sociologists include both men and women, who come from a variety of ethnic, national, and religious origins. In their work, sociologists seek to draw conclusions that speak to all people—not just the affluent or powerful. Doing so is not always easy. Insights into how a corporation can increase its profits tend to attract more attention and financial support than do, say, the merits of a needle exchange program for low-income inner-city residents. Yet today more than ever, sociology seeks to better understand the experiences of all people.

Sociologists have noted, for example, that the huge tsunami that hit South Asia in 2004 affected men and women differently. When the waves hit, mothers and grandmothers were at home

Sociology in the Global Community

BOX 4-1

Your Morning Cup of Coffee

When you drink a cup of coffee, do you give much thought to where the coffee beans came from, or do you think more about the pleasure you get from the popular beverage? Coffee certainly is popular—as an import, it is second only to petroleum, the most traded commodity in the world.

Although the coffee trade has been globalized, the customs of coffee drinking still vary from place to place. Starbucks, which now has 4,500 locations outside the United States, has over 1,000 locations in Europe. Managers find that in European countries, where the coffeehouse culture originated, 80

> The typical coffee picker works in a developing nation near the equator, receiving for a day's wages an amount that matches the price of a single cup of coffee in North America.

percent of their customers sit down to drink their coffee. In the United States, 80 percent of Starbucks' customers leave the store immediately, taking their coffee with them.

Today, the coffee trade relies on the exploitation of cheap labor. Coffee is a labor-intensive crop: there is little that technology can do to ease the coffee picker's burden. The typical coffee picker works in a developing nation near the equator, receiving for a day's wages an amount that matches the price of a single cup of coffee in North America. In the 1940s, advocacy groups began to promote the sale of certified *fair trade coffee*, which gives a living wage to those who harvest the crop, allowing them to become economically self-sufficient. But as of late 2009, fair trade coffee accounted for only 2.5 percent of the coffee that was bought and sold in the United States. Recently, a similar movement has begun to promote fair trade in the global clothing industry, reported on by Kelsey Timmerman in his book *Where Am I Wearing?*

Ecological activists have drawn attention to what they see as the coffee industry's contribution to the trend toward global warming.

The need to make room for more coffee fields, they charge, has encouraged the destruction of rain forests. The same criticism can be aimed at much of the consumption in industrial nations. Of all the products that emerge from developing nations, however, few have as singular a place in many people's daily ritual as that morning cup of joe. The drink in your hand is your tangible link to rural workers in some of the poorest areas of the world.

LET'S DISCUSS

1. Do you enjoy coffee? Would you willingly pay more for a cup of coffee if you knew that the worker who picked the beans would benefit from the higher price?

2. The coffee trade has been blamed for perpetuating social inequality and global warming. Can you think of any positive effects of the coffee trade? Who benefits most from this economic activity?

Sources: Adamy 2008; Fieser 2009; Jaffee 2007; Luttinger and Dicum 2006; E. Marx 2009; Pendergrast 1999; Ritzer 2011:218–227.

MODULE **4** | Recap and Review

Summary

Studying sociology allows you many ways to exercise your sociological imagination.

1. **Applied** and **clinical sociology** use the discipline of sociology to solve practical problems in human behavior and organizations. In contrast, **basic sociology** is sociological inquiry that seeks only a deeper knowledge of the fundamental aspects of human phenomena.

2. This textbook makes use of the sociological imagination by showing theory in practice and in current research: by thinking globally; by focusing on the significance of **social inequality;** by speaking across racial, gender, and religious boundaries; and by highlighting social policy around the world.

Thinking Critically

1. What issues facing your local community would you like to address with applied sociological research? Do you see any global connections to these issues?

2. In what specific ways does globalization affect your everyday life? Do you think the impact of globalization is primarily positive or negative?

Key Terms

Applied sociology

Basic sociology

Clinical sociology

Globalization

Social inequality

Appendix **Careers in Sociology**

For the past two decades the number of U.S. college students who have graduated with a degree in sociology has risen steadily (Figure A-1). In this appendix we'll consider some of the options these students have after completing their undergraduate education.

How do students first learn about the sociological perspective on society? Some may take a sociology course in high school. Others may study sociology at community college, where 40 percent of all college students in the United States are enrolled. Indeed, many future sociology majors first develop their sociological imaginations at a community college.

An undergraduate degree in sociology doesn't just serve as excellent preparation for future graduate work in sociology. It also provides a strong liberal arts background for entry-level positions in business, social services, foundations, community organizations, not-for-profit groups, law enforcement, and many government jobs. A number of fields—among them marketing, public relations, and broadcasting—now require investigative skills and an understanding of the diverse groups found in today's multiethnic and multinational environment. Moreover, a sociology degree requires accomplishment in oral and written communication, interpersonal skills, problem solving, and critical thinking—all job-related skills that may give sociology graduates an advantage over those who pursue more technical degrees.

Consequently, while few occupations specifically require an undergraduate degree in sociology, such academic training can be an important asset in entering a wide range of occupations. To emphasize this point, a number of chapters in this book highlight a real-life professional who describes how the study of sociology has helped in his or her career. For example, in Module 20 a Taking Sociology to Work box explains how a college graduate uses her training in sociology as a social media manager for nonprofit organizations. And in Module 48, another Taking Sociology to Work box shows how a recent graduate uses the skill set he acquired as a sociology major in his role as a government analyst.

Figure A-2 summarizes the sources of employment for those with BA or BS degrees in sociology. It shows that the areas of nonprofit organizations, education, business, and government offer major career opportunities for sociology graduates. Undergraduates who know where their career interests lie are well advised to enroll in sociology courses and specialties best suited to those interests. For example, students hoping to become health planners would take a class in medical sociology; students seeking employment as social science research assistants

FIGURE A-1 **Sociology Degrees Conferred in the United States by Gender**

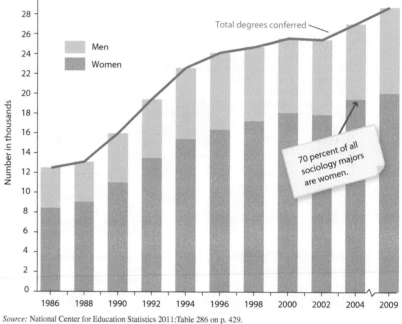

Source: National Center for Education Statistics 2011:Table 286 on p. 429.

would focus on courses in statistics and methods. Internships, such as placements at city planning agencies and survey research organizations, afford another way for sociology students to prepare for careers. Studies show that students who choose an internship placement have less trouble finding jobs, obtain better jobs, and enjoy greater job satisfaction than students without internship placements.

Finally, students should expect to change fields during their first five years of employment after graduation—for example, from sales and marketing to management (American Sociological Association 2009; Salem and Grabarek 1986; Spalter-Roth and Van Vooren 2010).

Many college students view social work as the field most closely associated with sociology. Traditionally, social workers received their undergraduate training in sociology and allied fields such as psychology and counseling. After some practical experience, social workers would generally seek a master's degree in social work (MSW) to be considered for supervisory or administrative positions. Today, however, some students choose (where it is available) to pursue a bachelor's

Did you know that as a student at Princeton University, Michelle Obama majored in sociology? She used that degree as a stepping-stone to Harvard Law School. Read her senior thesis at www.politico.com/news/stories/0208/8642.html.

degree in social work (BSW). This degree prepares graduates for direct service positions, such as caseworker or group worker.

Many students continue their sociological training beyond the bachelor's degree. More than 250 universities in the United States have graduate programs in sociology that offer PhD and/or master's degrees. These programs differ greatly in their areas of specialization, course requirements, costs, and the research and teaching opportunities available to graduate students. About 71 percent of the graduates are women (American Sociological Association 2005, 2010a).

Higher education is an important source of employment for sociologists with graduate degrees. About 83 percent of recent PhD recipients in sociology seek employment in colleges and universities. These sociologists teach not only majors who are committed to the discipline but also students hoping to become doctors, nurses, lawyers, police officers, and so forth (American Sociological Association 2005).

Sociologists who teach in colleges and universities may use their knowledge and training to influence public policy. For example, sociologist Andrew Cherlin (2003) has commented on the debate over proposed federal funding to promote marriage among welfare recipients. Citing the results of two of his studies, Cherlin questioned the potential effectiveness of such a policy in strengthening low-income families. Because many single mothers choose to marry someone other than the father of their children—sometimes for good reason—their children often grow up in stepfamilies. Cherlin's research shows that children who are raised in stepfamilies are no better off than those in single-parent families. He sees government efforts to promote marriage as a politically motivated attempt to foster traditional social values in a society that has become increasingly diverse.

For sociology graduates who are interested in academic careers, the road to a PhD (or doctorate) can be long and difficult. This degree symbolizes competence in original research; each candidate must prepare a book-length study known as a dissertation. Typically, a doctoral student in sociology will engage in four to seven years of intensive work, including the time required to complete the dissertation. Yet even this effort is no guarantee of a job as a sociology professor.

The good news is that over the next 10 years, the demand for instructors is expected to increase because of high rates of retirement among faculty from the baby boom generation, as well as the anticipated slow but steady growth in the college student population in the United States. Nonetheless, anyone who launches an academic career must be prepared for considerable uncertainty and competition in the college job market (American Sociological Association 2009).

Of course, not all people who work as sociologists teach or hold doctoral degrees. Take government, for example. The Census Bureau relies on people with sociological training to interpret data for other government agencies and the general public. Virtually every agency depends on survey research—a field in which sociology students can specialize—in order to assess everything from community needs to the morale of the agency's workers. In addition, people with sociological training can put their academic knowledge to effective use in probation and parole, health sciences, community development, and recreational services. Some people working in government or

FIGURE A-2 **Occupations of Graduating Sociology Majors**

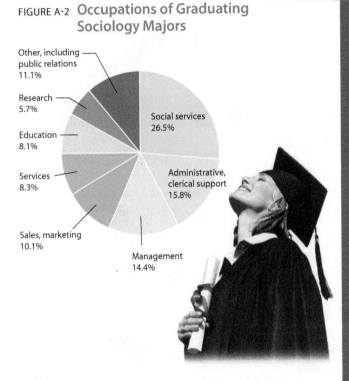

Other, including public relations 11.1%
Research 5.7%
Education 8.1%
Services 8.3%
Sales, marketing 10.1%
Social services 26.5%
Administrative, clerical support 15.8%
Management 14.4%

Note: Based on a national survey conducted in early 2007 of 1,800 sociology majors who graduated in 2005.
Source: Spalter-Roth and Van Vooren 2008a, p. 3.

private industry have a master's degree (MA or MS) in sociology; others have a bachelor's degree (BA or BS).

Currently, about 15 percent of the members of the American Sociological Association use their sociological skills outside the academic world, whether in social service agencies or in marketing positions for business firms. Increasing numbers of sociologists with graduate degrees are employed by businesses, industry, hospitals, and nonprofit organizations. Studies show that many sociology graduates are making career changes from social service areas to business and commerce. For an undergraduate major, sociology is excellent preparation for employment in many parts of the business world (Spalter-Roth and Van Vooren 2008b).

Whether you take a few courses in sociology or complete a degree, you will benefit from the critical thinking skills developed in this discipline. Sociologists emphasize the value of being able to analyze, interpret, and function within a variety of working situations—an asset in virtually any career. Moreover, given rapid technological change and the expanding global economy, all of us will need to adapt to substantial social change, even in our own careers. Sociology provides a rich conceptual framework that can serve as a foundation for flexible career development and assist you in taking advantage of new employment opportunities.

Mastering This Chapter: Understanding Sociology

taking sociology with you

1 Research! Find out who makes the sports apparel sold at your school's bookstore. What can you learn (perhaps from a company website) about where such products are manufactured and what the working conditions are?

2 In what ways have you been affected by the recent spate of home mortgage foreclosures? Has the widespread loss of home ownership made you and others more aware of the problem of homelessness, or has it pushed the issue out of sight?

3 Consider some group or organization that you participate in. Using Robert Merton's concepts, list its manifest and latent functions.

key terms

Anomie The loss of direction felt in a society when social control of individual behavior has become ineffective.

Applied sociology The use of the discipline of sociology with the specific intent of yielding practical applications for human behavior and organizations.

Basic sociology Sociological inquiry conducted with the objective of gaining a more profound knowledge of the fundamental aspects of social phenomena. Also known as *pure sociology*.

Clinical sociology The use of the discipline of sociology with the specific intent of altering social relationships or restructuring social institutions.

Conflict perspective A sociological approach that assumes that social behavior is best understood in terms of tension between groups over power or the allocation of resources, including housing, money, access to services, and political representation.

Cultural capital Noneconomic goods, such as family background and education, which are reflected in a knowledge of language and the arts.

Double consciousness The division of an individual's identity into two or more social realities.

Dramaturgical approach A view of social interaction in which people are seen as theatrical performers.

Dysfunction An element or process of a society that may disrupt the social system or reduce its stability.

Feminist perspective A sociological approach that views inequity in gender as central to all behavior and organization.

Functionalist perspective A sociological approach that emphasizes the way in which the parts of a society are structured to maintain its stability.

Globalization The worldwide integration of government policies, cultures, social movements, and financial markets through trade and the exchange of ideas.

Ideal type A construct or model for evaluating specific cases.

Interactionist perspective A sociological approach that generalizes about everyday forms of social interaction in order to explain society as a whole.

Latent function An unconscious or unintended function that may reflect hidden purposes.

Macrosociology Sociological investigation that concentrates on large-scale phenomena or entire civilizations.

Manifest function An open, stated, and conscious function.

Microsociology Sociological investigation that stresses the study of small groups, often through experimental means.

Natural science The study of the physical features of nature and the ways in which they interact and change.

Nonverbal communication The sending of messages through the use of gestures, facial expressions, and postures.

Science The body of knowledge obtained by methods based on systematic observation.

Social capital The collective benefit of social networks, which are built on reciprocal trust.

Social inequality A condition in which members of society have differing amounts of wealth, prestige, or power.

Social science The study of the social features of humans and the ways in which they interact and change.

Sociological imagination An awareness of the relationship between an individual and the wider society, both today and in the past.

Sociology The scientific study of social behavior and human groups.

Theory In sociology, a set of statements that seeks to explain problems, actions, or behavior.

Verstehen The German word for "understanding" or "insight"; used to stress the need for sociologists to take into account the subjective meanings people attach to their actions.

self-quiz

Read each question carefully and then select the best answer.

1. Sociology is
   a. very narrow in scope.
   b. concerned with what one individual does or does not do.
   c. the systematic study of social behavior and human groups.
   d. an awareness of the relationship between an individual and the wider society.

2. Which of the following thinkers introduced the concept of the sociological imagination?
   a. Émile Durkheim
   b. Max Weber
   c. Karl Marx
   d. C. Wright Mills

3. Émile Durkheim's research on suicide suggested that
   a. people with religious affiliations had a higher suicide rate than those who were unaffiliated.
   b. suicide rates seemed to be higher in times of peace than in times of war and revolution.
   c. civilians were more likely to take their lives than soldiers.
   d. suicide is a solitary act, unrelated to group life.

4. Max Weber taught his students that they should employ which of the following in their intellectual work?
   a. anomie
   b. *verstehen*
   c. the sociological imagination
   d. microsociology

5. Robert Merton's contributions to sociology include
   a. successfully combining theory and research.
   b. producing a theory that is one of the most frequently cited explanations of deviant behavior.
   c. an attempt to bring macro-level and micro-level analyses together.
   d. all of the above

6. Which sociologist made a major contribution to society through his in-depth studies of urban life, including both Blacks and Whites?
   a. W. E. B. DuBois
   b. Robert Merton
   c. Auguste Comte
   d. Charles Horton Cooley

7. In the late 19th century, before the term *feminist perspective* was even coined, the ideas behind this major theoretical approach appeared in the writings of
   a. Karl Marx.
   b. Ida Wells-Barnett.
   c. Charles Horton Cooley.
   d. Pierre Bourdieu.

8. Thinking of society as a living organism in which each part of the organism contributes to its survival is a reflection of which theoretical perspective?
   a. the functionalist perspective
   b. the conflict perspective
   c. the feminist perspective
   d. the interactionist perspective

9. Karl Marx's view of the struggle between social classes inspired the contemporary
   a. functionalist perspective.
   b. conflict perspective.
   c. interactionist perspective.
   d. dramaturgical approach.

10. Erving Goffman's dramaturgical approach, which postulates that people present certain aspects of their personalities while obscuring other aspects, is a derivative of what major theoretical perspective?
    a. the functionalist perspective
    b. the conflict perspective
    c. the feminist perspective
    d. the interactionist perspective

11. While the findings of sociologists may at times seem like common sense, they differ because they rest on _____ analysis of facts.

12. Within sociology, a(n) _____ is a set of statements that seeks to explain problems, actions, or behavior.

13. In _____ _____ 's hierarchy of the sciences, sociology was the "queen," and its practitioners were "scientist-priests."

14. In *Society in America*, originally published in 1837, English scholar _____ _____ examined religion, politics, child rearing, and immigration in the young nation.

15. _____ _____ adapted Charles Darwin's evolutionary view of the "survival of the fittest" by arguing that it is "natural" that some people are rich while others are poor.

16. Sociologist Max Weber coined the term _____ in referring to a construct or model that serves as a measuring rod against which actual cases can be evaluated.

17. In *The Communist Manifesto*, _____ _____ and _____ _____ argued that the masses of people who have no resources other than their labor (the proletariat) should unite to fight for the overthrow of capitalist societies.

18. _____ _____, an early female sociologist, cofounded the famous Chicago settlement house called Hull House and also tried to establish a juvenile court system.

19. The university's role in certifying academic competence and excellence is an example of a(n) _____ function.

20. The _____ _____ draws on the work of Karl Marx and Friedrich Engels in that it often views women's subordination as inherent in capitalist societies.

thinking about movies

We Were Here

In the 1980s, in response to the onset of the AIDS crisis, people came together to ameliorate suffering and strengthen a community.

When the Levees Broke

Spike Lee directs this documentary about the social costs of Hurricane Katrina.

Frozen River

Two working-class women overcome racial prejudice to form an unlikely friendship.

Sociological Research

2

Sociological Research

MODULE 5 — What Is the Scientific Method?

MODULE 6 — Major Research Designs

MODULE 7 — Ethics of Research

MODULE 8 — Development of Methodology

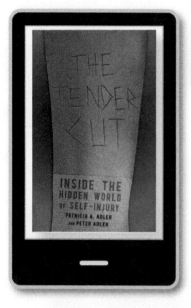

Did you ever wonder how researchers study behaviors that are private and personal?

Sociologists Patricia Adler and Peter Adler went on the Internet to study people who injure themselves. Read on to see what they learned.

❝ Self-injury has existed for nearly all of recorded history. Although it has been defined and regarded in various ways over time, its rise in the 1990s and early 2000s has taken a specific, although contested, form and meaning. We focus in this book on the deliberate, nonsuicidal destruction of one's own body tissue, incorporating practices such as self-cutting, burning, branding, scratching, picking at skin. . . . Our goal here is to discuss the form of this latest incarnation of self-injury, now often regarded as a typical behavior among adolescents, describing and analyzing it through the voices and from the perspective of those who practice it. . . .

Many self-injurers were driven to this behavior by nothing more serious than the minor stresses typically associated with normal adolescence. . . . People cited upsets with their friends, romantic relationships, and family members as having led them to self-injury. Mike was a scruffy-looking college student who always wore a stocking cap. He started cutting and burning himself between the ages of 12 and 14. When he was in high school Mike's girlfriend broke up with him, leaving him devastated. He reflected, "Yeah, I thought every relationship was the end of the world. I kept getting further and further depressed, and I just needed something to where I could vent and rage without having any outward signs so that anybody could tell

Mike was a scruffy-looking college student who always wore a stocking cap. He started cutting and burning himself between the ages of 12 and 14.

anything was wrong." He turned to cutting to assuage his feelings of sadness. . . .

Over the years that we were actively involved in the self-injury cyber world, it took several twists and turns. The earliest of the sites we discovered probably originated during the late 1990s. At that time, most sites were privately owned and unmonitored. Participants often used the term *self-mutilation*, and it was not uncommon to find graphic details and pictures of injuries. Sites had names such as "bleed me," "ruin your life," "bioetchings," "bleeding to ease the pain," "cut it out," and "gallery of pain." Their main purpose, it appeared, was to offer fellowship to self-harmers so they would know they were not alone. . . .

Over the course of our research we also collected tens of thousands (in the range of 30,000–40,000) of Internet messages and emails, including those posted publicly and those written to and by us. In 2006 we enlisted the aid of three student coders to help us sort and analyze the emails and postings from the Internet groups. At this time we were working on one paper, and the students helped us find posts and emails pertinent to our specific focus. We repeated this process again in 2008 with ten more student coders, expanding the project greatly. Each student took one set of emails we had collected from a group, board, or chat room and poured[sic] through the years of postings we had assembled. We divided the students into groups of five and met with each group biweekly. At each session the students submitted notes and memos about the material they had scanned, and we brainstormed for sociological codes, categories, concepts, trends, and patterns. ❞

(P. Adler and P. Adler 2011:1, 43, 44, 54–55) Additional information about this excerpt can be found on the Online Learning Center at www.mhhe.com/schaefermod2e.

---

n this excerpt from Patricia A. Adler and Peter Adler's book *The Tender Cut: Inside the Hidden World of Self-Injury,* the authors describe their extensive research on a little-known behavior and its social underpinnings. The Adlers conducted lengthy, emotionally intense interviews with self-injurers, becoming friends with many. They met others through Internet-based support groups and web postings. "Rather than remaining strictly detached from our subjects, we became involved in their lives, helping them and giving voice to their experiences and beliefs" (2007:542; 2011).

Though many people would like to ignore the phenomenon of self-injury, believing that those who practice it will eventually "grow out of it," the Adlers' research allows us to consider it intelligently and scientifically, within the social context. Self-injurers,

the Adlers found, are a diverse group, whose behavior is carefully planned and considered. Surprisingly, members often begin to injure themselves in the company of others. They have recently begun to coalesce as a subculture (2007:559–560).

This chapter will examine the research process used in conducting sociological studies. How do sociologists go about setting up a research project? How do they ensure that the results of the research are reliable and accurate? Can they carry out their research without violating the rights of those they study?

We will look first at the steps that make up the scientific method. Then we will look at various techniques used in sociological research, such as experiments, observations, and surveys. We will pay particular attention to the ethical challenges sociologists face in studying human behavior, and to the debate raised by Max

Weber's call for "value neutrality" in research. We will also examine feminist methodology and the role technology plays in research today. The Social Policy section that closes this chapter describes the difficulties and challenges of researching closely guarded sexual behaviors.

Whatever the area of sociological inquiry and whatever the perspective of the sociologist—whether functionalist, conflict, feminist, interactionist, or any other—there is one crucial requirement: imaginative, responsible research that meets the highest scientific and ethical standards.

Like all of us, sociologists are interested in the central questions of our time: Is the family falling apart? Why is there so much crime in the United States? Can the world feed a growing population? Such issues concern most people, whether or not they have academic training. However, unlike the typical citizen, the sociologist has a commitment to use the **scientific method** in studying society. The scientific method is a systematic, organized series of steps that ensures maximum objectivity and consistency in researching a problem.

Many of us will never actually conduct scientific research. Why, then, is it important that we understand the scientific method? The answer is that it plays a major role in the workings of our society. Residents of the United States are constantly bombarded with "facts" or "data." A television news report informs us that "one in every two marriages in this country now ends in divorce," yet Module 41 will show that this assertion is based on misleading statistics. Almost daily, advertisers cite supposedly scientific studies to prove that their products are superior. Such claims may be accurate or exaggerated. We can better evaluate such information—and will not be fooled so easily—if we are familiar with the standards of scientific research.

These standards are quite stringent, and they demand as strict adherence as possible. The scientific method requires precise preparation in developing research. Otherwise, the research data collected may not prove accurate. Sociologists and other researchers follow five basic steps in the scientific method: (1) defining the problem, (2) reviewing the literature, (3) formulating the hypothesis, (4) selecting the research design and then collecting and analyzing data, and (5) developing the conclusion (Figure 5-1). We'll use an actual example to illustrate the scientific method.

Defining the Problem

Does it "pay" to go to college? Some people make great sacrifices and work hard to get a college education. Parents borrow money for their children's tuition. Students work part-time jobs or even take full-time positions while attending evening or weekend classes. Does it pay off? Are there monetary returns for getting that degree?

The first step in any research project is to state as clearly as possible what you hope to investigate—that is, *define the problem.* In this instance, we are interested in knowing how schooling relates to income. We want to find out the earnings of people with different levels of formal schooling.

FIGURE 5-1 **The Scientific Method**

The scientific method allows sociologists to objectively and logically evaluate the data they collect. Their findings can suggest ideas for further sociological research.

Early on, any social science researcher must develop an operational definition of each concept being studied. An **operational definition** is an explanation of an abstract concept that is specific enough to allow a researcher to assess the concept. For example, a sociologist interested in status might use membership in exclusive social clubs as an operational definition of status. Someone studying prejudice might consider a person's unwillingness to hire or work with members of minority groups as an operational definition of prejudice. In our example, we need to develop two operational definitions—education and earnings—in order to study whether it pays to get an advanced educational degree. We'll define *education* as the number of years of schooling a person has achieved and *earnings* as the income a person reports having received in the past year.

Initially, we will take a functionalist perspective (although we may end up incorporating other perspectives). We will argue that opportunities for more earning power are related to level of schooling, and that schools prepare students for employment.

Reviewing the Literature

By conducting a *review of the literature*—relevant scholarly studies and information—researchers refine the problem under study, clarify possible techniques to be used in collecting data, and eliminate or reduce avoidable mistakes. In our example, we would examine information about the salaries for different occupations. We would see if jobs that require more academic training are better rewarded. It would also be appropriate to review other studies on the relationship between education and income.

The review of the literature would soon tell us that many factors besides years of schooling influence earning potential. For example, we would learn that the children of rich parents are more likely to go to college than those of poor parents, so we might consider the possibility that rich parents may later help their children to secure better-paying jobs.

We might also look at macro-level data, such as state-by-state comparisons of income and educational levels. In one macrolevel study based on census data, researchers found that in states whose residents have a relatively high level of education, household income levels are high as well (Figure 5-2). This finding suggests that schooling may well be related to income, though it does not speak to the micro-level relationship we are interested in. That is, we want to know whether *individuals* who are well educated are also well paid.

Formulating the Hypothesis

After reviewing earlier research and drawing on the contributions of sociological theorists, the researchers may then *formulate the hypothesis.* A **hypothesis** is a speculative statement about the relationship between two or more factors known as variables. Income, religion, occupation, and gender can all serve as variables in a study. We can define a **variable** as a measurable trait or characteristic that is subject to change under different conditions.

Researchers who formulate a hypothesis generally must suggest how one aspect of human behavior influences or affects another. The variable hypothesized to cause or influence another is called the **independent variable.** The other variable is termed the **dependent variable** because its action *depends* on the influence of the independent variable. In other words, the researcher believes that the independent variable predicts or causes change in the dependent variable. For example, a researcher in sociology might anticipate that the availability of affordable housing (the independent variable, *x*) affects the level of homelessness in a community (the dependent variable, *y*).

Our hypothesis is that the higher one's educational degree, the more money one will earn. The independent variable that is to be measured is the level of education. The variable that is thought to depend on it—income—must also be measured.

Identifying independent and dependent variables is a critical step in clarifying cause-and-effect relationships. As shown in Figure 5-3, **causal logic** involves the relationship between a condition or variable and a particular consequence, with one leading to the other. For instance, being less integrated into society may be directly related to, or produce a greater likelihood of, suicide.

It seems reasonable that these graduates of Fort Bethold Community College on the Fort Bethold Reservation, North Dakota, will earn more income than high school graduates. How would you go about testing that hypothesis?

Similarly, the time students spend reviewing material for a quiz may be directly related to, or produce a greater likelihood of, getting a high score on the quiz.

A **correlation** exists when a change in one variable coincides with a change in the other. Correlations are an indication that causality *may* be present; they do not necessarily indicate causation. For example, data indicate that people who prefer to watch televised news programs are less knowledgeable than those who read newspapers and newsmagazines. This correlation between people's relative knowledge and their choice of news media seems to make sense, because it agrees with the common belief that television dumbs down information. But the correlation between the two variables is actually caused by a third variable, people's relative ability to comprehend large amounts of information. People with poor reading skills are much more likely than others to get their news from television, while those who are more educated or skilled turn more often to the print media. Though television viewing is *correlated* with lower news comprehension, then, it does not *cause* it. Sociologists seek to identify the *causal* link between variables; the suspected causal link is generally described in the hypothesis (Neuman 2009).

Collecting and Analyzing Data

How do you test a hypothesis to determine if it is supported or refuted? You need to collect information, using one of the research designs described later in the chapter. The research design guides the researcher in collecting and analyzing data.

Selecting the Sample

In most studies, social scientists must carefully select what is known as a sample. A **sample** is a selection from a larger population that is statistically representative of that population. There are many kinds of samples, but the one social scientists

MAPPING LIFE NATIONWIDE

FIGURE 5-2 Educational Level and Household Income In the United States

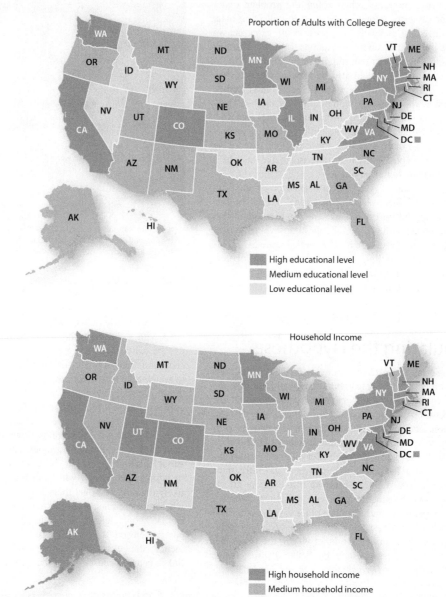

Notes: Cutoffs for high/medium and medium/low educational levels in 2009 were 29.7 percent and 24.5 percent of the population with a college degree, respectively; median for the entire nation was 27.9 percent. Cutoffs for high/medium and medium/low household income levels in 2010 were $53,900 and $43,000, respectively; national median household income was $50,046 in 2010.
Source: 2010 American Community Survey in Bureau of the Census 2011b:Table S1903; 2011a:Table 233.

use most frequently is the random sample. In a **random sample,** every member of an entire population being studied has the same chance of being selected. Thus, if researchers want to examine the opinions of people listed in a city directory (a book that, unlike the telephone directory, lists all households), they might use a computer to randomly select names from the directory.

The results would constitute a random sample. The advantage of using specialized sampling techniques is that sociologists do not need to question everyone in a population (Igo 2007).

In some cases, the subjects researchers want to study are hard to identify, either because their activities are clandestine or because lists of such people are not readily available. How do

FIGURE 5-3 Causal Logic

Independent variable	Dependent variable
x	y
Level of educational degree	Level of income
Degree of lack of integration into society	Likelihood of suicide
Availability of affordable housing	Level of homelessness
Parents' church attendance	Children's church attendance
Time spent preparing for quiz	Performance on quiz
Parents' income	Likelihood of children's enrolling in college

Think about It

Identify two or three dependent variables that might be influenced by this independent variable: number of alcoholic drinks ingested.

researchers create a sample of illegal drug users, for instance, or of women whose husbands are at least 10 years younger than they are? In such cases, researchers employ what are called *snowball* or *convenience samples*—that is, they recruit participants through word of mouth or by posting notices on the Internet. With the help of special statistical techniques, researchers can draw conclusions from such nonrandom samples.

It is all too easy to confuse the careful scientific techniques used in representative sampling with the many *nonscientific* polls that receive much more media attention. For example, website viewers are often encouraged to register their views on headline news or political contests. Such polls reflect nothing more than the views of those who happened to visit the website and took the

time, perhaps at some cost, to register their opinions. These data do not necessarily reflect (and indeed may distort) the views of the broader population. Not everyone has access to a computer on a regular basis, or the means and/or inclination to register their opinions. Even when these techniques include answers from tens of thousands of people, they will be far less accurate than a carefully selected representative sample of 1,500 respondents.

For the purposes of our research example, we will use information collected in the Current Population Survey conducted by the Bureau of the Census. Each year, the Census Bureau surveys approximately 77,000 households across the United States. Technicians at the bureau then use the data to estimate the nation's entire population.

Ensuring Validity and Reliability

The scientific method requires that research results be both valid and reliable. **Validity** refers to the degree to which a measure or scale truly reflects the phenomenon under study. A valid measure of income depends on the gathering of accurate data. Various studies show that people are reasonably accurate in reporting how much money they earned in the most recent year. If a question is written unclearly, however, the resulting data might not be accurate. For example, respondents to an unclear question about income might report their parents' or spouse's income instead of their own.

Reliability refers to the extent to which a measure produces consistent results. Some people may not disclose accurate information, but most do. In the Current Population Survey, some people refuse to give their income, or even to participate. Periodically, the Census Bureau follows up with a personal visit to nonrespondents, to ensure that their data do not differ significantly from data obtained from those who do cooperate (Bureau of the Census 2004b).

● Developing the Conclusion

Scientific studies, including those conducted by sociologists, do not aim to answer all the questions that can be raised about a particular subject. Therefore, the conclusion of a research study represents both an end and a beginning. Although it terminates a specific phase of the investigation, it should also generate ideas for future study.

Supporting Hypotheses

In our example, we find that the data support our hypothesis: people with more formal schooling *do* earn more money than others. Those with a high school diploma earn more than those who failed to complete high school, but those with an associate's degree earn more than high school graduates. The relationship continues through more advanced levels of schooling, so that those with graduate degrees earn the most.

The relationship is not perfect, however. Some people who drop out of high school end up with high incomes, and some with advanced degrees earn modest incomes, as shown in Figure 5-4. A successful entrepreneur, for example, might not have much formal schooling, while the holder of a doctorate may choose to work for a low-paying nonprofit institution. Sociologists are interested in both the general pattern that emerges from their data and exceptions to the pattern.

Sociological studies do not always generate data that support the original hypothesis. Many times, a hypothesis is refuted, and researchers must reformulate their conclusions. Unexpected results may also lead sociologists to reexamine their methodology and make changes in the research design.

Controlling for Other Factors

A **control variable** is a factor that is held constant to test the relative impact of an independent variable. For example, if researchers wanted to know how adults in the United States feel about restrictions on smoking in public places, they would probably attempt to use a respondent's smoking behavior as a control variable. That is, how do smokers versus nonsmokers feel about smoking in public places? The researchers would compile separate statistics on how smokers and nonsmokers feel about antismoking regulations.

Our study of the influence of education on income suggests that not everyone enjoys equal educational opportunities, a disparity that is one of the causes of social inequality. Since education affects a person's income, we may wish to call on the conflict perspective to explore this topic further. What impact does a person's race or gender have? Is a woman with a college degree likely to earn as much as a man with similar schooling? Later in this textbook we will consider these other factors and variables.

FIGURE 5-4 **Impact of a College Education on Income**

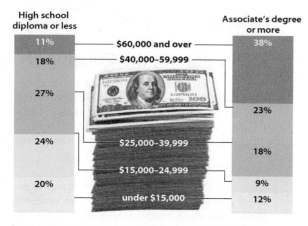

Source: Author's analysis of DeNavas-Walt et al. 2011, Detailed Table PINC-03. Forty-four percent of people with a high school diploma or less (left) earn under $25,000 a year, while only 29 percent earn $40,000 or more. In contrast, only 21 percent of those with an associate's degree or higher (right) earn less than $25,000, while 61 percent earn $40,000 or more.

Think about It

What kinds of knowledge and skills do people with an associate's degree or higher possess, compared to those with a high school education or less? Why would employers value those kinds of knowledge and skills?

trend|spotting

Overcounting and Undercounting in the U.S. Census

Every 10 years, as required by the Constitution, the U.S. government conducts a census to determine how many congressional representatives each state is allowed. Besides determining the states' political power, these data are used for a myriad of other purposes, from distributing federal aid to education to researching the market for breakfast cereal.

Despite concerns about government intrusion into people's private lives, U.S. citizens are relatively compliant with the head count. About three-quarters of households fill out and return the form or answer face-to-face questions from a census worker. Other industrial countries have much less success than the United States. Because of strong concerns about privacy, for example, the Netherlands has not had a door-to-door census since 1971.

With detailed knowledge of three out of every four households in the United States, census workers can use statistical techniques to estimate data for the other quarter. Still, officials have long recognized that the count is more likely to miss certain groups of people than others. This tendency, called *undercounting,* applies especially to low-income people, non-English speakers, and the homeless. Those who have good reason to avoid census workers, such as illegal immigrants and families who crowd together in inadequate housing, also swell the ranks of the undercounted.

Recently, however, concern has been growing about *overcounting,* or the tendency to count some people twice. College students who live at school rather than at home with their parents, "snowbirds" (retirees who move to warmer climes during the winter), active military personnel, and children whose parents share their custody all are likely to be overcounted.

Census officials estimate that the 2000 Census overcounted the nation's population by 11.6 million people. To correct the problem, the Bureau sought to identify people who had been listed twice, and by 2010 had reduced the overcount to just 36,000. In the 2010 Census, the undercount—that is, people who were not counted—was about 16 million, similar to the proportion of the population that was missed in 2000. Blacks, Hispanics, young children, and renters were more likely than others to be overlooked. Given the importance of accuracy in the nation's population count, officials will continue to address these issues in the 2020 Census.

That is, we will examine the impact that education has on income while controlling for variables such as gender and race.

In Summary: The Scientific Method

Let us briefly summarize the process of the scientific method through a review of the example. We *defined a problem* (the question of whether it pays to get a higher educational degree). We *reviewed the literature* (other studies of the relationship between education and income) and *formulated a hypothesis* (the higher one's educational degree, the more money one will earn). We *collected and analyzed the data,* making sure the sample was representative and the data were valid and reliable. Finally, we *developed the conclusion:* the data do support our hypothesis about the influence of education on income.

MODULE 5 | Recap and Review

Summary

Sociologists are committed to the use of the **scientific method** in their research efforts. In this module we examine the basic principles of the scientific method.

1. There are five basic steps in the scientific method: define the problem, review the literature, formulate a hypothesis, collect and analyze data, and develop the conclusion.

2. Whenever researchers wish to study abstract concepts, such as intelligence or prejudice, they must develop workable **operational definitions.**

3. A **hypothesis** states a possible relationship between two or more **variables.**

4. By using a **sample**, sociologists avoid having to test everyone in a population.

5. According to the scientific method, research results must possess both **validity** and **reliability.**

Thinking Critically

1. What might be the effects of a college education on society as a whole? Think of some potential effects on the family, government, and the economy.

2. Suppose that two researchers used different operational definitions for the same term. Could both researchers' results be reliable and valid? Explain your answer.

Key Terms

Causal logic

Control variable

Correlation

Dependent variable

Hypothesis

Independent variable

Operational definition

Random sample

Reliability

Sample

Scientific method

Validity

Variable

MODULE 6   Major Research Designs

An important aspect of sociological research is deciding *how* to collect the data. A **research design** is a detailed plan or method for obtaining data scientifically. Selection of a research design is often based on the theories and hypotheses the researcher starts with (Merton 1948). The choice requires creativity and ingenuity, because it directly influences both the cost of the project and the amount of time needed to collect the data. Research designs that sociologists regularly use to generate data include surveys, ethnography, experiments, and existing sources.

Surveys

Almost all of us have responded to surveys of one kind or another. We may have been asked what kind of detergent we use, which presidential candidate we intend to vote for, or what our favorite television program is. A **survey** is a study, generally in the form of an interview or questionnaire, that provides researchers with information about how people think and act. As anyone who watches the news during presidential campaigns knows, surveys have become a staple of political life.

When you think of surveys, you may recall seeing online polls that offer instant results. Although such polls can be highly interesting, they reflect only the opinions of those who visit the website and choose to respond online. As we have seen, a survey must be based on precise, representative sampling if it is to genuinely reflect a broad range of the population. Box 6-1 describes the challenges of conducting a public opinion survey over the telephone.

In preparing to conduct a survey, sociologists must not only develop representative samples; they must also exercise great care in the wording of questions. An effective survey question must be simple and clear enough for people to understand. It must also be specific enough so that there are no problems in interpreting the results. Open-ended questions ("What do you think of the programming on educational television?") must be carefully phrased to solicit the type of information desired. Surveys can be indispensable sources of information, but only if the sampling is done properly and the questions are worded accurately and without bias.

In wording questions, researchers must also pay careful attention to changes in society. In December 2010, officials at the Bureau of Labor Statistics recognized the effects of an extended recession by changing a decades-old practice. In the past, multiple-choice questions about how long a respondent had been unemployed had ended with a maximum of "99 weeks or over." By the end of 2010, joblessness had become so chronic that the bureau increased the number of choices, ending with "290 weeks or longer."

Think about It

What would constitute a less biased question for a survey on smoking?

Doonesbury

BY GARRY TRUDEAU

Research Today

BOX 6-1

Surveying Cell Phone Users

"Can you hear me now?" This question, familiar to cell phone callers everywhere, could be used to characterize a debate among researchers in sociology. Until recently, calling people on the telephone was a common way for survey takers to reach a broad range of people. Though not everyone owns a telephone—particularly not low-income people—researchers managed to account for that relatively small portion of the population in other ways.

However, the fact that many people now have a cell phone but no landline presents a serious methodological problem to scholars who depend on surveys and public opinion polling. As of 2012, 32 percent of households in the United States could be reached only by cell phone, and the proportion was rising. Among those under 30, the abandonment of landlines was nearly three times as common. These cell phone subscribers are more likely than others to be male and to earn a modest income.

Scholars are reluctant to rely only on landline-based surveys. They are concerned about the potential for misleading results, such as underestimates of the prevalence of health problems. For example, 38 percent of cell phone–only households have a binge drinker, compared to only 17 percent of landline households. And 28 percent of cell phone–only households do not have health insurance, compared to 14 percent of landline households.

> As of 2012, 32 percent of households in the United States could be reached only by cell phone, and the proportion was rising.

Unfortunately, surveying cell phone users has its own problems. In general, cell phone users are more likely than landline users to screen incoming calls or ignore them. And studies show that because cell phone users often take calls while they are involved in other activities, they are much more likely to break off a call midsurvey than someone who is speaking on a landline. Thus, it takes an average of nine calls to a working cell phone number to complete one survey, compared to five calls to a working landline number. Furthermore, federal law requires that calls to cell phones be hand-dialed; the use of automatic dialers, a standard tool of survey firms, is illegal. Survey takers have also found that calling cell phone numbers means they will reach a higher proportion of nonadults than when calling landline numbers. Finally, there are some ethical issues involved in randomly dialing cell phone users, who may be driving a motor vehicle or operating dangerous machinery when they answer.

Researchers are taking steps to stay abreast of technological change. For example, they are making allowances for people who communicate without any kind of telephone, using their personal computers and the Internet. And by drawing on historical data that suggest what kinds of people tend to adopt other wireless technologies, researchers are projecting which people are likely to abandon their landlines in the near future.

LET'S DISCUSS

1. Are you a cell phone–only user? If so, do you generally accept calls from unknown numbers? Aside from underestimating certain health problems and distorting the degree of support for certain politicians, what other problems might result from excluding cell phone–only users from survey research?

2. Apply what you have just learned to the task of surveying Internet users. Which of the problems that arise during telephone surveys might also arise during Internet surveys? Might Internet surveys involve some unique problems?

Sources: Blumberg and Luke 2007; David Brown 2009; Goldman 2012; Harrisinteractive 2008; Keeter and Kennedy 2006; Lavrakas et al. 2007.

There are two main forms of the survey: the **interview,** in which a researcher obtains information through face-to-face, telephone, or online questioning, and the **questionnaire,** in which the researcher uses a printed or written form to obtain information from a respondent. Each of these has its own advantages. An interviewer can obtain a higher response rate, because people find it more difficult to turn down a personal request for an interview than to throw away a written questionnaire. In addition, a skillful interviewer can go beyond written questions and probe for a subject's underlying feelings and reasons. On the other hand, questionnaires have the advantage of being cheaper, especially in large samples.

Why do people have sex? A straightforward question, but until recently it was rarely investigated scientifically, despite its significance to public health, marital counseling, and criminology. In a study published in 2007, researchers interviewed nearly 2,000 undergraduates at the University of Texas at Austin.

To develop the question for the interview, they first asked a random sample of 400 students to list all the reasons why they had ever had sex. The explanations were highly diverse, ranging from "I was drunk" to "I wanted to feel closer to God." The team then asked another sample of 1,500 students to rate the importance of each of the 287 reasons given by the first group. Table 6-1 ranks the results. Nearly every reason was rated most important by at least some respondents. Though there were some gender differences in the replies, there was significant consensus between men and women on the top 10 reasons (Meston and Buss 2007).

Table **6-1**   Top Reasons Why Men and Women Had Sex

Reason	Men	Women
I was attracted to the person	1	1
It feels good	2	3
I wanted to experience the physical pleasure	3	2
It's fun	4	8
I wanted to show my affection to the person	5	4
I was sexually aroused and wanted the release	6	6
I was "horny"	7	7
I wanted to express my love for the person	8	5
I wanted to achieve an orgasm	9	14
I wanted to please my partner	10	11
I realized I was in love	17	9
I was "in the heat of the moment"	13	10

Source: Meston and Buss 2007:506.

Studies have shown that the characteristics of the interviewer have an impact on survey data. For example, female interviewers tend to receive more feminist responses from female subjects than do male interviewers, and Black interviewers tend to receive more detailed responses about race-related issues from Black subjects than do White interviewers. The possible impact of gender and race indicates again how much care social research requires (D. W. Davis and Silver 2003).

The survey is an example of **quantitative research,** which collects and reports data primarily in numerical form. Most of the survey research discussed so far in this book has been quantitative. While this type of research can make use of large samples, it can't offer great depth and detail on a topic. That is why researchers also make use of **qualitative research,** which relies on what is seen in field and naturalistic settings, and often focuses on small groups and communities rather than on large groups or whole nations. The most common form of qualitative research is ethnography, or observation, which we consider next. Throughout this book you will find examples of both quantitative and qualitative research, since both are used widely. Some sociologists prefer one type of research to the other, but we learn most when we draw on many different research designs and do not limit ourselves to a particular type of research.

Ethnography

Investigators often collect information or test hypotheses through firsthand studies. **Ethnography** is the study of an entire social setting through extended systematic fieldwork. **Observation,** or direct participation in closely watching a group or organization, is the basic technique of ethnography. However, ethnographic research also includes the collection of historical information and the conduct of in-person interviews. Although ethnography may seem a relatively informal method compared to surveys or experiments, ethnographic researchers are careful to take detailed notes while observing their subjects.

Carnegie Mellon University's Data Truck lets researchers go where their subjects are—from nightclubs to marathon races. Equipped with the latest technology, the truck allows social scientists to enter the responses to their community surveys into their databases on site. It also gives them access to online social networks in the area, and even lets them videotape street activity.

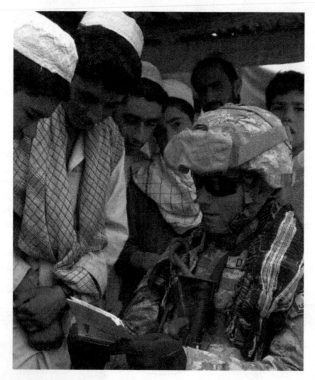

Sergeant Britt Damon, a social scientist on the U.S. Army Human Terrain Team, chats with Afghani children during a search operation. The participation of social scientists in the Army program, which some see as a violation of scholarly detachment, has proved controversial.

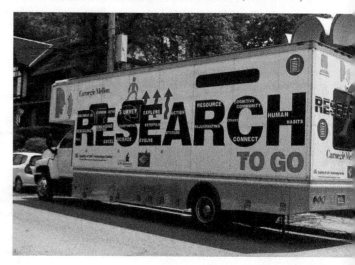

Research Today

BOX 6-2

Gender Messages in Scouting

Nearly 5 million children in the United States participate in scouting. What gender messages do these young people receive during their time as Scouts?

A key form of guidance not just for Scouts but for their leaders is the Scout's handbook. Sociologist Kathleen Denny did a content analysis of the Boy Scouts' *Webelos Handbook* and the *Junior Girl Scout Handbook*. Focusing specifically on material for Scouts in the fourth and fifth grades, she found that both handbooks delivered traditional gender messages. Girl Scout activities were more likely than Boy Scout activities to be communal or other-oriented; Boy Scout activities were more likely to be solo undertakings.

Denny found that the names of merit badges also conveyed traditional gender messages. Girl Scout badge names often include

> The most gender-specific aspect of the Girl Scout handbook is the subjects of the badges themselves. Many refer to stereotypically feminine activities.

puns or other forms of word play; Boy Scout badges do not. For example, the Boy Scout badge for studying rocks and geology is called simply the Geologist badge; the comparable Girl Scout badge is called the Rocks Rock badge. Boy Scout badges more often have career-oriented names—Engineer, Craftsman, Scientist; Girl Scout badge names have less of a career orientation—Sky Search instead of Astronomer, Car Care instead of Mechanic.

The most gender-specific aspect of the Girl Scout handbook is the subjects of the badges themselves. Many refer to stereotypically feminine activities: Caring for Children, Looking Your Best, Sew Simple. Besides personal hygiene and healthy eating, the Looking Your Best badge includes an "Accessory Party," which

requires Scouts to "experiment to see how accessories highlight your features and your outfit." Needless to say, such badges are not offered in the Boy Scouts. The most nearly comparable one in the Boy Scout handbook is the Fitness badge, which includes activities such as keeping a food diary and warning a relative about the dangers of drugs and alcohol.

Denny acknowledges that Scout handbooks are not the only influence on gender roles in scouting. How are gender messages communicated in person during troop or pack meetings and ceremonies, for example? How do parents reinforce or mediate the gender themes in scouting? And how do children adjust to, accept, or rebel against the gender messages they receive as Scouts? Denny's research suggests the need for further research on gender socialization in the Boy Scouts and Girl Scouts.

LET'S DISCUSS

1. Did you participate in scouting as a child? If so, were you aware of the gender messages you were receiving as part of the scouting experience? How did you react?

2. If you were a Scout leader yourself, what kind of gender model would you attempt to be? How would you become that kind of model?

Merit badges for boys (left) and girls (right)

Sources: Boy Scouts of America 2010; K. Denny 2011; Girl Scouts of the USA 2001:39; World Association of Girl Guides and Girl Scouts 2011.

In some cases, the sociologist actually joins a group for a period, to get an accurate sense of how it operates. This approach is called *participant observation*. In Barbara Ehrenreich's widely read book *Nickel and Dimed: On (Not) Getting By in America*, the author was a participant observer. Disguising herself as a divorced, middle-aged housewife without a college degree, Ehrenreich set out to see what life was like for low-wage workers. Her book chronicles her own and others' experiences trying to make ends meet on a minimum wage (Ehrenreich 2001).

During the late 1930s, in a classic example of participant-observation research, William F. Whyte moved into a low-income Italian neighborhood in Boston. For nearly four years he was a member of the social circle of "corner boys" that he describes in *Street Corner Society*. Whyte revealed his identity to these men and joined in their conversations, bowling, and other leisure-time activities. His goal was to gain greater insight into the community that these men had established. As Whyte (1981:303) listened to Doc, the leader of the group, he "learned the answers

to questions I would not even have had the sense to ask if I had been getting my information solely on an interviewing basis." Whyte's work was especially valuable, since at the time the academic world had little direct knowledge of the poor, and tended to rely for information on the records of social service agencies, hospitals, and courts (P. Adler et al. 1992).

The initial challenge that Whyte faced—and that every participant observer encounters—was to gain acceptance into an unfamiliar group. It is no simple matter for a college-trained sociologist to win the trust of a religious cult, a youth gang, a poor Appalachian community, or a circle of skid row residents. It requires a great deal of patience and an accepting, nonthreatening type of personality on the part of the observer.

Ethnographic research poses other complex challenges for the investigator. Sociologists must be able to fully understand what they are observing. In a sense, then, researchers must learn to see the world as the group sees it in order to fully comprehend the events taking place around them. This raises a delicate issue. If the research is to be successful, the observer cannot allow the close associations or even friendships that inevitably develop to influence the subjects' behavior or the conclusions of the study. Even while working hard to gain acceptance from the group being studied, the participant observer *must* maintain some degree of detachment.

Recently, the issue of detachment became a controversial one for social scientists embedded with the U.S. military in Afghanistan and Iraq. Among other studies, the academicians participated in the creation of the Army's Human Terrain System, a $4 million effort to identify the customs, kinship structures, and internal social conflicts in the two countries. The intention was to provide military leaders with information that would help them to make better decisions. Although the idea of scholars cooperating in any way with soldiers struck many people as inappropriate, others countered that the information they developed would help the military to avoid needless violence and might even facilitate the withdrawal of troops from the region (Glenn 2007; Human Terrain System 2011).

Experiments

When sociologists want to study a possible cause-and-effect relationship, they may conduct experiments. An **experiment** is an artificially created situation that allows a researcher to manipulate variables.

In the classic method of conducting an experiment, two groups of people are selected and matched for similar characteristics, such as age or education. The researchers then assign the subjects to one of two groups: the experimental or the control group. The **experimental group** is exposed to an independent variable; the **control group** is not. Thus, if scientists were testing a new type of antibiotic, they would administer the drug to an experimental group but not to a control group.

In some experiments, just as in observation research, the presence of a social scientist or other observer may affect the behavior of the people being studied. Sociologists have used the term **Hawthorne effect** to refer to the unintended influence that observers of experiments can have on their subjects. The term originated as the result of an experiment conducted at the Hawthorne plant of the Western Electric Company during the 1920s and 1930s. Researchers found that *every* change they made in working conditions—even reduced lighting—seemed to have a positive effect on workers' productivity. They concluded that workers had made a special effort to impress their observers. Though the carefully constructed study did identify some causes for changes in the workers' behavior that did not have to do with their being observed, the term *Hawthorne effect* has become synonymous with a placebo or guinea pig effect (Franke and Kaul 1978).

Use of Existing Sources

Sociologists do not necessarily need to collect new data in order to conduct research and test hypotheses. The term **secondary analysis** refers to a variety of research techniques that make use of previously collected and publicly accessible information and data. Generally, in conducting secondary analysis, researchers use data

in ways that were unintended by the initial collectors of information. For example, census data are compiled for specific uses by the federal government but are also valuable to marketing specialists in locating everything from bicycle stores to nursing homes. Box 6-2 describes a content study of gender differences in the way Boy Scouts and Girl Scouts earn merit badges.

Sociologists consider secondary analysis to be *nonreactive*—that is, it does not influence people's behavior. For example, Émile Durkheim's statistical analysis of suicide neither increased nor decreased human self-destruction. Researchers, then, can avoid the Hawthorne effect by using secondary analysis.

There is one inherent problem, however: the researcher who relies on data collected by someone else may not find exactly what is needed. Social scientists who are studying family violence can use statistics from police and social service agencies on *reported* cases of spouse abuse and child abuse, but how many cases are not reported? Government bodies have no precise data on *all* cases of abuse.

Many social scientists find it useful to study cultural, economic, and political documents, including newspapers, periodicals, radio and television tapes, the Internet, scripts, diaries, songs, folklore, and legal papers (Table 6-2). In examining these sources, researchers employ a technique known as **content analysis,** which is the systematic coding and objective recording of data, guided by some rationale.

Table **6-2** **Existing Sources Used in Sociological Research**

Most Frequently Used Sources
Census data
Crime statistics
Birth, death, marriage, divorce, and health statistics

Other Sources
Newspapers and periodicals
Personal journals, diaries, e-mail, and letters
Records and archival material of religious organizations, corporations, and other organizations
Transcripts of radio programs
Videotapes of motion pictures and television programs
Web pages, blogs, and chat rooms
Song lyrics
Scientific records (such as patent applications)
Speeches of public figures (such as politicians)
Votes cast in elections or by elected officials on specific legislative proposals
Attendance records for public events
Videos of social protests and rallies
Literature, including folklore

summingup

Think about It

Which of these sources do you access to collect information?

Table **6-3**   Major Research Designs   **summingup**

Method	Examples	Advantages	Limitations
Survey	Questionnaires, interviews	Yields information about specific issues	Can be expensive and time-consuming
Ethnography	Observation	Yields detailed information about specific groups or organizations	Involves months if not years of labor-intensive data
Experiment	Deliberate manipulation of people's social behavior	Yields direct measures of people's behavior	Ethical limitations on the degree to which subjects' behavior can be manipulated
Existing sources/ Secondary analysis	Analysis of census or health data Analysis of films or TV commercials	Cost-efficiency	Limited to data collected for some other purpose

Content analysis can be revealing. We might think that in the 21st century, blatant favoritism in media representations of men versus women is a thing of the past. However, research suggests otherwise. An analysis of hundreds of characters in children's coloring books shows that males are more likely than females to be shown taking an active role. Gender-stereotyped behavior dominates, with only 3 percent of males engaged in stereotypically female behavior, and only 6 percent of females engaged in stereotypically male behavior (Fitzpatrick and McPherson 2010).

Similarly, despite women's participation in all sports, content analysis of televised sports coverage shows that even when a men's sport is out of season (for example, men's basketball in late summer), it gets more coverage than women's sports in season (for example, women's basketball in July). Furthermore, coverage of female cheerleaders and athletes' wives exceeds coverage of the female athletes who compete in sports (Messner and Cooky 2010).

Table 6-3 summarizes the major research designs, along with their advantages and limitations.

use your **sociological imagination**

Imagine you are a legislator or government policymaker working on a complex social problem. What might happen if you were to base your decision on faulty research?

MODULE 6 | Recap and Review

Summary

In this module we focus on **research designs**, or the types of plans sociologists use to collect data.

1. Sociologists use four major research designs: surveys, **observation**, experiments, and existing sources.
2. The two principal forms of **survey** research are the **interview** and the **questionnaire**.
3. **Ethnography** allows sociologists to study certain behaviors and communities that cannot be investigated through other research methods.
4. When sociologists wish to study a cause-and-effect relationship, they may conduct an **experiment**.
5. Sociologists may also make use of existing sources in **secondary analysis** and **content analysis**.

Thinking Critically

1. How would you set up an experiment to measure the effect of TV watching on school-age children's grades?
2. Suppose your sociology instructor has asked you to study homelessness in your community. Which research technique would you find most useful? How would you use that technique?

Key Terms

Content analysis
Control group
Ethnography
Experiment
Experimental group
Hawthorne effect
Interview
Observation
Qualitative research
Quantitative research
Questionnaire
Research design
Secondary analysis
Survey

MODULE 7 | Ethics of Research

A biochemist cannot inject a drug into a human being unless it has been thoroughly tested and the subject agrees to the shot. To do otherwise would be both unethical and illegal. Sociologists, too, must abide by certain specific standards in conducting research, called a **code of ethics.** The professional society of the discipline, the American Sociological Association (ASA), first published the society's *Code of Ethics* in 1971 and revised it most recently in 1997. It puts forth the following basic principles:

1. Maintain objectivity and integrity in research.
2. Respect the subject's right to privacy and dignity.
3. Protect subjects from personal harm.
4. Preserve confidentiality.
5. Seek informed consent when data are collected from research participants or when behavior occurs in a private context.
6. Acknowledge research collaboration and assistance.
7. Disclose all sources of financial support (American Sociological Association 1999).

These basic principles probably seem clear-cut. How could they lead to any disagreement or controversy? Yet many delicate ethical questions cannot be resolved simply by reading these seven principles. For example, should a sociologist who is engaged in participant-observation research always protect the confidentiality of subjects? What if the subjects are members of a religious cult allegedly involved in unethical and possibly illegal activities? What if the sociologist is interviewing political activists and is questioned by government authorities about the research?

Because most sociological research uses *people* as sources of information—as respondents to survey questions, subjects of ethnography, or participants in experiments—these sorts of questions are important. In all cases, sociologists need to be certain they are not invading their subjects' privacy. Generally, they do so by assuring subjects of anonymity and by guaranteeing the confidentiality of personal information. In addition, research proposals that involve human subjects must now be overseen by a review board, whose members seek to ensure that subjects are not placed at an unreasonable level of risk. If necessary, the board may ask researchers to revise their research designs to conform to the code of ethics.

We can appreciate the seriousness of the ethical problems researchers confront by considering the experience of sociologist Rik Scarce, described in the next section. Scarce's vow to protect his subjects' confidentiality got him into considerable trouble with the law.

Confidentiality

Like journalists, sociologists occasionally find themselves subject to questions from law enforcement authorities because of knowledge they have gained in the course of their work. This uncomfortable situation raises profound ethical questions.

In May 1993, Rik Scarce, a doctoral candidate in sociology at Washington State University, was jailed for contempt of court. Scarce had declined to tell a federal grand jury what he knew—or even whether he knew anything—about a 1991 raid on a university research laboratory by animal rights activists. At the time, Scarce was conducting research for a book about environmental protesters and knew at least one suspect in the break-in. Curiously, although he was chastised by a federal judge, Scarce won respect from fellow prison inmates, who regarded him as a man who "wouldn't snitch" (Monaghan 1993:A8).

The American Sociological Association supported Scarce's position when he appealed his sentence. Scarce maintained his silence. Ultimately the judge ruled that nothing would be gained by further incarceration, and Scarce was released after serving 159 days in jail. In January 1994, the U.S. Supreme Court declined to hear Scarce's case on appeal. The Court's failure to consider his case led Scarce (2005) to argue that federal legislation is needed to clarify the right of scholars and members of the press to preserve the confidentiality of those they interview.

Conflict of Interest

Sometimes disclosing all the sources of funding for a study, as required in principle 7 of the ASA's *Code of Ethics,* is not a sufficient guarantee of ethical conduct. Especially in the case of both corporate and government funding, money given ostensibly for the support of basic research may come with strings attached. Accepting funds from a private organization or even a government agency that stands to benefit from a study's results can call into question a researcher's objectivity and integrity (principle 1). The controversy surrounding the involvement of social scientists in the U.S. Army's Human Terrain System is one example of this conflict of interest.

Another example is the Exxon Corporation's support for research on jury verdicts. In 1989, the Exxon oil tanker *Valdez* hit a reef off the coast of Alaska, spilling more than 11 million gallons of oil into Prince William Sound. Five years later a federal court ordered Exxon to pay $5.3 billion in damages for the accident. Exxon appealed the verdict and began approaching

A floating containment barrier (or boom) encircles the Exxon oil tanker *Valdez* after its grounding on a reef off the coast of Alaska. Exxon was found negligent in the environmental disaster and was ordered to pay $5.3 billion for the cleanup. On appeal, the company managed to reduce the damages to $500 million based on academic research that it had funded—research that some scholars believe involved a conflict of interest.

legal scholars, sociologists, and psychologists who might be willing to study jury deliberations. The corporation's objective was to develop academic support for its lawyers' contention that the punitive judgments in such cases result from faulty deliberations and do not have a deterrent effect.

Some scholars have questioned the propriety of accepting funds under these circumstances, even if the source is disclosed. In at least one case, an Exxon employee explicitly told a sociologist that the corporation offers financial support to scholars who have shown the tendency to express views similar to its own. An argument can also be made that Exxon was attempting to set scholars' research agendas with its huge war chest. Rather than funding studies on the improvement of cleanup technologies or the assignment of long-term environmental costs, Exxon chose to shift scientists' attention to the validity of the legal awards in environmental cases.

The scholars who accepted Exxon's support deny that it influenced their work or changed their conclusions. Some received support from other sources as well, such as the National Science Foundation and Harvard University's Olin Center for Law, Economics, and Business. Many of their findings were published in respected academic journals after review by a jury of peers. Still, at least one researcher who participated in the studies refused monetary support from Exxon to avoid even the suggestion of a conflict of interest.

Exxon has spent roughly $1 million on the research, and at least one compilation of studies congenial to the corporation's point of view has been published. As ethical considerations require, the academics who conducted the studies disclosed Exxon's role in funding them. Nevertheless, the investment appears to have paid off. In 2006, drawing on these studies, Exxon's lawyers succeeded in persuading an appeals court to reduce the corporation's legal damages from $5.3 to $2.5 billion. In 2008 Exxon appealed that judgment to the Supreme Court, which further reduced the damages to $500 million. The final award, which is to be shared by about 32,000 plaintiffs, will result in payments of about $15,000 to each person (Freudenburg 2005; Liptak 2008).

Value Neutrality

The ethical considerations of sociologists lie not only in the methods they use and the funding they accept, but also in the way they interpret their results. Max Weber ([1904] 1949) recognized that personal values would influence the questions that sociologists select for research. In his view, that was perfectly acceptable, but under no conditions could a researcher allow his or her personal feelings to influence the *interpretation* of data. In Weber's phrase, sociologists must practice **value neutrality** in their research.

As part of this neutrality, investigators have an ethical obligation to accept research findings even when the data run counter to their personal views, to theoretically based explanations, or to widely accepted beliefs. For example, Émile Durkheim challenged popular conceptions when he reported that social (rather than supernatural) forces were an important factor in suicide.

Although some sociologists believe that neutrality is impossible, ignoring the issue would be irresponsible. Let's consider what might happen if researchers brought their own biases to the investigation. A person investigating the impact of intercollegiate sports on alumni contributions, for example, might focus only on the highly visible revenue-generating sports of football and basketball and neglect the so-called minor sports, such as tennis or soccer, which are more likely to involve women athletes. Despite the early work of W. E. B. DuBois and Jane Addams, sociologists still need to be reminded that the discipline often fails to adequately consider all people's social behavior.

In her book *The Death of White Sociology* (1973), Joyce Ladner called attention to the tendency of mainstream sociology to treat the lives of African Americans as a social problem. More recently, feminist sociologist Shulamit Reinharz (1992) has argued that sociological research should be not only inclusive but also open to bringing about social change and to drawing on relevant research by nonsociologists. Both Ladner and Reinharz maintain that researchers should always analyze whether women's unequal social status has affected their studies in any way. For example, one might broaden the study of the impact of education on income to consider the implications of the unequal pay status of men and women. The issue of value neutrality does not mean that sociologists can't have opinions, but it does mean that they must work to overcome any biases, however unintentional, that they may bring to their analysis of research.

Sociologist Peter Rossi (1987) admits to having liberal inclinations that direct him to certain fields of study. Yet in line with Weber's view of value neutrality, Rossi's commitment to rigorous research methods and objective interpretation of data has sometimes led him to controversial findings that are not necessarily supportive of his liberal values. For example, his measure of the extent of homelessness in Chicago in the mid-1980s fell far below the estimates of the Chicago Coalition for the Homeless.

Coalition members bitterly attacked Rossi for hampering their social reform efforts by minimizing the extent of homelessness. Rossi (1987:79) concluded that "in the short term, good social research will often be greeted as a betrayal of one or another side to a particular controversy."

MODULE 7 | Recap and Review

Summary

Sociologists must abide by certain ethical principles when conducting research.

1. The *Code of Ethics* of the American Sociological Association calls for objectivity and integrity in research, confidentiality, and disclosure of all sources of financial support.
2. Max Weber urged sociologists to practice value neutrality in their research by ensuring that their personal feelings do not influence their interpretation of data.

Thinking Critically

1. If you were planning to do research on human sexuality, which of the seven principles in the ASA's *Code of Ethics* would particularly concern you? What ethical problems might arise in such a study, and how would you attempt to prevent them?
2. Why did Max Weber specify the need for neutrality in the interpretation of data? Is complete value neutrality possible in sociological research? To what extent should researchers try to overcome their own biases?

Key Terms

Code of ethics
Value neutrality

MODULE 8 | Development of Methodology

Feminist Methodology

Of the four theoretical approaches to sociology introduced in Chapter 1, the feminist perspective has had the greatest impact on the current generation of social researchers. How might this perspective influence research? Although researchers must be objective, their theoretical orientation may influence the questions they ask—or just as important, the questions they fail to ask. Until recently, for example, researchers frequently studied work and the family separately. Yet feminist theorists see the two spheres of activity as being closely integrated. Similarly, work and leisure, paid and unpaid domestic work may be seen not as two separate spheres, but as two sides of the same coin.

Recently, feminist scholars have become interested in self-injury, a practice described at the beginning of this chapter. Research shows that 85 percent of self-injurers are female; feminist researchers seek to explain why women predominate in this population. Rather than treat the behavior as a medical disorder, they note that society encourages women much more than men to attend to their bodies through hair removal, skin treatments, and depigmentation. Given this heightened attention to the female body, feminists suggest that specific instances of victimization can lead women to self-injure. They also seek to better understand male self-injurers, and are testing the hypothesis that among men, self-injury is a manifestation of hypermasculinity in the tolerance of pain (P. Adler and P. Adler 2011:25–27, 35–36).

The feminist perspective has also had an impact on global research. To feminist theorists, the traditional distinction between industrial nations and developing nations overlooks the close relationship between these two supposedly separate worlds. Feminist theorists have called for more research on the special role that immigrant women play in maintaining their households; on the use of domestic workers from less developed nations by households in industrial nations; and on the global trafficking of sex workers (Cheng 2003; Cooper et al. 2007; Sprague 2005).

Taking Sociology to Work

Dave Eberbach, *Associate Director, Iowa Institute for Community Alliances*

Dave Eberbach is a people person who has been working with computers most of his career. In 1994 he was hired as a research coordinator by the United Way of Central Iowa. In that position he helped to create and implement Iowa's Homeless Management Information System (HMIS), which coordinates data on housing and homeless service providers. Eberbach also collaborated with the Human Service Planning Alliance to create and maintain a "data warehouse" of social statistics from diverse sources. As a research coordinator, he found that the data helped him to identify small pockets of poverty that were generally hidden in state and county statistics.

Today, Eberbach works at the Iowa Institute for Community Alliances, a small nonprofit organization that offers computerized client management and on-site program monitoring to homeless and housing service providers. As Associate Director, Eberbach oversees a staff of seven and meets with clients who are working to improve service delivery to vulnerable people. "As fewer resources are being spent on social programs, it has been imperative to make sure that the focus of programs is on client success, not maintaining systems," he explains.

Eberbach went to Grinnell College, where he took a variety of social sciences courses before settling on sociology as a major. While there, he benefited from the presence of several visiting professors, who exposed him to a variety of racial and cultural perspectives. He found that his personal acquaintance with them complemented the concepts he was learning in his sociology classes. Today, Eberbach draws on his college experiences in his work, which brings him into contact with a diverse group of people.

As a student, Eberbach recalls, he never thought he would use statistics in his career, and didn't work very hard in the course. "As it turned out," he says, "I use it nearly every day.

Understanding data and statistics and being able to explain numbers to others has been very important in my job." The reverse has also been true, however: having a background in sociology has been helpful to him in systems design. "Understanding that systems need to work for a variety of groups of people, not just folks that grew up like I did," he explains, has been very helpful. "The world is not a computer problem or a math problem to be solved," he continues, "but rather a complex environment where groups of people continually bump into one another."

LET'S DISCUSS

1. Do you know what you want to be doing 10 years from now? If so, how might a knowledge of statistics help you in your future occupation?

2. What kinds of statistics, specifically, might you find in the Human Service Planning Alliance's data warehouse? Where would they come from?

Feminist theorists see the global trafficking of sex workers as a sign of the close relationship between the supposedly separate worlds of industrial nations and dependent developing nations.

Feminist researchers tend to involve and consult their subjects more than other researchers, and they are more oriented toward seeking change, raising the public consciousness, and influencing policy. They are particularly open to a multidisciplinary approach, such as making use of historical evidence or legal studies (T. Baker 1999; L. Lofland 1975; Reinharz 1992).

The Data-Rich Future

Advances in technology have affected all aspects of our lives, and sociological research is no exception. Massive increases in available data have allowed sociologists to undertake research that was virtually impossible just a decade ago. In the recent past, only people with grants or major institutional support could work easily with large amounts of data. Now anyone with a computer can access huge amounts of data and learn more about social behavior. Moreover, data from foreign countries are sometimes as available as information from the United States.

Research Today

BOX 8-1

Lying for Love Online

Today, about 40 million people seek love online, and according to one estimate, 21 percent of heterosexual couples and 61 percent of same-sex couples meet online. But do these people tell the truth in their online postings? Not always, and not often.

Data gathered from online dating sites like Match.com, OkCupid, and Yahoo reveals both truthfulness and deception in people's online postings:

- In their profiles, people often describe an idealized self—for example, "I rock climb."

> Men are more likely than women to say they are younger, taller, and wealthier than they really are.

- Women typically describe themselves as 8.5 pounds heavier than they really are; men, as 2 pounds lighter.
- Men are more likely than women to say they are younger, taller, and wealthier than they really are.
- Less attractive people often post enhanced or retouched photos.
- Women post photos that are an average of 1.5 years old; men post photos that are 6 months old.

- Men are more likely than women to lie about their occupation, education, and marginally, their relationship status.

Although much of the time these deceptions may be small, their widespread nature has made them an almost expected part of the game. In one study, a man who posted a five-year-old photograph said he looked the "same" now except that he had a beard. In another case, a woman saw no problem in listing her occupation as "marketing" rather than retail sales. After all, she explained, "it's not like me saying I'm a janitor, and then lying and saying that I'm a CEO." That, she concluded, would be unacceptable.

Little wonder that research shows daters like the personalities they meet online better than the ones they meet in person.

LET'S DISCUSS

1. Have you tried using an online dating service? If so, were you truthful in describing yourself online? Did the people you were matched with turn out to be truthful?

2. Why do you think online daters engage in deception if they are hoping eventually to meet someone face-to-face?

Sources: N. Ellison et al. 2012; R. Epstein 2009; Gelles 2011; Rosenbloom 2011; Toma et al. 2008; Toma and Hancock 2010.

In the latter part of 2009, the world experienced an intense burst of influenza initially referred to as "swine flu," but later identified as the H1N1 flu strain. How did medical researchers track the virus's spread across a nation, much less the world? Epidemiologists typically rely on reports that originate in doctors' offices and are funneled through government agencies. Data collection is a time-consuming process, with many days passing between the detection of symptoms and the publication of official statistics. However, public health researchers found a way to track contagious diseases using Google. By monitoring the topics people search for and compensating for the relative access to computers in different countries (high in Sweden and low in Nigeria, for example), they can monitor the spread of disease almost in real time (Dukić et al. 2011).

Similarly, in the past sociologists had to rely on victims' complaints or police reports to understand crime patterns. Now they are beginning to access real-time, geocoded (that is, location-specific) incident reports. These new data will offer sociologists much more information, which they can interpret and relate to other aspects of the social environment (G. King 2011). Box 8-1 describes some new opportunities the Internet offers to researchers who study dating and mate selection (and who once were confined to surveying undergraduates).

One ethical concern raised by all these data involves individual privacy. Sociologists now have access to information about people's real estate transactions, campaign contributions, online product purchases, and even travel along tollways. What steps should they take to protect the privacy of the individuals whose data they are using? This is not an academic question. Today, 87 percent of the people in the United States can be personally identified given only their gender, date of birth, and ZIP code (G. King 2011).

We have seen that researchers rely on a number of tools, from time-tested observational research and use of existing sources to the latest in computer technologies. The Social Policy section that follows will describe researchers' efforts to survey the general population about a controversial aspect of social behavior: human sexuality. (For more on human sexuality, see Chapter 12, The Family and Intimate Relationships.) This investigation was complicated by its potential social policy implications. Because in the real world, sociological research can have far-reaching consequences for public policy and public welfare, many of the modules in this book will close with a Social Policy section.

social policy | Studying Human Sexuality

How can researchers study human sexual behavior? Neuroscientists Ogi Ogas and Sai Gaddam (2011) studied millions of web searches, websites, and videos related to sex. They found that women and men differ decidedly in their preferences, but very little (if any) distinction between heterosexuals and homosexuals, other than their sexual orientation. This type of research has significant limitations, however. Ogas and Gaddam could not distinguish between online fantasies and rational desires, or between a single search and one of many repeated searches by the same person. Nevertheless, this cyber study is a step forward in the effort to understand human sexual behavior, the subject of this policy section (Bartlett 2011).

Looking at the Issue

In this age of devastating sexually transmitted diseases, there is no time more important to increase our scientific understanding of human sexuality. As we will see, however, this is a difficult topic to research, not only because of privacy concerns but because of all the preconceptions, myths, and beliefs people bring to the subject of sexuality. Many people actively oppose research on human sexuality. How does one carry out scientific research on such a controversial and personal topic?

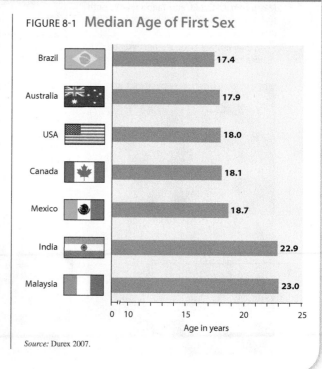

FIGURE 8-1 **Median Age of First Sex**

Country	Age in years
Brazil	17.4
Australia	17.9
USA	18.0
Canada	18.1
Mexico	18.7
India	22.9
Malaysia	23.0

Source: Durex 2007.

—Continued

Sex may sell, but persuading legislators to fund research on human sexual behavior is still a challenge.

Applying Sociology

Sociologists have little reliable national data on patterns of sexual behavior in the United States. Until the 1990s, the only comprehensive study of sexual behavior was the famous two-volume *Kinsey Report,* prepared in the 1940s (Kinsey et al. 1948, 1953; see also Igo 2007). Although the *Kinsey Report* is still widely quoted, the volunteers interviewed for the report were not representative of the nation's adult population.

In part, we lack reliable data on patterns of sexual behavior because it is difficult for researchers to obtain accurate information about this sensitive subject. Moreover, until AIDS emerged in the 1980s, there was little scientific demand for data on sexual behavior, except for specific concerns such as contraception. And even though the AIDS crisis has reached dramatic proportions (as will be discussed in Module 53), government funding for studies of sexual behavior is still controversial and therefore difficult to obtain.

The controversy surrounding research on human sexual behavior raises the issue of value neutrality, which becomes especially delicate when one considers the relationship of sociology to the government. The federal government has become the major source of funding for sociological research. Yet Max Weber urged that sociology remain an autonomous discipline and not become unduly influenced by any one segment of society. According to Weber's ideal of value neutrality, sociologists must remain free to reveal information that is embarrassing to the government, or for that matter, supportive of government institutions.

Initiating Policy

In 1987 the National Institute of Child Health and Human Development sought proposals for a national survey of sexual behavior. Sociologists responded with various plans that a review panel of scientists approved for funding. However,

in 1991, the U.S. Senate voted to forbid funding any survey of adult sexual practices. Despite the vote, sociologists developed the National Health and Social Life Survey (NHSLS) to better understand the sexual practices of adults in the United States. The researchers raised $1.6 million of *private* funding to make their study possible (Laumann et al. 1994a, 1994b).

The authors of the NHSLS believe that their research is important. They argue that data from their survey allow interest groups to more easily address public policy issues such as AIDS, sexual harassment, welfare reform, sex discrimination, abortion, teenage pregnancy, and family planning. Moreover, the research findings help to counter some commonsense notions. For instance, contrary to the popular beliefs that women regularly use abortion for birth control and that poor teens are the most likely socioeconomic group to have abortions, researchers found that three-fourths of all abortions are the first for the woman, and that well-educated and affluent women are more likely to have abortions than poor teens (Sweet 2001).

The usefulness of the NHSLS in addressing public policy issues has proved influential. As Figure 8-1 shows, scholars around the world are now studying human sexual behavior, in an effort to reduce the occurrence of HIV/AIDS.

TAKE THE ISSUE WITH YOU

1. Do you see any merit in the position of those who oppose government funding for research on sexual behavior? Explain your reasoning.

2. Exactly how could the results of research on human sexual behavior be used to control sexually transmitted diseases?

3. Compare the issue of value neutrality in government-funded research to the same issue in corporate-funded research. Are concerns about conflict of interest more or less serious in regard to government funding?

MODULE 8 | Recap and Review

Summary

Feminist theory and technological change have had important impacts on sociological research.

1. The feminist perspective has affected the questions sociologists ask, what groups they choose to study, the methods they use, and how globalization influences research.

2. Technology plays an important role in sociological research, whether it be a computer database or information obtained from the Internet.

3. Despite failure to obtain government funding, researchers developed the National Health and Social Life Survey (NHSLS) to better understand the sexual practices of adults in the United States.

Thinking Critically

1. Even if women are represented in a study, could the researcher's gender influence the data that are collected? If so, how? How might the problem be prevented?

2. Male sociologists once overlooked women in their studies of city life. What other groups could easily be overlooked in today's research, and why?

3. Suppose that you are a sociologist. You are trying to obtain funding for a study of adult sexual behavior from a government source. What arguments would you make to convince the government to fund your study?

In their effort to better understand social behavior, sociologists rely heavily on numbers and statistics. How have attitudes toward the legalization of marijuana changed over the past 40 years? A quick look at the results of 12 national surveys shows that while support for legalization of the drug has increased, it remains relatively weak (Figure A-3).

Using Statistics

The most common summary measures used by sociologists are percentages, means, modes, and medians. A **percentage** is a portion of 100. Use of percentages allows us to compare groups of different sizes. For example, if we were comparing financial contributors to a town's Baptist and Roman Catholic churches, the absolute numbers of contributors in each group could be misleading if there were many more Baptists than Catholics in the town. By using percentages, we could obtain a more meaningful comparison, showing the proportion of persons in each group who contribute to churches.

The **mean**, or *average,* is a number calculated by adding a series of values and then dividing by the number of values. For example, to find the mean of the numbers 5, 19, and 27, we would add them together (for a total of 51), divide by the number of values (3), and discover that the mean is 17.

The **mode** is the single most common value in a series of scores. Suppose we were looking at the following scores on a 10-point quiz:

   10 10 9 9 8 8 7 7 7 6 5

The mode—the most frequent score on the quiz—is 7. While the mode is easier to identify than other summary measures, it tells sociologists little about all the other values. Hence, you will find much less use of the mode in this book than of the mean and the median.

The **median** is the midpoint or number that divides a series of values into two groups of equal numbers of values. For the quiz just discussed, the median, or central value, is 8. The mean, or average, would be 86 (the sum of all scores) divided by 11 (the total number of scores), or 7.8.

Some of these statistics may seem confusing at first. But think how difficult it is to comb through an endless list of numbers to identify a pattern or central tendency. Percentages, means, modes, and medians are essential time-savers in sociological research and analysis.

Reading Graphs

Tables and figures (that is, graphs) allow social scientists to display data and develop their conclusions more easily. In 2010, the Gallup poll interviewed 1,025 people in the United States, age 18 and over.

FIGURE A-3 **Changing Attitudes toward the Legalization of Marijuana**

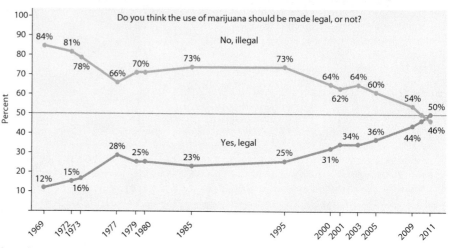

Source: Gallup 2011; see Newport 2011b in references.

Each respondent was asked, "Do you think the use of marijuana should be made legal, or not?" Without some type of summary, there is no way that analysts could examine the hundreds of individual responses to this question and reach firm conclusions. One type of summary sociologists use, a **cross-tabulation**, shows the relationship between two or more variables. Through the cross-tabulations presented graphically in Figure A-4, we can quickly see that older people are less likely to favor the legalization of marijuana than younger people, and that women are less supportive of legalization than men.

Graphs, like tables, can be quite useful to sociologists. And illustrations are often easier for the general public to understand, whether in newspapers or in PowerPoint presentations. Still, as with all data, we need to be careful how they are presented.

FIGURE A-4 **People Who Favor Legalization of Marijuana by Gender and Age, 2011**

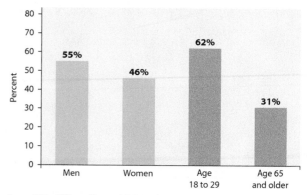

Source: Gallup 2011; see Newport 2011b in references.

Appendix II Writing a Research Report

Let's say you have decided to write a report on cohabitation (unmarried couples living together). How do you go about doing the necessary library research? Students must follow procedures similar to those used by sociologists in conducting original research. For your first step you must define the problem that you wish to study—perhaps in this case, how much cohabitation occurs and what its impact is on later marital happiness. The next step is to review the literature, which generally requires library research.

Finding Information

The following steps will be helpful in finding information:

1. Check this textbook and other textbooks that you own. Don't forget to begin with the materials closest at hand, including the website associated with this textbook, www.mhhe.com/schaefer10e.

2. Use the library's online catalog. Computerized library systems now access not only the college library's collection but also books and magazines from other libraries, available through interlibrary loans. These systems allow you to search for books by author or title. You can use title searches to locate books by subject as well. For example, if you search the title base for the keyword *cohabitation,* you will learn where books with that word in the title are located in the library's stacks. Near those books will be other works on cohabitation, which may not happen to have that word in the title. You may also want to search other, related keywords, such as *unmarried couples.*

3. Investigate using computerized periodical indexes, if they are available in your library. *Sociological Abstracts* online covers most sociological writing since 1963. In 2012, a search of just this one database found more than 2,233 documents having either *cohabitation* or *unmarried couples* as keywords. Some dealt with laws about cohabitation, while others focused on trends in other countries. If you limited your topic to same-sex couples, you would find 2,039 citations. Other electronic databases cover general-interest periodicals (*Time, Ms., National Review, Atlantic Monthly,* and so forth), reference materials, or newspapers. These electronic systems may be connected to a printer, allowing you to produce a printout complete with bibliographic information, and sometimes even complete copies of articles.

4. Examine government documents. The U.S. government, states and cities, and the United Nations publish information on virtually every subject of interest to social science researchers. Publications of the Census Bureau, for example, include tables showing the number of unmarried couples living together and some social characteristics of those households.

5. Use newspapers. Major newspapers publish annual or even weekly indexes that are useful in locating information about specific events or issues. Lexis-Nexis is an electronic index to U.S. and international newspapers.

6. Ask people, organizations, and agencies concerned with the topic for information and assistance. Be as specific as possible in making requests. You might receive very different information on the issue of cohabitation from talking with marriage counselors and with clergy from different religions.

7. If you run into difficulties, consult the instructor or the reference librarian at your college library.

A word of caution: be extremely careful in using the Internet to do research. Much of the information on the Internet is simply incorrect—even if it looks authoritative, is accompanied by impressive graphics, or has been widely circulated. Unlike the information in a library, which must be screened by a highly qualified librarian, "information" on the Internet can be created and posted by anyone with a computer. Check the sources for the information and note the Web page sponsor. Is the author qualified to write on the subject? Is the author even identified? Is the Web page sponsor likely to be biased? Whenever possible, try to confirm what you have read on the Internet through a well-known, reputable source or organization. If the accuracy of the information could be affected by how old it is, check the date on which the page or article was created or updated. Used intelligently, the Internet is a wonderful tool that offers students access to many of the reliable print sources noted earlier, including government documents and newspaper archives extending back over a century.

Writing the Report

Once you have completed all your research, you can begin writing the report. Here are a few tips:

- Be sure the topic you have chosen is not too broad. You must be able to cover it adequately in a reasonable amount of time and a reasonable number of pages.

- Develop an outline for your report. You should have an introduction and a conclusion that relate to each other, and the discussion should proceed logically throughout the paper. Use headings within the paper if they will improve clarity and organization.

- Do not leave all the writing until the last minute. It is best to write a rough draft, let it sit for a few days, and then take a fresh look before beginning revisions.

- If possible, read your paper aloud. Doing so may be helpful in locating sections or phrases that don't make sense.

Remember that you *must* cite all information you have obtained from other sources, including the Internet. Plagiarism is a serious academic offense, for which the penalties are severe. If you use an author's exact words, it is essential that you place them in quotation marks. Even if you reworked someone else's ideas, you must indicate the source of those ideas.

Mastering This Chapter: Sociological Research

taking sociology with you

1 Think about a job you are interested in. How can you see yourself using research techniques—surveys, observation, experiments, or existing sources—in that occupation?

2 How can a sociologist genuinely maintain value neutrality while studying a group that he or she finds repugnant (for example, a White supremacist organization, a satanic cult, or a group of convicted rapists)?

3 New technologies have benefited sociological research by facilitating surveys and statistical analysis. Can you think of any potential drawbacks these new technologies might have for sociological investigation?

key terms

Causal logic The relationship between a condition or variable and a particular consequence, with one leading to the other.

Code of ethics The standards of acceptable behavior developed by and for members of a profession.

Content analysis The systematic coding and objective recording of data, guided by some rationale.

Control group The subjects in an experiment who are not introduced to the independent variable by the researcher.

Control variable A factor that is held constant to test the relative impact of an independent variable.

Correlation A relationship between two variables in which a change in one coincides with a change in the other.

Cross-tabulation A table or matrix that shows the relationship between two or more variables.

Dependent variable The variable in a causal relationship that is subject to the influence of another variable.

Ethnography The study of an entire social setting through extended systematic fieldwork.

Experiment An artificially created situation that allows a researcher to manipulate variables.

Experimental group The subjects in an experiment who are exposed to an independent variable introduced by a researcher.

Hawthorne effect The unintended influence that observers of experiments can have on their subjects.

Hypothesis A speculative statement about the relationship between two or more variables.

Independent variable The variable in a causal relationship that causes or influences a change in another variable.

Interview A face-to-face, telephone, or online questioning of a respondent to obtain desired information.

Mean A number calculated by adding a series of values and then dividing by the number of values.

Median The midpoint or number that divides a series of values into two groups of equal numbers of values.

Mode The single most common value in a series of scores.

Observation A research technique in which an investigator collects information through direct participation, by closely watching a group or community.

Operational definition An explanation of an abstract concept that is specific enough to allow a researcher to assess the concept.

Percentage A portion of 100.

Qualitative research Research that relies on what is seen in field or naturalistic settings more than on statistical data.

Quantitative research Research that collects and reports data primarily in numerical form.

Questionnaire A printed or written form used to obtain information from a respondent.

Random sample A sample for which every member of an entire population has the same chance of being selected.

Reliability The extent to which a measure produces consistent results.

Research design A detailed plan or method for obtaining data scientifically.

Sample A selection from a larger population that is statistically representative of that population.

Scientific method A systematic, organized series of steps that ensures maximum objectivity and consistency in researching a problem.

Secondary analysis A variety of research techniques that make use of previously collected and publicly accessible information and data.

Survey A study, generally in the form of an interview or questionnaire, that provides researchers with information about how people think and act.

Validity The degree to which a measure or scale truly reflects the phenomenon under study.

Value neutrality Max Weber's term for objectivity of sociologists in the interpretation of data.

Variable A measurable trait or characteristic that is subject to change under different conditions.

self-quiz

Read each question carefully and then select the best answer.

1. The first step in any sociological research project is to
   a. collect data.
   b. define the problem.
   c. review previous research.
   d. formulate a hypothesis.

2. An explanation of an abstract concept that is specific enough to allow a researcher to measure the concept is a(n)
   a. hypothesis.
   b. correlation.
   c. operational definition.
   d. variable.

3. The variable hypothesized to cause or influence another is called the
   a. dependent variable.
   b. hypothetical variable.
   c. correlation variable.
   d. independent variable.

4. A correlation exists when
   a. one variable causes something to occur in another variable.
   b. two or more variables are causally related.
   c. a change in one variable coincides with a change in another variable.
   d. a negative relationship exists between two variables.

5. Through which type of research technique does a sociologist ensure that data are statistically representative of the population being studied?
   a. sampling
   b. experiments
   c. ethnography
   d. control variables

6. In order to obtain a random sample, a researcher might
   a. administer a questionnaire to every fifth woman who enters a business office.
   b. examine the attitudes of residents of a city by interviewing every 20th name in the city's telephone book.

c. study the attitudes of registered Democratic voters by choosing every 10th name found on a city's list of registered Democrats.
   d. do all of the above.

7. A researcher can obtain a higher response rate by using which type of survey?
   a. an interview
   b. a questionnaire
   c. representative samples
   d. ethnographic techniques

8. In the 1930s, William F. Whyte moved into a low-income Italian neighborhood in Boston. For nearly four years, he was a member of the social circle of "corner boys" that he describes in *Street Corner Society*. His goal was to gain greater insight into the community established by these men. What type of research technique did Whyte use?
   a. experiment
   b. survey
   c. secondary analysis
   d. participant observation

9. When sociologists want to study a possible cause-and-effect relationship, they may engage in what kind of research technique?
   a. ethnography
   b. survey research
   c. secondary analysis
   d. experiment

10. Émile Durkheim's statistical analysis of suicide was an example of what kind of research technique?
    a. ethnography
    b. observation research
    c. secondary analysis
    d. experimental research

11. Unlike the typical citizen, the sociologist has a commitment to use the _____ method in studying society.

12. A(n) _____ is a speculative statement about the relationship between two or more factors known as variables.

13. _____ refers to the degree to which a measure or scale truly reflects the phenomenon under study.

14. In order to obtain data scientifically, researchers need to select a research _____.

15. If scientists were testing a new type of toothpaste in an experimental setting, they would administer the toothpaste to a(n) _____ group, but not to a(n) _____ group.

16. The term _____ _____ refers to the unintended influence that observers of experiments can have on their subjects.

17. Using census data in a way unintended by its initial collectors would be an example of _____ _____.

18. Using _____ _____, researchers conducted a study of gender-stereotyped behavior in children's coloring books.

19. The American Sociological Association's *Code of* _____ requires sociologists to maintain objectivity and integrity and to preserve the confidentiality of their subjects.

20. As part of their commitment to _____ neutrality, investigators have an ethical obligation to accept research findings even when the data run counter to their personal views or to widely accepted beliefs.

thinking about movies

Gasland

This documentary investigates the possible health effects of a new technique for drilling natural gas, called *hydraulic fracturing* ("fracking").

An Inconvenient Truth

In this documentary about global warming, Al Gore makes the case that certain social groups are already paying the price for climate change.

Kinsey

Researchers confront the ethical challenges of studying human behavior in this film about the *Kinsey Report*.

Culture

3 Culture

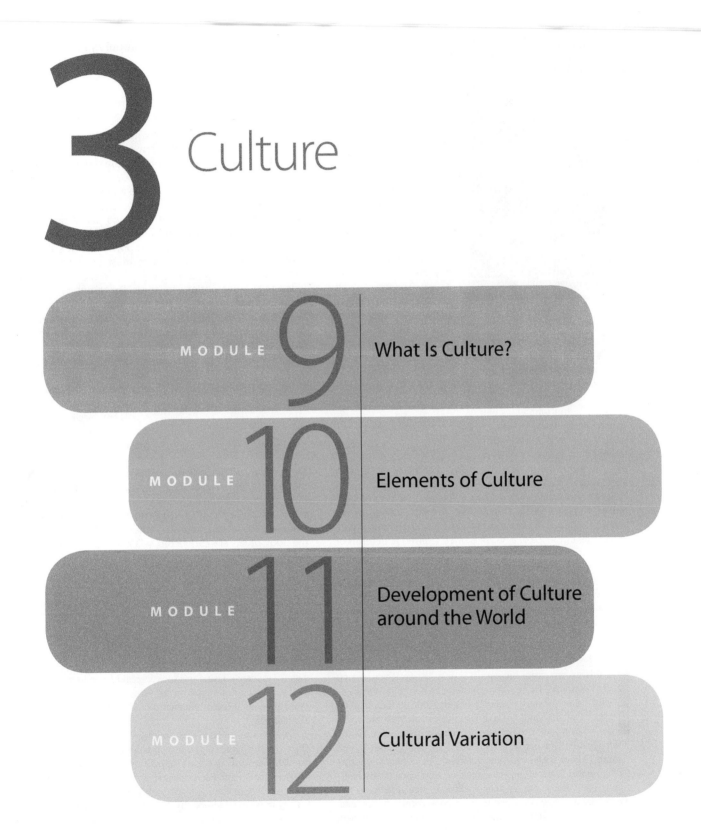

MODULE 9 — What Is Culture?

MODULE 10 — Elements of Culture

MODULE 11 — Development of Culture around the World

MODULE 12 — Cultural Variation

What do you think of the society described here by anthropologist Horace Miner?

Could you live in such a culture?

66 Nacirema culture is characterized by a highly developed market economy which has evolved in a rich natural habitat. While much of the people's time is devoted to economic pursuits, a large part of the fruits of these labors and a considerable portion of the day are spent in ritual activity. The focus of this activity is the human body, the appearance and health of which loom as a dominant concern in the ethos of the people. While such a concern is certainly not unusual, its ceremonial aspects and associated philosophy are unique.

The fundamental belief underlying the whole system appears to be that the human body is ugly and that its natural tendency is to debility and disease. Incarcerated in such a body, man's only hope is to avert these characteristics through the use of the powerful influences of ritual and ceremony. Every household has one or more shrines devoted to this purpose. The more powerful individuals in the society have several shrines in their houses and, in fact, the opulence of a house is often referred to in terms of the number of such ritual centers it possesses. Most houses are of wattle and daub construction, but the shrine rooms of the more wealthy are walled with stone. Poorer families imitate the rich by applying pottery plaques to their shrine walls.

While each family has at least one such shrine, the rituals associated with it are not family ceremonies but are private and secret. The rites are normally only discussed with children, and then only during the period when they are being initiated into these mysteries. I was able, however, to establish sufficient rapport with the natives to examine these shrines and to have the rituals described to me.

The focal point of the shrine is a box or chest which is built into the wall. In this chest are kept the many charms and magical potions without which no native believes he could live. These preparations are secured from a variety of specialized practitioners. The most powerful of these are the medicine men, whose assistance must be rewarded with substantial gifts. However, the medicine men do not provide the curative potions for their clients, but decide what the ingredients should be and then write them down in an ancient and secret language. This writing is understood only by the medicine men and by the herbalists who, for another gift, provide the required charm.

The charm is not disposed of after it has served its purpose, but is placed in the charm-box of the household shrine. As these magical materials are specific for certain ills, and the real or imagined maladies of the people are many, the charm-box is usually full to overflowing. The magical packets are so numerous that people forget what their purposes were and fear to use them again. While the natives are very vague on this point, we can only assume that the idea in retaining all the old magical materials is that their presence in the charm-box, before which the body rituals are conducted, will in some way protect the worshipper. 99

The focal point of the shrine is a box or chest which is built into the wall. In this chest are kept the many charms and magical potions without which no native believes he could live.

(Miner 1956:503–504) Additional information about this excerpt can be found on the Online Learning Center at www.mhhe.com/schaefermod2e.

I n this excerpt from his journal article "Body Ritual among the Nacirema," Horace Miner casts an anthropologist's observant eye on the intriguing rituals of an exotic culture. If some aspects of this culture seem familiar to you, you are right, for what Miner is describing is actually the culture of the United States ("Nacirema" is "American" spelled backward). The "shrine" Miner writes of is the bathroom; he correctly informs us that in this culture, one measure of wealth is how many bathrooms one's home has. In their bathroom rituals, he goes on, the Nacirema use charms and magical potions (beauty products and prescription drugs) obtained from specialized practitioners (such as hair stylists), herbalists (pharmacists), and medicine

men (physicians). Using our sociological imaginations, we could update Miner's description of the Nacirema's charms, written in 1956, by adding tooth whiteners, anti-aging creams, Waterpiks, and hair gel.

When we step back and examine a culture thoughtfully and objectively, whether it is our own culture in disguise or another less familiar to us, we learn something new about society. Take Fiji, an island in the Pacific where a robust, nicely rounded body has always been the ideal for both men and women. This is a society in which traditionally, "You've gained weight" has been considered a compliment, and "Your legs are skinny," an insult. Yet a recent study shows that for the first time, eating disorders have been showing up among young people in Fiji. What has happened to change their body image? Since the introduction of cable television in 1995, many Fiji islanders, especially young women, have begun to emulate not their mothers and aunts, but the small-waisted stars of television programs currently airing there, like *Gossip Girl* and *Modern Family*. Studying culture in places like Fiji, then, sheds light on our society as well (A. Becker 2007; Fiji TV 2012).

In these four modules we will study the development of culture around the world, including the cultural effects of the worldwide trend toward globalization. We will see just how basic the study of culture is to sociology. Our discussion will focus both on general cultural practices found in all societies and on the wide variations that can distinguish one society from another. We will define and explore the major aspects of culture, including language, norms, sanctions, and values. We will see how cultures develop a dominant ideology, and how functionalist and conflict theorists view culture. We'll also see what can happen when a major corporation ignores cultural variations. Then, in the Social Policy section, we will look at the conflicts in cultural values that underlie current debates over bilingualism.

MODULE 9 | What Is Culture?

Culture is the totality of learned, socially transmitted customs, knowledge, material objects, and behavior. It includes the ideas, values, and artifacts (for example, DVDs, comic books, and birth control devices) of groups of people. Patriotic attachment to the flag of the United States is an aspect of culture, as is a national passion for the tango in Argentina.

Sometimes people refer to a particular person as "very cultured" or to a city as having "lots of culture." That use of the term *culture* is different from our use in this textbook. In sociological terms, culture does not refer solely to the fine arts and refined intellectual taste. It consists of *all* objects and ideas within a society, including slang words, ice-cream cones, and rock music. Sociologists consider both a portrait by Rembrandt and the work of graffiti spray painters to be aspects of culture. A tribe that cultivates soil by hand has just as much culture as a people that relies on computer-operated machinery. Each people has a distinctive culture with its own characteristic ways of gathering and preparing food, constructing homes, structuring the family, and promoting standards of right and wrong.

The fact that you share a similar culture with others helps to define the group or society to which you belong. A fairly large number of people are said to constitute a **society** when they live in the same territory, are relatively independent of people outside their area, and participate in a common culture. Metropolitan Los Angeles is more populous than at least 150 nations, yet sociologists do not consider it a society in its own right. Rather, they see it as part of—and dependent on—the larger society of the United States.

A society is the largest form of human group. It consists of people who share a common heritage and culture. Members of the society learn this culture and transmit it from one generation to the next. They even preserve their distinctive culture through literature, art, video recordings, and other means of expression.

Sociologists have long recognized the many ways in which culture influences human behavior. Through what has been termed a tool kit of habits, skills, and styles, people of a common culture construct their acquisition of knowledge, their interactions with kinfolk, their entrance into the job market—in short, the way in which they live. If it were not for the social transmission of culture, each generation would have to reinvent television, not to mention the wheel (Swidler 1986).

Having a common culture also simplifies many day-to-day interactions. For example, when you buy an airline ticket, you know you don't have to bring along hundreds of dollars in cash. You can pay with a credit card. When you are part of a society, you take for granted many small (as well as more important)

Navigating cultural differences can be a challenge. During a visit to Tokyo, President Obama was criticized for his deep bow to Emperor Akihito. And at the 2010 Winter Olympics, Russian ice dancers Domnina and Shabalin were criticized for their interpretation of Aboriginal dress. Favored to win, they took third place.

cultural patterns. You assume that theaters will provide seats for the audience, that physicians will not disclose confidential information, and that parents will be careful when crossing the street with young children. All these assumptions reflect basic values, beliefs, and customs of the culture of the United States.

Today, when text, sound, and video can be transmitted around the world instantaneously, some aspects of culture transcend national borders. The German philosopher Theodor Adorno and others have spoken of the worldwide **culture industry** that standardizes the goods and services demanded by consumers. Adorno contends that globally, the primary effect of popular culture is to limit people's choices. Yet others have shown that the culture industry's influence does not always permeate international borders. Sometimes the culture industry is embraced; at other times, soundly rejected (Adorno [1971] 1991:98–106; Horkheimer and Adorno [1944] 2002).

Cultural Universals

All societies have developed certain common practices and beliefs, known as **cultural universals.** Many cultural universals are, in fact, adaptations to meet essential human needs, such as the need for food, shelter, and clothing. Anthropologist George Murdock (1945:124) compiled a list of cultural universals, including athletic sports, cooking, dancing, visiting, personal names, marriage, medicine, religious ritual, funeral ceremonies, sexual restrictions, and trade.

The cultural practices Murdock listed may be universal, but the manner in which they are expressed varies from culture to culture. For example, one society may let its members choose their marriage partners; another may encourage marriages arranged by the parents.

Not only does the expression of cultural universals vary from one society to another; within a society, it may also change dramatically over time. Each generation, and each year for that matter, most human cultures change and expand.

Ethnocentrism

Many everyday statements reflect our attitude that our culture is best. We use terms such as *underdeveloped, backward,* and *primitive* to refer to other societies. What "we" believe is a religion; what "they" believe is superstition and mythology.

It is tempting to evaluate the practices of other cultures on the basis of our perspectives. Sociologist William Graham Sumner (1906) coined the term **ethnocentrism** to refer to the tendency to assume that one's own culture and way of life represent the norm or are superior to all others. The ethnocentric person sees his or her group as the center or defining point of culture and views all other cultures as deviations from what is "normal." Westerners who think cattle are to be used for food might look down on India's Hindu religion and culture, which view the cow as sacred. Or people in one culture may dismiss as unthinkable the mate selection or child-rearing practices of another culture. In sum, our view of the world is dramatically influenced by the society in which we were raised.

Ethnocentrism is hardly limited to citizens of the United States. Visitors from many African cultures are surprised at the disrespect that children in the United States show their parents. People from India may be repelled by our practice of living in the same household with dogs and cats. Many Islamic fundamentalists in the Arab world and Asia view the United States as corrupt, decadent, and doomed to destruction. All these people may feel comforted by membership in cultures that in their view are superior to ours.

Cultural Relativism

While ethnocentrism means evaluating foreign cultures using the familiar culture of the observer as a standard of correct behavior, **cultural relativism** means viewing people's behavior from the perspective of their own culture. It places a priority on understanding other cultures, rather than dismissing them as "strange" or "exotic." Unlike ethnocentrists, cultural relativists employ the kind of value neutrality in scientific study that Max Weber saw as so important.

Cultural relativism stresses that different social contexts give rise to different norms and values. Thus, we must examine practices such as polygamy, bullfighting, and monarchy within the particular contexts of the cultures in which they are found. Although cultural relativism does not suggest that we must unquestionably accept every cultural variation, it does require a serious and unbiased effort to evaluate norms, values, and customs in light of their distinctive culture.

Consider the practice of children marrying adults. Most people in North America cannot fathom the idea of a 12-year-old girl marrying. The custom, which is illegal in the United States, is common in West Africa and South Asia. Should the United States respect such marriages? The apparent answer is no. In 2006 the U.S. government spent $623 million to discourage the practice in many of the countries with the highest child-marriage rates (Figure 9-1).

From the perspective of cultural relativism, we might ask whether one society should spend its resources to dictate the norms of another. However, federal officials have defended the government's actions. They contend that child marriage deprives girls of education, threatens their health, and weakens public health efforts to combat HIV/AIDS (Jain and Kurz 2007; B. Slavin 2007).

Sociobiology and Culture

While sociology emphasizes diversity and change in the expression of culture, another school of thought, sociobiology, stresses the universal aspects of culture. **Sociobiology** is the systematic study of how biology affects human social behavior. Sociobiologists assert that many of the cultural traits humans display, such as the almost universal expectation that women will be nurturers and men will be providers, are not learned but are rooted in our genetic makeup.

Sociobiology is founded on the naturalist Charles Darwin's (1859) theory of evolution. In traveling the world, Darwin had noted small variations in species—in the shape of a bird's beak, for example—from one location to another. He theorized that over hundreds of generations, random variations in genetic

FIGURE 9-1 **Countries with High Child Marriage Rates**

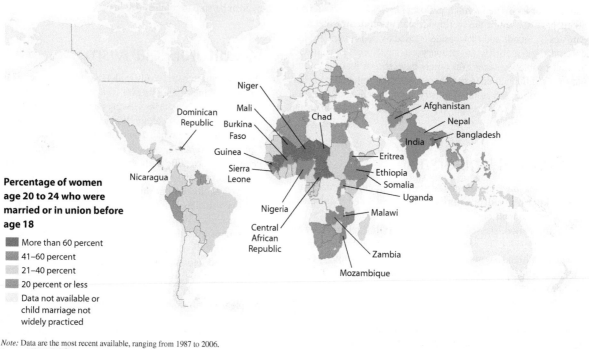

Percentage of women age 20 to 24 who were married or in union before age 18

- More than 60 percent
- 41–60 percent
- 21–40 percent
- 20 percent or less
- Data not available or child marriage not widely practiced

Note: Data are the most recent available, ranging from 1987 to 2006.
Source: UNICEF 2010.

In 21 countries, 40 percent or more of the women under 18 are married.

makeup had helped certain members of a species to survive in a particular environment. A bird with a differently shaped beak might have been better at gathering seeds than other birds, for instance. In reproducing, these lucky individuals had passed on their advantageous genes to succeeding generations. Eventually, given their advantage in survival, individuals with the variation began to outnumber other members of the species. The species was slowly adapting to its environment. Darwin called this process of adaptation to the environment through random genetic variation *natural selection.*

Sociobiologists apply Darwin's principle of natural selection to the study of social behavior. They assume that particular forms of behavior become genetically linked to a species if they contribute to its fitness to survive (van den Berghe 1978). In its extreme form, sociobiology suggests that *all* behavior is the result of genetic or biological factors, and that social interactions play no role in shaping people's conduct.

Sociobiologists do not seek to describe individual behavior on the level of "Why is Fred more aggressive than Jim?" Rather, they focus on how human nature is affected by the genetic composition of a *group* of people who share certain characteristics (such as men or women, or members of isolated tribal bands). In general, sociobiologists have stressed the basic genetic heritage that *all* humans share and have shown little interest in speculating about alleged differences between racial groups or nationalities. A few researchers have tried to trace specific behaviors, like criminal activity, to certain genetic markers, but those markers are not deterministic. Family cohesiveness, peer group behavior, and other social factors can override genetic influences on behavior (Guo et al. 2008; E. Wilson 1975, 1978).

Certainly most social scientists would agree that there is a biological basis for social behavior. But there is less support for the extreme positions taken by certain advocates of sociobiology. Like interactionists, conflict theorists and functionalists believe that people's behavior rather than their genetic structure defines social reality. Conflict theorists fear that the sociobiological approach could be used as an argument against efforts to assist disadvantaged people, such as schoolchildren who are not competing successfully (Freese 2008; Machalek and Martin 2010; E. Wilson 2000).

MODULE 9 | Recap and Review

Summary

Culture is the totality of learned, socially transmitted customs, knowledge, material objects, and behavior. This module examines the social practices common to all cultures.

1. A shared culture helps to define the group or **society** to which we belong.

2. Anthropologist George Murdock compiled a list of **cultural universals,** or common practices found in every culture, including marriage, sports, cooking, medicine, and sexual restrictions.

3. People who assume their own culture is superior to other cultures engage in **ethnocentrism.** In contrast, **cultural relativism** is the practice of viewing other people's behavior from the perspective of their own culture.

Thinking Critically

1. Select three cultural universals from George Murdock's list and analyze them from a functionalist perspective. Why are these practices found in every culture? What functions do they serve?

2. What are some problems with looking at social behavior from a sociobiological point of view? What are some benefits? How useful do you find this perspective?

Key Terms

Cultural relativism

Cultural universal

Culture

Culture industry

Ethnocentrism

Society

Sociobiology

Role of Language

Language is one of the major elements of culture that underlie cultural variations. It is also an important component of cultural capital. Recall from Module 2 that Pierre Bourdieu used the term *cultural capital* to describe noneconomic assets, such as family background and past educational investments, which are reflected in a person's knowledge of language and the arts.

Members of a society generally share a common language, which facilitates day-to-day exchanges with others. When you ask a hardware store clerk for a flashlight, you don't need to draw a picture of the instrument. You share the same cultural term for a small, portable, battery-operated light. However, if you were in England and needed this item, you would have to ask for an electric torch. Of course, even within the same society, a term can have a number of different meanings. In the United States, *pot* signifies both a container that is used for cooking and an intoxicating drug. In this section we will examine the cultural influence of language, which includes both the written and spoken word and nonverbal communication.

Language: Written and Spoken

Seven thousand languages are spoken in the world today—many more than the number of countries. For the speakers of each one, whether they number 2,000 or 200 million, language is fundamental to their shared culture.

The English language, for example, makes extensive use of words dealing with war. We speak of "conquering" space, "fighting" the "battle" of the budget, "waging war" on drugs, making a "killing" on the stock market, and "bombing" an examination; something monumental or great is "the bomb." An observer from an entirely different and warless culture could gauge the importance that war and the military have had in our lives simply by recognizing the prominence that militaristic terms have in our language. Similarly, the Sami people of northern Norway and Sweden have a rich diversity of terms for snow, ice, and reindeer (Haviland et al. 2008; Magga 2006).

Language is, in fact, the foundation of every culture. **Language** is an abstract system of word meanings and symbols for all aspects of culture. It includes speech, written characters, numerals, symbols, and nonverbal gestures and expressions. Because language is the foundation of every culture, the ability to speak other languages is crucial to intercultural relations. Throughout the Cold War era, beginning in the 1950s and continuing well into the 1970s, the U.S. government encouraged the study of Russian by developing special language schools for diplomats and

military advisers who dealt with the Soviet Union. And following September 11, 2001, the nation recognized how few skilled translators it had for Arabic and other languages spoken in Muslim countries. Language quickly became a key not only to tracking potential terrorists, but also to building diplomatic bridges with Muslim countries willing to help in the war against terrorism.

Language does more than simply describe reality; it also serves to *shape* the reality of a culture. For example, most people in the United States cannot easily make the verbal distinctions concerning snow and ice that are possible in the Sami culture. As a result, they are less likely to notice such differences.

The **Sapir-Whorf hypothesis,** named for two linguists, describes the role of language in shaping our interpretation of reality. According to Sapir and Whorf, because people can

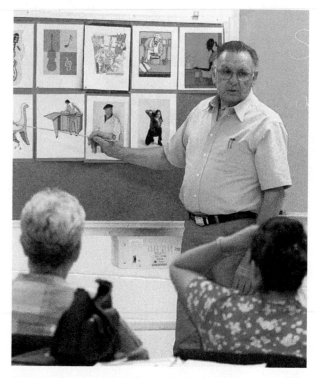

A native speaker trains instructors from the Oneida Nation of New York in the Berlitz method of language teaching. As of 2012, there were 527 speakers of the Oneida language. Many Native American tribes are taking similar steps to recover their seldom used languages, realizing that language is the essential foundation of any culture.

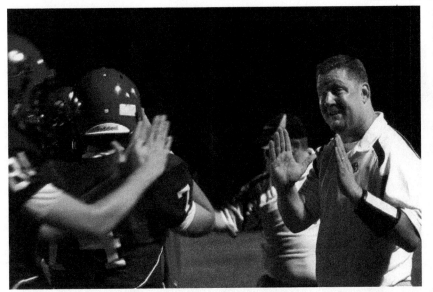

Using American Sign Language, a form of nonverbal communication, a football coach discusses a play with his team. The Silent Warriors, four-time national champions and the pride of the Alabama School for the Deaf, have defeated both hearing and nonhearing teams.

conceptualize the world only through language, language *precedes* thought. Thus, the word symbols and grammar of a language organize the world for us. The Sapir-Whorf hypothesis also holds that language is not a

given. Rather, it is culturally determined, and it encourages a distinctive interpretation of reality by focusing our attention on certain phenomena (Sapir 1929).

For decades, the Navajo have referred to cancer as *lood doo na'dziihii*. Now, through a project funded by the National Cancer Institute, the tribal college is seeking to change the phrase. Why? Literally, the phrase means "the sore that does not heal," and health educators are concerned that tribal members who have been diagnosed with cancer view it as a death sentence. Their effort to change the Navajo language, not easy in itself, is complicated by the Navajo belief that to talk about the disease is to bring it on one's people (Fonseca 2008).

Similarly, feminists have noted that gender-related language can reflect—although in itself it does not determine—the traditional acceptance of men and women in certain occupations. Each time we use a term such as *mailman, policeman,* or *fireman,* we are implying (especially to young children) that these occupations can be filled only by males. Yet many women work as *mail carriers, police officers,* and *firefighters*—a fact that is being increasingly recognized and legitimized through the use of such nonsexist language.

Language can shape how we see, taste, smell, feel, and hear. It also influences the way we think about the people, ideas, and objects around us. Language communicates a culture's most important norms, values, and sanctions. That's why the decline of an old language or the introduction of a new one is such a sensitive issue in many parts of the world (see the Social Policy section at the end of Module 12).

trend|spotting

Linguistic Isolation

In 2006, a severe winter storm hit the northwest United States, knocking out electrical power in many communities. Residents turned on their generators, some without heeding warnings about the risk of carbon monoxide poisoning. Although local media ran public service announcements about the need for adequate ventilation of the generators, six people died and several others fell ill from exposure to carbon monoxide. Investigators later determined that the victims had been unable to understand the English-only warnings. In response to the discovery, the *Seattle Times* took the unprecedented step of publishing the front-page story in six languages: English, Vietnamese, Chinese, Spanish, Russian, and Somali.

Although most immigrants can communicate effectively in English, language does isolate a small percentage of them. In the United States, social scientists use the term *linguistic isolation* to refer to households in which all members age 14 and older speak a non-English language and at the same time do not speak English very well. They have found that the proportion of the U.S. population that is linguistically isolated has been increasing steadily, from 3.2 percent in 2000 to 4.7 percent in 2009.

Studies show that those who are linguistically isolated are cut off from many public services. For example, public health professionals find that even after controlling for education and income, members of linguistically isolated households are less likely than others to receive adequate health care, or even to participate in basic health screening. And as the 2006 power outage in the Northwest showed, in some cases linguistic isolation can be deadly.

Nonverbal Communication

If you don't like the way a meeting is going, you might suddenly sit back, fold your arms, and turn down the corners of your mouth. When you see a friend in tears, you may give a quick hug. After winning a big game, you probably high-five your teammates. These are all examples of *nonverbal communication,* the use of gestures, facial expressions, and other visual images to communicate.

We are not born with these expressions. We learn them, just as we learn other forms of language, from people who share our same culture. This statement is as true for the basic expressions of happiness and sadness as it is for more complex emotions, such as shame or distress (Fridlund et al. 1987).

Like other forms of language, nonverbal communication is not the same in all cultures. For example, sociological research done at the micro level documents that people from various cultures differ in the degree to which they touch others during the

Sociology in the Global Community

BOX 10-1

Symbolizing 9/11

On September 11, 2001, the World Trade Center's twin towers took only minutes to collapse. Nearly a decade later, the creator of the memorial to those lost that day was still perfecting the site plan. Thirty-four-year-old architect Michael Arad, the man who submitted the winning design, had drawn two sunken squares, measuring an acre each, in the footprints left by the collapsed towers. His design, "Reflecting Absence," places each empty square in a reflecting pool surrounded by cascading water. Today, as visitors to the massive memorial stand at the edge of the site, they are struck by both the sound of the thundering water and the absence of life.

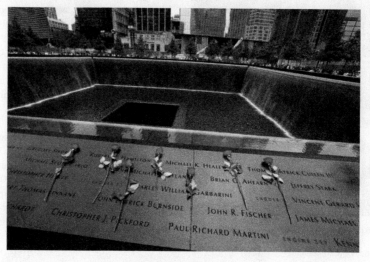

The memorial does not encompass the entire area destroyed in the attack, as some had wanted. In one of the great commercial capitals of the world, economic forces demanded that some part of the property produce income. Others had argued against constructing a memorial of any kind on what they regarded as hallowed ground. "Don't build on my sister's grave," one of them pleaded. They too had to compromise. On all sides of the eight-acre memorial site, new high rises have been and continue to be built. When construction is finished, the site will also accommodate a new underground transit hub.

Originally, the architect's plans called for the 2,982 victims of the attack to be listed elsewhere on the site. Today, in a revised plan, the names are displayed prominently along the sides of the reflecting pool. Arad had suggested that they be placed randomly, to symbolize the "haphazard brutality of life." Survivors objected, perhaps because they worried about locating their loved ones' names. In a compromise, the names were chiseled into the bronze walls of the memorial in groups that Arad calls "meaningful adjacencies": friends and co-workers; fellow passengers on the two downed aircraft, arranged by seat number; and first responders, grouped by their agencies or fire companies. Suggestions that would give first responders special recognition were set aside. The list includes victims of the simultaneous attack on the Pentagon in Washington, D.C., and passengers on the flight headed for the White House, who were attempting to thwart the attack when the plane crashed in a field in Pennsylvania. The six people who perished in the 1993 truck bombing at the World Trade Center are also memorialized.

Away from Ground Zero, symbols of 9/11 abound. Numerous small monuments and simple plaques grace intersections throughout metropolitan New York, particularly those that had a direct line of sight to the twin towers. In hundreds of cities worldwide, scraps of steel from the twisted buildings and remnants of destroyed emergency vehicles have been incorporated into memorials. And the USS *New York*, whose bow was forged from seven and a half tons of steel debris salvaged from the towers, has served as a working symbol of 9/11 since its commissioning in 2009.

> Numerous small monuments and simple plaques grace intersections throughout metropolitan New York, particularly those that had a direct line of sight to the twin towers.

LET'S DISCUSS

1. What does the 9/11 memorial symbolize to you? Explain the meaning of the cascading water, the reflecting pools, and the empty footprints. What does the placement of the victims' names suggest?

2. If you were designing a 9/11 memorial, what symbol or symbols would you incorporate? Use your sociological imagination to predict how various groups would respond to your design.

Sources: Blais and Rasic 2011; Kennicott 2011; Needham 2011.

course of normal social interactions. Even experienced travelers are sometimes caught off guard by these differences. In Saudi Arabia, a middle-aged man may want to hold hands with a partner after closing a business deal. In Egypt, men walk hand in hand in the street; in cafés, they fall asleep while lounging in each other's arms. These gestures, which would shock an American businessman, are considered compliments in those cultures. The meaning of hand signals is another form of nonverbal communication that can differ from one culture to the next. In Australia, the thumbs-up sign is considered rude (Passero 2002; Vaughan 2007).

A related form of communication is the use of symbols to convey meaning to others. **Symbols** are the gestures, objects, and words that form the basis of human communication. The thumbs-up gesture, a gold star sticker, and the smiley face in an e-mail are all symbols. Often deceptively simple, many symbols are rich in meaning and may not convey the same meaning in all social contexts. Around someone's neck, for example, a cross can symbolize religious reverence; over a grave site, a belief in everlasting life; or set in flames, racial hatred. Box 10-1 describes the delicate task of designing an appropriate symbol for the 9/11 memorial at New York's former World Trade Center—one that would have meaning for everyone who lost loved ones there, regardless of nationality or religious faith.

Norms and Values

"Wash your hands before dinner." "Thou shalt not kill." "Respect your elders." All societies have ways of encouraging and enforcing what they view as appropriate behavior while discouraging and punishing what they consider to be inappropriate behavior. They also have a collective idea of what is good and desirable in life—or not. In this section we will learn to distinguish between the closely related concepts of norms and values.

Norms

Norms are the established standards of behavior maintained by a society. For a norm to become significant, it must be widely shared and understood. For example, in movie theaters in the United States, we typically expect that people will be quiet while the film is shown. Of course, the application of this norm can vary, depending on the particular film and type of audience. People who are viewing a serious artistic film will be more likely to insist on the norm of silence than those who are watching a slapstick comedy or horror movie.

One persistent social norm in contemporary society is that of heterosexuality. Children are socialized to accept this norm from a very young age. Overwhelmingly, parents describe adult romantic relationships to their children exclusively as heterosexual relationships. That is not necessarily because they consider same-sex relationships unacceptable, but more likely because they see heterosexuality as the norm in marital partnerships. According to a national survey of mothers of three- to six-year-olds, one in five mothers teaches her young children that homosexuality is wrong. The same survey showed that parenting reflects the dominant ideology, in which homosexuality is treated as a rare exception. Most parents assume that their children are heterosexual; only one in four has even considered whether his or her child might grow up to be gay or lesbian (K. Martin 2009).

Types of Norms   Sociologists distinguish between norms in two ways. First, norms are classified as either formal or informal. **Formal norms** generally have been written down and specify strict punishments for violators. In the United States, we often formalize norms into laws, which are very precise in defining proper and improper behavior. Sociologist Donald Black (1995) has termed **law** "governmental social control," meaning that laws are formal norms enforced by the state. Laws are just one example of formal norms. The requirements for a college major and the rules of a card game are also considered formal norms.

In contrast, **informal norms** are generally understood but not precisely recorded. Standards of proper dress are a common example of informal norms. Our society has no specific punishment, or *sanction*, for a person who comes to school, say, wearing a monkey suit. Making fun of the nonconforming student is usually the most likely response.

Norms are also classified by their relative importance to society. When classified in this way, they are known as *mores* and *folkways*. **Mores** (pronounced MOR-ays) are norms deemed highly necessary to the welfare of a society, often because they embody the most cherished principles of a people. Each society demands obedience to its mores; violation can lead to severe penalties. Thus, the United States has strong mores against murder, treason, and child abuse, which have been institutionalized into formal norms.

Folkways are norms governing everyday behavior. Folkways play an important role in shaping the daily behavior of members of a culture. Society is less likely to formalize folkways than mores, and their violation raises comparatively little concern. For example, walking up a down escalator in a department store challenges our standards of appropriate behavior, but it will not result in a fine or a jail sentence.

💡 use your **sociological imagination**

You are a high school principal. What norms would you want to govern the students' behavior? How might those norms differ from norms appropriate for college students?

Acceptance of Norms   People do not follow norms, whether mores or folkways, in all situations. In some cases, they can evade a norm because they know it is weakly enforced. It is illegal for U.S. teenagers to drink alcoholic beverages, yet drinking by minors is common throughout the nation. (In fact, teenage alcoholism is a serious social problem.)

In some instances, behavior that appears to violate society's norms may actually represent adherence to the norms of a particular group. Teenage drinkers are conforming to the standards of their peer group when they violate norms that condemn underage drinking. Similarly, business executives who use shady accounting techniques may be responding to a corporate culture that demands the maximization of profits at any cost, including the deception of investors and government regulatory agencies.

Norms are violated in some instances because one norm conflicts with another. For example, suppose that you live in an apartment building and one night hear the screams of the woman next door, who is being beaten by her husband. If you decide to intervene by ringing their doorbell or calling the police, you are violating the norm of minding your own business, while following the norm of assisting a victim of violence.

Acceptance of norms is subject to change as the political, economic, and social conditions of a culture are transformed. Until the 1960s, for example, formal norms throughout much of the United States prohibited the marriage of people from different racial groups. Over the past half century, however, such legal prohibitions were cast aside. The process of change can be seen today in the increasing acceptance of single parents and growing support for the legalization of marriage between same-sex couples (see Module 38).

When circumstances require the sudden violation of long-standing cultural norms, the change can upset an entire population. In Iraq, where Muslim custom strictly forbids touching by strangers for men and especially for women, the war that began in 2003 brought numerous daily violations of the norm. Outside important mosques, government offices, and other facilities likely to be targeted by terrorists, visitors had to be patted down and have their bags searched by Iraqi security guards. To reduce the discomfort caused by the procedure, women were searched by female guards and men by male guards. Despite that concession, and the fact that many Iraqis admitted or even insisted on the need for such measures, people still winced at the invasion of their personal privacy. In reaction to the searches, Iraqi women began to limit the contents of the bags they carried or simply to leave them at home (Rubin 2003).

Sanctions

Suppose a football coach sends a 12th player onto the field. Imagine a college graduate showing up in shorts for a job interview at a large bank. Or consider a driver who neglects to put money in a parking meter. These people have violated widely shared and understood norms. So what happens? In each of these situations, the person will receive sanctions if his or her behavior is detected.

Sanctions are penalties and rewards for conduct concerning a social norm. Note that the concept of *reward* is included in this definition. Conformity to a norm can lead to positive sanctions such as a pay raise, a medal, a word of gratitude, or a pat on the back. Negative sanctions include fines, threats, imprisonment, and stares of contempt.

Table 10-1 summarizes the relationship between norms and sanctions. As you can see, the sanctions that are associated with formal norms (which are written down and codified) tend to be formal as well. If a college football coach sends too many players onto the field, the team will be penalized 15 yards. The driver who fails to put money in the parking meter will receive a ticket and have to pay a fine. But sanctions for violations of informal norms can vary. The college graduate who goes to the bank interview in shorts will probably lose any chance of getting the job; on the other hand, he or she might be so brilliant that bank officials will overlook the unconventional attire.

The entire fabric of norms and sanctions in a culture reflects that culture's values and priorities. The most cherished values will be most heavily sanctioned; matters regarded as less critical will carry light and informal sanctions.

Table 10-1   Norms and Sanctions

Norms	Sanctions	
	Positive	**Negative**
Formal	Salary bonus	Demotion
	Testimonial dinner	Firing from a job
	Medal	Jail sentence
	Diploma	Expulsion
Informal	Smile	Frown
	Compliment	Humiliation
	Cheers	Bullying

Values

Though we each have a personal set of values—which may include caring or fitness or success in business—we also share a general set of values as members of a society. Cultural **values** are these collective conceptions of what is considered good, desirable, and proper—or bad, undesirable, and improper—in a culture. They indicate what people in a given culture prefer as well as what they find important and morally right (or wrong). Values may be specific, such as honoring one's parents and owning a home, or they may be more general, such as health, love, and democracy. Of course, the members of a society do not uniformly share its values. Angry political debates and billboards promoting conflicting causes tell us that much.

Values influence people's behavior and serve as criteria for evaluating the actions of others. The values, norms, and sanctions of a culture are often directly related. For example, if a culture places a high value on the institution of marriage, it may have norms (and strict sanctions) that prohibit the act of adultery or make divorce difficult. If a culture views private property as a basic value, it will probably have stiff laws against theft and vandalism.

The values of a culture may change, but most remain relatively stable during any one person's lifetime. Socially shared, intensely felt values are a fundamental part of our lives in the United States. Sociologist Robin Williams (1970) has offered a list of basic values. It includes achievement, efficiency, material comfort, nationalism, equality, and the supremacy of science and reason over faith. Obviously, not all 309 million people in this country agree on all these values, but such a list serves as a starting point in defining the national character.

Each year more than 200,000 entering college students at nearly 300 of the nation's four-year colleges fill out a questionnaire about their values. Because this survey focuses on an array of issues, beliefs, and life goals, it is commonly cited as a barometer of the nation's values. The respondents are asked what values are personally important to them. Over the past half century, the value of "being very well-off financially" has shown the strongest gain in popularity; the proportion of first-year college students who endorse this value as "essential" or "very important" rose from 42 percent in 1966 to 80 percent in 2011 (Figure 10-1).

In contrast, the value that has shown the most striking decline in endorsement by students is "developing a meaningful philosophy of life." While this value was the most popular in the

FIGURE 10-1 Life Goals of First-Year College Students in the United States, 1966–2011

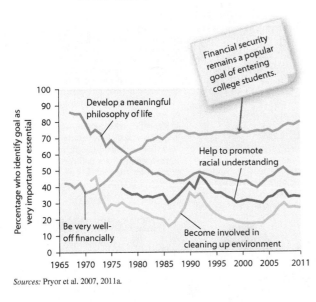

Sources: Pryor et al. 2007, 2011a.

Think about It

Why do you think values have shifted among college students in the past few decades? Which of these values is important to you?

1967 survey, endorsed by 85 percent of the respondents, it had fallen to seventh place on the list by 2011, when it was endorsed by less than 47 percent of students entering college.

During the 1980s and 1990s, support for values having to do with money, power, and status grew. At the same time, support for certain values having to do with social awareness and altruism, such as "helping others," declined. According to the 2011 nationwide survey, only 42 percent of first-year college students stated that "influencing social values" was an "essential" or "very important" goal. The proportion of students for whom "helping to promote racial understanding" was an essential or very important goal reached a record high of 46 percent in 1992, then fell to 34 percent in 2011. Like other aspects of culture, such as language and norms, a nation's values are not necessarily fixed.

Whether the slogan is "Think Green" or "Reduce Your Carbon Footprint," students have been exposed to values associated with environmentalism. How many of them accept those values? Poll results over the past 40 years show fluctuations, with a high of nearly 46 percent of students indicating a desire to become involved in cleaning up the environment. By the 1980s, however, student support for embracing this objective had dropped to around 20 percent or even lower (see Figure 10-1). Even with recent attention to global warming, the proportion remains level at only 26 percent of first-year students in 2011.

Recently, cheating has become a hot issue on college campuses. Professors who take advantage of computerized services that can identify plagiarism, such as the search engine Google, have been shocked to learn that many of the papers their students hand in are plagiarized in whole or in part. Box 10-2 examines the shift in values that underlies this decline in academic integrity.

Another value that has begun to change recently, not just among students but among the public in general, is the right to privacy. Americans have always valued their privacy and resented government intrusions into their personal lives. In the aftermath of the terrorist attacks of September 11, 2001, however, many citizens called for greater protection against the threat of terrorism. In response, the U.S. government broadened its surveillance powers and increased its ability to monitor people's behavior without court approval. In 2001, shortly after the attacks, Congress passed the Patriot Act, which empowers the FBI to access individuals' medical, library, student, and phone records without informing them or obtaining a search warrant.

Values can also differ in subtle ways not just among individuals and groups, but from one culture to another. For example, in Japan, young children spend long hours working with tutors, preparing for entrance exams required for admission to selective schools. No stigma is attached to these services, known as "cram schools"; in fact, they are highly valued. Yet in South Korea, people have begun to complain that cram schools give affluent students an unfair advantage. Since 2008, the South Korean government has regulated the after-school tutoring industry, limiting its hours and imposing fees on the schools. Some think this policy has lowered their society's expectations of students, describing it as an attempt to make South Koreans "more American" (Ramstad 2011; Ripley 2011).

Another example of cultural differences in values is public opinion regarding the treatment of different racial and ethnic groups. As Figure 10-2 shows, opinion on the need for equal treatment of different racial and ethnic groups varies dramatically from one country to another.

Global Culture War

For almost a generation, public attention in the United States has focused on **culture war,** or the polarization of society over controversial cultural elements. Originally, in the 1990s, the term referred to political debates over heated issues such as abortion, religious expression, gun control, and sexual orientation. Soon, however, it took on a global meaning—especially after 9/11, as Americans wondered, "Why do they hate us?" Through 2000, global studies of public opinion had reported favorable views of the United States in countries as diverse as Morocco and Germany. But after the United States established a military presence in Iraq and Afghanistan, foreign opinion of the United States became quite negative (J. Hunter 1991; Kohut et al. 2005, 2007).

In the past 30 years, extensive efforts have been made to compare values in different nations, recognizing the challenges in interpreting value concepts in a similar manner across cultures.

Sociology on Campus

BOX 10-2

A Culture of Cheating?

On November 21, 2002, after issuing several warnings, officials at the U.S. Naval Academy seized the computers of almost 100 midshipmen suspected of downloading movies and music illegally from the Internet. Officers at the school may have taken the unusually strong action to avoid liability on the part of the U.S. government, which owns the computers students were using. But across the nation, college administrators have been trying to restrain students from downloading pirated entertainment for free. The practice is so widespread, it has been slowing down the high-powered computer networks colleges and universities depend on for research and admissions.

Illegal downloading is just one aspect of the growing problem of copyright violation, both on campus and off. Now that students can use personal computers to surf the Internet, most do their research online. Apparently, the temptation to cut and paste passages from website postings and pass them off as one's own is irresistible to many. In 2010, 59 percent of high school students admitted cheating on a test, 34 percent of them more than twice. One in three high school students admitted using the Internet to plagiarize an assignment.

Research suggests that the proportion of students who cheat is even higher among college students. The Center for Academic Integrity estimates that at most colleges and universities, more than 75 percent of the students

> The Center for Academic Integrity estimates that at most colleges and universities, more than 75 percent of the students engage in some form of cheating.

engage in some form of cheating. Students not only cut passages from the Internet and paste them into their papers without citing the source; they share questions and answers on exams, collaborate on assignments they are supposed to do independently, and even falsify the results of their laboratory experiments.

To address what they consider an alarming trend, many colleges are rewriting or adopting new academic honor codes. Observers contend that the increase in student cheating reflects widely publicized instances of cheating in public life, which have served to create an alternative set of values in which the end justifies the means. When young people see sports heroes, authors, entertainers, and corporate executives exposed for cheating in one form or another, the message seems to be "Cheating is okay, as long as you don't get caught."

LET'S DISCUSS

1. Do you know anyone who has engaged in Internet plagiarism? What about cheating on tests or falsifying laboratory results? If so, how did the person justify these forms of dishonesty?

2. Even if cheaters aren't caught, what negative effects does their academic dishonesty have on them? What effects does it have on students who are honest? Could an entire college or university suffer from students' dishonesty?

Sources: Argetsinger and Krim 2002; Bartlett 2009; Center for Academic Integrity 2006; Josephson Institute 2011; R. Thomas 2003; Toppo 2011; Zernike 2002.

Psychologist Shalom Schwartz has measured values in more than 60 countries. Around the world, certain values are widely shared, including benevolence, which is defined as "forgiveness and loyalty." In contrast, power, defined as "control or dominance over people and resources," is a value that is endorsed much less often (Hitlin and Piliavin 2004; S. Schwartz and Bardi 2001).

Despite this evidence of shared values, some scholars have interpreted the terrorism, genocide, wars, and military occupations of the early 21st century as a "clash of civilizations." According to this thesis, cultural and religious identities, rather than national or political loyalties, are becoming the prime source of international conflict. Critics of this thesis point out that conflict over values is nothing new; only our ability to create havoc and violence has grown. Furthermore, speaking of a clash of "civilizations" disguises the sharp divisions that exist within large groups. Christianity, for example, runs the gamut from Quaker-style pacifism to certain elements of the Ku Klux Klan's ideology (Berman 2003; Huntington 1993; Said 2001).

Culture and the Dominant Ideology

Functionalist and conflict theorists agree that culture and society are mutually supportive, but for different reasons. Functionalists maintain that social stability requires a consensus and the support of society's members; strong central values and common norms provide that support. This view of culture became popular in sociology beginning in the 1950s. It was borrowed from British anthropologists who saw cultural traits as a stabilizing element in a culture. From a functionalist perspective, a cultural trait or practice will persist if it performs functions that society seems to need or contributes to overall social stability and consensus.

Conflict theorists agree that a common culture may exist, but they argue that it serves to maintain the privileges of certain groups. Moreover, while protecting their self-interest, powerful

FIGURE 10-2 **Valuing Ethnicity by Country**

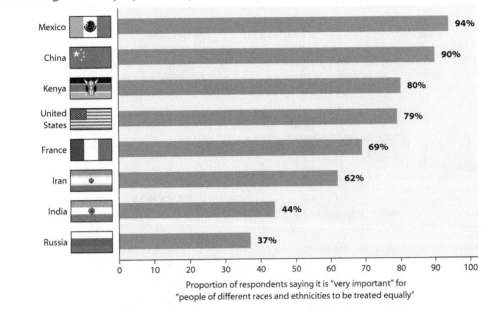

Source: Council on Foreign Relations 2009.

groups may keep others in a subservient position. The term **dominant ideology** describes the set of cultural beliefs and practices that helps to maintain powerful social, economic, and political interests. This concept was first used by Hungarian Marxist Georg Lukacs (1923) and Italian Marxist Antonio Gramsci (1929), but it did not gain an audience in the United States until the early 1970s. In Karl Marx's view, a capitalist society has a dominant ideology that serves the interests of the ruling class.

From a conflict perspective, the dominant ideology has major social significance. Not only do a society's most powerful groups and institutions control wealth and property; even more important, they control the means of producing beliefs about reality through religion, education, and the media. Feminists would also argue that if all a society's most important institutions tell women they should be subservient to men, that dominant ideology will help to control women and keep them in a subordinate position. Table 10-2 summarizes the major sociological perspectives on culture.

A growing number of social scientists believe that it is not easy to identify a core culture in the United States. For support,

Table **10-2**　Sociological Perspectives on Culture　　**Tracking** Sociological Perspectives

	Functionalist Perspective	Conflict Perspective	Feminist Perspective	Interactionist Perspective
Cultural Variation	Subcultures serve the interests of subgroups	Countercultures question the dominant social order; ethnocentrism devalues groups	Cultural relativism respects variations in the way men and women are viewed in different societies	Customs and traditions are transmitted through intergroup contact and through the media
Norms	Reinforce societal standards	Reinforce patterns of dominance	Reinforce roles of men and women	Are maintained through face-to-face interaction
Values	Are collective conceptions of what is good	May perpetuate social inequality	May perpetuate men's dominance	Are defined and redefined through social interaction
Culture and Society	Culture reflects a society's strong central values	Culture reflects a society's dominant ideology	Culture reflects society's view of men and women	A society's core culture is perpetuated through daily social interactions
Walmart	Provides goods and services to customers	Opposes labor unions; slow to provide employee health benefits, promote women	Limits role of women in leadership	Has been insensitive to cultural variations in store–customer relationships

they point to the lack of consensus on national values, the diffusion of cultural traits, the diversity within our culture, and the changing views of young people (look again at Figure 10-1). Instead, they suggest that the core culture provides the tools that people of all persuasions need to develop strategies for social change. Still, there is no denying that certain expressions of values have greater influence than others, even in as complex a society as the United States (Swidler 1986).

How one views a culture—whether from an ethnocentric point of view or through the lens of cultural relativism—can have serious consequences in business, as the following case study on Walmart demonstrates. It also has important implications for social policy. Should a nation accommodate non-native-language speakers by sponsoring bilingual programs, for example? We'll take a close look at this controversial issue in the Social Policy section at the end of Module 12.

MODULE 10 | Recap and Review

Summary

This module discusses the major elements that all cultures share: **language**, **norms**, and **values**.

1. **Language** includes speech, written characters, numerals, and **symbols**, as well as gestures and other forms of nonverbal communication. Language both describes culture and shapes it.

2. Sociologists distinguish between **norms** in two ways, classifying them as **formal** or **informal** and as **mores** or **folkways.**

3. The formal norms of a culture will carry the heaviest **sanctions**; informal norms will carry light sanctions.

4. The **dominant ideology** of a culture is the set of cultural beliefs and practices that help to maintain powerful social, economic, and political interests.

Thinking Critically

1. In the United States, is the norm of heterosexuality a formal norm or an informal norm? Would you categorize it with mores or folkways? Explain your reasoning.

2. Do you think the United States has a dominant ideology? If so, how would you describe it? Whose interests does it serve?

Key Terms

Culture war

Dominant ideology

Folkway

Formal norm

Informal norm

Language

Law

Mores

Norm

Sanction

Sapir-Whorf hypothesis

Symbol

Value

MODULE 11 | Development of Culture around the World

We've come a long way from our prehistoric heritage. The human species has produced such achievements as the novels of Leo Tolstoy, the art of Pablo Picasso, and the films of Ang Lee. A decade into the new millennium, we can transmit an entire book around the world via the Internet, clone cells, and prolong lives through organ transplants. We can peer into the outermost reaches of the universe or analyze our innermost feelings. In this section we will examine two of the social processes that make these remarkable achievements possible: innovation and the diffusion of culture through globalization and technology.

Innovation

The process of introducing a new idea or object to a culture is known as **innovation.** Innovation interests sociologists because of the social consequences of introducing something new. There are two forms of innovation: discovery and invention. **Discovery** involves making known or sharing the existence of an aspect of reality. The finding of the structure of the DNA molecule and the identification of a new moon of Saturn are both acts of discovery. A significant factor in the process of discovery is the sharing of newfound knowledge with others. In contrast, an **invention** results when existing cultural items are combined into a form that did not exist before. The bow and arrow, the automobile, and the television are all examples of inventions, as are Protestantism and democracy.

💡 use your **sociological imagination**

If you grew up in your parents' generation—without computers, e-mail, MP3 players, and cell phones—how would your daily life differ from the one you lead today?

Globalization, Diffusion, and Technology

The recent emergence of Starbucks, the worldwide chain of coffeehouses, is just one illustration of the rapidly escalating trend toward globalization (see Module 4). While people in Asia are beginning to enjoy coffee, people in North America are discovering sushi. Some have become familiar with the *bento box,* a small lunchbox that is often used to serve sushi. A trademark Japanese cuisine, sushi has evolved from a once-exotic dish in the United States to a mainstream food commonly found in supermarket refrigerators. Yet its move across the Pacific has changed the delicacy. Americans tend to treat sushi as a take-out or menu item. The authentic way to eat sushi is to sit at a bar and engage the chef in conversation about the day's catch before choosing which fish or shellfish to eat.

More and more cultural expressions and practices are crossing national borders and having an effect on the traditions and customs of the societies exposed to them. Sociologists use the term **diffusion** to refer to the process by which a cultural item spreads from group to group or society to society. Diffusion can occur through a variety of means, among them exploration, military conquest, missionary work, and the influence of the mass media, tourism, and the Internet (Box 11-1). It has also been hastened by the spread of the fast-food restaurant.

Sociologist George Ritzer coined the term *McDonaldization of society* to describe how the principles of fast-food restaurants, developed in the United States, have come to dominate more and more sectors of societies throughout the world (see Module 19). For example, hair salons and medical clinics now take walk-ins. In Hong Kong, sex selection clinics offer a menu of items, from fertility enhancement to methods of increasing the likelihood of having a child of the desired sex. And religious groups—from evangelical preachers on local stations or websites to priests at the Vatican Television Center—use marketing techniques similar to those that are used to sell Happy Meals.

McDonaldization is associated with the melding of cultures, through which we see more and more similarities in cultural expression. In Japan, for example, African entrepreneurs have found a thriving market for hip-hop fashions popularized by teens in the United States. Similarly, the familiar Golden Arches of McDonald's can be seen around the world. Yet corporations like McDonald's have had to make some adjustments of their own. Until 2001, McDonald's ran its *overseas* operations from corporate headquarters in suburban Chicago. After a few false starts, executives recognized the need to develop the restaurant's menus and marketing strategies overseas, relying on advice from local people. Now, at over 3,700 restaurants in Japan, customers can enjoy the Mega Tamago Burger—beef, bacon, and fried egg with special sauces. In India, patrons who don't eat beef can order a double chicken-patty sandwich known as the Maharaja Mac. In France, baguettes have been added to the menu. And in Austria, the locals' love of coffee, cake, and conversation has inspired the McCafé (Hughlett 2008; Ritzer 2002, 2011). When a company pays attention to local culture, globalization can succeed. Sometimes, however, lack of concern for cultural differences can result in problems, as the Case Study illustrates.

Sociology in the Global Community

BOX 11-1

Life in the Global Village

Imagine a "borderless world" in which culture, trade, commerce, money, and even people move freely from one place to another. Popular culture is widely shared, whether it be Japanese sushi or U.S. running shoes, and the English speaker who answers questions over the telephone about your credit card account is as likely to be in India or Ireland as in the United States. In this world, even the sovereignty of nations is at risk, challenged by political movements and ideologies that span nations.

> *Even* Pirates of the Caribbean *movies and Lady Gaga may be seen as threats to native cultures.*

What caused this great wave of cultural diffusion? First, sociologists take note of advances in communications technology. Satellite TV, cell phones, the Internet, and the like allow information to flow freely across the world, linking global markets. In 2008, this process reached the point where consumers could view videos on handheld devices and surf the Internet on their wireless cell phones, shopping online at Amazon.com, eBay, and other commercial

websites from cars, airports, and cafeterias. Second, corporations in the industrial nations have become multinational, with both factories and markets in developing countries. Business leaders welcome the opportunity to sell consumer goods in populous countries such as China. Third, these multinational firms have cooperated with global financial institutions, organizations, and governments to promote free trade—unrestricted or lightly restricted commerce across national borders.

Globalization is not universally welcomed. Many critics see the dominance of "businesses without borders" as benefiting the rich, particularly the very wealthy in industrial countries, at the expense of the poor in less developed nations. They consider globalization to be a successor to the imperialism and colonialism that oppressed Third World nations for centuries.

Another criticism of globalization comes from people who feel overwhelmed by global culture. Embedded in the concept of globalization is the notion of the cultural domination of developing nations by more affluent nations. Simply put, people lose their traditional values and begin to identify with the culture of dominant nations. They may discard or neglect their native languages and dress as they attempt to copy the icons of mass-market entertainment and fashion. Even *Pirates of the Caribbean*

movies and Lady Gaga may be seen as threats to native cultures, if they dominate the media at the expense of local art forms. As Sembene Ousmane, one of Africa's most prominent writers and filmmakers, noted, "[Today] we are more familiar with European fairy tales than with our own traditional stories" (World Development Forum 1990:4).

Globalization has its positive side, too. Many developing nations are taking their place in the world of commerce and bringing in much needed income. The communications revolution helps people to stay connected and gives them access to knowledge that can improve living standards and even save lives.

LET'S DISCUSS

1. How are you affected by globalization? Which aspects of globalization do you find advantageous and which objectionable?

2. How would you feel if the customs and traditions you grew up with were replaced by the culture or values of another country? How might you try to protect your culture?

Sources: Dodds 2000; Giddens 1991; Hirst and Thompson 1996; D. Martin et al. 2006; Ritzer 2004; Sernau 2001; Tedeschi 2006.

Technology in its many forms has increased the speed of cultural diffusion and broadened the distribution of cultural elements. Sociologist Gerhard Lenski has defined **technology** as "cultural information about the ways in which the material resources of the environment may be used to satisfy human needs and desires" (Nolan and Lenski 2009:357). Today's technological developments no longer await publication in journals with limited circulation. Press conferences, often carried simultaneously on the Internet, trumpet the new developments.

Technology not only accelerates the diffusion of scientific innovations but also transmits culture. The English language and North American culture dominate the Internet and World Wide Web. Such control, or at least dominance, of technology influences the direction of cultural diffusion. For example, websites cover even the most superficial aspects of U.S. culture but offer little information about the pressing issues faced by citizens of other nations. People all over the world find it easier to visit electronic chat rooms about the latest reality TV shows than to learn about their own governments' policies on day care or infant nutrition.

Sociologist William F. Ogburn (1922) made a useful distinction between the elements of *material* and *nonmaterial culture*. **Material culture** refers to the physical or technological aspects of our daily lives, including food, houses, factories,

and raw materials. **Nonmaterial culture** refers to ways of using material objects, as well as to customs, beliefs, philosophies, governments, and patterns of communication. Generally, the

Members of Big Toe Crew, a Vietnamese hip-hop group, rehearse for a performance. Through tourism and the mass media, music and dance spread from one culture to another in a process called diffusion.

When a society's nonmaterial culture (its values and laws) does not keep pace with rapid changes in its material culture, people experience an awkward period of maladjustment called *culture lag*. The transition to nuclear power generation that began in the second half of the 20th century brought widespread protests against the new technology, as well as serious accidents that government officials were poorly prepared to deal with. Tensions over the controversial technology have not run as high in some countries as in others, however. France, where this nuclear power plant is situated, generates 78 percent of all its electricity through nuclear power. The technology is not as controversial there as in the United States and Canada, which generate less than 20 percent of their electricity through nuclear reaction.

nonmaterial culture is more resistant to change than the material culture. Consequently, Ogburn introduced the term **culture lag** to refer to the period of maladjustment when the nonmaterial culture is still struggling to adapt to new material conditions. For example, in 2010, manufacturers introduced electronic cigarettes, battery-powered tubes that turn nicotine-laced liquid into a vapor mist. The innovation soon had officials at airlines (which ban smoking) and the Food and Drug Administration scrambling to respond to the latest technology (Kesmodel and Yadron 2010; Swidler 1986).

Resistance to technological change can lead not only to culture lag, but to some real questions of cultural survival (Box 11-2).

Sociology in the Global Community

BOX 11-2

Cultural Survival in Brazil

When the first Portuguese ships landed on the coast of what we now know as Brazil, more than 2 million people inhabited the vast, mineral-rich land. The natives lived in small, isolated settlements, spoke a variety of languages, and embraced many different cultural traditions.

Today, over five centuries later, Brazil's population has grown to more than 192 million, only about 650,000 of whom are indigenous peoples descended from the original inhabitants. Over 200 different indigenous groups

> In Mato Grosso, a heavily forested state near the Amazon River, loggers have been clear-cutting the land at a rate that alarms the Bororo.

have survived, living a life tied closely to the land and the rivers, just as their ancestors did. But over the past two generations, their numbers have dwindled as booms in mining, logging, oil drilling, and agriculture have encroached on their land and their settlements.

Many indigenous groups were once nomads, moving around from one hunting or fishing ground to another. Now they are hemmed in on the reservations the government confined them to, surrounded by huge farms or ranches whose owners deny their right to live off the land. State officials may insist that laws restrict the development of indigenous lands, but indigenous peoples tell a different story. In Mato Grosso, a heavily forested state near the Amazon River, loggers have been clear-cutting the land at a rate that alarms the Bororo, an indigenous group that has lived in the area for centuries. According to one elder, the Bororo are now confined to six small reservations of about 500 square miles—much less than the area officially granted them in the 19th century.

In the face of dwindling resources, indigenous groups like the Bororo struggle to maintain their culture. Though the tribe still observes the traditional initiation rites for adolescent boys, members are finding it difficult to continue their hunting and fishing rituals, given the scarcity of game and fish in the area. Pesticides in the runoff from nearby farms have poisoned the water they fish and bathe in, threatening both their health and their culture's survival.

LET'S DISCUSS

1. Compare the frontier in Brazil today to the American West in the 1800s. What similarities do you see?

2. What does society lose when indigenous cultures die?

Sources: Brazier and Hamed 2007; H. Chu 2005; Survival International 2012.

case study | Culture at Walmart

By some measures, Walmart is the largest corporation in the world. By other measures, it is the world's 14th largest economy. Indeed, the Bentonville, Arkansas–based retailer's annual revenue—over one-third of a trillion dollars—surpasses the total value of goods and services produced in many countries, such as Sweden.

Walmart's rise to the status of an economic superpower has not been without criticism. To keep prices low, the corporation pays store clerks as little as possible, and in North America, has determinedly shut out labor organizers who seek to better the clerks' wages. Given Walmart's wage levels, a large proportion of employees simply cannot afford health insurance, even if the corporation offers it. Also, Walmart has been noted for its lack of commitment to equal opportunity: very few women occupy managerial positions at the company (Barbaro 2008).

Although U.S. consumers have embraced Walmart's "everyday low prices," the reaction has not been as positive in countries where consumers hold different cultural values. The company, now located in 16 countries, has not been an unqualified success abroad. Consider the following missteps in three very different countries. In 2006, the company sold all its facilities in South Korea, where its warehouse-style stores were not appreciated by shoppers accustomed to more elegant surroundings. Today, Walmart is learning not to impose its corporate culture on foreign customers and employees. No longer do managers plan to sell golf clubs in Brazil, where the game is rarely played, or ice skates in Mexico, where skating rinks are hard to find. More important, the corporate giant has begun to study the culture and social patterns of potential customers (Landler and Barbaro 2006; Saporito 2007; Walmart 2010; A. Zimmerman and Nelson 2006).

Walmart also pulled out of Germany, due in part to its failure to adjust to the national culture. German shoppers, accustomed to no-nonsense, impersonal service, found Walmart employees' smiling, outgoing style off-putting. The company's "ten-foot attitude"—a salesperson who comes within 10 feet of a customer must look the person in the eye, greet the person, and ask if he or she needs help—simply did not play well there. Food shoppers, used to bagging their own groceries, were turned off by Walmart's practice of allowing clerks to handle their purchases. Furthermore, German employees, who had grown up in a culture that accepts workplace romances, found the company's prohibition against on-the-job relationships bizarre.

In China, where people are used to small mom-and-pop shops whose owners will haggle with customers over prices, Walmart's 353 stores have struggled. By comparison, Walmart's insistence on fixed prices—even if those fixed prices are lower—seems heavy-handed and impersonal (Burkitt 2011).

Today, rather than risk another mistake abroad, Walmart is considering buying Massmart, a retailer with 288 existing stores in Africa. Time will tell whether the proposed takeover is welcomed, or if Walmart is again rejected as the "Beast of Bentonville," as critics in Germany and South Africa called it (Maylie 2011).

MODULE 11 | Recap and Review

Summary

In this module we examine the ways in which culture changes and spreads.

1. Human culture is constantly expanding through the process of **innovation**, which includes both **discovery** and **invention**.

2. **Diffusion**—the spread of cultural items from one place to another—has fostered globalization. Still, people resist ideas that seem too foreign, as well as those they perceive as threatening to their own values and beliefs.

Thinking Critically

1. Name one culturally significant discovery and one culturally significant invention that occurred in your lifetime. Explain how these innovations have changed your culture.

2. Describe one positive example and one negative of McDonaldization that you have experienced.

Key Terms

Culture lag

Diffusion

Discovery

Innovation

Invention

Material culture

Nonmaterial culture

Technology

MODULE 12 | ## Cultural Variation

Each culture has a unique character. Inuit tribes in northern Canada, wrapped in furs and dieting on whale blubber, have little in common with farmers in Southeast Asia, who dress for the heat and subsist mainly on the rice they grow in their paddies. Cultures adapt to meet specific sets of circumstances, such as climate, level of technology, population, and geography. Thus, despite the presence of cultural universals such as courtship and religion, great diversity exists among the world's many cultures. Moreover, even *within* a single nation, certain segments of the populace develop cultural patterns that differ from the patterns of the dominant society.

Subcultures

Rodeo riders, residents of a retirement community, workers on an offshore oil rig—all are examples of what sociologists refer to as *subcultures*. A **subculture** is a segment of society that shares a distinctive pattern of customs, rules, and traditions that differs from the pattern of the larger society. In a sense, a subculture can be thought of as a culture existing within a larger, dominant culture. The existence of many subcultures is characteristic of complex societies such as the United States.

Members of a subculture participate in the dominant culture while engaging in unique and distinctive forms of behavior. Frequently, a subculture will develop an **argot,** or specialized language, that distinguishes it from the wider society. Athletes who play *parkour,* an extreme sport that combines forward running with fence leaping and the vaulting of walls, water barriers, and even moving cars, speak an argot they devised especially to describe their feats. Parkour runners talk about doing *King Kong vaults*—diving arms first over a wall or grocery cart and landing in a standing position. They may follow this maneuver with a *tic tac*—kicking off a wall to overcome some kind of obstacle (Tschorn 2010).

Such argot allows insiders—the members of the subculture—to understand words with special meanings. It also establishes patterns of communication that outsiders can't understand. Sociologists associated with the interactionist perspective emphasize that language and symbols offer a powerful way for a subculture to feel cohesive and maintain its identity.

In India, a new subculture has developed among employees at the international call centers established by multinational corporations. To serve customers in the United States and Europe, the young men and women who work there must

Employees of an international call center in India socialize after their shift has ended. Call center employees, whose odd working hours isolate them from others, tend to form tight-knit subcultures.

Members of the militia group Ohio Defense Force engage in paramilitary exercises, imagining they are destroying a threatening Muslim stronghold in the United States.

be fluent speakers of English. But the corporations that employ them demand more than proficiency in a foreign language; they expect their Indian employees to adopt Western values and work habits, including the grueling pace U.S. workers take for granted. In return they offer perks such as Western-style dinners, dances, and coveted consumer goods. Significantly, they allow employees to take the day off only on U.S. holidays, like Labor Day and Thanksgiving—not on Indian holidays like Diwali, the Hindu festival of lights. While most Indian families are home celebrating, call center employees see only each other; when they have the day off, no one else is free to socialize with them. As a result, these employees have formed a tight-knit subculture based on hard work and a taste for Western luxury goods and leisure-time pursuits.

Another shared characteristic among some employees at Indian call centers is their contempt for the callers they serve. In performing their monotonous, repetitive job day after day, hundreds of thousands of these workers have come to see the faceless Americans they deal with as slow, often rude customers. Such shared understandings underpin this emerging subculture (Bhagat 2007; Gentleman 2006; Patel 2010).

Functionalist and conflict theorists agree that variation exists within cultures. Functionalists view subcultures as variations of particular social environments and as evidence that differences can exist within a common culture. However, conflict theorists suggest that variations often reflect the inequality of social arrangements within a society. A conflict theorist would view the challenges to dominant social norms by African American activists, the feminist movement, and the gay rights movement as reflections of inequity based on race, gender, and sexual orientation. Conflict theorists also argue that subcultures sometimes emerge when the dominant society unsuccessfully tries to suppress a practice, such as the use of illegal drugs.

Countercultures

By the end of the 1960s, an extensive subculture had emerged in the United States, composed of young people turned off by a society they believed was too materialistic and technological. The group included primarily political radicals and hippies who had dropped out of mainstream social institutions. These young men and women rejected the pressure to accumulate cars, homes, and an endless array of material goods. Instead, they expressed a desire to live in a culture based on more humanistic values, such as sharing, love, and coexistence with the environment. As a political force, this subculture opposed the United States' involvement in the war in Vietnam and encouraged draft resistance (Flacks 1971; Roszak 1969).

When a subculture conspicuously and deliberately opposes certain aspects of the larger culture, it is known as a **counterculture.** Countercultures typically thrive among the young, who have the least investment in the existing culture. In most cases, a 20-year-old can adjust to new cultural standards more easily than someone who has spent 60 years following the patterns of the dominant culture (Zellner 1995).

In the last decade, counterterrorism experts have become concerned about the growth of ultraconservative militia groups in the United States. Secretive and well armed, members of these countercultural groups tend to be antigovernment, and they often tolerate racism in their midst. Watchdogs estimate that 127 militias are operating in the United States today (Southern Poverty Law Center 2010).

Culture Shock

Anyone who feels disoriented, uncertain, out of place, or even fearful when immersed in an unfamiliar culture may be experiencing **culture shock.** For example, a resident of the United States who visits certain areas in China and wants local meat for dinner may be stunned to learn that the specialty is dog meat. Similarly, someone from a strict Islamic culture may be shocked by the comparatively provocative dress styles and open displays of affection common in the United States and various European cultures.

All of us, to some extent, take for granted the cultural practices of our society. As a result, it can be surprising and even disturbing to realize that other cultures do not follow our way of life. The fact is, customs that seem strange to us may be considered normal and proper in other cultures, which may see our social practices as odd.

💡 use your **sociological imagination**

You arrive in a developing African country as a Peace Corps volunteer. What aspects of a very different culture do you think would be the hardest to adjust to? What might the citizens of that country find shocking about your culture?

social policy and Culture | Bilingualism

Looking at the Issue

All over the world, nations face the challenge of how to deal with minorities who speak a different language from that of mainstream culture. Because languages know no political boundaries, minority languages are common. In India, for example, Hindi is the most widely spoken language, while English is used widely for official purposes. Yet 18 other languages are officially recognized in this nation of about 1 billion people.

Throughout the world, then, schools must deal with incoming students who speak many languages. **Bilingualism** refers to the use of two languages in a particular setting, such as the workplace or schoolroom, treating each language as equally legitimate. Thus, a teacher of bilingual education may instruct children in their native language while gradually introducing them to the language of the host society. If the curriculum is also bicultural, children will learn about the mores and folkways of both the dominant culture and the subculture.

To what degree should schools in the United States present the curriculum in a language other than English? This issue has prompted a great deal of debate among educators and policymakers. According to the Bureau of the Census, 59 million U.S. residents over age five—that's about 20 percent of the population—spoke a language other than English as their primary language at home in 2009 (Figure 12-1). Indeed, 23 other languages are each spoken by at least 200,000 U.S. residents (Shin and Kominski 2010).

Do bilingual programs help the children of these families to learn English? It is difficult to reach firm conclusions, because bilingual programs in general vary so widely in their quality and approach. They differ in the length of the transition to English and in how long they allow students to remain in bilingual classrooms. Moreover, results have been mixed. In the years since California effectively dismantled its bilingual education program, reading and math scores of students with limited English proficiency rose dramatically, especially

MAPPING LIFE NATIONWIDE

FIGURE 12-1 Comparing Percentage of People Who Speak a Language Other Than English at Home, by State

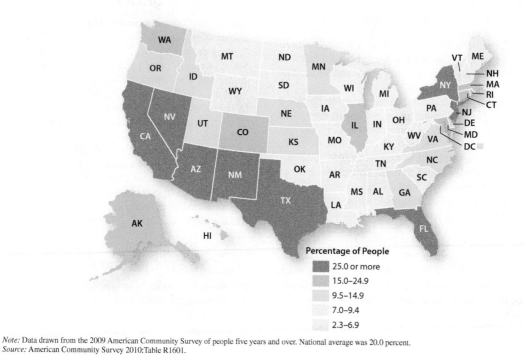

Note: Data drawn from the 2009 American Community Survey of people five years and over. National average was 20.0 percent.
Source: American Community Survey 2010:Table R1601.

—*Continued*

in the lower grades. Yet a major overview of 17 studies, done at Johns Hopkins University, found that students who are offered lessons in both English and their home languages make better progress than similar students who are taught only in English (R. Slavin and Cheung 2003).

Applying Sociology

For a long time, people in the United States demanded conformity to a single language. This demand coincided with the functionalist view that language serves to unify members of a society. Little respect was granted to immigrants' cultural traditions.

Recent decades have seen challenges to this pattern of forced obedience to the dominant ideology. Beginning in the 1960s, active movements for Black pride and ethnic pride insisted that people regard the traditions of all racial and ethnic subcultures as legitimate and important. Conflict theorists explain this development as a case of subordinated language minorities seeking opportunities for self-expression. Partly as a result of these challenges, people began to view bilingualism as an asset. It seemed to provide a sensitive way of assisting millions of non-English-speaking people in the United States to *learn* English in order to function more effectively within the society.

The perspective of conflict theory also helps us to understand some of the attacks on bilingual programs. Many of them stem from an ethnocentric point of view, which holds that any deviation from the majority is bad. This attitude tends to be expressed by those who wish to stamp out foreign influence wherever it occurs, especially in our schools. It does not take into account that success in bilingual education may actually have beneficial results, such as decreasing the number of high school dropouts and increasing the number of Hispanics in colleges and universities.

Initiating Policy

Bilingualism has policy implications largely in two areas: efforts to maintain language purity and programs to enhance bilingual education. Nations vary dramatically in their tolerance for a variety of languages. China continues to tighten its cultural control over Tibet by extending instruction of Mandarin, a Chinese dialect, from high school into the elementary schools there, which will now be bilingual along with Tibetan. In contrast, nearby Singapore establishes English as the medium of instruction but allows students to take their mother tongue as a second language, be it Chinese, Malay, or Tamil.

One bilingual hot spot is Québec, the French-speaking province of Canada. The Québécois, as they are known, represent 83 percent of the province's population, but only 25 percent of Canada's total population. A law implemented in 1978 mandated education in French for all Québec's children except those whose parents or siblings had learned English elsewhere in Canada. While special laws like this one have advanced French in the province, dissatisfied Québécois have tried to form their own separate country. In 1995, the people of Québec indicated their preference of remaining united with Canada by only the narrowest of margins (50.5 percent). Language and language-related cultural areas both unify and divide this nation of 33 million people (*The Economist* 2005b; R. Schaefer 2011).

Policymakers in the United States have been somewhat ambivalent in dealing with the issue of bilingualism. In 1965, the Elementary and Secondary Education Act (ESEA) provided for bilingual, bicultural education. In the 1970s, the federal government took an active role in establishing the proper form for bilingual programs. However, more recently, federal policy has been less supportive of bilingualism, and local school districts have been forced to provide an increased share of funding for their bilingual programs. Yet bilingual programs are an expense that many communities and states are unwilling to pay for and are quick to cut back. In 1998, voters in California approved a proposition that all but eliminated bilingual education: it requires instruction in English for 1.4 million children who are not fluent in the language.

In the United States, repeated efforts have been made to introduce a constitutional amendment declaring English as the nation's official language. As of 2012, 31 states had declared English their official language—an action that is now more symbolic than legislative in its significance.

Public concern over a potential decline in the use of English appears to be overblown. In reality, most immigrants and their offspring quickly become fluent in English and abandon their mother tongue. Nevertheless, many people are impatient with those immigrants who continue to use their mother tongue. The release in 2006 of *"Nuestro Himno,"* the Spanish-language version of the "Star-Spangled Banner," produced a strong public reaction: 69 percent of those who were surveyed on the topic said the anthem should be sung only in English. In reaction against the Spanish version, at least one congressman defiantly sang the national anthem in English—with incorrect lyrics. And the proprietor of a restaurant in Philadelphia posted signs advising patrons that he would accept orders for his famous steak sandwiches only in English. Throughout the year, passions ran high as policymakers debated how much support to afford people who speak other languages (J. Carroll 2006; U.S. English 2012).

—*Continued*

—Continued

In the end, the immigrant's experience is not only about learning a new language. It is about learning a whole new culture—a new totality of socially transmitted customs, knowledge, material objects, and behavior (Viramontes 2007).

TAKE THE ISSUE WITH YOU

1. Have you attended a school with students for whom English is a second language? If so, did the school set up a special bilingual program? Was it effective? What is your opinion of such programs?

2. The ultimate goal of both English-only and bilingual programs is for foreign-born students to become proficient in English. Why should the type of program students attend matter so much to so many people? List all the reasons you can think of for supporting or opposing such programs. What do you see as the primary reason?

3. Besides bilingualism, can you think of another issue that has become controversial recently because of a clash of cultures? If so, analyze the issue from a sociological point of view.

MODULE 12 | Recap and Review

Summary

Each human culture has unique characteristics that evolve to meet specific circumstances of climate, geography, technological development, and population.

1. A **subculture** is a small culture that exists within a larger, dominant culture. **Countercultures** are subcultures that deliberately oppose aspects of the larger culture.

2. A person who becomes immersed in an unfamiliar culture may experience **culture shock**.

3. The social policy of **bilingualism** calls for the use of two or more languages, treating each as equally legitimate. It is supported by those who want to ease the transition of non-native-language speakers into a host society, but opposed by those who adhere to a single cultural tradition and language.

Thinking Critically

1. To what subcultures do you belong? How do they function in relation to the larger society?

2. Why do people experience culture shock? What does this phenomenon reveal about the role of culture and of everyday customs?

Key Terms

Argot

Bilingualism

Counterculture

Culture shock

Subculture

Mastering This Chapter: Culture

taking sociology with you

1 Locate ethnocentrism. For two days, bearing in mind what sociologists mean by *ethnocentrism*, systematically record the places where you see or hear evidence of it.

2 Document a subculture. For two days, record the norms, values, sanctions, and argot evident in a subculture you are familiar with.

3 Study popular culture. For two days, record whatever evidence of the dominant culture you see on the Internet or in literature, music, movies, theater, television programs, and sporting events.

key terms

Argot Specialized language used by members of a group or subculture.

Bilingualism The use of two languages in a particular setting, such as the workplace or schoolroom, treating each language as equally legitimate.

Counterculture A subculture that deliberately opposes certain aspects of the larger culture.

Cultural relativism The viewing of people's behavior from the perspective of their own culture.

Cultural universal A common practice or belief found in every culture.

Culture The totality of learned, socially transmitted customs, knowledge, material objects, and behavior.

Culture industry The worldwide media industry that standardizes the goods and services demanded by consumers.

Culture lag A period of maladjustment when the nonmaterial culture is still struggling to adapt to new material conditions.

Culture shock The feeling of surprise and disorientation that people experience when they encounter cultural practices that are different from their own.

Culture war The polarization of society over controversial cultural elements.

Diffusion The process by which a cultural item spreads from group to group or society to society.

Discovery The process of making known or sharing the existence of an aspect of reality.

Dominant ideology A set of cultural beliefs and practices that helps to maintain powerful social, economic, and political interests.

Ethnocentrism The tendency to assume that one's own culture and way of life represent the norm or are superior to all others.

Folkway A norm governing everyday behavior whose violation raises comparatively little concern.

Formal norm A norm that has been written down and that specifies strict punishments for violators.

Informal norm A norm that is generally understood but not precisely recorded.

Innovation The process of introducing a new idea or object to a culture through discovery or invention.

Invention The combination of existing cultural items into a form that did not exist before.

Language An abstract system of word meanings and symbols for all aspects of culture; includes gestures and other nonverbal communication.

Law Governmental social control.

Material culture The physical or technological aspects of our daily lives.

Mores Norms deemed highly necessary to the welfare of a society.

Nonmaterial culture Ways of using material objects, as well as customs, beliefs, philosophies, governments, and patterns of communication.

Norm An established standard of behavior maintained by a society.

Sanction A penalty or reward for conduct concerning a social norm.

Sapir-Whorf hypothesis A hypothesis concerning the role of language in shaping our interpretation of reality. It holds that language is culturally determined.

Society A fairly large number of people who live in the same territory, are relatively independent of people outside their area, and participate in a common culture.

Sociobiology The systematic study of how biology affects human social behavior.

Subculture A segment of society that shares a distinctive pattern of customs, rules, and traditions that differs from the pattern of the larger society.

Symbol A gesture, object, or word that forms the basis of human communication.

Technology Cultural information about the ways in which the material resources of the environment may be used to satisfy human needs and desires.

Value A collective conception of what is considered good, desirable, and proper—or bad, undesirable, and improper—in a culture.

self-quiz

Read each question carefully and then select the best answer.

1. Which of the following is an aspect of culture?
   a. a comic book
   b. patriotic attachment to the flag of the United States
   c. slang words
   d. all of the above

2. People's adaptations to meet the needs for food, shelter, and clothing are examples of what George Murdock referred to as
   a. norms.
   b. folkways.
   c. cultural universals.
   d. cultural practices.

3. What term do sociologists use to refer to the process by which a cultural item spreads from group to group or society to society?
   a. diffusion
   b. globalization
   c. innovation
   d. cultural relativism

4. The appearance of Starbucks coffeehouses in China is a sign of what aspect of culture?
   a. innovation
   b. globalization
   c. diffusion
   d. cultural relativism

5. Which of the following statements is true according to the Sapir-Whorf hypothesis?
   a. Language simply describes reality.
   b. Language does not transmit stereotypes related to race.
   c. Language precedes thought.
   d. Language is not an example of a cultural universal.

6. Which of the following statements about norms is correct?
   a. People do not follow norms in all situations. In some cases, they evade a norm because they know it is weakly enforced.
   b. In some instances, behavior that appears to violate society's norms may actually represent adherence to the norms of a particular group.
   c. Norms are violated in some instances because one norm conflicts with another.
   d. all of the above

7. Which of the following statements about values is correct?
   a. Values never change.
   b. The values of a culture may change, but most remain relatively stable during any one person's lifetime.
   c. Values are constantly changing; sociologists view them as being very unstable.
   d. all of the above

8. Which of the following terms describes the set of cultural beliefs and practices that help to maintain powerful social, economic, and political interests?
   a. mores
   b. dominant ideology
   c. consensus
   d. values

9. Terrorist groups are examples of
   a. cultural universals.
   b. subcultures.
   c. countercultures.
   d. dominant ideologies.

10. What is the term used when one places a priority on understanding other cultures, rather than dismissing them as "strange" or "exotic"?
    a. ethnocentrism
    b. culture shock
    c. cultural relativism
    d. cultural value

11. _____ are gestures, objects, and/or words that form the basis of human communication.

12. _____ is the process of introducing a new idea or object to a culture.

13. The bow and arrow, the automobile, and the television are all examples of _____.

14. Sociologists associated with the _____ perspective emphasize that language and symbols offer a powerful way for a subculture to maintain its identity.

15. "Put on some clean clothes for dinner" and "Thou shalt not kill" are both examples of _____ found in U.S. culture.

16. The United States has strong _____ against murder, treason, and other forms of abuse that have been institutionalized into formal norms.

17. From a(n) _____ perspective, the dominant ideology has major social significance. Not only do a society's most powerful groups and institutions control wealth and property—more important, they control the means of production.

18. Countercultures (e.g., hippies) are typically popular among the _____, who have the least investment in the existing culture.

19. A person experiences _____ when he or she feels disoriented, uncertain, out of place, even fearful when immersed in an unfamiliar culture.

20. From the _____ perspective, subcultures are evidence that differences can exist within a common culture.

Answers

1 (d); 2 (c); 3 (a); 4 (b); 5 (c); 6 (d); 7 (b); 8 (b); 9 (c); 10 (c); 11 Symbols; 12 Innovation; 13 inventions; 14 interactionist; 15 norms; 16 mores; 17 conflict; 18 young; 19 culture shock; 20 functionalist

thinking about movies

Attack the Block

A subculture's values are put to the test in this sophisticated science fiction film, which takes place in a low-income housing project in London.

Smoke Signals

Members of the Coeur d'Alene Indian tribe hold to their own norms and values.

Sugar

A baseball player from the Dominican Republic copes with culture shock after being drafted into the U.S. Major Leagues.

Socialization and the Life Course

4 Socialization and the Life Course

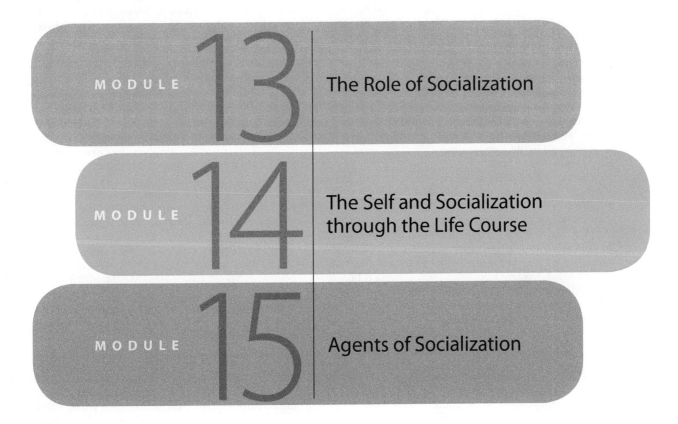

MODULE **13** The Role of Socialization

MODULE **14** The Self and Socialization through the Life Course

MODULE **15** Agents of Socialization

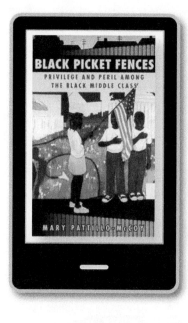

Who introduced you to your culture? Who made you feel that you belong?

In Groveland, a Chicago neighborhood, the list includes parents and relatives, friends and neighbors, teachers and church members.

❝ Charisse ... is sixteen and lives with her mother and younger sister, Deanne, across the street from St. Mary's Catholic Church and School. Charisse's mother is a personnel assistant at a Chicago university, and is taking classes there to get her bachelor's degree. Mr. Baker is a Chicago firefighter. While her father and mother are separated, Charisse sees her father many times a week at the after-school basketball hour that he supervises at St. Mary's gym. He and Charisse's mother are on very good terms, and Charisse has a loving relationship with both parents. Mr. Baker is as active as any parent could be, attending the father/daughter dances at Charisse's high school, never missing a big performance, and visiting his daughters often.

Charisse and her sister are being raised by the neighborhood family in addition to their biological parents. "We [are] real close. Like all our neighbors know us because my dad grew up over here. Since the '60s." Charisse is a third-generation Grovelandite just like Neisha Morris. Her grandparents moved into Groveland with Charisse's then-teenage father when the neighborhood first opened to African Americans. . . . Now Charisse is benefiting from the friends her family has made over their years of residence in Groveland, especially the members of St. Mary's church, who play the role of surrogate parents. When Charisse was in elementary school at St. Mary's, her late paternal grandmother

Charisse is a third-generation Grovelandite just like Neisha Morris. Her grandparents moved into Groveland with Charisse's then-teenage father when the neighborhood first opened to African Americans.

was the school secretary, and so the Baker girls were always under the watchful eye of their grandmother as well as the staff, who were their grandmother's friends. And in the evenings Charisse's mother would bring her and her sister to choir practice, where they accumulated an ensemble of mothers and fathers.

After St. Mary's elementary school, Charisse went on to St. Agnes Catholic High School for girls, her father's choice. St. Agnes is located in a suburb of Chicago and is a solid, integrated Catholic school where 100 percent of the girls graduate and over 95 percent go on to college. . . .

Most of Charisse's close friends went to St. Mary's and now go to St. Agnes with her, but her choice of boyfriends shows modest signs of rebellion. . . . Many of Charisse's male interests are older than she, and irregularly employed—although some are in and out of school. She meets many of them hanging out at the mall. One evening, members of the church's youth choir sat around talking about their relationships. Charisse cooed while talking about her present boyfriend, who had just graduated from high school but did not have a job and was uncertain about his future. But in the middle of that thought, Charisse spontaneously changed her attentions to a new young man that she had just met. "Charisse changes boyfriends like she changes her clothes," her sister joked, indicating the impetuous nature of adolescent relationships.

While these young men are not in gangs or selling drugs, many of them do not seem to share Charisse's strong career goals and diligence in attaining them. Some of them would not gain the approval of her parents. However, this full list of boyfriends has not clouded Charisse's focus. ❞

(Pattillo-McCoy 1999:100–102) Additional information about this excerpt can be found on the Online Learning Center at www.mhhe.com/schaefermod2e.

T his excerpt from *Black Picket Fences: Privilege and Peril among the Black Middle Class* describes the upbringing of a young resident of Groveland, a close-knit African American community in Chicago. The author, sociologist Mary Pattillo-McCoy, became acquainted with Charisse while living in the Groveland neighborhood, where she was doing ethnographic research. Charisse's childhood is similar to that of other youths in many respects. Regardless of race or social class, a young person's development involves a host of influences, from parents, grandparents, and siblings to friends and classmates, teachers and school administrators, neighbors and churchgoers—even youths who frequent the local mall. Yet in some ways, Charisse's development is specifically influenced by her race and social class. Contact with family and community members, for instance, has undoubtedly prepared her to deal with prejudice and the scarcity of positive images of African Americans in the media (W. Wilson et al. 2006).

Sociologists are interested in the patterns of behavior and attitudes that emerge *throughout* the life course, from infancy to old age. These patterns are part of the lifelong process of *socialization,* in which people learn the attitudes, values, and behaviors appropriate for members of a particular culture. In these three modules we will examine the role of socialization in human development. We will begin by analyzing the interaction of heredity with environmental factors. We will pay particular attention to how people develop perceptions, feelings, and beliefs about themselves. We will also explore the lifelong nature of the socialization process, as well as important agents of socialization, among them the family, schools, peers, the media, and technology. Finally, the Social Policy section will focus on the socialization experience of group child care for young children.

MODULE 13 | The Role of Socialization

Sociologists are interested in the process of **socialization,** through which people learn the attitudes, values, and behaviors appropriate for members of their culture. Socialization occurs through human interactions that begin in infancy and continue throughout life. We learn a great deal from those people who are most important in our lives—immediate family members, best friends, and teachers. But we also learn from people we see on the street, on television, on the Internet, and in films and magazines. From a microsociological perspective, socialization helps us discover how to behave "properly" and what to expect from others if we follow (or challenge) society's norms and values. From a macrosociological perspective, socialization provides for the transmission of a culture from one generation to the next and thereby for the long-term continuance of society. Socialization also shapes our self-images. For example, in the United States, a person who is viewed as "too heavy" or "too short" does not conform to the ideal cultural standard of physical attractiveness.

This kind of unfavorable evaluation can significantly influence the person's self-esteem. In this sense, socialization experiences can help shape our personalities. In everyday speech, the term **personality** refers to a person's typical patterns of attitudes, needs, characteristics, and behavior.

How much of a person's personality is shaped by culture, as opposed to inborn traits? In other words, what makes us who we are? Is it the genes we are born with, or the environment in which we grow up? Researchers have traditionally clashed over the relative importance of biological inheritance and environmental factors in human development—a conflict called the *nature versus nurture* (or *heredity versus environment*) debate. Today, most social scientists have moved beyond this debate, acknowledging instead the *interaction* of these variables in shaping human development. We can best appreciate how heredity and environmental factors interact and influence the socialization process if we first examine situations in which one factor operates almost entirely without the other (Homans 1979).

Social Environment: The Impact of Isolation

In the 1994 movie *Nell,* Jodie Foster played a young woman hidden from birth by her mother in a backwoods cabin. Raised without normal human contact, Nell crouches like an animal, screams wildly, and speaks or sings in a language all her own. This movie was drawn from the actual account of an emaciated 16-year-old boy who appeared mysteriously in 1828 in the town square of Nuremberg, Germany (Lipson 1994).

Isabelle and Genie: Two Cases

Some viewers may have found the story of Nell difficult to believe, but the painful childhood of Isabelle was all too real. For the first six years of her life, Isabelle lived in almost total seclusion in a darkened room. She had little contact with other people, with the exception of her mother, who could neither speak nor hear. Isabelle's mother's parents had been so deeply ashamed of Isabelle's illegitimate birth that they kept her hidden away from the world. Ohio authorities finally discovered the child in 1938, when Isabelle's mother escaped from her parents' home, taking her daughter with her.

When she was discovered at age six, Isabelle could not speak; she could merely make various croaking sounds. Her only communications with her mother were simple gestures. Isabelle had been largely deprived of the typical interactions and socialization experiences of childhood. Since she had seen few people, she showed a strong fear of strangers and reacted almost like a wild animal when confronted with an unfamiliar person. As she became accustomed to seeing certain individuals, her reaction changed to one of extreme apathy. At first, observers believed that Isabelle was deaf, but she soon began to react to nearby sounds. On tests of maturity, she scored at the level of an infant rather than a six-year-old.

Specialists developed a systematic training program to help Isabelle adapt to human relationships and socialization. They sought to overcome the several years when Isabelle has been left in seclusion in a dark room shut off from family members. She did come in contact with her mother but she was unable to speak or hear so nobody interacted or played with her in a way most young children experience. Lack of exposure to the outdoors and an inadequate diet had left her in poor health as well.

After a week of intensive effort, she made her first attempt to verbalize. Although she started slowly, Isabelle quickly passed through six years of development. In a little over two months she was speaking in complete sentences. Nine months later she could identify both words and sentences in books. Before Isabelle reached age nine, she was ready to attend school with other children. By age 14 she was in sixth grade, doing well in school, and emotionally well adjusted.

Yet without an opportunity to experience socialization in her first six years, Isabelle had been hardly human in the social sense when she was first discovered. Her inability to communicate at the time of her discovery—despite her physical and cognitive potential to learn—and her remarkable progress over the next few years underscore the impact of socialization on human development (K. Davis 1940, 1947).

The conclusion of this case study is that human children need socialization in the form of love, care, and affection. Absent of that, humans cannot learn to speak and interact in a manner that is expected. Of course, this need for positive social interaction does not end with childhood but continues throughout our lives. Unfortunately, other children who have been locked away or severely neglected have not fared so well as Isabelle. In many instances, the consequences of social isolation have proved much more damaging.

Isabelle's and Genie's experiences are important to researchers because there are only a few cases of children reared in total isolation. Unfortunately, however, there are many cases of children raised in extremely neglectful social circumstances. In the 1990s, public attention focused on infants and young children from orphanages in the formerly communist countries of Eastern Europe. In Romanian orphanages, babies once lay in their cribs for 18 to 20 hours a day, curled against their feeding bottles and receiving little adult care. Such minimal attention continued for the first five years of their lives. Many of them were fearful of human contact and prone to unpredictable anti-social behavior.

This situation came to light as families in North America and Europe began adopting thousands of the children. The adjustment problems for about 20 percent of them were often so dramatic that the adopting families suffered guilty fears of being ill-fit adoptive parents. Many of them have asked for assistance in dealing with the children. Slowly, efforts are being made to introduce the deprived youngsters to feelings of attachment that they have never experienced before (Groza et al. 1999; Craig Smith 2006).

Can you become human if you have had little human contact? Jodie Foster directed the motion picture Nell in which she played the title role of a girl discovered in a remote North Carolina backwoods cottage by a local doctor. While not based on a true story, it did draw upon cases of children raised in isolation like Isabelle. With significant intervention, Nell shows great progress in the several years covered in the movie, but still displays behavior reflective of her lack of childhood socialization.

Increasingly, researchers are emphasizing the importance of the earliest socialization experiences for children who grow up in more normal environments. We now know that it is not enough to care for an infant's physical needs; parents must also concern themselves with children's social development. If, for example, children are discouraged from having friends even as toddlers, they will miss out on social interactions with peers that are critical for emotional growth.

Despite the striking physical resemblance between these identical twins, there are undoubtedly many differences between them. Research points to some behavioral similarities between twins, but little beyond the likenesses found among nontwin siblings.

Primate Studies

Studies of animals raised in isolation also support the importance of socialization in development. Harry Harlow (1971), a researcher at the primate laboratory of the University of Wisconsin, conducted tests with rhesus monkeys that had been raised away from their mothers and away from contact with other monkeys. As was the case with Isabelle, the rhesus monkeys raised in isolation were fearful and easily frightened. They did not mate, and the females who were artificially inseminated became abusive mothers. Apparently, isolation had had a damaging effect on the monkeys.

A creative aspect of Harlow's experimentation was his use of "artificial mothers." In one such experiment, Harlow presented monkeys raised in isolation with two substitute mothers—one cloth-covered replica and one covered with wire that had the ability to offer milk. Monkey after monkey went to the wire mother for the life-giving milk, yet spent much more time clinging to the more motherlike cloth model. It appears that the infant monkeys developed greater social attachments from their need for warmth, comfort, and intimacy than from their need for milk.

While the isolation studies just discussed may seem to suggest that heredity can be dismissed as a factor in the social development of humans and animals, studies of twins provide insight into a fascinating interplay between hereditary and environmental factors.

use your **sociological imagination**

What events in your life have had a strong influence on who you are?

The Influence of Heredity

Identical twins Oskar Stohr and Jack Yufe were separated soon after their birth and raised on different continents, in very different cultural settings. Oskar was reared as a strict Catholic by his maternal grandmother in the Sudetenland of Czechoslovakia. As a member of the Hitler Youth movement in Nazi Germany, he learned to hate Jews. In contrast, his brother Jack was reared in Trinidad by the twins' Jewish father. Jack joined an Israeli kibbutz (a collective settlement) at age 17 and later served in the Israeli army. When the twins were reunited in middle age, however, some startling similarities emerged: They both wore wire-rimmed glasses and mustaches. They both liked spicy foods and sweet liqueurs, were absentminded, flushed the toilet before using it, stored rubber bands on their wrists, and dipped buttered toast in their coffee (Holden 1980).

The twins also differed in many important respects: Jack was a workaholic; Oskar enjoyed leisure-time activities. Oskar was a traditionalist who was domineering toward women; Jack was a political liberal who was much more accepting of feminism. Finally, Jack was extremely proud of being Jewish, whereas Oskar never mentioned his Jewish heritage (Holden 1987).

Oskar and Jack are prime examples of the interplay of heredity and environment. For a number of years, the Minnesota Twin Family Study has been following 137 sets of identical twins reared apart to determine what similarities, if any, they show in personality traits, behavior, and intelligence. Preliminary results from the available twin studies indicate that *both* genetic factors *and* socialization experiences are influential in human development. Certain characteristics, such as temperaments, voice patterns, and nervous habits, appear to be strikingly similar even in twins reared apart, suggesting that these qualities may be linked to hereditary causes. However, identical twins reared apart differ far more in their attitudes, values, chosen mates, and even drinking habits; these qualities, it would seem, are influenced by environmental factors. In examining clusters of personality traits among such twins, researchers have found marked similarities in their tendency toward leadership or dominance, but significant differences in their need for intimacy, comfort, and assistance.

trend|spotting

Multiple Births

The birth of identical twins or triplets is a rare event—only about 1 in every 250 births. Recently, however, multiple births have increased dramatically. There is some evidence that fertility treatments may be contributing to the increase, as they did with Kate and Jon Gosselin's sextuplets, born in 2004, and the Suleman octuplets, born in 2009. However, multiple births in general seem to be on the rise. Over the quarter century from 1980 to 2009, the birthrate for triplets and other multiples, identical or not, increased more than fourfold, from 37 to 154 of every 100,000 births.

quite differently on intelligence tests—a finding that supports the impact of socialization on human development (Joseph 2004; Kronstadt 2008a; McGue and Bouchard 1998; P. Miller 2012; Minnesota Center for Twin and Family Research 2012).

We need to be cautious in reviewing studies of twin pairs and other relevant research. Widely broadcast findings have often been based on preliminary analysis of extremely small samples. For example, one study (not involving twin pairs) was frequently cited as confirming genetic links with behavior. Yet the researchers had to retract their conclusions after they increased the sample and reclassified two of the original cases. After those changes, the initial findings were no longer valid.

Critics add that studies of twin pairs have not provided satisfactory information concerning the extent to which separated identical twins may have had contact with each other, even though they were raised apart. Such interactions—especially if they were extensive—could call into question the validity of the twin studies. As this debate continues, we can certainly anticipate numerous efforts to replicate the research and clarify the interplay between heredity and environmental factors in human development (Horgan 1993; Plomin 1989).

Researchers have also been impressed with the similar scores on intelligence tests of twins reared apart in *roughly similar* social settings. Most of the identical twins register scores even closer than those that would be expected if the same person took a test twice. At the same time, however, identical twins brought up in *dramatically different* social environments score

---

MODULE 13 | Recap and Review

Summary

Socialization is the process through which people learn the attitudes, values, and actions appropriate for members of a particular culture.

1. Socialization affects the overall cultural practices of a society; it also shapes the images we hold of ourselves.

2. Heredity and environmental factors interact in influencing the socialization process.

Thinking Critically

1. What might be some ethical concerns regarding research on the influences of heredity and environment?

2. What are some social policy implications of research on the effects of early socialization experiences?

Key Terms

Personality

Socialization

MODULE 14 | The Self and Socialization through the Life Course

We all have various perceptions, feelings, and beliefs about who we are and what we are like. How do we come to develop them? Do they change as we age?

We were not born with these understandings. Building on the work of George Herbert Mead (1964b), sociologists recognize that our concept of who we are, the *self*, emerges as we interact with others. The **self** is a distinct identity that sets us apart from others. It is not a static phenomenon, but continues to develop and change throughout our lives.

Sociologists and psychologists alike have expressed interest in how the individual develops and modifies the sense of self as a result of social interaction. The work of sociologists Charles Horton Cooley and George Herbert Mead, pioneers of the interactionist approach, has been especially useful in furthering our understanding of these important issues.

● Sociological Approaches to the Self

Cooley: Looking-Glass Self

In the early 1900s, Charles Horton Cooley advanced the belief that we learn who we are by interacting with others. Our view of ourselves, then, comes not only from direct contemplation of our personal qualities but also from our impressions of how others

perceive us. Cooley used the phrase **looking-glass self** to emphasize that the self is the product of our social interactions.

The process of developing a self-identity or self-concept has three phases. First, we imagine how we present ourselves to others—to relatives, friends, even strangers on the street. Then we imagine how others evaluate us (attractive, intelligent, shy, or strange). Finally, we develop some sort of feeling about ourselves, such as respect or shame, as a result of these impressions (Cooley 1902; M. Howard 1989).

A subtle but critical aspect of Cooley's looking-glass self is that the self results from an individual's "imagination" of how others view him or her. As a result, we can develop self-identities based on *incorrect* perceptions of how others see us. A student may react strongly to a teacher's criticism and decide (wrongly) that the instructor views the student as stupid. This misperception may be converted into a negative self-identity through the following process: (1) the teacher criticized me, (2) the teacher must think that I'm stupid, (3) I *am* stupid. Yet self-identities are also subject to change. If the student receives an A at the end of the course, he or she will probably no longer feel stupid.

Mead: Stages of the Self

George Herbert Mead continued Cooley's exploration of interactionist theory. Mead (1934, 1964a) developed a useful model of the process by which the self emerges, defined by three distinct stages: the preparatory stage, the play stage, and the game stage.

The Preparatory Stage   During the *preparatory stage,* children merely imitate the people around them, especially family members with whom they continually interact. Thus, a small child will bang on a piece of wood while a parent is engaged in carpentry work, or will try to throw a ball if an older sibling is doing so nearby.

As they grow older, children become more adept at using symbols, including the gestures and words that form the basis of human communication. By interacting with relatives and friends, as well as by watching cartoons on television and looking at picture books, children in the preparatory stage begin to understand symbols. They will continue to use this form of communication throughout their lives.

The Play Stage   Mead was among the first to analyze the relationship of symbols to socialization. As children develop skill in communicating through symbols, they gradually become more aware of social relationships.

Socialization can be negative as well as positive. When the very young come to view harmful behaviors like smoking or illegal drug use as "normal," socialization is negative. In Yemen, this child soldier has learned to use an automatic weapon.

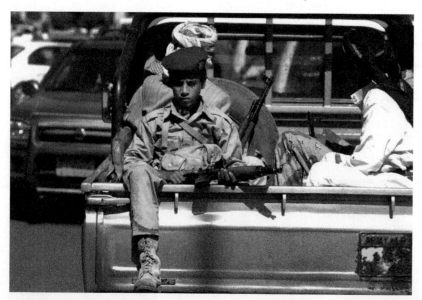

As a result, during the play stage, they begin to pretend to be other people. Just as an actor "becomes" a character, a child becomes a doctor, parent, superhero, or ship captain.

Mead, in fact, noted that an important aspect of the play stage is role-playing. **Role taking** is the process of mentally assuming the perspective of another and responding from that imagined viewpoint. For example, through this process a young child will gradually learn when it is best to ask a parent for favors. If the parent usually comes home from work in a bad mood, the child will wait until after dinner, when the parent is more relaxed and approachable.

The Game Stage   In Mead's third stage, the *game stage,* the child of about age eight or nine no longer just plays roles but begins to consider several tasks and relationships simultaneously. At this point in development, children grasp not only their own social positions but also those of others around them—just as in a football game the players must understand their own and everyone else's positions. Consider a girl or boy who is part of a Scout troop out on a weekend hike in the mountains. The child must understand what he or she is expected to do but must also recognize the responsibilities of other Scouts as well as the leaders. This is the final stage of development under Mead's model; the child can now respond to numerous members of the social environment.

Mead uses the term **generalized other** to refer to the attitudes, viewpoints, and expectations of society as a whole that a child takes into account in his or her behavior. Simply put, this concept suggests that when an individual acts, he or she takes into account an entire group of people. For example, a child will not act courteously merely to please a particular parent. Rather, the child comes to understand that courtesy is a widespread social value endorsed by parents, teachers, and religious leaders.

Table 14-1 summarizes the three stages of self outlined by George Herbert Mead.

Mead: Theory of the Self

Mead is best known for his theory of the self. According to Mead (1964b), the self begins at a privileged, central position in a person's world. Young children picture themselves as the focus of everything around them and find it difficult to consider the perspectives of others. For example, when shown a mountain scene and asked to describe what an observer on the opposite side of the mountain might see (such as a lake or hikers), young children

describe only objects visible from their vantage point. This childhood tendency to place ourselves at the center of events never entirely disappears. Many people with a fear of flying automatically assume that if any plane goes down, it will be the one they are on. And who reads the horoscope section in the paper without looking at their own horoscope first? Why else do we buy lottery tickets, if we do not imagine ourselves winning?

Nonetheless, as people mature, the self changes and begins to reflect greater concern about the reactions of others. Parents, friends, co-workers, coaches, and teachers are often among those who play a major role in shaping a person's self. The term **significant others** is used to refer to those individuals who are most important in the development of the self. Many young people, for example, find themselves drawn to the same kind of work their parents engage in (H. Sullivan [1953] 1968).

💡 use your **sociological imagination**

How do you view yourself as you interact with others around you? How do you think you formed this view of yourself?

Goffman: Presentation of the Self

How do we manage our "self"? How do we display to others who we are? Erving Goffman, a sociologist associated with the interactionist perspective, suggested that many of our daily activities involve attempts to convey impressions of who we are. His observations help us to understand the sometimes subtle yet critical ways in which we learn to present ourselves socially. They also offer concrete examples of this aspect of socialization.

Early in life, the individual learns to slant his or her presentation of the self in order to create distinctive appearances and satisfy particular audiences. Goffman (1959) referred to this altering of the presentation of the self as **impression management.** Box 14-1 describes an everyday example of this concept—the way students behave after receiving their exam grades.

In analyzing such everyday social interactions, Goffman makes so many explicit parallels to the theater that his view has been termed the **dramaturgical approach.** According to this perspective, people resemble performers in action. For example, a clerk may try to appear busier than he or she actually is if a supervisor happens to be watching. A customer in a singles' bar may try to look as if he or she is waiting for a particular person to arrive.

Table **14-1**   **Mead's Stages of the Self**   **summingup**

Stage	Self Present?	Definition	Example
Preparation	No	Child imitates the actions of others.	When adults laugh and smile, child laughs and smiles.
Play	Developing	Child takes the role of a single other, as if he or she were the other.	Child first takes the role of doctor, then the role of patient.
Game	Yes	Child considers the roles of two or more others simultaneously.	In game of hide-and-seek, child takes into account the roles of both hider and seeker.

Sociology on Campus

BOX 14-1

Impression Management by Students

When you and fellow classmates get an exam back, you probably react differently depending on the grades that you and they earned. This distinction is part of *impression management*. Researchers have found that students' reactions differ depending on the grades that others received, compared to their own. These encounters can be divided into three categories: those in which all students earned high grades (Ace–Ace encounters); those between Aces and students who received low or failing grades (Ace–Bomber encounters); and those between students who all got low grades (Bomber–Bomber encounters).

Ace–Ace encounters occur in a rather open atmosphere, because there is comfort in sharing a high mark with another high achiever. It is even acceptable to violate the norm of modesty and brag when among other Aces, since as one student admitted, "It's much easier to admit a high mark to someone who has done better than you, or at least as well."

Ace–Bomber encounters are often sensitive. Bombers generally attempt to avoid such exchanges, because "you . . . emerge looking

> When forced into interactions with Aces, Bombers work to appear gracious and congratulatory.

like the dumb one" or "feel like you are lazy or unreliable." When forced into interactions with Aces, Bombers work to appear gracious and congratulatory. For their part, Aces offer sympathy and support to the dissatisfied Bombers and even rationalize their own "lucky" high scores. To help Bombers save face, Aces may emphasize the difficulty and unfairness of the examination.

Bomber–Bomber encounters tend to be closed, reflecting the group effort to wall off the feared disdain of others. Yet within the safety of these encounters, Bombers openly share their disappointment and engage in expressions of mutual self-pity that they themselves call "pity parties." They devise face-saving excuses for

their poor performance, such as "I wasn't feeling well all week" or "I had four exams and two papers due that week."

Of course, grade comparisons are not the only occasion when students engage in impression management. Another study has shown that students' perceptions of how often fellow students work out can also influence their social encounters. In athletic terms, a bomber would be someone who doesn't work out; an ace would be someone who works hard at physical fitness.

LET'S DISCUSS

1. How do you react to those who have received higher or lower grades than you? Do you engage in impression management? How would you like others to react to your grade?

2. What social norms govern students' impression management strategies?

Sources: Albas and Albas 1988, 1996; C. Austin 2009; M. Mack 2003.

Goffman (1959) also drew attention to another aspect of the self, **face-work.** How often do you initiate some kind of face-saving behavior when you feel embarrassed or rejected? In response to a rejection at the singles' bar, a person may engage in face-work by saying, "There really isn't an interesting person in this entire crowd." We feel the need to maintain a proper image of the self if we are to continue social interaction.

People judge us by our appearance, attire, body language, demeanor, and mannerisms. Knowing that they do, most of us alter the way we present ourselves to others, a strategy that Goffman called impression management.

Face-work is a necessity for those who are unemployed. In an economic downturn like the recent recession, unemployment affects people of all social classes, many of whom are unaccustomed to being jobless. A recent ethnographic study found the newly unemployed redefining what it means to be out of work. They were focusing more than in the past on what they were accomplishing, and had begun to value volunteer work more since they had become volunteers themselves. Participants in this study engaged in both impression management and face-work (Garrett-Peters 2009).

Goffman's work on the self represents a logical progression of sociological studies begun by Cooley and Mead on how personality is acquired through socialization and how we manage the presentation of the self to others. Cooley stressed the process by which we create a self; Mead focused on how the self develops as we learn to interact with others; Goffman emphasized the ways in which we consciously create images of ourselves for others.

Psychological Approaches to the Self

Psychologists have shared the interest of Cooley, Mead, and other sociologists in the development of the self. Early work in psychology, such as that of Sigmund Freud (1856–1939), stressed the role of inborn drives—among them the drive for sexual gratification—in channeling human behavior. More recently, psychologists such as Jean Piaget have emphasized the stages through which human beings progress as the self develops.

Like Charles Horton Cooley and George Herbert Mead, Freud believed that the self is a social product, and that aspects of one's personality are influenced by other people (especially one's parents). However, unlike Cooley and Mead, he suggested that the self has components that work in opposition to each other. According to Freud, our natural impulsive instincts are in constant conflict with societal constraints. Part of us seeks limitless pleasure, while another part favors rational behavior. By interacting with others, we learn the expectations of society and then select behavior most appropriate to our culture. (Of course, as Freud was well aware, we sometimes distort reality and behave irrationally.)

Research on newborn babies by the Swiss child psychologist Jean Piaget (1896–1980) has underscored the importance of social interactions in developing a sense of self. Piaget found that newborns have no self in the sense of a looking-glass image. Ironically, though, they are quite self-centered; they demand that all attention be directed toward them. Newborns have not yet separated themselves from the universe of which they are a part. For these babies, the phrase "you and me" has no meaning; they understand only "me." However, as they mature, children are gradually socialized into social relationships, even within their rather self-centered world.

In his well-known **cognitive theory of development,** Piaget (1954) identified four stages in the development of children's thought processes. In the first, or *sensorimotor,* stage, young children use their senses to make discoveries. For example, through touching they discover that their hands are actually a part of themselves. During the second, or *preoperational,* stage, children begin to use words and symbols to distinguish objects and ideas. The milestone in the third, or *concrete operational,* stage is that children engage in more logical thinking. They learn that even when a formless lump of clay is shaped into a snake, it is still the same clay. In the fourth, or *formal operational,* stage, adolescents become capable of sophisticated abstract thought and can deal with ideas and values in a logical manner.

According to Piaget, social interaction is the key to development. As children grow older, they pay increasing attention to how other people think and why they act in particular ways. In order to develop a distinct personality, each of us needs opportunities to interact with others. As we saw earlier, Isabelle was deprived of the chance for normal social interactions, and the consequences were severe (Kitchener 1991).

We have seen that a number of thinkers considered social interaction the key to the development of an individual's sense of self. As is generally true, we can best understand this topic by drawing on a variety of theory and research. Table 14-2 summarizes the rich literature, both sociological and psychological, on the development of the self.

Socialization throughout the Life Course

The Life Course

Among the Kota people of the Congo in Africa, adolescents paint themselves blue. Mexican American girls go on a daylong religious retreat before dancing the night away. Egyptian mothers step over their newborn infants seven times, and graduating students at the Naval Academy throw their hats in the air. These are all ways of celebrating **rites of passage,** a means of dramatizing and validating changes in a person's status. Rites of passage can mark a separation, as in a graduation ceremony, or an incorporation, as in an initiation into an organization (Van Gennep [1909] 1960).

Rites of passage are a worldwide social phenomenon. The Kota rite marks the passage to adulthood. The color blue, viewed as the color of death, symbolizes the death of childhood. Hispanic girls celebrate reaching womanhood with a *quinceañera* ceremony at age 15. In the Cuban American community of Miami, the popularity of the *quinceañera* supports a network of party planners, caterers, dress designers, and the Miss Quinceañera Latina pageant. For thousands of years, Egyptian mothers have welcomed their newborns to the world in the Soboa ceremony by stepping over the seven-day-old infant seven times.

Table **14-2** **Theoretical Approaches to Development of the Self**

Tracking Sociological Perspectives

Scholar	Key Concepts and Contributions	Major Points of Theory
Charles Horton Cooley 1864–1929 sociologist (USA)	Looking-glass self	Stages of development not distinct; feelings toward ourselves developed through interaction with others
George Herbert Mead 1863–1931 sociologist (USA)	The self Generalized other	Three distinct stages of development; self develops as children grasp the roles of others in their lives
Erving Goffman 1922–1982 sociologist (USA)	Impression management Dramaturgical approach Face-work	Self developed through the impressions we convey to others and to groups
Sigmund Freud 1856–1939 psychotherapist (Austria)	Psychoanalysis	Self influenced by parents and by inborn drives, such as the drive for sexual gratification
Jean Piaget 1896–1980 child psychologist (Switzerland)	Cognitive theory of development	Four stages of cognitive development

These specific ceremonies mark stages of development in the life course. They indicate that the process of socialization continues through all stages of the life cycle. In fact, some researchers have chosen to concentrate on socialization as a lifelong process. Sociologists and other social scientists who take such a **life course approach** look closely at the social factors that influence people throughout their lives, from birth to death, including gender and income. They recognize that biological changes mold but do not dictate human behavior.

Several life events mark the passage to adulthood. Of course, these turning points vary from one society and even one generation to the next. In the United States, the key event seems to be the completion of formal schooling (Table 14-3). On average, Americans expect this milestone to occur by a person's 23rd birthday. Other major events in the life course, such as getting married or becoming a parent, are expected to follow three or four years later. Interestingly, comparatively few survey respondents identified marriage and parenthood as important milestones (Furstenberg, et al. 2004).

One result of these staggered steps to independence is that in the United States, unlike some other societies, there is no clear dividing line between adolescence and adulthood. Nowadays, few young people finish school, get married, and leave home at about the same age, clearly establishing their transition to adulthood. The terms *youthhood, emerging adulthood,* and *not quite adult* have been coined to describe the prolonged ambiguous status that young people in their 20s experience (Côté 2000; Settersten and Ray 2011; Christian Smith 2007).

Anticipatory Socialization and Resocialization

The development of a social self is literally a lifelong transformation that begins in the crib and continues as one prepares for death. Two types of socialization occur at many points throughout the life course: anticipatory socialization and resocialization.

Anticipatory socialization refers to processes of socialization in which a person rehearses for future positions, occupations, and social relationships. A culture can function more efficiently and smoothly if members become acquainted with the norms, values, and behavior associated with a social position before actually assuming that status. Preparation for many aspects of adult life begins with anticipatory socialization during childhood and adolescence, and continues throughout our lives as we prepare for new responsibilities.

You can see the process of anticipatory socialization take place when high school students start to consider what colleges they may attend. Traditionally, this task meant looking at

Table **14-3**   **Milestones in the Transition to Adulthood**

Life Event	Expected Age	Percentage of People Who View Event as Extremely/ Quite Important
Financial independence from parents/guardians	20.9 years	80.9%
Separate residence from parents	21.1	57.2
Full-time employment	21.2	83.8
Completion of formal schooling	22.3	90.2
Capability of supporting a family	24.5	82.3
Marriage	25.7	33.2
Parenthood	26.2	29.0

Note: Based on the 2002 General Social Survey of 1,398 people.
Source: T. Smith 2003.

Think about It

Why did so few respondents consider marriage and parenthood to be important milestones? Which milestones do you think are most important?

A young Apache woman undergoes a mudding ceremony traditionally used in rites of passage, such as puberty and in some cases weddings.

Socialization continues throughout the life course. When the Internet opened to commercial traffic, adults who are now in their 80s were over age 65. They were 75 when broadband became available.

publications received in the mail or making campus visits. However, with new technology, more and more students are using the web to begin their college experience. Colleges are investing more time and money in developing attractive websites through which students can take virtual campus tours and hear audio clips of everything from the college anthem to a sample zoology lecture.

Occasionally, assuming a new social or occupational position requires us to *unlearn* an established orientation. **Resocialization** refers to the process of discarding former behavior patterns and accepting new ones as part of a transition in one's life. Often resocialization occurs during an explicit effort to transform an individual, as happens in reform schools, therapy groups, prisons, religious conversion settings, and political indoctrination

camps. The process of resocialization typically involves considerable stress for the individual—much more so than socialization in general, or even anticipatory socialization (Gecas 2004).

Resocialization is particularly effective when it occurs within a total institution. Erving Goffman (1961) coined the term **total institution** to refer to an institution that regulates all aspects of a person's life under a single authority, such as a prison, the military, a mental hospital, or a convent. Because the total institution is generally cut off from the rest of society, it provides for all the needs of its members. Quite literally, the crew of a merchant vessel at sea becomes part of a total institution. So elaborate are its requirements, so all-encompassing its activities, a total institution often represents a miniature society.

Goffman (1961) identified four common traits of total institutions:

- All aspects of life are conducted in the same place under the control of a single authority.

- Any activities within the institution are conducted in the company of others in the same circumstances—for example, army recruits or novices in a convent.

- The authorities devise rules and schedule activities without consulting the participants.

- All aspects of life within a total institution are designed to fulfill the purpose of the organization. Thus, all activities in a monastery might be centered on prayer and communion with God (C. Davies 1989; P. Rose et al. 1979).

People often lose their individuality within total institutions. For example, a person entering prison may experience the humiliation of a **degradation ceremony** as he or she is stripped of clothing, jewelry, and other personal possessions. From this point on, scheduled daily routines allow for little or no personal initiative. The individual becomes secondary and rather invisible in the overbearing social environment (Garfinkel 1956).

MODULE 14 | Recap and Review

Summary

This module examines sociological and psychological views of the development of the **self.**

1. In the early 1900s, Charles Horton Cooley advanced the belief that we learn who we are by interacting with others, a phenomenon he called the **looking-glass self.**

2. George Herbert Mead, best known for his theory of the self, proposed that as people mature, their selves begin to reflect their concern about reactions from others, both **generalized others** and **significant others.**

3. Erving Goffman has shown that in many of our daily activities, we try to convey distinct impressions of who we are, a process he called **impression management.**

4. According to Jean Piaget's **cognitive theory of development,** social interaction is the key to psychological development.

5. Socialization proceeds throughout the life course. Some societies mark stages of development with formal **rites of passage.** In the culture of the United States, significant events such as marriage and parenthood serve to change a person's status.

Thinking Critically

1. Use Erving Goffman's dramaturgical approach to describe impression management among members of one of the following groups: athletes, college instructors, parents, physicians, or politicians.

2. What are some similarities between Mead's stages of the self and Piaget's cognitive development stages? What are some differences?

Key Terms

Anticipatory socialization

Cognitive theory of development

Degradation ceremony

Dramaturgical approach

Face-work

Generalized other

Impression management

Life course approach

Looking-glass self

Resocialization

Rites of passage

Role taking

Self

Significant other

Total institution

MODULE 15 | Agents of Socialization

As we have seen, the culture of the United States is defined by rather gradual movements from one stage of socialization to the next. The continuing and lifelong socialization process involves many different social forces that influence our lives and alter our self-images.

The family is the most important agent of socialization in the United States, especially for children. In this chapter, we'll also discuss six other agents of socialization: the school, the peer group, the mass media and technology, the workplace, religion, and the state. We'll explore the role of religion in socializing young people into society's norms and values more fully in Chapter 15.

Family

The lifelong process of learning begins shortly after birth. Since newborns can hear, see, smell, taste, and feel heat, cold, and pain, they are constantly orienting themselves to the surrounding world. Human beings, especially family members, constitute an important part of their social environment. People minister to the baby's needs by feeding, cleaning, carrying, and comforting the baby.

All families engage in socialization, but the way that Amish families encourage their children to accept their community's subculture is particularly striking. Box 15-1 describes their tolerance for the period of rebellion known as *rumspringa*, during which Amish children flirt with the adolescent subculture of mainstream American society.

In the United States, social development also includes exposure to cultural assumptions regarding gender and race. Black parents, for example, have learned that children as young as age two can absorb negative messages about Blacks in children's books, toys, and television shows—all of which are designed primarily for White consumers. At the same time, Black children are exposed more often than others to the inner-city youth gang culture. Because most Blacks, even those who are middle class, live near very poor neighborhoods, children such as Charisse (see the chapter-opening excerpt) are susceptible to these influences, despite their parents' strong family values (Linn and Poussaint 1999; Pattillo-McCoy 1999).

The term **gender role** refers to expectations regarding the proper behavior, attitudes, and activities of males and females. For example, we traditionally think of "toughness" as masculine—and desirable only in men—while we view "tenderness" as feminine. As we will see in Module 34, other cultures do not necessarily assign these qualities to each gender in the way that our culture does. The existence of gender roles does not imply that inevitably, males and females will assume certain roles, nor does it imply that those roles are quite distinct from one another. Rather, gender roles emphasize the fact that males and females are not genetically predetermined to occupy certain roles.

As the primary agents of childhood socialization, parents play a critical role in guiding children into those gender roles deemed appropriate in a society. Other adults, older siblings, the mass media, and religious and educational institutions also have a noticeable impact on a child's socialization into feminine and masculine norms. A culture or subculture may require that one sex or the other take primary responsibility for the socialization of children, economic support of the family, or religious or intellectual leadership. In some societies, girls are socialized mainly by their mothers and boys by their fathers—an arrangement that may prevent girls from learning critical survival skills. In South Asia, fathers teach their sons to swim to prepare them for a life as fishermen; girls typically do not learn to swim. When a deadly tsunami hit the coast of South Asia in 2004, many more men survived than women.

A daughter learns how to weave fabric from her mother in Guatemala. The family is the most important agent of socialization.

Research Today

BOX 15-1

Rum Springa: Raising Children Amish Style

All families face challenges raising their children, but what if your parents expected you not to dance, listen to music, watch television, or access the Internet? This is the challenge faced by Amish teens and their parents, who embrace a lifestyle of the mid-1800s. Amish youths—boys in particular—often rebel against their parents' strict morals by getting drunk, behaving disrespectfully, and indulging in "worldly" activities, such as buying a car. At times even the girls may become involved, to

> All families face challenges raising their children, but what if your parents expected you not to dance, listen to music, watch television, or access the Internet?

their families' dismay. As one scholar puts it, "The rowdiness of Amish youth is an embarrassment to church leaders and a stigma in the larger community" (Kraybill 2001:138).

Yet the strong pull of mainstream American culture has led Amish parents to routinize, almost to accept, some of their children's worldly activities. They expect adolescents to test their subculture's boundaries during a period of discovery called *rum springa,* a German term meaning "running around." A common occurrence during which young people attend barn dances and break social norms

that forbid drinking, smoking, and driving cars, *rum springa* is definitely not supported by the Amish religion.

Parents often react to these escapades by looking the other way, sometimes literally. If they hear radio music coming from the barn, or a motorcycle driving onto their property in the middle of the night, they don't retaliate by punishing their offspring. Instead, they pretend not to notice, secure in the knowledge

that Amish children almost always return to the community's traditional values. Indeed, despite the flirtation with popular culture and modern technology that is common during the *rum springa,* the vast majority of Amish youths do return to the Amish community and become baptized. Scholars report that 85 to 90 percent of Amish children accept the faith as young adults.

To mainstream Americans, this little known and understood subculture became a source of entertainment when in 2004, UPN aired a 10-week reality program called *Amish in the City.* In the series, five Amish youths allegedly on *rum springa* moved in with six worldly wise young adults in Los Angeles. On behalf of the Amish community, some critics called the series exploitative, a sign of how vulnerable the Amish are. No similar series would be developed on the rebellion of Muslim or Orthodox Jewish youths, they charged.

LET'S DISCUSS

1. Do you or anyone you know come from a subculture that rejects mainstream American culture? If so, describe the community's norms and values. How do they resemble and how do they differ from Amish norms and values?

2. Why do you think so many Amish youths return to their families' way of life after rebelling against it?

Sources: Kraybill 2001; R. Schaefer and Zellner 2011; Shachtman 2006; Stevick 2007; Weinraub 2004.

School

Like the family, schools have an explicit mandate to socialize people in the United States—especially children—into the norms and values of our culture.

As conflict theorists Samuel Bowles and Herbert Gintis (1976) have observed, schools in this country foster competition through built-in systems of reward and punishment, such as grades and evaluations by teachers. Consequently, a child who is experiencing difficulty trying to learn a new skill can sometimes come to feel stupid and unsuccessful. However, as the self matures, children become capable of increasingly realistic assessments of their intellectual, physical, and social abilities.

Functionalists point out that schools, as agents of socialization, fulfill the function of teaching children the values and customs of the larger society. Conflict theorists agree, but add that schools can reinforce the divisive aspects of society, especially those of social class. For example, higher education in the United

States is costly despite the existence of financial aid programs. Students from affluent backgrounds therefore have an advantage in gaining access to universities and professional training. At the same time, less affluent young people may never receive the preparation that would qualify them for the best-paying and most prestigious jobs. The contrast between the functionalist and conflict views of education will be discussed in more detail in Module 43.

Peer Group

As a child grows older, the family becomes somewhat less important in social development. Instead, peer groups increasingly assume the role of Mead's significant others. Within the peer group, young people associate with others who are approximately their age, and who often enjoy a similar social status (Giordano 2003).

We can see how important peer groups are to young people when their social lives are strained by war or disaster. In Baghdad, the overthrow of Saddam Hussein has profoundly

♟ Taking Sociology to Work

Rakefet Avramovitz, *Program Administrator, Child Care Law Center*

Rakefet Avramovitz has been working at the Child Care Law Center in San Francisco since 2003. The center uses legal tools to foster the development of quality, affordable child care, with the goal of expanding child care options, particularly for low-income families. As a support person for the center's attorneys, she manages grants, oversees the center's publications, and sets up conferences and training sessions.

Avramovitz graduated from Dickinson College in 2000. She first became interested in sociology when she took a social analysis course. Though she enjoyed her qualitative courses most, she found her quantitative courses fun, "in that we got to do surveys

of people on campus. I've always enjoyed fieldwork," she notes. Avramovitz's most memorable course was one that gave her the opportunity to interact with migrant farmworkers for an entire semester. "I learned ethnography and how to work with people of different cultures. It changed my life," she says.

Avramovitz finds that the skills she learned in her sociology courses are a great help to her on the job. "Sociology taught me how to work with people . . . and how to think critically. It taught me how to listen and find the stories that people are telling," she explains. Before joining the Child Care Law Center, Avramovitz worked as a counselor for women who were facing difficult issues. "My background in ethnography helped me to talk to these women and listen effectively," she notes. "I was able to help many women by understanding and

being able to express their needs to the attorneys we worked with."

Avramovitz is enthusiastic about her work and her ability to make a difference in other people's lives. Maybe that is why she looks forward to summer at the center, when the staff welcomes several law students as interns. "It is really neat to see people learn and get jazzed about child care issues," she says.

LET'S DISCUSS

1. What might be some of the broad, long-term effects of the center's work to expand child care options? Explain.

2. Besides the law, what other professions might benefit from the skills a sociology major has to offer?

---

changed teenagers' worlds, casting doubt on their future. Some young people have lost relatives or friends; others have become involved with fundamentalist groups or fled with their families to safer countries. Those youths who are left behind can suffer intense loneliness and boredom. Confined to their homes by crime and terrorism, those fortunate enough to have computers turn to Internet chat rooms or immerse themselves in their studies. Through e-mail, they struggle to maintain old friendships interrupted by wartime dislocation (Sanders 2004).

Gender differences are noteworthy among adolescents. Boys and girls are socialized by their parents, peers, and the media to identify many of the same paths to popularity, but to different degrees. Table 15-1 compares male and female college students' reports of how girls and boys they knew became popular in high school. The two groups named many of the same paths to popularity but gave them a different order of importance. While neither men nor women named sexual activity, drug use, or alcohol

use as one of the top five paths, college men were much more likely than women to mention those behaviors as a means to becoming popular, for both boys and girls.

● Mass Media and Technology

In the past 80 years, media innovations—radio, motion pictures, recorded music, television, and the Internet—have become important agents of socialization. Television, and increasingly the Internet, are critical forces in the socialization of children in the United States (Figure 15-1). The Internet has become so pervasive that 95 percent of all teens ages 12 to 17 were online by 2011, and 80 percent of them used social media sites. These sites echo and amplify much of teens' socialization (Lenhart et al. 2011).

These media, however, are not always a negative socializing influence. Television programs and even commercials can

---

Table **15-1**   **High School Popularity**

What makes high school girls popular?		What makes high school boys popular?	
According to college men:	**According to college women:**	**According to college men:**	**According to college women:**
1. Physical attractiveness	1. Grades/intelligence	1. Participation in sports	1. Participation in sports
2. Grades/intelligence	2. Participation in sports	2. Grades/intelligence	2. Grades/intelligence
3. Participation in sports	3. General sociability	3. Popularity with girls	3. General sociability
4. General sociability	4. Physical attractiveness	4. General sociability	4. Physical attractiveness
5. Popularity with boys	5. Clothes	5. Car	5. School clubs/government

Note: Students at the following universities were asked in which ways adolescents in their high schools had gained prestige with their peers: Cornell University, Louisiana State University, Southeastern Louisiana University, State University of New York at Albany, State University of New York at Stony Brook, University of Georgia, and University of New Hampshire.
Source: Suitor et al. 2001:445.

introduce young people to unfamiliar lifestyles and cultures. Not only do children in the United States learn about life in "faraway lands," but inner-city children learn about the lives of farm children, and vice versa. The same thing happens in other countries.

Sociologists and other social scientists have begun to consider the impact of technology on socialization. They are particularly interested in the online friendship networks, like Facebook. Does this way of communicating resemble face-to-face interaction, or does it represent a new form of social interaction? Box 15-2 explores the significance of this social phenomenon.

Not just in industrial nations, but in Africa and other developing areas, people have been socialized into relying on new communications technologies. Not long ago, if Zadhe Iyombe wanted to talk to his mother, he had to make an eight-day trip from the capital city of Kinshasa up the Congo River by boat to the rural town where he was born. Now both he and his mother have access to a cell phone, and they send text messages to each other daily. Iyombe and his mother are not atypical. Although cell phones aren't cheap, 1.4 billion owners in developing countries have come to consider them a necessity. Today, there are more cell phones in developing nations than in industrial nations—the first time in history that developing nations have outpaced the developed world in the adoption of a telecommunications technology (K. Sullivan 2006).

● Workplace

Learning to behave appropriately in an occupation is a fundamental aspect of human socialization. It used to be that going to work began with the end of our formal schooling, but that is no longer the case, at least not in the United States. More and more young people work today, and not just for a parent or relative. Adolescents generally seek jobs in order to make spending money; 80 percent of high school seniors say that little or none of what they earn goes to family expenses. These teens rarely look on their employment as a means of exploring vocational interests or getting on-the-job training.

Some observers feel that the increasing number of teenagers who are working earlier in life and for longer hours are finding the workplace almost as important an agent of socialization as school. In fact, a number of educators complain that student time at work is adversely affecting schoolwork. The level of teenage employment in the United States is the highest among industrial countries, which may provide one explanation for why U.S. high school students lag behind those in other countries on international achievement tests.

Socialization in the workplace changes when it involves a more permanent shift from an after-school job to full-time employment. Occupational socialization can be most intense

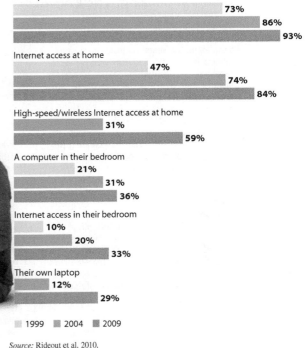

FIGURE 15-1 **The New Normal: Internet at Home**

Percentage of 8- to 18-year-olds with

A computer at home
- 73%
- 86%
- 93%

Internet access at home
- 47%
- 74%
- 84%

High-speed/wireless Internet access at home
- 31%
- 59%

A computer in their bedroom
- 21%
- 31%
- 36%

Internet access in their bedroom
- 10%
- 20%
- 33%

Their own laptop
- 12%
- 29%

■ 1999 ■ 2004 ■ 2009

Source: Rideout et al. 2010.

during the transition from school to job, but it continues throughout one's work history. Technological advances may alter the requirements of the position and necessitate some degree of resocialization. Today, men and women change occupations, employers, or places of work many times during their adult years. For example, the typical worker spends about four years with an employer. Occupational socialization continues, then, throughout a person's years in the labor market (Bialik 2010).

College students today recognize that occupational socialization is not socialization into one lifetime occupation. They

Research Today

BOX 15-2

Online Socializing: A New Agent of Socialization

Membership in the online social networks Facebook and MySpace has grown exponentially in recent years. At first, young adults monopolized these social networks. Indeed, Facebook was created in 2004 as a way for students on a single campus to become acquainted with one another before actually meeting.

Even in the brief history of online networking, sociologists can see social trends. For example, older people are now creating profiles on these sites. As the accompanying figure shows, there is still a clear correlation between age and online profiles: in a national survey of community college students, younger people were much more likely than older people to be online. However, the fastest-growing age groups are now those over 30, including those who are much older. As a result, online socializing is becoming much less age-specific—more like socializing in the real world. Moreover, this new agent of socialization can continue to influence people throughout the life course. Twitter is largely the exception to this trend; it is still a very age-specific method of social interaction.

Online networks—especially those that indicate how many "friends" an individual has—can also be seen in terms of social capital. In fact, "friending" is one, if not the, main activity on some online sites. Often the number of friends a person socializes with becomes the subject of boasting. By extension, individuals may use these sites to search for "friends" who may prove helpful to them in future endeavors. Becoming aware of new opportunities, either social or economic, through friends is a significant benefit of social capital.

Researchers have looked at the relationship between the display of friends online and the number of real-world friends people socialize with, and have proposed two competing hypotheses. According to the social enhancement hypothesis ("the rich get richer"), those

> Online networks—especially those that indicate how many "friends" an individual has—can also be seen in terms of social capital.

who are popular offline further increase their popularity through online networking sites. According to the social compensation hypothesis ("the poor get richer"), however, social network users try to increase their popularity online to compensate for inadequate popularity offline. The social compensation hypothesis, if correct, would be an example of impression management. Research supports elements of both hypotheses; neither hypothesis fully defines the participants in online networking sites.

Viewed from a societal perspective, socializing online can have both positive and negative functions. For members of some marginalized populations, it is a way to socialize with like-minded people. For example, Muslims in Great Britain connect with friends online to learn how to navigate through a society in which they form a distinct minority. For other people, such as members of neo-Nazi groups in Germany

and the Mafia in Italy, online networking is a way to proclaim allegiance to socially objectionable organizations. Governments frown on such online organizing, seeing it as dysfunctional, and periodically monitor these sites to see whether any laws have been violated. Little wonder that during the Arab Spring of 2011, which was marked by popular revolts against the central governments of Tunisia, Egypt, and Libya, authorities cracked down on citizens' access to social media.

Staying Connected: Community College Students

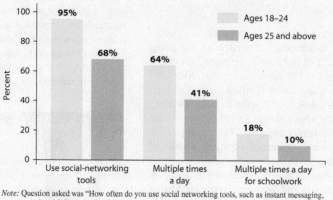

Note: Question asked was "How often do you use social networking tools, such as instant messaging, text messaging, MySpace and/or Facebook, Twitter, etc., for any purpose? (This does not include e-mail.)"
Source: Center for Community College Student Engagement 2009:8.

LET'S DISCUSS

1. Do you list your "friends" on an online social networking site? If so, what is your motivation for doing so? How much social capital do you think your list represents?

2. Do you think the advantages of online social networking outweigh the disadvantages?

Sources: Donadio 2009; N. Ellison et al. 2007; Facebook 2011; Gentile 2009; Hundley and Ramirez 2008; Lenhart 2009; Miyata and Kobayashi 2008; Zywica and Danowski 2008.

---

anticipate going through a number of jobs. The Bureau of Labor Statistics (2010) has found that from ages 18 to 42, the typical person has held 11 jobs. This high rate of turnover in employment applies to both men and women, and to those with a college degree as well as those with a high school diploma.

Religion and the State

Increasingly, social scientists are recognizing the importance of both religion and government ("the state") as agents of socialization, because of their impact on the life course.

Traditionally, family members have served as the primary caregivers in our culture, but in the 20th century, the family's protective function was steadily transferred to outside agencies such as hospitals, mental health clinics, and child care centers. Many of these agencies are run by groups affiliated with certain religions or by the state.

Both organized religion and government have impacted the life course by reinstituting some of the rites of passage once observed in agricultural communities and early industrial societies. For example, religious organizations stipulate certain traditional rites that may bring together all the members of an extended family, even if they never meet for any other reason. And government regulations stipulate the ages at which a person may drive a car, drink alcohol, vote in elections, marry without parental permission, work overtime, and retire. These regulations do not constitute strict rites of passage: most 18-year-olds choose not to vote, and most people choose their age of retirement without reference to government dictates.

In the Social Policy section at the end of this module, we will see that government is under pressure to become a provider of child care, which would give it a new and direct role in the socialization of infants and young children.

social policy and Socialization | Child Care around the World

Child care programs are not just babysitting services; they have an enormous influence on the development of young children—an influence that has been growing with the movement of more and more women into the paid labor force. The rise in single-parent families, increased job opportunities for women, and the need for additional family income have all propelled mothers of young children into the working world. Who should care for the children of working mothers during working hours?

Looking at the Issue

Preschoolers typically are not cared for by their parents. Seventy-three percent of employed mothers depend on others to care for their children, and 30 percent of mothers who aren't employed have regular care arrangements. In fact, children under age five are more likely to be cared for on a daily basis by their grandparents than by their parents. Over a third of them are cared for by nonrelatives in nursery schools, Head Start programs, day care centers, family day care, and other arrangements (Bureau of the Census 2008c).

Researchers have found that high-quality child care centers do not adversely affect the socialization of children; in fact, good day care benefits children. The value of preschool programs was documented in a series of studies conducted in the United States. Researchers found no significant differences in infants who had received extensive nonmaternal care compared with those who had been cared for solely by their mothers. They also reported that more and more infants in the United States are being placed in child care outside the home, and that overall, the quality of those arrangements is better than has been found in previous studies. It is difficult, however, to generalize about child care, since there is so much variability among day care providers, and even among government policies from one state to another (Loeb et al. 2004; Ludwig and Sawhill 2007; NICHD 2007).

Few people in the United States or elsewhere can afford the luxury of having a parent stay at home, or of paying for high-quality live-in child care. For millions of mothers and fathers, finding the right kind of child care is a challenge both to parenting and to the pocketbook. At present, the federal government supports child care through subsidized programs, which target low-income families, and income tax credits, which benefit families with moderate incomes. The annual expenditure to assist low-income parents is about $12 billion; the expenditure to support parents with moderate incomes is $58 billion (Cushing-Daniels and Zedlewski 2008).

Applying Sociology

Studies that assess the quality of child care outside the home reflect the micro level of analysis and the interest of interactionists in the impact of face-to-face interaction. These studies also explore macro-level implications for the functioning of social institutions like the family. Some of the issues surrounding day care have also been of interest to those who take the conflict perspective.

In the United States, high-quality day care is not equally available to all families. Parents in affluent communities have an easier time finding day care than those in poor or working-class communities. Finding *affordable* child care is also a problem. Viewed from a conflict perspective, child care costs are an especially serious burden for lower-class families. The poorest families spend 25 percent of their income for preschool child care, whereas families who are *not* poor pay only 6 percent or less of their income.

Feminist theorists echo the concern of conflict theorists that high-quality child care receives little government support

—Continued

—Continued

because it is regarded as "merely a way to let women work." Nearly all child care workers (97 percent) are women; many find themselves in low-status, minimum-wage jobs. Typically, food servers, messengers, and gas station attendants make more money than the 23 million child care workers in the United States, whose average annual salary of $19,605 puts them right at the poverty level for a family of three (Bureau of the Census 2011a; Ruiz 2010).

Initiating Policy

Policies regarding child care outside the home vary throughout the world. Most developing nations do not have the economic base to provide subsidized child care. Thus, working mothers rely largely on relatives or take their children to work. In the comparatively wealthy industrialized countries of western Europe, government provides child care as a basic service, at little or no expense to parents. But even those countries with tax-subsidized programs occasionally fall short of the need for high-quality child care.

Children play at the Communicare day care center in Perth, Australia. The Australian government subsidizes children's attendance at day care and afterschool programs from birth to age 12.

When policymakers decide that child care is desirable, they must determine the degree to which taxpayers should subsidize it. In Sweden and Denmark, one-half to two-thirds of preschoolers were in government-subsidized child care full-time in 2003. In the United States, annual fees for full-time child care of a four-year-old range from an average of $3,900 in Mississippi to an average of $11,678 in Massachusetts (Immervoll and Barber 2005; NACCRRA 2010).

We have a long way to go in making high-quality child care more affordable and accessible, not just in the United States but throughout the world as well. In an attempt to reduce government spending, France is considering cutting back the budgets of subsidized nurseries, even though waiting lists exist and the French public heartily disapproves of cutbacks. In Germany, reunification has reduced the options previously open to East German mothers, who had become accustomed to government-supported child care. Experts in child development view such reports as a vivid reminder of the need for greater government and private-sector support for child care (Hank 2001; L. King 1998).

TAKE THE ISSUE WITH YOU

1. Were you ever in a day care program? If so, do you recall the experience as good or bad? In general, do you think it is desirable to expose young children to the socializing influence of day care?

2. In the view of conflict theorists, child care receives little government support because it is "merely a way to let women work." Can you think of other explanations?

3. Should the costs of day care programs be paid by government, by the private sector, or entirely by parents?

MODULE 15 | Recap and Review

Summary

Important agents of socialization include the family, schools, peer groups, the mass media, the workplace, religious institutions, and the state.

1. As the primary agents of socialization, parents play a critical role in guiding children into those **gender roles** deemed appropriate in a society.

2. Like the family, schools in the United States have an explicit mandate to socialize people—especially children—into the norms and values of our culture.

3. Peer groups and the mass media, especially television and the Internet, are important agents of socialization for adolescents.

4. Socialization in the workplace begins with part-time employment while we are in school and continues as we work full-time and change jobs throughout our lives.

5. Religion and the state shape the socialization process by regulating the life course and influencing our views of appropriate behaviors at particular ages.

6. As more and more mothers of young children have entered the labor market, the demand for child care has increased dramatically, posing policy questions for many nations around the world.

Thinking Critically

1. How would functionalist and conflict theorists differ in their analysis of socialization by the mass media?

2. What sanctions limit participation in social networking? Describe the rules you have observed that limit the way people access and use online social networks. What are the purposes of such sanctions?

Key Term

Gender role

Mastering This Chapter: Socialization and the Life Course

taking sociology with you

1 Examine your looking-glass self. What was it like in high school? How did it change when you entered college, and who were the people who caused you to see yourself differently?

2 For two days, keep a record of your use of the mass media—television, the Internet, and so on—including what you watched, read, or communicated and your reasons for doing so. Then take the role of a sociologist and ask how you might have been socialized by the media you used. What norms and values were you exposed to, and how did they affect you?

3 Interview a person who has recently changed jobs. Ask about the process of resocialization required by the new job. Was the job change voluntary or involuntary, and how did it affect the person's adjustment? Which of the concepts you learned in this chapter seem relevant to the experience?

key terms

Anticipatory socialization Processes of socialization in which a person rehearses for future positions, occupations, and social relationships.

Cognitive theory of development The theory that children's thought progresses through four stages of development.

Degradation ceremony An aspect of the socialization process within some total institutions, in which people are subjected to humiliating rituals.

Dramaturgical approach A view of social interaction in which people are seen as theatrical performers.

Face-work The efforts people make to maintain the proper image and avoid public embarrassment.

Gender role Expectations regarding the proper behavior, attitudes, and activities of males and females.

Generalized other The attitudes, viewpoints, and expectations of society as a whole that a child takes into account in his or her behavior.

Impression management The altering of the presentation of the self in order to create distinctive appearances and satisfy particular audiences.

Life course approach A research orientation in which sociologists and other social scientists look closely at the social factors that influence people throughout their lives, from birth to death.

Looking-glass self A concept that emphasizes the self as the product of our social interactions.

Personality A person's typical patterns of attitudes, needs, characteristics, and behavior.

Resocialization The process of discarding former behavior patterns and accepting new ones as part of a transition in one's life.

Rite of passage A ritual marking the symbolic transition from one social position to another.

Role taking The process of mentally assuming the perspective of another and responding from that imagined viewpoint.

Self A distinct identity that sets us apart from others.

Significant other An individual who is most important in the development of the self, such as a parent, friend, or teacher.

Socialization The lifelong process in which people learn the attitudes, values, and behaviors appropriate for members of a particular culture.

Total institution An institution that regulates all aspects of a person's life under a single authority, such as a prison, the military, a mental hospital, or a convent.

self-quiz

Read each question carefully and then select the best answer.

1. Which of the following social scientists used the phrase *looking-glass self* to emphasize that the self is the product of our social interactions with other people?
   a. George Herbert Mead
   b. Charles Horton Cooley
   c. Erving Goffman
   d. Jean Piaget

2. In what he called the *play stage* of socialization, George Herbert Mead asserted that people mentally assume the perspectives of others, thereby enabling them to respond from that imagined viewpoint. This process is referred to as
   a. role taking.
   b. the generalized other.
   c. the significant other.
   d. impression management.

3. George Herbert Mead is best known for his theory of what?
   a. presentation of the self
   b. cognitive development
   c. the self
   d. impression management

4. Suppose a clerk tries to appear busier than he or she actually is when a supervisor happens to be watching. Erving Goffman would study this behavior from what approach?
   a. functionalist
   b. conflict
   c. psychological
   d. interactionist

5. According to child psychologist Jean Piaget's cognitive theory of development, children begin to use words and symbols to distinguish objects and ideas during which stage in the development of the thought process?
   a. the sensorimotor stage
   b. the preoperational stage
   c. the concrete operational stage
   d. the formal operational stage

6. On the first day of basic training in the army, a recruit has his civilian clothes replaced by army "greens," has his hair shaved off, loses his privacy, and finds that he must use a communal bathroom. All these humiliating activities are part of
   a. becoming a significant other.
   b. impression management.
   c. a degradation ceremony.
   d. face-work.

7. Which social institution is considered to be the most important agent of socialization in the United States, especially for children?
   a. the family
   b. the school
   c. the peer group
   d. the mass media

8. The term *gender role* refers to
   a. the biological fact that we are male or female.
   b. a role that is given to us by a teacher.
   c. a role that is given to us in a play.
   d. expectations regarding the proper behavior, attitudes, and activities of males and females.

9. Which sociological perspective emphasizes that schools in the United States foster competition through built-in systems of reward and punishment?
   a. the functionalist perspective
   b. the conflict perspective
   c. the interactionist perspective
   d. the psychological perspective

10. Which of the following statements about teenagers in Baghdad is true?
    a. They have lost much of their peer group due to death and relocation.
    b. They have lost peers who have joined fundamentalist groups.
    c. If they own a computer, they use it in an attempt to stay in contact with their pre-war peer group.
    d. all of the above

11. _____ is the term used by sociologists in referring to the lifelong process whereby people learn the attitudes, values, and behaviors appropriate for members of a particular culture.

12. In everyday speech, the term _____ is used to refer to a person's typical patterns of attitudes, needs, characteristics, and behavior.

13. Studies of twins raised apart suggest that both _____ and _____ influence human development.

14. A _____ _____ is an individual such as a parent, friend, or teacher who is most important in the development of the self.

15. Early work in _____, such as that by Sigmund Freud, stressed the role of inborn drives—among them the drive for sexual gratification—in channeling human behavior.

16. The Swiss psychologist Jean Piaget developed the _____ theory of development.

17. Preparation for many aspects of adult life begins with _____ socialization during childhood and adolescence and continues throughout our lives as we prepare for new responsibilities.

18. Resocialization is particularly effective when it occurs within a(n) _____ institution.

19. The _____ perspective emphasizes the role of schools in teaching the values and customs of the larger society.

20. As children grow older, the family becomes less important in social development, while _____ groups become more important.

Answers

1 (b); 2 (a); 3 (c); 4 (d); 5 (b); 6 (c); 7 (a); 8 (d); 9 (b); 10 (d); 11 Socialization; 12 personality; 13 heredity; environment; 14 significant other; 15 psychology; 16 cognitive; 17 anticipatory; 18 total; 19 functionalist; 20 peer.

thinking about movies

Pariah

A teenager comes of age in Brooklyn, New York, in this touching portrayal of the pressures of socialization.

The Wrestler

A professional wrestler who is past his prime tries to retire from the sport and return to mainstream society.

Grown Ups

Five childhood friends reunite and come to terms with the aging process.

Social Interaction, Social Structure, and Groups

Social Interaction, Social Structure, and Groups

MODULE **16**
Social Interaction and Social Structure

MODULE **17**
Social Structure in Global Perspective

MODULE **18**
Understanding Groups

MODULE **19**
Understanding Organizations

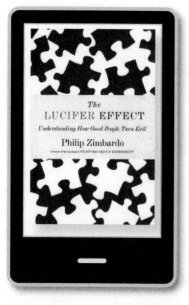

If you were a prison guard, would you mistreat the inmates?

To find the answer to this question, social psychologist Philip Zimbardo created a mock prison and enlisted college students to serve as the inmates and guards.

" As each of the blindfolded prisoners is escorted down the flight of steps in front of Jordan Hall into our little jail, our guards order them to strip and remain standing naked with their arms outstretched against the wall and legs spread apart. They hold that uncomfortable position for a long time as the guards ignore them because they are busy with last-minute chores, like packing away the prisoners' belongings for safekeeping, fixing up their guards quarters, and arranging beds in the three cells. Before being given his uniform, each prisoner is sprayed with powder, alleged to be a delouser, to rid him of lice that might be brought in to contaminate our jail.... The humiliation of being a prisoner has begun, much as it does in many institutions from military boot camps to prisons, hospitals, and low-level jobs....

The morning shift comes on in the middle of the night, 2 a.m....

The prisoners are sound asleep. Some are snoring in their dark, cramped cells. Suddenly the silence is shattered. Loud whistles shriek, voices yell, "Up and at 'em." "Wake up and get out here for the count!" "Okay, you sleeping beauties, it's time to see if you learned how to count." Dazed prisoners line up against the wall and count off mindlessly as the three guards alternate in coming up with new variations on count themes. The count and its attendant push-ups and jumping jacks for failures continue on and on for nearly a weary hour. Finally, the prisoners are ordered back to sleep—until reveille a few hours later....

[By Tuesday] our prisoners are looking raggedy and bleary-eyed, and our little prison is beginning to smell like a men's toilet in a New York subway station. Seems that some guards have made toilet visits a privilege to be awarded infrequently and never after lights out. During the night, prisoners have to urinate and defecate in buckets in their cells, and some guards refuse to allow them to be emptied till morning. Complaints are coming fast and furiously from many of the prisoners....

After less than three days into this bizarre situation, some of the students role-playing prison guards have moved far beyond mere playacting. They have internalized the hostility, negative affect, and mind-set characteristic of some real prison guards, as is evident from their shift reports, retrospective diaries, and personal reflections.

...

The depersonalization of the prisoners and the spreading extent of dehumanization are beginning to affect [one of the guards], too: "As I got angrier and angrier, I didn't question this behavior as much. I couldn't let it affect me, so I started hiding myself deeper behind my role. It was the only way of not hurting yourself. I was really lost on what was happening but didn't even think about quitting."

Blaming the victims for their sorry condition—created by our failure to provide adequate shower and sanitation facilities—became common among the staff. We see this victim blame in operation as [the guard] complains, "I got tired of seeing the prisoners in rags, smelling bad, and the prison stink. "

(Zimbardo 2007:40, 41, 52, 53, 80, 86) Additional information about this excerpt can be found on the Online Learning Center at www.mhhe.com/schaefermod2e.

> *After less than three days into this bizarre situation, some of the students role-playing prison guards have moved far beyond mere playacting. They have internalized the hostility, negative affect, and mind-set characteristic of some real prison guards.*

I n this study, directed and described by social psychologist Philip Zimbardo, college students adopted the patterns of social interaction expected of guards and prisoners when they were placed in a mock prison. Sociologists use the term *social interaction* to refer to the ways in which people respond to one another. In the mock prison, social interactions between guards and prisoners were highly impersonal. The guards addressed the prisoners by number rather than name, and they wore reflective sunglasses that made eye contact impossible.

As in many real-life prisons, the simulated prison had a social structure in which guards held virtually total control over prisoners. The term *social structure* refers to the way in which a society is organized into predictable relationships. The social structure of Zimbardo's mock prison influenced how the guards and prisoners interacted. Zimbardo and his colleagues (2009:516) note that it was a real prison "in the minds of the jailers and their captives." His simulated prison experiment, first conducted more than 30 years ago, has been repeated (with similar findings) both in the United States and in other countries.

In these modules we will study social structure and its effect on our social interactions. What determines a person's status in society? How do our social roles affect our social interactions? What is the place of social institutions such as the family, religion, and government in our social structure? How can we better understand and manage large organizations such as multinational corporations? We'll begin by considering how social interactions shape the way we view the world around us. Next, we'll focus on the six basic elements of social structure: statuses, social roles, groups, social networks, social institutions such as the family, religion, and government, and the mass media. We'll also touch on a new element of social network, *virtual worlds*. We'll see that functionalists, conflict theorists, and interactionists approach these institutions quite differently. We'll compare our modern social structure with simpler forms around the world. We'll note the differences between various types of groups, with particular attention to small groups. Next, we'll consider why formal organizations, such as corporations or the college you attend, came into existence, touching on Max Weber's model of the modern bureaucracy. The Social Policy section at the end of the chapter focuses on the recent concentration of the mass media in the hands of a few large corporations.

The prison experiment described in *The Lucifer Effect* took on new relevance during the Iraq War, in the wake of shocking revelations of prisoner abuse at the U.S.-run Abu Ghraib military facility. Graphic photos showed U.S. soldiers humiliating naked Iraqi prisoners and threatening to attack them with police dogs. The structure of the wartime prison, coupled with intense pressure on military intelligence officers to get information about terrorist plots, contributed to the breakdown in the guards' behavior. But the guards' depraved behavior could have been predicted on the basis of Zimbardo's research.

The two concepts of social interaction and social structure are central to sociology. **Social interaction,** the ways people respond to one another, and **social structure,** the way society is organized into predictable relationships, work together. Both concepts are closely related to socialization (see Module 13), the process through which people learn the attitudes, values, and behaviors appropriate to their society. When the students in Zimbardo's experiment entered the mock prison, they began a process of resocialization. In that process, they adjusted to a new social structure and learned new rules for social interaction.

Social Interaction and Reality

When someone in a crowd shoves you, do you automatically push back? Or do you consider the circumstances of the incident and the attitude of the instigator before you react? Chances are you do the latter. According to sociologist Herbert Blumer (1969:79), the distinctive characteristic of social interaction among people is that "human beings interpret or 'define' each other's actions instead of merely reacting to each other's actions." In other words, our response to someone's behavior is based on the *meaning* we attach to his or her actions. Reality is shaped by our perceptions, evaluations, and definitions.

These meanings typically reflect the norms and values of the dominant culture and our socialization experiences within that culture. As interactionists emphasize, the meanings that we attach to people's behavior are shaped by our interactions with them and with the larger society. Social reality is literally constructed from our social interactions (Berger and Luckmann 1966).

How do we define our social reality? Consider something as simple as how we regard tattoos. At one time, most of us in the United States considered tattoos weird or kooky. We associated them with fringe countercultural groups, such as punk rockers, biker gangs, and skinheads. Among many people, a tattoo elicited an automatic negative response. Now, however, so many people have tattoos—including society's trendsetters and major sports figures—and the ritual of getting a tattoo has become so legitimized, that mainstream culture regards tattoos differently. At this point, as a result of increased social interaction with tattooed people, tattoos look perfectly at home to us in a number of settings.

The nature of social interaction and what constitutes reality varies across cultures. In Western societies, with their emphasis on romantic love, couples see marriage as a relationship as well as a social status. From Valentine's Day flowers to more informal, everyday gestures, professions of love are an expected part of marriage. In Japan, however, marriage is considered more a social status than a relationship. Although many or most Japanese couples undoubtedly do love each other, saying "I love you" does not come easily to them, especially not to husbands. Nor do most husbands call their wives by name (they prefer "Mother") or look them in the eyes. In 2006, in an effort to change these restrictive customs, some Japanese men formed the Devoted Husband Organization, which has been sponsoring a new holiday, Beloved Wives Day. In 2008, this group organized an event called Shout Your Love from the Middle of a Cabbage Patch Day. Dozens of men stood in a cabbage patch north of Tokyo and shouted, "I love you!" to their wives, some of whom had never heard their husbands say those words. In another rare gesture, husbands pledged to be home by 8 p.m. that day (Japan Aisaika Organization 2012; Kambayashi 2008).

The ability to define social reality reflects a group's power within a society. In fact, one of the most crucial aspects of the relationship between dominant and subordinate groups is the ability of the dominant or majority group to define a society's values. Sociologist William I. Thomas (1923), an early critic of theories of racial and gender differences, recognized that the "definition of the situation" could mold the thinking and personality of the individual. Writing from an interactionist perspective, Thomas observed that people respond not only to the objective features of a person or situation but also to the *meaning* that person or situation has for them. For example, in Philip Zimbardo's mock prison experiment, student "guards" and "prisoners" accepted the definition of the situation (including the traditional roles and behavior associated with being a guard or prisoner) and acted accordingly.

As we have seen throughout the past 60 years—first in the civil rights movement of the 1950s and 1960s and since then among such groups as women, the elderly, gays and lesbians, and people with disabilities—an important aspect of the process of social change involves redefining or reconstructing social reality. Members of subordinate groups challenge traditional definitions and begin to perceive and experience reality in a new way.

Elements of Social Structure

All social interaction takes place within a social structure, including those interactions that redefine social reality. For purposes of study, we can break down any social structure into six elements: statuses, social roles, groups, social networks, virtual worlds, and social institutions. These elements make up social structure just as a foundation, walls, and ceilings make up a building's structure. The elements of social structure are developed through the lifelong process of socialization described in Module 14.

Statuses

We normally think of a person's *status* as having to do with influence, wealth, and fame. However, sociologists use the term **status** to refer to any of the full range of socially defined positions within a large group or society, from the lowest to the highest. Within our society, a person can occupy the status of president of the United States, fruit picker, son or daughter, violinist, teenager, resident of Minneapolis, dental technician, or neighbor. A person can hold a number of statuses at the same time.

Ascribed and Achieved Status   Sociologists view some statuses as *ascribed* and others as *achieved* (Figure 16-1). An **ascribed status** is assigned to a person by society without regard for the person's unique talents or characteristics. Generally, the assignment takes place at birth; thus, a person's racial background, gender, and age are all considered ascribed statuses. Though these characteristics are biological in origin, they are significant mainly because of the *social* meanings they have in our culture. Conflict theorists are especially interested in ascribed statuses, since they often confer privileges or reflect a person's membership in a subordinate group. The social meanings of race, ethnicity, and gender will be analyzed more fully in Modules 32 and 34.

In most cases, we can do little to change an ascribed status, but we can attempt to change the traditional constraints associated with it. For example, the Gray Panthers—an activist political group founded in 1971 to work for the rights of older people—have tried to modify society's negative and confining stereotypes of the elderly. As a result of their work and that of other groups supporting older citizens, the ascribed status of "senior citizen" is no longer as difficult for millions of older people.

An ascribed status does not necessarily have the same social meaning in every society. In a cross-cultural study, sociologist Gary Huang (1988) confirmed the long-held view that respect for the elderly is an important cultural norm in China. In many

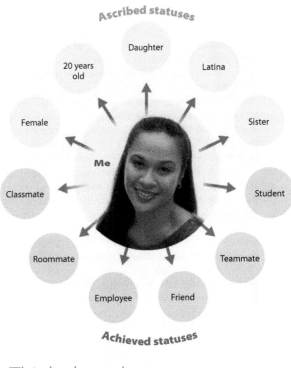

FIGURE 16-1 **Social Statuses**

Ascribed statuses

Daughter · Latina · 20 years old · Sister · Female · Me · Student · Classmate · Roommate · Teammate · Employee · Friend

Achieved statuses

Think about It

The young woman in this figure—"me"—occupies many positions in society, each of which involves distinct statuses. How would you define your statuses? Which have the most influence in your life?

cases, the prefix "old" is used respectfully: calling someone "old teacher" or "old person" is like calling a judge in the United States "your honor." Huang points out that positive age-seniority language distinctions are uncommon in the United States; consequently, we view the term *old man* as more of an insult than a celebration of seniority and wisdom.

Unlike ascribed statuses, an **achieved status** comes to us largely through our own efforts. Both "computer programmer" and "prison guard" are achieved statuses, as are "lawyer," "pianist," "sorority member," "convict," and "social worker." We must do something to acquire an achieved status—go to school, learn a skill, establish a friendship, invent a new product. But as we will see in the next section, our ascribed status heavily influences our achieved status. Being male, for example, would decrease the likelihood that we would consider child care as a career.

Master Status   Each person holds many different and sometimes conflicting statuses; some may connote higher social position and some, lower position. How, then, do others view one's overall social position? According to sociologist Everett Hughes

Ascribed status may intersect with a person's achieved status. This woman's achieved status as a low-income worker, combined with her minority ethnic status, contrast sharply with the high status of her customer.

(1945), societies deal with inconsistencies by agreeing that certain statuses are more important than others. A **master status** is a status that dominates others and thereby determines a person's general position in society. For example, Arthur Ashe, who died of AIDS in 1993, had a remarkable career as a tennis star, but at the end of his life, his status as a well-known personality with AIDS may have outweighed his statuses as a retired athlete, author, and political activist. Throughout the world, many people with disabilities find that their status as disabled receives undue weight, overshadowing their actual ability to perform successfully in meaningful employment (Box 16-1).

Our society gives such importance to race and gender that they often dominate our lives. These ascribed statuses frequently influence our achieved status. The Black activist Malcolm X (1925–1965), an eloquent and controversial advocate of Black power and Black pride during the early 1960s, recalled that his feelings and perspectives changed dramatically in middle school. Elected class president and finishing near the top of his class academically, he had developed a positive outlook. However, his teachers, all of them White, discouraged him from taking more challenging courses, which they felt were not appropriate for Black students. When his eighth-grade English teacher, a White man, advised him that his goal of becoming a lawyer was not realistic, and encouraged him instead to become a carpenter, Malcolm X concluded that his being a Black man (ascribed status) was an obstacle to his dream of becoming a lawyer (achieved status). In the United States, the ascribed statuses of race and gender can function as master statuses that have an important impact on one's potential to achieve a desired professional and social status (Malcolm X [1964] 1999:37; Marable 2011:36–38).

Social Roles

What Are Social Roles? Throughout our lives, we acquire what sociologists call social roles. A **social role** is a set of expectations for people who occupy a given social position or status. Thus, in the United States, we expect that cab drivers will know how to get around a city, that receptionists will be reliable in handling phone messages, and that police officers will take action if they see a citizen being threatened. With each distinctive social status—whether ascribed or achieved—come particular role expectations. However, actual performance varies from individual to individual. One secretary may assume extensive administrative responsibilities, while another may focus on clerical duties. Similarly, in Philip Zimbardo's mock prison experiment, some students were brutal and sadistic guards; others were not.

Roles are a significant component of social structure. Viewed from a functionalist perspective, roles contribute to a society's stability by enabling members to anticipate the behavior of others and to pattern their actions accordingly. Yet social roles can also be dysfunctional if they restrict people's interactions and relationships. If we view a person *only* as a "police officer" or "supervisor," it will be difficult to relate to him or her as a friend or neighbor.

Role Conflict Imagine the delicate situation of a woman who has worked for a decade on an assembly line in an electrical plant, and has recently been named supervisor of her unit. How is this woman expected to relate to her longtime friends and co-workers? Should she still go out to lunch with them, as she has done almost daily for years? Is it her responsibility to recommend the firing of an old friend who cannot keep up with the demands of the assembly line?

Role conflict occurs when incompatible expectations arise from two or more social positions held by the same person. Fulfillment of the roles associated with one status may directly violate the roles linked to a second status. In the example just given, the newly promoted supervisor will most likely experience a sharp conflict between her social and occupational roles. Such role conflicts call for important ethical choices. The new supervisor will have to make a difficult decision about how much allegiance she owes her friend and how much she owes her employers, who have given her supervisory responsibilities.

use your **sociological imagination**

If you were a male nurse, what aspects of role conflict might you experience? Now imagine you are a professional boxer and a woman. What conflicting role expectations might that involve? In both cases, how well do you think you would handle role conflict?

Another type of role conflict occurs when individuals move into occupations that are not common among people with their ascribed status. Male preschool teachers and female police officers experience this type of role conflict. In the latter case, female officers must strive to reconcile their workplace role

Research Today

BOX 16-1

Disability as a Master Status

Throughout history and around the world, people with disabilities have been subjected to cruel and inhuman treatment. For example, in the 20th century, the disabled were frequently viewed as subhuman creatures who were a menace to society. In Japan more than 16,000 women with disabilities were involuntarily sterilized with government approval from 1945 to 1995. Sweden apologized for the same action taken against 62,000 of its citizens in the 1970s.

Such blatantly hostile treatment of people with disabilities has given way to a *medical model*, in which the disabled are viewed as chronic patients. Increasingly, however, people concerned with the rights of the disabled have criticized this model as well. In their view, it is the unnecessary and discriminatory barriers present in the environment—both physical and attitudinal—that stand in the way of people with disabilities, more than any biological limitations. Applying a *civil rights model*, activists emphasize that those with disabilities face widespread prejudice, discrimination, and segregation. For example, most voting places are inaccessible to wheelchair users and fail to provide ballots that can be used by those unable to read print.

Drawing on the earlier work of Erving Goffman, contemporary sociologists have

suggested that society attaches a stigma to many forms of disability, a stigma that leads to prejudicial treatment. People with disabilities frequently observe that the nondisabled see them only as blind, wheelchair users, and so forth, rather than as complex human beings with individual strengths and weaknesses, whose blindness or use of a wheelchair is merely one aspect of their lives.

Although discrimination against the disabled occurs around the world, attitudes are

> In Japan more than 16,000 women with disabilities were involuntarily sterilized with government approval from 1945 to 1995.

changing. The African nation of Botswana has plans to assist its disabled, most of whom live in rural areas and need special services for mobility and economic development. In many countries, disability rights activists are targeting issues essential to overcoming this master status and becoming a full citizen, including

employment, housing, education, and access to public buildings.

LET'S DISCUSS

1. Does your campus present barriers to disabled students? If so, what kinds of barriers—physical, attitudinal, or both? Describe some of them.

2. Why do you think nondisabled people see disability as the most important characteristic of a disabled person? What can be done to help people see beyond the wheelchair and the Seeing Eye dog?

Sources: Albrecht 2004; Goffman 1963; D. Murphy 1997; *Newsday* 1997; R. Schaefer 2012; J. Shapiro 1993.

---

in law enforcement with the societal view of a woman's role, which does not embrace many skills needed in police work. And while female police officers encounter sexual harassment, as women do throughout the labor force, they must also deal with the "code of silence," an informal norm that precludes their implicating fellow officers in wrongdoing (Fletcher 1995; S. Martin 1994).

Role Strain   Role conflict describes the situation of a person dealing with the challenge of occupying two social positions simultaneously. However, even a single position can cause problems. Sociologists use the term **role strain** to describe the difficulty that arises when the same social position imposes conflicting demands and expectations.

People who belong to minority cultures may experience role strain while working in the mainstream culture. Criminologist Larry Gould (2002) interviewed officers of the Navajo Nation Police Department about their relations with conventional law enforcement officials, such as sheriffs and FBI agents. Besides enforcing the law, Navajo Nation officers practice an alternative form of justice known as Peacemaking, in which they seek reconciliation between the parties to a crime. The officers expressed great confidence in Peacemaking, but worried that if they did not make arrests, other law enforcement

officials would think they were too soft, or "just taking care of their own." Regardless of the strength of their ties to traditional Navajo ways, all felt the strain of being considered "too Navajo" or "not Navajo enough."

Role Exit   Often, when we think of assuming a social role, we focus on the preparation and anticipatory socialization a person undergoes for that role. Such is true if a person is about to become an attorney, a chef, a spouse, or a parent. Yet until recently, social scientists have given little attention to the adjustments involved in *leaving* social roles.

Sociologist Helen Rose Fuchs Ebaugh (1988) developed the term **role exit** to describe the process of disengagement from a role that is central to one's self-identity in order to establish a new role and identity. Drawing on interviews with 185 people—among them ex-convicts, divorced men and women, recovering alcoholics, ex-nuns, former doctors, retirees, and transexuals—Ebaugh (herself an ex-nun) studied the process of voluntarily exiting from significant social roles.

Ebaugh has offered a four-stage model of role exit. The first stage begins with *doubt*. The person experiences frustration, burnout, or simply unhappiness with an accustomed status and the roles associated with the social position. The second stage involves a *search for alternatives*. A person who is unhappy with

Taking Sociology to Work

Danielle Taylor, *Account Manager, Cash Cycle Solutions*

When Danielle Taylor entered Clemson University, she was planning to study medicine, but then she discovered that sociology was "ten times more interesting." Today she is an account manager with a company in Charlotte, North Carolina, that provides transaction processing services.

Taylor began her business career as a restaurant manager, a job that involved a good deal of interaction with the public. Sociology prepared her for a diverse work environment, she says, and helped her to handle customer complaints, allowing her to "defuse these often delicate situations more easily and with much less struggle" than managers without her background.

Taylor was managing a corporate restaurant when she made the connection that led to her present position as an account manager. "I was privy to meeting many people with lots of connections in other fields," she explains. "Networking is never as formal as it sounds and just simply conversing with my customers led to me finding a much better suited career."

Taylor thinks she is a more open and understanding person thanks to her sociological training. "I tend to judge less and analyze more," she says. She also sees the big picture that other people might miss. "Managing a restaurant with a degree in sociology was an eye-opening experience," she concludes.

LET'S DISCUSS

1. Before you read this box, would you have thought that a sociology major could be successful as a business manager? Why or why not?

2. Take the skills that Danielle Taylor gained from studying sociology and apply them to the job you hope to get when you graduate. Do they apply just as well to your chosen field?

According to sociologist Helen Rose Fuchs Ebaugh, role exit is a four-stage process. Is this transsexual in the first or the fourth stage of changing genders?

his or her career may take a leave of absence; an unhappily married couple may begin what they see as a temporary separation.

The third stage of role exit is the *action stage* or *departure*. Ebaugh found that the vast majority of her respondents could identify a clear turning point that made them feel it was essential to take final action and leave their jobs, end their marriages, or engage in another type of role exit. Twenty percent of respondents saw their role exit as a gradual, evolutionary process that had no single turning point.

The fourth stage of role exit involves the *creation of a new identity.* Many of you participated in a role exit when you made the transition from high school to college. You left behind the role of offspring living at home and took on the role of a somewhat independent college student living with peers in a dorm. Sociologist Ira Silver (1996) has studied the central role that material objects play in this transition. The objects students choose to leave at home (like stuffed animals and dolls) are associated with their prior identities. They may remain deeply attached to those objects, but do not want them to be seen as part of their new identities at college. The objects they bring with them symbolize how they now see themselves and how they wish to be perceived. iPods and wall posters, for example, are calculated to say, "This is me."

Groups

In sociological terms, a **group** is any number of people with similar norms, values, and expectations who interact with one another on a regular basis. The members of a women's basketball team, a hospital's business office, a synagogue, or a symphony orchestra constitute a group. However, the residents of a suburb would not be considered a group, since they rarely interact with one another at one time.

Groups play a vital part in a society's social structure. Much of our social interaction takes place within groups and is influenced by their norms and sanctions. Being a teenager or a retired person takes on special meanings when we interact within groups designed for people with that particular status. The expectations associated with many social roles, including those accompanying the statuses of brother, sister, and student, become more clearly defined in the context of a group.

Social Networks

Groups do not merely serve to define other elements of the social structure, such as roles and statuses; they also link the individual with the larger society. We all belong to a number of different groups, and through our acquaintances make connections with people in different social circles. These connections are known as a **social network**—a series of social relationships that links a person directly to others, and through them indirectly to still more people. Social networks are one of the five basic elements of social structure.

Social networks can center on virtually any activity, from sharing job information to exchanging news and gossip, or even sharing sex. Much of network analysis serves as an example of applied research. Box 16-2 describes a long-term study in which public health officials used network analysis to curb obesity.

Involvement in social networks—commonly known as *networking*—is especially valuable in finding employment. Albert Einstein was successful in finding a job only when a classmate's father put him in touch with his future employer. These kinds of contacts—even those that are weak and distant—can be crucial in establishing social networks and facilitating the transmission of information.

Q Research Today

BOX 16-2

Social Networks and Obesity

Over the past two generations, obesity has become a public health problem in the United States. To explain the trend toward excess weight, researchers have focused on Americans' nutritional practices, as well as on their genetic tendencies. Another variable that contributes to obesity, less obvious than diet and heredity, is social networking.

Researchers identified this last variable in the course of a long-term heart health survey, during which they tracked the weight of

> Weight gain in one person is often associated with weight gain in his or her friends, siblings, spouse, and neighbors.

12,067 respondents. At the same time, they mapped the social networks that respondents belonged to (see the accompanying figure). Over the three decades since the survey began, they have noted that weight gain in one person is often associated with weight gain in his or her friends, siblings, spouse, and neighbors. In fact, a person's chances of becoming obese increased by 57 percent if a friend became overweight during the same period. This association, they found, was attributable solely to selectivity in the choice of friends—that is, to people of a certain weight seeking out others of roughly the same weight.

This study shows that social networks do influence the way people behave. More important, the results suggest that networking could be exploited to spread positive health behaviors—for example, by recruiting friends to participate in a person's weight-loss plan.

A Network of the Obese

- ● Obese person
- ● Non-obese person
- — Friendship/marital ties

- ◐ Female
- ◐ Male
- — Familial ties

Larger circles represent heavier people.

Through a similar approach, health practitioners could include social networking in efforts to control smoking, drinking, and drug abuse.

LET'S DISCUSS

1. Have you ever tried to lose weight, and if so, did your cluster of friends and family help or hinder you? In your experience, do people who are overweight tend to cluster in separate groups from those of normal weight?

2. Besides public health campaigns, what applications can you think of for research on social networking?

Sources: Christakis and Fowler 2007, 2009; Haas et al. 2010.

During the recent economic downturn, electronic social networks have served a new purpose, encouraging the jobless. Websites and chat rooms that cannot locate jobs for those who have been thrown out of work concentrate instead on helping them to stick together, support one another, and maintain a positive attitude. For the unemployed, online conversations with friends or even strangers in the same predicament can be an invaluable morale booster (Scherer 2010b).

Research indicates, however, that both in person and online, not everyone participates equally in social networks. Women and racial and ethnic minorities are at a disadvantage when seeking new and better job opportunities or social contacts (Trimble and Kmec 2011).

Virtual Worlds

Today, with recent advances in technology, people can maintain their social networks electronically; they don't need face-to-face contacts. Whether through text-messaging, handheld devices, or social networking sites like Facebook, a significant amount of networking occurs online. Adolescents can now interact freely

case study | The Second Life Virtual World

E-mail, webcams, and blogs are only the first stage in the creation of alternative forms of social reality. Recently a whole new society, the Second Life® world, has sprung up in virtual space. Web-based and three-dimensional, the Second Life virtual world included over 19 million networked "players" as of 2012. In this game, players assume avatars that may represent looking-glass selves very different from their actual identities. Once equipped with an avatar, they go about their lives in the virtual world, establishing businesses, even buying and decorating homes.

Just like real worlds, virtual worlds have become politicized and commercialized. In 2007, Sweden became the first real-world country to place an "embassy" in the Second Life world. Elsewhere in this virtual world, virtual protesters have paraded on behalf of a far-right French group in a confrontation with anti-Nazi protesters. The Second Life virtual world is now open to real-world corporations that want to "build" their stores in it. Some corporations have even purchased "islands" to use for training sessions or employee conferences. Employees who attend these exclusive functions may show up in their finest avatar attire. The commercialization of these spaces has been met with a good deal of antagonism: Reebok

has weathered a virtual nuclear bomb attack, and "customers" have been "shot" outside the American Apparel store.

A more positive side of the Second Life virtual world is evident in Al-Andalus, a democratically run nonprofit community dedicated to interfaith understanding. Begun after 9/11, Al-Andalus has equal numbers of Jewish, Muslim, Christian, and atheist avatars. It even boasts a library to provide objective information on religion, run by an avatar who in real life is a librarian at the Smithsonian Institution.

Sociologist Manuel Castells views these emerging electronic social networks as fundamental to new organizations, and to the growth of existing businesses and associations. With other scholars, sociologists are now scrambling to understand these environments and their social processes. The Second Life world went public in 2003—a millennium ago in the world of cyberspace. Scholars worry that after the current period of transition, given the absence of a historical record, reconstructing these worlds as they existed when they were populated by only a hundred avatars, much less tens of thousands, will be impossible (Boellstorff 2008; Borrelli 2010; Castells 2010a, 2010b, 2010c; Gilsdorf 2010; Malaby 2009; Second Life 2010).

Virtual worlds have just begun to test our imaginations. On the left, a group of avatars interacts in the Second Life® world. On the right, in the blockbuster film *Avatar*, the Na'vi people interact in the screen-based virtual world of Pandora.

with distant friends, even under close scrutiny by parents or teachers. Without leaving their cubicles, employees with a taste for adventure can escape their work environments. In Box 15-2, we considered the impact of online social networks on the process of socialization.

Virtual networks also can help to preserve real-world networks interrupted by war and other dislocations. The recent deployment of U.S. troops in the Middle East and Afghanistan increased many people's reliance on e-mail. Today, digital photos and sound files accompany e-mail messages between soldiers and their families and friends. GIs can even view siblings' graduations or children's birthday parties live, via webcams. And U.S. soldiers have been posting their opinions of the war in Afghanistan in online journals called web logs, or blogs. Though critics are skeptical of the identity of some of the authors, these postings have become yet another source of news about the war (Faith 2005; O'Connor 2004; Sisson 2007).

use your **sociological imagination**

What features of the Second Life world would you like to investigate, and why? How would you go about doing so?

Social Institutions

The mass media, the government, the economy, the family, and the health care system are all examples of social institutions found in our society. **Social institutions** are organized patterns of beliefs and behavior centered on basic social needs, such as replacing personnel (the family) and preserving order (the government).

A close look at social institutions gives sociologists insight into the structure of a society. Consider religion, for example. The institution of religion adapts to the segment of society that it serves. Church work has very different meanings for ministers who serve a skid row area and those who serve a suburban middle-class community. Religious leaders assigned to a skid row mission will focus on tending to the ill and providing food and shelter. In contrast, clergy in affluent suburbs will be occupied with counseling those considering marriage and divorce, arranging youth activities, and overseeing cultural events (R. Schaefer 2008b).

Functionalist Perspective One way to understand social institutions is to see how they fulfill essential functions. Anthropologists and sociologists have identified five major tasks, or functional prerequisites, that a society or relatively permanent group must accomplish if it is to survive:

1. *Replacing personnel.* Any group or society must replace personnel when they die, leave, or become incapacitated. This task is accomplished through such means as immigration, annexation of neighboring groups, acquisition of slaves, or sexual reproduction. The Shakers,

a religious sect that came to the United States in 1774, are a conspicuous example of a group that has *failed* to replace personnel. Their religious beliefs commit the Shakers to celibacy; to survive, the group must recruit new members. At first, the Shakers proved quite successful in attracting members, reaching a peak of about 6,000 members in the United States during the 1840s. As of 2011, however, the only Shaker community left in this country was a farm in Maine with three members—one man and two women (R. Schaefer and Zellner 2011).

2. *Teaching new recruits.* No group or society can survive if many of its members reject the group's established behavior and responsibilities. Thus, finding or producing new members is not sufficient; the group or society must also encourage recruits to learn and accept its values and customs. Such learning can take place formally, within schools (where learning is a manifest function), or informally, through interaction in peer groups (where learning is a latent function).

3. *Producing and distributing goods and services.* Any relatively permanent group or society must provide and distribute desired goods and services to its members. Each society establishes a set of rules for the allocation of financial and other resources. The group must satisfy the needs of most members to some extent, or it will risk the possibility of discontent and ultimately disorder.

4. *Preserving order.* Throughout the world, indigenous and aboriginal peoples have struggled to protect themselves from outside invaders, with varying degrees of success. Failure to preserve order and defend against conquest leads to the death not only of a people, but of a culture as well.

5. *Providing and maintaining a sense of purpose.* In order to fulfill the first four requirements, people must feel motivated to continue as members of a group or society. Patriotism, tribal identities, religious values, or personal moral codes can help people to develop and maintain such a sense of purpose. Whatever the motivator, in any society there remains one common and critical reality: if an individual does not have a sense of purpose, he or she has little reason to contribute to a society's survival.

This list of functional prerequisites does not specify *how* a society and its corresponding social institutions will perform each task. For example, one society may protect itself from external attack by amassing a frightening arsenal of weaponry, while another may make determined efforts to remain neutral in world politics and to promote cooperative relationships with its neighbors. No matter what its particular strategy, any society or relatively permanent group must attempt to satisfy all these functional prerequisites for survival. If it fails on even one condition, the society runs the risk of extinction (Aberle et al. 1950; R. Mack and Bradford 1979).

Conflict Perspective   Conflict theorists do not agree with the functionalist approach to social institutions. Although proponents of both perspectives agree that social institutions are organized to meet basic social needs, conflict theorists object to the idea that the outcome is necessarily efficient and desirable.

From a conflict perspective, the present organization of social institutions is no accident. Major institutions, such as education, help to maintain the privileges of the most powerful individuals and groups within a society, while contributing to the powerlessness of others. To give one example, public schools in the United States are financed largely through property taxes. This arrangement allows more affluent areas to provide their children with better-equipped schools and better-paid teachers than low-income areas can afford. As a result, children from prosperous communities are better prepared to compete academically than children from impoverished communities. The structure of the nation's educational system permits and even promotes such unequal treatment of schoolchildren.

Conflict theorists argue that social institutions such as education have an inherently conservative nature. Without question, it has been difficult to implement educational reforms that promote equal opportunity—whether bilingual education, school desegregation, or mainstreaming of students with disabilities. From a functionalist perspective, social change can be dysfunctional, since it often leads to instability. However, from a conflict view, why should we preserve the existing social structure if it is unfair and discriminatory?

Social institutions also operate in gendered and racist environments, as conflict theorists, as well as feminists and interactionists, have pointed out. In schools, offices, and government institutions, assumptions about what people can do reflect the sexism and racism of the larger society. For instance, many people assume that women cannot make tough decisions—even those in the top echelons of corporate management. Others assume that all Black students at elite colleges represent affirmative action admissions. Inequality based on gender, economic status, race, and ethnicity thrives in such an environment—to which we might add discrimination based on age, physical disability, and sexual orientation. The truth of this assertion can be seen in routine decisions by employers on how to advertise jobs, as well as whether to provide fringe benefits such as child care and parental leave.

Interactionist Perspective   Social institutions affect our everyday behavior, whether we are driving down the street or waiting in a long shopping line. Sociologist Mitchell Duneier (1994a, 1994b) studied the social behavior of the word processors, all women, who worked in the service center of a large Chicago law firm. Duneier was interested in the informal social norms that emerged in this work environment and the rich social network these female employees created.

trend|spotting

The Growth of Online Societies

Sociologists and other scholars who study social structure are turning their attention to online societies. Why? These virtual societies have been growing exponentially. India and China, whose roots go back for thousands of years, both have well over a billion people—an enormous population compared to most other countries. By 2012, however, over 800 million people per month were active in Facebook, an online society that has existed for less than a decade. Twitter, with nearly 10 billion visits a month in the United States alone, had 200 million users—more than the population of Pakistan.

The Network Center, as it is called, is a single, windowless room in a large office building where the law firm occupies seven floors. The center is staffed by two shifts of word processors, who work either from 4:00 p.m. to midnight or from midnight to 8:00 a.m. Each word processor works in a cubicle with just enough room for her keyboard, terminal, printer, and telephone. Work assignments for the word processors are placed in a central basket and then completed according to precise procedures.

At first glance, we might think that these women labor with little social contact, apart from limited breaks and occasional conversations with their supervisor. However, drawing on the interactionist perspective, Duneier learned that despite working in a large office, these women find private moments to talk (often in the halls or outside the washroom) and share a critical view of the law firm's attorneys and day-shift secretaries. Indeed, the word processors routinely suggest that their assignments represent work that the "lazy" secretaries should have completed during the normal workday. Duneier (1994b) tells of one word processor who resented the lawyers' superior attitude and pointedly refused to recognize or speak with any attorney who would not address her by name.

Interactionist theorists emphasize that our social behavior is conditioned by the roles and statuses we accept, the groups to which we belong, and the institutions within which we function. For example, the social roles associated with being a judge occur within the larger context of the criminal justice system. The status of judge stands in relation to other statuses, such as attorney, plaintiff, defendant, and witness, as well as to the social institution of government. Although courts and jails have great symbolic importance, the judicial system derives its continued significance from the roles people carry out in social interactions (Berger and Luckmann 1966).

Table 16-1 summarizes the three major sociological perspectives on social institutions.

Table **16-1** Sociological Perspectives on Social Institutions

Tracking Sociological Perspectives

Perspective	Role of Social Institutions	Focus
Functionalist	Meeting basic social needs	Essential functions
Conflict	Meeting basic social needs	Maintenance of privileges and inequality
Interactionist	Fostering everyday behavior	Influence of the roles and statuses we accept

MODULE **16** | Recap and Review

Summary

Social interaction refers to the ways in which people respond to one another. **Social structure** refers to the way in which a society is organized into predictable relationships. This module examines the basic elements of social structure: **statuses, social roles, groups, social networks, virtual worlds,** and **social institutions.**

1. People shape their social reality based on what they learn through **social interactions.** Social change comes from redefining or reconstructing social reality.

2. An **ascribed status** is generally assigned to a person at birth, whereas an **achieved status** is attained largely through one's own effort. Some ascribed statuses, such as race and gender, can function as **master statuses** that affect one's potential to achieve a certain professional or social status.

3. With each distinctive status—whether ascribed or achieved—comes a particular **social role,** the set of expectations for people who occupy that status.

4. Much of our social behavior takes place in **groups.**

5. **Social institutions** fulfill essential functions, such as replacing personnel, training new recruits, and preserving order. The mass media, the government, the economy, the family, and the health care system are all examples of social institutions.

6. Virtual worlds are another important realm in which social interaction takes place and social networks form.

7. **Social networks** form linkages between individuals and groups and can center on virtually any activity.

Thinking Critically

1. Think back over the events of the past few days. Identify two occasions on which different people defined the same social reality differently.

2. Describe a specific master status and explain how it was established. Is it a negative status? If so, how would a person overcome it?

3. Describe some specific ways in which participation in virtual worlds is changing the nature of social groups.

Key Terms

Achieved status

Ascribed status

Group

Master status

Role conflict

Role exit

Role strain

Social institution

Social interaction

Social network

Social role

Social structure

Status

Modern societies are complex, especially compared to earlier social arrangements. Sociologists Émile Durkheim, Ferdinand Tönnies, and Gerhard Lenski developed ways to contrast modern societies with simpler forms of social structure.

Durkheim's Mechanical and Organic Solidarity

In his *Division of Labor* ([1893] 1933), Durkheim argued that social structure depends on the division of labor in a society—in other words, on the manner in which tasks are performed. Thus, a task such as providing food can be carried out almost totally by one individual, or it can be divided among many people. The latter pattern is typical of modern societies, in which the cultivation, processing, distribution, and retailing of a single food item are performed by literally hundreds of people.

In societies in which there is minimal division of labor, a collective consciousness develops that emphasizes group solidarity. Durkheim termed this collective frame of mind **mechanical solidarity,** implying that all individuals perform the same tasks. In this type of society, no one needs to ask, "What do your parents do?" since all are engaged in similar work. Each person prepares food, hunts, makes clothing, builds homes, and so forth. Because people have few options regarding what to do with their lives, there is little concern for individual needs. Instead, the group is the dominating force in society. Both social interaction and negotiation are based on close, intimate, face-to-face social contacts. Since there is little specialization, there are few social roles.

As societies become more advanced technologically, they rely on greater division of labor, so that no individual can go it alone. Dependence on others becomes essential for group survival. In Durkheim's terms, mechanical solidarity is replaced by **organic solidarity,** a collective consciousness resting on the need a society's members have for one another. Durkheim chose the term *organic solidarity* because in his view, individuals become interdependent in much the same way as organs of the human body.

Tönnies's *Gemeinschaft* and *Gesellschaft*

Ferdinand Tönnies (1855–1936) was appalled by the rise of an industrial city in his native Germany during the late 1800s. In his view, the city marked a dramatic change from the ideal of a close-knit community, which Tönnies termed a *Gemeinschaft,*

to that of an impersonal mass society, known as a *Gesellschaft* (Tönnies [1887] 1988).

The *Gemeinschaft* (pronounced guh-mine-shoft) is typical of rural life. It is a small community in which people have similar backgrounds and life experiences. Virtually everyone knows one another, and social interactions are intimate and familiar, almost as among kinfolk. In this community there is a commitment to the larger social group and a sense of togetherness among members. People relate to others in a personal way, not just as "clerk" or "manager." With this personal interaction comes little privacy, however: we know too much about everyone.

Social control in the *Gemeinschaft* is maintained through informal means such as moral persuasion, gossip, and even gestures. These techniques work effectively because people genuinely care how others feel about them. Social change is relatively limited in the *Gemeinschaft;* the lives of members of one generation may be quite similar to those of their grandparents.

In contrast, the *Gesellschaft* (pronounced guh-zell-shoft) is an ideal community that is characteristic of modern urban life. In this community most people are strangers who feel little in common with other residents. Relationships are governed by social roles that grow out of immediate tasks, such as purchasing a product or arranging a business meeting. Self-interest dominates, and there is little consensus concerning values or commitment to the group. As a result, social control must rest on more formal techniques, such as laws and legally defined punishments. Social change is an important aspect of life in the *Gesellschaft;* it can be strikingly evident even within a single generation.

"I'd like to think of you as a person, David, but it's my job to think of you as personnel."

In a *Gesellschaft*, people are likely to relate to one another in terms of their roles rather than their relationships.

Table **17-1**   Comparison of the *Gemeinschaft* and *Gesellschaft*   **summingup**

Gemeinschaft	*Gesellschaft*
Rural life typifies this form.	Urban life typifies this form.
People share a feeling of community that results from their similar backgrounds and life experiences.	People have little sense of commonality. Their differences appear more striking than their similarities.
Social interactions are intimate and familiar.	Social interactions are likely to be impersonal and task-specific.
People maintain a spirit of cooperation and unity of will.	Self-interest dominates.
Tasks and personal relationships cannot be separated.	The task being performed is paramount; relationships are subordinate.
People place little emphasis on individual privacy.	Privacy is valued.
Informal social control predominates.	Formal social control is evident.
People are not very tolerant of deviance.	People are more tolerant of deviance.
Emphasis is on ascribed statuses.	Emphasis is on achieved statuses.
Social change is relatively limited.	Social change is very evident, even within a generation.

Think about It

How would you classify the communities with which you are familiar? Are they more *Gemeinschaft* or *Gesellschaft*?

Table 17-1 summarizes the differences between the *Gemeinschaft* and the *Gesellschaft*. Sociologists have used these terms to compare social structures that stress close relationships with those that emphasize less personal ties. It is easy to view the *Gemeinschaft* with nostalgia, as a far better way of life than the rat race of contemporary existence. However, the more intimate relationships of the *Gemeinschaft* come at a price. The prejudice and discrimination found there can be quite confining; ascribed statuses such as family background often outweigh a person's unique talents and achievements. In addition, the *Gemeinschaft* tends to distrust individuals who seek to be creative or just to be different.

Lenski's Sociocultural Evolution Approach

Sociologist Gerhard Lenski takes a very different view of society and social structure. Rather than distinguishing between two opposite types of society, as Tönnies did, Lenski sees human societies as undergoing a process of change characterized by a dominant pattern known as **sociocultural evolution.** This term refers to long-term social trends resulting from the interplay of continuity, innovation, and selection (Nolan and Lenski 2009:361).

In Lenski's view, a society's level of technology is critical to the way it is organized. Lenski defines **technology** as "cultural information about the ways in which the material resources of the environment may be used to satisfy human needs and desires" (Nolan and Lenski 2009:357). The available technology does not completely define the form that a particular society and its social structure take. Nevertheless, a low level of technology may limit the degree to which a society can depend on such things as irrigation or complex machinery. As technology advances, Lenski writes, a community evolves from a preindustrial to an industrial and finally a postindustrial society.

Preindustrial Societies

How does a preindustrial society organize its economy? If we know that, we can categorize the society. The first type of preindustrial society to emerge in human history was the **hunting-and-gathering society,** in which people simply rely on whatever foods

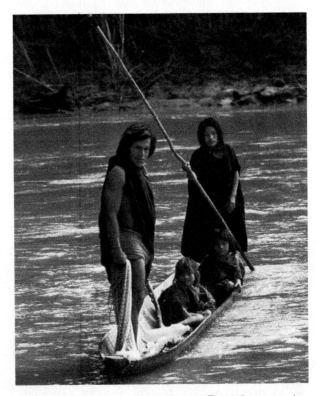

Preindustrial societies still exist in some remote areas. These indigenous people are from the Envira region of the Amazon rain forest, in Brazil.

Table **17-2**   **Stages of Sociocultural Evolution**   summing**up**

Societal Type	First Appearance	Characteristics
Hunting-and-gathering	Beginning of human life	Nomadic; reliance on readily available food and fibers
Horticultural	About 12,000 years ago	More settled; development of agriculture and limited technology
Agrarian	About 5,000 years ago	Larger, more stable settlements; improved technology and increased crop yields
Industrial	1760–1850	Reliance on mechanical power and new sources of energy; centralized workplaces; economic interdependence; formal education
Postindustrial	1960s	Reliance on services, especially the processing and control of information; expanded middle class
Postmodern	Latter 1970s	High technology; mass consumption of consumer goods and media images; cross-cultural integration

and fibers are readily available. Technology in such societies is minimal. Organized into groups, people move constantly in search of food. There is little division of labor into specialized tasks.

Hunting-and-gathering societies are composed of small, widely dispersed groups. Each group consists almost entirely of people who are related to one another. As a result, kinship ties are the source of authority and influence, and the social institution of the family takes on a particularly important role. Tönnies would certainly view such societies as examples of the *Gemeinschaft.*

Social differentiation within the hunting-and-gathering society is based on ascribed statuses such as gender, age, and family background. Since resources are scarce, there is relatively little inequality in terms of material goods. By the close of the 20th century, hunting-and-gathering societies had virtually disappeared (Nolan and Lenski 2009).

Horticultural societies, in which people plant seeds and crops rather than merely subsist on available foods, emerged about 12,000 years ago. Members of horticultural societies are much less nomadic than hunters and gatherers. They place greater emphasis on the production of tools and household objects. Yet technology remains rather limited in these societies, whose members cultivate crops with the aid of digging sticks or hoes (Wilford 1997).

Believe it or not, this photograph was taken in Japan, at Universal Studios theme park in Osaka. In a postmodern society, people consume goods, information, and media images en masse. Universal's park is popularizing U.S. media images abroad, illustrating another characteristic of postmodern societies, globalization.

The last stage of preindustrial development is the **agrarian society,** which emerged about 5,000 years ago. As in horticultural societies, members of agrarian societies engage primarily in the production of food. However, technological innovations such as the plow allow farmers to dramatically increase their crop yields. They can cultivate the same fields over generations, allowing the emergence of larger settlements.

The agrarian society continues to rely on the physical power of humans and animals (as opposed to mechanical power). Nevertheless, its social structure has more carefully defined roles than that of horticultural societies. Individuals focus on specialized tasks, such as the repair of fishing nets or blacksmithing. As human settlements become more established and stable, social institutions become more elaborate and property rights more important. The comparative permanence and greater surpluses of an agrarian society allow members to create artifacts such as statues, public monuments, and art objects and to pass them on from one generation to the next.

Table 17-2 summarizes Lenski's three stages of sociocultural evolution, as well as the stages that follow, described next.

Industrial Societies

Although the Industrial Revolution did not topple monarchs, it produced changes every bit as significant as those resulting from political revolutions. The Industrial Revolution, which took place largely in England during the period 1760 to 1830, was a scientific revolution focused on the application of nonanimal (mechanical) sources of power to labor tasks. An **industrial society** is a society that depends on mechanization to produce its goods and services. Industrial societies rely on new inventions that facilitate agricultural and industrial production, and on new sources of energy, such as steam.

As the Industrial Revolution proceeded, a new form of social structure emerged. Many societies underwent an irrevocable shift from an agrarian-oriented economy to an industrial base. No longer did an individual or a family typically make an entire product. Instead, specialization of tasks and manufacturing of goods became increasingly common. Workers, generally men but also women and even children, left their family homesteads to work in central locations such as factories.

Postindustrial and Postmodern Societies

When Lenski first proposed the sociocultural evolutionary approach in the 1960s, he paid relatively little attention to how maturing industrialized societies may change with the emergence of even more advanced forms of technology. More recently, he and other sociologists have studied the significant changes in the occupational structure of industrial societies as they shift from manufacturing to service economies. In the 1970s, sociologist Daniel Bell wrote about the technologically advanced **postindustrial society,** whose economic system is engaged primarily in the processing and control of information. The main output of a postindustrial society is services rather than manufactured goods. Large numbers of people become involved in occupations devoted to the teaching, generation, or dissemination of ideas. Jobs in fields such as advertising, public relations, human resources, and computer information systems would be typical of a postindustrial society (D. Bell [1973] 1999). The Social Policy section in Module 19 describes an important example of these postindustrial organizations—the media industry.

Bell views the transition from industrial to postindustrial society as a positive development. He sees a general decline in organized working-class groups and a rise in interest groups concerned with national issues such as health, education, and the environment. Bell's outlook is functionalist, because he portrays the postindustrial society as basically consensual. As organizations and interest groups engage in an open and competitive process of decision making, Bell believes, the level of conflict between diverse groups will diminish, strengthening social stability.

Conflict theorists take issue with Bell's functionalist analysis of the postindustrial society. For example, Michael Harrington (1980), who alerted the nation to the problems of the poor in his book *The Other America,* questioned the significance that Bell attached to the growing class of white-collar workers. Harrington conceded that scientists, engineers, and economists are involved in important political and economic decisions, but he disagreed with Bell's claim that they have a free hand in decision making, independent of the interests of the rich. Harrington followed in the tradition of Marx by arguing that conflict between social classes will continue in the postindustrial society.

Sociologists have gone beyond discussion of the postindustrial society to the ideal of the postmodern society. A **postmodern society** is a technologically sophisticated society that is preoccupied with consumer goods and media images (Brannigan 1992). Such societies consume goods and information on a mass scale. Postmodern theorists take a global perspective, noting the ways that culture crosses national boundaries. For example, residents of the United States may listen to reggae music from Jamaica, eat sushi and other Japanese foods, and wear clogs from Sweden. And online social networks know no national boundaries.

The emphasis of postmodern theorists is on observing and describing newly emerging cultural forms and patterns of social interaction. Within sociology, the postmodern view offers support for integrating the insights of various theoretical perspectives—functionalism, conflict theory, feminist theory, and interactionism—while incorporating other contemporary approaches. Feminist sociologists argue optimistically that with its indifference to hierarchies and distinctions, the postmodern society will discard traditional values of male dominance in favor of gender equality. Yet, others contend that despite new technologies, postindustrial and postmodern societies can be expected to display the same problems of inequality that plague industrial societies (Denzin 2004; Smart 1990; B. Turner 1990; van Vucht Tijssen 1990).

Durkheim, Tönnies, and Lenski present three visions of society's social structure. While they differ, each is useful, and this textbook will draw on all three. The sociocultural evolutionary approach emphasizes a historical perspective. It does not picture different types of social structure coexisting within the same society. Consequently, one would not expect a single society to include hunters and gatherers along with a postmodern culture. In contrast, Durkheim's and Tönnies's theories allow for the existence of different types of community—such as a *Gemeinschaft* and a *Gesellschaft*—in the same society. Thus, a rural New Hampshire community located 100 miles from Boston can be linked to the city by modern information technology. The main difference between these two theories is a matter of emphasis. While Tönnies emphasized the overriding concern in each type of community—one's own self-interest or the well-being of the larger society—Durkheim emphasized the division (or lack of division) of labor.

The work of these three thinkers reminds us that a major focus of sociology has been to identify changes in social structure and the consequences for human behavior. At the macro level, we see society shifting to more advanced forms of technology. The social structure becomes increasingly complex, and new social institutions emerge to assume some functions that once were performed by the family. On the micro level, these changes affect the nature of social interactions. Each individual takes on multiple social roles, and people come to rely more on social networks and less on kinship ties. As the social structure becomes more complex, people's relationships become more impersonal, transient, and fragmented.

MODULE 17 | Recap and Review

Summary

Sociologists have developed classification systems that help us contrast complex modern societies with simpler forms of social structure.

1. Émile Durkheim thought that social structure depends on the division of labor in a society. According to Durkheim, societies with minimal division of labor have a collective consciousness called **mechanical solidarity.**

Those with greater division of labor show an interdependence called **organic solidarity.**

2. Ferdinand Tönnies distinguished the close-knit community of *Gemeinschaft* from the impersonal mass society known as *Gesellschaft.*

3. Gerhard Lenski thinks that a society's social structure changes as its culture and technology become more sophisticated, a process he calls **sociocultural evolution.**

Thinking Critically

1. According to Lenski, technology is the key to sociocultural evolution. What social factors are most likely to influence whether a society's culture evolves to a new stage of sociocultural evolution?

2. How are Durkheim's and Tönnies's classifications similar? How are they different?

3. Describe any personal experiences you have had with a nonindustrial, or developing, society. If you have not had that kind of experience, how do you think you would prepare for it?

Key Terms

Agrarian society

Gemeinschaft

Gesellschaft

Horticultural society

Hunting-and-gathering society

Industrial society

Mechanical solidarity

Organic solidarity

Postindustrial society

Postmodern society

Sociocultural evolution

Technology

MODULE 18 | Understanding Groups

Most of us use the term *group* loosely to describe any collection of individuals, whether three strangers sharing an elevator or hundreds attending a rock concert. However, in sociological terms a **group** is any number of people with similar norms, values, and expectations who interact with one another on a regular basis. College sororities and fraternities, dance companies, tenants' associations, and chess clubs are all considered groups. The important point is that members of a group share some sense of belonging. This characteristic distinguishes groups from mere *aggregates* of people, such as passengers who happen to be together on an airplane flight, or from *categories* of people, such as those who share a common feature (such as being retired) but otherwise do not act together.

Consider the case of a college singing group. It has agreed-on values and social norms. All members want to improve their singing skills and schedule lots of performances. In addition, like many groups, the singing ensemble has both a formal and an informal structure. The members meet regularly to rehearse; they choose leaders to run the rehearsals and manage their affairs. At the same time, some group members may take on unofficial leadership roles by coaching new members in singing techniques and performing skills.

The study of groups has become an important part of sociological investigation because they play such a key role in the transmission of culture. As we interact with others, we pass on our ways of thinking and acting—from language and values to ways of dressing and leisure activities.

Types of Groups

Sociologists have made a number of useful distinctions between types of groups—primary and secondary groups, in-groups and out-groups, reference groups, and coalitions.

Primary and Secondary Groups

Charles Horton Cooley (1902) coined the term **primary group** to refer to a small group characterized by intimate, face-to-face association and cooperation. The members of a street gang constitute a primary group; so do members of a family living in the same household, as do a group of "sisters" in a college sorority.

Primary groups play a pivotal role both in the socialization process (see Module 13) and in the development of roles and statuses (see Module 16). Indeed, primary groups can be instrumental in a person's day-to-day existence. When we find ourselves identifying closely with a group, it is probably a primary group.

We also participate in many groups that are not characterized by close bonds of friendship, such as large college classes

A pizza delivery crew is an example of a *secondary group*—a formal, impersonal group in which there is little social intimacy or mutual understanding. While waiting for the next delivery, members of this crew in Surrey, England, will become well enough acquainted to distinguish those who see the job as temporary from those who view it as permanent. They will learn who looks forward to deliveries in perceived high-risk areas and who does not. They may even spend time together after work, joking or boasting about their exploits on the job, but their friendships typically will not develop beyond that point.

and business associations. The term **secondary group** refers to a formal, impersonal group in which there is little social intimacy or mutual understanding (Table 18-1). Secondary groups often emerge in the workplace among those who share special understandings about their occupation. The distinction between primary and secondary groups is not always clear-cut, however.

Table **18-1** Comparison of Primary and Secondary Groups

Primary Group	Secondary Group
Generally small	Usually large
Relatively long period of interaction	Relatively short duration, often temporary
Intimate, face-to-face association	Little social intimacy or mutual understanding
Some emotional depth to relationships	Relationships generally superficial
Cooperative, friendly	More formal and impersonal

summingup

Some social clubs may become so large and impersonal that they no longer function as primary groups.

A considerable amount of sociological research has been done on people's behavior in groups. Box 18-1 describes the findings of one well-known but short-lived group: the jury.

In-Groups and Out-Groups

A group can hold special meaning for members because of its relationship to other groups. For example, people in one group sometimes feel antagonistic toward or threatened by another group, especially if that group is perceived as being different, either culturally or racially. To identify these "we" and "they" feelings, sociologists use two terms first employed by William Graham Sumner (1906): *in-group* and *out-group*.

An **in-group** can be defined as any group or category to which people feel they belong. Simply put, it comprises everyone who is regarded as "we" or "us." The in-group may be as narrow as a teenage clique or as broad as an entire society. The very existence of an in-group implies that there is an out-group that is viewed as "they" or "them." An **out-group** is a group or category to which people feel they do *not* belong.

In-group members typically feel distinct and superior, seeing themselves as better than people in the out-group. Proper behavior for the in-group is simultaneously viewed as unacceptable behavior for the out-group. This double standard enhances the sense of superiority. Sociologist Robert Merton (1968) described this process as the conversion of "in-group virtues" into "out-group vices." We can see this differential standard operating in worldwide discussions of terrorism. When a group or a nation takes aggressive actions, it usually justifies them as necessary, even if civilians are hurt or killed. Opponents are quick to label such actions with the emotion-laden term of *terrorist* and appeal to the world community for condemnation. Yet these same people may themselves retaliate with actions that hurt civilians, which the first group will then condemn.

💡 use your **sociological imagination**

Try putting yourself in the shoes of an out-group member. What does your in-group look like from that perspective?

Conflict between in-groups and out-groups can turn violent on a personal as well as a political level. In 1999 two disaffected students at Columbine High School in Littleton, Colorado, launched an attack on the school that left 15 students and teachers dead, including themselves. The gunmen, members of an

🔍 Research Today

BOX 18-1

The Drinking Rape Victim: Jury Decision Making

She was heavily intoxicated. He had drunk a few beers. They had sex. She said she was raped. He said it was consensual. The jury deliberated, and the verdict was. . . .

This is not an actual case, but an experiment in group decision making. Few small groups have received as much attention from sociologists over the past decade and a half as juries. Scholars have used several research methods to investigate juries' decision making: interviews with jury members after they have reached a verdict; observation of jurors as they sit through and react to courtroom events; observation of actual jury deliberations, which presiding judges have permitted in a few instances; and experiments involving mock juries. The findings indicate that jurors do not always make decisions the way they are supposed to. How do jurors form impressions in rape cases, especially those that involve intoxication?

To find out, legal scholars Emily Finch and Vanessa Munro simulated a rape trial in which intoxication was an issue. The two researchers varied the story to see what the effect might be on the verdict. In one version the alleged victim was drunk; in another she was drugged by a third person; in another she was drugged by the defendant.

Finch and Munro found that male or female, the mock jurors in their study followed a double standard. The more intoxicated the *defendant* was said to have been, the less likely jurors were to regard him as culpable. They were far more likely to regard a *victim* who had drunk too much as having contributed to her rape. This finding applied even in cases in which the victim's drink had been spiked. In short, before jurors could summon up much sympathy for the victim, the defendant had to engage in a great deal of bad behavior.

Today, research on juries is expanding to deal with generational changes in the experience of being a juror. Some jurors arrive at court expecting to see the kind of sophisticated DNA analysis or

> *Finch and Munro found that male or female, the mock jurors in their study followed a double standard.*

investigative methods featured on televised crime shows, such as *CSI*. Improved methods of documenting crime scenes, including the use of computer-generated re-creations, mean that today's jurors are more likely than past jurors to be exposed to images of graphic violence and gore.

LET'S DISCUSS

1. Have you ever served on a jury? If so, were you aware of jurors who made up their minds early in the trial, despite the judge's instructions? Did you experience stress from being exposed to graphic images of violence and bloodshed?

2. Is a jury a typical group? Why or why not?

Sources: S. Diamond and Rose 2005; Finch and Munro 2005, 2007, 2008; McGlynn and Munro 2010.

out-group that other students referred to as the Trenchcoat Mafia, apparently resented taunting by an in-group referred to as the Jocks. Similar episodes have occurred in schools across the nation, where rejected adolescents, overwhelmed by personal and family problems, peer group pressure, academic responsibilities, or media images of violence, have struck out against more popular classmates.

Reference Groups

Both primary groups and in-groups can dramatically influence the way an individual thinks and behaves. Sociologists call any group that individuals use as a standard for evaluating themselves and their own behavior a **reference group.** For example, a high school student who aspires to join a social circle of hip-hop music devotees will pattern his or her behavior after that of the group. The student will begin dressing like these peers, listening to the same downloads and DVDs, and hanging out at the same stores and clubs.

At a powwow, a drum circle breathes spirit into an ancient tribal tradition. These accomplished ceremonial musicians may serve as a reference group for onlookers who want to know more about drumming.

Reference groups have two basic purposes. They serve a normative function by setting and enforcing standards of conduct and belief. The high school student who wants the approval of the hip-hop crowd will have to follow the group's dictates, at least to some extent. Reference groups also perform a comparison function by serving as a standard against which people can measure themselves and others. An actor will evaluate himself or herself against a reference group composed of others in the acting profession (Merton and Kitt 1950).

Reference groups may help the process of anticipatory socialization. For example, a college student majoring in finance may read the *Wall Street Journal,* study the annual reports of corporations, and listen to midday stock market news on the radio. Such a student is using financial experts as a reference group to which he or she aspires.

Often, two or more reference groups influence us at the same time. Our family members, neighbors, and co-workers all shape different aspects of our self-evaluation. In addition, reference group attachments change during the life cycle. A corporate executive who quits the rat race at age 45 to become a social worker will find new reference groups to use as standards for evaluation. We shift reference groups as we take on different statuses during our lives.

Coalitions

As groups grow larger, coalitions begin to develop. A **coalition** is a temporary or permanent alliance geared toward a common goal. Coalitions can be broad-based or narrow and can take on many different

objectives. Sociologist William Julius Wilson (1999) has described community-based organizations in Texas that include Whites and Latinos, working class and affluent, who have banded together to work for improved sidewalks, better drainage systems, and comprehensive street paving. Out of this type of coalition building, Wilson hopes, will emerge better interracial understanding.

Can you outwit, outplay, outlast your competition? Maybe a coalition can help. In *Survivor: One World,* filmed on an island in Samoa, coalition building continued to be a key to success in the long-running television series, now in its 24th season.

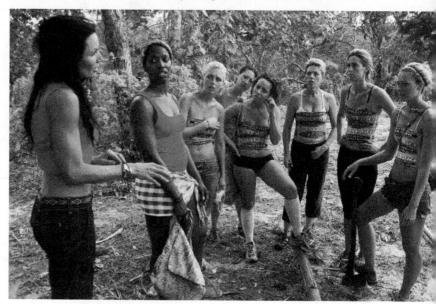

Some coalitions are intentionally short-lived. For example, short-term coalition building is a key to success in popular TV programs like *Survivor*. In the program's first season, *Survivor: Borneo,* broadcast in 2000, the four members of the "Tagi alliance" banded together to vote fellow castaways off the island. The political world is also the scene of many temporary coalitions. For example, in 1997 big tobacco companies joined with antismoking groups to draw up a settlement for reimbursing states for tobacco-related medical costs. Soon after the settlement was announced the coalition members returned to their decades-long fight against each other (Pear 1997).

use your **sociological imagination**

Describe an experience you have had with coalition building, or one that you have read about—perhaps in politics. Was the coalition effective? What problems did the members need to overcome?

MODULE 18 | **Recap and Review**

Summary

Much of our social behavior takes place in groups.

1. When we find ourselves identifying closely with a group, it is probably a primary group. A secondary group is more formal and impersonal.

2. People tend to see the world in terms of in-groups and out-groups, a perception often fostered by the very groups to which they belong.

3. Reference groups set and enforce standards of conduct and serve as a source of comparison for people's evaluations of themselves and others.

4. Interactionist researchers have noted that groups allow coalitions to form and serve as links to social networks and their vast resources.

Thinking Critically

1. Describe an example of coalition building you have experienced or read about (perhaps in the political realm). Was the coalition effective? What problems had to be overcome?

2. Think of a primary and secondary group to which you belong. Under what circumstances might the primary group become a secondary group, or the secondary group become a primary group?

Key Terms

Coalition

Group

In-group

Out-group

Primary group

Reference group

Secondary group

Formal Organizations and Bureaucracies

As contemporary societies have shifted to more advanced forms of technology and their social structures have become more complex, our lives have become increasingly dominated by large secondary groups referred to as *formal organizations*. A **formal organization** is a group designed for a special purpose and structured for maximum efficiency. The U.S. Postal Service, McDonald's, and the Boston Pops orchestra are examples of formal organizations. Though organizations vary in their size, specificity of goals, and degree of efficiency, they are all structured to facilitate the management of large-scale operations. They also have a bureaucratic form of organization, described in the next section.

In our society, formal organizations fulfill an enormous variety of personal and societal needs, shaping the lives of every one of us. In fact, formal organizations have become such a dominant force that we must create organizations to supervise other organizations, such as the Securities and Exchange Commission (SEC) to regulate brokerage companies. Although it sounds more exciting to say that we live in the "computer age" than to say that we live in the "age of formal organization," the latter is probably a more accurate description (Azumi and Hage 1972; Etzioni 1964).

Ascribed statuses such as gender, race, and ethnicity can influence how we see ourselves within formal organizations. For example, a study of female lawyers in the nation's largest law firms found significant differences in the women's self-images, depending on the relative presence or absence of women in positions of power. In firms in which less than 15 percent of partners were women, the female lawyers were likely to believe that "feminine" traits were strongly devalued and that "masculine" traits were equated with success. As one female attorney put it, "Let's face it: this is a man's environment, and it's sort of Jock City, especially at my firm." Women in firms where female lawyers were better represented in positions of power had a stronger desire for and higher expectations of promotion (Ely 1995:619).

Characteristics of a Bureaucracy

A **bureaucracy** is a component of formal organization that uses rules and hierarchical ranking to achieve efficiency. Rows of desks staffed by seemingly faceless people, endless lines and forms, impossibly complex language, and frustrating encounters with red tape—all these unpleasant images have combined to make *bureaucracy* a dirty word and an easy target in political campaigns. As a result, few people want to identify their occupation as "bureaucrat," despite the fact that all of us perform various bureaucratic tasks. In an industrial society, elements of bureaucracy enter into almost every occupation.

Max Weber ([1913–1922] 1947) first directed researchers to the significance of bureaucratic structure. In an important sociological advance, Weber emphasized the basic similarity of structure and process found in the otherwise dissimilar enterprises of religion, government, education, and business. Weber saw bureaucracy as a form of organization quite different from the family-run business. For analytical purposes, he developed an ideal type of bureaucracy that would reflect the most characteristic aspects of all human organizations. By **ideal type** Weber meant a construct or model for evaluating specific cases. In actuality, perfect bureaucracies do not exist; no real-world organization corresponds exactly to Weber's ideal type.

Weber proposed that whether the purpose is to run a church, a corporation, or an army, the ideal bureaucracy displays five basic characteristics. A discussion of those characteristics, as well as the dysfunctions of a bureaucracy, follows.

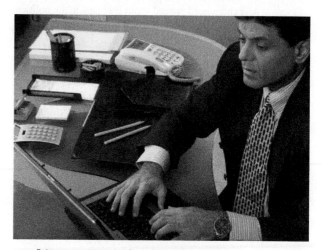

Being an accountant in a large corporation may be a relatively high-paying occupation. In Marxist terms, however, accountants are vulnerable to alienation, since they are far removed from the product or service that the corporation creates.

1. **Division of labor.** Specialized experts perform specific tasks. In your college bureaucracy, the admissions officer does not do the job of registrar; the guidance counselor does not see to the maintenance of buildings. By working at a specific task, people are more likely to become highly skilled and carry out a job with maximum efficiency. This emphasis on specialization is so basic a part of our lives that we may not realize it is a fairly recent development in Western culture.

The downside of division of labor is that the fragmentation of work into smaller and smaller tasks can divide workers and remove any connection they might feel to the overall objective of the bureaucracy. In *The Communist Manifesto* (written in 1848), Karl Marx and Friedrich Engels charged that the capitalist system reduces workers to a mere "appendage of the machine" (Tucker 1978). Such a work arrangement, they wrote, produces extreme **alienation**—a condition of estrangement or dissociation from the surrounding society. According to both Marx and conflict theorists, restricting workers to very small tasks also weakens their job security, since new employees can easily be trained to replace them.

Although division of labor has certainly enhanced the performance of many complex bureaucracies, in some cases it can lead to **trained incapacity;** that is, workers become so specialized that they develop blind spots and fail to notice obvious problems. Even worse, they may not care about what is happening in the next department. Some observers believe that such developments have caused workers in the United States to become less productive on the job.

In some cases, the bureaucratic division of labor can have tragic results. In the wake of the coordinated attacks on the World Trade Center and the Pentagon on September 11, 2001, Americans wondered aloud how the FBI and CIA could have failed to detect the terrorists' elaborately planned operation. The problem, in part, turned out to be the division of labor between the FBI, which focuses on domestic matters, and the CIA, which operates overseas. Officials at these intelligence-gathering organizations, both of which are huge bureaucracies, are well known for jealously guarding information from one another. Subsequent investigations revealed that they knew about Osama bin Laden and his Al-Qaeda terrorist network in the early 1990s. Unfortunately, five federal agencies—the CIA, FBI, National Security Agency, Defense Intelligence Agency, and National Reconnaissance Office—failed to share their leads on the network. Although the hijacking of the four commercial airliners used in the massive attacks may not have been preventable, the bureaucratic division of labor definitely hindered efforts to defend against terrorism, undermining U.S. national security.

2. **Hierarchy of authority.** Bureaucracies follow the principle of hierarchy; that is, each position is under the supervision of a higher authority. A president heads a college bureaucracy; he or she selects members of the administration, who in turn hire their own staff. In the Roman Catholic Church, the pope is the supreme authority; under him are cardinals, bishops, and so forth.

3. **Written rules and regulations.** What if your sociology professor gave your classmate an A for having such a friendly smile? You might think that wasn't fair, that it was against the rules. Through written rules and regulations, bureaucracies generally offer employees clear standards for an adequate (or exceptional) performance. In addition, procedures provide a valuable sense of continuity in a bureaucracy. Individual workers will come and go, but the structure and past records of the organization give it a life of its own that outlives the services of any one bureaucrat.

Of course, rules and regulations can overshadow the larger goals of an organization to the point that they become dysfunctional. What if a hospital emergency room physician failed to treat a seriously injured person because he or she had no valid proof of U.S. citizenship? If blindly applied, rules no longer serve as a means to achieving an objective, but instead become important (and perhaps too important) in their own right. Robert Merton (1968) used the term **goal displacement** to refer to overzealous conformity to official regulations.

4. **Impersonality.** Max Weber wrote that in a bureaucracy, work is carried out *sine ira et studio,* "without hatred or passion." Bureaucratic norms dictate that officials perform their duties without giving personal consideration to people as individuals. Although this norm is intended to guarantee equal treatment for each person, it also contributes to the often cold and uncaring feeling associated with modern organizations. We typically think of big government and big business when we think of impersonal bureaucracies. In some cases, the impersonality that is associated with a bureaucracy can have tragic results. More frequently, bureaucratic impersonality produces frustration and disaffection. Today, even small firms filter callers with electronic menus.

5. **Employment based on technical qualifications.** Within the ideal bureaucracy, hiring is based on technical qualifications rather than on favoritism, and performance is measured against specific standards. Written personnel policies dictate who gets promoted, and people often have a right to appeal if they believe that particular rules have been violated. Such procedures protect bureaucrats against arbitrary dismissal, provide a measure of security, and encourage loyalty to the organization.

Although ideally, any bureaucracy will value technical and professional competence, personnel decisions do not always follow that ideal pattern. Dysfunctions within bureaucracy have become well publicized, particularly because of the work of Laurence J. Peter. According to the **Peter principle,** every employee within a hierarchy tends to rise to his or her level of incompetence (Peter and Hull 1969). This hypothesis, which has not been directly or systematically tested, reflects a possible dysfunctional outcome of advancement on the basis of merit. Talented people receive promotion after promotion, until sadly, some of them finally achieve positions that they cannot handle with their usual competence.

Table 19-1 summarizes the five characteristics of bureaucracy. These characteristics, developed by Max Weber more than 80 years ago, describe an ideal type rather than an actual

Table **19-1**   Characteristics of a Bureaucracy   **summingup**

| | | Negative Consequence | |
	Positive Consequence	For the Individual	For the Organization
Division of labor	Produces efficiency in a large-scale corporation	Produces trained incapacity	Produces a narrow perspective
Hierarchy of authority	Clarifies who is in command	Deprives employees of a voice in decision making	Permits concealment of mistakes
Written rules and regulations	Let workers know what is expected of them	Stifle initiative and imagination	Lead to goal displacement
Impersonality	Reduces bias	Contributes to feelings of alienation	Discourages loyalty to company
Employment based on technical qualifications	Discourages favoritism and reduces petty rivalries	Discourages ambition to improve oneself elsewhere	Fosters Peter principle

bureaucracy. Not every formal organization will possess all five of Weber's characteristics. In fact, wide variation exists among actual bureaucratic organizations.

Bureaucracy pervades modern life; through McDonaldization, it has reached new heights. As Box 19-1 shows, the McDonald's organization provides an excellent illustration of Weber's concept of bureaucracy (Ritzer 2011).

 use your sociological imagination

Your school or workplace suddenly ceases to exhibit one of the five characteristics of bureaucracy. Which characteristic is it, and what are the consequences?

Bureaucratization as a Process

Have you ever had to speak to 10 or 12 individuals in a corporation or government agency just to find out which official has jurisdiction over a particular problem? Ever been transferred from one department to another until you finally hung up in disgust? Sociologists have used the term **bureaucratization** to refer to the process by which a group, organization, or social movement becomes increasingly bureaucratic.

Normally, we think of bureaucratization in terms of large organizations. But bureaucratization also takes place within small-group settings. Sociologist Jennifer Bickman Mendez (1998) studied domestic houseworkers employed in central California by a nationwide franchise. She found that housekeeping tasks were minutely defined, to the point that employees had to follow 22 written steps for cleaning a bathroom. Complaints and special requests went not to the workers, but to an office-based manager.

Oligarchy: Rule by a Few

Conflict theorists have examined the bureaucratization of social movements. The German sociologist Robert Michels (1915) studied socialist parties and labor unions in Europe before World War I and found that such organizations were becoming increasingly bureaucratic. The emerging leaders of the organizations—even some of the most radical—had a vested interest in clinging to power. If they lost their leadership posts, they would have to return to full-time work as manual laborers.

Through his research, Michels originated the idea of the **iron law of oligarchy**, which describes how even a democratic organization will eventually develop into a bureaucracy ruled by a few, called an oligarchy. Why do oligarchies emerge? People who achieve leadership roles usually have the skills, knowledge, or charismatic appeal (as Weber noted) to direct, if not control, others. Michels argued that the rank and file of a movement or organization look to leaders for direction and thereby reinforce the process of rule by a few. In addition, members of an oligarchy are strongly motivated to maintain their leadership roles, privileges, and power.

Bureaucracy and Organizational Culture

How does bureaucratization affect the average individual who works in an organization? The early theorists of formal organizations tended to neglect this question. Max Weber, for example,

focused on the management personnel in bureaucracies, but had little to say about workers in industry or clerks in government agencies.

According to the **classical theory** of formal organizations, or **scientific management approach,** workers are motivated almost entirely by economic rewards. This theory stresses that only the physical constraints on workers limit their productivity. Therefore, workers may be treated as a resource, much like the machines that began to replace them in the 20th century. Under the scientific management approach, management attempts to achieve maximum work efficiency through scientific planning,

Sociology in the Global Community

BOX 19-1

McDonald's and the Worldwide Bureaucratization of Society

In his book *The McDonaldization of Society,* sociologist George Ritzer notes the enormous influence of a well-known fast-food organization on modern-day culture and social life.

Not surprisingly, Max Weber's five characteristics of bureaucracy are apparent in McDonald's restaurants, as well as in the global corporation behind them. Food preparation and order-taking reflect a painstaking *division of labor,* implemented by a *hierarchy of authority* that stretches from the food workers up to the store operator, and ultimately to the corporate board of directors. Store operators learn McDonald's *written rules and regulations,* which govern even the amount of ketchup or mustard placed on a hamburger, at McDonald's Hamburger University. Little bonding occurs between servers and customers, creating a pervasive sense of *impersonality.* Finally, employees are expected to have specific *technical qualifications,* although most of the skills they need to perform routine tasks can be learned in a brief training period.

The real significance of McDonaldization is that it is not confined to the food-service industry or to coffee shops like Starbucks. Worldwide, McDonald's brand of predictability, efficiency, and dependence on nonhuman technology have become customary in a number of services, ranging from medical care to wedding planning to education. Even sporting events reflect the influence of bureaucratization. Around the world, stadiums are becoming increasingly similar, both physically and in the way they present the sport to spectators. All seats offer spectators an unrestricted view, and a big screen guarantees them access to instant replays. Scores, player statistics, and attendance figures are updated automatically by computer and displayed on an automated scoreboard or fed to people's smartphones. Spectator enthusiasm is manufactured through digital displays urging

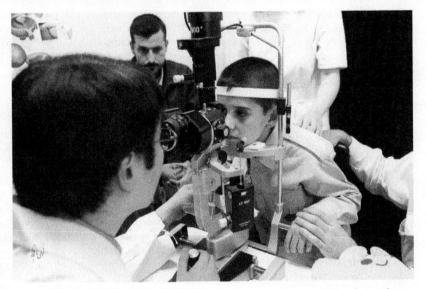

The worldwide success of highly efficient fast-food operations has led to the bureaucratization of many other services, including eye care and other forms of medical treatment.

> Worldwide, McDonald's brand of predictability, efficiency, and dependence on nonhuman technology have become customary in a number of services, ranging from medical care to wedding planning to education.

applause or rhythmic chanting. And of course, the merchandising of teams' and even players' names and images is highly controlled.

McDonald's reliance on the five characteristics of bureaucracy is not revolutionary. What is new is the bureaucratization of services and life events that once were highly individualized, at times even spontaneous. More and more, society itself is undergoing McDonaldization.

LET'S DISCUSS

1. What features of fast-food restaurants do you appreciate? Do you have any complaints about them?

2. Analyze life at your college using Weber's model of bureaucracy. What elements of McDonaldization do you see? Do you wish life were less McDonaldized?

Sources: Ormond 2005; Ritzer 2008, 2011.

established performance standards, and careful supervision of workers and production. Planning involves efficiency studies but not studies of workers' attitudes or job satisfaction.

Not until workers organized unions—and forced management to recognize that they were not objects—did theorists of formal organizations begin to revise the classical approach. Social scientists became aware that along with management and administrators, informal groups of workers have an important impact on organizations. An alternative way of considering bureaucratic dynamics, the **human relations approach,** emphasizes the role of people, communication, and participation in a bureaucracy. This type of analysis reflects the interest of interactionist theorists in small-group behavior. Unlike planning under the scientific management approach, planning based on the human relations approach focuses on workers' feelings, frustrations, and emotional need for job satisfaction.

The gradual move away from a sole focus on the physical aspects of getting the job done—and toward the concerns and needs of workers—led advocates of the human relations approach to stress the less formal aspects of bureaucratic structure. Informal groups and social networks within organizations develop partly as a result of people's ability to create more direct forms of communication than under the formal structure. Charles Page (1946) used the term *bureaucracy's other face* to refer to the unofficial activities and interactions that are such a basic part of daily organizational life.

Today, research on formal organizations is following new avenues. Among them are

- The recent arrival of a small number of women and minority group members in high-level management;
- In large corporations, the decision-making role of groups that lie outside the top ranks of leadership;
- The loss of fixed boundaries in organizations that have outsourced key functions; and
- The role of the Internet and virtual worlds in influencing business and consumer preferences.

Though research on organizations still embraces Max Weber's insights, then, it has gone well beyond them (Hamm 2007; Kleiner 2003; W. Scott and Davis 2007).

social policy and Social Structure | Media Concentration

One of the most pervasive social institutions in our society, the mass media encompass information outlets ranging from printed leaflets to online virtual worlds. Perhaps more than any other institution, they exemplify our postmodern society. According to Lenski's theory of sociocultural evolution, all societies undergo continual change, whether rapid or slow. In today's postmodern world, one of the more noticeable changes—and a potentially undesirable one—is the trend toward control of the media by fewer and fewer corporations.

Looking at the Issue

Who owns the media production and distribution process? Increasingly, the answer is a small number of very large corporations. The social consequence of this trend toward the concentration of media ownership is a reduction in the number of information outlets.

True, the United States still has thousands of independent media outlets—small-town newspapers, radio stations, and television broadcasters—but the clear trend in the media industry is toward the consolidation of ownership. The fact is, a few multinational corporations dominate the publishing, broadcasting, and film industries, although their influence may be hard

to identify, since global conglomerates manage many different product names. Consider Time Warner (HBO, CNN, AOL, *Time* and *People* magazines); Rupert Murdoch's News Corporation, founded in Australia (Fox Network Television, several book publishers, numerous newspapers and magazines, Dow Jones, and 20th Century Fox); Sony of Japan (Columbia Pictures, IMAX, CBS Records, and Columbia

—*Continued*

Records); and Viacom/CBS (Paramount, DreamWorks SKG, MTV, and Black Entertainment Television), and the extent of their power becomes clear.

Similar concerns have been raised about the situation in countries such as China, Cuba, Iraq, and North Korea, where the ruling party owns and controls the media. The difference, which is considerable, is that in the United States the gate-keeping process lies in the hands of private individuals, whose main desire is to maximize profits. In totalitarian countries, the gatekeeping process belongs to political leaders, whose desire is to maintain control of the government.

We should note one significant exception to the central-ization and concentration of the media: the Internet. Today, more and more people receive their media content through the Internet. The World Wide Web is now accessible to millions of producers of media content, through independent outlets. Obviously, the producer must be technologically proficient and must have access to a computer, but compared to other media outlets, the Internet is much more readily available. Media conglomerates, well aware of the Internet's potential, are already delivering their material via the web. But for now, the Internet is the only medium that allows the average individ-ual to become a media entrepreneur with a potential audience of millions. Some media scholars warn, however, that it is only a matter of time before corporate giants like AT&T and Com-cast begin to dominate the Internet (Noam 2009; Wu 2010).

Applying Sociology

Concentration of ownership is not unique to the media (think about aircraft and automobile manufacturers). However, the media deserve special attention given the way they filter our view of reality. New media technologies also form the basis for group membership and networking, making them a power-ful influence on today's society.

Functionalists see media concentration—or the consoli-dation of any business—as a step toward greater economic efficiency. In their view, consolidation reduces the cost of operations, freeing capital for the development of new cre-ative outlets. Furthermore, they believe that global trade in the media facilitates the free exchange of intellectual prop-erty, which is often hampered by arbitrary local restrictions (Croteau and Hoynes 2006).

Conflict theorists believe that media concentration stifles opportunities for minority ownership. According to the most recent FCC data, less than 4 percent of television stations in the United States are owned by racial and ethnic minorities; less than 5 percent are owned by women. Minority owners are underrepresented even in markets where minorities make up the majority of the audience. This issue is particularly troubling not just to politicians but to all of society, because as sociolo-gist Manuel Castells has observed, communicative power can shape human behavior. As such, it lies at the heart of the social structure (Castells 2009; S. Turner and Cooper 2006).

Interactionists see a change in the way people get their news, although not in their interest in it. In the past people may have met or called one another to discuss the latest epi-sode of *Survivor;* now they share the latest Internet news via e-mail or buddy list. Why wait for the evening news when online sources are at your fingertips? Because savvy media users can seek out the media they consume, interactionists suggest that warnings about media concentration may be overdone (Bielby and Harrington 2008).

Initiating Policy

Any discussion of media regulation must begin with the Tele-communications Act of 1996, which marked the first overhaul of media policy since the early 1930s. The act, which covers everything from cable service to social issues such as obscenity and violence, made a significant distinction between informa-tion services, such as the Internet, and promoters of telecom-munications service—that is, traditional telephone and wireless phone companies, as well as cable companies that offer phone service. Nevertheless, rapid technological development has ren-dered the act obsolete in many people's minds. With the conver-gence of telephone service, videocasting, and the Internet, not to mention the delivery of motion pictures online, such distinc-tions became archaic only a decade after the act was passed.

Significantly, the act eliminated most restrictions on media ownership; those that remain appear to be on their way out, as well. In 2007 the Federal Communications Commis-sion went even further by allowing the consolidation of news-paper and television ownership in cities with only one local newspaper and one local television station. Critics worried that once the transition to digital television was completed in 2009, a single local media outlet could transmit a dozen sig-nals *and* deliver the daily newspaper (Rice 2008).

The lack of governmental restraint of media concentration—indeed, the move toward deregulation of the media under several recent administrations—has been ascribed to the unique rela-tionship politicians have with the media industry, compared to other industries. Elected leaders fear the impact that the media may have on their careers, given the control the media exercise over the flow of information to voters (McChesney 2008).

TAKE THE ISSUE WITH YOU

1. Are you aware of who owns or manages the media you watch or listen to? If not, find out.
2. Do concerns about media concentration differ from concerns over the monopoly of certain products or services? Explain.
3. Does the trend toward media concentration affect traditional media outlets (print, radio, and broadcast television) differently from the Internet? Why or why not?

MODULE 19 | Recap and Review

Summary

As societies become larger and more complex, daily life is increasingly dominated by large **formal organizations.**

1. Max Weber argued that in its ideal form, a **bureaucracy** has five basic characteristics: division of labor, hierarchical authority, written rules and regulations, impersonality, and employment based on technical qualifications. Carefully constructed bureaucratic policies can be either undermined or redefined by an organization's informal structure.

2. The **scientific management approach** to management considers workers to be economic resources. In contrast, the **human relations approach** emphasizes the role of people, communications, and participation.

3. The Internet is the one significant exception to the trend toward media concentration, allowing millions of people to produce their own media content.

Thinking Critically

1. Select an organization that is familiar to you—for example, your college, workplace, religious institution, or civic association—and apply Weber's five characteristics of bureaucracy to it. To what degree does it correspond to Weber's ideal type of bureaucracy?

2. What are some of the benefits and drawbacks of large formal organizations?

Key Terms

Alienation

Bureaucracy

Bureaucratization

Classical theory

Formal organization

Goal displacement

Human relations approach

Ideal type

Iron law of oligarchy

Peter principle

Scientific management approach

Trained incapacity

Mastering This Chapter: Social Interaction, Social Structure, and Groups

taking sociology with you

1 Interview a professional in a field of your choice. What role conflicts does a professional in that field commonly experience? What guidance does the profession's code of conduct offer regarding such conflicts?

2 Enter the Second Life virtual world and create an avatar for yourself. Then take a look around. What evidence do you see of social status and social roles?

What groups and networks reside in this virtual world? Do you recognize any formal organizations?

3 Talk with two or three business students or businesspeople about the bureaucratization of business. On balance, do they see bureaucratization as a positive or negative trend? What bureaucratic dysfunctions are common in business, and how do managers attempt to counteract them?

key terms

Achieved status A social position that a person attains largely through his or her own efforts.

Agrarian society The most technologically advanced form of preindustrial society. Members engage primarily in the production of food, but increase their crop yields through technological innovations such as the plow.

Alienation A condition of estrangement or dissociation from the surrounding society.

Ascribed status A social position assigned to a person by society without regard for the person's unique talents or characteristics.

Bureaucracy A component of formal organization that uses rules and hierarchical ranking to achieve efficiency.

Bureaucratization The process by which a group, organization, or social movement becomes increasingly bureaucratic.

Classical theory An approach to the study of formal organizations that views workers as being motivated almost entirely by economic rewards.

Coalition A temporary or permanent alliance geared toward a common goal.

Formal organization A group designed for a special purpose and structured for maximum efficiency.

Gemeinschaft A close-knit community, often found in rural areas, in which strong personal bonds unite members.

Gesellschaft A community, often urban, that is large and impersonal, with little commitment to the group or consensus on values.

Goal displacement Overzealous conformity to official regulations of a bureaucracy.

Group Any number of people with similar norms, values, and expectations who interact with one another on a regular basis.

Horticultural society A preindustrial society in which people plant seeds and crops rather than merely subsist on available foods.

Human relations approach An approach to the study of formal organizations that emphasizes the role of people, communication, and participation in a bureaucracy and tends to focus on the informal structure of the organization.

Hunting-and-gathering society A preindustrial society in which people rely on whatever foods and fibers are readily available in order to survive.

Ideal type A construct or model for evaluating specific cases.

Industrial society A society that depends on mechanization to produce its goods and services.

In-group Any group or category to which people feel they belong.

Iron law of oligarchy A principle of organizational life under which even a democratic organization will eventually develop into a bureaucracy ruled by a few individuals.

Master status A status that dominates others and thereby determines a person's general position in society.

Mechanical solidarity A collective consciousness that emphasizes group solidarity, characteristic of societies with minimal division of labor.

Organic solidarity A collective consciousness that rests on mutual interdependence, characteristic of societies with a complex division of labor.

Out-group A group or category to which people feel they do not belong.

Peter principle A principle of organizational life according to which every employee within a hierarchy tends to rise to his or her level of incompetence.

Postindustrial society A society whose economic system is engaged primarily in the processing and control of information.

Postmodern society A technologically sophisticated society that is preoccupied with consumer goods and media images.

Primary group A small group characterized by intimate, face-to-face association and cooperation.

Reference group Any group that individuals use as a standard for evaluating themselves and their own behavior.

Role conflict The situation that occurs when incompatible expectations arise from two or more social positions held by the same person.

Role exit The process of disengagement from a role that is central to one's self-identity in order to establish a new role and identity.

Role strain The difficulty that arises when the same social position imposes conflicting demands and expectations.

Scientific management approach Another name for the classical theory of formal organizations.

Secondary group A formal, impersonal group in which there is little social intimacy or mutual understanding.

Social institution An organized pattern of beliefs and behavior centered on basic social needs.

Social interaction The ways in which people respond to one another.

Social network A series of social relationships that links a person directly to others, and through them indirectly to still more people.

Social role A set of expectations for people who occupy a given social position or status.

Social structure The way in which a society is organized into predictable relationships.

Sociocultural evolution Long-term social trends resulting from the interplay of continuity, innovation, and selection.

Status A term used by sociologists to refer to any of the full range of socially defined positions within a large group or society.

Technology Cultural information about the ways in which the material resources of the environment may be used to satisfy human needs and desires.

Trained incapacity The tendency of workers in a bureaucracy to become so specialized that they develop blind spots and fail to notice obvious problems.

self-quiz

Read each question carefully and then select the best answer.

1. In the United States, we expect that cab drivers will know how to get around a city. This expectation is an example of which of the following?
   a. role conflict
   b. role strain
   c. social role
   d. master status

2. What occurs when incompatible expectations arise from two or more social positions held by the same person?
   a. role conflict
   b. role strain
   c. role exit
   d. both a and b

3. In sociological terms, what do we call any number of people with similar norms, values, and expectations who interact with one another on a regular basis?
   a. a category
   b. a group
   c. an aggregate
   d. a society

4. The Shakers, a religious sect that came to the United States in 1774, has seen their group's membership diminish significantly due to their inability to
   a. teach new recruits.
   b. preserve order.
   c. replace personnel.
   d. provide and maintain a sense of purpose.

5. Which sociological perspective argues that the present organization of social institutions is no accident?
   a. the functionalist perspective
   b. the conflict perspective
   c. the interactionist perspective
   d. the global perspective

6. The U.S. Postal Service, the Boston Pops orchestra, and the college or university in which you are currently enrolled as a student are all examples of
   a. primary groups.
   b. reference groups.
   c. formal organizations.
   d. triads.

7. One positive consequence of bureaucracy is that it reduces bias. Reduction of bias results from which characteristic of a bureaucracy?
   a. impersonality
   b. hierarchy of authority
   c. written rules and regulations
   d. employment based on technical qualifications

8. According to the Peter principle,
   a. all bureaucracies are notoriously inefficient.
   b. if something *can* go wrong, it *will*.
   c. every employee within a hierarchy tends to rise to his or her level of incompetence.
   d. all line workers get burned in the end.

9. Social control in what Ferdinand Tönnies termed a *Gemeinschaft* community is maintained through all but which of the following means?
   a. moral persuasion
   b. gossip
   c. legally defined punishment
   d. gestures

10. Sociologist Daniel Bell uses which of the following terms to refer to a society whose economic system is engaged primarily in the processing and control of information?
    a. postmodern
    b. horticultural
    c. industrial
    d. postindustrial

11. The term _____ refers to the way in which a society is organized into predictable relationships.

12. The African American activist Malcolm X wrote in his autobiography that his position as a Black man, a(n) _____ status, was an obstacle to his dream of becoming a lawyer, a(n) _____ status.

13. Sociologist Helen Rose Fuchs Ebaugh developed the term _____ to describe the process of disengagement from a role that is central to one's self-identity in order to establish a new role and identity.

14. _____ groups often emerge in the workplace among those who share special understandings about their occupation.

15. In many cases, people model their behavior after groups to which they may not belong. These groups are called _____ groups.

16. In studying the social behavior of word processors in a Chicago law firm, sociologist Mitchell Duneier drew on the _____ perspective.

17. Max Weber developed a(n) _____ of bureaucracy, which reflects the most characteristic aspects of all human organizations.

18. According to Émile Durkheim, societies with a minimal division of labor are characterized by _____ solidarity, while societies with a complex division of labor are characterized by _____ solidarity.

19. In Gerhard Lenski's theory of sociocultural evolution, a society's level of _____ is critical to the way it is organized.

20. A(n) _____ society is a technologically sophisticated society that is preoccupied with consumer goods and media images.

Answers

1 (c); 2 (a); 3 (b); 4 (c); 5 (b); 6 (c); 7 (a); 8 (c); 9 (c); 10 (d); 11 social structure; 12 ascribed, achieved; 13 role exit; 14 Secondary; 15 reference; 16 interactionist; 17 ideal type; 18 mechanical, organic; 19 technology; 20 postmodern

thinking about movies

Restrepo

In this documentary, a U.S. Army platoon stationed in Afghanistan attempts to gain the trust of the local people as they clear the area of armed insurgents.

The Town

A career criminal tries to leave his life of crime, but his membership in a local gang complicates the attempt.

The Miners' Hymns

This documentary, set in the north of England, illustrates the difficulty of organizing coal miners into a union.

Deviance, Crime, and Social Control

7 Deviance, Crime, and Social Control

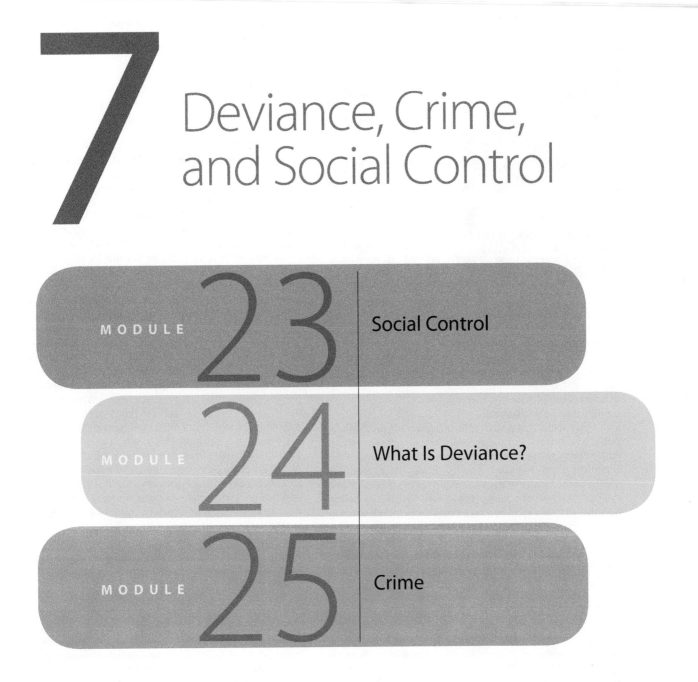

MODULE 23 Social Control

MODULE 24 What Is Deviance?

MODULE 25 Crime

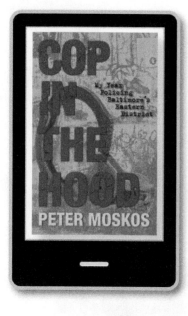

What do you think (or know) life is like in a high-crime area?

To learn about crime firsthand, sociologist Peter Moskos became a Baltimore police officer.

❝ Living in Baltimore City, I was required to carry my gun both on and off duty. I never fired a shot outside of training. Only rarely was my service weapon—a charged semi-automatic nine-millimeter Glock-17 with no safety and a seventeen-round clip—pointed at somebody. But in my police duties, my gun was very routinely removed from its holster, probably every other shift. I did occasionally chase people down alleys and wrestled a few suspects. I maced one person, but did not hit anybody. As a police officer, I tried to speak softly and carry a big stick. The department issued a twenty-nine-inch straight wooden baton just for this purpose. I brought it along to all my calls.

In any account of police work, inevitably the noncriminal public, the routine, and the working folks all get short shrift. Police don't deal with a random cross-section of society, even within the areas they work. And this book reflects that. The ghetto transcends stereotypes. Families try to make it against the odds. Old women sweep the streets. People rise before dawn to go to work. On Sundays, ladies go to church wearing beautiful hats and preachers preach to the choir. But if you're looking for stereotypes, they're there. Between the vacant and abandoned buildings you'll find liquor stores, fast food, Korean corner stores, and a Jewish pawn shop. Living conditions are worse than third-world shanty towns: children in filthy apartments without plumbing or electricity, entire homes put out on eviction day, forty-five-year-old great-grand parents, junkies not raising their kids, drug dealers, and everywhere signs of violence and despair.

As a middle-class white man policing the ghetto, I should address the charge of "exoticism," that I use poor residents for my own advantage. I plead no-contest. If you're not from the ghetto, and though it may not be politically correct to say so, the ghetto *is* exotic. One field-training officer accused me of being "*fascinated* by the ghetto." I am. There are very few aspects of urban life that don't fascinate me. But it is not my intent to sensationalize the ghetto. This is a book about police.

If you want to read about the ghetto, good books are out there. Ghettos are diverse and encompass many cultures and classes. Some object to the very term ghetto. I use the word because it is the vernacular of police officers and many (though by no means all) of the residents. If you really want to learn about the ghetto, go there. There's probably one near you. Visit a church; walk down the street; buy something from the corner store; have a beer; eat. But most importantly, talk to people. That's how you learn. When the subject turns to drugs and crime, you'll hear a common refrain: "It just don't make sense."

Twenty months in Baltimore wasn't very long, but it was long enough to see five police officers killed in the line of duty. And there were other cops, friends of mine, who were hurt, shot, and lucky to live. A year after I quit the force, my friend and academy classmate became the first Baltimore police woman killed in the line of duty, dying in a car crash on the way to back up another police officer. ❞

Twenty months in Baltimore wasn't very long, but it was long enough to see five police officers killed in the line of duty.

(Moskos 2008:15–17) Additional information about this excerpt can be found on the Online Learning Center at www.mhhe.com/schaefermod2e.

Peter Moskos's route to becoming a sworn police officer was unusual. None of his friends or relatives were on the force: his father was a sociologist. During his graduate studies, however, Moskos persuaded Baltimore's police commissioner to let him attend the police academy, as both a student and a sociologist. On the second day of class, the commissioner was ousted from office, to be replaced by a new commissioner who questioned Moskos's motives. "Why don't you want to be a cop for real?" he challenged. That was the beginning of Moskos's 20-month tour of duty with the Baltimore Police Department. In this excerpt from his book *Cop in the Hood: My Year Policing Baltimore's Eastern District*, Moskos describes his beat as seen through the eyes of a sociologist, taking sociology with him to the academy, the station house, and the street. Moskos notes that the residents he served could not fathom the crime that plagued their inner-city neighborhood. What does explain it? Although drug dealing, prostitution, and selling stolen goods are illegal, they provide some stability to those who live on the edge. Only a thin line separates their *deviant behavior*—behavior that violates social norms—from their illegal activities.

Crime is functional in their subculture, even if it is socially unacceptable to the rest of the neighborhood.

Another example of a behavior that can be seen as either socially acceptable or socially unacceptable is binge drinking. On the one hand, we can view binge drinking as *deviant,* violating a school's standards of conduct and endangering a person's health. On the other hand, we can see it as *conforming,* or complying with peer culture.

These modules examine the relationship between conformity, deviance, and social control. When does conformity verge on deviance? How does a society control its members? What are the consequences of deviance? We will begin by distinguishing between conformity and obedience and then look at an experiment on obedience to authority. Next, we will analyze the informal and formal mechanisms societies use to encourage conformity and discourage deviance and focus on theoretical explanations for deviance. The final module focuses on crime, a specific type of deviant behavior subject to official, written norms. We will look at various types of crime found in the United States, the ways crime is measured, and international crime rates, and will consider the controversial topic of the death penalty.

MODULE 23 | Social Control

As we saw in Module 12, each culture, subculture, and group has distinctive norms governing appropriate behavior. Laws, dress codes, organizational bylaws, course requirements, and the rules of sports and games all express social norms.

How does a society bring about acceptance of basic norms? The term **social control** refers to the techniques and strategies for preventing deviant human behavior in any society. Social control occurs on all levels of society. In the family, we are socialized to obey our parents simply because they are our parents. Peer groups introduce us to informal norms, such as dress codes, that govern the behavior of their members. Colleges establish standards they expect of students. In bureaucratic organizations, workers encounter a formal system of rules and regulations. Finally, the government of every society legislates and enforces social norms.

Most of us respect and accept basic social norms and assume that others will do the same. Even without thinking, we obey the instructions of police officers, follow the day-to-day rules at our jobs, and move to the rear of elevators when people enter. Such behavior reflects an effective process of socialization to the dominant standards of a culture. At the same time, we are well aware that individuals, groups, and institutions *expect* us to act "properly." This expectation carries with it **sanctions,** or penalties and rewards for conduct concerning a social norm. If we fail to live up to the norm, we may face punishment through informal sanctions such as fear and ridicule or formal sanctions such as jail sentences or fines.

The challenge to effective social control is that people often receive competing messages about how to behave. While the state or government may clearly define acceptable behavior, friends or fellow employees may encourage quite different behavior patterns. Historically, legal measures aimed at blocking discrimination based on race, religion, gender, age, and sexual orientation have been difficult to implement, because many people tacitly encourage the violation of such measures.

Functionalists maintain that people must respect social norms if any group or society is to survive. In their view, societies literally could not function if massive numbers of people defied standards of appropriate conduct. In contrast, conflict theorists contend that the successful functioning of a society will consistently benefit the powerful and work to the disadvantage of other groups. They point out that in the United States, widespread resistance to social norms was necessary to win our independence from England, to overturn the institution of slavery, to allow women to vote, to secure civil rights, and to force an end to the war in Vietnam.

Conformity and Obedience

Techniques for social control operate on both the group level and the societal level. People we think of as peers or equals influence us to act in particular ways; the same is true of people who

In Finland (left), a young man relaxes in his prison cell, which resembles a college dorm room. In the United States (right), prisoners at a super-maximum-security prison watch television in cages that prevent them from making physical contact with guards or other prisoners. The rate of imprisonment in Finland is less than one-half that of England and one-fourth that of the United States.

hold authority over us or occupy awe-inspiring positions. Social psychologist Stanley Milgram (1975) made a useful distinction between these two levels of social control.

The Milgram Experiment

Milgram used the term **conformity** to mean going along with peers—individuals of our own status who have no special right to direct our behavior. In contrast, **obedience** is compliance with higher authorities in a hierarchical structure. Thus, a recruit entering military service will typically *conform* to the habits and language of other recruits and *obey* the orders of superior officers. Students will *conform* to the drinking behavior of their peers and *obey* the requests of campus security officers.

If ordered to do so, would you comply with an experimenter's instruction to administer increasingly painful electric shocks to a subject? Most people would say no; yet Milgram's research (1963, 1975) suggests that most of us *would* obey such orders. In his words (1975:xi), "Behavior that is unthinkable in an individual . . . acting on his own may be executed without hesitation when carried out under orders."

Milgram placed advertisements in New Haven, Connecticut, newspapers to recruit subjects for a learning experiment at Yale University. Participants included postal clerks, engineers, high school teachers, and laborers. They were told that the purpose of the research was to investigate the effects of punishment on learning. The experimenter, dressed in a gray technician's coat, explained that in each test, one subject would be randomly selected as the "learner," while another would function as the "teacher." However, the experiment was rigged so that the real subject would always be the teacher, while an associate of Milgram's served as the learner.

At this point, the learner's hand was strapped to an electric apparatus. The teacher was taken to an electronic "shock generator" with 30 levered switches labeled from 15 to 450 volts. Before beginning the experiment, all subjects received sample shocks of 45 volts, to convince them of the authenticity of the experiment. The experimenter then instructed the teacher to apply shocks of increasing voltage each time the learner gave an incorrect answer on a memory test. Teachers were told that "although the shocks can be extremely painful, they cause no permanent tissue damage." In reality, the learner did not receive any shocks.

In a prearranged script, the learner deliberately gave incorrect answers and expressed pain when "shocked." For example, at 150 volts, the learner would cry out, "Get me out of here!" At 270 volts, the learner would scream in agony. When the shock reached 350 volts, the learner would fall silent. If the teacher wanted to stop the experiment, the experimenter would insist that the teacher continue, using such statements as "The experiment requires that you continue" and "You have no other choice; you *must* go on" (Milgram 1975:19–23).

Reflecting on the Milgram Experiment

The results of this unusual experiment stunned and dismayed Milgram and other social scientists. A sample of psychiatrists had predicted that virtually all subjects would refuse to shock innocent victims. In their view, only a "pathological fringe" of less than 2 percent would continue administering shocks up to the maximum level. Yet almost *two-thirds* of participants fell into the category of "obedient subjects."

Why did these subjects obey? Why were they willing to inflict seemingly painful shocks on innocent victims who had never done them any harm? There is no evidence that these subjects were unusually sadistic; few seemed to enjoy administering the shocks. Instead, in Milgram's view, the key to obedience was the experimenter's social role as a "scientist" and "seeker of knowledge."

Milgram pointed out that in the modern industrial world, we are accustomed to submitting to impersonal authority figures whose status is indicated by a title (professor, lieutenant, doctor) or by a uniform (the technician's coat). Because we view the authority as larger and more important than the individual, we shift responsibility for our behavior to the authority figure. Milgram's subjects frequently stated, "If it were up to me, I would not have administered shocks." They saw themselves as merely doing their duty (Milgram 1975).

From a conflict perspective, our obedience may be affected by the value we place on those whom our behavior affects. While Milgram's experiment shows that in general, people are willing to obey authority figures, other studies show that they are even more willing to obey if they feel the "victim" is deserving of punishment. Sociologist Gary Schulman (1974) re-created Milgram's experiment and found that White students were significantly more likely to shock Black learners than White learners. By a margin of 70 percent to 48 percent, they imposed more shocks on the Black learners than on the White learners.

In one of Stanley Milgram's experiments, the learner supposedly received an electric shock from a shock plate when he answered a question incorrectly. At the 150-volt level, the learner would demand to be released and would refuse to place his hand on the shock plate. The experimenter would then order the actual subject, the teacher, to force the hand onto the plate, as shown in the photo. Though 40 percent of the true subjects stopped complying with Milgram at this point, 30 percent did force the learner's hand onto the shock plate, despite his pretended agony.

From an interactionist perspective, one important aspect of Milgram's findings is the fact that subjects in follow-up studies were less likely to inflict the supposed shocks as they were moved physically closer to their victims. Moreover, interactionists emphasize the effect of *incrementally* administering additional dosages of 15 volts. In effect, the experimenter negotiated with the teacher and convinced the teacher to continue inflicting higher levels of punishment. It is doubtful that anywhere near the two-thirds rate of obedience would have been reached had the experimenter told the teachers to administer 450 volts immediately (B. Allen 1978; Katovich 1987).

Milgram launched his experimental study of obedience to better understand the involvement of Germans in the annihilation of 6 million Jews and millions of other people during World War II. In an interview conducted long after the publication of his study, he suggested that "if a system of death camps were set up in the United States of the sort we had seen in Nazi Germany, one would be able to find sufficient personnel for those camps in any medium-sized American town." Though many people questioned his remark, the revealing photos taken at Iraq's Abu Ghraib prison in 2004, showing U.S. military guards humiliating if not torturing Iraqi prisoners, recalled the experiment Milgram had done two generations earlier. Under conducive circumstances, otherwise normal people can and often do treat one another inhumanely (CBS News 1979:7–8; Hayden 2004; Zimbardo 2007a).

How willing would participants in this experiment be to shock learners today? Although many people may be skeptical of the high levels of conformity Milgram found, recent replications of his experiment confirm his findings. In 2006, using additional safeguards to protect participants' welfare, psychologist Jerry Burger (2009) repeated part of Milgram's experiment with college undergraduates. To avoid biasing the participants, Burger was careful to screen out students who had heard of Milgram's study. The results of the replication were startlingly similar to Milgram's: participants showed a high level of willingness to shock the learner, just as the participants in Milgram's experiment had almost half a century earlier. At the most comparable point in the two studies, Burger measured a rate of 70 percent full obedience—lower, but not significantly so, than the rate of 82.5 percent measured two generations earlier.

💡 use your **sociological imagination**

If you were a participant in Milgram's research on conformity, how far do you think you would go in carrying out orders? Do you see any ethical problem with the experimenter's manipulation of the subjects?

● Informal and Formal Social Control

The sanctions that are used to encourage conformity and obedience—and to discourage violation of social norms—are carried out through both informal and formal social control. As the term implies, people use **informal social control** casually to enforce norms. Examples include smiles, laughter, a raised eyebrow, and ridicule.

In the United States and many other cultures, adults often view spanking, slapping, or kicking children as a proper and necessary means of informal social control. Child development specialists counter that such corporal punishment is inappropriate because it teaches children to solve problems through violence. They warn that slapping and spanking can escalate into more serious forms of abuse. Yet, despite a policy statement by the American Academy of Pediatrics that corporal punishment is not effective and can indeed be harmful, 59 percent of pediatricians support the use of corporal punishment, at least in certain situations. Our culture widely accepts this form of informal social control (Chung et al. 2009).

Formal social control is carried out by authorized agents, such as police officers, judges, school administrators, employers, military officers, and managers of movie theaters. It can serve as a last resort when socialization and informal sanctions do not bring about desired behavior. Sometimes, informal social control can actually undermine formal social control, encouraging people to violate social norms. Box 23-1 examines binge drinking

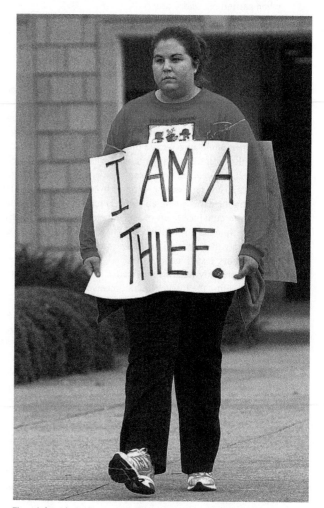

Though formal social control usually involves fines, probation, or incarceration, some judges have used public humiliation as a sanction.

Sociology on Campus

BOX 23-1

Binge Drinking

About 1,700 college students die each year of unintentional alcohol-related injuries. According to a study published by the Harvard School of Public Health, 44 percent of college students indulge in binge drinking (defined as at least five drinks in a row for men and four in a row for women). These numbers represent an increase from 1990s data, despite efforts on many campuses across the nation to educate students about the risks of binge drinking.

The problem is not confined to the United States—Britain, Russia, and South Africa all report regular "drink till you drop" alcoholic consumption among young people. According to a study that compared data from 22 countries, however, college students in the United States have the highest rate of drinking and driving. Nor does binge drinking begin in college. A national study found that over a 30-day period, 29 percent of high school students engaged in binge drinking.

Binge drinking on campus presents a difficult social problem. On the one hand, it can be regarded as *deviant,* violating the standards of conduct expected of those in an academic setting. In fact, Harvard researchers consider binge drinking the most serious public health hazard facing colleges. On the other hand, binge drinking represents *conformity* to the peer culture, especially in fraternities and sororities, which serve as social centers on many campuses. Most students seem to take an "everybody does it—no big deal" attitude toward the behavior.

Some colleges and universities are taking steps to make binge drinking a bit less "normal" by means of *social control*—banning kegs, closing fraternities and sororities, encouraging

Forty-four percent of college students indulge in binge drinking.

liquor retailers not to sell in high volume to students, and expelling students after three alcohol-related infractions. Despite privacy laws, many schools are notifying parents whenever their underage children are caught drinking. Even with these measures, however, curbing underage drinking is a challenge.

LET'S DISCUSS

1. Why do you think most college students regard binge drinking as a normal rather than a deviant behavior?

2. Which do you think would be more effective in stopping binge drinking on your campus, informal or formal social control?

Sources: Bernstein 2007; Centers for Disease Control and Prevention 2010, 2012a; J. Miller et al. 2007; National Center on Addiction and Substance Abuse at Columbia University 2007; Outside the Classroom 2009; Parker-Pope 2012; Wechsler et al. 2002, 2004.

among college students, who receive conflicting messages about the acceptability of the behavior from sources of social control.

An increasingly significant means of formal social control in the United States is to imprison people. During the course of a year, over 7 million adults undergo some form of correctional supervision—jail, prison, probation, or parole. Put another way, almost 1 out of every 30 adult Americans is subject to this very formal type of social control every year (Sabol et al. 2009).

In 2007, in the wake of the mass shootings at Virginia Tech, many college officials reviewed security measures on their campuses. Administrators were reluctant to end or even limit the relative freedom of movement students on their campuses enjoyed. Instead, they concentrated on improving emergency communications between campus police and students, faculty, and staff. Reflecting a reliance on technology to maintain social control, college leaders called for replacement of the "old" technology of e-mail with instant alerts that could be sent to people's cell phones via instant messaging.

In the aftermath of September 11, 2001, new measures of social control became the norm in the United States. Some of them, such as stepped-up security and surveillance at airports and high-rise buildings, were highly visible to the public. The federal government has also publicly urged citizens to engage in informal social control by watching for and reporting people whose actions seem suspicious (Monahan 2011).

Many people think this kind of social control goes too far. Civil rights advocates worry that the government's request for information on suspicious activities may encourage negative stereotyping of Muslims and Arab Americans. Clearly, there is a trade-off between the benefits of surveillance and the right to privacy.

Law and Society

Some norms are so important to a society that they are formalized into laws regarding people's behavior. **Law** may be defined as governmental social control (Black 1995). Some laws, such as the prohibition against murder, are directed at all members of society. Others, such as fishing and hunting regulations, affect particular categories of people. Still others govern the behavior of social institutions (for instance, corporate law and laws regarding the taxing of nonprofit enterprises).

Sociologists see the creation of laws as a social process. Because laws are passed in response to a perceived need for formal social control, sociologists have sought to explain how and why such a perception arises. In their view, law is not merely a static body of rules handed down from generation to generation. Rather, it reflects continually changing standards of what is right and wrong, of how violations are to be determined, and of what sanctions are to be applied (Schur 1968).

Sociologists representing varying theoretical perspectives agree that the legal order reflects the values of those in a position to exercise authority. Therefore, the creation of civil and criminal law can be a most controversial matter. Should it be against the law to employ illegal immigrants, to have an abortion (see Module 35), to allow prayer in public schools, or to smoke on an airplane? Such issues have been bitterly debated, because they require a choice among competing values. Not surprisingly, laws that are unpopular—such as the one-time prohibition of alcohol under the Eighteenth Amendment and the widespread establishment of a 55-mile-per-hour speed limit on highways—become difficult to enforce when there is no consensus supporting the norms.

One current and controversial debate over laws governing behavior is whether people should be allowed to use marijuana legally, for medical purposes. Although the majority of adults polled in national surveys support such a use, the federal government continues to regard all uses of marijuana as illegal. In 2005 the Supreme Court upheld the federal government's position. Nevertheless, 15 states and the District of Columbia have granted citizens the right to use marijuana for medical purposes—even if that privilege rests on dubious legal grounds (Figure 23-1).

Socialization is the primary source of conforming and obedient behavior, including obedience to law. Generally, it is not external pressure from a peer group or authority figure that makes us go along with social norms. Rather, we have internalized such norms as valid and desirable and are committed to observing them. In a profound sense, we want to see ourselves (and to be seen) as loyal, cooperative, responsible, and respectful of others. In the United States and other societies around the world, people are socialized both to want to belong and to fear being viewed as different or deviant.

Control theory suggests that our connection to members of society leads us to systematically conform to society's norms. According to sociologist Travis Hirschi and other control theorists, our bonds to family members, friends, and peers induce us to follow the mores and folkways of our society. We give little conscious thought to whether we will be sanctioned if we fail to conform. Socialization develops our self-control so well that

In Singapore, a custodian removes a bit of litter from an otherwise spotless floor. Strict social controls prevail in the city-state, where the careless disposal of a cigarette butt or candy wrapper carries a $200 fine.

we don't need further pressure to obey social norms. Although control theory does not effectively explain the rationale for every conforming act, it nevertheless reminds us that while the media may focus on crime and disorder, most members of most societies conform to and obey basic norms (Brewis et al. 2011; Gottfredson and Hirschi 1990; Hirschi 1969).

trend|spotting

Incarceration Nation

Since 1980, through prosperity and recession, war and peace, the United States has been sending more and more people to prison. Today, about 1.6 million people reside in federal or state institutions. That number is higher than the population of the fifth largest U.S. city, Phoenix.

Both the number of prisoners and the rate of incarceration have grown steadily. From 1980 through the end of 2010, the prison population increased from just over 1 in 1,000 to 1 in 231. If only adults are counted, the current proportion is 1 in every 33. The trend becomes even more disturbing when we consider the growing reliance on early-release programs. If cash-strapped states were not using electronic monitoring devices, like ankle bracelets, to lower their prison populations, the statistics would be even more dismal.

Internationally, the United States' incarceration rate stands out as one of the highest in the world—more than three times as high as that of Mexico or Canada. Even China with its huge population does not have as many people behind bars as the United States.

MAPPING LIFE NATIONWIDE

FIGURE 23-1 **The Status of Medical Marijuana**

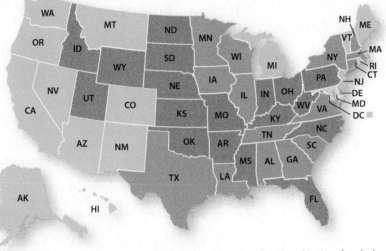

- 16 states and the District of Columbia have laws that allow the cultivation of medical marijuana and that protect patients who possess medical marijuana (with their doctors' recommendations or certifications) from criminal penalties.

- Maryland protects medical marijuana patients from jail, but not from the threat of arrest.

- 15 states have laws that recognize marijuana's medical value, but these laws are ineffective because they rely on federal cooperation.

- 18 states have no provisions for medical marijuana.

Source: NORML 2012.
The actions some states have taken to legalize marijuana are largely symbolic. Federal law still prohibits doctors from writing prescriptions for marijuana, and pharmacies from distributing the substance. Although patients can still be prosecuted by the federal government for possessing or using marijuana, the Obama administration has decided not to prosecute medical marijuana users who comply with state laws.

MODULE 23 | Recap and Review

Summary

This module examines the relationship between conformity and mechanisms of **social control.**

1. A society uses **social control** to encourage the acceptance of basic norms.

2. Stanley Milgram defined **conformity** as going along with one's peers; **obedience** is compliance with higher authorities in a hierarchical structure.

3. Some norms are so important to a society that they are formalized into **laws.** Socialization is a primary source of conforming and obedient behavior, including obedience to laws.

Thinking Critically

1. Think about a job you once held. How did your employer exercise social control over the employees?

How did you, as an employee, use social control in relating to those around you?

2. Should some illegal drugs be decriminalized? Why or why not?

Key Terms

Conformity

Control theory

Formal social control

Informal social control

Law

Obedience

Sanction

Social control

For sociologists, the term *deviance* does not mean perversion or depravity. **Deviance** is behavior that violates the standards of conduct or expectations of a group or society. In the United States, alcoholics, compulsive gamblers, and the mentally ill would all be classified as deviants. Being late for class is categorized as a deviant act; the same is true of wearing jeans to a formal wedding. On the basis of the sociological definition, we are all deviant from time to time. Each of us violates common social norms in certain situations (Best 2004).

Is being overweight an example of deviance? In the United States and many other cultures, unrealistic standards of appearance and body image place a huge strain on people—especially women and girls—based on how they look. Journalist Naomi Wolf (1992) has used the term *beauty myth* to refer to an exaggerated ideal of beauty, beyond the reach of all but a few females, which has unfortunate consequences. In order to shed their "deviant" image and conform to unrealistic societal norms, many women and girls become consumed with adjusting their appearances. Yet what is deviant in one culture may be celebrated in another.

Deviance involves the violation of group norms, which may or may not be formalized into law. It is a comprehensive concept that includes not only criminal behavior but also many actions that are not subject to prosecution. The public official who takes a bribe has defied social norms, but so has the high school student who refuses to sit in an assigned seat or cuts class. Of course, deviation from norms is not always negative, let alone criminal. A member of an exclusive social club who speaks out against a traditional policy of not admitting women, Blacks, and Jews is deviating from the club's norms. So is a police officer who blows the whistle on corruption or brutality within the department.

From a sociological perspective, deviance is hardly objective or set in stone. Rather, it is subject to social definition within a particular society and at a particular time. For that reason, what is considered deviant can shift from one social era to another. In most instances, those individuals and groups with the greatest status and power define what is acceptable and what is deviant. For example, despite serious medical warnings against the dangers of tobacco, made since 1964, cigarette smoking continued to be accepted for decades—in good part because of the power of tobacco farmers and cigarette manufacturers. Only after a long campaign led by public health and anticancer activists did cigarette smoking become more of a deviant activity. Today, many state and local laws limit where people can smoke.

Deviance and Social Stigma

A person can acquire a deviant identity in many ways. Because of physical or behavioral characteristics, some people are unwillingly cast in negative social roles. Once assigned a deviant role, they have trouble presenting a positive image to others and may even experience lowered self-esteem. Whole groups of people—for instance, "short people" or "redheads"—may be labeled in this way. The interactionist Erving Goffman coined the term **stigma** to describe the labels society uses to devalue members of certain social groups (Goffman 1963; Heckert and Best 1997).

Prevailing expectations about beauty and body shape may prevent people who are regarded as ugly or obese from advancing as rapidly as their abilities permit. Both overweight and anorexic people are assumed to be weak in character, slaves to their appetites or to media images. Because they do not conform to the beauty myth, they may be viewed as "disfigured" or "strange" in appearance, bearers of what Goffman calls a "spoiled identity." However, what constitutes disfigurement is a matter of interpretation. Of the 17 million cosmetic procedures done every year in the United States alone, many are performed on women who

In 2009, baseball fans were shocked by the revelation that, like several other baseball greats, superstar Alex Rodriguez had used banned substances and lied about it.

Think about It

If your friends or teammates violate a social norm, is their behavior deviant?

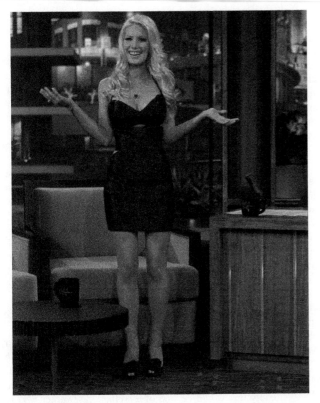

Deviant or normal? Television personality and recording artist Heidi Montag shocked fans in 2010 by revealing that she had undergone 10 plastic surgery procedures in a single day. Montag had already undergone breast augmentation, collagen lip injections, and rhinoplasty. Would you consider her behavior deviant?

would be defined objectively as having a normal appearance. And while feminist sociologists have accurately noted that the beauty myth makes many women feel uncomfortable with themselves, men too lack confidence in their appearance. The number of males who choose to undergo cosmetic procedures has risen sharply in recent years (American Academy of Cosmetic Surgery 2010).

Often people are stigmatized for deviant behaviors they may no longer engage in. The labels "compulsive gambler," "ex-convict," "recovering alcoholic," and "ex–mental patient" can stick to a person for life. Goffman draws a useful distinction between a prestige symbol that draws attention to a positive aspect of one's identity, such as a wedding band or a badge, and a stigma symbol that discredits or debases one's identity, such as a conviction for child molestation. While stigma symbols may not always be obvious, they can become a matter of public knowledge. Starting in 1994, many states required convicted sex offenders to register with local police departments. Some communities publish the names and addresses, and in some instances even the pictures, of convicted sex offenders on the web.

While some types of deviance will stigmatize a person, other types do not carry a significant penalty. Examples of socially tolerated forms of deviance can be found in the world of high technology.

Deviance and Technology

Technological innovations such as pagers and voice mail can redefine social interactions and the standards of behavior related to them. When the Internet was first made available to the general public, no norms or regulations governed its use. Because online communication offers a high degree of anonymity, uncivil behavior—speaking harshly of others or monopolizing chat room space—quickly became common. Online bulletin boards designed to carry items of community interest became littered with commercial advertisements. Such deviant acts are beginning to provoke calls for the establishment of formal rules for online behavior. For example, policymakers have debated whether to regulate the content of websites featuring hate speech and pornography.

Some deviant uses of technology are criminal, though not all participants see it that way. On the street, the for-profit pirating of software, motion pictures, and music has become a big business. On the Internet, the downloading of music by individual listeners, which is typically forbidden by copyright, is widely accepted. The music and motion picture industries have waged much publicized campaigns to stop these illegal uses of their products, yet among many people, no social stigma attaches to them. Deviance, then, is a complex concept. Sometimes it is trivial, sometimes profoundly harmful. Sometimes it is accepted by society and sometimes soundly rejected.

Sociological Perspectives on Deviance

Why do people violate social norms? We have seen that deviant acts are subject to both informal and formal social control. The nonconforming or disobedient person may face disapproval, loss of friends, fines, or even imprisonment. Why, then, does deviance occur?

Early explanations for behavior that deviated from societal expectations blamed supernatural causes or genetic factors (such as "bad blood" or evolutionary throwbacks to primitive ancestors). By the 1800s, substantial research efforts were being made to identify biological factors that lead to deviance, and especially to criminal activity. Though such research was discredited in the 20th century, contemporary studies, primarily by biochemists, have sought to isolate genetic factors that suggest a likelihood of certain personality traits. Although criminality (much less deviance) is hardly a personality characteristic, researchers have focused on traits that might lead to crime, such as aggression. Of course, aggression can also lead to success in the corporate world, in professional sports, or in other walks of life.

The contemporary study of the possible biological roots of criminality is but one aspect of the larger debate over sociobiology. In general, sociologists reject any emphasis on the genetic roots of crime and deviance. The limitations of current knowledge, the possibility of reinforcing racist and sexist assumptions, and the disturbing implications for the rehabilitation of criminals have led sociologists to draw largely on other approaches to explain deviance (Sagarin and Sanchez 1988).

Functionalist Perspective

According to functionalists, deviance is a common part of human existence, with positive as well as negative consequences for social stability. Deviance helps to define the limits of proper behavior. Children who see one parent scold the other for belching at the dinner table learn about approved conduct. The same is true of the driver who receives a speeding ticket, the department store cashier who is fired for yelling at a customer, and the college student who is penalized for handing in papers weeks overdue.

Durkheim's Legacy Émile Durkheim ([1895] 1964) focused his sociological investigations mainly on criminal acts, yet his conclusions have implications for all types of deviant behavior. In Durkheim's view, the punishments established within a culture (including both formal and informal mechanisms of social control) help to define acceptable behavior and thus contribute to stability. If improper acts were not sanctioned, people might stretch their standards of what constitutes appropriate conduct.

Sociologist Kai Erikson (1966) illustrated the boundary-maintenance function of deviance in his study of the Puritans of 17th-century New England. By today's standards, the Puritans placed tremendous emphasis on conventional morals. Their persecution and execution of women as witches represented a continuing attempt to define and redefine the boundaries of their community. In effect, their changing social norms created crime waves, as people whose behavior was previously acceptable suddenly faced punishment for being deviant (R. Schaefer and Zellner 2011).

Durkheim ([1897] 1951) introduced the term **anomie** into sociological literature to describe the loss of direction felt in a society when social control of individual behavior has become ineffective. Anomie is a state of normlessness that typically occurs during a period of profound social change and disorder, such as a time of economic collapse. People become more aggressive or depressed, which results in higher rates of violent crime and suicide. Since there is much less agreement on what constitutes proper behavior during times of revolution, sudden prosperity, or economic depression, conformity and obedience become less significant as social forces. It also becomes much more difficult to state exactly what constitutes deviance.

Merton's Theory of Deviance What do a mugger and a teacher have in common? Each is "working" to obtain money that can then be exchanged for desired goods. As this example illustrates, behavior that violates accepted norms (such as mugging) may be based on the same basic objectives as the behavior of people who pursue more conventional lifestyles.

On the basis of this kind of analysis, sociologist Robert Merton (1968) adapted Durkheim's notion of anomie to explain why people accept or reject the goals of a society, the socially approved means of fulfilling their aspirations, or both. Merton maintained that one important cultural goal in the United States is success, measured largely in terms of money. In addition to providing this goal for people, our society offers specific instructions on how to pursue success—go to school, work hard, do not quit, take advantage of opportunities, and so forth.

What happens to individuals in a society with a heavy emphasis on wealth as a basic symbol of success? Merton reasoned that people adapt in certain ways, either by conforming to or by deviating from such cultural expectations. His **anomie theory of deviance** posits five basic forms of adaptation (Table 24-1).

Conformity to social norms, the most common adaptation in Merton's typology, is the opposite of deviance. It involves acceptance of both the overall societal goal ("become affluent") and the approved means ("work hard"). In Merton's view, there must be some consensus regarding accepted cultural goals and the legitimate means for attaining them. Without such a consensus, societies could exist only as collectives of people rather than as unified cultures, and might experience continual chaos.

The other four types of behavior represented in Table 24-1 all involve some departure from conformity. The "innovator" accepts the goals of society but pursues them with means that are regarded as improper. For instance, a safecracker may steal money to buy consumer goods and expensive vacations.

In Merton's typology, the "ritualist" has abandoned the goal of material success and become compulsively committed to the institutional means. Work becomes simply a way of life rather than a means to the goal of success. An example would be the bureaucratic official who blindly applies rules and regulations without remembering the larger goals of the organization. Certainly that would be true of a welfare caseworker who refuses to assist a homeless family because their last apartment was in another district.

The "retreatist," as described by Merton, has basically retreated (or withdrawn) from both the goals and the means of society. In the United States, drug addicts and vagrants are typically portrayed as retreatists. Concern has been growing that adolescents who are addicted to alcohol will become retreatists at an early age.

The final adaptation identified by Merton reflects people's attempts to create a *new* social structure. The "rebel" feels alienated from the dominant means and goals and may seek a dramatically different social order. Members of a revolutionary political organization, such as a militia group, can be categorized as rebels according to Merton's model.

Table **24-1**   Modes of Individual Adaptation

Mode	Institutionalized Means (hard work)	Societal Goal (acquisition of wealth)
Nondeviant	Accept	Accept
Conformity		
Deviant		
Innovation	Reject	Accept
Ritualism	Accept	Reject
Retreatism	Reject	Reject
Rebellion	Replace with new means	Replace with new goals

Source: Adapted from Merton 1968:194.

Research Today

BOX 24-1

Does Crime Pay?

A driver violates the speed limit to get to a job interview on time. A financially strapped parent shoplifts goods that her family needs. These people may feel justified in violating the law because they do so to meet a reasonable objective. In Robert Merton's terms, they are *innovators*—people who violate social norms to achieve a commonly shared societal goal. Although their actions are criminal and potentially hurtful to others, from their own short-term perspective, their actions are functional.

Carried to its logical conclusion, innovation can and does become a career for some people. Yet from a purely economic point of view, even considering the fact that crime may pay is controversial, because doing so may seem to tolerate or encourage rule violation. Nothing is more controversial than the suggestion that gang-run drug deals are profitable and produce "good jobs." Although some people may see drug dealers as a cross between MBA-educated professionals and streetwise entrepreneurs, society in general does not admire these innovators.

Sociologist Sudhir Venkatesh collected detailed data on the illegal drug trade during his observation research on a Chicago street gang. Working with economist Steven Levitt,

coauthor of the best seller *Freakonomics*, to analyze the business of selling crack cocaine, he found that less than 5 percent of even the gang leaders earned $100,000 per year. The rest of the leaders and virtually all the rank and file earned less than the minimum wage. In fact, most were unpaid workers seeking to move up in the gang hierarchy. (Thus the title of a chapter in Levitt's book, "Why Do Drug Dealers Still Live with Their Moms?") As Levitt notes, the drug gang is like most corporations: the top 2 percent of workers take home most of the money.

Why, from a sociological *and* an economic perspective, do these nonprofitable practices persist, especially considering that one in every four members of drug-oriented

> Less than 5 percent of even the gang leaders earned $100,000 per year. The rest of the leaders and virtually all the rank and file earned less than the minimum wage.

street gangs is eventually killed? One reason, of course, is the public's almost insatiable demand for illegal drugs. And from the drug peddler's perspective, few legitimate jobs are available to young adults in poverty-stricken areas, urban or rural. Functionally, these youths are contributing to their household incomes by dealing drugs.

Scholars see a need for further research on Merton's concept of innovation. Why, for example, do some disadvantaged groups have lower rates of reported crime than others? Why do many people who are caught in adverse circumstances reject criminal activity as a viable alternative? Merton's theory of deviance does not easily answer such questions.

LET'S DISCUSS

1. Do you know anyone who has stolen out of need? If so, did the person feel justified in stealing, or did he or she feel guilty? How long did the theft continue?
2. Economically, profit is the difference between revenues and costs. What are the costs of the illegal drug trade, both economic and social? Is this economic activity profitable for society?

Sources: Clinard and Miller 1998; Kingsbury 2008; S. Levitt and Dubner 2006; S. Levitt and Venkatesh 2000; Rosen and Venkatesh 2008; Venkatesh 2008.

Merton made a key contribution to the sociological understanding of deviance by pointing out that deviants such as innovators and ritualists share a great deal with conforming people. The convicted felon may hold many of the same aspirations as people with no criminal background. The theory helps us to understand deviance as a socially created behavior rather than as the result of momentary pathological impulses. However, this theory of deviance has not been applied systematically to real-world crime. Box 24-1 examines scholars' efforts to confirm the theory's validity.

Interactionist Perspective

The functionalist approach to deviance explains why rule violations continue to happen despite pressure to conform and obey. However, functionalists do not indicate how a given person comes to commit a deviant act or why on some occasions crimes do or do not occur. The emphasis on everyday behavior that is the focus of the interactionist perspective offers two explanations of crime: cultural transmission and routine activities theory.

Cultural Transmission In the course of studying graffiti writing by gangs in Los Angeles, sociologist Susan A. Phillips (1999) discovered that the writers learned from one another. In

fact, Phillips was surprised by how stable their focus was over time. She also noted how other ethnic groups built on the models of the African American and Chicano gangs, superimposing Cambodian, Chinese, or Vietnamese symbols.

Humans *learn* how to behave in social situations, whether properly or improperly. There is no natural, innate manner in which people interact with one another. These simple ideas are not disputed today, but such was not the case when sociologist Edwin Sutherland (1883–1950) first advanced the idea that an individual undergoes the same basic socialization process in learning conforming and deviant acts.

Sutherland's ideas have been the dominating force in criminology. He drew on the **cultural transmission** school, which emphasizes that one learns criminal behavior by interacting with others. Such learning includes not only the techniques of lawbreaking (for example, how to break into a car quickly and quietly) but also the motives, drives, and rationalizations of the criminal. The cultural transmission approach can also be used to explain the behavior of those who habitually abuse alcohol or drugs.

Sutherland maintained that through interactions with a primary group and significant others, people acquire definitions of proper and improper behavior. He used the term

differential association to describe the process through which exposure to attitudes *favorable* to criminal acts leads to the violation of rules. Research suggests that this view of differential association also applies to noncriminal deviant acts, such as smoking, truancy, and early sexual behavior.

Sutherland offers the example of a boy who is sociable, outgoing, and athletic and who lives in an area with a high rate of delinquency. The youth is very likely to come into contact with peers who commit acts of vandalism, fail to attend school, and so forth, and may come to adopt such behavior. However, an introverted boy who lives in the same neighborhood may stay away from his peers and avoid delinquency. In another community, an outgoing and athletic boy may join a Little League baseball team or a scout troop because of his interactions with peers. Thus, Sutherland views improper behavior as the result of the types of groups to which one belongs and the kinds of friendships one has.

According to critics, the cultural transmission approach may explain the deviant behavior of juvenile delinquents or graffiti artists, but it fails to explain the conduct of the first-time impulsive shoplifter or the impoverished person who steals out of necessity. While it is not a precise statement of the process through which one becomes a criminal, differential association theory does direct our attention to the paramount role of social interaction in increasing a person's motivation to engage in deviant behavior (Harding 2009; Sutherland et al. 1992).

Social Disorganization Theory The social relationships that exist in a community or neighborhood affect people's behavior. Philip Zimbardo (2007a:24–25), author of the mock prison experiment described in Chapter 5, once did an experiment that demonstrated the power of communal relationships. He abandoned a car in each of two different neighborhoods, leaving its hood up and removing its hub caps. In one neighborhood, people started to strip the car for parts before Zimbardo had finished setting up a remote video camera to record their behavior. In the other neighborhood, weeks passed without the car being touched, except for a pedestrian who stopped to close the hood during a rainstorm.

Under cover of darkness, drag racers await the start signal on a deserted Los Angeles street. Sutherland's concepts of differential association and cultural transmission would both apply to the practice of drag racing on city streets.

What accounts for the strikingly different outcomes of Zimbardo's experiment in the two communities? According to **social disorganization theory,** increases in crime and deviance can be attributed to the absence or breakdown of communal relationships and social institutions, such as the family, school, church, and local government. This theory was developed at the University of Chicago in the early 1900s to describe the apparent disorganization that occurred as cities expanded with rapid immigration and migration from rural areas. Using the latest survey techniques, Clifford Shaw and Henry McKay literally mapped the distribution of social problems in Chicago. They found high rates of social problems in neighborhoods where buildings had deteriorated and the population had declined. Interestingly, the patterns persisted over time, despite changes in the neighborhoods' ethnic and racial composition.

This theory is not without its critics. To some, social disorganization theory seems to "blame the victim," leaving larger societal forces, such as the lack of jobs or high-quality schools, unaccountable. Critics also argue that even troubled neighborhoods have viable, healthy organizations, which persist despite the problems that surround them.

More recently, social disorganization theorists have taken to emphasizing the effect of social networks on communal bonds. These researchers acknowledge that communities are not isolated islands. Residents' bonds may be enhanced or weakened by their ties to groups outside the immediate community (Jensen 2005; Sampson and Graves 1989; Shaw and McKay 1942).

Labeling Perspective

The Saints and the Roughnecks were groups of high school males who were continually engaged in excessive drinking, reckless driving, truancy, petty theft, and vandalism. There the similarity ended. None of the Saints was ever arrested, but every Roughneck was frequently in trouble with police and townspeople. Why the disparity in their treatment? On the basis of observation research in their high school, sociologist William Chambliss (1973) concluded that social class played an important role in the varying fortunes of the two groups.

The Saints hid behind a facade of respectability. They came from "good families," were active in school organizations, planned on attending college, and received good grades. People generally viewed their delinquent acts as a few isolated cases of sowing wild oats. The Roughnecks had no such aura of respectability. They drove around town in beat-up cars, were generally unsuccessful in school, and aroused suspicion no matter what they did.

We can understand such discrepancies by using an approach to deviance known as **labeling theory.** Unlike Sutherland's work, labeling theory does not focus on why some individuals come to commit deviant acts. Instead, it attempts to explain why certain people (such as the Roughnecks) are *viewed* as deviants, delinquents, bad kids, losers, and criminals, whereas others whose behavior is similar (such as the Saints) are not seen in such harsh terms. Reflecting the contribution of interactionist theorists, labeling theory emphasizes how a person comes to be labeled as deviant or to accept that label. Sociologist Howard Becker (1963:9; 1964), who popularized this approach, summed it up with this statement: "Deviant behavior is behavior that people so label."

Labeling theory is also called the **societal-reaction approach,** reminding us that it is the *response* to an act, not the behavior itself, that determines deviance. For example, studies have shown that some school personnel and therapists expand educational programs designed for learning-disabled students to include those with behavioral problems. Consequently, a "troublemaker" can be improperly labeled as "learning-disabled," and vice versa (Grattet 2011).

Labeling and Agents of Social Control   Traditionally, research on deviance has focused on people who violate social norms. In contrast, labeling theory focuses on police, probation officers, psychiatrists, judges, teachers, employers, school officials, and other regulators of social control. These agents, it is argued, play a significant role in creating the deviant identity by designating certain people (and not others) as deviant. An important aspect of labeling theory is the recognition that some individuals or groups have the power to *define* labels and *apply* them to others. This view ties into the conflict perspective's emphasis on the social significance of power.

In recent years the practice of *racial profiling,* in which people are identified as criminal suspects purely on the basis of their race, has come under public scrutiny. Studies confirm the public's suspicions that in some jurisdictions, police officers are much more likely to stop Black males than White males for routine traffic violations, in the expectation of finding drugs or guns in their cars. Civil rights activists refer to these cases sarcastically as DWB (Driving While Black) violations. Beginning in 2001, profiling took a new turn as people who appeared to be Arab or Muslim came under special scrutiny. (Racial profiling will be examined in more detail in Chapter 10).

The popularity of labeling theory is reflected in the emergence of a related perspective, called social constructionism. According to the **social constructionist perspective,** deviance is the product of the culture we live in. Social constructionists focus specifically on the decision-making process that creates the deviant identity. They point out that "child abductors," "deadbeat dads," "spree killers," and "date rapists" have always been with us, but at times have become *the* major social concern of policymakers because of intensive media coverage (Liska and Messner 1999; E. R. Wright et al. 2000).

How do certain behaviors come to be viewed as a problem? Cigarette smoking, which was once regarded as a polite, gentlemanly activity, is now considered a serious health hazard, not only to the smoker but also to others nearby who don't smoke. Recently, people have become concerned about the danger, especially to children, posed by *thirdhand smoke*—smoke-related chemicals that cling to clothes and linger in rooms, cars, even elevators (Winickoff et al. 2009).

use your **sociological imagination**

You are a teacher. What labels, freely used in education, might you attach to your students?

Conflict Perspective

Conflict theorists point out that people with power protect their interests and define deviance to suit their needs. Sociologist Richard Quinney (1974, 1979, 1980) was a leading exponent of the view that the criminal justice system serves the interests of the powerful. Crime, according to Quinney (1970), is a definition of conduct created by authorized agents of social control—such as legislators and law enforcement officers—in a politically organized society. He and other conflict theorists argue that lawmaking is often an attempt by the powerful to coerce others into their morality (see also Spitzer 1975).

This theory helps to explain why our society has laws against gambling, drug use, and prostitution, many of which are violated on a massive scale. (We will examine these "victimless crimes" later in the chapter.) According to conflict theorists, criminal law does not represent a consistent application of societal values, but instead reflects competing values and interests. Thus, the U.S. criminal code outlaws marijuana because of its alleged harm to users, yet cigarettes and alcohol—both of which can be harmful to users—are sold legally almost everywhere.

In the 1930s, the Federal Bureau of Narcotics launched a campaign to portray marijuana as a dangerous drug rather than a pleasure-inducing substance. From a conflict perspective, those in power often use such tactics to coerce others into adopting a different point of view.

Table **24-2**   Sociological Perspectives on Deviance   **Tracking Sociological Perspectives**

Approach	Theoretical Perspective	Proponents	Emphasis
Anomie	Functionalist	Émile Durkheim Robert Merton	Adaptation to societal norms
Cultural transmission/ Differential association	Interactionist	Edwin Sutherland	Patterns learned through others
Social disorganization	Interactionist	Clifford Shaw Henry McKay	Communal relationships
Labeling/Social constructionist	Interactionist	Howard Becker	Societal response to acts
Conflict	Conflict	Richard Quinney	Dominance by authorized agents Discretionary justice
Feminist	Conflict/Feminist	Freda Adler Meda Chesney-Lind	Role of gender Women as victims and perpetrators

In fact, conflict theorists contend that the entire criminal justice system in the United States treats suspects differently based on their racial, ethnic, or social-class background. In many cases, officials in the system use their own discretion to make biased decisions about whether to press charges or drop them, whether to set bail and how much, whether to offer parole or deny it. Researchers have found that this kind of **differential justice**—differences in the way social control is exercised over different groups—puts African Americans and Latinos at a disadvantage in the justice system, both as juveniles and as adults. On average, White offenders receive shorter sentences than comparable Latino and African American offenders, even when prior arrest records and the relative severity of the crime are taken into consideration (Brewer and Heitzeg 2008; Sandefur 2008; Schlesinger 2011).

The perspective advanced by conflict and labeling theorists forms quite a contrast to the functionalist approach to deviance. Functionalists see standards of deviant behavior as merely reflecting cultural norms; conflict and labeling theorists point out that the most powerful groups in a society can shape laws and standards and determine who is (or is not) prosecuted as a criminal. These groups would be unlikely to apply the label "deviant" to the corporate executive whose decisions lead to large-scale environmental pollution. In the opinion of conflict theorists, agents of social control and other powerful groups can impose their own self-serving definitions of deviance on the general public.

Feminist Perspective

Feminist criminologists such as Freda Adler and Meda Chesney-Lind have suggested that many of the existing approaches to deviance and crime were developed with only men in mind. For example, in the United States, for many years any husband who forced his wife to have sexual intercourse—without her consent and against her will—was not legally considered to have committed rape. The law defined rape as pertaining only to sexual relations between people who were not married to each other, reflecting the overwhelmingly male composition of state legislatures at the time.

It took repeated protests by feminist organizations to get changes in the criminal law defining rape. Beginning in 1993, husbands in all 50 states could be prosecuted under most circumstances for the rape of their wives. There remain alarming exceptions in no fewer than 30 states, however. For example, the husband is exempt when he does not need to use force because his wife is asleep, unconscious, or mentally or physically impaired. These interpretations still rest on the notion that the marriage contract entitles a husband to sex (Bergen 2006).

In the future, feminist scholarship can be expected to grow dramatically. Particularly on topics such as white-collar crime, drinking behavior, drug abuse, and differential sentencing rates between the genders, as well as on the fundamental question of how to define deviance, feminist scholars will have much to say.

We have seen that over the past century, sociologists have taken many different approaches in studying deviance, arousing some controversy in the process. Table 24-2 summarizes the various theoretical approaches to this topic.

MODULE 24 | **Recap and Review**

Summary

Deviant behavior is behavior that violates social norms. A very wide range of behavior may be classified as deviant, and everyone violates social norms in some situations.

1. Some forms of **deviance** carry a negative social **stigma,** while other forms are more or less accepted.

2. From a functionalist point of view, deviance and its consequences help to define the limits of proper behavior.

3. Some interactionists maintain that people learn criminal behavior by interacting with others (**cultural transmission**). To them, deviance results from exposure to attitudes that are favorable to criminal acts (**differential association**).

4. Other interactionists attribute increases in crime and deviance to the absence or breakdown of communal relationships and social institutions, such as the family, school, church, and local government (**social disorganization theory**).

5. An important aspect of **labeling theory** is the recognition that some people are viewed as deviant, while others who engage in the same behavior are not.

6. From the conflict perspective, laws and punishments are a reflection of the interests of the powerful.

7. The feminist perspective emphasizes cultural attitudes and differential economic relationships to help explain gender differences in deviance and crime.

Thinking Critically

1. Do some research on a culture you are unfamiliar with. Do any of the customs seem deviant to you? Which of your own customs might seem deviant to members of that culture?

2. Using examples drawn from work or college life, illustrate each of Merton's five modes of individual adaptation.

3. Explain the presence of both criminals and law-abiding citizens in an inner-city neighborhood in terms of the interactionist perspective.

Key Terms

Anomie

Anomie theory of deviance

Cultural transmission

Deviance

Differential association

Differential justice

Labeling theory

Social constructionist perspective

Social disorganization theory

Societal-reaction approach

Stigma

MODULE 25 | Crime

Crime is on everyone's mind. Until recently, college campuses were viewed as havens from crime. But as Box 25-1 shows, at today's colleges and universities, crime goes well beyond cheating and senior class pranks.

Crime is a violation of criminal law for which some governmental authority applies formal penalties. It represents a deviation from formal social norms administered by the state. Laws divide crimes into various categories, depending on the severity of the offense, the age of the offender, the potential punishment, and the court that holds jurisdiction over the case.

Types of Crime

Rather than relying solely on legal categories, sociologists classify crimes in terms of how they are committed and how society views the offenses. In this section we will examine six types of crime differentiated by sociologists: victimless crimes, professional crime, organized crime, white-collar and technology-based crime, hate crimes, and transnational crime.

Victimless Crimes

When we think of crime, we tend to think of acts that endanger people's economic or personal well-being against their will (or without their direct knowledge). In contrast, sociologists use the term **victimless crime** to describe the willing exchange among adults of widely desired but illegal goods and services, such as prostitution (Schur 1965, 1985).

Some activists are working to decriminalize many of these illegal practices. Supporters of decriminalization are troubled by the attempt to legislate a moral code for adults. In their view, prostitution, drug abuse, gambling, and other victimless crimes are impossible to prevent. The already overburdened criminal justice system should instead devote its resources to street crimes and other offenses with obvious victims.

Despite widespread use of the term *victimless crime,* however, many people object to the notion that there is no victim other than the offender in such crimes. Excessive drinking, compulsive gambling, and illegal drug use contribute to an enormous amount of personal and property damage. A person with a drinking problem may become abusive to a spouse or children; a compulsive gambler or drug user may steal to pursue his or her obsession. And feminist sociologists contend that prostitution, as well as the more disturbing aspects of pornography, reinforce the misconception that women are "toys" who can be treated as objects rather than people. According to critics of decriminalization, society must not give tacit approval to conduct that has such harmful consequences (Melissa Farley and Malarek 2008).

The controversy over decriminalization reminds us of the important insights of labeling and conflict theorists presented earlier. Underlying this debate are two questions: Who has the power to label gambling, prostitution, and public drunkenness as "crimes"? and Who has the power to label such behaviors as "victimless"? The answer is generally the state legislatures, and in some cases, the police and the courts.

Professional Crime

Although the adage "Crime doesn't pay" is familiar, many people do make a career of illegal activities. A **professional criminal,** or *career criminal,* is a person who pursues crime as a day-to-day occupation, developing skilled techniques and enjoying a certain degree of status among other criminals. Some professional criminals specialize in burglary, safecracking, hijacking of cargo, pickpocketing, and shoplifting. Such people have acquired skills that reduce the likelihood of arrest, conviction, and imprisonment. As a result, they may have long careers in their chosen professions.

Edwin Sutherland (1937) offered pioneering insights into the behavior of professional criminals by publishing an annotated account written by a professional thief. Unlike the person who engages in crime only once or twice, professional thieves make a business of stealing. They devote their entire working time to planning and executing crimes, and sometimes travel across the nation to pursue their "professional duties." Like people in regular occupations, professional thieves consult with their colleagues concerning the demands of work, becoming part of a subculture of similarly occupied individuals. They exchange information on places to burglarize, on outlets for unloading stolen goods, and on ways of securing bail bonds if arrested.

Organized Crime

A 1976 government report devotes three pages to defining the term *organized crime.* For our purposes, we will consider **organized crime** to be the work of a group that regulates relations among criminal enterprises involved in illegal activities,

Sociology on Campus

BOX 25-1

Campus Crime

According to a national survey released in 2008, 72 percent of college students consider campus safety "very important" in selecting a college. A generation earlier, would campus crime have been uppermost in the minds of prospective students?

Research on crime in college has focused on interpersonal violence ("date rape," as it is sometimes trivialized) and the way in which colleges handle such incidents. In 2007, two very different events brought campus crime to national attention. First, there was the April 16, 2007, rampage at Virginia Tech. In its aftermath, observers questioned whether campus officials should have notified students and employees of the first shootings, at a dormitory, during the two hours that passed before the gunman's second attack in a classroom building. The federal law known as the Clery Act, passed in 1990, requires timely warnings of campus crime, but how they should be delivered and how specific they should be (for example, whether the names of alleged assailants should be revealed) is unclear.

The second incident, the death of a girl in her dormitory room at Eastern Michigan University, led to the resignation of the university's president. For two months, officials had assured her parents that she died a natural death. Later, her family learned that she had been raped and murdered, and that her body had been missing for three days.

These and other less publicized incidents have prompted colleges to become more forthcoming about campus crime and to provide better security. However, the growing trend toward living (and partying) off campus poses a challenge to their efforts. Student safety at internship sites and study-abroad programs is even more difficult to ensure.

Making judgments about campus crime based on the reports mandated by the Clery Act is difficult. Because these documents include only reported incidents, they may or may not be accurate. The latest data from the University of California, which has over 20,000 students, for example, show that the total number of forcible sex offenses per year ranges from 2 to more than 62.

> The federal law known as the Clery Act, passed in 1990, requires timely warnings of campus crime, but how they should be delivered and how specific they should be is unclear.

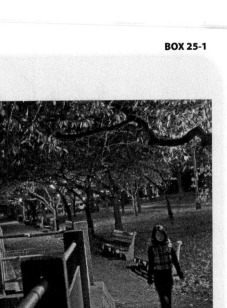

campus, and how does it compare to crime rates at other schools? Relate what you have learned to sociological theory.

2. What have officials at your college done to discourage campus crime?

LET'S DISCUSS

1. Do some research on campus crime. What is the crime rate on your college

Sources: Department of Justice 2009; Interface Group Report (Virginia Tech) 2007; Lipka 2009; National Institute of Justice 2005; *New York Times* 2007, 2008; Security on Campus 2008.

---

including prostitution, gambling, and the smuggling and sale of illegal drugs. Organized crime dominates the world of illegal business just as large corporations dominate the conventional business world. It allocates territory, sets prices for goods and services, and acts as an arbitrator in internal disputes. A secret, conspiratorial activity, it generally evades law enforcement. It takes over legitimate businesses, gains influence over labor unions, corrupts public officials, intimidates witnesses in criminal trials, and even "taxes" merchants in exchange for "protection" (National Advisory Commission on Criminal Justice 1976).

Organized crime serves as a means of upward mobility for groups of people struggling to escape poverty. Sociologist Daniel Bell (1953) used the term *ethnic succession* to describe the sequential passage of leadership from Irish Americans in the early part of the 20th century to Jewish Americans in the 1920s and then to Italian Americans in the early 1930s. Ethnic succession has become more complex, reflecting the diversity of the nation's latest immigrants. Colombian, Mexican, Russian,

Chinese, Pakistani, and Nigerian immigrants are among those who have begun to play a significant role in organized crime activities (Chin 1996; Kleinknecht 1996).

White-Collar and Technology-Based Crime

Income tax evasion, stock manipulation, consumer fraud, bribery and extraction of kickbacks, embezzlement, and misrepresentation in advertising—these are all examples of **white-collar crime,** illegal acts committed in the course of business activities, often by affluent, "respectable" people. Edwin Sutherland (1949, 1983) likened these crimes to organized crime because they are often perpetrated through occupational roles.

A new type of white-collar crime has emerged in recent decades: computer crime. The use of high technology allows criminals to carry out embezzlement or electronic fraud, often leaving few traces, or to gain access to a company's inventory without leaving home. According to a study by the FBI and the

"KICKBACKS, EMBEZZLEMENT, PRICE-FIXING, BRIBERY... THIS IS AN EXTREMELY HIGH-CRIME AREA."

National White Collar Crime Center, over 300,000 Internet crimes are reported every year, ranging from scams on online auction sites to identity theft (Internet Crime Complaint Center 2011).

When Charles Horton Cooley spoke of the self and Erving Goffman of impression management, surely neither scholar could have envisioned the insidious crime of identity theft. Each year about 14 percent of all adults find that their personal information has been misused for criminal purposes. Unfortunately, with our society's growing reliance on electronic financial transactions, assuming someone else's identity has become increasingly easy (Vamosi et al. 2010).

Identity theft does not necessarily require technology. A criminal can obtain someone's personal information by pickpocketing or by intercepting mail. However, the widespread exchange of information online has allowed criminals to access large amounts of personal information. Public awareness of the potential harm from identity theft took a giant leap in the aftermath of September 11, 2001, when investigations revealed that several hijackers had used fraudulent IDs to open bank accounts, rent apartments, and board planes. A law enacted in 2004 makes identity theft punishable by a mandatory prison sentence if it is linked to other crimes. Still, unauthorized disclosures of information, even if accidental, persist (Brubaker 2008).

Sutherland (1940) coined the term *white-collar crime* in 1939 to refer to acts by individuals, but the term has been broadened more recently to include offenses by businesses and corporations as well. *Corporate crime,* or any act by a corporation that is punishable by the government, takes many forms and includes individuals, organizations, and institutions among its victims. Corporations may engage in anticompetitive behavior, environmental

pollution, medical fraud, tax fraud, stock fraud and manipulation, accounting fraud, the production of unsafe goods, bribery and corruption, and health and safety violations (J. Coleman 2006).

For many years, corporate wrongdoers got off lightly in court by documenting their long history of charitable contributions and agreeing to help law enforcement officials find other white-collar criminals. Unfortunately, that is still the case. The highly visible jailing of multimedia personality Martha Stewart in 2004, as well as recent disclosures of "Wall Street greed," may lead the casual observer to think that government is cracking down on white-collar crime. However, an independent analysis found that from 2000 through 2009, the number of white-collar crimes that were prosecuted increased only modestly (Transactional Records Access Clearinghouse 2009).

The leniency shown to white-collar criminals is not limited to the United States. Japan did not level a fine for insider trading on a major financial corporation until 2012. The profit from the crime was about $119,000; the penalty was $600 (Fukase and Inagaki 2012).

Even when a person is convicted of corporate crime, the verdict generally does not harm his or her reputation and career aspirations nearly so much as conviction for street crime would. Apparently, the label "white-collar criminal" does not carry the stigma of the label "felon convicted of a violent crime." Conflict theorists don't find such differential treatment surprising. They argue that the criminal justice system largely disregards the crimes of the affluent, focusing on crimes committed by the poor. Generally, if an offender holds a position of status and influence, his or her crime is treated as less serious, and the sanction is much more lenient.

Hate Crime

In contrast to other crimes, hate crimes are defined not only by the perpetrators' actions, but by the purpose of their conduct. The government considers an ordinary crime to be a **hate crime** when the offender is motivated to choose a victim based on race, religion, ethnic group, national origin, or sexual orientation, and when evidence shows that hatred prompted the offender to commit the crime. Hate crimes are sometimes referred to as *bias crimes* (Department of Justice 2008).

In 1990, Congress passed the Hate Crimes Statistics Act, which created a national mandate to identify crimes based on race, religion, ethnic group, and national origin. (Before that time, only 12 states had monitored such crimes.) Since then the act has been broadened to include disabilities, both physical and mental, and sexual orientation. In addition, some jurisdictions impose harsher sanctions (jail time or fines) for hate crimes than for other crimes. For example, if the penalty for assault is a year in jail, the penalty for an assault identified as a hate crime might be two years.

In 2011, law enforcement agencies submitted data on hate crimes to the federal government. The statistics included official reports of more than 7,600 hate crimes and bias-motivated incidents. As Figure 25-1 shows, race was the apparent motivation in approximately 47 percent of the reports. Although vandalism and intimidation were the most common crimes, 40 percent of the incidents involved assault, rape, or murder.

FIGURE 25-1 **Categorization of Reported Hate Crimes**

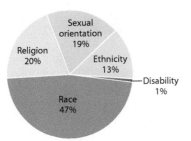

Source: Incidents reported for 2010 in 2011. Department of Justice 2011b.

The vast majority of hate crimes, although not all of them, are committed by members of the dominant group against those who are relatively powerless. One in every six racially based hate crimes is an anti-White incident. Except for the most horrific hate crimes, these offenses receive little media attention; anti-White incidents probably receive even less. Clearly, hostility based on race knows no boundaries (Department of Justice 2011b).

Transnational Crime

More and more, scholars and police officials are turning their attention to **transnational crime,** or crime that occurs across multiple national borders. In the past, international crime was often limited to the clandestine shipment of goods across the border between two countries. But increasingly, crime is no more restricted by such borders than is legal commerce. Rather than concentrating on specific countries, international crime now spans the globe.

Historically, probably the most dreadful example of transnational crime has been slavery. At first, governments did not regard slavery as a crime, but merely regulated it as they would the trade in goods. In the 20th century, transnational crime grew to embrace trafficking in endangered species, drugs, and stolen art and antiquities.

Transnational crime is not exclusive of some of the other types of crime we have discussed. For example, organized criminal networks are increasingly global. Technology definitely facilitates their illegal activities, such as trafficking in child pornography. Beginning in the 1990s, the United Nations began to categorize transnational crimes; Table 25-1 lists some of the more common types.

Bilateral cooperation in the pursuit of border criminals such as smugglers has been common for many years. The first global effort to control international crime was the International Criminal Police Organization (Interpol), a cooperative network of European police forces founded to stem the movement of political revolutionaries across borders. While such efforts to fight transnational crime may seem lofty—an activity with which any government should cooperate—they are complicated by sensitive legal and security issues. Most nations that have signed protocols issued by the United Nations, including the United States, have expressed concern over potential encroachments on their national judicial systems, as well as concern over their national

security. Thus, they have been reluctant to share certain types of intelligence data. The terrorist attacks of September 11, 2001, increased both the interest in combating transnational crime and sensitivity to the risks of sharing intelligence data (Deflem 2005; Felson and Kalaitzidis 2005).

💡 use your **sociological imagination**

As the editor of an online news service, how might you treat stories on corporate or white-collar crime differently from those on violent crime?

⬤ Crime Statistics

Crime statistics are not as accurate as social scientists would like, especially since they deal with an issue of grave concern to the people of the United States. Unfortunately, they are frequently cited as if they were completely reliable. Such data do serve as an indicator of police activity, as well as an approximate indication of the level of certain crimes. Yet it would be a mistake to interpret these data as an exact representation of the incidence of crime.

Index Crimes and Victimization Surveys

Typically, the crime data reported in the United States are based on **index crimes,** or the eight types of crime tabulated each year by the Federal Bureau of Investigation (FBI). This category of criminal behavior generally consists of those serious offenses that people think of when they express concern about the nation's crime problem. Index crimes include murder, rape, robbery, and assault—all of which are violent crimes committed against people—as well as the property crimes of burglary, larceny-theft, motor vehicle theft, and arson (Table 25-2). The crime index is published annually by the FBI as part of the *Uniform Crime Reports.*

Table **25-1** **Types of Transnational Crime**

Bankruptcy and insurance fraud
Computer crime (treating computers as both a tool and a target of crime)
Corruption and bribery of public officials
Environmental crime
Hijacking of airplanes (skyjacking)
Illegal drug trade
Illegal money transfers (money laundering)
Illegal sales of firearms and ammunition
Infiltration of legal businesses
Intellectual property crime
Networking of criminal organizations
Sea piracy
Terrorism
Theft of art and cultural objects
Trafficking in body parts (includes illegal organ transplants)
Trafficking in human beings (includes sex trade)

Source: Compiled and updated by the author based on Mueller 2001 and United Nations Office on Drugs and Crime 2010.

Table **25-2** National Crime Rates and Percentage Change

Crime Index Offenses in 2010	Number Reported	Rate per 100,000 Inhabitants	Percentage Change in Rate since 2001
Violent crime			
Murder	14,748	5	−15
Forcible rape	84,767	28	−14
Robbery	367,832	119	−20
Aggravated assault	778,901	252	−21
Total	1,246,248	404	−20
Property crime			
Burglary	2,159,878	700	−6
Larceny-theft	6,185,867	2,004	−19
Motor vehicle theft	737,142	239	−40
Total	9,082,887	2,942	−20

Notes: Arson was designated an index offense beginning in 1979; data on arson were still incomplete as of 2012. Because of rounding, the offenses may not add to totals.
Source: Department of Justice 2011a: Tables 1, 1a.

Obviously, many serious offenses, such as white-collar crimes, are not included in this index (although they are recorded elsewhere). In addition, the crime index is disproportionately devoted to property crimes, whereas most citizens are more worried about violent crimes. Thus, a significant decrease in the number of rapes and robberies could be overshadowed by a slightly larger increase in the number of automobiles stolen, leading to the mistaken impression that *personal* safety is more at risk than before.

The most serious limitation of official crime statistics is that they include only those crimes actually *reported* to law enforcement agencies. Because members of racial and ethnic minority groups often distrust law enforcement agencies, they may not contact the police. Feminist sociologists and others have noted that many women do not report rape or spousal abuse out of fear they will be blamed for the crime.

Partly because of these deficiencies in official statistics, the National Crime Victimization Survey was initiated in 1972. The Bureau of Justice Statistics, in compiling this annual report, seeks information from law enforcement agencies, but also interviews households across the nation and asks if they were victims of a specific set of crimes during the preceding year. In general, those who administer **victimization surveys** question ordinary people, not police officers, to determine whether they have been victims of crime.

Taking Sociology to Work

Stephanie Vezzani, *Special Agent, U.S. Secret Service*

Stephanie Vezzani wasn't sure what she wanted to major in when she entered the University of Akron, but she did know what she wanted to do with her life: she wanted a career as a crime fighter. Vezzani began as an accounting major, but switched to sociology when she discovered the department offered a special concentration in law enforcement.

Vezzani is now an agent with the U.S. Secret Service, whose twofold mission is to protect high-ranking officials and their families and to investigate financial crimes, including counterfeiting, identity theft, and computer-based attacks on the financial, banking, and telecommunications industries. She has tackled both aspects of the job. For her, a typical week would include working on a criminal investigation in a field office or traveling around the country with a government official in need of protection.

Vezzani finds that travel is one of the most exciting aspects of her job. Over the past six years she has visited Russia, Turkey, Jordan, Vietnam, and South Korea. She also attended the 2002 Winter Olympics in Salt Lake City, where she provided protection for the athletes living in the Olympic Village. Vezzani relishes meeting people from different cultures, and of course she loves the sights she gets to see. "The architecture in St. Petersburg, Russia, was amazing," she says.

Vezzani uses her training in sociology on a daily basis, as she interviews suspects, witnesses, and victims of crime. "It is critical in the field of law enforcement to have an understanding of people's relationships and the beliefs and value systems that contribute to their decision making," she explains. "Sociology has provided me the knowledge to speak to and listen to people with different values and cultures in order to complete my job at the highest level possible."

LET'S DISCUSS

1. Besides an awareness of different beliefs, values, and cultures, what else might sociology offer to those who serve in law enforcement?

2. Law enforcement is a relatively new career option for women. What special strengths do you think a woman might bring to police work?

Unfortunately, like other crime data, victimization surveys have particular limitations. They require that victims understand what has happened to them and are willing to disclose such information to interviewers. Fraud, income tax evasion, and blackmail are examples of crimes that are unlikely to be reported in victimization studies.

Crime Trends

Crime fills the news reports on television, over the Internet, and in the newspaper. As a result, the public regards crime as a major social problem. Yet there has been a significant decline in violent crime in the United States in recent years, after many years of increases.

How much has crime declined? Consider this: the rate of crime being reported in 2012 was comparable to what it was back when gasoline cost 29 cents a gallon and the average person earned less than $6,000 a year. That was 1963.

Dramatic declines have occurred within the last decade. As Table 25-2 shows, both violent crime and property crime dropped 20 percent in the last 10 years. Although a tragic 14,748 people were murdered in 2010, in 1991 that number was a staggering 24,700. Declines have also been registered in victimization surveys (Figure 25-2).

What explains these declines in both index crimes and victimization rates? Possible explanations include the following:

- Community-oriented policing and crime prevention programs
- New gun control laws
- A massive increase in the prison population, which at least prevents inmates from committing crimes outside prison
- New surveillance technologies
- The decline of the crack cocaine epidemic, which soared in the late 1980s
- The aging of the population, as the number of people in their 50s increased and the number in their 20s decreased

No single explanation could account for such a marked change in crime rates. Taken together, however, these changes in public policy, public health, technology, and demographics may well explain it (Eckberg 2006:5- 223; Florida 2011; James Q. Wilson 2011; Wood 2012; Zimring 2007).

Feminist scholars draw our attention to one significant countertrend: the proportion of major crimes committed by women has increased. However, violent crimes committed by women, which have never been common, have declined. Despite the "mean girls" headlines in the tabloid magazines, every reliable measure shows that among women, fights, weapons possession, assaults, and violent injuries have plunged over the last decade (Males and Lind 2010).

International Crime Rates

If developing reliable crime data is difficult in the United States, making useful cross-national comparisons is even more difficult.

FIGURE 25-2 **Victimization Rates, 1973–2010**

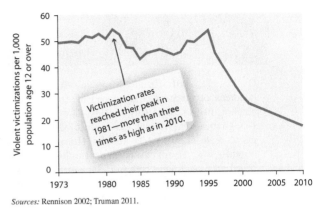

Sources: Rennison 2002; Truman 2011.

Nevertheless, with some care, we can offer preliminary conclusions about how crime rates differ around the world.

During the 1980s and 1990s, violent crimes were much more common in the United States than in western Europe. Murders, rapes, and robberies were reported to the police at much higher rates in the United States. Yet the incidence of certain other types of crime appears to be higher elsewhere. For example, England, Italy, Australia, and New Zealand all have higher rates of car theft than the United States. Developing nations have significant rates of reported homicide due to civil unrest and political conflict among civilians (International Crime Victim Survey 2004; World Bank 2003).

A particularly worrisome development has been the rapid escalation in homicide rates in developing countries that supply drugs to industrialized countries, especially the United States. The huge profits generated by cocaine exports to North America and Europe have allowed drug gangs to arm themselves to the point of becoming illegal armies. Homicide rates in Mexico are now about twice as high as those in the United States. Honduras, Guatemala, Venezuela, and El Salvador's homicide rates are three to five times those of Mexico (*The Economist* 2010c).

Why are rates of violent crime generally so much higher in the United States than in western Europe? Sociologist Elliot Currie (1985, 1998) has suggested that our society places greater emphasis on individual economic achievement than other societies. At the same time, many observers have noted that the culture of the United States has long tolerated, if not condoned, many forms of violence. Coupled with sharp disparities between poor and affluent citizens, significant unemployment, and substantial alcohol and drug abuse, these factors combine to produce a climate conducive to crime.

In the United States, high rates of violent crime, especially in the cities, have long fueled calls for greater use of the death penalty. We will take a close look at the controversy over the ultimate penalty in the Social Policy section that follows.

social policy and Social control | The Death Penalty in the United States and Worldwide

On June 11, 2001, Timothy McVeigh—the man who killed hundreds of innocent people when he bombed the federal building in Oklahoma City in 1995—was executed by the U.S. government. McVeigh was the first federal prisoner to be put to death in nearly four decades. His execution, and that of others who received the death penalty for their crimes, has raised many questions, both from supporters and from critics of capital punishment. How can the government prevent the execution of innocent men and women? Is it right to resort to a punishment that imitates the crime it seeks to condemn? Is life in prison enough of a punishment for a truly heinous crime?

Looking at the Issue

Historically, execution has been a significant form of punishment, both for deviance from social norms and for criminal behavior. In North America, the death penalty has been used for centuries to punish murder, alleged witchcraft, and a few other crimes. Yet for most of that time, little thought was given to its justification; capital punishment was simply assumed to be morally and religiously right. Today, the death penalty is still on the books in most states, where it is used to a greater or lesser extent (Figure 25-3).

In other parts of the world, serious thought has been given to the ethical implications of the ultimate penalty. As of 2012, 97 nations had abolished capital punishment; many more use it only sparingly, if at all (Figure 25-4).

Applying Sociology

Traditionally, the debate over the death penalty has focused on its appropriateness as a form of punishment and its value in deterring crime. Viewed from Émile Durkheim's functionalist perspective, sanctions against deviant acts help to reinforce society's standards of proper behavior. Supporters of capital punishment insist that fear of execution will prevent at least some criminals from committing serious offenses. Moreover, even if it does not serve as a deterrent, they still see the death penalty as justified, because they believe the worst criminals deserve to die for their crimes.

The death penalty also creates some dysfunctions, however. Although many citizens are concerned that the alternative to execution, life in prison, is unnecessarily expensive, sentencing a person to death is not cheap. According to a recent analysis, in California, prosecuting death penalty cases costs $184 million more per year than prosecuting cases involving life without parole. Housing, health care, and legal representation also cost more for convicts on death row than for other inmates (Alarcón et al. 2011).

Conflict theorists counter that the persistence of social inequality in today's society puts poor people at a disadvantage in the criminal justice system. Simply put, the poor cannot

MAPPING LIFE NATIONWIDE

FIGURE 25-3 **Executions by State since 1976**

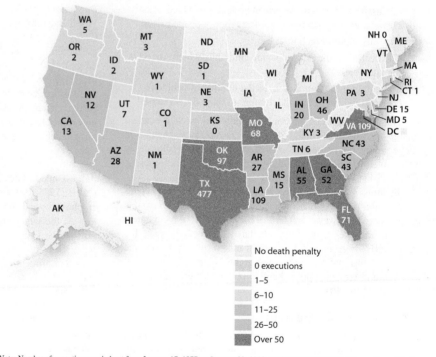

Legend:
- No death penalty
- 0 executions
- 1–5
- 6–10
- 11–25
- 26–50
- Over 50

Note: Number of executions carried out from January 17, 1977, to January 23, 2012, not including three federal executions. Illinois carried out 12 executions before abolishing the death penalty.
Source: Death Penalty Information Center 2012.

—Continued

—Continued

MAPPING LIFE NATIONWIDE

FIGURE 25-4 **Death Penalty Status by Country**

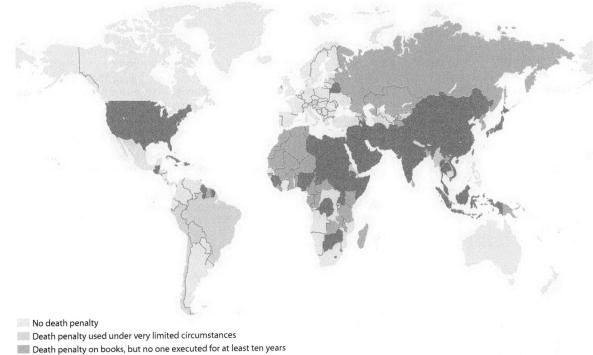

  No death penalty
  Death penalty used under very limited circumstances
  Death penalty on books, but no one executed for at least ten years
  Death penalty in use

Source: Amnesty International 2011.

afford to hire the best lawyers, but must rely instead on court-appointed attorneys, who typically are overworked and underpaid. This unequal access to legal resources may mean the difference between life and death for poor defendants. Indeed, the American Bar Association (1997) has repeatedly expressed concern about the limited defense most defendants who face the death penalty receive. As of late 2010, DNA analysis and other new technologies had exonerated 17 death row inmates.

Another issue of crucial concern to conflict theorists and researchers is the possibility of racial discrimination. Numerous studies show that defendants are more likely to be sentenced to death if their victims were White rather than Black. About 76 percent of the victims in death penalty cases are White, even though only 50 percent of all murder victims are White. And there is some evidence that Black defendants, who constituted 42 percent of all death row inmates in 2012, are more likely to face execution than Whites in the same legal circumstance. About 60 percent of the 289 who have been exonerated for any reason,

including poor legal defense, are members of minority groups. Evidence exists, too, that capital defendants receive poor legal services because of the racist attitudes of their own defense counsel. While racism is never acceptable, it is particularly devastating in the criminal justice system, where the legal process can result in an execution (Death Penalty Information Center 2012; Innocence Project 2012; Petrie and Coverdill 2010).

Initiating Policy

Many people hesitate to endorse the death penalty, yet when confronted with a horrendous crime, they feel the death penalty should be available, at least in some cases. In most people's minds, for example, Timothy McVeigh's sentence would be an appropriate use of the death penalty, although opinion on this point has fluctuated. In 2011, support for the death penalty was 62 percent—about the same level as when the question was first posed in 1936, in a national survey (Pew Research Center for the People and the Press 2012).

—Continued

—Continued

Recently, policy initiatives have moved in two different directions. In several death penalty states, legislators are considering broadening the range of offenses for which convicted criminals may be sentenced to execution. In these states, child molesters who did not murder their victims could become eligible for the death penalty, along with certain repeat offenders. The countertrend, a movement away from the death penalty, is based on doubts about whether an execution can be carried out humanely.

Legal action has been taken on behalf of those convicted to die, especially by lethal injection, which is used in virtually all death penalty jurisdictions. Concerns about lethal injection range from medical ethics (the injection must be administered by a medical technician) to the effectiveness of the technique, which sometimes takes a long time to cause death. In 2008, the Supreme Court ruled that Kentucky's procedures were constitutional, but specified protocols for the use of chemicals, personnel training, medical supervision, and error risk that apply in all 35 states that use lethal injection (L. Greenhouse 2008).

Surprisingly, only about 40 to 50 death sentences are handed out for the more than 15,000 reported murders that occur every year. Courts continue to address the question of how this ultimate penalty can be administered in a judicially fair manner. Policymakers, however, do not seem concerned with such questions. In recent years, federal and state legislatures have declared additional crimes to be punishable by death, curtailed appeals by death row inmates, and reimbursed far fewer lawyers for their defense of condemned criminals.

Internationally, attention has focused on those nations where executions are relatively common, such as China and Iran. Foes of the death penalty see these nations as violators of human rights. In the United States, which usually regards itself as a champion of human rights, pressure to abolish capital punishment has grown both at home and abroad.

TAKE THE ISSUE WITH YOU

1. Does the death penalty deter crime? If so, why are crime rates in the United States high compared to those in other nations?
2. What is your position on the death penalty—should it be legal or should it be abolished? Explain your reasoning.
3. Should youths who have been convicted of violent crimes be subject to the death penalty? Why or why not?

MODULE 25 | Recap and Review

Summary

Crime is deviation from formal social norms administered by the state.

1. Sociologists differentiate among **victimless crimes** (such as drug use and prostitution), crime committed by **professional criminals, organized crime, white-collar crime,** and **transnational crime.**

2. Crime statistics are among the least reliable social data, partly because so many crimes are not reported to law enforcement agencies. Rates of violent crime are higher in the United States than in other Western societies, although they have been dropping.

3. The death penalty is the ultimate sanction, one that functionalists believe deters serious crime. However, it is applied disproportionately to the economically disadvantaged and to racial minorities. Worldwide, many countries have renounced the death penalty

Thinking Critically

1. Why is it useful to sociologists to have victimization surveys in addition to reported crime data?

2. Apply at least two of the theories discussed in Module 24 to the problem of professional crime. Which theory seems to provide the best explanation?

Key Terms

Crime
Hate crime
Index crime
Organized crime
Professional criminal
Transnational crime
Victimization survey
Victimless crime
White-collar crime

Mastering This Chapter: Deviance, Crime, and Social Control

taking sociology with you

1 Describe the mechanisms of social control, both formal and informal, on your campus. Which is more effective, formal or informal control?

2 Explain the presence of both criminals and law-abiding citizens in an inner-city neighborhood in terms of the interactionist perspective.

3 Pay a visit to your local courthouse and observe a trial by jury from the point of view of a sociologist. Then describe what you saw and heard using sociological concepts.

key terms

Anomie Durkheim's term for the loss of direction felt in a society when social control of individual behavior has become ineffective.

Anomie theory of deviance Robert Merton's theory of deviance as an adaptation of socially prescribed goals or of the means governing their attainment, or both.

Conformity Going along with peers—individuals of our own status who have no special right to direct our behavior.

Control theory A view of conformity and deviance that suggests that our connection to members of society leads us to systematically conform to society's norms.

Crime A violation of criminal law for which some governmental authority applies formal penalties.

Cultural transmission A school of criminology that argues that criminal behavior is learned through social interactions.

Deviance Behavior that violates the standards of conduct or expectations of a group or society.

Differential association A theory of deviance that holds that violation of rules results from exposure to attitudes favorable to criminal acts.

Differential justice Differences in the way social control is exercised over different groups.

Formal social control Social control that is carried out by authorized agents, such as police officers, judges, school administrators, and employers.

Hate crime A criminal offense committed because of the offender's bias against a race, religion, ethnic group, national origin, or sexual orientation. Also referred to as *bias crime*.

Index crimes The eight types of crime tabulated each year by the FBI in the *Uniform Crime Reports*: murder, rape, robbery, assault, burglary, theft, motor vehicle theft, and arson.

Informal social control Social control that is carried out casually by ordinary people through such means as laughter, smiles, and ridicule.

Labeling theory An approach to deviance that attempts to explain why certain people are viewed as deviants while others engaged in the same behavior are not.

Law Governmental social control.

Obedience Compliance with higher authorities in a hierarchical structure.

Organized crime The work of a group that regulates relations among criminal enterprises involved in illegal activities, including prostitution, gambling, and the smuggling and sale of illegal drugs.

Professional criminal A person who pursues crime as a day-to-day occupation, developing skilled techniques and enjoying a certain degree of status among other criminals.

Sanction A penalty or reward for conduct concerning a social norm.

Social constructionist perspective An approach to deviance that emphasizes the role of culture in the creation of the deviant identity.

Social control The techniques and strategies for preventing deviant human behavior in any society.

Social disorganization theory The theory that crime and deviance are caused by the absence or breakdown of communal relationships and social institutions.

Societal-reaction approach Another name for *labeling theory*.

Stigma A label used to devalue members of certain social groups.

Transnational crime Crime that occurs across multiple national borders.

Victimization survey A questionnaire or interview given to a sample of the population to determine whether people have been victims of crime.

Victimless crime A term used by sociologists to describe the willing exchange among adults of widely desired but illegal goods and services.

White-collar crime Illegal acts committed by affluent, "respectable" individuals in the course of business activities.

self quiz

Read each question carefully and then select the best answer.

1. Society brings about acceptance of basic norms through techniques and strategies for preventing deviant human behavior. This process is termed
   a. stigmatization.
   b. labeling.
   c. law.
   d. social control.

2. Which sociological perspective argues that people must respect social norms if any group or society is to survive?
   a. the conflict perspective
   b. the interactionist perspective
   c. the functionalist perspective
   d. the feminist perspective

3. Stanley Milgram used the word *conformity* to mean
   a. going along with peers.
   b. compliance with higher authorities in a hierarchical structure.
   c. techniques and strategies for preventing deviant human behavior in any society.
   d. penalties and rewards for conduct concerning a social norm.

4. Which sociological theory suggests that our connection to members of society leads us to conform systematically to society's norms?
   a. feminist theory
   b. control theory
   c. interactionist theory
   d. functionalist theory

5. Which of the following statements is true of deviance?
   a. Deviance is always criminal behavior.
   b. Deviance is behavior that violates the standards of conduct or expectations of a group or society.
   c. Deviance is perverse behavior.
   d. Deviance is inappropriate behavior that cuts across all cultures and social orders.

6. Which sociologist illustrated the boundary-maintenance function of deviance in his study of Puritans in 17th-century New England?
   a. Kai Erikson
   b. Émile Durkheim
   c. Robert Merton
   d. Edwin Sutherland

7. Which of the following is *not* one of the basic forms of adaptation specified in Robert Merton's anomie theory of deviance?
   a. conformity
   b. innovation
   c. ritualism
   d. hostility

8. Which sociologist first advanced the idea that an individual undergoes the same basic socialization process whether learning conforming or deviant acts?
   a. Robert Merton
   b. Edwin Sutherland
   c. Travis Hirschi
   d. William Chambliss

9. Which of the following theories contends that criminal victimization increases when communal relationships and social institutions break down?
   a. labeling theory
   b. conflict theory
   c. social disorganization theory
   d. differential association theory

10. Which of the following conducted observation research on two groups of high school males (the Saints and the Roughnecks) and concluded that social class played an important role in the varying fortunes of the two groups?
    a. Richard Quinney
    b. Edwin Sutherland
    c. Émile Durkheim
    d. William Chambliss

11. If we fail to respect and obey social norms, we may face punishment through informal or formal _____.

12. Police officers, judges, administrators, employers, military officers, and managers of movie theaters are all instruments of _____ social control.

13. Some norms are considered so important by a society that they are formalized into _____ controlling people's behavior.

14. It is important to underscore the fact that _____ is the primary source of conformity and obedience, including obedience to law.

15. _____ is a state of normlessness that typically occurs during a period of profound social change and disorder, such as a time of economic collapse.

16. Labeling theory is also called the _____ _____ approach.

17. _____ theorists view standards of deviant behavior as merely reflecting cultural norms, whereas _____ and _____ theorists point out that the most powerful groups in a society can shape laws and standards and determine who is (or is not) prosecuted as a criminal.

18. Feminists contend that prostitution and some forms of pornography are not _____ crimes.

19. Daniel Bell used the term _____ _____ to describe the process during which leadership of organized crime was transferred from Irish Americans to Jewish Americans and later to Italian Americans and others.

20. Consumer fraud, bribery, and income tax evasion are considered _____ _____ crimes.

Answers
1 (d); 2 (c); 3 (a); 4 (b); 5 (b); 6 (a); 7 (d); 8 (b); 9 (c); 10 (d); 11 sanctions; 12 formal; 13 laws; 14 socialization; 15 Anomie; 16 societal-reaction; 17 Functionalist, conflict, labeling; 18 victimless; 19 ethnic succession; 20 white-collar

thinking about movies

Temple Grandin

An autistic woman fights for animal rights.

Shame

A man struggles to keep his life together while coping with a sex addiction.

American Gypsy

This documentary sheds light on the Romani, a minority group whose members are often stereotyped as criminals.

Stratification and Social Mobility in the United States

8

Stratification and Social Mobility in the United States

MODULE **26** Systems of Stratification

MODULE **27** Stratification by Social Class

MODULE **28** Poverty and Social Mobility

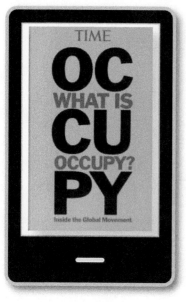

What does the Occupy Wall Street (OWS) movement say about American society?

Rana Foroohar, Assistant Managing Editor at *Time*, thinks that the movement voices our fear and anger over the loss of the American dream.

❝ America's story, our national mythology, is built on the idea of being an opportunity society. From the tales of Horatio Alger to the real lives of Henry Ford and Mark Zuckerberg, we have defined our country as a place where everyone, if he or she works hard enough, can get ahead. We may be poor today, but as long as there's a chance that we can be rich tomorrow, things are O.K.

But does America still work like that? The suspicion that the answer is no inspires not only the Occupy Wall Street (OWS) protests that have spread across the nation and beyond but also a movement as seemingly divergent as the Tea Party. While OWS may focus its anger on rapacious bankers, and the Tea Party on spendthrift politicians, both would probably agree that there's a cabal of entitled elites on Wall Street and in Washington who have somehow loaded the dice and made it impossible for average people to get ahead. The American Dream, like our economy, has become bifurcated.

Certainly the numbers support the idea that for most people, it's harder to get ahead than it's ever been in the postwar era. Inequality in the U.S., always high compared with that in other developed countries, is rising. The 1% decried by OWS takes home 21% of the country's income and accounts for 35% of its wealth. Wages, which have stagnated in real terms since the 1970s, have been falling for much of 2011, in part because of pervasively high unemployment. For the first time in 20 years, the percentage of the population employed in the U.S. is lower than in the U.K., Germany and the Netherlands.

We don't peg ourselves to our parents; we peg ourselves to the Joneses. . . . By that standard, we aren't doing very well at all.

The obvious question is, What happened? The answers, like social mobility itself, are nuanced and complex. You can argue about what kind of mobility really matters. Many conservatives, for example, would be inclined to emphasize absolute mobility, which means the extent to which people are better off than their parents were at the same age. That's a measure that focuses mostly on how much economic growth has occurred, and by that measure, the U.S. does fine. Two-thirds of 40-year-old Americans live in households with larger incomes, adjusted for inflation, than their parents had at the same age (though the gains are smaller than they were in the previous generation).

But just as we don't feel grateful to have indoor plumbing or multichannel digital cable television, we don't necessarily feel grateful that we earn more than our parents did. That's because we don't peg ourselves to our parents; we peg ourselves to the Joneses. Behavioral economics tells us that our sense of well-being is tied not to the past but to how we are doing compared with our peers. Relative mobility matters. By that standard, we aren't doing very well at all. Having the right parents increases your chances of ending up middle to upper middle class by a factor of three or four.

There are many reasons for the huge and growing wealth divide in our country. The rise of the money culture and bank deregulation in the 1980s and '90s certainly contributed to it. As the financial sector grew in relation to the rest of the economy (it's now at historic highs of about 8%), a winner-take-all economy emerged. Wall Street was less about creating new businesses—entrepreneurship has stalled as finance has become a bigger industry—but it did help set a new pay band for top talent. In the 1970s, corporate chiefs earned about 40 times as much as their lowest-paid worker (closer to the norm in many parts of Europe). Now they earn more than 400 times as much. ❞

(Foroohar 2011:77, 78, 79, 80) Additional information about this excerpt can be found on the Online Learning Center at www.mhhe.com/schaefermod2e.

The Occupy Wall Street movement began in Vancouver, Canada, after the editors of *Adbusters* magazine suggested a protest against "corporate rule" in lower Manhattan. Their call to action went out in a tweet ending with "#occupywallstreet."

On the first day of the movement, September 17, 2011, the 2,000 protesters who assembled in New York claimed to represent the vast majority of Americans. In their words, they were "the 99 percent" who had suffered as the wealthiest 1 percent—those earning roughly $500,000 a year—flourished. In the next few weeks, their movement spread across the United States to Honolulu and then throughout the world (Peralta 2011; M. Scherer 2011).

What did Americans make of this new movement? Opinions ran the gamut, from former New York City mayor Rudy Giuliani's sarcastic "How about you occupy a job?" to sociologist Craig Calhoun's comparison to student protests in China. The police response to Occupy Wall Street, Calhoun wrote, was "reminiscent of the Chinese government ousting protesters from Tiananmen." Native Americans observed that their land has been occupied for over five centuries without much notice from White protesters. And the homeless marveled over the sudden concern for people (protesters) sleeping in city parks (Calhoun 2011; K. Lawler 2011).

But is social inequality inescapable? How does government policy affect the life chances of the working poor? Is this country still a place where a hardworking person can move up the social ladder? These modules focus on the unequal distribution of socially valued rewards and its consequences. We will begin by examining four general systems of stratification, including the one most familiar to us, the social class system. We will examine three sociological perspectives on stratification, paying particular attention to the theories of Karl Marx and Max Weber. We'll also ask whether stratification is universal and see what sociologists have to say about that question. We will see how sociologists define social class and examine the consequences of class for people's wealth and income, safety, and educational opportunities. Then we will take a close look at poverty, particularly the question of who belongs to the underclass and why. And we will confront the question of social mobility, both upward and downward. Finally, in the Social Policy section, we will examine the issue of executive compensation—the huge salaries and bonuses that corporate executives earn even when their companies are losing money and employees are losing their jobs.

Ever since people began to speculate about the nature of human society, they have wondered about the differences between individuals and groups. The term **social inequality** describes a situation where different people have different amounts of wealth, prestige, or power.

When a system of social inequality is based on a hierarchy of groups, sociologists refer to it as **stratification:** a structured ranking of entire groups of people that perpetuates unequal economic rewards and power in a society. These unequal rewards are evident, not only in the distribution of wealth and income, but even in the distressing mortality rates of impoverished communities. Stratification involves the ways in which one generation passes on social inequalities to the next, producing groups of people arranged in rank order, from low to high.

Stratification is a crucial subject of sociological investigation because of its pervasive influence on human interactions and institutions. It results inevitably in social inequality, because certain groups of people stand higher in social rankings, control scarce resources, wield power, and receive special treatment. As we will see in Module 27, the consequences of stratification are evident in the unequal distribution of both income and wealth in industrial societies.

Sociologists consider stratification on many levels, ranging from its impact on the individual to worldwide patterns of inequality. No matter where we look, however, disparities in wealth and income are substantial. Take income and poverty patterns in the United States, for example. As the top part of Figure 26-1 shows, in many states the median household income is 25 percent higher than that in other states. And as the bottom part of the figure shows, the poverty rate in many states is 200 percent that of other states. Later in this chapter we will address the meaning of such statistics. We'll begin our discussion here with an overview of the four basic systems of stratification. Then we'll see what sociologists have had to say on the subject of social inequality.

Look at the four general systems of stratification examined here—slavery, castes, estates, and social classes—as ideal types useful for purposes of analysis. Any stratification system may include elements of more than one type. For example, prior to the Civil War, you could find in the southern states of the United States both social classes dividing Whites from Whites and the institutionalized enslavement of Blacks.

To understand these systems better, it may be helpful to review the distinction between *achieved status* and *ascribed status,* explained in Module 16. **Ascribed status** is a social position assigned to a person by society without regard for the person's

unique talents or characteristics. In contrast, **achieved status** is a social position that a person attains largely through his or her efforts. The two are closely linked. The nation's most affluent families generally inherit wealth and status, while many members of racial and ethnic minorities inherit disadvantaged status. Age and gender, as well, are ascribed statuses that influence a person's wealth and social position.

Four Forms of Stratification

Slavery

The most extreme form of legalized social inequality for both individuals and groups is **slavery.** What distinguishes this oppressive system of stratification is that enslaved individuals are *owned* by other people, who treat these human beings as property, just as if they were household pets or appliances.

Slavery has varied in the way it has been practiced. In ancient Greece, the main source of slaves was piracy and captives of war. Although succeeding generations could inherit slave status, it was not necessarily permanent. A person's status might change, depending on which city-state happened to triumph in a military conflict. In effect, all citizens had the potential to become slaves or receive freedom, depending on the circumstances of history. In contrast, in the United States and Latin America, where slavery was an ascribed status, racial and legal barriers prevented the freeing of slaves.

Today, the Universal Declaration of Human Rights, which is binding on all members of the United Nations, prohibits slavery in all its forms. Yet more people are enslaved today than at any point in world history. In many developing countries, bonded laborers are imprisoned in virtual lifetime employment; in some countries, human beings are owned outright. But a form of slavery also exists in Europe and the United States, where guest workers and illegal immigrants have been forced to labor for years under terrible conditions, either to pay off debts or to avoid being turned over to immigration authorities.

Both these situations are likely to involve the transnational crime of trafficking in humans. Each year an estimated 600,000 to 800,000 men, women, and children are transported across international borders for slavery or sexual exploitation. In 2000, the U.S. Congress passed the Trafficking Victims Protection Act, which established minimum standards for the elimination of human trafficking. The act requires the State Department to monitor other countries' efforts to vigorously investigate, prosecute, and convict

MAPPING LIFE NATIONWIDE

FIGURE 26-1   **The 50 States: Contrasts in Income and Poverty Levels**

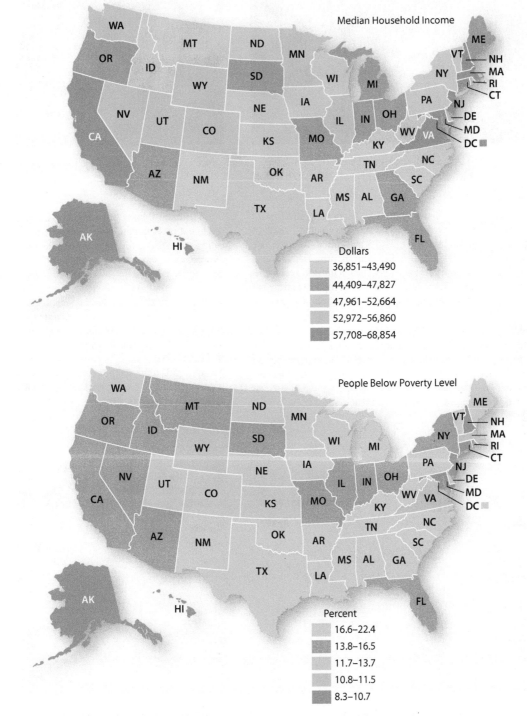

Median Household Income

Dollars

36,851–43,490
44,409–47,827
47,961–52,664
52,972–56,860
57,708–68,854

People Below Poverty Level

Percent

16.6–22.4
13.8–16.5
11.7–13.7
10.8–11.5
8.3–10.7

Note: National median household income was $51,914; national poverty rate, 13.9 percent.

Source: 2010 census data presented in American Community Survey 2011:Tables B19013, S1701.

Reactions to the Occupy movement varied with people's socioeconomic status. "How about you occupy a job?" former New York City mayor Rudy Giuliani (left) retorted. At the other extreme, Native American leaders observed that their lands have been occupied for five centuries.

individuals who participate in trafficking—including government officials. Each year, the department reports its findings, some of which are shown in Table 26-1. Tier 1 and Tier 2 countries are thought to be largely in compliance with the act. Tier 2 Watch countries are making efforts to comply, though trafficking remains a significant concern. Tier 3 countries are not compliant and are not making significant efforts to comply (Bernat and Zhilina 2011).

Castes

Castes are hereditary ranks that are usually religiously dictated and that tend to be fixed and immobile. Caste membership is an ascribed status (at birth, children automatically assume the same position as their parents). Each caste is quite sharply defined, and members are expected to marry within that caste.

The caste system is generally associated with Hinduism in India and other countries. In India there are four major castes, called *varnas*. A fifth category of outcastes, referred to as the *untouchables,* represents 16 percent of the population; its members are considered so lowly and unclean as to have no place within this stratification system. In an effort to avoid perpetuating the historical stigma these people bear, the government now refers to the untouchables as *scheduled castes.* The untouchables themselves prefer *Dalit* ("the repressed"), a term that communicates their desire to overcome their disadvantaged status (P. Smith 2008).

In 1950, after gaining independence from Great Britain, India adopted a new constitution that formally outlawed the caste system. Over the past decade or two, however, urbanization and

Table **26-1**   **Human Trafficking Report**

Tier 1 Full Compliance	Tier 2 Significant Effort	Tier 2 Watch List Some Effort, but Trafficking Remains a Concern	Tier 3 Noncompliant, No Effort
Australia	Bolivia	Afghanistan	Burma
Canada	Brazil	Bahamas	Congo (Dem. Rep.)
Colombia	Cambodia	China	Cuba
Denmark	Chile	Dominican Republic	Iran
France	Greece	Fiji	Mauritania
Germany	India	Malaysia	North Korea
Great Britain	Japan	Panama	Papua New Guinea
Norway	Mexico	Russia	Saudi Arabia
Poland	Philippines	Syria	Sudan
South Korea	South Africa	Ukraine	Venezuela
Spain	Turkey	Vietnam	Zimbabwe

Note: Table is incomplete; each tier lists only a sample of all nations classified. Since the *Human Trafficking Report* is created by the State Department, the level of compliance by the United States is considered to be "full compliance."

Source: Department of State 2011b.

Taking Sociology to Work

Jessica Houston Su, *Research Assistant, Joblessness and Urban Poverty Research Program*

Jessica Houston Su chose sociology as her major "because it was the first class that appealed to my desire to understand the roots of inequality." It also helped her to make sense of what was going on around her at Dartmouth College. "I grew up in a rural, working-class community," she explains, "it was quite a culture shock to attend an affluent, Ivy League college." Learning about social structures and institutions helped Su to navigate through a new environment filled with people from many different backgrounds.

Su went through several potential majors before taking a sociology course and realizing that she was interested in almost every course the department offered. When she was hired for a work-study job in the department, she "soon realized that I was spending a lot of time reading all of the articles I was supposed to be photocopying," she jokes. "It became very obvious to me that I had found my major."

Su works with Harvard University's John F. Kennedy School of Government on a research program directed by the well-known sociologist William Julius Wilson. She is currently assigned to a large-scale longitudinal study of welfare reform in Boston, Chicago, and San Antonio. Her primary responsibility is to analyze the qualitative data from the study, gathered through ethnographic interviews with families who are affected by welfare reform, by searching for themes that might help to explain the study's quantitative data. She finds it exciting to be able to follow the same families over a long period. "I feel like I almost know some of the people," she explains.

Of all the things she learned as a sociology major, Su thinks one of the most important was the concept of social construction. "We consider many things to simply be facts of life," she explains, "but upon further investigation it is clear that most things have been socially constructed in some way." The concept of social construction has helped her to look more carefully at the world around her: "My worldview is much more nuanced and I've gained a much better understanding of how society works, both the good and the bad."

Su uses the research methods she learned in her sociology courses all the time. "I love going to work each day," she says. "I am challenged academically and I feel fulfilled knowing that I am working on something that will benefit society and perhaps influence future policy."

LET'S DISCUSS

1. Did you experience a sense of culture shock when you entered college and were exposed to students from different social classes? If so, has studying sociology helped you to adjust to the diversity in students' backgrounds?

2. Have you begun to see the world differently since you learned about the social construction of reality? If so, what in particular do you see in a different light?

---

technological advances have brought more change to India's caste system than the government or politics has in more than half a century. The anonymity of city life tends to blur caste boundaries, allowing the *Dalit* to pass unrecognized in temples, schools, and places of employment. And the globalization of high technology has opened up India's social order, bringing new opportunities to those who possess the skills and ability to capitalize on them.

Worried about home foreclosures? Not the wealthy. The rich now spend $50,000 to $250,000 on their children's playhouses and tree houses.

The term *caste* can also be applied in recent historical contexts outside India. For example, the system of stratification that characterized the southern United States from the end of the Civil War through the 1960s resembled a caste system. So did the rigid system of segregation that prevailed in the Republic of South Africa under apartheid, from 1948 through the 1990s. In both cases, race was the defining factor that placed a person in the social hierarchy.

Estates

A third type of stratification system, called *estates,* was associated with feudal societies during the Middle Ages. The **estate system**, or *feudalism,* required peasants to work land leased to them by nobles in exchange for military protection and other services. The basis for the system was the nobles' ownership of land, which was critical to their superior and privileged status. As in systems based on slavery and caste, inheritance of one's position largely defined the estate system. The nobles inherited their titles and property; the peasants were born into a subservient position within an agrarian society.

As the estate system developed, it became more differentiated. Nobles began to achieve varying degrees of authority. By the 12th century, a priesthood had emerged in most of Europe, along with classes of merchants and artisans. For the first time there were groups of people whose wealth did not depend on land ownership or agriculture. This economic change had profound social consequences as the estate system ended and a class system of stratification came into existence.

Social Classes

A **class system** is a social ranking based primarily on economic position in which achieved characteristics can influence social mobility. In contrast to slavery and caste systems, the boundaries between classes are imprecisely defined, and one can move from one stratum, or level, of society to another. Even so, class systems maintain stable stratification hierarchies and patterns of class division, and they, too, are marked by unequal distribution of wealth and power. Class standing, although it is achieved, is heavily dependent on family and ascribed factors, such as race and ethnicity.

Sociologist Daniel Rossides (1997) uses a five-class model to describe the class system of the United States: the upper class, the upper-middle class, the lower-middle class, the working class, and the lower class. Although the lines separating social classes in his model are not so sharp as the divisions between castes, members of the five classes differ significantly in ways other than just income level.

Upper and Lower Classes   Rossides characterizes about 1 to 2 percent of the people of the United States as *upper class*. This group is limited to the very wealthy, who associate in exclusive clubs and social circles. In contrast, the *lower class,* consisting of approximately 20 to 25 percent of the population, disproportionately consists of Blacks, Hispanics, single mothers with dependent children, and people who cannot find regular work or must make do with low-paying work. This class lacks both wealth and income and is too weak politically to exercise significant power.

Both these classes, at opposite ends of the nation's social hierarchy, reflect the importance of ascribed status and achieved status. Ascribed statuses such as race and disability clearly influence a person's wealth and social position. People with disabilities are particularly vulnerable to unemployment, are often poorly paid, and tend to occupy the lower rungs of the occupational ladder. Regardless of their actual performance on the job, the disabled are stigmatized as not earning their keep. Such are the effects of ascribed status. We will look again at the plight of the lower class when we consider poverty and welfare policies.

The economist John Kenneth Galbraith (1977:44) observed that "of all classes the rich are the most noticed and the least studied." The poor receive a good deal of attention from reporters, social activists, and policymakers seeking to alleviate their poverty, but the very affluent, who live apart from the rest of the population, are largely a mystery. Since Galbraith's comment, moreover, the residential separation of the rich has grown. The newspaper's society page may give us a peek at members of this class, but we know very little about their everyday lives. Statistically, over 2 million households in the United States are worth more than $10 million each. Less than 10 percent of these people inherited their money, and very few of them are celebrities (Massey 2007).

Middle Class   Sandwiched between the upper and lower classes in this model are the upper-middle class, the lower-middle class, and the working class. The *upper-middle class,* about 10 to 15 percent of the population, includes professionals such as doctors,

lawyers, and architects. They participate extensively in politics and take leadership roles in voluntary associations. The *lower-middle class,* about 30 to 35 percent of the population, includes less affluent professionals (such as elementary school teachers and nurses), owners of small businesses, and a sizable number of clerical workers. While not all members of the middle class hold degrees from a college, they share the goal of sending their children there.

The middle class is currently under a great deal of economic pressure. Close analysis indicates that of those who lost their middle-class standing during the latter 20th century, about half rose to a higher ranking in the social class system, while half dropped to a lower position. These data mean that the United States is moving toward a "bipolar income distribution." That is, a broadly based middle class is slowly being replaced by two growing groups of rich and poor.

Sociologists and other scholars have identified several factors that have contributed to the shrinking size of the middle class:

- *Disappearing opportunities for those with little education.* Today, most jobs require formal schooling, yet less than a third of adults between ages 35 and 44 have prepared themselves with a college degree.

- *Global competition and rapid advances in technology.* These two trends, which began several decades ago, mean that workers are more easily replaced now than they were in the past. Increasingly, globalization and technological advances are affecting the more complex jobs that were once the bread and butter of middle-class workers.

- *Growing dependence on the temporary workforce.* For those workers who have no other job, temporary positions are tenuous at best, because they rarely offer health care coverage or retirement benefits.

Today, the once broadly based middle class is on the defensive and is slowly being squeezed by two growing groups, the rich and the poor.

- *The rise of new growth industries and nonunion workplaces, like fast-food restaurants.* Industries may have added employment opportunities, but they are at the lower end of the wage scale.

Middle-class families want comfortable homes, college degrees for their children, occasional family vacations, affordable health care—the cost of which has been growing faster than inflation—and retirement security. The answer, for many people, is either to go without or to work longer hours at multiple jobs (Billitteri 2009; Blank 2010, 2011; Massey 2007; Thurow 1984).

Working Class Rossides describes the *working class*—about 40 to 45 percent of the population—as people who hold regular manual or blue-collar jobs. Certain members of this class, such as electricians, may have higher incomes than people in the lower-middle class. Yet even if they have achieved some degree of economic security, they tend to identify with manual workers and their long history of involvement in the labor movement of the United States. Of the five classes, the working class is declining noticeably in size. In the economy of the United States, service and technical jobs are replacing those involved in the actual manufacturing or transportation of goods.

Social class is one of the independent or explanatory variables most frequently used by social scientists to shed light on social issues. In later chapters, we will analyze the relationships between social class and child rearing (Module 40), religious affiliation (Module 42), and formal schooling (Module 48), as well as other relationships in which social class is a variable.

Class Warfare With Occupy Wall Street in the headlines, political leaders began to speak of class conflict. To some, the Occupy movement's call for a reduction in social inequality seemed a reply to the federal government's favorable tax treatment of the affluent. Before the recession began, the Bush administration had lowered the income tax rate paid by high-income filers. In 2009, the Tea Party pushed Congress to maintain that tax cut, despite a growing deficit. Others insisted that the affluent actually paid less in taxes than the average citizen, given the many loopholes—offshore bank accounts, and so on—available to them. In Congress, the suggestion that the rich should pay the same effective tax rate as other citizens was met with an angry charge of class warfare.

As we will see shortly, by any statistical measure, the gulf between the rich and everyone else in the United States has grown over the last decade—indeed, over the last 50 years. Yet people do not tend to identify with or see themselves as members of a specific social class. Still, as the rhetoric heated up during the 2012 presidential campaign, and the Occupy Wall Street

movement remained visible, a growing share of the population thought they saw evidence of class conflict. In December 2011, 66 percent of the public (compared to 47 percent in 2009) said they perceived "strong" conflict between the rich and the poor. Younger adults, women, and African Americans were most likely to hold this view. Interestingly, personal income had little to do with such perceptions: the rich were just as likely as the poor to agree with the existence of class conflict (Archer and Orr 2011; Pew Social and Demographic Trends 2012; Skocpol and Williamson 2012).

Sociological Perspectives on Stratification

Sociologists have hotly debated stratification and social inequality and have reached varying conclusions. No theorist stressed the significance of class for society—and for social change—more strongly than Karl Marx. Marx viewed class differentiation as the crucial determinant of social, economic, and political inequality. In contrast, Max Weber questioned Marx's emphasis on the overriding importance of the economic sector, arguing that stratification should be viewed as having many dimensions.

Karl Marx's View of Class Differentiation

Karl Marx was concerned with stratification in all types of human society, beginning with primitive agricultural tribes and continuing into feudalism. However, his main focus was on the effects of economic inequality on all aspects of 19th-century Europe. The plight of the working class made him feel that it was imperative to strive for changes in the class structure of society.

In Marx's view, social relations during any period of history depend on who controls the primary mode of economic production, such as land or factories. Differential access to scarce resources shapes the relationship between groups. Thus, under the feudal estate system, most production was agricultural, and the land was owned by the nobility. Peasants had little choice but to work according to terms dictated by those who owned the land.

Using this type of analysis, Marx examined social relations within **capitalism**—an economic system in which the means of production are held largely in private hands and the main incentive for economic activity is the accumulation of profits. Marx focused on the two classes that began to emerge as the feudal estate system declined, the bourgeoisie and the proletariat. The **bourgeoisie,** or capitalist class, owns the means of production, such as factories and machinery; the **proletariat** is the working class. In capitalist societies, the members of the bourgeoisie maximize profit in competition with other firms. In the process, they exploit workers, who must exchange their labor for subsistence wages. In Marx's view, members of each class share a distinctive culture. Marx was most interested in the culture of the proletariat, but he also examined the ideology of the bourgeoisie, through which that class justifies its dominance over workers.

According to Marx, exploitation of the proletariat will inevitably lead to the destruction of the capitalist system, because the workers will revolt. But first, the working class must develop **class consciousness**—a subjective awareness of common vested interests and the need for collective political action to bring about social change. Often, workers must overcome what Marx termed **false consciousness,** or an attitude held by members of a class that does not accurately reflect their objective position. A worker with false consciousness may adopt an individualistic viewpoint toward capitalist exploitation ("*I* am being exploited by *my* boss"). In contrast, the class-conscious worker realizes that all workers are being exploited by the bourgeoisie and have a common stake in revolution.

For Marx, class consciousness was part of a collective process in which the proletariat comes to identify the bourgeoisie as the source of its oppression. Revolutionary leaders will guide the working class in its struggle. Ultimately, the proletariat will overthrow the rule of both the bourgeoisie and the government (which Marx saw as representing the interests of capitalists) and will eliminate private ownership of the means of production. In Marx's rather utopian view, classes and oppression will cease to exist in the postrevolutionary workers' state.

How accurate were Marx's predictions? He failed to anticipate the emergence of labor unions, whose power in collective bargaining weakens the stranglehold that capitalists maintain over workers. Moreover, as contemporary conflict theorists note, he did not foresee the extent to which political liberties and relative prosperity could contribute to false consciousness. Many workers came to view themselves as individuals striving for improvement within free societies that offer substantial mobility, rather than as downtrodden members of a social class who face a collective fate. Even today, "class warfare" seems to refer more to diminished individual expectations than to a collective identity. Finally, Marx did not predict that Communist Party

A miner peers into the dark at the Logan Orion coal mine in West Virginia's Logan County. Karl Marx would identify coal miners as members of the proletariat, or working class. Even today, miners are poorly compensated for the considerable dangers they face. Such exploitation of the working class is a core principle of Marxist theory.

rule would be established and later overthrown in the former Soviet Union and throughout Eastern Europe. Still, the Marxist approach to the study of class is useful in stressing the importance of stratification as a determinant of social behavior and the fundamental separation in many societies between two distinct groups, the rich and the poor

use your **sociological imagination**

Have you ever been unaware of your true position in society—that is, have you experienced false consciousness? Explain.

Max Weber's View of Stratification

Unlike Karl Marx, Max Weber ([1913–1922] 1947) insisted that no single characteristic (such as class) totally defines a person's position within the stratification system. Instead, writing in 1916, he identified three distinct components of stratification: class, status, and power.

Weber used the term **class** to refer to a group of people who have a similar level of wealth and income. For example, certain workers in the United States try to support their families through minimum-wage jobs. According to Weber's definition, these wage earners constitute a class because they share the same economic position and fate. Although Weber agreed with Marx on the importance of this economic dimension of stratification, he argued that the actions of individuals and groups cannot be understood *solely* in economic terms.

Weber used the term **status group** to refer to people who have the same prestige or lifestyle. An individual gains status through membership in a desirable group, such as the medical

With Mt. Everest in the background, a wealthy golfer plays a shot in a remote location, which he reached by helicopter. Traveling to exotic places to indulge in sports that most people play at home is an example of Thorstein Veblen's concept of conspicuous consumption, a spending pattern common to those at the very top of the social ladder.

profession. But status is not the same as economic class standing. In our culture, a successful pickpocket may belong to the same income class as a college professor. Yet the thief is widely regarded as holding low status, whereas the professor holds high status.

For Weber, the third major component of stratification has a political dimension. **Power** is the ability to exercise one's will over others. In the United States, power stems from membership in particularly influential groups, such as corporate boards of directors, government bodies, and interest groups. Conflict theorists generally agree that two major sources of power—big business and government—are closely interrelated. For instance, many of the heads of major corporations also hold powerful positions in the government or military. The Social Policy section at the end of this chapter examines the executive compensation that the powerful heads of corporations in the United States enjoy.

To summarize, in Weber's view, each of us has not one rank in society but three. Our position in a stratification system reflects some combination of class, status, and power. Each factor influences the other two, and in fact the rankings on these three dimensions often tend to coincide. John F. Kennedy came from an extremely wealthy family, attended exclusive preparatory schools, graduated from Harvard University, and went on to become president of the United States. Like Kennedy, many people from affluent backgrounds achieve impressive status and power.

Interactionist Perspective

Both Karl Marx and Max Weber looked at inequality primarily from a macrosociological perspective, considering the entire society or even the global economy. Marx did suggest the importance of a more microsociological analysis, however, when he stressed the ways in which individuals develop a true class consciousness.

Interactionists, as well as economists, have long been interested in the importance of social class in shaping a person's lifestyle. The theorist Thorstein Veblen (1857–1929) noted that those at the top of the social hierarchy typically convert part of their wealth into **conspicuous consumption**—that is, they purchase goods not to survive but to flaunt their superior wealth and social standing. For example, they may purchase more automobiles than they can reasonably use, or build homes with more rooms than they can possibly occupy. In an element of conspicuous consumption called *conspicuous leisure*, they may jet to a remote destination, staying just long enough to have dinner or view a sunset over some historic locale (Veblen [1899] 1964).

At the other end of the spectrum, behavior that is judged to be typical of the lower class is subject not only to ridicule but even to legal action. Communities have, from time to time, banned trailers from people's front yards and sofas from their front porches. In some communities, it is illegal to leave a pickup truck in front of the house overnight.

Is Stratification Universal?

Must some members of society receive greater rewards than others? Do people need to feel socially and economically superior to others? Can social life be organized without structured inequality? These questions have been debated for centuries, especially among political activists. Utopian socialists, religious minorities, and members of recent countercultures have all attempted to establish communities that to some extent or other would abolish inequality in social relationships.

Social scientists have found that inequality exists in all societies—even the simplest. For example, when anthropologist Gunnar Landtman ([1938] 1968) studied the Kiwai Papuans of New Guinea, at first he noticed little differentiation among them. Every man in the village did the same work and lived in similar housing. However, on closer inspection, Landtman observed that certain Papuans—men who were warriors, harpooners, and sorcerers—were described as "a little more high" than others. In contrast, villagers who were female, unemployed, or unmarried were considered "down a little bit" and were barred from owning land.

Stratification is universal in that all societies maintain some form of social inequality among members. Depending on its values, a society may assign people to distinctive ranks based on their religious knowledge, skill in hunting, physical attractiveness, trading expertise, or ability to provide health care. But why has such inequality developed in human societies? And how much differentiation among people, if any, is actually essential?

Functionalist and conflict sociologists offer contrasting explanations for the existence and necessity of social stratification. Functionalists maintain that a differential system of rewards and punishments is necessary for the efficient operation of society. Conflict theorists argue that competition for scarce resources results in significant political, economic, and social inequality.

Functionalist Perspective

Would people go to school for many years to become physicians if they could make as much money and gain as much respect working as street cleaners? Functionalists say no, which is partly why they believe that a stratified society is universal.

In the view of Kingsley Davis and Wilbert Moore (1945), society must distribute its members among a variety of social positions. It must not only make sure that these positions are filled but also see that they are filled by people with the appropriate talents and abilities. Rewards, including money and prestige, are based on the importance of a position and the relative scarcity of qualified personnel. Yet this assessment often devalues work performed by certain segments of society, such as women's work in the home or in occupations traditionally filled by women, or low-status work in fast-food outlets.

Davis and Moore argue that stratification is universal and that social inequality is necessary so that people will be motivated to fill functionally important positions. But critics say that unequal rewards are not the only means of encouraging people to fill critical positions and occupations. Personal pleasure, intrinsic satisfaction, and value orientations also motivate people to enter particular careers. Functionalists agree, but they note that society must use some type of reward to motivate people to enter unpleasant or dangerous jobs and professions that require a long training period. This response does not address stratification systems in which status is largely inherited, such as slave or caste societies. Moreover, even if stratification is inevitable, the functionalist explanation for differential rewards does not explain the wide disparity between the rich and the poor (R. Collins 1975; Kerbo 2012).

Conflict Perspective

The writings of Karl Marx lie at the heart of conflict theory. Marx viewed history as a continuous struggle between the oppressors and the oppressed, which ultimately would culminate in an egalitarian, classless society. In terms of stratification, he argued that under capitalism, the dominant class—the bourgeoisie—manipulates the economic and political systems in order to maintain control over the exploited proletariat. Marx did not believe that stratification was inevitable, but he did see inequality and oppression as inherent in capitalism (E. O. Wright et al. 1982; E. O. Wright 2011).

Like Marx, contemporary conflict theorists believe that human beings are prone to conflict over scarce resources such as wealth, status, and power. However, Marx focused primarily on class conflict; more recent theorists have extended the analysis to include conflicts based on gender, race, age, and other dimensions. British sociologist Ralf Dahrendorf (1929–2009) is one of the most influential contributors to the conflict approach.

Dahrendorf (1959) has modified Marx's analysis of capitalist society to apply to modern capitalist societies. For Dahrendorf, social classes are groups of people who share common interests resulting from their authority relationships. In identifying the most powerful groups in society, he includes not only the bourgeoisie—the owners of the means of production—but also the managers of industry, legislators, the judiciary, heads of the government bureaucracy, and others. In that respect, Dahrendorf has merged Marx's emphasis on class conflict with Weber's recognition that power is an important element of stratification (Cuff et al. 1990).

Conflict theorists, including Dahrendorf, contend that the powerful of today, like the bourgeoisie of Marx's time, want society to run smoothly so that they can enjoy their privileged positions. Because the status quo suits those with wealth, status, and power, they have a clear interest in preventing, minimizing, or controlling societal conflict.

One way for the powerful to maintain the status quo is to define and disseminate the society's dominant ideology. The term **dominant ideology** describes a set of cultural beliefs and practices that helps to maintain powerful social, economic, and political

As the reality television series *Ice Road Truckers* suggests, long-haul truck drivers take pride in their low-prestige job. According to the conflict perspective, the cultural beliefs that form a society's dominant ideology, such as the popular image of the truck driver as hero, help the wealthy to maintain their power and control at the expense of the lower classes.

interests. For Marx, the dominant ideology in a capitalist society served the interests of the ruling class. From a conflict perspective, the social significance of the dominant ideology is that not only do a society's most powerful groups and institutions control wealth and property; even more important, they control the means of producing beliefs about reality through religion, education, and the media (Abercrombie et al. 1980, 1990; Robertson 1988).

The powerful, such as leaders of government, also use limited social reforms to buy off the oppressed and reduce the danger of challenges to their dominance. For example, minimum-wage laws and unemployment compensation unquestionably give some valuable assistance to needy men and women. Yet these reforms also serve to pacify those who might otherwise rebel. Of course, in the view of conflict theorists, such maneuvers can never entirely eliminate conflict, since workers will continue to demand equality, and the powerful will not give up their control of society.

Conflict theorists see stratification as a major source of societal tension and conflict. They do not agree with Davis and Moore that stratification is functional for a society or that it serves as a source of stability. Rather, conflict sociologists argue that stratification will inevitably lead to instability and social change (R. Collins 1975; L. Coser 1977).

Table 26-2 summarizes and compares the three major perspectives on social stratification.

Lenski's Viewpoint

Let's return to the question posed earlier—Is stratification universal?—and consider the sociological response. Some form of differentiation is found in every culture, from the most primitive to the most advanced industrial societies of our time. Sociologist Gerhard Lenski, in his sociocultural evolution approach, described how economic systems change as their level of technology becomes more complex, beginning with hunting and gathering and culminating eventually with industrial society.

In subsistence-based hunting-and-gathering societies, people focus on survival. While some inequality and differentiation are evident, a stratification system based on social class does not emerge because there is no real wealth to be claimed. As a society advances technologically, it becomes capable of producing a considerable surplus of goods. The emergence of surplus resources greatly expands the possibilities for inequality in status, influence, and power, allowing a well-defined, rigid social class system to develop. To minimize strikes, slowdowns, and industrial sabotage, the elites may share a portion of the economic surplus with the lower classes, but not enough to reduce their own power and privilege.

As Lenski argued, the allocation of surplus goods and services controlled by those with wealth, status, and power reinforces the social inequality that accompanies stratification systems. While this reward system may once have served the overall purposes of society, as functionalists contend, the same cannot be said for the large disparities separating the haves from the have-nots in current societies. In contemporary industrial society, the degree of social and economic inequality far exceeds what is needed to provide for goods and services (Lenski 1966; Nolan and Lenski 2009).

Table 26-2   Sociological Perspectives on Social Stratification

Tracking Sociological Perspectives

	Functionalist	Conflict	Interactionist
Purpose of social stratification	Facilitates filling of social positions	Facilitates exploitation	Influences people's lifestyles
Attitude toward social inequality	Necessary to some extent	Excessive and growing	Influences intergroup relations
Analysis of the wealthy	Talented and skilled, creating opportunities for others	Use the dominant ideology to further their own interests	Exhibit conspicuous consumption and conspicuous leisure

MODULE 26 | Recap and Review

Summary

Stratification is the structured ranking of entire groups of people that perpetuates unequal economic rewards and **power** in a society.

1. Some degree of **social inequality** characterizes all cultures.

2. Systems of social stratification include **slavery, castes,** the **estate system,** and social classes.

3. Karl Marx saw that differences in access to the means of production created social, economic, and political inequality, as well as two distinct classes, owners and laborers.

4. Max Weber identified three analytically distinct components of stratification: **class, status group,** and **power.**

5. Functionalists argue that stratification is necessary to motivate people to fill society's important positions. Conflict theorists see stratification as a major source of societal tension and conflict. Interactionists stress the importance of social class in determining a person's lifestyle.

Thinking Critically

1. What are the differences between slavery and caste systems? What are the similarities?

2. Give some examples of conspicuous consumption among your fellow college students. Which are obvious and which more subtle?

3. In your view, is the extent of social inequality in the United States helpful or harmful to society as a whole? Explain.

Key Terms

Achieved status

Ascribed status

Bourgeoisie

Capitalism

Caste

Class

Class consciousness

Class system

Conspicuous consumption

Dominant ideology

Estate system

False consciousness

Power

Proletariat

Slavery

Social inequality

Status group

Stratification

We continually assess how wealthy people are by looking at the cars they drive, the houses they live in, the clothes they wear, and so on. Yet it is not so easy to locate an individual within our social hierarchies as it would be in slavery or caste systems of stratification. To determine someone's class position, sociologists generally rely on the objective method.

Measuring Social Class

In the **objective method** of measuring social class, class is viewed largely as a statistical category. Researchers assign individuals to social classes on the basis of criteria such as occupation, education, income, and place of residence. The key to the objective method is that the *researcher,* rather than the person being classified, identifies an individual's class position.

The first step in using this method is to decide what indicators or causal factors will be measured objectively, whether wealth, income, education, or occupation. The prestige ranking of occupations has proved to be a useful indicator of a person's class position. For one thing, it is much easier to determine accurately than income or wealth. The term **prestige** refers to the respect and admiration that an occupation holds in a society. "My daughter, the physicist" connotes something very different from "my daughter, the waitress." Prestige is independent of the particular individual who occupies a job, a characteristic that distinguishes it from esteem. **Esteem** refers to the reputation that a specific person has earned within an occupation. Therefore, one can say that the position of president of the United States has high prestige, even though it has been occupied by people with varying degrees of esteem. A hairdresser may have the esteem of his clients, but he lacks the prestige of a corporate executive.

Table 27-1 ranks the prestige of a number of well-known occupations. In a series of national surveys, sociologists assigned prestige rankings to about 500 occupations, ranging from surgeon to panhandler. The highest possible prestige score was 100; the lowest was 0. Surgeon, physician, lawyer, dentist, and college professor were the most highly regarded occupations. Sociologists have used such data to assign prestige rankings to virtually all jobs and have found a stability in rankings from 1925 to the present. Similar studies in other countries have also developed useful prestige rankings of occupations (Nakao and Treas 1994).

Gender and Occupational Prestige

For many years, studies of social class tended to neglect the occupations and incomes of *women* as determinants of social rank.

With more than half of all married women now working outside the home (see Module 35), this approach seems outmoded. How should we judge class or status in dual-career families—by the occupation regarded as having greater prestige, the average, or some other combination of the two? Sociologists—in particular, feminist sociologists in Great Britain—are drawing on new approaches to assess women's social class standing. One approach is to focus on the individual (rather than the family or household) as the basis for categorizing a woman's class position. Thus, a woman would be classified according to her own occupational status rather than that of her spouse (O'Donnell 1992).

Another feminist effort to measure the contribution of women to the economy reflects a more clearly political agenda. International Women Count Network, a global grassroots feminist organization, has sought to give a monetary value to women's unpaid work. Besides providing symbolic recognition of women's role in labor, this value would also be used to calculate pension and other benefits, which are usually based on wages received. The United Nations has placed an $11 trillion price tag on unpaid labor by women, largely in child care, housework, and agriculture. Whatever the figure, the continued undercounting of many workers' contributions to a family and to an entire economy means that virtually all measures of stratification are in need of reform (United Nations Development Programme 1995; United Nations Economic and Social Council 2010; Wages for Housework Campaign 1999).

Multiple Measures

Another complication in measuring social class is that advances in statistical methods and computer technology have multiplied the factors used to define class under the objective method. No longer are sociologists limited to annual income and education in evaluating a person's class position. Today, studies use as criteria the value of homes, sources of income, assets, years in present occupations, neighborhoods, and considerations regarding dual careers. Adding these variables will not necessarily paint a different picture of class differentiation in the United States, but it does allow sociologists to measure class in a more complex and multidimensional way. When researchers use multiple measures, they typically speak of **socioeconomic status (SES),** a measure of social class that is based on income, education, and occupation. To determine the socioeconomic status of a young person, such as a college student under age 25, they use *parental* income, education, and occupation.

Whatever the technique used to measure class, the sociologist is interested in real and often dramatic differences in power, privilege, and opportunity in a society. The study of

Table **27-1**   **Prestige Rankings of Occupations**

Occupation	Score	Occupation	Score
Physician	86	Bank teller	50
College professor	78	Electrician	49
Lawyer	76	Farm manager	48
Dentist	74	Insurance agent	47
Banker	72	Secretary	46
Architect	71	Mail carrier	42
Airline pilot	70	Farmer	41
Clergy	69	Correctional officer	40
Registered nurse	66	Carpenter	40
High school teacher	63	Receptionist	39
Dental hygienist	61	Barber	38
Legislator	61	Child care worker	36
Pharmacist	61	Hotel clerk	32
Elementary school teacher	60	Bus driver	32
Veterinarian	60	Auto body repairer	31
Police officer or detective	60	Truck driver	30
Prekindergarten teacher	60	Salesworker (shoes)	28
Accountant	57	Waiter and waitress	28
Librarian	55	Cook (short-order)	28
Firefighter	53	Bartender	25
Funeral director	52	Garbage collector	17
Social worker	52	Janitor	16
Optician	51	Newspaper vendor	15

Note: 100 is the highest and 0 the lowest possible prestige score.
Source: General Social Survey 2012.

Think about It

Can you name what you think are two more high-prestige occupations? Two more low-prestige occupations?

stratification is a study of inequality. Nowhere is the truth of that statement more evident than in the distribution of income and wealth.

Income and Wealth

By all measures, in the United States **income,** a term that refers to salaries and wages, is distributed unevenly. Nobel Prize–winning economist Paul Samuelson has described the situation in the following words: "If we made an income pyramid out of building blocks, with each layer portraying $500 of income, the peak would be far higher than Mount Everest, but most people would be within a few feet of the ground" (Samuelson and Nordhaus 2010:324).

Recent data support Samuelson's analogy. In 2010, the median household income in the United States was $49,445. In other words, half of all households had higher incomes that year and half had lower incomes. However, this fact does not fully convey the income disparities in our society. We can get some sense of income inequality by contrasting this median (middle) income with the mean arithmetic average, which in 2010 was $67,530. The mean is so much higher than the median because some people make a lot more money than others, which draws the mean up. Thus, the mean is a less useful statistic than the median for describing the average, or typical, income (DeNavas-Walt et al. 2011:33–34).

We can gain additional insight into income inequality in the United States by looking at the relative placement of households within the income distribution. One of the most common ways of doing so is to line up all income-earning households from low to high and then break them into quintiles, or fifths. Because there

FIGURE 27-1 **Mean Household Income by Quintile**

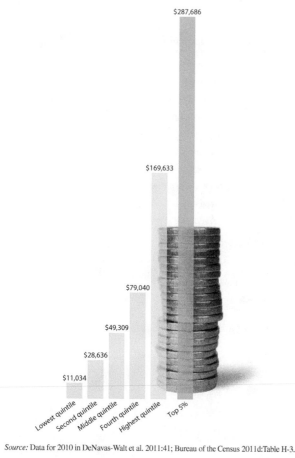

$287,686

$169,633

$79,040

$49,309

$28,636

$11,034

Lowest quintile   Second quintile   Middle quintile   Fourth quintile   Highest quintile   Top 5%

Source: Data for 2010 in DeNavas-Walt et al. 2011:41; Bureau of the Census 2011d:Table H-3.

tax policies favored the affluent. Moreover, while the salaries of highly skilled workers and professionals have continued to rise, the wages of less skilled workers have *decreased* when controlled for inflation.

Just how dramatic has this growth in inequality been? Consider the period between 1984 and 2008. In just 25 years, the following changes occurred in real household income (adjusted for inflation):

- For the lowest 20 percent of the population, income rose 9 percent.
- For the next lowest 20 percent of the population, income rose 10 percent.
- For the middle 20 percent of the population, income rose 13 percent.
- For the next highest 20 percent of the population, income rose 20 percent.
- For the top 20 percent of the population, income rose a whopping 40 percent.

The pattern is clear. Though income has increased for all segments of the population, by far the biggest winners have been the affluent.

Careful economic analysis has shown that over the past 30 years, federal and state tax policies have tended to accentuate the trend toward income inequality. During one 25-year period, the top 1 percent of income earners *after taxes* saw their incomes rise 228 percent, compared to only 21 percent for households in the middle quintile. Little wonder that the middle class is shrinking (Billitteri 2009; Sherman 2007).

trend|spotting

are approximately 118 million households in the United States, each quintile includes an equal number of about 23.4 million households. This method gives us a sense of the average income within each quintile, along with the percentage of the nation's total income earned in each quintile.

As Figure 27-1 shows, looking at the population in this way reveals a significant degree of income inequality. The mean income for households in the lowest quintile is $11,034; in the top quintile, it is $169,633. Those households in the top 5 percent—the ones most responsible for bringing up the arithmetic mean—average a staggering $287,686 in annual income. If we were to move up even higher in the income distribution, we would find that the top 0.01 percent of taxpayers—about 15,000 households—make incomes of at least $11.5 million a year. Collectively, they control 6 percent of the nation's total income (Sloan 2009:27).

There has been a modest redistribution of income in the United States over the past 80 years, but not always to the benefit of the poor or even the middle class. From 1929 through 1970, the government's economic and tax policies shifted some income to the poor. However, in the past four decades—especially in the 1980s and in the decade from 2001 through 2010—federal

Women as Wage Earners

In 2010, for the first time, women outnumbered men in the U.S. workforce. The historic reversal was caused by long-term changes in women's roles that began four decades ago. In the 2008 recession, massive job losses among men tipped the balance.

This change in the trend reflects the growing importance of women as wage earners, although on average, women still work fewer hours than men. They also hold more part-time jobs than men, and they earn only 77 percent of what men make. And of course, men still dominate the higher-paying executive levels of the workforce.

Women's share of the once heavily male labor force has been growing for nearly a century. Big expansions occurred during the Great Depression, when payrolls were limited, and World War II, when millions of men left their jobs to join the service. In 2008, the boost to women's employment came from a severe economic slowdown that hit hard at male-dominated occupations, such as construction and manufacturing.

Although women's outnumbering of men in the labor force may be temporary—an artifact of the recent recession—their transformation of the U.S. workplace is permanent. There are no signs of a countertrend to their participation in the workforce.

Globalization is often blamed for this growing inequality, because it has forced less skilled workers to compete with lower-paid foreign-born workers. While that is true, research suggests that the number of displaced workers who are reemployed at similarly paid or even higher-paid jobs roughly equals the number of workers whose earnings drop (S. Zimmerman 2008a).

Wealth, an inclusive term encompassing all a person's material assets (including land, stocks, and other types of property), is distributed much more unevenly than income in the United States. A 2009 Federal Reserve Bank study showed that half the population controls 2.5 percent of the nation's wealth; the other half controls over 97 percent (Figure 27-2). Put another way, the wealth of the top 1 percent exceeds the collective wealth of the bottom 90 percent.

Researchers have also found a dramatic disparity in the wealth of African Americans and Hispanics compared to that of Whites. The median wealth of White households is now 18 times the median wealth of Latino households and 20 times that of Blacks. Furthermore, evidence suggests that the gap is widening (Pew Social and Demographic Trends 2011; Shapiro et al. 2010).

FIGURE 27-2 **Distribution of Wealth in the United States**

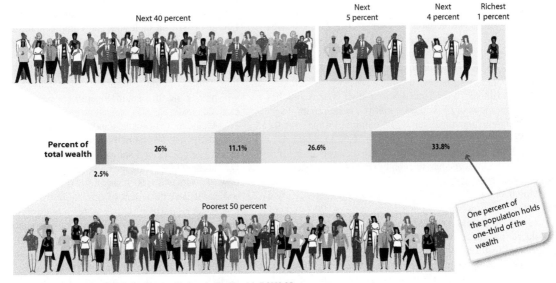

Source: Data for 2007, as reported in a 2009 Federal Reserve Bank study. See Kennickell 2009:35.

MODULE 27 | **Recap and Review**

Summary

One consequence of social class in the United States is that both **income** and **wealth** are distributed unevenly.

1. Sociologists use the **objective method** of measuring social class, which uses criteria such as occupation, education, and income. **Socioeconomic status (SES)** is an objective measure based on these criteria.

2. Regardless of the measure used, income inequality rose from the late 1960s to the end of the 20th century.

Thinking Critically

1. To what degree are students motivated by the prestige of their future occupations?

2. What does the pattern of income distribution in the United States tell you about your own future income? How much can you expect it to grow over the years?

Key Terms

Esteem

Income

Objective method

Prestige

Socioeconomic status (SES)

Wealth

Approximately one out of every nine people in the United States lives below the poverty line established by the federal government. In 2012, no fewer than 46.2 million people were living in poverty. The economic boom of the 1990s passed these people by. A Bureau of the Census report shows that one in five households has trouble meeting basic needs, from paying the utility bills to buying dinner (Bauman 1999; DeNavas-Walt et al. 2011).

One contributor to the United States' high poverty rate has been the large number of workers employed at minimum wage. The federal government has raised the minimum wage over the past half century from 75 cents in 1950 to $6.55 in 2008 and to $7.25 in 2009. But in terms of its real value adjusted for inflation, the minimum wage has frequently failed to keep pace with the cost of living.

Moreover, raising the minimum wage does not remedy other difficulties that low-wage workers encounter. A 2009 survey of workers in various low-wage occupations, such as apparel manufacturing, child care (see Module 15), and discount retailing, showed that these workers lose about 15 percent of the pay that is due them through employers' wage violations. Typically, employers limit workers' wages by pressuring them not to file for workers' compensation after on-the-job injuries, requiring them to work off the clock, and paying the straight hourly wage rate for overtime hours. Women are far more likely than men to be cheated in this way (Bernhardt et al. 2009).

Sociologists have long had an interest in the impact of substandard work on society, beginning with the writings of Karl Marx, Émile Durkheim, and Max Weber. Their interest increased with the global economic decline that began in 2008, which trapped many people in jobs they did not want or left them unemployed. Box 28-1 considers recent sociological work on *precarious work.*

In this section, we'll consider just how social scientists define *poverty.* We'll also take a closer look at the people who fall into that category—including the working poor.

Studying Poverty

The efforts of sociologists and other social scientists to better understand poverty are complicated by the difficulty of defining it. This problem is evident even in government programs that conceive of poverty in either absolute or relative terms. **Absolute poverty** refers to a minimum level of subsistence that no family should be expected to live below.

One commonly used measure of absolute poverty is the federal government's *poverty line,* a money income figure that is adjusted annually to reflect the consumption requirements of families based on their size and composition. The poverty line serves as an official definition of which people are poor. In 2010, for example, any family of four (two adults and two children) with a combined income of $22,113 or less fell below the poverty line. This definition determines which individuals and families will be eligible for certain government benefits (DeNavas-Walt et al. 2011:61).

Although by absolute standards, poverty has declined in the United States, it remains higher than in many other industrial nations. As Figure 28-1 shows, a comparatively high proportion of U.S. households is poor, meaning that they are unable to purchase basic consumer goods. If anything, this cross-national comparison understates the extent of poverty in the United States, since U.S. residents are likely to pay more for housing, health care, child care, and education than residents of other countries, where such expenses are often subsidized (Smeeding 2008).

In contrast, **relative poverty** is a floating standard of deprivation by which people at the bottom of a society, whatever their lifestyles, are judged to be disadvantaged *in comparison with the nation as a whole.* Therefore, even if the poor of 2012 are better off in absolute terms than the poor of the 1930s or 1960s, they are still seen as deserving of special assistance.

Debate has been growing over the accuracy of the federal government's measure of poverty, which has remained largely unchanged since 1963. If noncash benefits such as Medicare, Medicaid, tax credits, food stamps, public housing, and health care and other employer-provided fringe benefits were included, the reported poverty rate would be lower. On the other hand, if out-of-pocket medical expenses and mandatory work expenses for transportation and child care were included, the poverty rate would be higher. Although the current poverty measure does consider family size, it does not consider a household's location, whether in a relatively expensive city like New York or in a less expensive rural area. Nor does it consider whether a householder pays rent or a mortgage installment, lives at home or with someone else. To address some of these shortcomings, in 2010 the federal government launched a second statistic called the Supplemental Poverty Measure (SPM), which will be used to estimate economic hardship. The SPM is a relative poverty measure that is based on a broad range of changing household resources and expenses. It will be calculated beginning in late 2011, but will not replace the poverty line in determining a household's eligibility for benefits (Blank 2011; Wimer et al. 2011).

Research Today

BOX 28-1

Precarious Work

In 2008 Jim Marshall, age 39, lost his job in Detroit's faltering auto industry. Figuring that job prospects had to be better elsewhere, he moved to Florida. But by May 2009 Jim was homeless, living in a tent city just north of St. Petersburg. "My parents always taught me to work hard in school, graduate high school, go to college, get a degree and you'll do fine. You'll do better than your parents' generation," Marshall says. "I did all those things. . . . For a while, I did have that good life, but nowadays that's not the reality" (Bazar 2009:A2).

Jim's story is all too common. He is one of the millions of Americans who have been reduced to doing **precarious work**— employment that is poorly paid, and from the worker's perspective, insecure and unprotected. People who engage in precarious work often cannot support a household, and they are vulnerable to falling into poverty.

Even before economists recognized the economic downturn in 2009, there was ample statistical evidence that precarious work was increasing, despite the fact that the unemployment rate remained steady. In his presidential address to the ASA, Arne L. Kalleberg offered the following five social indicators:

1. *A decline in the average length of time workers remain with an employer.* This trend has been especially noticeable among older White men, who in the past were protected by employers.

2. *An increase in long-term unemployment.* The proportion of workers who remained unemployed after six months rose in the 2000s, when the number of manufacturing jobs shrank and fewer new jobs were created.

3. *A decrease in job security.* Given the increase in long-term unemployment and the decrease in average time spent with an employer, workers became

increasingly insecure about their ability to replace a lost job.

4. *An increase in outsourcing and temporary work.* To meet cyclical fluctuations in supply and demand, employers have turned more and more to nontraditional labor sources. Today, virtually any job can be outsourced, including accounting, legal, and military services.

> To meet cyclical fluctuations in supply and demand, employers have turned more and more to nontraditional labor sources. Today, virtually any job can be outsourced, including accounting, legal, and military services.

5. *A shift in risk from employers to employees.* Few companies offer traditional pensions anymore. Employees are being asked to shoulder at least part of the cost and risk not only of their retirement investments, but of their health insurance plans as well.

Although precarious work is becoming more common, people differ in their vulnerability to it. Members of racial and ethnic minorities are more likely than others to be engaged in precarious work. Immigrants, including those who are in the United States legally, are also more likely than others to be precariously employed. Around the world—in the United States, other industrial countries, and developing nations—women are much more likely than men to do precarious work.

What can be done to revitalize labor markets so that fewer workers end up doing substandard work—or at least, so that those who do will suffer less from it? Denmark is one country that has tried to deal with the problem. Although the government there cannot make jobs more secure, it does provide significant assistance to the unemployed. Help finding a job, significant income compensation (90 percent of a worker's previous wage for one year, without conditions), and subsidized education and training are all available to Danish workers who have lost their jobs.

LET'S DISCUSS

1. Has the trend toward increasing reliance on precarious work touched your family or friends? Has anyone you know been unemployed longer than six months? If so, did that person or persons belong to one or more of the groups that are particularly vulnerable to precarious work?

2. Looking forward to your own career, can you think of a strategy for avoiding precarious work, frequent job loss, and long-term unemployment?

Sources: Bazar 2009; European Metalworkers' Federation 2010; Fudge and Owens 2006; Kalleberg 2009; McDowell et al. 2009; Somavla 2008; Westergaard-Nielsen 2008.

Who Are the Poor?

Not only does the category of the poor defy any simple definition; it counters the common stereotypes about "poor people." For example, many people in the United States believe that the vast majority of the poor are able to work but will not. Yet many poor adults do work outside the home, although only a small portion of them work full-time throughout the year. In 2010, about 40 percent of all poor working adults worked full-time, compared to 65 percent of all adults. Of those poor adults who do not work, most are ill or disabled, or are occupied in maintaining a home (DeNavas-Walt et al. 2011:15).

Though many of the poor live in urban slums, a majority live outside those poverty-stricken areas. Poverty is no stranger in rural areas, from Appalachia to hard-hit farming regions to Native American reservations. Table 28-1 provides additional statistical information regarding low-income people in the United States.

Feminization of Poverty

Since World War II, an increasing proportion of the poor people of the United States have been women, many of whom are divorced or never-married mothers. In 1959, female householders accounted for 26 percent of the nation's poor; by 2010, that figure had risen to 51 percent (see Table 28-1). This alarming trend, known as the **feminization of poverty,** is evident not just in the United States but around the world.

FIGURE 28-1 **Poverty in Selected Countries**

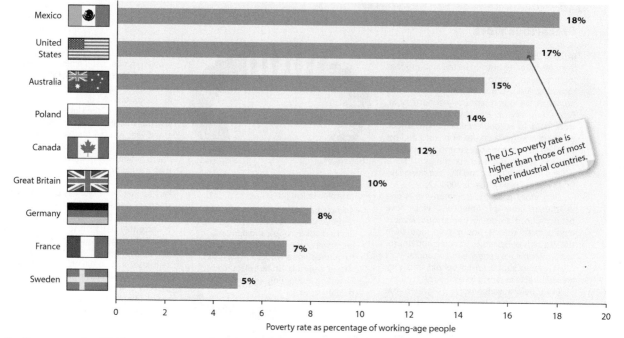

Note: Data are averages for mid-2000s, as reported in 2012. Poverty threshold is 50 percent of a nation's median household income.
Source: Organisation for Economic Co-operation and Development 2012a.

About half of all women living in poverty in the United States are in transition, coping with an economic crisis caused by the departure, disability, or death of a husband. The other half tend to be economically dependent either on the welfare system or on friends and relatives living nearby. A major factor in the feminization of poverty has been the increase in families with women as single heads of the household (see Module 40). Conflict theorists and other observers trace the higher rates of poverty among women to three distinct factors: the difficulty in finding affordable child care, sexual harassment, and sex discrimination in the labor market (Burns 2010).

The Underclass

In 2010, 42 percent of poor people in the United States were living in central cities. These highly visible urban residents are the focus of most government efforts to alleviate poverty. Yet according to many observers, the plight of the urban poor is growing worse, owing to the devastating interplay of inadequate education and limited employment prospects. Traditional employment opportunities in the industrial sector are largely closed to the unskilled poor. Past and present discrimination heightens these problems for those low-income urban residents who are Black or Hispanic.

Along with other social scientists, sociologist William Julius Wilson

Even if this single parent works her way up the chain of command, supporting her family will still be difficult.

(1980, 1987, 1996) and his colleagues (2004) have used the term **underclass** to describe the long-term poor who lack training and skills. According to an analysis of census data, 8.7 million people live in extremely impoverished areas. Although not all of them are poor, living in such disadvantaged neighborhoods means limited educational opportunities, greater exposure to crime and health risks, reduced access to private investment, and higher prices for goods and services. About 45 percent of the population in these neighborhoods is Black, 34 percent Hispanic, and 17 percent White (Kneebone et al. 2011).

Those statistics may sound high, but they could climb higher. Some scholars are predicting that the recent economic downturn may swell the ranks of the underclass, increasing the proportion of the U.S. population that they represent. Indeed, the recession seems to have accelerated the demise of less efficient, less profitable firms. When the downturn is over, jobs will not return to declining industries.

Analyses of the poor in general reveal that they are not a static social class. The overall composition of the poor changes continually, because some individuals and families near the top edge of poverty move above the poverty level after a year or two, while others slip below it.

Still, hundreds of thousands of people remain in poverty for many years at a time. Blacks and Latinos are more likely than Whites to be persistently poor. Both Latinos and Blacks are less likely than Whites to leave the welfare rolls as a result of welfare reform (Jäntti 2009).

Explaining Poverty

Why is it that poverty pervades a nation of such vast wealth? Sociologist Herbert Gans (1995), who has applied functionalist analysis to the existence of poverty, argues that various segments of society actually *benefit* from the existence of the poor. Gans has identified a number of social, economic, and political functions that the poor perform for society:

- The presence of poor people means that society's dirty work—physically dirty or dangerous, dead-end and underpaid, undignified and menial jobs—will be performed at low cost.

- Poverty creates jobs for occupations and professions that serve the poor. It creates both legal employment (public health experts, welfare caseworkers) and illegal jobs (drug dealers, numbers runners).

- The identification and punishment of the poor as deviants upholds the legitimacy of conventional social norms and mainstream values regarding hard work, thrift, and honesty.

- Within a relatively hierarchical society, the existence of poor people guarantees the higher status of the rich. As psychologist William Ryan (1976) noted, affluent people may justify inequality (and gain a measure of satisfaction) by *blaming the victims* of poverty for their disadvantaged condition.

- Because of their lack of political power, the poor often absorb the costs of social change. Under the policy of deinstitutionalization, mental patients released from long-term hospitals have been transferred primarily to low-income communities and neighborhoods. Similarly, halfway houses for rehabilitated drug abusers, rejected by more affluent communities, often end up in poorer neighborhoods.

In Gans's view, then, poverty and the poor actually satisfy positive functions for many nonpoor groups in the United States.

Life Chances

Max Weber saw class as being closely related to people's **life chances**—that is, their opportunities to provide themselves with material goods, positive living conditions, and favorable life experiences (Gerth and Mills 1958). Life chances are reflected in measures such as housing, education, and health. Occupying a higher social class in a society improves your life chances and brings greater access to social rewards. In contrast, people in the lower social classes are forced to devote a larger proportion of their limited resources to the necessities of life. In some cases, life chances are a

Table 28-1   Who Are the Poor in the United States?

Group	Percentage of the Population of the United States	Percentage of the Poor of the United States
Age		
Under 18 years old	24%	35%
18 to 64 years old	63	57
65 years and older	13	8
Race-Ethnicity		
Whites (non-Hispanic)	64	43
Blacks	13	23
Hispanics	16	28
Asians and Pacific Islanders	5	4
Family Composition		
Married couples with male householders	74	39
Female householders	19	51
People with Disabilities	8	16

Source: Data for 2010, as reported by the Bureau of the Census; DeNavas-Walt et al. 2011:15–16.

matter of life and death. According to a medical study published in 2011, in the United States, approximately 133,000 deaths a year can be attributed to individual poverty, and another 119,000 to income inequality. That is over a quarter million deaths per year caused by severely limited resources (Galea et al. 2011).

In times of danger, the affluent and powerful have a better chance of surviving than people of ordinary means. When the supposedly unsinkable British ocean liner *Titanic* hit an iceberg in 1912, it was not carrying enough lifeboats to accommodate all passengers. Plans had been made to evacuate only first- and second-class passengers. About 62 percent of the first-class passengers survived the disaster. Despite a rule that women and children would go first, about a third of those passengers were male. In contrast, only 25 percent of the third-class passengers survived. The first attempt to alert them to the need to abandon ship came well after other passengers had been notified. In an ironic demonstration of continuing social inequality, a luxury travel organization called Bluefish recently charged passengers $60,000 each to view the underwater remains of the *Titanic* from a deep-sea submersible (Butler 1998; Crouse 1999; Dickler 2011; Riding 1998).

Class position also affects people's vulnerability to natural disasters. When Hurricane Katrina hit the Gulf Coast of the United States in 2005, affluent and poor people alike became its victims. However, poor people who did not own automobiles (100,000 of them in New Orleans alone) were less able than others to evacuate in advance of the storm. The poor who survived its fury had no nest egg to draw on, and thus were more likely than others to accept relocation wherever social service agencies could place them—sometimes hundreds or thousands of miles from home. Those who were able to return are still dealing with the toxic debris left behind (Bullard and Wright 2009).

Class position affects people's vulnerability to disasters. When the ill-fated *Titanic* sank in 1912, many more first-class passengers than third-class passengers survived. This photograph, taken recently on the ocean floor, shows the remains of a first-class cabin on the luxury liner.

use your **sociological imagination**

Imagine a society in which there are no social classes—no differences in people's wealth, income, and life chances. What would such a society be like? Would it be stable, or would its social structure change over time?

Wealth, status, and power may not ensure happiness, but they certainly provide additional ways of coping with problems and disappointments. For this reason, the opportunity for advancement—for social mobility—is of special significance to those on the bottom of society. Most people want the rewards and privileges that are granted to high-ranking members of a culture. What can society do to increase their social mobility? One strategy is to offer financial aid to college students from low-income families, on the theory that education lifts people out of poverty. Yet such programs are not having as great an effect as their authors once hoped (Box 28-2).

Social Mobility

In the movie *Maid in Manhattan,* Jennifer Lopez plays the lead in a modern-day Cinderella story, rising from the lowly status of chambermaid in a big-city hotel to a company supervisor and the girlfriend of a well-to-do politician. The ascent of a person from a poor background to a position of prestige, power, or financial reward is an example of social mobility. Formally defined, the term **social mobility** refers to the movement of individuals or groups from one position in a society's stratification system to another. But how significant—how frequent, how dramatic—is mobility in a class society such as the United States?

Open versus Closed Stratification Systems

Sociologists use the terms *open stratification system* and *closed stratification system* to indicate the degree of social mobility in

a society. An **open system** implies that the position of each individual is influenced by his or her *achieved* status. Such a system encourages competition among members of society. The United States is moving toward this ideal type as the government attempts to reduce the barriers faced by women, racial and ethnic minorities, and people born in lower social classes. Even in the midst of the economic downturn of 2008–2009, nearly 80 percent of people in the United States felt they could get ahead (Economic Mobility Project 2009).

At the other extreme of social mobility is the **closed system,** which allows little or no possibility of individual social mobility. The slavery and caste systems of stratification are examples of closed systems. In such societies, social placement is based on *ascribed* statuses, such as race or family background, which cannot be changed.

Types of Social Mobility

An elementary school teacher who becomes a police officer moves from one social position to another of the same rank. Each occupation has the same prestige ranking: 60 on a scale ranging from a low of 0 to a high of 100 Table 27-1. Sociologists call this kind of movement **horizontal mobility.** However, if the teacher were to become a lawyer (prestige ranking of 76), he or she would experience **vertical mobility,** the movement of an individual from one social position to another of a different rank. Vertical mobility can also involve moving *downward* in a society's stratification system, as would be the case if the teacher became a bank teller (ranking of 50). Pitirim Sorokin ([1927] 1959) was the first sociologist to distinguish between horizontal and vertical mobility. Most sociological analysis, however, focuses on vertical rather than horizontal mobility.

One way of examining vertical social mobility is to contrast its two types, intergenerational and intragenerational mobility. **Intergenerational mobility** involves changes in the social position of children relative to their parents. Thus, a plumber whose father was a physician provides an example of downward intergenerational mobility. A film star whose parents were both factory workers illustrates upward intergenerational mobility. Because education contributes significantly to upward mobility, any barrier to the pursuit of advanced degrees can definitely limit intergenerational mobility (see Box 28-2; Isaacs 2007a; Isaacs et al. 2008; Sawhill and Morton 2007).

Figure 28-2 shows intergenerational mobility based on income. In 1978–1980, a national survey looked at the family income of 6,000 young people. Two decades later, in 1997–2003, researchers followed up on those young adults and their income. The results showed a strong stickiness in both the bottom and top quintiles, or fifths, of the income distribution. Just over 33 percent of those whose parents were in the bottom quintile and 37 percent of those who were in the top quintile remained in the same quintile as adults. Yet the study also showed mobility: almost 66 percent of those in the bottom quintile moved up, and over 60 percent of those at the top experienced downward mobility.

Among men born in the 1960s, this consistent intergenerational mobility resulted largely from economic growth. On

Sociology on Campus

BOX 28-2

Social Class and Financial Aid

Today's young people have been dubbed Generation Y, but a more appropriate name for them might be Generation Debt. In 2011, young people graduating from college with student loans left school carrying an average of $27,200 in debt, up 12 percent in just two years.

Every year, millions of prospective college students and their parents struggle through the intricate and time-consuming process of applying for financial aid. Originally, financial aid programs were intended to level the playing field—to allow qualified students from all walks of life to attend college, regardless of the cost. But have these programs fulfilled their promise?

> Statistics that show the educational level in the United States rising overall obscure the widening gap between the advantaged and the less advantaged.

In 2004, 40 percent of first-year students at major state universities came from families with incomes of more than $100,000 a year. In other words, close to half of all students came from high-income families. For students from families with the lowest incomes, the cost can be prohibitive. Only 11 percent of children from the poorest families in the United States have earned college degrees, compared to 53 percent of children from families in the top fifth of the population.

Community colleges, with their low tuition, are often regarded as a hedge against the high costs of higher education. Although these two-year commuter colleges may be cheaper than four-year residential schools, they are not inexpensive. In the academic year 2009–2010, the annual cost of attending community college was more than $14,000. For students at these schools, a greater proportion of their expenses goes to transportation and child care than for students who live on campus at four-year schools.

Besides the spiraling cost of an education, the widespread difficulty in paying for college stems from three trends. First, over the past few decades, colleges and universities have been moving away from making outright grants, such as scholarships, to deserving students, and toward low-interest student loans. Second, much of the assistance schools offer in the form of loans is not based strictly on need. Third, interest rates on federally guaranteed loans have risen steadily, increasing the burden of repayment.

These trends in financial aid for higher education are closely tied to trends in social inequality. As noted earlier in this chapter, over the past half century, rather than declining, inequality in income and wealth has actually increased. In a variation on the truism that the rich tend to get richer while the poor get poorer, the rich are getting better educations and the poor are getting poorer educations. Statistics that show the educational level in the

United States rising overall obscure the widening gap between the advantaged and the less advantaged.

LET'S DISCUSS

1. How important are student loans to you and your friends? Without them, would you be able to cover your college expenses?

2. Aside from a reduction in individual social mobility, what might be the long-term effects of the shortage of need-based financial aid? Relate your answer to the trend toward globalization.

Sources: Boushey 2005; Campbell et al. 2005; College Board 2009; Isaacs et al. 2008; Kamenetz 2006; Leonhardt 2004; Lewin 2011; Michals 2003; Trumbull 2006.

---

average, these men earned more than their fathers did at the same age; their family incomes improved as well. However, the trend did not continue into the next generation. Currently, young men are earning less than their fathers did at the same age—about 12 percent less. Family incomes are slightly higher than in the last generation, but only because women have moved into the paid labor force to supplement their husbands' earnings. With so few women left to join the labor force, most families will need to increase their wages to raise their incomes further (Sawhill and Haskins 2009).

Intragenerational mobility involves changes in social position within a person's adult life. A woman who begins work as a teacher's aide and eventually becomes superintendent of the school district experiences upward intragenerational mobility. A man who becomes a taxicab driver after his accounting firm goes bankrupt undergoes downward intragenerational mobility.

Social Mobility in the United States

The belief in upward mobility is an important value in our society. Does that mean that the United States is indeed the land of opportunity? Not unless such ascriptive characteristics as race, gender, and family background have ceased to be significant in determining one's future prospects. We can see the impact of these factors in the occupational structure.

Occupational Mobility Two sociological studies conducted a decade apart offer insight into the degree of mobility in the nation's occupational structure (Blau and Duncan 1967; Featherman and Hauser 1978). Taken together, these investigations lead to several noteworthy conclusions. First, occupational mobility (both intergenerational and intragenerational) has been common among males. Approximately 60 to 70 percent of sons are employed in higher-ranked occupations than their fathers.

FIGURE 28-2 **Intergenerational Income Mobility**

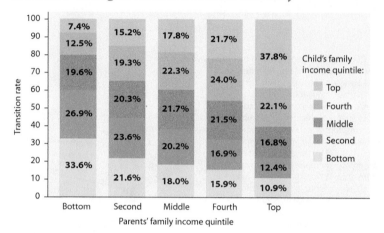

Source: Mazumder 2008:10.

Over a 25-year period, adult children often end up in the same income bracket as their parents. About 7 percent of those who begin in the bottom quintile reach the top quintile as adults; their story is one of rags to riches. About 11 percent of those who start in the top quintile fall to the bottom.

Second, although there is a great deal of mobility in the United States, much of it is minor. That is, people who reach an occupational level above or below that of their parents usually advance or fall back only one or two out of a possible eight occupational levels. Thus, the child of a laborer may become an artisan or a technician, but he or she is less likely to become a manager or professional. The odds against reaching the top are extremely high unless one begins from a relatively privileged position.

The Impact of Education Another conclusion of both studies is that education plays a critical role in social mobility. The impact of formal schooling on adult status is even greater than that of family background (although as we have seen, family background influences the likelihood that one will receive higher education). Furthermore, education represents an important means of intergenerational mobility. A person who was born into a poor family but who graduates from college has a one in five chance of entering the top fifth of all income earners as an adult (Isaacs et al. 2008).

The impact of education on mobility has diminished somewhat in the past decade, however. An undergraduate degree—a BA or a BS—serves less as a guarantee of upward mobility now than it did in the past, simply because more and more entrants into the job market hold such a degree. Moreover, intergenerational mobility is declining, since there is no longer such a stark difference between generations. In earlier decades, many high school–educated parents successfully sent their children to college, but today's college students are increasingly likely to have college-educated parents (Sawhill and Morton 2007).

The Impact of Race and Ethnicity Sociologists have long documented the fact that the class system is more rigid for African Americans than it is for members of other racial groups. African American men who have good jobs, for example, are less

likely than White men to see their adult children attain the same status. The cumulative disadvantage of discrimination plays a significant role in the disparity between the two groups' experiences. Compared to White households, the relatively modest wealth of African American households means that adult African American children are less likely than adult White children to receive financial support from their parents. Indeed, young African American couples are much more likely than young White couples to be assisting their parents—a sacrifice that hampers their social mobility (Favreault 2008).

Not surprisingly, African Americans are more likely than Whites to experience downward intergenerational mobility, and less likely to move up the social ladder. A study of the income data for people born between 1955 and 1970 shows that four in five Black children who began in the top quintile experienced downward mobility, compared to just two in five White children. Similarly, three in five White children who began in the bottom two quintiles experienced upward social mobility, compared to one in four Black children (Sharkey 2009).

The African American middle class has grown over the past few decades, due to economic expansion and the benefits of the civil rights movement of the 1960s. Yet many of these middle-class households have little savings, a fact that puts them in danger during times of crisis. We noted earlier that recession hits Black and Latino households harder than White households. Studies have consistently shown that downward mobility is significantly higher for Blacks than it is for Whites (Conley 2010; Oliver and Shapiro 2006; Sernau 2001; W. Wilson 1996).

The Latino population is not doing much better. The typical Hispanic has less than 10 percent of the wealth that a White person has. One study suggests that in recent years, Latinos have

If this lawyer were the son of a car mechanic, his rise to the upper-middle class would illustrate intergenerational mobility. If he had begun as a paralegal and worked his way up the occupational ladder, his career would illustrate intragenerational mobility.

After beginning her career at General Electric, Ellen Kullman joined DuPont chemical company, where she became CEO in 2009. Despite equal opportunity laws, occupational barriers still limit women's climb to the top of the corporate ladder. Just 12 Fortune 500 companies are now run by women.

even lost ground. Their continuing immigration accounts for part of the disparity: most of the new arrivals are destitute. But even the wealthiest 5 percent of Latino households have only a third as much net worth as the top 5 percent of White households (Kochhar 2008).

The Impact of Gender   Studies of mobility, even more than those of class, have traditionally ignored the significance of gender, but some research findings are now available that explore the relationship between gender and mobility.

Women's employment opportunities are much more limited than men's (as Module 35 will show). Moreover, according to recent research, women whose skills far exceed the jobs offered them are more likely than men to withdraw entirely from the paid labor force. Their withdrawal violates an assumption common to traditional mobility studies: that most people will aspire to upward mobility and seek to make the most of their opportunities.

In contrast to men, women have a rather large range of clerical occupations open to them. But the modest salary ranges and few prospects for advancement in many of these positions limit the possibility of upward mobility. Self-employment as shopkeepers, entrepreneurs, independent professionals, and the like—an important road to upward mobility for men—is more difficult for women, who find it harder to secure the necessary financing. Although sons commonly follow in the footsteps of their fathers, women are unlikely to move into their fathers' positions. Consequently, gender remains an important factor in shaping social mobility. Women in the United States (and in other parts of the world) are especially likely to be trapped in poverty, unable to rise out of their low-income status (Beller 2009; Heilman 2001).

On the positive side, though today's women lag behind men in employment, their earnings have increased faster than their mothers' did at a comparable age, so that their incomes are substantially higher. The one glaring exception to this trend is the daughters of low-income parents. Because these women typically care for children—many as single parents—and sometimes for other relatives as well, their mobility is severely restricted (Isaacs 2007b).

social policy and Stratification | Executive Compensation

Few topics in the news today have led to such public outrage as the compensation received by top executives in the private sector. In the wake of recent corporate meltdowns, such as those involving several huge mortgage lending institutions, executive salaries and bonuses that run into the millions of dollars have begun to strike people as inappropriate. Is multimillion-dollar compensation really necessary, much less desirable, to attract talented corporate leaders?

Looking at the Issue

Over the period from 2000 to 2010, Barry Diller, CEO of Expedia, received a staggering $1.14 billion in compensation—despite the fact that the company's shares *lost* 22 percent of their value. Over an eight-year period, United Health's top executive, William McGuire, took home $453 million, even though the company's stockholders lost 99 percent of their investment. In defense, spokesmen for the two men claimed that their compensation reflected the stocks' solid performance during earlier periods (Thurm 2010).

Although executive pay has always been high in the United States, in recent years it has grown dramatically. The corporate executives who head private companies now earn the highest incomes in the nation. In fact, the gap between their salaries and those of average workers has widened significantly over

—Continued

—*Continued*

time. In 1965, top executives earned only 24 times the average worker's pay. By 2010, the gap had widened to 325 times the average (S. Anderson et al. 2011).

Applying Sociology

From a functionalist perspective, such generous compensation seems reasonable given the potential for gain that a talented executive brings to a corporation. Today, even a small increase in a multibillion-dollar company's performance can add hundreds of millions of dollars to its bottom line. Not surprisingly, then, competition to attract top-performing executives to a company is fierce. Not all these executives are successful all the time, however; sometimes their leadership reduces profits. Critics point out that during the last decade, 7 of the top 25 highly paid executives presided over companies that lost money (Frank 2010; Thurm 2010).

Conflict theorists question not only the relatively high levels of executive compensation, but also the process through which executives' pay is determined. The board of directors, which holds the responsibility for determining executives' pay, has an incentive to go along with arrangements that are favorable to top executives. Board members themselves earned an average of about $228,000 in 2009, so they have a natural desire to avoid conflict over high salaries (Bebchuk and Fried 2010; Strauss 2011).

Taking an almost interactionist approach, sociologist Thomas DiPrete and his colleagues have observed that today, corporations must report executives' compensation relative to their peer group's compensation—that is, to the compensation received by leaders of similar businesses of similar size. Although members of such peer groups do not interact in the way that members of a primary group or even a secondary group would, they do form a social network. Thus, public comparisons of executive compensation within particular industries may influence board members' decisions, prompting them to tie executives' compensation more directly to their performance (DiPrete et al. 2010).

Initiating Policy

Although policymakers have long been concerned about executive compensation, until recently hard data have been difficult to obtain. Before 1992, corporations were required to disclose executives' pay, but not in a uniform manner. Many companies disguised the dollar amounts by literally spelling the words out in the midst of long, densely written documents. Today, the law mandates that companies publish "summary compensation tables." In 2006, reporting requirements were expanded to cover retirement packages, including the "golden parachute" clauses that protect executives who bail out of failing companies (Bebchuk and Fried 2010).

In 2011, as the U.S. economy began to pull out of a deep, long-lasting recession, corporate executives were still earning huge salaries and bonuses—despite the fact that many workers remained jobless.

During the economic downturn that began in 2008, the value of the stock that top executives received as part of their compensation packages did decline. Yet overall, CEOs' salaries in the 500 largest corporations still rose 3 percent in 2009. In response, the White House appointed a Treasury Department official, whom reporters quickly dubbed the "pay czar," to look into executive compensation. Given the deferred stock payments, expense accounts, and other perquisites executives typically receive, the assignment was a difficult one (D. Jones and Hansen 2009).

In the short time the pay czar has been in office, results have been mixed. Critics complain the office hasn't made significant progress in curbing executive pay, while companies claim that the government is hampering their ability to compete. Although the czar has managed to change some compensation practices, critics worry that companies may develop new ways to inflate executives' pay (Congressional Oversight Panel 2011; Edmans and Gabaix 2010; Grusky and Wimer 2010; Reuters 2010).

TAKE THE ISSUE WITH YOU

1. Should corporate executives earn high salaries even when their companies are losing money? Explain. How do you think functionalists would defend such a practice?

2. What do you think of the "golden parachute" clauses that allow executives to bail out of failing companies unharmed? What might be the effect of such clauses on executives' performance? On shareholders and on lower-level employees?

3. Relate the increases in executive compensation over the past half century to changes in U.S. social structure during that time. How have those changes affected you and your family?

MODULE 28 | Recap and Review

Summary

Poverty is difficult to explain or define, although its effects are obvious and pervasive.

1. Many of those who live in poverty are full-time workers who struggle to support their families at minimum-wage jobs. The long-term poor—those who lack the training and skills to lift themselves out of poverty—form an **underclass.**

2. Functionalists find that the poor satisfy positive functions for many of the nonpoor in the United States.

3. One's **life chances** —opportunities for obtaining material goods, positive living conditions, and favorable life experiences—are related to one's social class. Occupying a high social position improves a person's life chances.

4. **Social mobility** is more likely to be found in an **open system** that emphasizes achieved status than in a **closed system** that emphasizes ascribed status. Race, gender, and family background are important factors in social mobility.

5. During the past half century, the gap between executive compensation and the average worker's pay has increased to 325 to 1. Although corporations claim that talented leaders enhance their performance, making executive pay packages well worth the money, they have gone to some trouble to disguise the expense from public scrutiny.

Thinking Critically

1. How do you identify areas of poverty in your own community or one nearby? Do you consider residents' achieved or ascribed characteristics?

2. How do people's life chances affect society as a whole?

3. Which factor—occupation, education, race and ethnicity, or gender—do you expect will have the greatest impact on your own social mobility? Explain.

Key Terms

Absolute poverty
Closed system
Feminization of poverty
Horizontal mobility
Intergenerational mobility
Intragenerational mobility
Life chances
Open system
Precarious work
Relative poverty
Social mobility
Underclass
Vertical mobility

Mastering This Chapter: Stratification and Social Mobility in the United States

taking sociology with you

1 Do some research on the educational and occupational levels in the city or town where you live. Based on what you have learned, describe the social-class stratification of your community.

2 Use census data to create a map showing the median income levels and/or property values in the geographic areas surrounding your home. What patterns does it show?

3 Talk with a parent or grandparent about your family's history. What can you learn about your forebears' life chances? About their social mobility? How do you hope to fit into the story?

key terms

Absolute poverty A minimum level of subsistence that no family should be expected to live below.

Achieved status A social position that a person attains largely through his or her own efforts.

Ascribed status A social position assigned to a person by society without regard for the person's unique talents or characteristics.

Bourgeoisie Karl Marx's term for the capitalist class, comprising the owners of the means of production.

Capitalism An economic system in which the means of production are held largely in private hands and the main incentive for economic activity is the accumulation of profits.

Caste A hereditary rank, usually religiously dictated, that tends to be fixed and immobile.

Class A group of people who have a similar level of wealth and income.

Class consciousness In Karl Marx's view, a subjective awareness held by members of a class regarding their common vested interests and the need for collective political action to bring about social change.

Class system A social ranking based primarily on economic position in which achieved characteristics can influence social mobility.

Closed system A social system in which there is little or no possibility of individual social mobility.

Conspicuous consumption Purchasing goods not to survive but to flaunt one's superior wealth and social standing.

Dominant ideology A set of cultural beliefs and practices that helps to maintain powerful social, economic, and political interests.

Estate system A system of stratification under which peasants were required to work land leased to them by nobles in exchange for military protection and other services. Also known as *feudalism.*

Esteem The reputation that a specific person has earned within an occupation.

False consciousness A term used by Karl Marx to describe an attitude held by members of a class that does not accurately reflect their objective position.

Feminization of poverty A trend in which women constitute an increasing proportion of the poor people of both the United States and the world.

Horizontal mobility The movement of an individual from one social position to another of the same rank.

Income Salaries and wages.

Intergenerational mobility Changes in the social position of children relative to their parents.

Intragenerational mobility Changes in social position within a person's adult life.

Life chances The opportunities people have to provide themselves with material goods, positive living conditions, and favorable life experiences.

Objective method A technique for measuring social class that assigns individuals to classes on the basis of criteria such as occupation, education, income, and place of residence.

Open system A social system in which the position of each individual is influenced by his or her achieved status.

Power The ability to exercise one's will over others.

Precarious work Employment that is poorly paid, and from the worker's perspective, insecure and unprotected.

Prestige The respect and admiration that an occupation holds in a society.

Proletariat Karl Marx's term for the working class in a capitalist society.

Relative poverty A floating standard of deprivation by which people at the bottom of a society, whatever their lifestyles, are judged to be disadvantaged *in comparison with the nation as a whole.*

Slavery A system of enforced servitude in which some people are owned by other people.

Social inequality A condition in which members of society have differing amounts of wealth, prestige, or power.

Social mobility Movement of individuals or groups from one position in a society's stratification system to another.

Socioeconomic status (SES) A measure of social class that is based on income, education, and occupation.

Status group People who have the same prestige or lifestyle, independent of their class positions.

Stratification A structured ranking of entire groups of people that perpetuates unequal economic rewards and power in a society.

Underclass The long-term poor who lack training and skills.

Vertical mobility The movement of an individual from one social position to another of a different rank.

Wealth An inclusive term encompassing all a person's material assets, including land, stocks, and other types of property.

self-quiz

Read each question carefully and then select the best answer.

1. Which of the following describes a condition in which members of a society have different amounts of wealth, prestige, or power?
   a. stratification
   b. status inconsistency
   c. slavery
   d. social inequality

2. In Karl Marx's view, the destruction of the capitalist system will occur only if the working class first develops
   a. bourgeois consciousness.
   b. false consciousness.
   c. class consciousness.
   d. caste consciousness.

3. Which of the following were viewed by Max Weber as analytically distinct components of stratification?
   a. conformity, deviance, and social control
   b. class, status, and power
   c. class, caste, and age
   d. class, prestige, and esteem

4. Which sociological perspective argues that stratification is universal and that social inequality is necessary so that people will be motivated to fill socially important positions?
   a. the functionalist perspective
   b. the conflict perspective
   c. the interactionist perspective
   d. the labeling perspective

5. British sociologist Ralf Dahrendorf views social classes as groups of people who share common interests resulting from their authority relationships. Dahrendorf's ideology aligns best with which theoretical perspective?
   a. the functionalist perspective
   b. the conflict perspective
   c. the interactionist perspective

   d. sociocultural evolution

6. The respect or admiration that an occupation holds in a society is referred to as
   a. status.
   b. esteem.
   c. prestige.
   d. ranking.

7. Approximately how many out of every nine people in the United States live(s) below the poverty line established by the federal government?
   a. one
   b. two
   c. three
   d. four

8. Which sociologist has applied functionalist analysis to the existence of poverty and argues that various segments of society actually benefit from the existence of the poor?
   a. Émile Durkheim
   b. Max Weber
   c. Karl Marx
   d. Herbert Gans

9. A measure of social class that is based on income, education, and occupation is known as
   a. the objective method.
   b. stratification.
   c. socioeconomic status.
   d. the open system.

10. A plumber whose father was a physician is an example of
   a. downward intergenerational mobility.
   b. upward intergenerational mobility.
   c. downward intragenerational mobility.
   d. upward intragenerational mobility.

11. _____ is the most extreme form of legalized social inequality for individuals or groups.

12. In the _____ system of stratification, or feudalism, peasants were required to work land leased to them by nobles in exchange for military protection and other services.

13. Karl Marx viewed _____ differentiation as the crucial determinant of social, economic, and political inequality.

14. _____ _____ is the term Thorstein Veblen used to describe the extravagant spending patterns of those at the top of the class hierarchy.

15. _____ poverty is the minimum level of subsistence that no family should be expected to live below.

16. _____ poverty is a floating standard of deprivation by which people at the bottom of a society, whatever their lifestyles, are judged to be disadvantaged in comparison with the nation as a whole.

17. Sociologist William Julius Wilson and other social scientists have used the term _____ to describe the long-term poor who lack training and skills.

18. Max Weber used the term _____ _____ to refer to people's opportunities to provide themselves with material goods, positive living conditions, and favorable life experiences.

19. An open class system implies that the position of each individual is influenced by the person's _____ status.

20. _____ mobility involves changes in social position within a person's adult life.

Answers

1 (d); 2 (c); 3 (b); 4 (a); 5 (b); 6 (c); 7 (a); 8 (d); 9 (c); 10 (a); 11 Slavery; 12 estate; 13 class; 14 Conspicuous consumption; 15 Absolute; 16 Relative; 17 underclass; 18 life chances; 19 achieved; 20 Intragenerational

thinking about movies

The Fighter

Two working-class brothers strive for upward mobility in the world of professional boxing.

Jumping the Broom

When two families come together to celebrate a wedding, social-class differences cause tension.

Dark Days

In this documentary, a community of homeless people in New York City copes with extreme poverty by living underground near a railroad station.

Global Inequality

Global Inequality

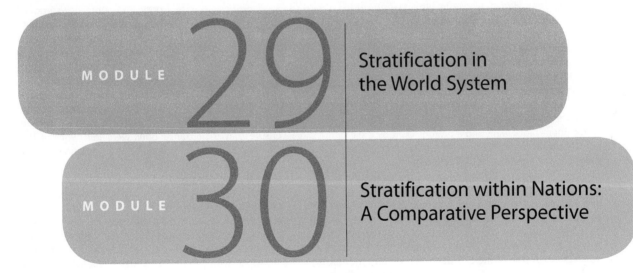

MODULE 29 Stratification in the World System

MODULE 30 Stratification within Nations: A Comparative Perspective

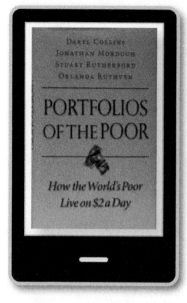

Could you live on less than $2 a day, including your rent or campus housing?

When a team of researchers asked poor people in developing countries how they spent their meager incomes, the results were surprising.

“To get a first sense of what the financial diaries [of the poor] reveal, consider Hamid and Khadeja. The couple married in a poor coastal village of Bangladesh where there was very little work for a poorly educated and unskilled young man like Hamid. Soon after their first child was born they gave up rural life and moved, as so many hundreds of thousands had done before them, to the capital city, Dhaka, where they settled in a slum. After spells as a cycle-rickshaw driver and construction laborer and many days of unemployment, Hamid, whose health was not good, finally got taken on as a reserve driver of a motorized rickshaw. That's what he was doing when we first met Hamid and Khadeja in late 1999, while Khadeja stayed home to run the household, raise their child, and earn a little from taking in sewing work. Home was one of a strip of small rooms with cement block walls and a tin roof, built by their landlord on illegally occupied land, with a toilet and kitchen space shared by the eight families that lived there.

In an average month they lived on the equivalent of $70, almost all of it earned by Hamid, whose income arrived in unpredictable daily amounts that varied according to whether he got work that day (he was only the reserve driver) and, if he did get work, how much business he attracted, how many hours he was allowed to keep his vehicle, and how often it broke down. A fifth of the $70 was spent on rent (not always paid on time), and much of the rest went toward the most basic necessities of life—food and the means to prepare it. By the couple's own reckoning, which our evidence agrees with, their income put them among the poor of Bangladesh, though not among the very poorest. By global standards they would fall into the bottom two-fifths of the world's income distribution tables.

An unremarkable poor household: a partly educated couple trying to stay alive, bring up a child, run a one-room home, and keep Ha-mid's health in shape—on an uncertain $0.78 per person per day. You wouldn't expect them to have much of a financial life. Yet the diversity of instruments in their year-end household balance sheet shows that Hamid and Khadeja, as part of their struggle to survive within their slim means, were active money managers.

Far from living hand-to-mouth, consuming every taka as soon as it arrived, Hamid and Khadeja had built up reserves in six different instruments, ranging from $2 kept at home for minor day-to-day shortfalls to $30 sent for safe-keeping to his parents, $40 lent out to a relative, and $76 in a life insurance savings policy. In addition, Hamid always made sure he had $2 in his pocket to deal with anything that might befall him on the road.

In addition to saving, borrowing, and repaying *money*, Hamid and Khadeja, like nearly all poor and some not-so-poor households, also saved, borrowed, and repaid in kind. Khadeja, sharing a crude kitchen with seven other wives, would often swap small amounts of rice or lentils or salt with her neighbors. She would keep a note of the quantities in her head, and so would her partners in these exchanges, to ensure that their transactions were fair over the long haul. Virtually all of the rural Bangladeshi households followed the well-established tradition of *musti chaul*—of keeping back one fistful of dry rice each time a meal was cooked, to hold against lean times, to have ready when a beggar called, or to donate to the mosque or temple when called on to do so. For rural respondents in India and Bangladesh, the intermediation of goods and services rather than cash was common, and included borrowing grain to be repaid after the harvest, repaying a loan with one's labor, or using labor to buy farm inputs. We recorded much of this activity.”

An unremarkable poor household: a partly educated couple trying to stay alive, bring up a child, run a one-room home, and keep Hamid's health in shape—on an uncertain $0.78 per person per day. You wouldn't expect them to have much of a financial life.

(D. Collins et al. 2009:7–8, 10–11) Additional information about this excerpt can be found on the Online Learning Center at www.mhhe.com/schaefermod2e.

Well over 2.5 billion people live on less than $2 a day—the widely recognized definition of poverty in the developing world. Incredibly, over 50 percent of them live on less than the extreme poverty level of $1.25 a day (World Bank 2012a:41). To find out how these poor households survive, four researchers conducted an intensive study of 250 families in Bangladesh, India, and South Africa. Daryl Collins, Jonathan Morduch, Stuart Rutherford, and Orlanda Ruthven wanted to know how best to use *microfinance*—small lending—to assist poor families in the developing world. As explained in the book *Portfolios of the Poor: How the World's Poor Live on $2 a Day*, rather than simply interviewing the families, Collins and his colleagues asked them to maintain financial diaries for a year.

Through the diaries, the research team discovered that the families were quite adept at managing their income. Because the stakes were high—there is no room for error on $1 or $2 a day—these mostly uneducated people had surprisingly sophisticated methods for managing their resources.

In developing countries like Bangladesh, most but not all the people are poor. Even in the poorest countries, the poor rub shoulders with the very wealthy. Inequality, then, exists within all countries, not just within the United States. On a global scale, inequality also exists *between* developing and developed nations, which is why a living allowance of $2 a day is so difficult for those of us in the developed world to comprehend. In these modules we will consider social inequality both within developing nations and between the developing and developed worlds.

What economic and political conditions explain the divide between rich nations and poor? Within developing nations, how are wealth and income distributed, and how much opportunity does the average worker have to move up the social ladder? How do race and gender affect social mobility in these countries? In Module 29 we will focus on global inequality, beginning with the global divide. We will consider the impact of colonialism and neocolonialism, globalization, the rise of multinational corporations, and the trend toward modernization. Then we will focus on stratification within nations, in terms of the distribution of wealth and income as well as social mobility. In a special case study, we will look closely at social stratification in Mexico, including the social impact of race and gender and the economic effects of industrialization. The chapter closes with a Social Policy section on welfare reform in Europe and North America.

The Global Divide

In some parts of the world, the people who have dedicated their lives to fighting starvation refer to what they call "coping mechanisms"—ways in which the desperately poor attempt to control their hunger. Eritrean women will strap flat stones to their stomachs to lessen their hunger pangs. In Mozambique, people eat the grasshoppers that have destroyed the crops, calling them "flying shrimp." Though dirt eating is considered a pathological condition (called *pica*) among the well-fed, the world's poor eat dirt to add minerals to their diet. And in many countries, mothers have been known to boil stones in water, to convince their hungry children that supper is almost ready. As they hover over the pot, these women hope that their malnourished children will fall asleep (McNeil 2004).

Around the world, inequality is a significant determinant of human behavior, opening doors of opportunity to some and closing them to others. Indeed, disparities in life chances are so extreme that in some places, the poorest of the poor may not be aware of them. Western media images may have circled the globe, but in extremely depressed rural areas, those at the bottom of society are not likely to see them.

A few centuries ago, such vast divides in global wealth did not exist. Except for a very few rulers and landowners, everyone in the world was poor. In much of Europe, life was as difficult as it was in Asia or South America. This was true until the Industrial Revolution and rising agricultural productivity produced explosive economic growth. The resulting rise in living standards was not evenly distributed across the world.

Figure 29-1 compares the industrialized nations of the world to the developing nations. Using total population as a yardstick, we see that the developing countries have more than their fair share of rural population, as well as of total births, disease, and childhood deaths. At the same time, the industrialized nations of the world, with a much smaller share of total population, have much more income and exports than the developing nations. Industrialized nations also spend more on health and the military than other nations, and they emit more carbon dioxide (CO_2; Sachs 2005; Sutcliffe 2002).

Although the divide between industrialized and developing nations is sharp, sociologists recognize a continuum of nations, from the richest of the rich to the poorest of the poor. For example, in 2008, the average value of goods and services produced per citizen (or per capita gross national income) in the industrialized countries of the United States, the Netherlands, Switzerland, France, and Norway was more than $47,000. In at least 39 poorer countries, the value was just $1,000 or less. However, most countries fell somewhere between those extremes, as Figure 29-2 shows.

Still, the contrasts are stark. Three forces discussed here are particularly responsible for

FIGURE 29-1 **Fundamental Global Inequality**

Note: In this comparison, industrialized nations include the United States and Canada, Japan, western Europe, and Australasia. Developing nations include Africa, Asia (except for Japan), Latin America, eastern Europe, the Caribbean, and the Pacific.

Source: Adapted from Sutcliffe 2002:18.

Think about It

What is the relationship between health spending, disease, and deaths of children? Between CO_2 emissions, income, and exports?

MAPPING LIFE WORLDWIDE

FIGURE 29-2   Gross National Income per Capita

GNI per capita in 2010

- Below $3,100
- $3,100–$7,995
- $8,000–$19,100
- Over $19,200
- No available data

Note: Country sizes and incomes based on 2010 estimates. Includes only those countries with 3 million or more people.
Sources: Haub 2010; Weeks 2012.

This stylized map reflects the relative population sizes of the world's nations. The color for each country shows the gross national income (the total value of goods and services produced by the nation in a given year) per capita.

What do we stand in line for? People's needs and desires differ dramatically depending on where they live. On the left, eager customers line up outside a store in New York City to purchase the newly released iPhone 4S. On the right, residents of Ethiopia line up to receive water.

the domination of the world marketplace by a few nations: the legacy of colonialism, the advent of multinational corporations, and modernization.

The Legacy of Colonialism

Colonialism occurs when a foreign power maintains political, social, economic, and cultural domination over a people for an extended period. In simple terms, it is rule by outsiders. The long reign of the British Empire over much of North America, parts of Africa, and India was an example of colonial domination. The same can be said of French rule over Algeria, Tunisia, and other parts of North Africa. Relations between the colonial nation and colonized people are similar to those between the dominant capitalist class and the proletariat, as described by Karl Marx.

By the 1980s, colonialism had largely disappeared. Most of the nations that were colonies before World War I had achieved political independence and established their own governments. However, for many of those countries, the transition to genuine self-rule was not yet complete. Colonial domination had established patterns of economic exploitation that continued even after nationhood was achieved—in part because former colonies were unable to develop their own industry and technology. Their dependence on more industrialized nations, including their former colonial masters, for managerial and technical expertise, investment capital, and manufactured goods kept former colonies in a subservient position. Such continuing dependence and foreign domination are referred to as **neocolonialism.**

The economic and political consequences of colonialism and neocolonialism are readily apparent. Drawing on the conflict perspective, sociologist Immanuel Wallerstein (1974, 1979a, 2000, 2012) views the global economic system as being divided between nations that control wealth and nations from which resources are taken. Through his **world systems analysis,** Wallerstein has described an interdependent global economy resting on unequal economic and political relationships. Critical to his analysis is the understanding that by themselves, nations do not, nor have they

ever, constituted whole systems. Instead, they exist within a larger, global social context.

In Wallerstein's view, certain industrialized nations (among them the United States, Japan, and Germany) and their global corporations dominate the *core* of this system (Figure 29-3). At the *semiperiphery* of the system are countries with marginal economic status, such as Israel, Ireland, and South Korea. Wallerstein suggests that the poor developing countries of Asia, Africa, and Latin America are on the *periphery* of the world economic system. The key to Wallerstein's macro-level analysis is the exploitative relationship of *core* nations toward *non-core* nations. Core nations and their corporations control and

trend|spotting

Feeding the World

As we saw in the last chapter, life chances are the opportunities (or lack of them) individuals have to improve their quality of life. One of the most basic life chances—and a growing concern around the world—is the opportunity to eat an adequate amount of food. For years, food prices have been rising, a trend that is expected to continue. Bad weather, poor crop yields, and the high cost of fuel have always affected the price of food. Now, production of biofuels like ethanol is reducing the supply of grain that is available for human consumption. Moreover, as incomes have risen in developing countries like China and India, people's dietary preferences have begun to shift from the relatively inexpensive cereals to pricier meat and vegetables. These environmental and economic pressures have reduced the amount of food available for distribution to the malnourished and starving.

Although worldwide, population growth is slowing, the outlook is far from rosy. Farmers may be able to feed the world for the foreseeable future, but charities and government organizations are falling behind in their efforts to distribute food fairly and to eliminate waste. Today, as the world's population passes the seven-billion mark, finding adequate food is becoming more—not less—of a challenge for more and more people.

FIGURE 29-3 World Systems Analysis

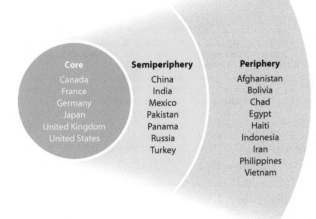

Core	Semiperiphery	Periphery
Canada	China	Afghanistan
France	India	Bolivia
Germany	Mexico	Chad
Japan	Pakistan	Egypt
United Kingdom	Panama	Haiti
United States	Russia	Indonesia
	Turkey	Iran
		Philippines
		Vietnam

Note: Figure shows only a partial listing of countries, selected by the author.

exploit noncore nations' economies. Unlike other nations, they are relatively independent of outside control (Chase-Dunn and Grimes 1995).

The division between core and periphery nations is significant and remarkably stable. A study by the International Monetary Fund (2000) found little change over the course of the *past 100 years* for the 42 economies that were studied. The only changes were Japan's movement up into the group of core nations and China's movement down toward the margins of the semiperiphery nations. Yet Immanuel Wallerstein (2012:9) speculates that the world system as we currently understand it may soon undergo unpredictable changes. The world is becoming increasingly urbanized, a trend that is gradually eliminating the large pools of low-cost workers in rural areas. In the future, core nations will have to find other ways to reduce their labor costs. Exhaustion of land and water resources through clearcutting and pollution is also driving up the costs of production.

Wallerstein's world systems analysis is the most widely used version of **dependency theory.** According to this macro-level theory, even as developing countries make economic advances, they remain weak and subservient to core nations and corporations in an increasingly intertwined global economy. This interdependency allows industrialized nations to continue to exploit developing countries. In a sense, dependency theory applies the conflict perspective on a global scale.

In the view of world systems analysts and dependency theorists, a growing share of the human and natural resources of developing countries is being redistributed to the core industrialized nations. This redistribution happens in part because developing countries owe huge sums of money to industrialized nations as a result of foreign aid, loans, and trade deficits. The global debt crisis has intensified the Third World dependency begun under colonialism, neocolonialism, and multinational investment. International financial institutions are pressuring indebted countries to take severe measures to meet their interest payments. The result is that developing nations may be forced to devalue their currencies, freeze workers' wages, increase the privatization of industry, and reduce government services and employment.

Closely related to these problems is **globalization,** the worldwide integration of government policies, cultures, social movements, and financial markets through trade and the exchange of ideas. Because world financial markets transcend governance by conventional nation-states, international organizations such as the World Bank and the International Monetary Fund have emerged as major players in the global economy. The function of these institutions, which are heavily funded and influenced by core nations, is to encourage economic trade and development and to ensure the smooth operation of international financial markets. As such, they are seen as promoters of globalization and defenders primarily of the interests of core nations.

Critics call attention to a variety of issues, including violations of workers' rights, the destruction of the environment, the

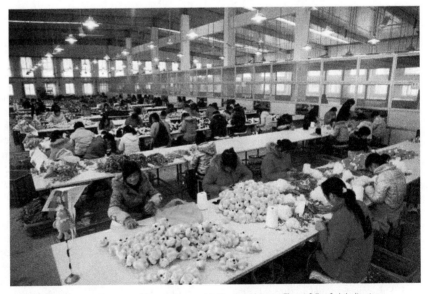

In a factory in China, workers assemble toys for export to the United States. The pitfalls of globalization were brought home—literally—to U.S. consumers in 2007, when U.S. companies were forced to recall toys manufactured in China because they were finished with lead-based paint.

Sociology in the Global Community

BOX 29-1

Income Inequality: A Global Perspective

Just how do incomes compare across the globe? Within nations? Sociologists Roberto Korzeniewicz and Timothy Moran faced these questions head-on and obtained some dramatic answers.

To simplify the task of comparing incomes across billions of people, the two researchers divided residents of each country into 10 deciles, or groups of 10 percent, based on per capita incomes. Then they ranked each set of deciles from the highest (Decile 10) to the lowest (Decile 1). Finally, they did the same for the world as a whole, dividing the world's population into deciles based on income.

Korzeniewicz and Moran found that in Norway and Switzerland, members of Decile 10 made slightly more income than members of the same decile in Denmark, Canada, and Germany. Outside Europe and North America, however, inequality became more apparent, both between and within nations. In the United States, members of Decile 4—that is, those people with incomes in the bottom 31 to 40 percent—fell within the top decile for the world as a whole. That is, in the United States (or Germany or France, for that matter), members of Decile 4 were better off than members of Decile 10 in Brazil, Malaysia, Poland, and Russia.

You might think you would rather be in the richest decile in Poland than in the seventh richest decile in the United States. However, in Poland an engineer or doctor may earn a salary equivalent to a factory worker's salary in the United States. Although the Polish professor may enjoy a relatively high status, he or she may not be able to afford to own a home or to go away on vacation. Similarly, the average income of a food service worker in Decile 2 in the United States may exceed the earnings of a middle-class worker in China, Romania, or Mexico. From the perspective of a U.S. resident, income inequality within the nation may be sharp, but from a global perspective it is not nearly as dramatic as income inequality in a world where hundreds of millions of people struggle just to survive.

> The American Pet Products Manufacturers Association estimates the average annual expenditure on a dog in the United States at around $1,400—a figure comparable to human incomes in nations like Paraguay and Egypt.

The degree of global inequality becomes even more apparent if we compare the resources consumed by dogs in the United States to the incomes of people around the world. The American Pet Products Manufacturers Association estimates the average annual expenditure on a dog in the United States at around $1,400—a figure comparable to human incomes in nations like Paraguay and Egypt. U.S. dogs, in fact, are better off than 40 percent of the world's people. Their health care expenditures alone exceed those of 80 percent of the world's humans.

LET'S DISCUSS

1. Does your family have a pet? If so, how much money do you think you spend on your pet every year? How does that figure compare to the average annual income in China or India?

2. By itself, do you think Korzeniewicz and Moran's income-based measure is a sufficient indicator of global inequality? If not, what other kinds of information would you want to consider?

Sources: Korzeniewicz and Moran 2009; Therborn 2010.

---

loss of cultural identity, and discrimination against minority groups in periphery nations. The impact of globalization appears to be most problematic for developing countries in Latin America and Africa. In Asia, developing nations seem to do better. Foreign investment there involves the high-tech sector, which produces more sustainable economic growth (Kerbo 2006). Even there, however, globalization definitely has not reduced income disparities, either between nations or within countries (Box 29-1).

Some observers see globalization and its effects as the natural result of advances in communications technology, particularly the Internet and worldwide transmission of the mass media. Others view it more critically, as a process that allows multinational corporations to expand unchecked, as we will see shortly (Chase-Dunn et al. 2000).

use your sociological imagination

You are traveling through a developing country. What evidence do you see of neocolonialism and globalization?

Poverty Worldwide

In developing countries, any deterioration of the economic well-being of those who are least well off threatens their very survival. By U.S. standards, even those who are well-off in the developing world are poor. Those who are poor in developing countries are truly destitute.

What would a map of the world look like if we drew it to a scale that reflects the number of *poor* people in each country instead of the number of people, as in Figure 29-2? As Figure 29-4 shows, when we focus on the poverty level rather than the population, the world looks quite different. Note the huge areas of poverty in Africa and Asia, and the comparatively small areas of affluence in industrialized North America and Europe. Poverty is a worldwide problem that blights the lives of billions of people.

How do social scientists measure global poverty? As we saw in Module 28, there is significant disagreement over where to draw the poverty line in the United States. Adding the rest of the world to the equation further complicates the task. Individually, many developing nations define poverty based on the minimum income a person needs to survive—an amount that typically ranges from a low of $1 a day to a high of $2 a day. Zambia defines poverty in terms of the inability to afford specific foods in a subsistence diet (Oxford Poverty and Human Development Initiative 2012).

In 2000 the United Nations launched the Millennium Project, whose objective is to eliminate extreme poverty worldwide by the year 2015. Although 15 years may seem a long time, the challenge is great. To reach the project's goal, planners estimated that industrialized nations must set aside 0.51 percent of their *gross national income*—that is, the total value of a nation's goods and services (GNP), plus or minus income received from and sent to other nations—to aid developing countries (Landler and Sanger 2009; Sachs 2005; United Nations 2005).

At the time the Millennium Project was launched, only five countries were giving at that target rate: Denmark,

Luxembourg, the Netherlands, Norway, and Sweden. As of 2010, the United States would need to multiply its present aid level by 150 percent to match the Millennium target of 0.51 percent of gross national income. Although in dollar terms the U.S. government delivers far more aid to foreign countries and multinational organizations than any other nation, the amount is not impressive considering the nation's tremendous wealth relative to other countries. In terms of the percentage of gross national income, the United States' contribution is among the lowest of the 22 most advanced industrialized countries, on a par with Japan's (Figure 29-5).

Privileged people in industrialized nations tend to assume that the world's poor lack significant assets. Yet again and again, observers from these countries have been startled to discover how far even a small amount of capital can go. Numerous microfinance programs, which involve relatively small grants or loans, have encouraged marginalized people to invest not in livestock, which

MAPPING LIFE WORLDWIDE

FIGURE 29-4 **Poverty Worldwide**

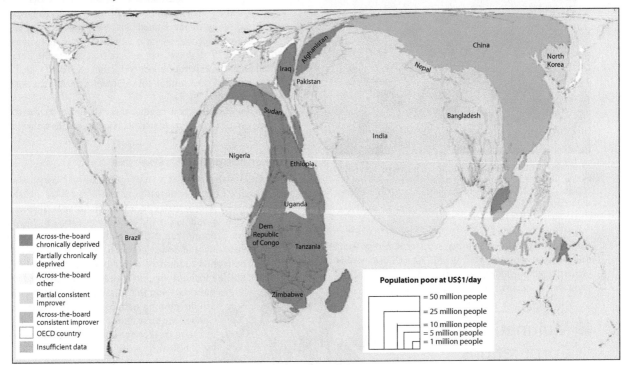

Source: Chronic Poverty Research Centre 2009.
The scale of this map is based on the number of people in each region who are chronically poor. The colors represent the income levels of those who are poorest. In OECD countries—those that belong to the Organisation for Economic Co-Operation and Development (white)—chronic poverty is not a nationwide issue.

Think about It

To what degree does this map minimize those countries you have studied or might want to visit?
To what degree does it emphasize parts of the world about which you know very little?

Open displays of social inequality are apparent in every nation. In Mumbai, India, billionaire Mukesh Ambani built this 27-story home for his wife and three children, complete with three helicopter pads and a 160-vehicle garage. To run the building, Ambani employs a staff of 600.

may die, or jewelry, which may be stolen, but in technological improvements such as small stoves. We will discuss this topic in greater depth in Modules 48 through 51, on the government and the economy.

◉ Multinational Corporations

We have seen that globalization has not necessarily improved the lives of the poor in the developing world. Another trend that does not always serve developing countries well has been the rise of multinational corporations. Worldwide, corporate giants play a key role in neocolonialism. The term **multinational corporations** refers to commercial organizations that are headquartered in one country but do business throughout the world. Such private trade and lending relationships are not new; merchants have conducted business abroad for hundreds of years, trading gems, spices, garments, and other goods. However, today's multinational giants are not merely buying and selling overseas; they are also *producing* goods all over the world (Wallerstein 1974).

Moreover, today's "global factories" (factories throughout the developing world that are run by multinational corporations) may soon have the "global office" sitting alongside them. Multinationals based in core countries are beginning to establish reservation services and centers for processing data and insurance claims in periphery nations. As service industries become a more important part of the international marketplace, many companies are concluding that the low costs of overseas operations more than offset the expense of transmitting information around the world.

Do not underestimate the size of these global corporations. As Figure 29-6 shows, the total revenues of multinational businesses are on a par with the total value of goods and services exchanged in *entire nations*. Foreign sales represent an important source of profit for multinational corporations, which are constantly seeking to expand into other countries (in many cases, developing nations). The economy of the United States depends heavily on foreign commerce, much of which is conducted by multinationals. Over 12 percent of all goods and services produced in the United States relates to the export of goods to foreign countries, which supports an estimated 10.3 million jobs (Office of the United States Trade Representative 2012).

Functionalist and conflict theorists differ on the social and economic effects of multinational corporations, as we will see next.

Functionalist Perspective

Functionalists believe that multinational corporations can actually help the developing nations of the world. They bring jobs and industry to areas where subsistence agriculture once served as the only means of survival. Multinationals also promote rapid development through the diffusion of inventions and innovations from industrialized nations. Viewed from a functionalist perspective, the combination of skilled technology and management provided by multinationals and the relatively cheap labor available in developing nations is ideal for a global enterprise. Multinationals can take maximum advantage of technology while reducing costs and boosting profits.

Through their international ties, multinational corporations also make the nations of the world more interdependent. These ties may prevent certain disputes from reaching the point of serious conflict. A country cannot afford to sever diplomatic relations or engage in warfare with a nation that is the headquarters for its main business suppliers or a key outlet for its exports.

FIGURE 29-5 Foreign Aid per Capita in Nine Countries

Total aid in $ millions

Country	Total aid in $ millions	Aid as percentage of gross national income
Japan	11.0	0.20%
USA	30.4	0.21%
Australia	3.8	0.32%
Canada	5.2	0.34%
Ireland	.9	0.52%
Great Britain	13.1	0.57%
Netherlands	6.4	0.81%
Sweden	4.5	0.97%
Norway	4.6	1.10%

Aid as percentage of gross national income

Note: Actual net development assistance in 2010.
Source: Organisation for Economic Co-operation and Development 2012a.

Conflict Perspective

Conflict theorists challenge this favorable evaluation of the impact of multinational corporations. They emphasize that multinationals exploit local workers to maximize profits. Starbucks—the international coffee retailer based in Seattle—gets some of its coffee from farms in Guatemala. But to earn enough money to buy a pound of Starbucks coffee, a Guatemalan farmworker would have to pick 500 pounds of beans, representing five days of work: see Box 4-1, (Entine and Nichols 1996).

The pool of cheap labor in the developing world prompts multinationals to move factories out of core countries. An added bonus for the multinationals is that the developing world discourages strong trade unions. In industrialized countries, organized labor insists on decent wages and humane working conditions, but governments seeking to attract or keep multinationals may develop a "climate for investment" that includes repressive antilabor laws which restrict union activity and collective bargaining. If labor's demands become too threatening, the multinational firm will simply move its plant elsewhere, leaving a trail of unemployment behind. Nike, for example, moved its factories from the United States to Korea to Indonesia to Vietnam in search of the lowest labor costs. Conflict theorists conclude that on the whole, multinational corporations have a negative social impact on workers in *both* industrialized and developing nations.

Several sociologists who have surveyed the effects of foreign investment by multinationals conclude that although it may at first contribute to a host nation's wealth, it eventually increases economic inequality within developing nations. This conclusion holds true for both income and land ownership. The upper and middle classes benefit most from economic expansion; the lower classes benefit least. As conflict theorists point out, multinationals invest in limited economic sectors and restricted regions of a nation. Although certain sectors of the host nation's economy expand, such as hotels and expensive restaurants, their very expansion appears to retard growth in agriculture and other economic sectors. Moreover, multinational corporations often buy out or force out local entrepreneurs and companies, thereby increasing economic and cultural dependence (Chase-Dunn and Grimes 1995; Kerbo 2012; Wallerstein 1979b).

💡 use your **sociological imagination**

Think of something you bought recently that was made by a multinational corporation. How do you know the maker was a multinational?

● Modernization

Globalization and the rise of multinational corporations have affected developing countries not just economically, but culturally. Around the world, millions of people are witnessing a revolutionary transformation of their day-to-day life. Contemporary social scientists use the term **modernization** to describe the far-reaching process through which periphery nations move from traditional or less developed institutions to those characteristic of more developed societies.

Sociologist Wendell Bell (1981), whose definition of modernization we are using, notes that modern societies tend to be urban, literate, and industrial. These societies have sophisticated transportation and media systems. Their families tend to be organized within the nuclear family model rather than the extended-family model (see Module 40). Thus, members of societies that undergo modernization must shift their allegiance from traditional authorities, such as parents and priests, to newer authorities, such as government officials.

Many sociologists are quick to note that terms such as *modernization* and even *development* contain an ethnocentric bias. The unstated assumption behind these terms is that "they" (people living in developing nations) are struggling to become more like "us" (people in core industrialized nations). Viewed from a conflict perspective, these terms perpetuate the dominant ideology of capitalist societies.

The term *modernization* also suggests positive change. Yet change, if it comes, often comes slowly, and when it does it tends to serve the affluent segments of industrialized nations. This truism seems to apply to the spread of the latest electronic technologies to the developing world Box 20-2.

A similar criticism has been made of **modernization theory,** a functionalist approach that proposes that modernization and development will gradually improve the lives of people in developing nations. According to this theory, even though nations develop at uneven rates, the development of peripheral nations will be assisted by innovations transferred from the industrialized world. Critics of modernization theory, including dependency theorists, counter that any such technology transfer only increases the dominance of core nations over developing nations and facilitates further exploitation.

When we see all the Coca-Cola and IBM signs going up in developing nations, it is easy to assume that globalization and economic change are effecting cultural change. But that is not always the case, researchers note. Distinctive cultural traditions, such as a particular religious orientation or a nationalistic identity, often persist and can soften the impact of modernization on a developing nation. Some contemporary sociologists emphasize that both industrialized and developing countries are "modern." Increasingly, researchers gauge modernization using a series of social indicators—among them degree of urbanization, energy use, literacy, political democracy, and use of birth control. Clearly, some of these are subjective indicators; even in industrialized nations, not everyone would agree that wider use of birth control is an example of progress (Armer and Katsillis 1992; Hedley 1992; Inglehart and Baker 2000).

Current modernization studies generally take a convergence perspective. Using the indicators just noted, researchers focus on how societies are moving closer together, despite traditional differences. From a conflict perspective, the modernization of developing nations often perpetuates their dependence on and continued exploitation by industrialized nations. Conflict theorists view such continuing dependence on foreign powers as an example of contemporary neocolonialism.

Table 29-1 summarizes the three major approaches to global inequality.

FIGURE 29-6 **Multinational Corporations Compared to Nations**

Corporate revenue — Gross national income

- 440 **Walmart** (USA)
- 437 Saudi Arabia
- 392 **Royal Dutch Shell** (Britain/Netherlands)
- 394 Argentina and Morocco
- 363 **ExxonMobil (USA)**
- 347 Singapore and Chile
- 297 **BP British Petroleum** (Britain)
- 286 Venezuela
- 236 **Chevron** (USA)
- 233 Portugal
- 229 **Toyota** (Japan)
- 228 Colombia
- 187 **Conoco Phillips** (USA)
- 185 Nigeria
- 165 **Volkswagen** (Germany)
- 170 Pakistan
- 150 **AXA** (France)
- 154 Algeria
- 147 **General Electric** (USA)
- 142 **Vietnam and Ecuador**
- 106 **Bank of America** (USA)
- 110 Kazakhstan

Sources: Ranking prepared by author. Revenue from corporate quarterly report statements for 2011. GNI from Bureau of the Census 2011a:Table 1348 on page 846.

Think about It

What happens to society when corporations grow richer than countries and spill across international borders?

Where am I wearing? This UNICEF poster reminds affluent Western consumers that the brand-name jeans they wear may be produced by exploited workers in developing countries. In sweatshops throughout the developing world, nonunion garment workers—some of them children—labor long hours for what we would consider extremely low wages—even if for the workers in those semiperiphery countries, wages are relatively high.

Tracking Sociological Perspectives

Table **29-1** Sociological Perspectives on Global Inequality

Approach	Sociological Perspective	Explanation
World systems analysis	Functionalist and conflict	Unequal economic and political relationships maintain sharp divisions between nations.
Dependency theory	Conflict	Industrialized nations exploit developing nations through colonialism and multinational corporations.
Modernization theory	Functionalist	Developing nations move away from traditional cultures and toward the cultures of industrialized nations.

MODULE 29 | Recap and Review

Summary

Worldwide, stratification can be seen both in the gap between rich and poor nations and in the inequality within countries. This module examines the global divide and stratification within nations as well as the impact of **globalization, modernization,** and **multinational corporations** on developing countries.

1. Developing nations account for most of the world's population and most of its births, but they also bear the burden of most of its poverty, disease, and childhood deaths.

2. Former colonized nations are kept in a subservient position, subject to foreign domination, through the process of **neocolonialism.**

3. Drawing on the conflict perspective, Immanuel Wallerstein's **world systems analysis** views the global economic system as divided between nations that control wealth (core nations) and those from which capital is taken (periphery nations).

4. According to **dependency theory,** even as developing countries make economic advances, they remain weak and subservient to core nations and corporations in an increasingly integrated global economy.

5. **Globalization,** the worldwide integration of government policies, cultures, social movements, and financial markets through trade and the exchange of ideas, is a controversial trend that critics blame for contributing to the cultural domination of periphery nations by core nations.

6. **Multinational corporations** bring jobs and industry to developing nations, but they also tend to exploit workers in order to maximize profits.

7. Sociologists note that terms such as **modernization** and even *development* carry an ethnocentric bias. **Modernization theory** suggests that the development of periphery countries will be assisted by innovations transferred from the industrialized world.

Thinking Critically

1. Relate Durkheim's, Tönnies's, and Lenski's theories of social structure to the global divide that exists today. Could sociocultural evolution have something to do with the global divide?

2. Relate modernization theory to dependency theory. Do you agree with critics that modernization will increase the dominance of core nations? Why or why not?

Key Terms

Colonialism
Dependency theory
Globalization
Modernization
Modernization theory
Multinational corporation
Neocolonialism
World systems analysis

MODULE 30

Stratification within Nations: A Comparative Perspective

At the same time that the gap between rich and poor nations is widening, so too is the gap between rich and poor citizens *within* nations. As discussed earlier, stratification in developing nations is closely related to their relatively weak and dependent position in the global economy. Local elites work hand in hand with multinational corporations and prosper from such alliances. At the same time, the economic system creates and perpetuates the exploitation of industrial and agricultural workers. That is why foreign investment in developing countries tends to increase economic inequality. As Box 30-1 makes clear, inequality within a society is evident in Latin America's most populous nation, Brazil.

Distribution of Wealth and Income

Global inequality is staggering. Worldwide, the richest 2 percent of adults own more than 50 percent of the world's household wealth. In at least 22 nations around the world, the most affluent 10 percent

of the population receives at least 40 percent of all income. The list includes the African nation of Namibia (the leader, at 65 percent of all income), as well as Nicaragua, Thailand, and South Africa. Figure 30-1 compares the distribution of income in selected industrialized and developing nations (World Bank 2011:68–70).

use your **sociological imagination**

Imagine that the United States borders a country with a much higher standard of living. In this neighboring country, the salaries of workers with a college degree start at $120,000 a year. What is life in the United States like?

Social Mobility

Mobility in Industrial Nations

Studies of intergenerational mobility in industrialized nations have found the following patterns:

1. Substantial similarities exist in the ways that parents' positions in the stratification system are transmitted to their children.

2. As in the United States, mobility opportunities in other nations have been influenced by structural factors, such as labor market changes that lead to the rise or decline of an occupational group within the social hierarchy.

3. Immigration continues to be a significant factor in shaping a society's level of intergenerational mobility.

Cross-cultural studies suggest that intergenerational mobility has been increasing over the past 50 years in most but not all countries. In particular, researchers have noted a common pattern of movement away from agriculture-based occupations. However, they are quick to point out that growth in mobility does not necessarily bring growth in equality. Indeed, despite the evidence of steady upward mobility, their studies show that the gap between the rich and the poor has

FIGURE 30-1 **Distribution of Income in Nine Nations**

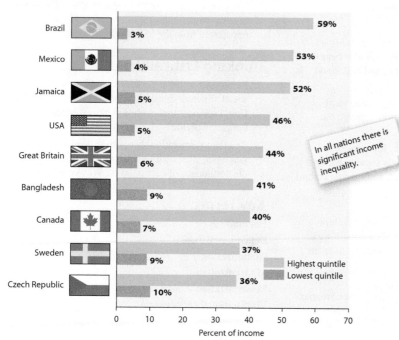

Nation	Highest quintile	Lowest quintile
Brazil	59%	3%
Mexico	53%	4%
Jamaica	52%	5%
USA	46%	5%
Great Britain	44%	6%
Bangladesh	41%	9%
Canada	40%	7%
Sweden	37%	9%
Czech Republic	36%	10%

In all nations there is significant income inequality.

Note: Data are considered comparable although based on statistics covering 1996 to 2010.
Source: World Bank 2012a:74–76.

Sociology in the Global Community

BOX 30-1

Stratification in Brazil

Brazil conjures up exotic images: dazzling beaches, tropical foliage, colorful *Carnival* in Rio de Janeiro. Deep, grinding poverty and persistent inequality may not spring to mind, yet they are as much a part of South America's largest nation and economy as the expensive tourist resorts. Brazil has been described as three nations in one: a rich country with a population the size of Canada's; a poor country with a population equal to Mexico's; and a third nation of indigents—totally impoverished people with no income at all—whose population equals Argentina's.

> As in the United States, Brazil's social inequality is compounded by racial distinctions that originated in slavery.

Not until 1988 did Brazil's government begin to consider a redistribution of wealth or land to remedy these inequities. The resulting program did not get under way until 2003. Since then, the gap between rich and poor has narrowed only a bit.

As in the United States, Brazil's social inequality is compounded by racial distinctions that originated in slavery. However, race is not socially constructed as it is in the United States. In Brazil, unlike the United States, dark skin color has never been a measure of innate inferiority.

Still, Brazil is no racial paradise. Rather, it is a multitiered racist society, one whose government has acknowledged the existence of racism. A country that once prided itself on its freedom from racial intolerance, Brazil has now outlawed

Income by Race, Brazil and the United States

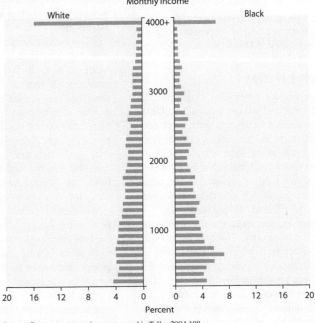

Source: Government agencies, as reported in Telles 2004:108.

discrimination against people of color. Opinion is divided over the effectiveness of the legislation.

Today, the Brazilian economy shows a significant degree of racially related income disparity. As the accompanying figure shows, people of color are clustered disproportionately on the lowest levels of the income pyramid. To remedy this entrenched inequality, Brazil's government has instituted a quota-based affirmative action program that ensures access to higher education for people of color. Because of the lack of clear-cut racial categories in Brazil—Brazilians recognize many different color gradients—charges of reverse racism and complaints about inexplicable classifications have been common. As in the United States, finding solutions to the twin problems of racism and inequality is a challenge.

LET'S DISCUSS

1. Look at the bottom of each of the accompanying graphs. Which income distribution, Brazil's or the United States', appears to be more unequal? Now look at the top of each graph. Which income distribution appears to be more unequal? What aspect of these graphs do you find most striking?

2. Race-based college admissions quotas have been the subject of hot debate in the United States. Why do you think they have been accepted as law in Brazilian society?

Sources: Ash 2007; Daniel 2006; Dzidzienyo 1987; Fiola 2008; Margolis 2009; Santos 2006; SustainAbility 2006; Telles 2004.

In developing countries, people who hope to rise out of poverty often move from the country to the city, where employment prospects are better. The jobs available in industrialized urban areas offer perhaps the best means of upward mobility. This woman works in an electronics factory in Kuala Lumpur, Malaysia.

grown. Over the past 20 years, poverty levels in the 30 largest industrial economies have remained relatively constant (Organisation for Economic Co-operation and Development 2008).

Mobility in Developing Nations

Mobility patterns in industrialized countries are usually associated with both intergenerational and intragenerational mobility. However, in developing nations, macro-level social and economic changes often overshadow micro-level movement from one occupation to another. For example, there is typically a substantial wage differential between rural and urban areas, which leads to high levels of migration to the cities. Yet the urban industrial sectors of developing countries generally cannot provide sufficient employment for all those seeking work.

In large developing nations, the most socially significant mobility is the movement out of poverty. This type of mobility is difficult to measure and confirm, however, because economic trends can differ from one area of a country to another. For instance, China's rapid income growth has been accompanied by a growing disparity in income between urban and rural areas and among different regions. Similarly, in India during the 1990s, poverty declined in urban areas but may have remained static at best in rural areas. Around the world, downward social mobility

is also dramatically influenced by catastrophes such as crop failure and warfare.

Despite the continuing struggles of massive numbers of people, the global economic situation is not entirely bleak. Although economists have documented the stubborn persistence of poverty around the world, they have also noted some growth in the number of people who enjoy a middle-class lifestyle. At the beginning of the 21st century, millions of people entered the middle class in the populous nations of China, India, Russia, Brazil, and Mexico. Entrepreneurship, microfinancing, merchandising, and in some countries, a growing, relatively well-paid government sector have fostered this increase in upward social mobility (R. Adler 2008; *The Economist* 2009a).

Gender Differences in Mobility

Women in developing countries find life especially difficult. Karuna Chanana Ahmed, an anthropologist from India who has studied women in developing nations, calls women the most exploited of oppressed people. Beginning at birth women face sex discrimination. They are commonly fed less than male children, are denied educational opportunities, and are often hospitalized only when they are critically ill. Inside or outside the home, women's work is devalued. When economies fail, as they did in Asian countries in the late 1990s, women are the first to be laid off from work (J. Anderson and Moore 1993; Kristof 1998).

Surveys show a significant degree of *female infanticide* (the killing of baby girls) in China and rural areas of India. Only one-third of Pakistan's sexually segregated schools are for women, and one-third of those schools have no buildings. In Kenya and Tanzania, it is illegal for a woman to own a house. In Saudi Arabia, women are prohibited from driving, walking alone in public, and socializing with men outside their families. We will explore women's second-class status throughout the world more fully in Module 36.

Only recently have researchers begun to investigate the impact of gender on the mobility patterns of developing nations. Many aspects of the development process—especially modernization in rural areas and the rural-to-urban migration just described—may result in the modification or abandonment of traditional cultural practices and even marital systems. The effects on women's social standing and mobility are not necessarily positive. As a country develops and modernizes, women's vital role in food production deteriorates, jeopardizing both their autonomy and their material well-being. Moreover, the movement of families to the cities weakens women's ties to relatives who can provide food, financial assistance, and social support (Lawson 2008).

In the Philippines, however, women have moved to the forefront of the indigenous peoples' struggle to protect their ancestral land from exploitation by outsiders. Having established their right to its rich minerals and forests, members of indigenous groups had begun to feud among themselves over the way in which the land's resources should be developed. Aided by the United Nations Partners in Development Programme, women volunteers established the Pan-Cordillera Women's Network for Peace and Development, a coalition of women's groups dedicated to resolving local disputes. The women mapped boundaries,

case study | **Stratification in Mexico**

Since 1994, when the United States began beefing up patrols along the 2,000-mile border with Mexico, more than 6,000 Mexicans—about 1 every 24 hours—have died attempting to cross the border illegally. Why do Mexicans risk their lives crossing the dangerous desert that lies between the two countries?

The answer to this question can be found in the income disparity between the two nations— one an industrial giant and the other a partially developed country still recovering from a history of colonialism and neocolonialism. In this section we will look in some detail at the dynamics of stratification in Mexico, a country of 108 million people. Since the early 20th century there has been a close cultural, economic, and political relationship between Mexico and the United States, one in which the United States is the dominant party. According to Immanuel Wallerstein's analysis, the United States is at the core while neighboring Mexico is still on the semiperiphery of the world economic system (Jimenez 2009).

A gardener tends the grounds at the opulent Hacienda Temozon hotel in Yucatán State, near Mérida, Mexico. Although international tourism is a major industry in Mexico, most Mexicans have not benefited much from it. Hotel workers earn low wages, and their jobs are jeopardized by the travel industry's frequent boom and bust cycles.

Mexico's Economy

While the faltering U.S. economy is no longer a magnet for foreigners seeking work, Mexico's economy has faltered even more. Many out-of-work Mexicans have begun to return home from the United States, increasing the ranks of the unemployed in Mexico. Those who remain in the United States are less likely than they once were to send money back to their families in Mexico (Jordan 2009).

Although Mexico is unquestionably a poor country, the gap between its richest and poorest citizens is one of the widest in the world (refer back to Figure 30-1). The World Bank has reported that in 2012, 4.9 percent of Mexico's population survived on $2 per day. At the same time, the wealthiest 10 percent of Mexico's people accounted for 37 percent of the entire nation's income. According to *Forbes* magazine's 2011 portrait of the world's wealthiest individuals, that year Mexico was home to the wealthiest person in the world, telecom tycoon Carlos Slim Helu, worth $69 billion. *Forbes'* story also mentioned many other Mexicans who had become wealthy through banking, mining, and retail merchandising ventures (Kroll and Dolan 2012; World Bank 2012a:70, 75).

Political scientist Jorge Castañeda (1995:71) calls Mexico a "polarized society with enormous gaps between rich and poor, town and country, north and south, white and brown (or *criollos* and *mestizos*)." He adds that the country is also divided along lines of class, race, religion, gender, and age.

We will examine stratification within Mexico by focusing on race relations and the plight of Mexican Indians; the status of Mexican women; and emigration to the United States and its impact on the U.S.–Mexican borderlands.

Race Relations in Mexico: The Color Hierarchy

Mexico's indigenous Indians account for an estimated 14 percent of the nation's population. More than 90 percent of them live in houses without sewers, compared with 21 percent of the population as a whole. And whereas just 10 percent of Mexican adults are illiterate, the proportion for Mexican Indians is 44 percent (Boudreaux 2002; *The Economist* 2004; G. Thompson 2001).

The subordinate status of Mexico's Indians is but one reflection of the nation's color hierarchy, which links social class to the appearance of racial purity. At the top of this hierarchy are the *criollos*, the 10 percent of the population who are typically White, well-educated members of the business and intellectual elites, with familial roots in Spain. In the middle is the large, impoverished *mestizo* majority, most of whom have brown skin and a mixed racial lineage as a result of intermarriage. At the bottom of the color hierarchy are the destitute, full-blooded Mexican Indian minority and a small number of Blacks, some descended from 200,000 African slaves brought to Mexico. This color hierarchy is an important part of day-to-day life—enough so that some Mexicans in the cities use hair dyes, skin lighteners, and blue or green contact lenses to appear White and European. Ironically, however, nearly all Mexicans are considered part Indian because of centuries of intermarriage (Castañeda 1995; Stahler-Sholk 2008).

Many observers take note of widespread denial of prejudice and discrimination against people of color in Mexico. Schoolchildren are taught that the election of Benito Juárez, a Zapotec Indian, as president of Mexico in the 19th century proves that all Mexicans are equal. Yet there has been a marked growth in the past decade of formal organizations and voluntary associations representing indigenous Indians (Escárcega 2008; Muñoz 2008).

The Status of Women in Mexico

In 1975, Mexico City hosted the first international conference on the status of women, convened by the United Nations. Much of the discussion concerned the status of women in developing countries; in that regard, the situation is mixed. Women now constitute 48 percent of the labor force—an increase from 34 percent in 1980, but still less than in industrialized countries. Unfortunately, Mexican women are even more mired in the lowest-paying jobs than their counterparts in industrialized nations (Bureau of the Census 2011a:Table 1368).

Feminist sociologists emphasize that even when Mexican women work outside the home, they often are not recognized as active and productive household members, whereas men are typically viewed as heads of the household. As one consequence, women find it difficult to obtain credit and technical assistance in many parts of the country, and to inherit land in rural areas. Within manufacturing and service industries, women generally receive little training and tend to work in the least-automated and least-skilled jobs—in good part because there is little expectation that women will pursue career advancement, organize for better working conditions, or become active in labor unions.

In recent decades, Mexican women have begun to organize to address an array of economic, political, and health issues. Since women continue to serve as the household managers for their families, even when they work outside the home, they are well aware of the consequences of the inadequate public services in lower-income urban neighborhoods. In Mexico's cities, they have organized to improve the quality of water service. And because women are often victimized by criminals on public transport, they have pioneered "pink taxis," women-only buses, and women-only spaces in the subway (Bennett et al. 2005; Llana 2009).

The Borderlands

Growing recognition of the borderlands reflects the increasingly close and complex relationship between Mexico and the United States. The term **borderlands** refers to the area of common culture along the border between these two countries. Legal and illegal emigration from Mexico to the United States, day laborers crossing the border regularly to go to jobs in the United States, the implementation of the North American Free Trade Agreement (NAFTA), and the exchange of media across the border all make the notion of separate Mexican and U.S. cultures obsolete in the borderlands.

The economic position of the borderlands is rather complicated, as we can see in the emergence of *maquiladoras* on the Mexican side (Figure 30-2). These are foreign-owned factories established just across the border in Mexico, where the companies that own them do not have to pay taxes or provide insurance and benefits to workers. The *maquiladoras* have attracted manufacturing jobs from other parts of North America to Mexico. However, they are now experiencing the same challenge from global trade as U.S. manufacturing plants. Beginning in 2001, some companies began shifting their operations to China. While Mexican labor costs (wages plus benefits) are typically $8 to $16 per day, Chinese labor costs are much lower—$2.05 an hour at most. Of the 700,000 new *maquiladora* jobs created by NAFTA, 75 percent were eliminated between 2000 and 2011 (Archibold 2011; Cañas et al. 2007; Rabinovitch 2011).

The social impact of emigration to the United States is felt throughout Mexico. According to sociological research, the earliest emigrants were typically married men of working age who came from the middle of the stratification system. They had enough financial resources to afford the costs and risks of emigration, yet were experiencing enough financial strain that entering the United States was attractive to them. Over time, kinship ties to migrants multiplied and emigration became less class-selective, with entire families making the trek to the United States. More recently, the occupational backgrounds of Mexican emigrants have widened further, reflecting not only changes in U.S. immigration policy but the continuing crisis in the Mexican economy as well (Massey 1998, 2008).

Many Mexicans who have come to the United States send some part of their earnings back across the border to family members still in Mexico. This substantial flow of money, sometimes referred to as **remittances** or *migradollars,* is estimated at a minimum of $24 billion a year and is surpassed only by oil as a source of income. If these funds went solely into the purchase of consumer goods, they would underscore the view of dependency theory, that Mexico's economy is little more than an extension of the economy of the United States. In fact, however, some of these migradollars are used by Mexicans

—Continued

case study | —Continued

MAPPING LIFE WORLDWIDE

FIGURE 30-2 **The Borderlands**

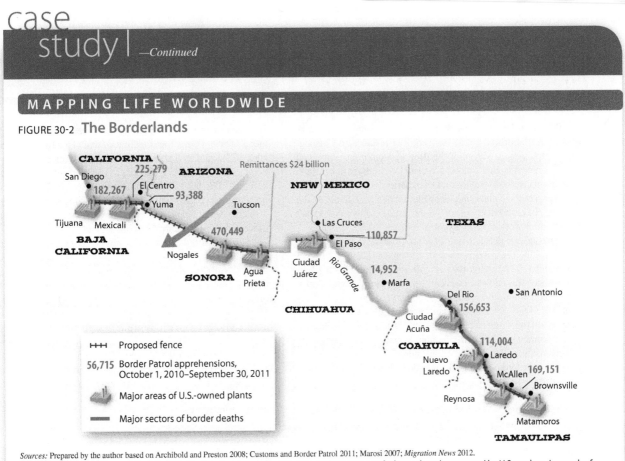

Sources: Prepared by the author based on Archibold and Preston 2008; Customs and Border Patrol 2011; Marosi 2007; *Migration News* 2012.
Maquiladoras located just south of the U.S.–Mexican border employ Mexican workers at wages far lower than those earned by U.S. workers. In search of higher wages, undocumented Mexicans often attempt to cross the border illegally, risking their lives in the process. Mexicans who do reach the United States send large amounts of money, called remittances, back to family in Mexican communities.

Think about It

Do U.S. consumers benefit from the buildup of factories along the U.S.–Mexican border? How or how not?

to establish and maintain small business enterprises, such as handicraft workshops and farms. Consequently, the transfer of migradollars does stimulate the local and national economies of Mexico (*Migration News* 2012).

We have seen that inequality is a problem not just in Mexico, but throughout the world. We turn now to a comparison of the welfare systems that countries have established to help those at the bottom of the social ladder.

prepared development plans, and negotiated more than 2,000 peace pacts among community members. They have also run in elections, campaigned against social problems, and organized residents to work together for the common good (United Nations Development Programme 2000:87).

Studies of the distribution of wealth and income within various countries, together with cross-cultural research on mobility, consistently reveal stratification based on class, gender, and other factors within a wide range of societies. Clearly, a worldwide view of stratification must include not only the sharp contrast

between wealthy and impoverished nations but also the layers of hierarchy *within* industrialized nations and developing nations.

💡 use your **sociological imagination**

Imagine a day when the border between the United States and Mexico is completely open. What would the two countries' economies be like? What would their societies be like?

social policy and Global Inequality | Rethinking Welfare in Europe and North America

In Pasadena, Denise Sims-Bowles, who has been out of work for more than three years, has sent 273 résumés to prospective employers. A victim of the deep economic recession and jobless recovery that followed the stock market crash of 2008, she has more than two decades of experience as a white-collar worker, yet she cannot find an opening. She is not alone. At the end of 2011, about 45 percent of the nation's unemployed had been out of work for half a year or more.

In a suburb in Spain not far from Madrid, Mari Cruz, who used to dine out each week with her husband, eats at a soup kitchen to save money for her children's meals. Both Mari, who once worked for a catering firm, and her husband, Antonio, a construction worker, are unemployed. Once prosperous enough to buy a home, cars, and designer clothes, the couple is now on the verge of poverty, unable to pay the mortgage on their home with their only income, Antonio's unemployment compensation. Hundreds of thousands of families in Spain are in the same predicament, thrown out of work by the global recession.

In Athens, Greece, where the economic collapse was so bad that the nation had to be bailed out by the European Union, the story is even worse. Anargyros D., reluctant to give his last name, has lost everything—his father's business, his home, his personal possessions. Among men his age, the unemployment rate has more than doubled since 2008. His father is supporting him now, on a government pension that has been cut by a third. Looking broken, Anargyros says he has entertained thoughts of suicide. He is not alone. Calls to a local suicide help line have doubled in the last two years (Hay 2009; Scherer 2010a, 2010c; L. Thomas Jr. 2011; Wessel 2011).

These are the faces of people living on the edge. In a time of economic stress and growing need, governments in all parts of the world are searching for the right solution to welfare: How much subsidy should they provide? How much responsibility should fall on the shoulders of the poor?

Looking at the Issue

In the 1990s, an intense debate took place in the United States over the issue of welfare. Welfare programs were costly, and concern was widespread (however unfounded) that welfare payments discouraged recipients from seeking jobs. Both Democrats and Republicans vowed to "end welfare as we know it."

In late 1996, in a historic shift in federal policy, Congress passed the Personal Responsibility and Work Opportunity Reconciliation Act, ending the long-standing federal guarantee of assistance to every poor family that meets eligibility requirements. The law set a lifetime limit of five years of welfare benefits, and required all able-bodied adults to work after receiving two years of benefits (although hardship exceptions were allowed). The federal government would give block grants to the states to use as they wished in assisting poor and needy residents, and it would permit states to experiment with ways to move people off welfare (Seccombe 2011).

In the United States, the government safety net now falls far short of that in Europe, even after recent cutbacks there. Available data indicate that in Great Britain and Sweden, 84 percent of health expenditures are paid for by the government; in Canada, 71 percent; but in the United States, only 53 percent. In fact, most industrialized nations devote higher proportions of their expenditures to housing, social security, welfare, health care, and unemployment compensation than the United States does. As U.S. economist Dean Baker declared recently, "The increase in social spending is still relatively modest given the severity of the downturn. We're not France" (Cauchon 2009; World Bank 2012a:100–102).

Applying Sociology

Many sociologists tend to view the debate over welfare reform in industrialized nations from a conflict perspective: the "haves" in positions of policymaking listen to the interests of other "haves," while the cries of the "have-nots" are drowned out. Critics of welfare reform believe that the nation's economic problems are unfairly blamed on welfare spending and the poor. From a conflict perspective, this backlash against welfare recipients reflects deep fears and hostility toward the nation's urban, predominantly African American and Hispanic underclass.

Those who are critical of the backlash note that "welfare scapegoating" conveniently ignores the lucrative federal handouts that go to *affluent* individuals and families. For example, while federal housing aid to the poor was cut drastically in the 1980s, tax deductions for mortgage interest and property taxes more than doubled.

Conflict theorists have noted an oft-ignored aspect of the welfare system, administrative sanctions. The law allows administrators to end welfare payments if clients fail to complete job-readiness classes, community work, or job searches. A great deal of discretion is used in applying sanctions. According to one study, Black clients are more likely to be sanctioned than White clients (Schram et al. 2009).

—Continued

—Continued

Those who take a conflict perspective also urge policymakers and the general public to look closely at **corporate welfare**—the tax breaks, bailouts, direct payments, and grants that the government gives to corporations—rather than looking closely at the comparatively small allowances being given to mothers and their children. Yet any suggestion to curtail such corporate welfare brings a strong response from special-interest groups that are much more powerful than any coalition on behalf of the poor. One example of corporate welfare is the huge federal bailouts given to distressed financial institutions in fall 2008 and to bankrupt automobile companies in 2009. Although the outlay of hundreds of billions of dollars was vital to the nation's economic recovery, the measure received relatively little scrutiny

In northern and western Europe, following the deep worldwide recession that began in 2008, countries with strong social safety nets were forced to cut back benefits. These civil servants in Granada, Spain, are protesting salary cutbacks.

from Congress. Just a few months later, however, when legislation was proposed to extend the safety net for laid-off workers—unemployment compensation, food stamps, subsidized child care, assistance to the homeless, disability support, and infant nutrition—it met with loud demands for the monitoring of expenditures (DeParle 2009; Piven and Cloward 1996).

Initiating Policy

The government likes to highlight welfare-reform success stories. Though many people who once depended on tax dollars are now working and paying taxes themselves, it is much too soon to see if "workfare" will be successful. The new jobs that were generated by the booming economy of the late 1990s were an unrealistic test of the system. Prospects have faded for the hard-core jobless—people who are difficult to train or are encumbered by drug or alcohol abuse, physical disabilities, or child care needs—since that boom passed.

True, fewer people remain on the rolls since welfare reform was enacted in August 1996. By November 2011 just under 1.9 million families were still on the rolls, down 65 percent from a high of 5.1 million in 1994. But while those families that have left the rolls are modestly better off now, most of their breadwinners continue to hold low-paying, unskilled jobs. For them, the economic downturn that was well in place by 2009 made finding work tougher than ever. Of those adults who remain on welfare, nearly 60 percent are not in school or in welfare-to-work

programs, as the law requires them to be. This group tends to face the greatest challenges—substance abuse, mental illness, or a criminal record (Bitler and Hoynes 2010; Danziger 2010; Department of Health and Human Services 2012a).

European governments have encountered many of the same citizen demands as in North America: keep our taxes low, even if it means reducing services to the poor. However, nations in eastern and central Europe have faced a special challenge since the end of communism. Though governments in those nations traditionally provided an impressive array of social services, they differed from capitalist systems in several important respects. First, the communist system was premised on full employment, so there was no need to provide unemployment insurance; social services focused on the old and the disabled. Second, subsidies for housing and even utilities played an important role. With new competition from the West and tight budgets, some of these countries are beginning to realize that universal coverage is no longer affordable and must be replaced with targeted programs.

The reduction in state assistance to the unemployed is not limited to the former Soviet bloc. Even Sweden, despite its long history of social welfare programs, is feeling the pinch. Welfare payments have been reduced there over the past two years, and the number of sick days and other employment benefits trimmed. Yet by any standard, the European safety net is still significantly stronger than that of the United States (*The Economist* 2010d; Petrášová 2006; M. Walker and Thurow 2009).

—Continued

This decline in public assistance has not escaped public attention. Erik O. Wright, 2012 president of the American Sociological Society, has observed that the Occupy Wall Street movement (described at the beginning of Chapter 8) "is not a uniquely American event . . . it is part of a global wave of protests." Wright senses rising concern that "harsh inequalities" are becoming "increasingly illegitimate. It would appear the present trends in welfare policy are doing little to address these concerns" (E. O. Wright 2011).

TAKE THE ISSUE WITH YOU

1. Do you personally know anyone who has had to depend on public assistance, such as food stamps? If so, what were the circumstances? Would you yourself need government assistance under such circumstances?

2. Do you think welfare recipients should be required to work? If so, what kind of support should they receive? Should any exceptions be granted to the work requirement?

3. Why do you think western and northern European countries have more generous welfare programs than the United States?

MODULE 30 | Recap and Review

Summary

This module examines the effects of stratification within nations. The global economic system creates and perpetuates the gap between the rich and poor in developing nations.

1. Although Mexico is unquestionably a poor country, the gap between its richest and poorest citizens is one of the widest in the world.

2. The subordinate status of Mexico's Indians is but one reflection of the nation's color hierarchy, which links social class to the appearance of racial purity.

3. Growing recognition of the **borderlands** reflects the increasingly close and complex relationship between Mexico and the United States.

Thinking Critically

1. Contrast social mobility in developing and industrial nations. Do you think the differences will eventually disappear? Why or why not?

2. How do the borderlands increase social mobility within Mexico? How do they hinder it?

Key Terms

Borderlands

Corporate Welfare

Remittances

Mastering This Chapter: Global Inequality

taking sociology with you

1 Pick a multinational corporation whose products you are familiar with and look up its financial statements. In which countries does the corporation produce products and in which does it sell products? In which country does the corporation pay taxes? To which country do its profits flow? Why should the answers to these questions matter to you?

2 Choose a foreign country that you are interested in and do some research on social stratification in that country. How equally or unequally are wealth and income distributed there, in comparison to the United States? How extensive is social mobility? Explain the reasons for any differences in stratification.

3 Choose a European country and a developing country and do some research on their welfare systems. How do the two systems differ? How does each reflect the culture and society it serves?

key terms

Borderlands The area of common culture along the border between Mexico and the United States.

Colonialism The maintenance of political, social, economic, and cultural domination over a people by a foreign power for an extended period.

Corporate welfare Tax breaks, bailouts, direct payments, and grants that the government gives to corporations.

Dependency theory An approach that contends that industrialized nations continue to exploit developing countries for their own gain.

Globalization The worldwide integration of government policies, cultures, social movements, and financial markets through trade and the exchange of ideas.

Modernization The far-reaching process through which periphery nations move from traditional or less developed institutions to those characteristic of more developed societies.

Modernization theory A functionalist approach that proposes that modernization and development will gradually improve the lives of people in developing nations.

Multinational corporation A commercial organization that is headquartered in one country but does business throughout the world.

Neocolonialism Continuing dependence of former colonies on foreign countries.

Remittances The monies that immigrants return to their families of origin. Also called *migradollars*.

World systems analysis The global economy as an interdependent system of economically and politically unequal nations.

self-quiz

Read each question carefully and then select the best answer.

1. The maintenance of political, social, economic, and cultural domination over a people by a foreign power for an extended period is referred to as
   a. neocolonialism.
   b. government-imposed stratification.
   c. colonialism.
   d. dependency.

2. In viewing the global economic system as divided between nations that control wealth and those that are controlled and exploited, sociologist Immanuel Wallerstein draws on the
   a. functionalist perspective.
   b. conflict perspective.

   c. interactionist perspective.
   d. dramaturgical approach.

3. Which of the following nations would Immanuel Wallerstein classify as a *core* country within the world economic system?
   a. Germany
   b. South Korea
   c. Ireland
   d. Mexico

4. Which sociological perspective argues that multinational corporations can actually help the developing nations of the world?
   a. the interactionist perspective
   b. the feminist perspective

c. the functionalist perspective
d. the conflict perspective

5. Which of the following terms is used by contemporary social scientists to describe the far-reaching process by which peripheral nations move from traditional or less developed institutions to those characteristic of more developed societies?
   a. dependency
   b. globalization
   c. industrialization
   d. modernization

6. In at least 22 nations around the world, the most affluent 10 percent receives at least what percentage of all income?
   a. 20 percent
   b. 30 percent
   c. 40 percent
   d. 50 percent

7. Karuna Chanana Ahmed, an anthropologist from India who has studied developing nations, calls which group the most exploited of oppressed people?
   a. children
   b. women

c. the elderly
d. the poor

8. Which of the following terms is used to refer to Mexico's large, impoverished majority, most of whom have brown skin and a mixed racial lineage due to intermarriage?
   a. *criollo*
   b. *indio*
   c. *mestizo*
   d. *zapatista*

9. In Mexico, women now constitute what percentage of the labor force?
   a. 15 percent
   b. 23 percent
   c. 34 percent
   d. 48 percent

10. Which of the following terms refers to the foreign-owned factories established just across the border in Mexico, where the companies that own them don't have to pay taxes or provide insurance or benefits for their workers?
    a. *maquiladoras*
    b. *hombres*
    c. *mujeres*
    d. *toreadors*

11. Colonial domination established patterns of economic exploitation leading to former colonies remaining dependent on more industrialized nations. Such continuing dependence and foreign domination are referred to as _____.

12. According to Immanuel Wallerstein's analysis, the United States is at the _____ while neighboring Mexico is on the _____ of the world economic system.

13. Wallerstein's world systems analysis is the most widely used version of _____ theory.

14. _____ factories are factories found throughout the developing world that are run by multinational corporations.

15. As _____ industries become a more important part of the international marketplace, many companies have concluded that the low costs of overseas operations more than offset the expense of transmitting information around the world.

16. Viewed from a(n) _____ perspective, the combination of skilled technology and management provided by multinationals and the relatively cheap labor available in developing nations is ideal for a global enterprise.

17. In 2000 the United Nations launched the _____ _____; its objective is to eliminate extreme poverty worldwide by the year 2015.

18. Modernization theory reflects the _____ perspective.

19. At the top of the color hierarchy in Mexico are the _____, the 10 percent of the population who are typically White, well-educated members of the business and intellectual elites, and who have familial roots in Spain.

20. The term _____ refers to the area of a common culture along the border between Mexico and the United States.

thinking about movies

The End of Poverty?

This documentary asks whether we can close the gap between rich and poor nations by redistributing the world's wealth.

Hotel Rwanda

A hotel becomes a safe haven during the Rwandan genocide.

The Inheritors

Mexican agricultural laborers endure harsh working conditions in this documentary film.

Racial and Ethnic Inequality

10

Racial and Ethnic Inequality

MODULE **31** Minority, Racial, and Ethnic Groups

MODULE **32** Sociological Perspectives on Race and Ethnicity

MODULE **33** Race and Ethnicity in the United States

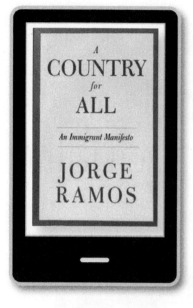

What kind of barriers to success have you faced in your life? Were they connected to your race, ethnicity, or citizenship status?

Many people have faced such barriers and overcome them, but few of them have risen as fast and as far as Alfredo Quiñones-Hinojosa.

" The life of Alfredo Quiñones-Hinojosa is an inspiring example of what an undocumented [illegal] immigrant can do in the United States when given the opportunity.

Alfredo came to the United States as an undocumented immigrant in 1987. He was just nineteen years old, and one of six children. "I was hopping back and forth," he told me, "between Calexico (in the United States) and Mexicali (in Mexico).... All I wanted to do back then was provide food and basic living essentials to a very poor Mexican family."

Alfredo crossed over the border without the aid of a coyote, or guide. His family didn't have the six-hundred-dollar going rate to hire one at the time.

His first job was as a farmhand, cultivating tomatoes, chili peppers, and cotton in central California's San Joaquin Valley. He earned $3.35 an hour. Later, he moved to a small city, where he tried his hand at other jobs: sweeping floors, shoeing horses, and soldering metal. That was where he learned English, and eventually he applied and was accepted to a local community college.

His next big step was when he accepted an offer to study at the University of California at Berkeley. Alfredo dreamed of becoming a doctor, and nothing was going to stop him.

After graduating from Berkeley, Alfredo was accepted to Harvard Medical School, where he graduated with honors. He then returned to California to complete his residency in neurosurgery at the University of California–San Francisco.

This young man, who started his working life harvesting cotton in the fields, now serves as the director of the brain tumor program at the Johns Hopkins Bayview campus.

After enduring a lengthy legal process, Alfredo became an American citizen in 1997. And in Boston, during his citizenship ceremony, he came to the realization that in a short time he had achieved something that takes most others an entire generation.

"The person who was speaking at the ceremony began to talk about how his great-grandfather had come here from Italy, and that his grandfather had worked hard so that his father could become a teacher, and how he eventually got to Harvard," he recalled. "And I realized that in less than ten years, I had jumped over all those generations."

As he told me, "A jump like that might seem incredible, but it's not impossible."

Today, Alfredo's expertise in treating spinal, brain stem, and brain tumors quite literally saves lives. Every single day. He is also heavily involved in researching the origins of tumors, and in developing new ways of treating brain cancer that might one day lead to a cure. "That would be my dream," he said. "Of course, many people consider that impossible. But that's also what people would have said about my life, back when I was only nineteen years old," and an undocumented farm worker.

There are many people like Dr. Quiñones-Hinojosa living among us, and with as much potential. But so many are not as lucky as he is.

These millions continue to live in the shadows. "

(Ramos 2010:xiii–xvi) Additional information about this excerpt can be found on the Online Learning Center at www.mhhe.com/schaefermod2e

His first job was as a farmhand, cultivating tomatoes, chili peppers, and cotton in central California's San Joaquin Valley. He earned $3.35 an hour.

I n this excerpt from *A Country for All: An Immigrant Manifesto,* journalist Jorge Ramos writes about the remarkable life of Dr. Alfredo Quiñones-Hinojosa, or Dr. Q, as he has come to be known. Few people, even those who are privileged, attend Harvard University and then go on to become neurosurgeons and brain researchers. On the face of it, Dr. Q's rise from immigrant farm laborer to eminent neurosurgeon suggests that the United States is a land of opportunity for all, despite race or ethnicity. Yet immigrants like Quiñones-Hinojosa, who crossed the Mexican border illegally at age 19, are exactly the people that government policymakers now want to exclude from the United States (Quiñones-Hinojosa with Rivas 2011).

What sense are we to make of the issues of race, ethnicity, and immigration in the 21st century? Today, unlike Dr. Q, millions of African Americans, Asian Americans, Hispanic Americans, and many other racial and ethnic minorities experience an often bitter contrast between the "American dream" and the grim realities of poverty, prejudice, and discrimination. Like class, the social definitions of race and ethnicity still affect people's place and status in a stratification system, not only in this country, but throughout the world. High incomes, a good command of English, and hard-earned professional credentials do not always override racial and ethnic stereotypes or protect those who fit them from the sting of racism.

What is prejudice, and how is it institutionalized in the form of discrimination? In what ways have race and ethnicity affected the experience of immigrants from other countries? What are the fastest-growing minority groups in the United States today? In this chapter we will focus on the meaning of race and ethnicity. We will begin by identifying the basic characteristics of a minority group and distinguishing between racial and ethnic groups. Then we will examine the dynamics of prejudice and discrimination. After considering four sociological perspectives on race and ethnicity, we'll take a look at common patterns of intergroup relations. The following section will describe the major racial and ethnic groups in the United States. Finally, in the Social Policy section we will explore the issue of global immigration.

MODULE 31 | Minority, Racial, and Ethnic Groups

Sociologists frequently distinguish between racial and ethnic groups. The term **racial group** describes a group that is set apart from others because of physical differences that have taken on social significance. Whites, African Americans, and Asian Americans are all considered racial groups in the United States. While race does turn on physical differences, it is the culture of a particular society that constructs and attaches social significance to those differences, as we will see later. Unlike racial groups, an **ethnic group** is set apart from others primarily because of its national origin or distinctive cultural patterns. In the United States, Puerto Ricans, Jews, and Polish Americans are all categorized as ethnic groups (Table 31-1).

Minority Groups

A numerical minority is any group that makes up less than half of some larger population. The population of the United States includes thousands of numerical minorities, including television actors, green-eyed people, tax lawyers, and descendants of the Pilgrims who arrived on the *Mayflower*. However, these numerical minorities are not considered to be minorities in the sociological sense; in fact, the number of people in a group does not necessarily determine its status as a social minority (or a dominant group). When sociologists define a minority group, they are concerned primarily with the economic and political power, or powerlessness, of that group. A **minority group** is a subordinate group whose members have significantly less control or power over their own lives than the members of a dominant or majority group have over theirs.

Sociologists have identified five basic properties of a minority group: unequal treatment, physical or cultural traits, ascribed status, solidarity, and in-group marriage (Wagley and Harris 1958):

1. Members of a minority group experience unequal treatment compared to members of a dominant group. For example, the management of an apartment complex may refuse to rent to African Americans, Hispanics, or Jews. Social inequality may be created or maintained by prejudice, discrimination, segregation, or even extermination.

2. Members of a minority group share physical or cultural characteristics that distinguish them from the dominant group. Each society arbitrarily decides which characteristics are most important in defining groups.

3. Membership in a minority (or dominant) group is not voluntary; people are born into the group. Thus, race and ethnicity are considered *ascribed* statuses.

4. Minority group members have a strong sense of group solidarity. William Graham Sumner, writing in 1906, noted that people make distinctions between members of their own group (the *in-group*) and everyone else (the *out-group*). When a group is the object of long-term prejudice and discrimination, the feeling of "us versus them" can and often does become extremely intense.

5. Members of a minority group generally marry others from the same group. A member of a dominant group is often unwilling to marry into a supposedly inferior minority group. In addition, the minority group's sense of solidarity encourages marriage within the group and discourages marriage to outsiders.

Race

Many people think of race as a series of biological classifications. However, research shows that is not a meaningful way of differentiating people. Genetically, there are no systematic differences between the races that affect people's social behavior and abilities. Instead, sociologists use the term *racial group* to refer to those minorities (and the corresponding dominant groups) who are set apart from others by obvious physical differences. But what is an "obvious" physical difference? Each society labels those differences that people consider important, while ignoring other characteristics that could serve as a basis for social differentiation.

Social Construction of Race

Because race is a social construction, the process of defining races typically benefits those who have more power and privilege than others. In the United States, we see differences in both skin color and hair color. Yet people learn informally that differences in skin color have a dramatic social and political meaning, whereas differences in hair color do not.

When observing skin color, many people in the United States tend to lump others rather casually into the traditional categories of "Black," "White," and "Asian." Subtle differences in skin color often go unnoticed. In many nations of Central America and South America, in contrast, people recognize color gradients on a continuum from light to dark skin color. Brazil has approximately 40 color groupings, while in other countries people may be described as "Mestizo Hondurans," "Mulatto Colombians," or "African Panamanians." What we see as "obvious" differences, then, are subject to each society's social definitions.

Table **31-1**   Racial and Ethnic Groups in the United States, 2010

Classification	Number in Thousands	Percentage of Total Population
Racial Groups		
Whites (non-Hispanic)	194,553	63.1%
Blacks/African Americans	34,658	11.2
Native Americans, Alaskan Natives	2,476	0.8
Asian Americans	15,899	5.2
Chinese	3,535	1.1
Asian Indians	2,919	1.0
Filipinos	2,650	0.9
Vietnamese	1,633	0.5
Koreans	1,464	0.5
Japanese	842	0.3
Pacific Islanders, Native Hawaiians, and other Asian Americans	2,856	0.9
Ethnic Groups		
White ancestry (single or mixed, non-Hispanic)		
Germans	49,345	16.0
Irish	35,664	11.6
English	26,874	8.7
Italians	17,491	5.7
Poles	9,757	3.2
French	9,159	3.0
Scottish and Scotch-Irish	9,122	3.0
Jews	6,452	2.1
Hispanics (or Latinos)	50,478	16.4
Mexican Americans	31,798	10.3
Puerto Ricans	4,624	1.5
Cubans	1,785	0.6
Salvadorans	1,648	0.5
Dominicans	1,415	0.5
Guatemalans	1,044	0.3
Other Hispanics	8,164	2.7
TOTAL (all groups)	**308,746**	

Note: All data for 2010. Percentages do not total 100 percent, and subheads do not add up to totals in major categories because of overlap between groups (e.g., Polish American Jews or people of mixed ancestry, such as Irish and Italian).

Sources: 2008–2010 3-year estimate from American Community Survey 2011:Tables B04003, B03001, C04006; Davidson and Pyle 2011:117; Ennis et al. 2011; Hoeffel et al. 2012; Humes et al. 2011.

The largest racial minorities in the United States are African Americans (or Blacks), Native Americans (or American Indians), and Asian Americans (Japanese Americans, Chinese Americans, and other Asian peoples). Figure 31-1 provides information about the population of racial and ethnic groups in the United States over the past five centuries.

Given current population patterns, it is clear that the nation's diversity will continue to increase. In 2011, for the first time ever, census data revealed that the majority of all children ages three and under are now either Hispanic or non-White. This turning point marks the beginning of a pattern in which the nation's minority population will slowly become the majority. By 2050, if not sooner, the majority of all school-age children in the United States will belong to racial or ethnic minority groups (Frey 2011).

Racial definitions are crystallized through what Michael Omi and Howard Winant (1994) have called **racial formation,** a sociohistorical process in which racial categories are created, inhabited, transformed, and destroyed. In this process, those who have power define groups of people according to a racist social structure. The creation of a reservation system for Native Americans in the late 1800s is one example of racial formation. Federal officials combined what were distinctive tribes into a single racial group, which we refer to today as Native Americans. The extent and frequency with which peoples are subject to racial formation is such that no one escapes it.

Another example of racial formation from the 1800s was known as the "one-drop rule." If a person had even a single drop of "Black blood," that person was defined and viewed as Black, even if he or she *appeared* to be White. Clearly, race had social significance, enough so that White legislators established official standards about who was "Black" and who was "White."

The one-drop rule was a vivid example of the *social construction of race*—the process by which people come to define a group as a race based in part on physical characteristics, but also on historical, cultural, and economic factors. For example, in the 1800s, immigrant groups such as Italian and Irish Americans were not at first seen as being "White," but as foreigners who were not necessarily trustworthy. The social construction of race is an ongoing process that is subject to debate, especially in a diverse society such as the United States, where each year increasing numbers of children are born to parents of different racial backgrounds.

Recognition of Multiple Identities

In 1900, in an address to the Anti-Slavery Union in London, scholar W. E. B. DuBois predicted that "the color line" would become the foremost problem of the 20th century. DuBois, born a free Black man in 1868, had witnessed prejudice and discrimination throughout the United States. His comment was prophetic. Today, over a century later, race and ethnicity still carry enormous weight in the United States (DuBois [1900] 1969).

The color line has blurred significantly since 1900, however. Interracial marriage is no longer forbidden by law and custom. Thus, Geetha Lakshmi-narayanan, a native of Ann Arbor, Michigan, is both White and Asian Indian. Often mistaken for a Filipina or Latina, she has grown accustomed to the blunt question "What are you?" (Navarro 2005).

In the late 20th century, with immigration from Latin America rising, the fluid nature of racial formation became evident.

FIGURE 31-1 Racial and Ethnic Groups in the United States, 1500–2100 (Projected)

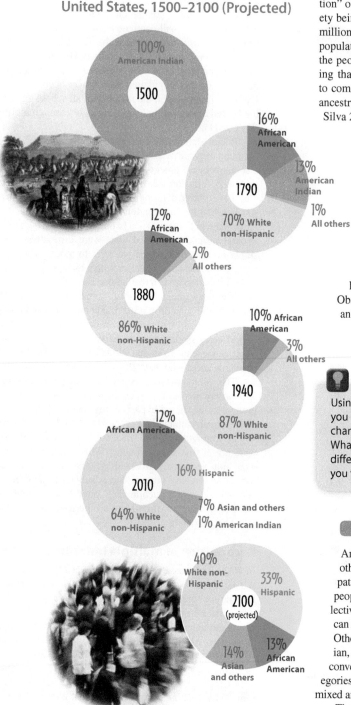

1500
100% American Indian

1790
16% African American
13% American Indian
1% All others
70% White non-Hispanic

1880
12% African American
2% All others
86% White non-Hispanic

1940
10% African American
3% All others
87% White non-Hispanic

2010
12% African American
16% Hispanic
7% Asian and others
1% American Indian
64% White non-Hispanic

2100 (projected)
40% White non-Hispanic
33% Hispanic
13% African American
14% Asian and others

Sources: Author's estimate; Bureau of the Census 2004a; Humes et al. 2011. Data for 2010 and 2100, African American and Asian and others, are for non-Hispanics.

The racial and ethnic composition of what is today the United States has been undergoing change not just for the past 50 years, but for the past 500. Five centuries ago the land was populated only by indigenous Native Americans.

Suddenly, people were speaking about the "Latin Americanization" of the United States, or about a biracial, Black/White society being replaced by a triracial one. In the 2010 Census, over 9 million people in the United States (or about 2.9 percent of the population) reported that they were of two or more races. Half the people classified as multiracial were under age 18, suggesting that this segment of the population will grow in the years to come. People who claimed both White and American Indian ancestry were the largest group of multiracial residents (Bonilla-Silva 2004; Humes et al. 2011).

This statistical finding of millions of multiracial people obscures how individuals are often asked to handle their identity. For example, the enrollment forms for government programs typically include only a few broad racial-ethnic categories. This approach to racial categorization is part of a long history that dictates single-race identities. Still, many individuals, especially young adults, struggle against social pressure to choose a single identity, and instead openly embrace multiple heritages. Public figures, rather than hide their mixed ancestry, now flaunt it. Singer Mariah Carey celebrates her Irish American background, and President Barack Obama speaks of being born in Hawaii to a Kenyan father and a White mother from Kansas. Tiger Woods, the world's best-known professional golfer, considers himself both Asian and African American.

use your **sociological imagination**

Using a TV remote control, how quickly do you think you could find a television show in which all the characters share your racial or ethnic background? What about a show in which all the characters share a different background from yours—how quickly could you find one?

Ethnicity

An ethnic group, unlike a racial group, is set apart from others because of its national origin or distinctive cultural patterns. Among the ethnic groups in the United States are peoples with a Spanish-speaking background, referred to collectively as *Latinos* or *Hispanics,* such as Puerto Ricans, Mexican Americans, Cuban Americans, and other Latin Americans. Other ethnic groups in this country include Jewish, Irish, Italian, and Norwegian Americans. Although these groupings are convenient, they serve to obscure differences *within* ethnic categories (as in the case of Hispanics), as well as to overlook the mixed ancestry of so many people in the United States.

The distinction between racial and ethnic minorities is not always clear-cut. Some members of racial minorities, such as Asian Americans, may have significant cultural differences from other racial groups. At the same time, certain ethnic minorities, such as Latinos, may have obvious physical differences that set them apart from other ethnic groups in the United States.

Despite categorization problems, sociologists continue to feel that the distinction between racial groups and ethnic groups is socially significant. In most societies, including the United States, socially constructed physical differences tend to be more visible than ethnic differences. Partly as a result of this fact, stratification along racial lines is more resistant to change than stratification along ethnic lines. Over time, members of an ethnic minority can sometimes become indistinguishable from the majority—although the process may take generations and may never include all members of the group. In contrast, members of a racial minority find it much more difficult to blend in with the larger society and gain acceptance from the majority.

The inauguration of President Barack Obama in 2009 was clearly historic. To put its significance in perspective, however, Obama's Senate seat was the only one held by a Black man when he left it to become president. More than half of White voters in the 2008 presidential election—57 percent—cast their ballots for candidates other than Obama

Prejudice and Discrimination

Looking at the United States in the 21st century, some people wonder aloud if race and ethnicity are still relevant to social stratification. After all, African Americans have served as secretary of state, secretary of defense, and chairman of the Joint Chiefs of Staff; the office of attorney general has been held by both an African American and a Hispanic. Most notably, an African American now serves as president. As historic as these leaders' achievements have been, however, in every case their elevation meant that they left behind a virtually all-White government department or assembly.

At the same time, college campuses across the United States have been the scene of bias-related incidents. Student-run newspapers and radio stations have ridiculed racial and ethnic minorities; threatening literature has been stuffed under the doors of

Today, some children of mixed-race families identify themselves as biracial or multiracial, rejecting efforts to place them in a single racial category.

minority students; graffiti endorsing the views of White supremacist organizations such as the Ku Klux Klan have been scrawled on university walls. In some cases, there have even been violent clashes between groups of White and Black students (Southern Poverty Law Center 2010). What causes such ugly incidents?

Prejudice

Prejudice is a negative attitude toward an entire category of people, often an ethnic or racial minority. If you resent your

roommate because he or she is sloppy, you are not necessarily guilty of prejudice. However, if you immediately stereotype your roommate on the basis of such characteristics as race, ethnicity, or religion, that is a form of prejudice. Prejudice tends to perpetuate false definitions of individuals and groups.

Sometimes prejudice results from **ethnocentrism**—the tendency to assume that one's own culture and way of life represent the norm or are superior to all others. Ethnocentric people judge other cultures by the standards of their group, which leads quite easily to prejudice against cultures they view as inferior.

One important and widespread ideology that reinforces prejudice is **racism,** the belief that one race is supreme and all others are innately inferior. When racism prevails in a society, members of subordinate groups generally experience prejudice, discrimination, and exploitation. In 1990, as concern mounted about racist attacks in the United States, Congress passed the Hate Crimes Statistics Act. As a result, **hate crimes** are now beginning to be reported and

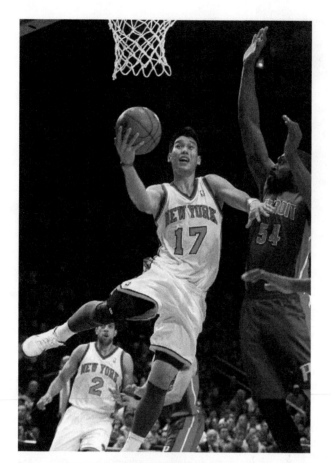

Even successful members of minority groups are subjected to ethnic slurs. "Chink in the Armor" proclaimed a headline on ESPN's website after Jeremy Lin, who had spearheaded the New York Knicks in a multigame winning streak, had a bad night. The network later apologized for the remark.

investigated in much the same way as conventional crimes against property and people (see Module 25).

Prejudice is also rooted in racial and ethnic **stereotypes**—unreliable generalizations about all members of a group that do not recognize individual differences within the group. The dominant or majority group creates these stereotypes through the process of racial formation. As the interactionist William I. Thomas (1923) noted, the dominant group's "definition of the situation" is often so powerful, it can mold the individual personality. That is, people respond not only to the objective features of a situation or person, but to the *social meaning* that situation or person carries. Thus, the false images or stereotypes created by the dominant group can become real in their consequences.

Color-Blind Racism

Over the past three generations, nationwide surveys have consistently shown growing support among Whites for integration, interracial dating, and the election of minority group members to public office—including the presidency of the United States. How can this trend be explained, given the persistence of residential segregation and the commission of thousands of hate crimes every year? The answer, to some extent, is that prejudice and discriminatory attitudes are no longer expressed as freely as they once were. Often, they are couched in terms of equal opportunity.

Color-blind racism is the use of the principle of race neutrality to defend a racially unequal status quo. Proponents of race neutrality claim they believe that everyone should be treated equally. However, the way they apply the principle to government policy is anything but neutral. Proponents of this approach oppose affirmative action (see page 260), public welfare assistance, and to a large extent, government-funded health insurance, all of which they see largely as favors to minority groups. Yet they do not object to practices that privilege Whites, such as college admissions criteria that give preference to the relatives of alumni. Nor do they oppose tax breaks for homeowners, most of whom are White, or government financial aid to college students, who are also disproportionately White. Though race neutrality is not based on theories of racial superiority or inferiority, then, the idea that society should be color-blind only perpetuates racial inequality.

Color-blind racism has also been referred to as "covert racism." Although its proponents rarely speak of racism, other indicators of social status, such as social class or citizenship, tend to become proxies for race. Thus, many White people can convince themselves that they are not racist—nor do they know anyone who is—and yet remain prejudiced against "welfare mothers" and "immigrants." They can conclude, mistakenly, that racial tolerance, or even racial and ethnic equality, has been achieved.

Researchers who have surveyed White attitudes toward African Americans over the past several decades have reached two inescapable conclusions. First, people's attitudes do change.

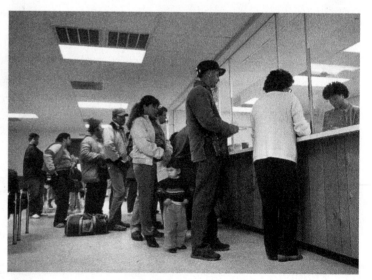

People in need of help crowd a government public assistance office. Those who oppose government welfare programs but support other forms of government assistance, such as financial aid to college students, may be exhibiting color-blind racism.

In periods of social upheaval, dramatic attitudinal shifts can occur within a single generation. Second, less racial progress was made in the late 20th and early 21st centuries than in the relatively brief period of the 1950s and 1960s. Today, economically disadvantaged groups such as African Americans and Latinos have become so closely associated with urban decay, homelessness, welfare, and crime that those problems are now viewed as racial issues, even if they are not labeled as such. The tendency to *blame the victims* of these social ills complicates their resolution (see the Social Policy section in Module 30), especially at a time when government's ability to address social problems is limited by recession, antitax initiatives, and concern over terrorism. In short, the color line is still in place, even if more and more people refuse to acknowledge its existence (Ansell 2008; Bonilla-Silva 2006; Coates 2008; M. King 2007:3–4; Quillian 2006; Winant 1994:106–108).

Discriminatory Behavior

Prejudice often leads to **discrimination,** the denial of opportunities and equal rights to individuals and groups because of prejudice or other arbitrary reasons. Say that a White corporate president with a prejudice against Asian Americans has to fill an executive position. The most qualified candidate for the job is a Vietnamese American. If the president refuses to hire this candidate and instead selects an inferior White candidate, he or she is engaging in an act of racial discrimination.

Prejudiced *attitudes* should not be equated with discriminatory *behavior.* Although the two are generally related, they are not identical; either condition can be present without the other. A prejudiced person does not always act on his or her biases.

The White corporate president, for example, might choose—despite his or her stereotypes—to hire the Vietnamese American. That would be prejudice without discrimination. On the other hand, a White corporate president with a completely respectful view of Vietnamese Americans might refuse to hire them for executive posts out of fear that biased clients would take their business elsewhere. In that case, the president's action would constitute discrimination without prejudice.

A field experiment by sociologist Devah Pager, then a doctoral candidate at the University of Wisconsin–Madison, documented racial discrimination in hiring. Pager sent four polite, well-dressed young men out to look for an entry-level job in Milwaukee, Wisconsin. All were 23-year-old college students, but they presented themselves as high school graduates with similar job histories. Two of the men were Black and two were White. One Black applicant and one White applicant claimed to have served 18 months in jail for a felony conviction—possession of cocaine with intent to distribute.

As one might expect, the four men's experiences with 350 potential employers were vastly different. Predictably, the White applicant with a purported prison record received only half as many callbacks as the other White applicant—17 percent compared to 34 percent. But as dramatic as the effect of his criminal record was, the effect of his race was more significant. Despite his prison record, he received slightly more callbacks than the Black applicant *with no criminal record* (17 percent compared to 14 percent). Race, it seems, was more of a concern to potential employers than a criminal background.

The implications of this research are not limited to any one city, such as Milwaukee. Similar studies have confirmed discriminatory handling of job applications in Chicago; New York City; Long Island, New York; San Diego; and Washington, D.C. Over time, the cumulative effect of such differential behavior by employers contributes to significant differences in income. Figure 31-2 vividly illustrates the income inequality between White men and almost everyone else (Pager 2007; Pager et al. 2009).

If race serves as a barrier, why do Asian American men earn slightly more income than White men (see Figure 31-2)? Not all Asian American men earn high incomes; indeed, some Asian American groups, such as Laotians and Vietnamese, have high levels of poverty. Nevertheless, a significant number of Asian Americans have advanced degrees that qualify them for highly paid jobs, and which raise the median income for the group as a whole. Although these highly educated Asian Americans earn a lot of money, they do not earn quite as much as their White counterparts, however. With a doctorate holder in the family, the typical Asian American household earns an estimated $130,000, compared to $140,000 for a White household.

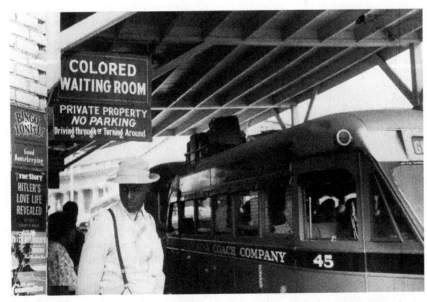

Before passage of the Civil Rights Act (1964), segregation of public accommodations was the norm throughout the South. Whites used the most up-to-date bathrooms, waiting rooms, and even drinking fountains, while Blacks ("Colored") were directed to older facilities in inferior condition. Such separate but unequal arrangements are a blatant example of discrimination.

Sometimes racial and ethnic discrimination is overt. Internet forums like Craigslist.org or Roommate.com feature classified ads that state "African Americans and Arabians tend to clash with me" or "Clean, Godly Christian men only." While anti-discrimination laws prevent such notices from being published in the newspapers, existing law has not caught up with online bigotry in hiring and renting (Liptak 2006).

Discrimination persists even for the most educated and qualified minority group members from the best family backgrounds. Despite their talents and experiences, they sometimes encounter attitudinal or organizational bias that prevents them from reaching their full potential. The term **glass ceiling** refers to an invisible barrier that blocks the promotion of a qualified individual in a work environment because of the individual's gender, race, or ethnicity (R. Schaefer 2012; Yamagata et al. 1997).

In early 1995, the federal Glass Ceiling Commission issued the first comprehensive study of barriers to promotion in the United States. The commission found that glass ceilings continue to block women and minority group men from top management positions in the nation's industries.

use your **sociological imagination**

How might online social networking maintain prejudice and discrimination?

The Privileges of the Dominant

One aspect of discrimination that is often overlooked is the privileges that dominant groups enjoy at the expense of others. For instance, we tend to focus more on the difficulty women have getting ahead at work and getting a hand at home than on the ease with which men manage to make their way in the world and avoid household chores. Similarly, we concentrate more on discrimination against racial and ethnic minorities than on the advantages members of the White majority enjoy. Indeed, most White people rarely think about their "Whiteness," taking their status for granted.

Sociologists and other social scientists are becoming increasingly interested in what it means to be "White," for White privilege is the other side of the proverbial coin of racial discrimination. In this context, **White privilege** refers to rights or immunities granted to people as a particular benefit or favor simply because they are White (Ferber and Kimmel 2008). This view of whiteness as a privilege echoes an observation by W. E. B. DuBois, that rather than wanting fair working conditions for all laborers, White workers had accepted the "public and psychological wage" of whiteness ([1935] 1962:700).

The feminist scholar Peggy McIntosh (1988) became interested in White privilege after noticing that most men would not acknowledge that there were privileges attached to being male—even if they would agree that being female had its disadvantages. Did White people suffer from a similar blind spot regarding their racial privilege? she wondered. Intrigued, McIntosh began to list all the ways in which she benefited from her Whiteness. She soon realized that the list of unspoken advantages was long and significant.

McIntosh found that as a White person, she rarely needed to step out of her comfort zone, no matter where she went. If she wished to, she could spend most of her time with people of her race. She could find a good place to live in a pleasant neighborhood, buy the foods she liked to eat from almost any grocery store, and get her hair styled in almost any salon. She could attend a public meeting without feeling that she did not belong, that she was different from everyone else.

McIntosh discovered, too, that her skin color opened doors for her. She could cash checks and use credit cards without suspicion, browse through stores without being shadowed by security guards. She could be seated without difficulty in a restaurant. If she asked to see the manager, she could assume he or she would be of her race. If she needed help from a doctor or a lawyer, she could get it.

McIntosh also realized that her Whiteness made the job of parenting easier. She did not need to worry about protecting her children from people who didn't like them. She could be sure that their schoolbooks would show pictures of people who looked like them, and that their history texts would describe White people's achievements. She knew that the television programs they watched would include White characters.

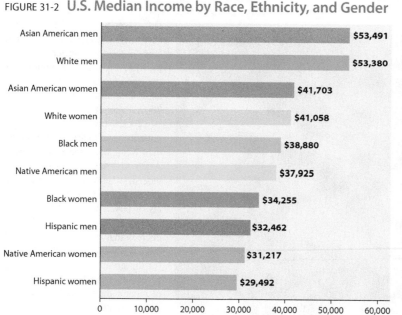

FIGURE 31-2 **U.S. Median Income by Race, Ethnicity, and Gender**

Group	Median income
Asian American men	$53,491
White men	$53,380
Asian American women	$41,703
White women	$41,058
Black men	$38,880
Native American men	$37,925
Black women	$34,255
Hispanic men	$32,462
Native American women	$31,217
Hispanic women	$29,492

Median income (dollars)

Note: Data released in 2011 for income earned in 2010. Median income is from all sources and is limited to year-round, full-time workers at least 25 years old. Data for White men and women are for non-Hispanics.
Sources: DeNavas-Walt et al. 2011:PINC-03; for Native Americans, author's estimate based on American Community Survey 2011:Tables B20017C, B20017H, and B20017I.

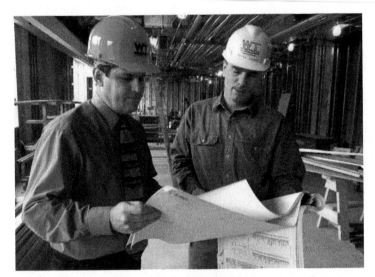

White people are accustomed to seeing other White people in professional positions and jobs with authority and prestige. Whiteness *does* have its privileges.

Finally, McIntosh had to admit that others did not constantly evaluate her in racial terms. When she appeared in public, she didn't need to worry that her clothing or behavior might reflect poorly on White people. If she was recognized for an achievement, it was seen as her achievement, not that of an entire race. And no one ever assumed that the personal opinions she voiced should be those of all White people. Because McIntosh blended in with the people around her, she wasn't always onstage.

These are not all the privileges White people take for granted as a result of their membership in the dominant racial group in the United States. As Devah Pager's study showed (see page 256), White job seekers enjoy a tremendous advantage over equally well-qualified—even better-qualified—Blacks. Whiteness *does* carry privileges—to a much greater extent than most White people realize (Fitzgerald 2008; Picca and Feagin 2007).

use your **sociological imagination**

How often do you think people are privileged because of their race or ethnicity? How about yourself—how often are you privileged?

Taking Sociology to Work

Prudence Hannis, *Associate Director, First Nations Post-Secondary Institution, Odanak, Québec*

Prudence Hannis is a First Nations (Native American) woman who belongs to the Abenaki tribe. As associate director of the First Nations Post-Secondary Institution, which opened in 2011, she is helping to establish a school "built for and by First Nations." Hannis sees the new institution as a significant step toward self-determination among First Nations peoples. Historically, graduation rates have been very low among Québec's First Nations, for political, cultural, social, and economic reasons. The First Nations Post-Secondary Institution was conceived to provide the kind of support that mainstream educational institutions don't offer First Nations students, including everything from day care services to academic support.

The school also offers social-emotional support to students who may not be comfortable in an academic environment. In the social sciences, students participate in weekly sharing circles, where they learn about the root causes of high dropout rates and are encouraged to become agents of change. In deciding to "step out of victimization," students exert a positive influence on the school, on their own future and that of generations to come, and on their peoples' relationship with mainstream society. Hannis is proud to report that in 2011, all the incoming students finished the first term (the dropout rate was zero). The next term, 19 additional students enrolled.

Before taking her current position, Hannis was a liaison officer at the National Institute of Science Research at the University of Québec, where she advised scholars wishing to do research on First Nations communities. She has also worked on women's health issues, first at the Centre of Excellence on Women's Health, Consortium Université de Montréal, and later as a researcher and community activist with Québec Native Women. Her job with Québec Native Women, she explains, was "to defend First Nations women's concerns, to be their spokesperson when needed, to analyze critical situations for our sisters, and mostly, to determine ways in which women can empower themselves, their families, and their communities."

Hannis received her BA in sociology from the University of Québec at Montréal in 2000.

"I have made good use of what I have learned concerning gender inequality, social class, racial and ethnic inequality (tensions, conflict, and struggles), domination, oppression, and social exclusion," she says. "These concepts allow for a better analysis of social problems First Nations are facing (high rates of unemployment, low graduation rates, greater health risks, ghettoization)." Hannis finds her studies have also helped in her work with government agencies, allowing her to raise public awareness of issues such as violence against native women and to identify possible solutions. "I have never been hired as a 'sociologist' per se," she explains, "but the work I was given always involved sociological analysis of issues relevant to First Nations."

LET'S DISCUSS

1. What is the dropout rate at your school? What political, cultural, social, and economic conditions might contribute to that dropout rate?

2. In speaking of empowering First Nations women, what sociological perspective do you think Hannis is drawing on?

Institutional Discrimination

Discrimination is practiced not only by individuals in one-to-one encounters but also by institutions in their daily operations. Social scientists are particularly concerned with the ways in which structural factors such as employment, housing, health care, and government operations maintain the social significance of race and ethnicity. **Institutional discrimination** refers to the denial of opportunities and equal rights to individuals and groups that results from the normal operations of a society. This kind of discrimination consistently affects certain racial and ethnic groups more than others.

The Commission on Civil Rights (1981:9–10) has identified various forms of institutional discrimination:

- Rules requiring that only English be spoken at a place of work, even when it is not a business necessity to restrict the use of other languages.
- Preferences shown by law and medical schools in the admission of children of wealthy and influential alumni, nearly all of whom are White.
- Restrictive employment-leave policies, coupled with prohibitions on part-time work, that make it difficult for the heads of single-parent families (most of whom are women) to obtain and keep jobs.

In some cases, even seemingly neutral institutional standards can have discriminatory effects. African American students at a midwestern state university protested a policy under which fraternities and sororities that wished to use campus facilities for a dance were required to pay a $150 security deposit to cover possible damages. They complained that the policy had a discriminatory impact on minority student organizations. Campus police countered that the university's policy applied to all student groups interested in using the facilities. However, since the overwhelmingly White fraternities and sororities at the school had their own houses, which they used for dances, the policy indeed affected only the African American and other minority organizations.

Significant potential for institutional discrimination exists in laws that govern voting. States have begun requiring voters to show a photo ID (see Figure 31-3), presumably to prevent voter fraud. However, there is little evidence that people have been impersonating eligible voters at the polls. Such laws disproportionately disenfranchise members of minority groups simply because these individuals do not have a driver's license. According to national surveys, 25 percent of African Americans and 16 percent of Latino citizens do not have a valid government-issued photo ID, compared to 8 percent of White citizens (Brennan Center 2006; Dade 2012).

Attempts have also been made to eradicate or compensate for other forms of discrimination in the United States. The 1960s saw the passage of many pioneering civil rights laws, including the landmark 1964 Civil Rights Act (which prohibits discrimination in public accommodations and publicly owned facilities on the basis of race, color, creed, national origin, and gender).

For more than 40 years, affirmative action programs have been instituted to overcome past discrimination. **Affirmative action** refers to positive efforts to recruit minority group members or women for jobs, promotions, and educational opportunities. Many people resent these programs, arguing that advancing one group's cause merely shifts the discrimination to another group. By giving priority to African Americans in admissions, for example, schools may overlook more qualified White candidates. In many parts of the country and many sectors of the economy, affirmative action is being rolled back, even though it was never fully implemented. We will discuss affirmative action in more detail in Module 44.

Discriminatory practices continue to pervade nearly all areas of life in the United States today. In part, that is because various individuals and groups actually *benefit* from racial and ethnic discrimination in terms of money, status, and influence. Discrimination permits members of the majority to enhance their wealth, power, and prestige at the expense of others. Less qualified people get jobs and promotions simply because they are members of the dominant group. Such individuals and groups will not surrender these advantages easily. We'll turn now to a closer look at this functionalist analysis, as well as the conflict, labeling, and interactionist perspectives on race and ethnicity.

trend|spotting

Members of the Board

Significant trends do not always involve dramatic shifts upward or downward. Sometimes, the *lack* of change can be socially significant. Such is the case with the elite individuals who meet in corporate boardrooms: collectively, their racial and ethnic makeup is not changing.

As a rule, the corporate board is and always has been White and male. Of the 1,219 individuals who currently sit on the boards of the *Fortune* 100 largest corporations, 1,031—that is, 85 percent—are White non-Hispanic males. In the most diverse companies, including PepsiCo, IBM, DuPont, and Hartland Financial Services, about 30 percent of the directors belong to minority groups—a proportion that matches that in the general population. No corporation's board exceeds the general population in diversity.

This static trend is significant. Not only do the directors of the nation's largest corporations interact with other economic elites, and in doing so influence major economic forces; they also serve as role models for those who hope to climb the corporate ladder. To the extent that their ranks do not include members of minority groups, their influence as role models will be limited to members of their own exclusive club: White males.

MAPPING LIFE NATIONWIDE

FIGURE 31-3 **Voter ID Requirements**

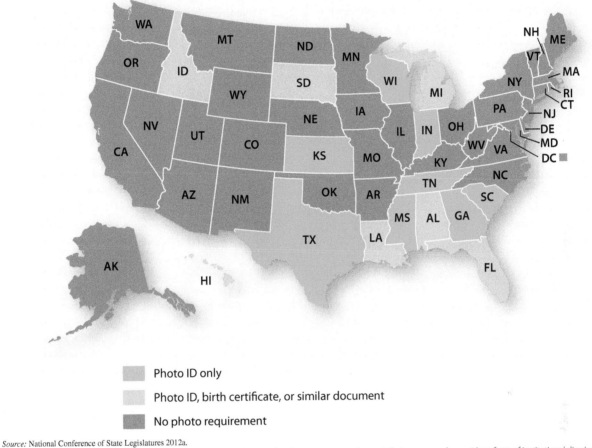

■ Photo ID only

■ Photo ID, birth certificate, or similar document

■ No photo requirement

Source: National Conference of State Legislatures 2012a.

Fifteen states demand that voters show a photo ID or similar document—a requirement that some people consider a form of institutional discrimination.

Think about It

Have you ever had to show a photo ID before voting?

MODULE 31 | Recap and Review

Summary

The social dimensions of race and ethnicity are important factors in shaping people's lives.

1. A **racial group** is set apart from others by physical differences; an **ethnic group** is set apart primarily by national origin or cultural patterns.

2. When sociologists define a **minority group,** they are concerned primarily with the economic and political power, or powerlessness, of the group.

3. The meaning people attach to the physical differences between races gives social significance to race, producing **stereotypes.**

4. **Prejudice** often but not always leads to **discrimination.** Sometimes, through **color-blind racism,** prejudiced people try to use the principle of racial neutrality to defend a racially unequal status quo.

5. **Institutional discrimination** results from the normal operations of a society.

Thinking Critically

1. Why does the social construction of race defy the traditional notion of race as a biological category?
2. Which would be more socially significant, the elimination of prejudice or the elimination of discrimination?

Key Terms

Affirmative action

Color-blind racism

Discrimination

Ethnic group

Ethnocentrism

Glass ceiling

Institutional discrimination

Minority group

Prejudice

Racial formation

Racial group

Racism

Stereotype

White privilege

MODULE 32 | Sociological Perspectives on Race and Ethnicity

Relations among racial and ethnic groups lend themselves to analysis from four major sociological perspectives. Viewing race from the macro level, functionalists observe that racial prejudice and discrimination serve positive functions for dominant groups. Conflict theorists see the economic structure as a central factor in the exploitation of minorities. Labeling theorists note the way in which minorities are singled out for differential treatment by law enforcement officers. On the micro level, interactionist researchers stress the manner in which everyday contact between people from different racial and ethnic backgrounds contributes to tolerance or hostility.

Functionalist Perspective

What possible use could racial bigotry have? Functionalist theorists, while agreeing that racial hostility is hardly to be admired, point out that it serves positive functions for those who practice discrimination.

Anthropologist Manning Nash (1962) has identified three functions of racially prejudiced beliefs for the dominant group:

1. Racist views provide a moral justification for maintaining an unequal society that routinely deprives a minority group of its rights and privileges. Southern Whites justified slavery by believing that Africans were physically and spiritually subhuman and devoid of souls.

2. Racist beliefs discourage the subordinate minority from attempting to question its lowly status, which would be to question the very foundations of society.

3. Racial myths suggest that any major societal change (such as an end to discrimination) would only bring greater poverty to the minority and lower the majority's standard of living. As a result, racial prejudice grows when a society's value system (one underlying a colonial empire or slavery, for example) is threatened.

Although racial prejudice and discrimination may serve the powerful, such unequal treatment can also be dysfunctional for a society, and even for the dominant group. Sociologist Arnold Rose (1951) has outlined four dysfunctions that are associated with racism:

1. A society that practices discrimination fails to use the resources of all individuals. Discrimination limits the search for talent and leadership to the dominant group.

2. Discrimination aggravates social problems such as poverty, delinquency, and crime, and places the financial burden of alleviating those problems on the dominant group.

3. Society must invest a good deal of time and money to defend its barriers to the full participation of all members.

4. Racial prejudice and discrimination often undercut goodwill and friendly diplomatic relations between nations.

Conflict Perspective

Conflict theorists would certainly agree with Arnold Rose that racial prejudice and discrimination have many harmful consequences for society. Sociologists such as Oliver Cox (1948), Robert Blauner (1972), and Herbert M. Hunter (2000) have used the **exploitation theory** (or *Marxist class theory*) to explain the basis of racial subordination in the United States. As we saw in Module 26, Karl Marx viewed the exploitation of the lower class as a basic part of the capitalist economic system. From a Marxist point of view, racism keeps minorities in low-paying jobs, thereby supplying the capitalist ruling class with a pool of cheap labor. Moreover, by forcing racial minorities to accept low wages, capitalists can restrict the wages of *all* members of the proletariat. Workers from the dominant group who demand

In U.S. retail stores, Black customers have different experiences from White customers. They are more likely than Whites to have their checks or credit cards refused and more likely to be profiled by security personnel.

U.S. employers' demand for low-paid labor fuels illegal immigration.

higher wages can always be replaced by minorities who have no choice but to accept low-paying jobs.

The conflict view of race relations seems persuasive in a number of instances. Japanese Americans were the object of little prejudice until they began to enter jobs that brought them into competition with Whites. The movement to keep Chinese immigrants out of the United States became most fervent during the latter half of the 19th century, when Chinese and Whites fought over dwindling work opportunities. Both the enslavement of Blacks and the extermination and removal westward of Native Americans were economically motivated.

However, the exploitation theory is too limited to explain prejudice in its many forms. Not all minority groups have been exploited to the same extent. In addition, many groups (such as the Quakers and the Mormons) have been victimized by prejudice for other than economic reasons. Still, as Gordon Allport (1979:210) concludes, the exploitation theory correctly "points a sure finger at one of the factors involved in prejudice, . . . rationalized self-interest of the upper classes."

Labeling Perspective

One practice that fits both the conflict perspective and labeling theory is racial profiling. **Racial profiling** is any arbitrary action initiated by an authority based on race, ethnicity, or national origin rather than on a person's behavior. Generally, racial profiling occurs when law enforcement officers, including customs officials, airport security, and police, assume that people who fit a certain description are likely to be engaged in illegal activities. Beginning in the 1980s with the emergence of the crack cocaine market, skin color became a key characteristic in racial profiling. This practice is often based on very explicit stereotypes. For example, one federal antidrug initiative encouraged officers to look specifically for people with dreadlocks and for Latino men traveling together.

Today, authorities continue to rely on racial profiling, despite overwhelming evidence that it is misleading. A recent

study showed that Blacks are still more likely than Whites to be frisked and handled with force when they are stopped. Yet Whites are more likely than Blacks to possess weapons, illegal drugs, or stolen property (A. Farrell and McDevitt 2010).

Research on the ineffectiveness of racial profiling, coupled with calls by minority communities to end the stigmatization, has led to growing demands to end the practice. But these efforts came to an abrupt halt after the September 11, 2001, terrorist attacks on the United States, when suspicions arose about Muslim and Arab immigrants. Foreign students from Arab countries were summoned for special questioning by authorities. Legal immigrants who were identified as Arab or Muslim were scrutinized for possible illegal activity and prosecuted for violations that authorities routinely ignored among immigrants of other ethnicities and faiths. National surveys have found little change since 2001 in public support for profiling of Arab Americans at airports. In 2010, 53 percent of Americans favored "ethnic and religious profiling" of air travelers—even those who are U.S. citizens—together with more intensive security checks of passengers who fit certain profiles (Zogby 2010).

Interactionist Perspective

A Hispanic woman is transferred from a job on an assembly line to a similar position working next to a White man. At first, the White man is patronizing, assuming that she must be incompetent. She is cold and resentful; even when she needs assistance, she refuses to admit it. After a week, the growing tension between the two leads to a bitter quarrel. Yet over time, each slowly comes to appreciate the other's strengths and talents. A year after they begin working together, these two workers become respectful friends. This story is an example of what interactionists call the *contact hypothesis* in action.

The **contact hypothesis** states that in cooperative circumstances, interracial contact between people of equal status will cause them to become less prejudiced and to abandon old stereotypes. People begin to see one another as individuals and discard the broad generalizations characteristic of stereotyping. Note the phrases *equal status* and *cooperative circumstances*. In the story just told, if the two workers had been competing for one vacancy as a supervisor, the racial hostility between them might have worsened (Allport 1979; Fine 2008).

As Latinos and other minorities slowly gain access to better-paying and more responsible jobs, the contact hypothesis may take on even greater significance. The trend in our society is toward increasing contact between individuals from dominant and subordinate groups. That may be one way of eliminating—or at least reducing—racial and ethnic stereotyping and prejudice. Another may be the establishment of interracial coalitions, an idea suggested by sociologist William Julius Wilson (1999). To work, such coalitions would obviously need to be built on an equal role for all members.

Table 32-1 summarizes the four major sociological perspectives on race. No matter what the explanation for racial and ethnic distinctions—functionalist, conflict, labeling, or

Tracking Sociological Perspectives

Table **32-1**   Sociological Perspectives on Race and Ethnicity

Perspective	Emphasis
Functionalist	The dominant majority benefits from the subordination of racial minorities.
Conflict	Vested interests perpetuate racial inequality through economic exploitation.
Labeling	People are profiled and stereotyped based on their racial and ethnic identity.
Interactionist	Cooperative interracial contacts can reduce hostility.

French police remove a member of the Roma minority who is resisting deportation to his home country. The expulsion of certain racial or ethnic groups is an extreme result of prejudice.

interactionist—these socially constructed inequalities can have powerful consequences in the form of prejudice and discrimination. In the next section, we will see how inequality based on the ascribed characteristics of race and ethnicity can poison people's interpersonal relations, depriving whole groups of opportunities others take for granted.

Spectrum of Intergroup Relations

Racial and ethnic groups can relate to one another in a wide variety of ways, ranging from friendships and intermarriages to hostility, from behaviors that require mutual approval to behaviors imposed by the dominant group.

One devastating pattern of intergroup relations is **genocide**—the deliberate, systematic killing of an entire people or nation. This term describes the killing of 1 million Armenians by Turkey beginning in 1915. It is most commonly applied to Nazi Germany's extermination of 6 million European Jews, as well as gays, lesbians, and the Roma ("Gypsies"), during World War II. The term *genocide* is also appropriate in describing the United States' policies toward Native Americans in the 19th century. In 1800, the Native American (or American Indian) population of the United States was about 600,000; by 1850, it had been reduced to 250,000 through warfare with the U.S. cavalry, disease, and forced relocation to inhospitable environments.

The *expulsion* of a people is another extreme means of acting out racial or ethnic prejudice. In 1979, for example, the government of Vietnam expelled nearly 1 million ethnic Chinese from the country. The action resulted partly from centuries of hostility between Vietnam and neighboring China.

More recently (beginning in 2009), France expelled over 10,000 ethnic Roma (or Gypsies) who had immigrated from their home countries of Bulgaria and Romania. The action appeared to violate the European Union's ban against targeting ethnic groups, as well as its policy of "freedom of movement" throughout the EU. In 2011, the EU withdrew the threat of legal action when

the French government modified its policy to apply only to those Roma who lived in "illegal camps." However, many observers saw the concession as a thinly veiled attempt to circumvent the EU's long-standing human rights policies.

In a variation of expulsion, called *secession,* failure to resolve an ethnic or racial conflict results in the drawing of formal boundaries between the groups. In 1947, India was partitioned into two separate countries in an attempt to end violent conflict between Hindus and Muslims. The predominantly Muslim areas in the north became the new country of Pakistan; the rest of India became predominantly Hindu.

Secession, expulsion, and genocide are extreme behaviors, clustered on the negative end of what is called the Spectrum of Intergroup Relations (Figure 32-1). More typical intergroup relations follow four identifiable patterns: (1) segregation, (2) amalgamation, (3) assimilation, and (4) pluralism. Each pattern defines the dominant group's actions and the minority group's responses. Intergroup relations are rarely restricted to only one of the four patterns, although invariably one does tend to dominate. Think of these patterns primarily as ideal types.

Segregation

Separate schools, separate seating on buses and in restaurants, separate washrooms, even separate drinking fountains—these were all part of the lives of African Americans in the South when segregation ruled early in the 20th century. **Segregation** refers to the physical separation of two groups of people in terms of residence, workplace, and social events. Generally, a dominant group imposes this pattern on a minority group. Segregation is rarely complete, however. Intergroup contact inevitably occurs, even in the most segregated societies.

From 1948 (when it received its independence) to 1990, the Republic of South Africa severely restricted the movement of Blacks and other non-Whites by means of a wide-ranging system of segregation known as **apartheid.** Apartheid even included the creation of separate homelands where Blacks were expected to live. However, decades of local resistance to apartheid, combined with international pressure, led to marked political changes in

FIGURE 32-1 **Spectrum of Intergroup Relations**

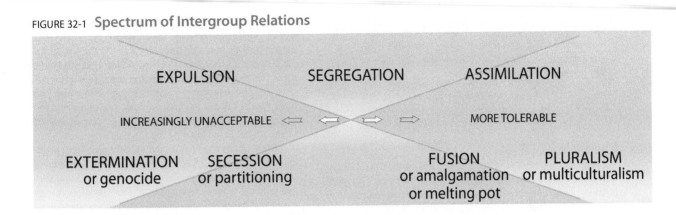

EXPULSION   SEGREGATION   ASSIMILATION

INCREASINGLY UNACCEPTABLE ⇐ ⇐ ⇒ ⇒ MORE TOLERABLE

EXTERMINATION   SECESSION   FUSION   PLURALISM
or genocide   or partitioning   or amalgamation   or multiculturalism
                                       or melting pot

the 1990s. In 1994, a prominent Black activist, Nelson Mandela, was elected South Africa's president in the first election in which Blacks (the majority of the nation's population) were allowed to vote. Mandela had spent almost 28 years in South African prisons for his anti-apartheid activities. His election was widely viewed as the final blow to South Africa's oppressive policy of segregation.

In contrast to the enforced segregation in South Africa, the United States exemplifies an unmandated but nevertheless persistent separation of the races. In their book *American Apartheid,* sociologists Douglas Massey and Nancy Denton (1993) described segregation in U.S. cities using 1990 census data. As the book's title suggests, the racial makeup of U.S. neighborhoods resembles the rigid government-imposed segregation that prevailed for so long in South Africa.

Analysis of more recent census data shows the continuing segregation of U.S. cities, despite the nation's growing racial and ethnic diversity. Across the board, the residential segregation of African Americans has declined only modestly since 2000; for Asian Americans and Latinos it has increased. Even allowing for social class, these patterns of residential segregation persist. One implication of this persistent segregation is that *affluent* Black and Latino households are much more likely than affluent White households to be located in or near poor neighborhoods. As a result, well-to-do minority group members have less immediate access than other groups to high-quality retail stores, restaurants, and services (Bureau of the Census 2010b; Farley 2004; Frey 2011; Logan 2011; Wilkes and Iceland 2004).

Amalgamation

Amalgamation happens when a majority group and a minority group combine to form a new group. Through intermarriage over several generations, various groups in society combine to form a new group. This pattern can be expressed as A + B + C → D, where A, B, and C represent different groups in a society, and D signifies the end result, a unique cultural-racial group unlike any of the initial groups (Newman 1973).

The belief in the United States as a "melting pot" became compelling in the first part of the 20th century, particularly since that image suggested that the nation had an almost divine mission to amalgamate various groups into one people. However, in actuality, many residents were not willing to include Native Americans, Jews, African Americans, Asian Americans, and Irish Roman Catholics in the melting pot. Therefore, this pattern does not adequately describe dominant–subordinate relations in the United States. There *has* been a significant increase in interracial marriage among Whites, Blacks, Asians, and Hispanics in recent years—a trend we will examine in Module 40.

Assimilation

In India, many Hindus complain about Indian citizens who copy the traditions and customs of the British. In France, people of Arab and African origin, many of them Muslim, complain they are treated as second-class citizens—a charge that provoked riots in 2005. In Australia, Aborigines who have become part of the dominant society refuse to acknowledge their darker-skinned grandparents on the street. And in the United States, some Italian Americans, Polish Americans, Hispanics, and Jews have changed their ethnic-sounding family names to names that are typically found among White Protestant families.

Assimilation is the process through which a person forsakes his or her cultural tradition to become part of a different culture. Generally, it is practiced by a minority group member who wants to conform to the standards of the dominant group. Assimilation can be described as a pattern in which A + B + C → A. The majority, A, dominates in such a way that members of minorities B and C imitate it and attempt to become indistinguishable from it (Newman 1973).

A recent comparison study of immigrant groups in the United States, Canada, and Europe found that for the most part, assimilation has progressed further in the United States than in Europe, although more slowly than in Canada. In the United States, the rate of assimilation has generally been constant across groups. However, the recent recession has hampered new groups' ability to move into a broad range of jobs (Myers and Pitkin 2011; Vigdor 2011).

use your **sociological imagination**

You have immigrated to another country with a very different culture. What steps might you take to assimilate?

Pluralism

In a pluralistic society, a subordinate group does not have to forsake its lifestyle and traditions to avoid prejudice or discrimination. **Pluralism** is based on mutual respect for one another's cultures among the various groups in a society. This pattern allows a minority group to express its own culture and still participate without prejudice in the larger society. Earlier, we described amalgamation as A + B + C → D, and assimilation as A + B + C → A. Using this same approach, we can conceive of pluralism as A + B + C → A + B + C. All the groups coexist in the same society (Newman 1973).

In the United States, pluralism is more of an ideal than a reality. There are distinct instances of pluralism—the ethnic neighborhoods in major cities, such as Koreatown, Little Tokyo, Andersonville (Swedish Americans), and Spanish Harlem—yet there are also limits to cultural freedom. To survive, a society must promote a certain consensus among its members regarding basic ideals, values, and beliefs. Thus, if a Hungarian immigrant to the United States wants to move up the occupational ladder, he or she cannot avoid learning the English language.

Switzerland exemplifies the modern pluralistic state. There, the absence of both a national language and a dominant religious faith leads to a tolerance for cultural diversity. In addition, various political devices safeguard the interests of ethnic groups in a way that has no parallel in the United States. In contrast, Great Britain has had difficulty achieving cultural pluralism in a multiracial society. East Indians, Pakistanis, and Blacks from the Caribbean and Africa experience prejudice and discrimination within the dominant White society there. Some British advocate cutting off all Asian and Black immigration, and a few even call for expulsion of those non-Whites currently living in Britain.

MODULE 32 | **Recap and Review**

Summary

Four major theoretical perspectives—functionalism, conflict theory, labeling theory, and interactionism—are useful for analyzing relations among racial and ethnic groups.

1. Functionalists point out that discrimination is both functional and dysfunctional for society.

2. Conflict theorists explain racial subordination through **exploitation theory.**

3. **Racial profiling** is any arbitrary action initiated by an authority based on race, ethnicity, or national origin rather than on a person's behavior. Based on false stereotypes of certain racial and ethnic groups, the practice is not an effective way to fight crime.

4. Interactionists pose the **contact hypothesis** as a means of reducing prejudice and discrimination.

5. Four patterns describe typical intergroup relations in North America and elsewhere: **amalgamation, assimilation, segregation,** and **pluralism.** Pluralism remains more of an ideal than a reality.

Thinking Critically

1. Describe an example of labeling that you are personally familiar with.

2. Give examples of amalgamation, assimilation, segregation, and pluralism that you have seen on your campus or in your workplace.

Key Terms

Amalgamation
Apartheid
Assimilation
Contact hypothesis
Exploitation theory
Genocide
Pluralism
Racial profiling
Segregation

MODULE 33 | Race and Ethnicity in the United States

Few societies have a more diverse population than the United States; the nation is truly a multiracial, multiethnic society. Of course, that has not always been the case. The population of what is now the United States has changed dramatically since the arrival of European settlers in the 1600s, as Figure 31-1 shows. Immigration, colonialism, and in the case of Blacks, slavery determined the racial and ethnic makeup of our present-day society.

Today, the largest racial minorities in the United States are African Americans, Native Americans, and Asian Americans.

The largest ethnic groups are Latinos, Jews, and the various White ethnic groups. Figure 33-1 shows where the major racial and ethnic minorities are concentrated.

African Americans

"I am an invisible man," wrote Black author Ralph Ellison in his novel *Invisible Man* (1952:3). "I am a man of substance, of flesh and

MAPPING LIFE NATIONWIDE

FIGURE 33-1 **The United States: The Image of Diversity**

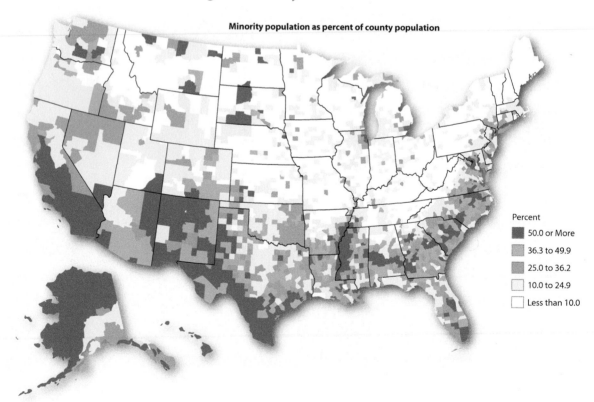

Minority population as percent of county population

Percent
- 50.0 or More
- 36.3 to 49.9
- 25.0 to 36.2
- 10.0 to 24.9
- Less than 10.0

Source: Humes et al. 2011:21.
Overall, 36.3 percent of the U.S. population belonged to a minority group in 2010. In four states (California, Hawai'i, New Mexico, and Texas) and the District of Columbia, minorities constitute the numerical majority. The 2010 Census also showed that 11 percent of the nation's counties already have become "majority minority"—less than 50 percent non-Hispanic white. Another 7 percent of the nation's counties have reached the "tipping point" toward becoming majority minority sometime in the next decade.

Think about It

The United States is a diverse nation. Why, in many parts of the country, can't people see that diversity in their towns?

bone, fiber and liquids—and I might even be said to possess a mind. I am invisible, understand, simply because people refuse to see me."

Over five decades later, many African Americans still feel invisible. Despite their large numbers, they have long been treated as second-class citizens. Currently, by the standards of the federal government, more than 1 out of every 4 African Americans—as opposed to 1 out of every 11 White non-Hispanics—is poor (DeNavas-Walt et al. 2011:15).

Contemporary institutional discrimination and individual prejudice against African Americans are rooted in the history of slavery in the United States. Many other subordinate groups had little wealth and income, but as sociologist W. E. B. DuBois ([1909] 1970) and others have noted, enslaved African Americans were in an even more oppressive situation, because by law they could not own property and could not pass on the benefits of their labor to their children. Today, increasing numbers of African Americans and sympathetic Whites are calling for *slave reparations* to compensate for the injustices of forced servitude. Reparations could include official expressions of apology from governments such as the United States, ambitious programs to improve African Americans' economic status, or even direct payments to descendants of slaves (D. Williams and Collins 2004).

The end of the Civil War did not bring genuine freedom and equality for Blacks. The Southern states passed Jim Crow laws to enforce official segregation, and the Supreme Court upheld them as constitutional in 1896. In addition, Blacks faced the danger of lynching campaigns, often led by the Ku Klux Klan, during the late 1800s and early 1900s. From a conflict perspective, Whites maintained their dominance formally through legalized segregation and informally by means of vigilante terror and violence (Franklin and Higginbotham 2011).

During the 1960s, a vast civil rights movement emerged, with many competing factions and strategies for change. The Southern Christian Leadership Conference (SCLC), founded by Dr. Martin Luther King Jr., used nonviolent civil disobedience to oppose segregation. The National Association for the Advancement of Colored People (NAACP) favored use of the courts to press for equality for African Americans. But many younger Black leaders, most notably Malcolm X, turned toward an ideology of Black power. Proponents of **Black power** rejected

the goal of assimilation into White middle-class society. They defended the beauty and dignity of Black and African cultures and supported the creation of Black-controlled political and economic institutions (Ture and Hamilton 1992).

Despite numerous courageous actions to achieve Black civil rights, Black and White citizens are still separate, still unequal. From birth to death, Blacks suffer in terms of their life chances. Life remains difficult for millions of poor Blacks, who must attempt to survive in ghetto areas shattered by high unemployment and abandoned housing. Today the median household income of Blacks is still 60 percent that of Whites, and the unemployment rate among Blacks is more than twice that of Whites.

Some African Americans—especially middle-class men and women—have made economic gains over the past 50 years. For example, data show that the number of African Americans in management increased nationally from 2.4 percent of the total in 1958 to 6.4 percent in 2010. Yet Blacks still represent only 7 percent or less of all physicians, engineers, scientists, lawyers, judges, and marketing managers (Bureau of the Census 2011a:Table 616).

Native Americans

Today, about 2.5 million Native Americans represent a diverse array of cultures distinguishable by language, family organization, religion, and livelihood. The outsiders who came to the United States—European settlers—and their descendants came to know these native peoples' forefathers as "American Indians." By the time the Bureau of Indian Affairs (BIA) was organized as part of the War Department in 1824, Indian–White relations had already included more than two centuries of hostile actions that had led to the virtual elimination of native peoples Figure 33-1. During the 19th century, many bloody wars wiped out a significant part of the Indian population. By the end of the century, schools for Indians—operated by the BIA or by church missions—prohibited the practice of Native American cultures. Yet at the same time, such schools did little to make the children effective members of White society.

Today, life remains difficult for members of the 554 tribal groups in the United States, whether they live in cities or on reservations. For example, one Native American teenager in six has attempted suicide—a rate four times higher than the rate for other teenagers. Traditionally, some Native Americans have chosen to assimilate and abandon all vestiges of their tribal cultures to escape certain forms of prejudice.

Native American artists often break new ground to represent their life experiences. Dunne-Za member Brian Jungen used Nike shoes to make this three-dimensional piece, which suggests both his Pacific Northwest culture and his family's practice of stretching their modest means by reusing everything.

However, by the 1990s, an increasing number of people in the United States were openly claiming a Native American identity. Since 1960, the federal government's count of Native Americans has tripled.

Native Americans have made some progress in redressing their past mistreatment. In 2009, the federal government settled a 13-year-old lawsuit for the recovery of lease payments due on tribal lands used by the government for oil and gas exploration and grazing. Although the $3.4 billion settlement was large, it was long overdue—some of the government's debts dated back to 1887—and from the perspective of tribal leaders, it was too little, too late. The United States is not the only country that has tried to redress the government's past actions toward indigenous peoples (Box 33-1).

The introduction of gambling on Indian reservations has transformed the lives of some Native Americans. Native Americans got into the gaming industry in 1988, when Congress passed the Indian Gambling Regulatory Act. The law stipulates that states must negotiate agreements with tribes interested in commercial gaming; they cannot prevent tribes from engaging in gambling operations, even if state law prohibits such ventures. The income from these lucrative operations is not evenly distributed, however. About two-thirds of recognized Indian tribes are not involved in gambling ventures. Those tribes that earn substantial revenues from gambling constitute a small fraction of Native Americans (Conner and Taggart 2009).

Like Native Americans, many native peoples living in the United States have successfully established their autonomy, gaining control over their resources and business enterprises. In Module 00, we will consider Native Hawaiians' continuing struggle for recognition of their rights.

💡 use your **sociological imagination**

You are a Native American whose tribe is about to open a reservation-based casino. Will the casino further the assimilation of your people into mainstream society or encourage pluralism?

🌐 Sociology in the Global Community

BOX 33-1

The Aboriginal People of Australia

The indigenous, or Aboriginal, people of Australia have inhabited their home continent continuously for at least 50,000 years. Today they make up about 2.4 percent of Australia's total population. Although their numbers are small, they are highly visible in Australian society.

The cultural practices of the Aboriginal people are quite diverse, given their many clans, language groups, and communities. Except for occasional connections between kin or trading partners, these groups have little social contact. When Europeans first arrived in Australia, the diversity of Aborigines was even greater: an estimated 600 to 700 different groups spoke 200 to 250 languages as distinct from each other as French is from German. The existence of many dialects, or variants of languages that were more or less understandable to others, increased the complexity.

Like the American Indians, Australia's Aboriginal population declined dramatically following European settlement. New diseases, some of which were not life-threatening to Europeans, had a devastating effect on Aboriginal communities, which lacked immunity to them. Mistreatment under the British colonial regime, dispossession of their land, and the disruption and disintegration of their culture also overwhelmed the Aboriginal people. Decades of protests and legal efforts regarding their land rights have brought little change.

Historically, the Aboriginal people received little legal recognition from Europeans. Only in 1967 did the government of Australia extend citizenship and voting rights to the Aboriginals, along with access to welfare and unemployment benefits. Yet it would be misleading to view the Aboriginal people as passive victims, either in colonial days or in more recent times. They have worked actively to secure their rights.

As in the United States, Whites' low regard for the Aboriginal people became the basis for an effort to stamp out their culture. From 1910 to 1970, thousands of Aboriginal children were forcibly removed from their families so they could be raised by Whites and impressed into the dominant culture. Between 10 to 30 percent of all Aboriginal children were affected by

> From 1910 to 1970, thousands of Aboriginal children were forcibly removed from their families so they could be raised by Whites and impressed into the dominant culture.

this program. Not until 2008 did the Australian government finally apologize to Aboriginals for "the Stolen Generations." The government has expressed its intention to improve the Aboriginal people's living conditions and their prospects for the future.

LET'S DISCUSS

1. Try to think of a situation in your culture in which the government might forcibly remove a child from his or her family. Do you know anyone who has had such an experience? If so, what were the repercussions?

2. What kind of reasoning do you think lay behind the Australian government's forced removal of Aboriginal children from their families? In sociological terms, what actually happened?

Sources: W. Anderson 2003; Attwood 2003; Australia 1997, 2008; R. Schaefer 2012.

Asian Americans

Asian Americans are a diverse group, one of the fastest-growing segments of the U.S. population (up 43 percent between 2000 and 2010). Among the many groups of Americans of Asian descent are Vietnamese Americans, Chinese Americans, Japanese Americans, and Korean Americans (Figure 33-2).

Asian Americans are also economically diverse. There are rich and poor Japanese Americans, rich and poor Filipino Americans, and so forth. In fact, Southeast Asians living in the United States have the highest rate of welfare dependency of any racial or ethnic group. According to a study published in 2011, poverty rates are particularly high among the adult children of Cambodian, Hmong, and Thai immigrants to the United States. Though Asian Americans have substantially more schooling than other ethnic groups, their median income is only slightly higher than Whites' income, and their poverty rate is higher. In 2010, for every Asian American household with an annual income of $150,000 or more, there was another earning less than $20,000 a year (DeNavas-Walt et al. 2011:38; Takei and Sakamoto 2011).

The fact that as a group, Asian Americans work in the same occupations as Whites suggests that they have been successful—and many have. However, there are some differences between the two groups. Asian immigrants, like other minorities and immigrants before them, are found disproportionately in low-paying service occupations. At the same time, better-educated Asian Americans are concentrated near the top in professional and managerial positions, although they rarely reach the pinnacle. Instead, they hit the glass ceiling, or try to "climb a broken ladder," as some put it.

Asian Americans rarely head the casts of motion pictures, unless those films feature the martial arts. Two exceptions to the rule are John Cho (left) and Kal Penn, who co-star in the successful Harold & Kumar movies. Penn is the stage name used by Kalpen Modi, the son of Asian Indian immigrants to the United States. In 2009, President Obama appointed Modi associate director of the Office of Public Engagement, where he served as a liaison to the Asian American and Pacific Islander communities.

FIGURE 33-2 Asian American and Pacific Islander Population by Origin

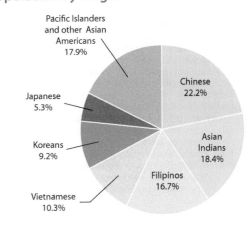

- Pacific Islanders and other Asian Americans 17.9%
- Chinese 22.2%
- Japanese 5.3%
- Asian Indians 18.4%
- Koreans 9.2%
- Filipinos 16.7%
- Vietnamese 10.3%

Source: Census 2010 in Hoeffel et al. 2012:Table 6.

Think about It

Do Asian Americans really have a common identity?

Ironically, Asian Americans are often held up as an unqualified success story. According to popular belief, they have succeeded in adapting to mainstream U.S. culture despite past prejudice and discrimination, and without resorting to confrontations with Whites. Box 33-2 compares this common conception with Asian Americans' actual experience.

Chinese Americans

Unlike African slaves and Native Americans, the Chinese were initially encouraged to immigrate to the United States. From 1850 to 1880, thousands of Chinese immigrated to this country, lured by job opportunities created by the discovery of gold. However, as employment possibilities decreased and competition for mining jobs grew, the Chinese became the target of a bitter campaign to limit their numbers and restrict their rights. Chinese laborers were exploited, then discarded.

In 1882, Congress enacted the Chinese Exclusion Act, which prevented Chinese immigration and even forbade Chinese in the United States to send for their families. As a result, the Chinese population declined steadily until after World War II. More recently, the descendants of the 19th-century immigrants have been joined by a new influx from Hong Kong and Taiwan. These groups

BOX 33-2

Asian Americans: A Model Minority?

Asian Americans are often held up as a **model**, or **ideal, minority group**, supposedly because they have succeeded economically, socially, and educationally, despite past prejudice and discrimination and without resorting to political and violent confrontations with Whites.. Proponents of this view add that because Asian Americans have achieved success, they are no longer disadvantaged. This portrayal of Asian Americans as a model minority ignores their economic diversity. Moreover, even those Asian Americans who are clustered at the high end of the social scale face some barriers to advancement.

The dramatic success of Asian Americans in the U.S. educational system has undoubtedly contributed to the model minority stereotype. Compared with their numbers in the population as a whole, Asian Americans are greatly overrepresented in the student bodies of the most prestigious universities, public and private. Their upward mobility in schooling can be attributed in part to a strong cultural belief in the value of education, to family pressure to succeed, and to the desire to escape discrimination through academic achievement.

The resulting perception of Asian Americans as academic stars does not always work to their advantage. Asian American students who do not excel in school may face criticism from parents or teachers for their failure to conform to the "whiz kid" image. In fact, the high school dropout rate among Asian Americans is increasing rapidly. In California's special program for low-income, academically disadvantaged students, Asian Americans make up 30 percent of the students, and their proportion of all students in the program is rising.

Some observers see Asian Americans' supposed success as a reaffirmation of the cherished belief that with talent and hard work, anyone can get ahead in the United States. This view of Asian Americans as a successful minority carries an implicit critique of Blacks, Hispanics, and other groups who have not fared as well as the model minority. The tacit assumption is that minorities who have been less successful than Asian Americans are completely responsible for their failure to get ahead. Viewed from a conflict perspective, this flip side to the Asian American stereotype is yet another instance of "blaming the victim" (see Explaining Poverty in Module 28, p. 000).

> This view of Asian Americans as a successful minority carries an implicit critique of Blacks, Hispanics, and other groups who have not fared as well as the model minority.

LET'S DISCUSS

1. Are Asian Americans seen as "whiz kids" at your school? If so, how close to reality do you think that stereotype is?

2. Talk with some Asian American students about their grades and their study habits. Do they all have the same work ethic? How does your own work ethic compare to theirs?

Sources: Ryan 1976; Tachibana 1990; Takei and Sakamoto 2011; Teranishi 2010.

---

may contrast sharply in their degree of assimilation, desire to live in Chinatowns, and feelings about this country's relations with the People's Republic of China.

Currently, over 3 million Chinese Americans live in the United States. Some Chinese Americans have entered lucrative occupations, yet many immigrants struggle to survive under living and working conditions that belie the model-minority stereotype. New York City's Chinatown district is filled with illegal sweatshops in which recent immigrants—many of them Chinese women—work for minimal wages. Outside of Chinatown, 23 percent of Asian Americans fall into the low-income category. At the other end of the income distribution, barely 5 percent of Chinatown's residents earn more than $100,000 a year, compared to 25 percent of Asian Americans who live elsewhere in New York City (Logan et al. 2002; Wong 2006).

Asian Indians

After Chinese Americans, the second-largest Asian American group, immigrants from India and their descendants, numbers over 2.9 million. It is difficult to generalize about Asian Indian Americans because Asian Indians are such a diverse population. India, a country of more than 1.2 billion people that is fast becoming the most populous nation in the world, is multiethnic. Perhaps because Asian Indian immigrants feel threatened by mainstream U.S. culture, religious orthodoxy is often stronger among first-generation immigrants to the United States than it is in India. New immigrants try to practice their religion just as they did in India rather than join congregations already established by other immigrant groups.

Maintaining family traditions is a major challenge for Asian Indian immigrants to the United States. Family ties remain strong despite their immigration—so much so that many Asian Indians feel more connected to their relatives in India than Americans do to relatives nearby. These *Desi* (pronounced day-see, colloquial for people who trace their ancestry to South Asia, especially India) are particularly concerned about the erosion of traditional family authority. Indian American children dress like their peers, go to fast-food restaurants, and even eat hamburgers, rejecting the vegetarian diet typical of both Hindus and many Asian Indian

Muslims. Sons do not feel the extent of responsibility to the family that tradition dictates. Daughters, whose occupations and marriage partners the family could control in India, assert their right to choose their careers, and even their husbands (Rangaswamy 2005).

Filipino Americans

Filipinos are the third-largest Asian American group in the United States, with over 2.6 million people. For geographic reasons, social scientists consider them to be of Asian extraction, but physically and culturally this group also reflects centuries of Spanish and U.S. colonial rule, as well as the more recent U.S. military occupation.

Filipinos began immigrating to the United States as American nationals when the U.S. government gained possession of the Philippine Islands at the end of the Spanish–American War (1899). When the Philippines gained their independence in 1948, Filipinos lost their unrestricted immigration rights, although farmworkers were welcome to work in Hawai'i's pineapple groves. Aside from this exception, immigration was restricted to 50 to 100 Filipinos a year until 1965, when the Immigration Act lifted the strict quotas.

Today, a significant percentage of Filipino immigrants are well-educated professionals who work in the field of health care. Although they are a valuable human resource in the United States, their immigration has long drained the medical establishment in the Philippines. When the U.S. Immigration and Naturalization Service stopped giving preference to physicians, Filipino doctors began entering the country as nurses—a dramatic illustration of the incredible income differences between the two countries. Like other immigrant groups, Filipino Americans save much of their income and send a significant amount of money, called *remittances,* back to their extended families (Zarembo 2004b).

For several reasons, Filipino Americans have not coalesced in a single formal social organization, despite their numbers. Their strong loyalty to the family (*sa pamilya*) and to the church—particularly Roman Catholicism—reduces their need for a separate organization. Moreover, their diversity complicates the task of uniting the Filipino American community, which reflects the same regional, religious, and linguistic distinctions that divide their homeland. Thus, the many groups that Filipino Americans have organized tend to be club-like or fraternal in nature. Because those groups do not represent the general population of Filipino Americans, they remain largely invisible to Anglos. Although Filipinos remain interested in events in their homeland, they also seek to become involved in broader, non-Filipino organizations and to avoid exclusive activities (Bonus 2000; Kang 1996; Lau 2006; Padilla 2008).

Vietnamese Americans

Vietnamese Americans came to the United States primarily during and after the Vietnam War—especially after U.S. withdrawal from the conflict in 1975. Refugees from the communist government in Vietnam, assisted by local agencies, settled throughout the United States, tens of thousands of them in small towns. Over time, however, Vietnamese Americans have gravitated toward the larger urban areas, establishing Vietnamese restaurants and grocery stores in their ethnic enclaves there.

In 1995, the United States resumed normal diplomatic relations with Vietnam. Gradually, the *Viet Kieu,* or Vietnamese living abroad, began to return to their old country to visit, but usually not to take up permanent residence. Today, more than 35 years after the end of the Vietnam War, sharp differences of opinion remain among Vietnamese Americans, especially the older ones, concerning the war and the present government of Vietnam (Pfeifer 2008).

Korean Americans

At over 1.4 million, the population of Korean Americans now exceeds that of Japanese Americans. Yet Korean Americans are often overshadowed by other groups from Asia.

Today's Korean American community is the result of three waves of immigration. The initial wave arrived between 1903 and 1910, when Korean laborers migrated to Hawai'i. The second wave followed the end of the Korean War in 1953; most of those immigrants were wives of U.S. servicemen and war orphans. The third wave, continuing to the present, has reflected the admissions priorities set up in the 1965 Immigration Act. These well-educated immigrants arrive in the United States with professional skills. Yet because of language difficulties and discrimination, many must settle at least initially for positions of lower responsibility than those they held in Korea and must suffer through a period of disenchantment. Stress, loneliness, and family strife may accompany the pain of adjustment.

In the early 1990s, the apparent friction between Korean Americans and another subordinate racial group, African Americans, attracted nationwide attention. Conflict between the two groups was dramatized in Spike Lee's 1989 movie *Do the Right Thing.* The situation stemmed from Korean Americans' position as the latest immigrant group to cater to the needs of inner-city populations abandoned by those who have moved up the economic ladder. This type of friction is not new; generations of Jewish, Italian, and Arab merchants have encountered similar hostility from what to outsiders seems an unlikely source—another oppressed minority (Kim 1999).

Japanese Americans

Approximately 842,000 Japanese Americans live in the United States. As a people, they are relatively recent arrivals. In 1880, only 148 Japanese lived in the United States, but by 1920 there were more than 110,000. Japanese immigrants—called the *Issei* (pronounced ee-say), or first generation—were usually males seeking employment opportunities. Many Whites saw them (along with Chinese immigrants) as a "yellow peril" and subjected them to prejudice and discrimination.

In 1941, the attack on Hawai'i's Pearl Harbor by Japan had severe repercussions for Japanese Americans. The federal government decreed that all Japanese Americans on the West Coast must leave their homes and report to "evacuation camps." In effect, Japanese Americans became scapegoats for the anger that other people in the United States felt concerning Japan's role in

World War II. By August 1943, in an unprecedented application of guilt by virtue of ancestry, 113,000 Japanese Americans had been forced into hastily built camps. In striking contrast, only a few German Americans and Italian Americans were sent to evacuation camps (Hosokawa 1969).

In 1983, a federal commission recommended government payments to all surviving Japanese Americans who had been held in detention camps. The commission reported that the detention was motivated by "race prejudice, war hysteria, and a failure of political leadership." It added that "no documented acts of espionage, sabotage, or fifth-column activity were shown to have been committed" by Japanese Americans. In 1988, President Ronald Reagan signed the Civil Liberties Act, which required the federal government to issue individual apologies for all violations of Japanese Americans' constitutional rights, and established a $1.25 billion trust fund to pay reparations to the approximately 77,500 surviving Japanese Americans who had been interned (Department of Justice 2000).

Arab Americans

Arab Americans are immigrants, and their descendants, from the 22 nations of the Arab world. As defined by the League of Arab States, these are the nations of North Africa and what is popularly known as the Middle East, including Lebanon, Syria, Palestine, Morocco, Iraq, Saudi Arabia, and Somalia. Not all residents

of those countries are Arab; for example, the Kurds, who live in northern Iraq, are not Arab. And some Arab Americans may have immigrated to the United States from non-Arab countries such as Great Britain or France, where their families have lived for generations.

The Arabic language is the single most unifying force among Arabs, although not all Arabs, and certainly not all Arab Americans, can read and speak Arabic. Moreover, the language has evolved over the centuries so that people in different parts of the Arab world speak different dialects. Still, the fact that the Koran (or Qur'an) was originally written in Arabic gives the language special importance to Muslims, just as the Torah's compilation in Hebrew gives that language special significance to Jews.

Estimates of the size of the Arab American community differ widely. By some estimates, up to 3 million people of Arab ancestry reside in the United States. Among those who identify themselves as Arab Americans, the most common country of origin is Lebanon, followed by Syria, Egypt, and Palestine. In 2000, these four countries of origin accounted for two-thirds of all Arab Americans. Their rising numbers have led to the development of Arab retail centers in several cities, including Dearborn and Detroit, Michigan; Los Angeles; Chicago; New York City; and Washington, D.C.

As a group, Arab Americans are extremely diverse. Many families have lived in the United States for several generations; others are foreign born. Their points of origin range from the metropolis of Cairo, Egypt, to the rural villages of Morocco. Despite the stereotype, most Arab Americans are *not* Muslim (Figure 33-3). Nor can Arab Americans be characterized as having a specific family type, gender role, or occupational pattern (David 2004, 2008).

Think about It

Do Hispanic Americans really have a common identity?

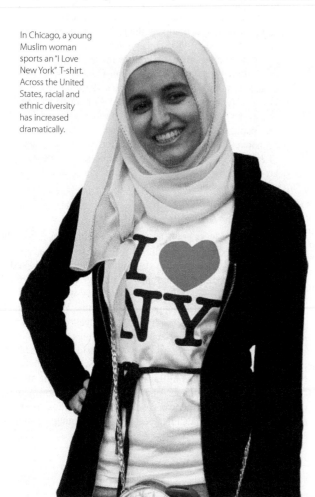

In Chicago, a young Muslim woman sports an "I Love New York" T-shirt. Across the United States, racial and ethnic diversity has increased dramatically.

FIGURE 33-3 Arab American Religious Affiliations

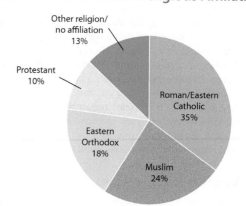

- Other religion/no affiliation 13%
- Protestant 10%
- Eastern Orthodox 18%
- Roman/Eastern Catholic 35%
- Muslim 24%

Notes: Roman/Eastern Catholic includes Roman Catholic, Maronite, and Melkite (Greek Catholic); Eastern Orthodox includes Antiochian, Syrian, Greek, and Coptic; Muslim includes Sunni, Shi'a, and Druze.
Source: Arab American Institute 2010, based on 2002 Zogby International Survey.
Unlike Arabs in other parts of the world, most Arab Americans are Christian.

In spite of this great diversity, profiling of potential terrorists at airports has put Arab and Muslim Americans under special surveillance. For years, a number of airlines and law enforcement authorities have used appearance and ethnic-sounding names to identify and take aside Arab Americans and search their belongings. After the terrorist attacks of September 2001, criticism of this practice declined as concern for the public's safety mounted.

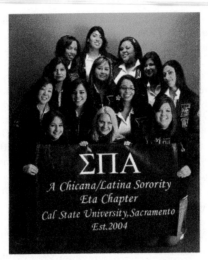

Latinos

Together, the various groups included under the general category *Latinos* represent the largest minority in the United States. There are more than 50 million Hispanics in this country, including 30 million Mexican Americans, more than 4 million Puerto Ricans, and smaller numbers of Cuban Americans and people of Central and South American origin (Figure 33-4). The latter group represents the fastest-growing and most diverse segment of the Hispanic community.

According to Census Bureau data, the Latino population now outnumbers the African American population in 6 of the 10 largest metropolitan areas of the United States: New York City, Los Angeles, Chicago, Dallas–Fort Worth, Houston, and Miami–Fort Lauderdale. The rise of the Hispanic population of the United States—fueled by comparatively high birthrates and immigration levels—has Latinos beginning to flex their muscles as voters. In the 2012 presidential election, Latinos accounted for more than 10 percent of eligible voters. As Hispanics age and immigrants become citizens, their presence in the voting booth will be felt even more strongly (Bureau of the Census 2011a:Table 23; Lopez 2011).

The various Latino groups share a heritage of Spanish language and culture, which can cause serious problems in their assimilation. An intelligent student whose first language is Spanish may be presumed slow or even unruly by English-speaking schoolchildren, and frequently by English-speaking teachers as well. The labeling of Latino children as underachievers, as learning disabled, or as emotionally disturbed can act as a self-fulfilling prophecy for some children. Bilingual education aims at easing the educational difficulties experienced by Hispanic children and others whose first language is not English.

The educational difficulties of Latino students certainly contribute to Hispanics' generally low economic status. In 2008, about 17 percent of all Hispanic households earned less than $15,000, compared to 11 percent of White non-Hispanic households; the poverty rate was 25.3 percent for Hispanics, compared to 9.4 percent for White non-Hispanics. Although, Latinos are not as affluent as White non-Hispanics, a middle class is beginning to emerge (DeNavas-Walt et al. 2010:15, 35, 38).

Mexican Americans

The largest Latino population is Mexican Americans, who can be further subdivided into those descended from residents of the territories annexed after the Mexican American War of 1848 and those who have immigrated from Mexico to the United States. The opportunity for a Mexican to earn in one hour what it would take an entire day to earn in Mexico has pushed millions of legal and illegal immigrants north.

Many people view Mexican Americans as primarily an immigrant group. Since at least 2000, however, the number of Mexican Americans who were born in the United States has far exceeded those who immigrated here. Overall, Mexican Americans accounted for 42 percent of the nation's population growth in the decade 2000–2010. Two-thirds of them were born here; the other third were new arrivals (Bureau of the Census 2011a:8; Pew Hispanic Center 2011).

Puerto Ricans

The second-largest segment of Latinos in the United States is Puerto Ricans. Since 1917, residents of Puerto Rico have held the status of American citizens; many have migrated to New York and other eastern cities. Unfortunately, Puerto Ricans have experienced serious poverty both in the United States and on the island. Those who live in the continental United States earn barely half the family income of Whites. As a result, a reverse migration began in the 1970s, when more Puerto Ricans were leaving for the island than were coming to the mainland (Torres 2008).

Politically, Puerto Ricans in the United States have not been as successful as Mexican Americans in organizing for their rights. For many mainland Puerto Ricans—as for many residents of the

FIGURE 33-4 Hispanic Population by Origin

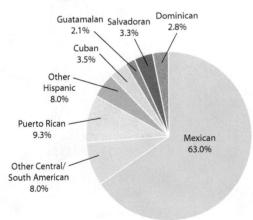

Note: "Other Hispanic" includes Spanish Americans and Latinos identified as being of mixed ancestry.
Source: 2010 Census data in Ennis et al. 2011:33.

island—the paramount political issue is the destiny of Puerto Rico itself: should it continue in its present commonwealth status, petition for admission to the United States as the 51st state, or attempt to become an independent nation? This question has divided Puerto Rico for decades and remains a central issue in Puerto Rican elections. In a 1998 referendum, voters supported a "none of the above" option, effectively favoring continuation of the commonwealth status over statehood or independence.

Cuban Americans

Cuban immigration to the United States dates back as far as 1831, but it began in earnest following Fidel Castro's assumption of power in the Cuban revolution (1959). The first wave of 200,000 Cubans included many professionals with relatively high levels of schooling; these men and women were largely welcomed as refugees from communist tyranny. However, more recent waves of immigrants have aroused growing concern, partly because they were less likely to be skilled professionals. Throughout these waves of immigration, Cuban Americans have been encouraged to locate around the United States. Nevertheless, many continue to settle in (or return to) metropolitan Miami, Florida, with its warm climate and proximity to Cuba.

The Cuban experience in the United States has been mixed. Some detractors worry about the vehement anticommunism of Cuban Americans and the apparent growth of an organized crime syndicate that engages in the drug trade and ganglike violence. Recently, Cuban Americans in Miami have expressed concern over what they view as the indifference of the city's Roman Catholic hierarchy. Like other Hispanics, Cuban Americans are underrepresented in leadership positions within the church. Also—despite many individual success stories—as a group, Cuban Americans in Miami remain behind Whites in income, rate of employment, and proportion of professionals (Masud-Piloto 2008).

Central and South Americans

Immigrants from Central and South America are a diverse population that has not been closely studied. Indeed, most government statistics treat members of this group collectively as "other," rarely differentiating among them by nationality. Yet people from Chile and Costa Rica have little in common other than their hemisphere of origin and the Spanish language—if that. The fact is, not all Central and South Americans speak Spanish. Immigrants from Brazil, for example, speak Portuguese; immigrants from French Guyana speak French; and immigrants from Suriname speak Dutch.

Racially, many of the nations of Central and South America follow a complex classification system that recognizes a multitude of color gradients. Experience with this multiracial system does not prepare immigrants to the United States for the stark Black–White racial divide that characterizes U.S. society. Beyond their diversity in color and language, immigrants from Central and South America are differentiated by social class distinctions, religious differences, urban or rural upbringings, and dialects. Some of them may come from indigenous populations, especially in Guatemala and Belize. If so, their social identity would be separate from any national allegiance.

In short, social relations among Central and South Americans, who collectively number nearly 7 million people, defy generalization. The same can be said about their relations with other Latinos and with non-Latinos. Central and South Americans do not form, nor should they be expected to form, a cohesive group. Nor do they easily form coalitions with Cuban Americans, Mexican Americans, or Puerto Ricans.

Jewish Americans

Jews constitute about 2 percent of the population of the United States. They play a prominent role in the worldwide Jewish community, because the United States has the world's largest concentration of Jews. Like the Japanese, many Jewish immigrants came to this country and became white-collar professionals in spite of prejudice and discrimination.

Anti-Semitism—that is, anti-Jewish prejudice—has often been vicious in the United States, although rarely so widespread and never so formalized as in Europe. In many cases, Jews have been used as scapegoats for other people's failures. Not surprisingly, Jews have not achieved equality in the United States. Despite high levels of education and professional training, they are still conspicuously absent from the top management of large corporations (except for the few firms founded by Jews). Nonetheless, a national survey in 2009 showed that one out of four people in the United States blames "the Jews" for the financial crisis. In addition, private social clubs and fraternal groups frequently continue to limit membership to Gentiles (non-Jews), a

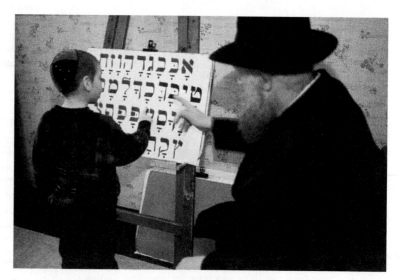

For practicing Jews, the Hebrew language is an important part of religious instruction. This young pupil learns the Hebrew alphabet with a Jewish teacher.

practice upheld by the Supreme Court in the 1964 case *Bell v. Maryland* (Malhotra and Margalit 2009).

The Anti-Defamation League (ADL) of B'nai B'rith coordinates an annual tally of reported anti-Semitic incidents. Although the number has fluctuated, in 2009 the tabulation of the total reported incidents of harassment, threats, vandalism, and assaults came to 1,211. Some incidents were inspired and carried out by neo-Nazi skinheads—groups of young people who champion racist and anti-Semitic ideologies. Such threatening behavior only intensifies the fears of many Jewish Americans, who remember the Holocaust—the extermination of 6 million Jews by the Nazi Third Reich during World War II (Anti-Defamation League 2010).

As is true for other minorities discussed in this chapter, Jewish Americans face the choice of maintaining ties to their long religious and cultural heritage or

White Americans often express their ethnicity with special celebrations, such as this Scandinavian Festival parade in Junction City, Oregon. Participants proudly display the flag of Denmark.

becoming as indistinguishable as possible from Gentiles. Many Jews have tended to assimilate, as is evident from the rise in marriages between Jews and Christians. In marriages that occurred in the 1970s, more than 70 percent of Jews married Jews or people who converted to Judaism. In marriages since 1996, that proportion has dropped to 53 percent. This trend means that today, American Jews are almost as likely to marry a Gentile as a Jew. For many, religion is a nonissue—neither parent practices religious rituals. Two-thirds of the children of these Jewish–Gentile marriages are not raised as Jews. Finally, in 2005, two-thirds of Jews felt that the biggest threat to Jewish life was anti-Semitism; only one-third named intermarriage as the biggest threat (American Jewish Committee 2005; Sanua 2007).

White Ethnics

A significant segment of the population of the United States is made up of White ethnics whose ancestors arrived from Europe within the past century. The nation's White ethnic population includes about 49 million people who claim at least partial German ancestry, 36 million Irish Americans, 17 million Italian Americans, and 10 million Polish Americans, as well as immigrants from other European nations. Some of these people continue to live in close-knit ethnic neighborhoods, whereas others have largely assimilated and left the "old ways" behind.

Many White ethnics today identify only sporadically with their heritage. **Symbolic ethnicity** refers to an emphasis on concerns such as ethnic food or political issues rather than on deeper ties to one's ethnic heritage. It is reflected in the occasional family trip to an ethnic bakery, the celebration of a ceremonial event such as St. Joseph's Day among Italian Americans, or concern about the future of Northern Ireland among Irish Americans.

Such practices are another example of the social construction of race and ethnicity. Except in cases in which new immigration reinforces old traditions, symbolic ethnicity tends to decline with each passing generation (Alba 1990; Winter 2008).

Although the White ethnic identity may be a point of pride to those who share it, they do not necessarily celebrate it at the expense of disadvantaged minorities. It is all too easy to assume that race relations are a zero-sum game in which one group gains at the expense of the other. Rather, the histories of several White ethnic groups, such as the Irish and the Italians, show that once marginalized people can rise to positions of prestige and influence (Alba 2009).

That is not to say that White ethnics and racial minorities have not been antagonistic toward one another because of economic competition—an interpretation that agrees with the conflict approach to sociology. As Blacks, Latinos, and Native Americans emerge from the lower class, they must compete with working-class Whites for jobs, housing, and educational opportunities. In times of high unemployment or inflation, any such competition can easily generate intense intergroup conflict.

In many respects, the plight of White ethnics raises the same basic issues as that of other subordinate people in the United States. How ethnic can people be—how much can they deviate from an essentially White, Anglo-Saxon, Protestant norm—before society punishes them for their willingness to be different? Our society does seem to reward people for assimilating, yet as we have seen, assimilation is no easy process. In the years to come, more and more people will face the challenge of fitting in, not only in the United States but around the world, as the flow of immigrants from one country to another continues to increase. In the Social Policy section that follows, we focus on global immigration and its implications for the future.

social
policy and Racial and Ethnic Inequality | **Global Immigration**

Worldwide, immigration is at an all-time high. Each year, about 191 million people move from one country to another—a number that is roughly the equivalent of the total populations of Russia and Italy. A million of these immigrants enter the United States legally, to join the 13 percent of the U.S. population who are foreign born. Perhaps more significantly, one-fourth of the U.S. labor force is foreign born—the largest proportion in at least 120 years (Passel and Cohn 2011).

Globally, these mass migrations have had a tremendous social impact. The constantly increasing numbers of immigrants and the pressure they put on job opportunities and welfare capabilities in the countries they enter raise troubling questions for many of the world's economic powers. Who should be allowed in? At what point should immigration be curtailed (United Nations 2009)?

Looking at the Issue

The migration of people is not uniform across time or space. At certain times, war or famine may precipitate large movements of people, either temporarily or permanently. Temporary dislocations occur when people wait until it is safe to return to their home areas. However, more and more migrants who cannot make an adequate living in their home nations are making permanent moves to developed nations. The major migration streams flow into North America, the oil-rich areas of the Middle East, and the industrial economies of western Europe and Asia. Currently, seven of the world's wealthiest nations (including Germany, France, the United Kingdom, and the United States) shelter about one-third of the world's migrant population, but less than one-fifth of the world's total population. As long as disparities in job opportunities exist among countries, there is little reason to expect this international trend to reverse.

One consequence of global immigration is the emergence of **transnationals**—immigrants who sustain multiple social relationships that link their societies of origin with the society of settlement. The industrial tycoons of the early 20th century, whose power outmatched that of many nation-states, were among the world's first transnationals. Today, millions of people, many of very modest means, move back and forth between countries much as commuters do between city and suburbs. More and more of these people have dual citizenship. Rather than being shaped by allegiance to one country, their identity is rooted in their struggle to survive—and in some instances prosper—by transcending international borders. We will take a closer look at these citizens of the world in the Social Policy section of Chapter 16 (Croucher 2004; Sassen 2005).

Countries that have long been a destination for immigrants, such as the United States, usually have policies regarding who has preference to enter. Often, clear racial and ethnic biases are built into these policies. In the 1920s, U.S. policy gave preference to people from western Europe, while making it difficult for residents of southern and eastern Europe, Asia, and Africa to enter the country. During the late 1930s and early 1940s, the federal government refused to lift or loosen restrictive immigration quotas in order to allow Jewish refugees to escape the terror of the Nazi regime. In line with this policy, the SS *St. Louis,* with more than 900 Jewish refugees on board, was denied permission to land in the United States in 1939. The ship was forced to sail back to Europe, where it is estimated that at least a few hundred of its passengers later died at the hands of the Nazis (Morse 1967; G. Thomas and Witts 1974).

Since the 1960s, U.S. policy has encouraged the immigration of relatives of U.S. residents as well as of people who have desirable skills. This change has significantly altered the pattern of sending nations. Previously, Europeans dominated, but for the past 40 years, immigrants have come primarily from Latin America and Asia. Thus, an ever-growing proportion of the U.S. population will be Asian or Hispanic (Figure 33-5). To a large degree, fear and resentment of growing racial and ethnic diversity is a key factor in opposition to immigration. In many nations, people are concerned that the new arrivals do not reflect their own cultural and racial heritage.

Applying Sociology

Research suggests that immigrants adapt well to life in the United States, becoming an asset to the nation's economy. In some areas, heavy immigration may drain a local community's resources, but in other areas it revitalizes the local economy.

Despite people's fears, immigration performs many valuable functions. For the receiving society, it alleviates labor shortages, as it does in health care and technology in the United States. For the sending nation, migration can relieve an economy unable to support large numbers of people. Often overlooked is the large amount of money *(remittances)* that immigrants send *back* to their home nations.

Immigration can be dysfunctional as well. Although studies generally show that it has a positive impact on the receiving nation's economy, areas that accept high concentrations of immigrants may find it difficult to meet short-term social service needs. And when migrants with skills or educational potential leave developing countries, their departure can be dysfunctional for those nations. No amount of payments sent back home can make up for the loss of valuable human resources from poor nations (Borjas et al. 2006; Kochhar 2006; Sum et al. 2006).

—Continued

—*Continued*

FIGURE 33-5 Legal Migration to the United States, 1820–2010

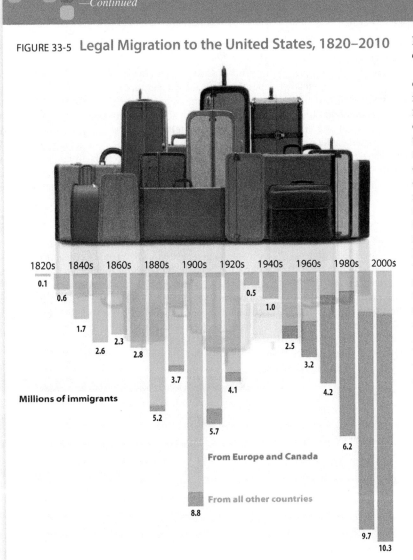

1820s 1840s 1860s 1880s 1900s 1920s 1940s 1960s 1980s 2000s

0.1
0.6
1.7
2.6 2.3
2.8
3.7
5.2
5.7
4.1
0.5
1.0
2.5
3.2
4.2
6.2
9.7
8.8
10.3

Millions of immigrants

From Europe and Canada

From all other countries

Source: Office of Immigration Statistics 2011.
For the past four decades, the majority of immigrants to the United States have come from outside Europe and Canada.

Conflict theorists note how much of the debate over immigration is phrased in economic terms. The debate intensifies when the arrivals are of a different racial or ethnic background from the host population. For example, Europeans often refer to "foreigners," but the term does not necessarily mean one of foreign birth. In Germany, "foreigners" refers to people of non-German ancestry, even if they were *born* in Germany; it does not refer to people of German ancestry born in another country, who may choose to return to their mother country.

Fear and dislike of "new" ethnic groups divides countries throughout the world.

The feminist perspective pays special attention to the role that women play in global immigration. Immigrant women face all the challenges that immigrant men do, and some additional ones. Typically, they bear the responsibility for obtaining services for their families, particularly their children. Because the men are likely to be consumed with work, the women are left to navigate through the bureaucratic tangle of schools, city services, and medical facilities, as well as the unfamiliar stores and markets they must visit to feed their families. Women who need special medical services or are victims of domestic violence are often reluctant to seek outside help. Yet they are more likely than the men to serve as the liaison between their households and community and religious associations. Also, because many new immigrants view the United States as a dangerous place to raise a family, women must be especially watchful over their children's lives (Hondagneu-Sotelo 2003).

Initiating Policy

The long border with Mexico provides ample opportunity for illegal immigration into the United States. Throughout the 1980s, the public perception that the United States had lost control of its borders grew. Feeling pressure for immigration control, Congress ended a decade of debate by approving the Immigration Reform and Control Act of 1986. The act marked a historic change in the nation's immigration policy. For the first time, the hiring of illegal aliens was outlawed, and employers caught violating the law became subject to fines and even prison sentences. Just as significant a change was the extension of amnesty and legal status to many illegal immigrants already living in the United States. More than 20 years later, however, the act appears to have had mixed results. Substantial numbers of illegal immigrants continue to enter the country each year, with an estimated 11 million or more present at any given time—a marked increase since 2000, when their number was estimated at close to 8 million (Passel and Cohn 2011).

—*Continued*

—Continued

In 2010, frustrated by the continuing flow of illegal immigrants across the Mexican border, Arizona enacted a law empowering police to detain without authorization people whom they reasonably suspect of being illegal immigrants and to verify their immigration status. Immediately, opponents charged that the new law would lead to racial profiling. Legal experts questioned whether state enforcement of immigration law was constitutional. Although implementation of the law has been problematic, it has highlighted the resolve of those seeking to tighten control of the nation's borders. It has also galvanized those seeking to reform the nation's immigration law.

Recently, immigrants have staged massive marches to pressure Congress to speed the naturalization process and develop ways for illegal immigrants to gain legal residency. Counterdemonstrations by those who oppose illegal immigration have called for more resources with which to detect and deport illegal immigrants and to strengthen the U.S.–Mexican border. Despite this widespread public dissatisfaction with the nation's immigration policy, little progress has been made. Congress has had difficulty reaching a bipartisan compromise that pleases both sides: both supporters of strict social control and those who would allow illegal immigrants to remain in the country legally, under some circumstances.

The entire world feels the overwhelming impact of globalization on immigration patterns. The European Union agreement of 1997 gave the governing commission authority to propose a Europe-wide policy on immigration. An EU policy that allows residents of one EU country to live and work in another EU country is expected to complicate efforts by sending nations, such as Turkey, to become members of the EU. Immigrants from Turkey's predominantly Muslim population are not welcome in many EU countries (Denny 2004).

In the wake of the attacks of September 11, 2001, on the World Trade Center and the Pentagon, immigration procedures were complicated by the need to detect potential terrorists. Illegal immigrants especially, but even legal immigrants, have felt increased scrutiny by government officials around the world. For would-be immigrants to many nations, the wait to receive the right to enter a country—even to join relatives—has increased substantially, as immigration officials scrutinize more closely what were once routine applications.

The intense debate over immigration reflects deep value conflicts in the cultures of many nations. One strand of our culture, for example, has traditionally emphasized egalitarian principles and a desire to help people in time of need. At the same time, hostility to potential immigrants and refugees—whether the Chinese in the 1880s, European Jews in the 1930s and 1940s, or Mexicans, Haitians, and Arabs today—reflects not only racial, ethnic, and religious prejudice, but a desire to maintain the dominant culture of the in-group by keeping out those viewed as outsiders.

TAKE THE ISSUE WITH YOU

1. Did you or your parents or grandparents immigrate to the United States from another nation? If so, when and where did your family come from, and why?

2. On balance, do the functions of immigration to the United States outweigh the dysfunctions?

3. Do you live, work, or study with recent immigrants to the United States? If so, are they well accepted in your community, or do they face prejudice and discrimination?

MODULE 33 | Recap and Review

Summary

The U.S. population is highly diverse, both racially and ethnically.

1. Contemporary prejudice and discrimination against African Americans are rooted in the history of slavery in the United States.

2. Asian Americans are commonly viewed as a **model** or **ideal minority,** a false stereotype that is not necessarily beneficial to members of that group.

3. The various groups included under the general term *Latinos* represent the largest ethnic minority in the United States.

4. Worldwide, immigration is at an all-time high, fueling controversy not only in the United States but also in the European Union. A new kind of immigrant, the **transnational,** moves back and forth across international borders in search of a better job or education.

Thinking Critically

1. Mexican culture seems alive in many Mexican American communities. Native Americans routinely display their tribal identities. Why do White ethnic identities seem more elusive?

2. To what extent has U.S. society achieved pluralism? Give examples from your own experience to support your viewpoint.

Key Terms

Anti-Semitism

Black power

Model, or **ideal, minority**

Symbolic ethnicity

Transnationals

Mastering This Chapter: Racial and Ethnic Inequality

taking sociology with you

1 Consider one or more jobs you have had, or an occupation you aspire to. How diverse is the staff you worked or would work with? What about your clients or customers? Do you expect racial and ethnic diversity to play an important role in your future career?

2 Talk with an older relative about your family's past. Did your ancestors experience prejudice or discrimination because of their race or ethnicity, and if so, in what way? Did they ever use racial or ethnic slurs to refer to

people of other races or ethnicities? Have your family's attitudes toward members of other groups changed over the years, and if so, why?

3 Look up the census statistics on the racial and ethnic composition of your community. What are the predominant racial and ethnic groups? How many other groups are represented? How many members of your community are immigrants, and where do they come from?

key terms

Affirmative action Positive efforts to recruit minority group members or women for jobs, promotions, and educational opportunities.

Amalgamation The process through which a majority group and a minority group combine to form a new group.

Anti-Semitism Anti-Jewish prejudice.

Apartheid A former policy of the South African government, designed to maintain the separation of Blacks and other non-Whites from the dominant Whites.

Assimilation The process through which a person forsakes his or her cultural tradition to become part of a different culture.

Black power A political philosophy, promoted by many younger Blacks in the 1960s, that supported the creation of Black-controlled political and economic institutions.

Color-blind racism The use of the principle of race neutrality to defend a racially unequal status quo.

Contact hypothesis An interactionist perspective which states that in cooperative circumstances, interracial contact between people of equal status will reduce prejudice.

Discrimination The denial of opportunities and equal rights to individuals and groups because of prejudice or other arbitrary reasons.

Ethnic group A group that is set apart from others primarily because of its national origin or distinctive cultural patterns.

Ethnocentrism The tendency to assume that one's own culture and way of life represent the norm or are superior to all others.

Exploitation theory A Marxist theory that views racial subordination in the United States as a manifestation of the class system inherent in capitalism.

Genocide The deliberate, systematic killing of an entire people or nation.

Glass ceiling An invisible barrier that blocks the promotion of a qualified individual in a work environment because of the individual's gender, race, or ethnicity.

Hate crime 255 Institutional discrimination The denial of opportunities and equal rights to individuals and groups that results from the normal operations of a society.

Minority group A subordinate group whose members have significantly less control or power over their own lives than the members of a dominant or majority group have over theirs.

Model, or ideal, minority A subordinate group whose members supposedly have succeeded economically, socially, and educationally despite past prejudice and discrimination, and without resorting to political and violent confrontations with Whites.

Pluralism Mutual respect for one another's cultures among the various groups in a society, which allows minorities to express their cultures without experiencing prejudice.

Prejudice A negative attitude toward an entire category of people, often an ethnic or racial minority.

Racial formation A sociohistorical process in which racial categories are created, inhabited, transformed, and destroyed.

Racial group A group that is set apart from others because of physical differences that have taken on social significance.

Racial profiling Any arbitrary action initiated by an authority based on race, ethnicity, or national origin rather than on a person's behavior.

Racism The belief that one race is supreme and all others are innately inferior.

Segregation The physical separation of two groups of people in terms of residence, workplace, and social events; often imposed on a minority group by a dominant group.

Stereotype An unreliable generalization about all members of a group that does not recognize individual differences within the group.

Symbolic ethnicity An ethnic identity that emphasizes concerns such as ethnic food or political issues rather than deeper ties to one's ethnic heritage.

Transnational An immigrant who sustains multiple social relationships that link his or her society of origin with the society of settlement.

White privilege Rights or immunities granted to people as a particular benefit or favor simply because they are White.

self-quiz

Read each question carefully and then select the best answer.

1. Sociologists have identified five basic properties of a minority group. Which of the following is *not* one of those properties?
   a. unequal treatment
   b. physical traits
   c. ascribed status
   d. cultural bias

2. The largest racial minority group in the United States is
   a. Asian Americans.
   b. African Americans.
   c. Native Americans.
   d. Jewish Americans.

3. Racism is a form of which of the following?
   a. ethnocentrism
   b. discrimination
   c. prejudice
   d. both b and c

4. Suppose that a White employer refuses to hire a qualified Vietnamese American but hires an inferior White applicant. This decision is an act of
   a. prejudice.
   b. ethnocentrism.
   c. discrimination.
   d. stigmatization.

5. Suppose that a workplace requires that only English be spoken, even when it is not a business necessity to restrict the use of other languages. This requirement would be an example of
   a. prejudice.
   b. scapegoating.
   c. a self-fulfilling prophecy.
   d. institutional discrimination.

6. Working together as computer programmers for an electronics firm, a Hispanic woman and a Jewish man overcome their initial prejudices and come to appreciate each other's strengths and talents. This scenario is an example of
   a. the contact hypothesis.
   b. a self-fulfilling prophecy.
   c. amalgamation.
   d. reverse discrimination.

7. Intermarriage over several generations, resulting in various groups combining to form a new group, would be an example of
   a. amalgamation.
   b. assimilation.
   c. segregation.
   d. pluralism.

8. Alphonso D'Abruzzo changed his name to Alan Alda. His action is an example of
   a. amalgamation.
   b. assimilation.
   c. segregation.
   d. pluralism.

9. In which of the following racial or ethnic groups has one teenager in every six attempted suicide?
   a. African Americans
   b. Asian Americans
   c. Native Americans
   d. Latinos

10. Advocates of *Marxist class theory* argue that the basis for racial subordination in the United States lies within the capitalist economic system. Another representation of this point of view is reflected in which of the following theories?
    a. exploitation
    b. functionalist
    c. interactionist
    d. contact

11. Sociologists consider race and ethnicity to be _____ statuses, since people are born into racial and ethnic groups.

12. The one-drop rule was a vivid example of the social _____ of race—the process by which people come to define a group as a race based in part on physical characteristics, but also on historical, cultural, and economic factors.

13. _____ are unreliable generalizations about all members of a group that do not recognize individual differences within the group.

14. Sociologists use the term _____ to refer to a negative attitude toward an entire category of people, often an ethnic or racial minority.

15. When White Americans can use credit cards without suspicion and browse through stores without being shadowed by security guards, they are enjoying _____ _____.

16. _____ _____ refers to positive efforts to recruit minority group members or women for jobs, promotions, and educational opportunities.

17. After the Civil War, the Southern states passed "_____ _____" laws to enforce official segregation, and the Supreme Court upheld them as constitutional in 1896.

18. In the 1960s, proponents of _____ _____ rejected the goal of assimilation into White, middle-class society. They defended the beauty and dignity of Black and African cultures and supported the creation of Black-controlled political and economic institutions.

19. Asian Americans are held up as a(n) _____ or _____ minority group, supposedly because despite past suffering from prejudice and discrimination, they have succeeded economically, socially, and educationally without resorting to political and violent confrontations with Whites.

20. Together, the various groups included under the general category _____ represent the largest minority group in the United States.

thinking about movies

Red Tails

During World War II, the Tuskegee Airmen overcome institutionalized segregation and racial prejudice to become the first African American pilots in the U.S. Army Air Corps.

Amreeka

A Palestinian family that has immigrated to the United States struggles with judgments against their ethnicity.

Crash

The lives of multiple characters collide, revealing layers of prejudice directed at a wide range of races and ethnicities.

The Family and Human Sexuality

13 The Family and Human Sexuality

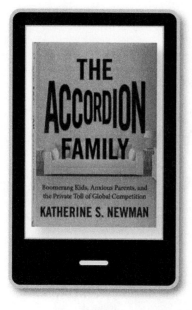

Do you know adult children in their 20s and 30s who continue to live at home or have returned to their parents' home? Are you one of them?

Some people call these families "accordion families" because they expand and contract as the adult children come and go.

" William Rollo and his wife arrived in Newton [Massachusetts] in 1989 after having lived in Seattle, Philadelphia, and Summit, New Jersey. A Brooklyn native, William married Janet at the age of twenty-two and set about completing a residency in podiatry. Their eldest son, John, grew up in Newton and did well enough in high school to attend the liberal arts college Williams, one of the nation's most selective. Even so, he beat it home after graduating and has lived with his parents for several years while preparing to apply to graduate school. "A lot of my friends are living at home to save money," he explains.

Tight finances are not all that is driving John's living arrangements. The young man had choices and decided he could opt for more of the ones he wanted if he sheltered under his parents' roof. John is saving money from his job in an arts foundation for a three-week trip to Africa, where he hopes to work on a mobile health-care project in a rural region. It's a strategic choice designed to increase his chances to be accepted into Harvard University's competitive graduate program in public health.

John needs to build up his credentials if he wants to enter a school like that. To get from here to there, he needs more experience working with patients in clinics or out in the field. It takes big bucks to travel to exotic locations, and a master's degree will cost him dearly, too. In order to make good on his

On his own, John could pay the rent on an apartment, especially if he had roommates. What he can't afford is to pay for both privacy and travel, to support himself and save for his hoped-for future.

aspirations, John needs his parents to cover him for the short run. On his own, John could pay the rent on an apartment, especially if he had roommates. What he can't afford is to pay for both privacy *and* travel, to support himself *and* save for his hoped-for future. Autonomy turns out to be the lesser priority, so he has returned to the bedroom he had before he left for college, and there he stays.

John sees few drawbacks to this arrangement. His parents don't nag him or curtail his freedom. Janet wonders if they should ask him to pay rent, to bring him down to earth a bit and teach him some life skills, like budgeting. William is not so sure. He enjoys his son's company and was happy when he moved back into his old bedroom....

. . .

If John had no goals, no sense of direction, William would not be at ease with this "boomerang arrangement." Hiding in the basement playing video games would not do. Happily, that is not on John's agenda. William is glad to help his son realize his ambitions. He approves of John's career plans and doesn't really care if they don't involve making a handsome living....

And it will cost this family, big time. William and Janet have invested nearly two hundred thousand dollars in John's education already. They will need to do more if John is going to become a public health specialist. They are easily looking at another fifty thousand dollars, even if John attends a local graduate program and continues to live with them. Fortunately, there are excellent options—some of the nation's finest—close by. Whatever it costs, they reason, the sacrifice is worth it. "

(Newman 2012:xv–xvii) Additional information about this excerpt can be found on the Online Learning Center at www.mhhe.com/schaefermod2e.

n this excerpt from *The Accordion Family: Boomerang Kids, Anxious Parents, and the Private Toll of Global Competition,* sociologist Katherine S. Newman describes one of the major trends in family life today. In the United States as well as in many other countries, parenthood is being extended as single adult children remain at home, or return home after college or a brief foray into the job market. In the United States in 2011, 31 percent of single men and 15 percent of single women between the ages of 25 and 34 lived with their parents. Some of those adult children were still pursuing an education, but in many cases financial difficulties underlay their living arrangements. For younger job seekers, employment is often short term

or low paying—not secure enough to support a separate household. And with many marriages now ending in divorce—most commonly in the first seven years—divorced sons and daughters often return to their parents, sometimes with their own children in tow (Bureau of the Census 2011e:Table A2).

This trend is an example of the increasing complexity of family life. The family of today is not what it was a century ago, or even a generation ago. New roles, new gender distinctions, new child-rearing patterns have all combined to create new forms of family life. Today, for example, more and more women are taking the breadwinner's role, whether married or as a single parent. Blended families—the result of divorce and remarriage—are almost the norm. And many people are seeking intimate relationships without being married, whether in gay partnerships or in cohabiting arrangements (Cherlin 2009, 2011). The word *family* is inadequate to describe some of these arrangements, including cohabiting partners, same-sex marriages, and single-parent households. In 2011, the nation crossed a major threshold: the majority of births to women under age 30 occurred outside of marriage (Cherlin 2011; Wildsmith et al. 2011).

These modules address family and human sexuality in the United States as well as other parts of the world. As we will see, family patterns differ from one culture to another and even within the same culture. Despite the differences, however, the family is universal—found in every culture.

What are families in different parts of the world like? How do people select their mates? How does divorce affect the children? What are the alternatives to the nuclear family, and how prevalent are they? We will look at the family and intimate relationships from the functionalist, conflict, interactionist, and feminist points of view. We'll examine variations in marital patterns and family life, including child rearing, paying particular attention to the increasing numbers of people in dual-income and single-parent families. We'll examine divorce in the United States and consider diverse lifestyles such as cohabitation and marriage without children. We'll conclude by considering the complexity of human sexual behavior, and the growing acceptance of lesbian and gay relationships. Finally, in the Social Policy section we'll confront the controversial issue of gay marriage.

Among Tibetans, a woman may be married simultaneously to more than one man, usually brothers. This system allows sons to share the limited amount of good land. Among the Betsileo of Madagascar, a man has multiple wives, each one living in a different village where he cultivates rice. Wherever he has the best rice field, that wife is considered his first or senior wife. Among the Yanomami of Brazil and Venezuela, it is considered proper to have sexual relations with your opposite-sex cousins if they are the children of your mother's brother or your father's sister. But if your opposite-sex cousins are the children of your mother's sister or your father's brother, the same practice is considered to be incest (Haviland et al. 2008; Kottak 2011).

Universal Principles

As these examples illustrate, there are many variations in the family from culture to culture. Yet the family as a social institution exists in all cultures. A **family** can be defined as a set of people related by blood, marriage, some other agreed-on relationship, or adoption, who share the primary responsibility for reproduction and caring for members of society. Moreover, certain general principles concerning its composition, kinship patterns, and authority patterns are universal.

Composition: What Is the Family?

If we were to take our information on what a family is from what we see on television, we might come up with some strange scenarios. The media do not always present a realistic view of the family. Moreover, many people still think of the family in very narrow terms—as a married couple and their unmarried children living together, like the family in the old *Cosby Show.* However, this is but one type of family, what sociologists refer to as a **nuclear family.** The term *nuclear family* is well chosen, since this type of family serves as the nucleus, or core, on which larger family groups are built.

Most people in the United States see the nuclear family as the preferred family arrangement. Yet by 2000, only about a third of the nation's family households fit this model. The proportion of households in the United States that is composed of married couples with children at home has decreased steadily over the past 40 years and is expected to continue shrinking. At the same time, the number of single-parent households has increased (Figure 39-1).

A family in which relatives—such as grandparents, aunts, or uncles—live in the same home as parents and their children is known as an **extended family.** Although not common, such living arrangements do exist in the United States. The structure of the extended family offers certain advantages over that of the nuclear family. Crises such as death, divorce, and illness put less strain on family members, since more people can provide assistance and emotional support. In addition, the extended family constitutes a larger economic unit than the nuclear family. If the family is engaged in a common enterprise—a farm or a small business—the additional family members may represent the difference between prosperity and failure.

In considering these different family types, we have limited ourselves to the form of marriage that is characteristic of the United States—monogamy. The term **monogamy** describes a form of marriage in which one woman and one man are married only to each other. Some observers, noting the high rate of divorce in the United States, have suggested that "serial monogamy" is a more accurate description of the form marriage takes in this country. In **serial monogamy,** a person may have several spouses in his or her lifetime, but only one spouse at a time.

Some cultures allow an individual to have several husbands or wives simultaneously. This form of marriage is known as **polygamy.** In fact, most societies throughout the world, past and present, have preferred polygamy to monogamy. Anthropologist George Murdock (1949, 1957) sampled 565 societies and found that in more than 80 percent, some type of polygamy was the preferred form. While polygamy declined steadily through most of the 20th century, in at least five countries in Africa 20 percent of men still have polygamous marriages (Population Reference Bureau 1996).

There are two basic types of polygamy. According to Murdock, the most common—endorsed by the majority of cultures he sampled—is *polygyny.* **Polygyny** refers to the marriage of a man to more than one woman at the same time. The wives are often sisters, who are expected to hold similar values and have already had experience sharing a household. In polygynous societies, relatively few men actually have multiple spouses. Most individuals live in monogamous families; having multiple wives is viewed as a mark of status.

The other principal variation of polygamy is **polyandry,** in which a woman may have more than one husband at the same time. Such is the case in the culture of the Nyinba, described in Box 39-1. Polyandry, however, is exceedingly rare today, though it is accepted in some extremely poor societies. Like many other societies, polyandrous cultures devalue the social worth of women (Zeitzen 2008).

FIGURE 39-1 U.S. Households by Family Type, 1940–2010

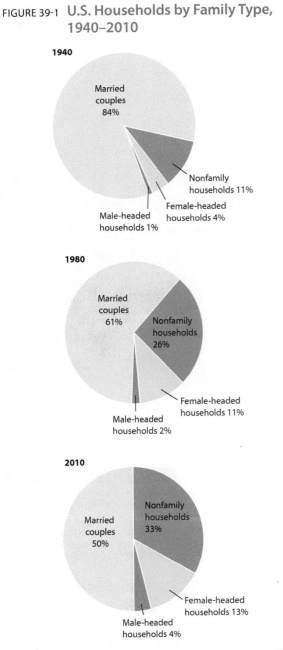

1940

Married couples 84%

Nonfamily households 11%

Female-headed households 4%

Male-headed households 1%

1980

Married couples 61%

Nonfamily households 26%

Female-headed households 11%

Male-headed households 2%

2010

Nonfamily households 33%

Married couples 50%

Female-headed households 13%

Male-headed households 4%

Note: Nonfamily households include women and men living alone or exclusively with people to whom they are not related, as in a college dormitory, homeless shelter, or military base.
Source: Bureau of the Census 2010b:Table HH1.

Kinship Patterns: To Whom Are We Related?

Many of us can trace our roots by looking at a family tree or by listening to elderly family members talk about their lives—and about the lives of ancestors who died long before we were born. Yet a person's lineage is more than simply a personal history; it also reflects societal patterns that govern descent. In every culture, children encounter relatives to whom they are expected to show an emotional attachment. The state of being related to others is called **kinship.** Kinship is culturally learned, however, and is not totally determined by biological or marital ties. For example, adoption creates a kinship tie that is legally acknowledged and socially accepted.

The family and the kin group are not necessarily one and the same. Whereas the family is a household unit, kin do not always live together or function as a collective body on a daily basis. Kin groups include aunts, uncles, cousins, in-laws, and so forth. In a society such as the United States, the kinship group may come together only rarely, for a wedding or funeral. However, kinship ties frequently create obligations and responsibilities. We may feel compelled to assist our kin, and we may feel free to call on them for many types of aid, including loans and babysitting.

How do we identify kinship groups? The principle of descent assigns people to kinship groups according to their relationship to a mother or father. There are three primary ways of determining descent. The United States follows the system of **bilateral descent,** which means that both sides of a person's family are regarded as equally important. For example, no higher value is given to the brothers of one's father than to the brothers of one's mother.

Most societies—according to George Murdock, 64 percent—give preference to one side of the family or the other in tracing descent. In **patrilineal** (from the Latin *pater,* "father") **descent,** only the father's relatives are significant in terms of property, inheritance, and emotional ties. Conversely, in societies that favor **matrilineal** (from the Latin *mater,* "mother") **descent,** only the mother's relatives are significant.

New forms of reproductive technology will necessitate a new way of looking at kinship. Today, a combination of biological and social processes can "create" a family member, requiring that more distinctions be made about who is related to whom.

💡 use your **sociological imagination**

In your family, which relatives do you have a significant relationship with? Which do you hardly ever see?

Authority Patterns: Who Rules?

Imagine that you have recently married and must begin to make decisions about the future of your new family. You and your spouse face many questions. Where will you live? How will you furnish your home? Who will do the cooking, the shopping, the cleaning? Whose friends will be invited to dinner? Each time a decision must be made, an issue is raised: Who has the power to make the decision? In simple terms, who rules the family? Conflict theorists examine these questions in the context of traditional gender stratification, under which men have held a dominant position over women.

Societies vary in the way power is distributed within the family. A society that expects males to dominate in all family decision making is termed a **patriarchy.** In patriarchal societies, such as Iran, the eldest male often wields the greatest

Sociology in the Global Community

BOX 39-1

One Wife, Many Husbands: The Nyinba

The Nyinba culture of Nepal and Tibet is an agrarian society located in the remote valleys of the Himalaya Mountains, more than 9,000 feet above sea level. Despite the Nyinba's isolation, they have been closely studied. Scholars from around the world have traveled to the Himalayas to observe this people, one of the few remaining cultures on earth to practice polyandry.

In the physically challenging environment of the Himalayas, polyandry seems to work well. Because the land and climate make it difficult to sustain crops, farming is labor-intensive: many Nyinba laborers must work the fields to support a single family. Thus, a typical marriage involving three brothers and one wife provides the necessary adult male laborers, yet minimizes the number of offspring—a necessity in a place where the food supply is limited.

While an outsider might suppose that Nyinba women dominate their families, in fact authority and inheritance rest on the husband or son. The birth of a son is celebrated; the birth of a daughter, regardless of who might be the father, brings disappointment. Paternity appears to be a nonissue in this culture, since households are shared by brothers from the same family. The literal head of the household is the oldest brother, who typically chooses a wife from outside his extended family.

A Nyinba family threshing buckwheat in the field. At left is the wife; in the center, one of her five husbands (with raised mallet); at right, her mother-in-law.

> Favoritism toward a particular husband is frowned on by the Nyinba. Thus, it is the wife's responsibility to see that each husband shares time with her in a rotational fashion.

Favoritism toward a particular husband is frowned on by the Nyinba. Thus, it is the wife's responsibility to see that each husband shares time with her in a rotational fashion. Often, over the morning meal, she will indicate which husband will sleep with her that night. To avoid any confusion, the chosen husband will place his shoes outside her bedroom door.

As in any society (for example, the United States), not all Nyinba households conform to the social norm. If a family has only one son, he must of necessity marry monogamously—an unfortunate outcome in this society. If a wife is unable to have children, a second wife, typically her sister or cousin, may be welcomed into the marriage.

LET'S DISCUSS

1. Why would a monogamous marriage be considered an unfortunate one in the Nyinba culture?
2. What might be some other ways for a society to handle the physical constraints of life in a mountainous terrain?

Sources: N. Levine 1988; Stockard 2002; Zeitzen 2008.

power, although wives are expected to be treated with respect and kindness. An Iranian woman's status is typically defined by her relationship to a male relative, usually as a wife or daughter. In many patriarchal societies, women find it more difficult to obtain a divorce than a man does. In contrast, in a **matriarchy**, women have greater authority than men. Matriarchies, which are very uncommon, emerged among Native American tribal societies and in nations in which men were absent for long periods because of warfare or food-gathering expeditions (Farr 1999).

In a third type of authority pattern, the **egalitarian family**, spouses are regarded as equals. That does not mean, however, that all decisions are shared in such families. Wives may hold authority in some spheres, husbands in others. Many sociologists believe the egalitarian family has begun to replace the patriarchal family as the social norm in the United States.

Sociological Perspectives on the Family

Do we really need the family? Over a century ago, Friedrich Engels ([1884] 1959), a colleague of Karl Marx, described the family as the ultimate source of social inequality because of its role in the transfer of power, property, and privilege. More

Although spouses in an egalitarian family may not share all their decisions, they regard themselves as equals. This pattern of authority is becoming more common in the United States.

recently, conflict theorists have argued that the family contributes to societal injustice, denies women opportunities that are extended to men, and limits freedom in sexual expression and mate selection. In contrast, the functionalist view focuses on the ways in which the family gratifies the needs of its members and contributes to social stability. The interactionist view considers the intimate, face-to-face relationships that occur in the family. And the feminist approach examines the role of the wife and mother, especially in the absence of an adult male.

Functionalist Perspective

The family performs six paramount functions, first outlined nearly 80 years ago by sociologist William F. Ogburn (Ogburn and Tibbits 1934):

1. **Reproduction.** For a society to maintain itself, it must replace dying members. In this sense, the family contributes to human survival through its function of reproduction.

2. **Protection.** In all cultures, the family assumes the ultimate responsibility for the protection and upbringing of children.

3. **Socialization.** Parents and other kin monitor a child's behavior and transmit the norms, values, and language of their culture to the child.

4. **Regulation of sexual behavior.** Sexual norms are subject to change both over time (for instance, in the customs for dating) and across cultures (compare strict Saudi Arabia to the more permissive Denmark). However, whatever the time period or cultural values of a soci-

ety, standards of sexual behavior are most clearly defined within the family circle.

5. **Affection and companionship.** Ideally, the family provides members with warm and intimate relationships, helping them to feel satisfied and secure. Of course, a family member may find such rewards outside the family—from peers, in school, at work—and may even perceive the home as an unpleasant or abusive setting. Nevertheless, we expect our relatives to understand us, to care for us, and to be there for us when we need them.

6. **Provision of social status.** We inherit a social position because of the family background and reputation of our parents and siblings. The family presents the newborn child with an ascribed status based on race and ethnicity that helps to determine his or her place within society's stratification system. Moreover, family resources affect children's ability to pursue certain opportunities, such as higher education.

Traditionally, the family has fulfilled a number of other functions, such as providing religious training, education, and recreational outlets. But Ogburn argued that other social institutions have gradually assumed many of those functions. Education once took place at the family fireside; now it is the responsibility of professionals working in schools and colleges. Even the family's traditional recreational function has been transferred to outside groups such as Little Leagues, athletic clubs, and Twitter.

Conflict Perspective

Conflict theorists view the family not as a contributor to social stability, but as a reflection of the inequality in wealth and power that is found within the larger society. Feminist and conflict theorists note that the family has traditionally legitimized and perpetuated male dominance. Throughout most of human history—and in a wide range of societies—husbands have exercised overwhelming power and authority within the family. Not until the first wave of contemporary feminism in the United States, in the mid-1800s, was there a substantial challenge to the historic status of wives and children as the legal property of husbands.

While the egalitarian family has become a more common pattern in the United States in recent decades—owing in good part to the activism of feminists beginning in the late 1960s and early 1970s—male dominance over the family has hardly disappeared. Sociologists have found that while married men are increasing their involvement in child care, their wives still perform a disproportionate amount of it. Furthermore, for every stay-at-home dad there are 38 stay-at-home moms. And unfortunately, many husbands reinforce their power and control over wives and children through acts of domestic violence (Fields 2004:11–12; Garcia-Moreno et al. 2005; Sayer et al. 2004).

Conflict theorists also view the family as an economic unit that contributes to societal injustice. The family is the basis for transferring power, property, and privilege from one generation to the next. Although the United States is widely viewed as a land of opportunity, social mobility is restricted in important ways. Children inherit the privileged or less-than-privileged social and economic status of their parents (and in some cases, of earlier generations). The social class of parents significantly influences children's socialization experiences and the degree of protection they receive. Thus, the socioeconomic status of a child's family will have a marked influence on his or her nutrition, health care, housing, educational opportunities, and in many respects, life chances as an adult. For this reason, conflict theorists argue that the family helps to maintain inequality.

Interactionist Perspective

Interactionists focus on the micro level of family and other intimate relationships. They are interested in how individuals interact with one another, whether they are cohabiting partners or longtime married couples. For example, in a study of both Black and White two-parent households, researchers found that when fathers are more involved with their children (reading to them, helping them with homework, or restricting their television viewing), the children have fewer behavior problems, get along better with others, and are more responsible (Mosley and Thomson 1995).

Interactionists are particularly interested in the ways in which parents relate to each other and to their children. The close and loving relationship illustrated here is one of the foundations of a strong family.

Another interactionist study might examine the role of the stepparent. The increased number of single parents who remarry has sparked an interest in those who are helping to raise other people's children. Studies have found that stepmothers are more likely than stepfathers to accept the blame for bad relations with their stepchildren. Interactionists theorize that stepfathers (like most fathers) may simply be unaccustomed to interacting directly with children when the mother isn't there (Bray and Kelly 1999; F. Furstenberg and Cherlin 1991).

Feminist Perspective

Because "women's work" has traditionally focused on family life, feminist sociologists have taken a strong interest in the family as a social institution. As we saw in Module 34, research on gender roles in child care and household chores has been extensive. Sociologists have looked particularly closely at how women's work outside the home impacts their child care and housework—duties Arlie Hochschild (1989, 1990, 2005) has referred to as the "second shift." Today, researchers recognize that for many women, the second shift includes the care of aging parents as well.

Feminist theorists have urged social scientists and social agencies to rethink the notion that families in which no adult male is present are automatically a cause for concern, or even dysfunctional. They have also contributed to research on single women, single-parent households, and lesbian couples. In the case of single mothers, researchers have focused on the resiliency of many such households, despite economic stress. According to Velma McBride Murray and her colleagues (2001) at the University of Georgia, such studies show that among African Americans, single mothers draw heavily on kinfolk for material resources, parenting advice, and social support. Considering feminist research on the family as a whole, one researcher concluded that the family is the "source of women's strength" (V. Taylor et al. 2009).

Finally, feminists who take the interactionist perspective stress the need to investigate neglected topics in family studies. For instance, in a growing number of dual-income households, the wife earns a higher income than the husband. In 2005, a study of 58 married couples revealed that 26 percent of the wives earned more than their husbands. In 1981, the proportion was just 16 percent. Yet beyond individual case studies, little research has been done on how these families may differ from those in which the husband is the major breadwinner (Wills and Risman 2006).

Table 39-1 summarizes the four major theoretical perspectives on the family.

Tracking Sociological Perspective

Table **39-1** Sociological Perspectives on the Family

Theoretical Perspective	Emphasis
Functionalist	The family as a contributor to social stability Roles of family members
Conflict	The family as a perpetuator of inequality Transmission of poverty or wealth across generations
Interactionist	Relationships among family members
Feminist	The family as a perpetuator of gender roles Female-headed households

MODULE 39 | Recap and Review

Summary

The family, in its many forms, is present in all human cultures.

1. Families vary from culture to culture and even within the same culture.

2. The structure of the **extended family** can offer certain advantages over that of the **nuclear family.**

3. Societies determine **kinship** by descent from both parents (**bilateral descent**), from the father only (**patrilineal descent**), or from the mother only (**matrilineal descent**).

4. Sociologists do not agree on whether the **egalitarian family** has replaced the patriarchal family in the United States.

5. William F. Ogburn outlined six basic functions of the family: reproduction, protection, socialization, regulation of sexual behavior, companionship, and the provision of social status.

6. Conflict theorists argue that male dominance of the family contributes to societal injustice and denies women opportunities. Interactionists focus on how individuals interact within the family and other intimate relationships. Feminists stress the need to broaden research on the family. Like conflict theorists, they see the family's role in socializing children as the primary source of sexism.

Thinking Critically

1. From a woman's point of view, what are the economic advantages and disadvantages of monogamous, polygamous, and polyandrous families? What are the advantages and disadvantages of each of these family situations for men?

2. How would functionalist, conflict, interactionist, and feminist theorists explain a polygamous family structure?

Key Terms

Bilateral descent

Egalitarian family

Extended family

Family

Kinship

Matriarchy

Matrilineal descent

Monogamy

Nuclear family

Patriarchy

Patrilineal descent

Polyandry

Polygamy

Polygyny

Serial monogamy

MODULE 40 | Marriage and Family

Currently, over 95 percent of all men and women in the United States marry at least once during their lifetimes. Historically, the most consistent aspect of family life in this country has been the high rate of marriage. In fact, despite the high rate of divorce, there are some indications of a miniboom in marriages of late.

In this part of the chapter, we will examine various aspects of love, marriage, and parenthood in the United States and contrast them with cross-cultural examples. Though we're used to thinking of romance and mate selection as strictly a matter of individual preference, sociological analysis tells us that social institutions and distinctive cultural norms and values also play an important role.

Courtship and Mate Selection

In the past, most couples met their partners through family, friends, or their neighborhood or workplace. Today, however, many couples meet on the Internet. According to a national survey done in 2010, the Internet is second only to friends as a source of romantic partners—ahead of family, workplace, and neighborhood. Significantly, online networking is just as important to mate-seekers in their 40s and 50s as to those under age 30. It is especially important to gays and lesbians, given the limited number of meeting places available to them: 61 percent of same-sex couples meet online, compared to 23 percent of heterosexual couples (Rosenfeld 2010).

Internet romance is only the latest courtship practice. In the central Asian nation of Uzbekistan and many other traditional cultures, courtship is defined largely through the interaction of two sets of parents, who arrange marriages for their children. Typically, a young Uzbekistani woman will be socialized to eagerly anticipate her marriage to a man whom she has met only once, when he is presented to her family at the time of the final inspection of her dowry. In the United States, in contrast, courtship is conducted primarily by individuals who have a romantic interest in each other. In our culture, courtship often requires these individuals to rely heavily on intricate games, gestures, and signals. Despite such differences, courtship—whether in the United States, Uzbekistan, or elsewhere—is influenced by the norms and values of the larger society (Carol J. Williams 1995).

One unmistakable trend in mate selection is that the process appears to be taking longer today than in the past. A variety of factors, including concerns about financial security and personal independence, has contributed to this delay in marriage. Most people are now well into their 20s before they marry, both in the United States and in other countries (Figure 40-1).

Aspects of Mate Selection

Many societies have explicit or unstated rules that define potential mates as acceptable or unacceptable. These norms can be distinguished in terms of endogamy and exogamy. **Endogamy** (from the Greek *endon,* "within") specifies the groups within which a spouse must be found and prohibits marriage with others. For example, in the United States, many people are expected to marry within their racial, ethnic, or religious group, and are strongly discouraged or even prohibited from marrying outside

trend spotting

Cougars on the Rise

Typically, people choose someone of the same age as a romantic partner. In the most common deviation from this pattern, the husband is older than the wife. Yet today, the number of marriages that involve a much older woman—at least 10 years older—is growing. In fact, there is at least one online dating service that is dedicated to matching older women, dubbed "cougars," with younger men. According to sociologist Andrew Beveridge, although this type of couple represents only 1.3 percent of all marriages, that percentage is double that of 1960.

A similar trend can be seen among dating couples. According to an AARP survey, 20 percent of single women ages 40 to 69 said they were dating or had recently dated a man who was at least five years younger. And an informal tally by one dating service, published in the *New York Times,* indicates a rapid increase in the percentage of women over 40 who want to date men much younger than they are.

Professor Sandra L. Caron of the University of Maine has studied the reasons for this new trend. She notes that unlike many younger women, mature women are self-sufficient and don't need to look for an older, better educated man to support them. She finds that in general, women who marry much younger men have happy marriages, although they may be insecure about their ages. That insecurity is probably misplaced. University of Washington sociologist Pepper Schwartz says she thinks young men are attracted to older women who are sexually free and don't make the demands that younger women do. As men become more accustomed to the idea of women earning more money than they do, the social barriers between young men and older women begin to melt away.

FIGURE 40-1 **Median Age at First Marriage in Eight Countries**

Country	Women	Men
Finland	30.2	32.3
Australia	28.7	30.9
Canada	26.8	29.6
United States	26.3	28.6
Poland	25.2	28.0
China	23.1	24.8
Mexico	22.7	25.0
India	19.9	24.9

Women
Men

Age: 0 10 20 30 40 50 60

Source: United Nations Statistics Division 2008.

Think about It

Why do people marry earlier in India than in Finland?

the group. Endogamy is intended to reinforce the cohesiveness of the group by suggesting to the young that they should marry someone "of their own kind."

Even in the United States, interracial and interethnic marriages are still the exception. According to a report released in 2012, among newly married White couples, about 9 percent marry someone of a different race or ethnicity. Among African American couples the proportion is 17 percent; among Latinos, 26 percent; and among Asian Americans, 28 percent (W. Wang 2012).

In contrast, **exogamy** (from the Greek *exo,* "outside") requires mate selection outside certain groups, usually one's family or certain kinfolk. The **incest taboo,** a social norm common to virtually all societies, prohibits sexual relationships between certain culturally specified relatives. For those of us in the United States, this taboo means that we must marry outside the nuclear family. We cannot marry our siblings, and in most states we cannot marry our first cousins.

Another factor that influences the selection of a marriage partner is **homogamy,** the conscious or unconscious tendency to select a mate with personal characteristics similar to one's own. The "like marries like" rule can be seen in couples with similar personalities and cultural interests. However, mate selection is unpredictable. Though some people may follow the homogamous pattern, others observe the "opposites attract" rule: one person is dependent and submissive—almost childishly so— while the other is dominant and controlling.

Recently, the concept of homogamy has been incorporated into the process of seeking a date or marital partner online. The Internet dating site eHarmony claims to be the first to use a "scientific approach" to matching people based on a variety of abilities and interests. As in real life, online searchers typically do not seek out people of a different race. According to one study of Yahoo daters, over 71 percent of women and 53 percent of men explicitly indicate their racial preferences (Robnett and Feliciano 2011).

The Love Relationship

Today's generation of college students seems more likely to hook up or cruise in large packs than to engage in the romantic dating relationships of their parents and grandparents. Still,

Although most interracial marriages are not as visible as Robert De Niro and Grace Hightower's, such unions are becoming increasingly common and accepted. They are also blurring the definitions of race. Will the children of these couples be considered Black or White? Why do you think so?

at some point in their adult lives, the great majority of today's students will meet someone they love and enter into a long-term relationship that focuses on creating a family.

Parents in the United States tend to value love highly as a rationale for marriage, so they encourage their children to develop intimate relationships based on love and affection. Songs, films, books, magazines, television shows, and even cartoons and comic books reinforce the theme of love. At the same time, our society expects parents and peers to help a person confine his or her search for a mate to "socially acceptable" members of the opposite sex.

Though most people in the United States take the importance of falling in love for granted, the coupling of love and marriage is by no means a cultural universal. Many of the world's cultures give priority in mate selection to factors other than romantic feelings. In societies with *arranged marriages* engineered by parents or religious authorities, economic considerations play a significant role. The newly married couple is expected to develop a feeling of love *after* the legal union is formalized, if at all (Dayananda 2006).

Throughout the world, even where marital arrangements differ from our own, new media technologies are changing the mating game. In a rural Turkish village, where a small minority of the population still practices polygyny, the search for a second wife has moved from neighboring Syria to an Internet café where local men can contact prospective brides in faraway Morocco. Moroccan women watch Turkish soap operas on television and tend to see Turkish men as more romantic than others. They have become familiar with Turkey's culture and religion, politics and economy through the international news media. With a weak economy at home, many of these women must look elsewhere for marriage, so they turn to the Arabic website Habibti.com ("Mydear.com") to find a traditional marriage in an untraditional way (Schleifer 2009).

💡 use your sociological imagination

Your parents and/or a matchmaker are going to arrange a marriage for you. What kind of mate will they select? Will your chances of having a successful marriage be better or worse than if you selected your own mate?

⬤ Variations in Family Life and Intimate Relationships

Within the United States, social class, race, and ethnicity create variations in family life. Studying these variations will give us a more sophisticated understanding of contemporary family styles in our country.

Social Class Differences

Various studies have documented the differences in family organization among social classes in the United States. In the upper class, the emphasis is on lineage and maintenance of family position. If you are in the upper class, you are not simply a member of a nuclear family, but rather a member of a larger family

tradition (think of the Rockefellers or the Kennedys). As a result, upper-class families are quite concerned about what they see as proper training for children.

Lower-class families do not often have the luxury of worrying about the "family name"; they must first struggle to pay their bills and survive the crises often associated with a life of poverty. Such families are more likely to have only one parent at home, which creates special challenges in child care and financial management. Children from lower-class families typically assume adult responsibilities—including marriage and parenthood—at an earlier age than children from affluent homes. In part, that is because they may lack the money needed to remain in school.

Social class differences in family life are less striking today than they once were. In the past, family specialists agreed that the contrasts in child-rearing practices were pronounced. Lower-class families were found to be more authoritarian in rearing children and more inclined to use physical punishment. Middle-class families were more permissive and more restrained in punishing their children. And compared to lower-class families, middle-class families tended to schedule more of their children's time, or even to overstructure it. However, these differences may have narrowed as more and more families from all social classes turned to the same books, magazines, and even television talk shows for advice on rearing children (Kronstadt and Favreault 2008; Luster et al. 1989; J. Sherman and Harris 2012).

Among the poor, women often play a significant role in the economic support of the family. Men may earn low wages, may be unemployed, or may be entirely absent from the family. In 2010, 32 percent of all families headed by women with no husband present fell below the federal government's poverty line. In comparison, the poverty rate for married couples was only 6.2 percent. The disproportionate representation of female-headed households among the poor is a persistent and growing trend, referred to by sociologists as the *feminization of poverty* (see Chapter 8; DeNavas-Walt et al. 2011:16).

Finally, in her book *The Accordion Family* (see the chapter-opening excerpt), Katherine S. Newman (2012) noted that the accordion or boomerang family differs by social class. An upper-middle-class family like the one described in the opening excerpt can afford to provide space to an adult child who is working toward an advanced degree. Less privileged families tend to hang on to their adult children for the labor or income they can contribute to the family's welfare.

Many racial and ethnic groups appear to have distinctive family characteristics. However, racial and class factors are often closely related. In examining family life among racial and ethnic minorities, keep in mind that certain patterns may result from class as well as cultural factors.

Racial and Ethnic Differences

The subordinate status of racial and ethnic minorities in the United States profoundly affects their family lives. For example, the lower incomes of African Americans, Native Americans, most Hispanic groups, and selected Asian American groups make creating and maintaining successful marital unions a difficult task. The economic restructuring of the past 60 years, described by sociologist William Julius Wilson (1996, 2009) and others, has especially affected people living in inner cities and desolate rural areas, such as reservations. Furthermore, the immigration policy of the United States has complicated the successful relocation of intact families from Asia and Latin America.

The African American family suffers from many negative and inaccurate stereotypes. It is true that in a significantly higher proportion of Black than White families, no husband is present in the home (Figure 40-2). Yet Black single mothers often belong to stable, functioning kin networks, which mitigate the pressures of sexism and racism. Members of these networks—predominantly female kin such as mothers, grandmothers, and aunts—ease financial strains by sharing goods and services. In addition to these strong kinship bonds, Black family life has emphasized deep religious commitment and high aspirations for achievement (DuBois [1909] 1970; F. Furstenberg 2007).

Like African Americans, Native Americans draw on family ties to cushion many of the hardships they face. On the Navajo reservation, for example, teenage parenthood is not regarded as the crisis that it is elsewhere in the United States. The Navajo trace their descent matrilineally. Traditionally, couples reside with the wife's family after marriage, allowing the grandparents to help with the child rearing. While the Navajo do not approve of teenage parenthood, the deep emotional commitment of their extended families provides a warm home environment for children, even when no father is present or involved (Dalla and Gamble 2001; John 2012).

Sociologists also have taken note of differences in family patterns among other racial and ethnic groups. For example, Mexican American men have been described as exhibiting a sense of virility, personal worth, and pride in their maleness that is called **machismo**. Mexican Americans are also described as being more familistic than many other subcultures. **Familism** (or *familismo*) refers to pride in the extended family, expressed through the maintenance of close ties and strong obligations to kinfolk outside the immediate family. Traditionally, Mexican Americans have placed proximity to their extended families above other needs and desires.

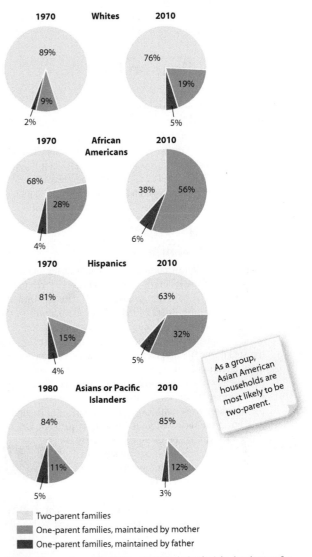

FIGURE 40-2 **Rise of Single-Parent Families in the United States, 1970–2010**

Note: Families are groups with children under 18. Early data for Asian Americans are for 1980. Hispanics can be of any race. Not included are unrelated people living together with no children present. All data exclude the 11 percent of children in nonparental households.
Sources: Bureau of the Census 2008a:56, 2010c:Table FG10.

Although familism is often seen as a positive cultural attribute, it may also have negative consequences. Sociologists who have studied the relatively low college application rates of Hispanic students have found they have a strong desire to stay at home. Even the children of college-educated parents express this preference, which diminishes the likelihood of their getting a four-year degree and dramatically reduces the possibility that they will apply to a selective college.

These family patterns are changing, however, in response to changes in Latinos' social class standing, educational achievements, and occupations. Like other Americans, career-oriented

Latinos in search of a mate but short on spare time are turning to Internet sites. As Latinos and other groups assimilate into the dominant culture of the United States, their family lives take on both the positive and negative characteristics associated with White households (Negroni 2012; Suárez and Perez 2012).

Child-Rearing Patterns

The Nayars of southern India acknowledge the biological role of fathers, but the mother's eldest brother is responsible for her children. In contrast, uncles play only a peripheral role in child care in the United States. Caring for children is a universal function of the family, yet the ways in which different societies assign this function to family members can vary significantly. Even within the United States, child-rearing patterns are varied. We'll take a look here at parenthood and grandparenthood, adoption, dual-income families, single-parent families, and stepfamilies.

Parenthood and Grandparenthood

The socialization of children is essential to the maintenance of any culture. Consequently, parenthood is one of the most important (and most demanding) social roles in the United States. Sociologist Alice Rossi (1968, 1984) has identified four factors that complicate the transition to parenthood and the role of socialization. First, there is little anticipatory socialization for the social role of caregiver. The normal school curriculum gives scant attention to the subjects most relevant to successful family life, such as child care and home maintenance. Second, only limited learning occurs during the period of pregnancy itself. Third, the transition to parenthood is quite abrupt. Unlike adolescence, it is not prolonged; unlike the transition to work, the duties of caregiving cannot be taken on gradually. Finally, in Rossi's view, our society lacks clear and helpful guidelines for successful parenthood. There is little consensus on how parents can produce happy and well-adjusted offspring—or even on what it means to be well adjusted. For these reasons, socialization for parenthood involves difficult challenges for most men and women in the United States.

In some homes, the full nest holds grandchildren. By 2009, 9 percent of White children, 17 percent of Black children, and 14 percent of Hispanic children lived with at least one grandparent. In about a third of these homes, no parent was present to assume responsibility for the youngsters. Special difficulties are inherent in such relationships, including legal custodial concerns, financial issues, and emotional problems for adults and youths alike. It is not surprising that support groups such as Grandparents as Parents have emerged to provide assistance (Kreider and Ellis 2011).

Adoption

In a legal sense, **adoption** is the transfer of the legal rights, responsibilities, and privileges of parenthood to a new legal parent or parents. In many cases, these rights are transferred from a biological parent or parents (often called birth parents) to an adoptive parent or parents. Every year, about 135,000 children are adopted (Child Welfare Information 2011).

Viewed from a functionalist perspective, government has a strong interest in encouraging adoption. Policymakers, in fact, have both a humanitarian and a financial stake in the process. In theory, adoption offers a stable family environment for children who otherwise might not receive satisfactory care. Moreover, government data show that unwed mothers who keep their babies tend to be of lower socioeconomic status and often require public assistance to support their children. The government can lower its social welfare expenses, then, if children are transferred to economically self-sufficient families. From an interactionist perspective, however, adoption may require a child to adjust to a very different family environment and parental approach to child rearing.

There are two legal methods of adopting an unrelated person: the adoption may be arranged through a licensed agency, or in some states it may be arranged through a private agreement sanctioned by the courts. Adopted children may come from the United States or from abroad. In 2011, over 9,300 children entered the United States as the adopted children of U.S. citizens (Bureau of Consular Affairs 2011).

Having a new child is a major adjustment for everyone in the family; adopting a child is an even bigger adjustment. If the adopted child comes from another culture and is racially or ethnically different from the adopting family, the challenge is that

When nine-year-old Blake Brunson shows up for a basketball game, so do his *eight* grandparents—the result of his parents' remarriages. Blended families can be very supportive to children, but what message do they send to them on the permanency of marriage?

much greater. Box 40-1 describes research on the adjustment that occurs when a U.S. family adopts a child from South Korea.

The 2010 earthquake in Haiti drew attention to the foreign perspective on international adoptions, which is not always positive. When well-meaning people from the United States arrived in Haiti to rescue alleged orphans and arrange for their adoption in other countries, government officials objected. Some of the children, it turned out, were not orphans; their parents were simply too poor to care for them. For the governments of overstressed developing nations, adoption can be both a solution and a problem.

Adoption is controversial not only abroad but at home as well. In some cases, those who adopt children are not married. In 1995, an important court decision in New York held that a couple does not need to be married to adopt a child. Under this ruling, unmarried heterosexual couples, lesbian couples, and gay couples can all adopt children in New York. Today, most states permit gay and lesbian couples to adopt. Significant restrictions or outright prohibitions exist in Florida, Michigan, Mississippi, Nebraska, and Utah (National Gay and Lesbian Task Force 2012).

Research Today

BOX 40-1

Transracial Adoption: The Experience of Children from Korea

Caleb Littell was born in South Korea and adopted by a White couple in the United States as an infant. He joined a loving family in the predominantly White suburb of Renton, Washington, just outside Seattle. Now in his 30s, Caleb always knew that he was loved and fiercely wanted by his parents. Still, he struggled with his identity. Why did he look different from his parents? Why was he adopted? What did it mean to be Korean? These questions didn't trouble him at home, but at school and in the wider community, where he was often teased for being "Oriental" or "Asian." His White parents, whom he identified with, didn't see him as different from themselves, he reasoned, yet people outside the family did—why? Caleb wasn't just hurt; he was confused.

This story, recounted by educator Mia Tuan and sociologist Jiannbin Lee Shiao, is all too familiar to children who have experienced **transracial adoption,** the adoption of a non-White child by White parents or a Hispanic child by non-Hispanics. According to a 2011 estimate, there are about 300,000 such children under age 16 in the United States today. Although this type of adoption has occurred for generations, it became more common in the 1990s with the increase in international adoptions. About 85 percent of international adoptions are transracial.

Although no single case is typical, the life-long socialization of the transracially adopted child does present some special challenges. In Chapter 5 we noted that a child's relationship to his or her parents is an ascribed status, as is ethnicity or race. Korean children who were adopted by White families find that when they move outside their protective nuclear families, their ascribed identities are immediately questioned. Sociologists and other researchers

> Now in his 30s, Caleb always knew that he was loved and fiercely wanted by his parents. Still, he struggled with his identity.

point out that their experience reflects contemporary racial and ethnic relations in the United States. That is to say, these children find acceptance and opportunity as well as intolerance and conflict in their new home country.

Assessing the long-term success of transracial adoption is difficult, since the outcomes of raising children in general are complex. The researcher must separate normal parenting problems from transracial parenting problems. One common transracial parenting problem is that White parents may lack the individual experiences, and at first the resources, to transmit positive identity messages to their adopted children. For advice, parents often turn to

support groups and online chat rooms. Some send their children to *heritage camps,* which have emerged over the last 30 years to immerse children in cultural experiences reflective of their cultural background, be it African, Asian, or Hispanic. Besides offering language instruction, such camps allow children to socialize with others who were transracially adopted. The degree and quality of support from other relatives and from the surrounding community is also important to the children's adjustment.

In terms of the children's adult identity, there is no single outcome. Adult Korean American adoptees may describe themselves as "Korean American," "Caucasian, except when looking in the mirror," or "Amerasian trying to be White." Research indicates that their identification with Korea is weak, although it has strengthened a bit among more recent adoptees, as support structures have improved. Few of them really learn to speak the Korean language or to truly enjoy Korean food.

LET'S DISCUSS

1. How well do you think transracially adopted children fit in with their peers? How might these children's ages and their new communities affect their adjustment?

2. Compare the experience of transracial adoption to the experience of entering a blended family. From the child's point of view, what might be the advantages and disadvantages of each? From the parents' point of view, what might be the challenges of each?

Sources: Freundlich and Lieberthal 2000; Kreider 2011; Randolph and Holtzman 2010; Tuan and Shiao 2011; Woon 2005.

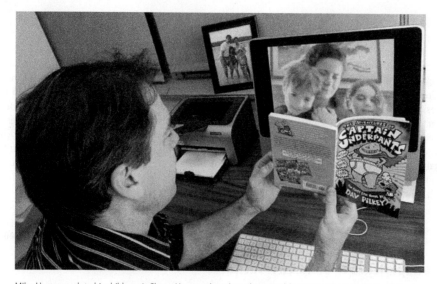

Miles Harvey reads to his children via Skype. Harvey, who is happily married, lives 900 miles from his family in Chicago. He accepted a job in New Orleans for economic reasons.

For every child who is adopted, many more remain the wards of state-sponsored child protective services. At any given time, around half a million children in the United States are living in foster care. Every year, about 57,000 of them are adopted; another 103,000 are eligible and waiting to be adopted (Department of Health and Human Services 2011b).

Dual-Income Families

The idea of a family consisting of a wage-earning husband and a wife who stays at home has largely given way to the dual-income household. Among married people between ages 25 and 34, 94 percent of the men and 69 percent of the women were in the labor force in 2010 (Bureau of the Census 2011a:Table 597 on page 384).

Why has there been such a rise in the number of dual-income couples? A major factor is economic need, coupled with a desire by both men *and* women to pursue their careers. Evidence of this trend can be found in the rise in the number of married couples living apart for reasons other than marital discord. The 3.6 million couples who now live apart represent 1 out of every 33 marriages. More than half of them live farther than 100 miles apart, and half of those live 1,000 or more miles apart. Of course, couples living apart are nothing new; men have worked at transient jobs for generations as soldiers, truck drivers, or traveling salesmen. Now, however, the woman's job is often the one that creates the separation. The existence of such household arrangements reflects an acceptance of the egalitarian family type (Higgins et al. 2010; Holmes 2009; Silverman 2009).

Single-Parent Families

The 2004 *American Idol* winner Fantasia Barrino's song "Baby Mama" offers a tribute to young single mothers—a subject she knows about. Barrino was 17 when she became pregnant with her daughter. Though critics charged that the song sends the wrong message to teenage girls, Barrino says it is not about encouraging teens to have sex. Rather, she sees the song as an anthem for young mothers courageously trying to raise their children alone (Cherlin 2006).

In recent decades, the stigma attached to unwed mothers and other single parents has significantly diminished. **Single-parent families,** in which only one parent is present to care for the children, can hardly be viewed as a rarity in the United States. In 2010, a single parent headed about 24 percent of White families with children under 18, 37 percent of Hispanic families with children, and 62 percent of African American families with children (Figure 40-2).

The lives of single parents and their children are not inevitably more difficult than life in a traditional nuclear family. It is as inaccurate to assume that a single-parent family is necessarily deprived as it is to assume that a two-parent family is always secure and happy. Nevertheless, life in a single-parent family can be extremely stressful, in both economic and emotional terms. A family headed by a single mother faces especially difficult problems when the mother is a teenager.

Why might low-income teenage women wish to have children and face the obvious financial difficulties of motherhood? Viewed from an interactionist perspective, these women tend to have low self-esteem and limited options; a child may provide a sense of motivation and purpose for a teenager whose economic worth in our society is limited at best. Given the barriers that many young women face because of their gender, race, ethnicity, and class, many teenagers may believe they have little to lose and much to gain by having a child.

According to a widely held stereotype, "unwed mothers" and "babies having babies" in the United States are predominantly African American. However, this view is not entirely accurate. African Americans account for a disproportionate share of births to unmarried women and teenagers, but the majority of all babies born to unmarried teenage mothers are born to White adolescents. Moreover, since 1980, birthrates among Black teenagers have generally declined (J. Martin et al. 2009).

Although 84 percent of single parents in the United States are mothers, the number of households headed by single fathers more than quadrupled from 1987 to 2011. Though single mothers often develop social networks, single fathers are typically more isolated. In addition, they must deal with schools and social service agencies that are more accustomed to women as custodial parents (Bureau of the Census 1994, 2011c).

use your **sociological imagination**

What personal experience do you have with child rearing by grandparents, dual-income families, or single-parent families? Describe what you observed using sociological concepts.

Stepfamilies

Approximately 45 percent of all people in the United States will marry, divorce, and then remarry. The rising rates of divorce and remarriage have led to a noticeable increase in stepfamily relationships.

The exact nature of blended families has social significance for adults and children alike. Certainly resocialization is required when an adult becomes a stepparent or a child becomes a step-child and stepsibling. Moreover, an important distinction must be made between first-time stepfamilies and households where there have been repeated divorces, breakups, or changes in custodial arrangements.

In evaluating the rise of stepfamilies, some observers have assumed that children would benefit from remarriage because they would be gaining a second custodial parent, and would potentially enjoy greater economic security. However, after reviewing many studies of stepfamilies, sociologist Andrew J. Cherlin (2010) concluded that children whose parents have remarried do not have higher levels of well-being than children in divorced single-parent families.

Stepparents can play valuable and unique roles in their stepchildren's lives, but their involvement does not guarantee an improvement in family life. In fact, standards may decline. Studies suggest that children raised in families with stepmothers are likely to have less health care, education, and money spent on their food than children raised by biological mothers. The measures are also negative for children raised by stepfathers, but only half as negative as in the case of stepmothers.

Most households In the United States do not consist of two parents living with their unmarried children.

These results don't mean that stepmothers are "evil"—it may be that the stepmother holds back out of concern for seeming too intrusive, or relies mistakenly on the biological father to carry out parental duties (Schmeeckle 2007; Schmeeckle et al. 2006).

💡 use your **sociological imagination**

What special challenges might stepfamilies face? What advantages might they enjoy? Explain using sociological concepts.

MODULE 40 | Recap and Review

Summary

People select mates in a variety of ways: in some societies, marriages are arranged, while in others, people select their own mates.

1. Some societies require mates to be chosen within a certain group (**endogamy**) or outside certain groups (**exogamy**). Consciously or unconsciously, many people look for a mate with similar personal characteristics (**homogamy**).

2. In the United States, family life varies with social class, race, and ethnicity.

3. Currently, in the majority of all married couples in the United States, both husband and wife work outside the home.

4. **Single-parent families** account for an increasing proportion of U.S. families.

Thinking Critically

1. How do both cultural and socioeconomic factors contribute to the following trends: later age of first marriage, the increasing number of extended-family households, and the boomerang generation?

2. Explain mate selection from the functionalist and interactionist perspectives.

Key Terms

Adoption

Endogamy

Exogamy

Familism

Homogamy

Incest taboo

Machismo

Single-parent family

Transracial adoption

MODULE 41 | Alternatives to Traditional Families

Divorce

In the United States, the pattern of family life includes commitments both to marriage and to self-expression and personal growth. Needless to say, the tension between those competing commitments can undermine a marriage, working against the establishment of a lasting relationship. This approach to family life is distinctive to the United States. In some nations, such as Italy, the culture strongly supports marriage and discourages divorce. In others, such as Sweden, people treat marriage the same way as cohabitation, and both arrangements are just as lasting (Cherlin 2009).

Statistical Trends in Divorce

Just how common is divorce? Surprisingly, this is not a simple question; divorce statistics are difficult to interpret. The media frequently report that one out of every two marriages ends in divorce, but that figure is misleading. It is based on a comparison of all divorces that occur in a single year (regardless of when the couples were married) with the number of new marriages in the same year.

In many countries, divorce began to increase in the late 1960s but then leveled off; since the late 1980s, it has declined by 30 percent. (Figure 41-1 shows the pattern in the United States.) This trend is due partly to the aging of the baby boomer population and the corresponding decline in the proportion of people of marriageable age. But it also indicates an increase in marital stability in recent years (Coontz 2006).

Getting divorced obviously does not sour people on marriage. About 63 percent of all divorced people in the United States have remarried. Women are less likely than men to remarry because many retain custody of their children after a divorce, which complicates a new adult relationship (Bianchi and Spain 1996; Saad 2004).

Some people regard the nation's high rate of remarriage as an endorsement of the institution of marriage, but it does lead to the new challenges of a kin network composed of both current and prior marital relationships. Such networks can be particularly complex if children are involved or if an ex-spouse remarries.

Factors Associated with Divorce

Perhaps the most important factor in the increase in divorce over the past hundred years has been the greater social *acceptance* of divorce. It is no longer considered necessary to endure an unhappy marriage. More important, various religious denominations have relaxed their negative attitudes toward divorce, so that most religious leaders no longer treat it as a sin.

The growing acceptance of divorce is a worldwide phenomenon. A decade ago, Sunoo, South Korea's foremost matchmaking service, had no divorced clients. Few Koreans divorced; those who did felt social pressure to resign themselves to the single life. But in one recent seven-year period, South Korea's divorce rate doubled. Today, 15 percent of Sunoo's membership are divorced (Onishi 2003; United Nations Statistics Division 2009:Table 23).

In the United States, several factors have contributed to the growing social acceptance of divorce:

- Most states have adopted more liberal divorce laws in the past three decades. No-fault divorce laws, which allow a couple to end their marriage without fault on either side (by specifying adultery, for instance), accounted for an initial surge in the divorce rate after they were introduced in the 1970s, but appear to have had little effect beyond that.

- Divorce has become a more practical option in newly formed families, since families tend to have fewer children now than in the past.

FIGURE 41-1 Trends in Marriage and Divorce in the United States, 1920–2010

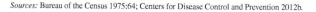

> The divorce rate has generally risen since 1920, while the marriage rate has declined.

Sources: Bureau of the Census 1975:64; Centers for Disease Control and Prevention 2012b.

- A general increase in family incomes, coupled with the availability of free legal aid to some poor people, has meant that more couples can afford costly divorce proceedings.

- As society provides greater opportunities for women, more and more wives are becoming less dependent on their husbands, both economically and emotionally. They may feel more able to leave a marriage if it seems hopeless.

Impact of Divorce on Children

Divorce is traumatic for all involved, but it has special meaning for the more than 1 million children whose parents divorce each year. Of course, for some of these children, divorce signals the welcome end to a very dysfunctional relationship. Perhaps that is why a national study that tracked 6,332 children both before and after their parents' divorce found that their behavior did not suffer from the marital breakups. Other studies have shown greater unhappiness among children who live amid parental conflict than among children whose parents are divorced. Still, it would be simplistic to assume that children are automatically better off following the breakup of their parents' marriage. The interests of the parents do not necessarily serve children well (H. Kim 2011; Zi 2007).

Diverse Lifestyles

Marriage is no longer the presumed route from adolescence to adulthood. Instead, it is treated as just one of several paths to maturity. As a result, the marriage ceremony has lost much of its social significance as a rite of passage. The nation's marriage rate has declined since 1960 because people are postponing marriage until later in life, and because more couples, including same-sex couples, are deciding to form partnerships without marriage (Haq 2011).

Cohabitation

In the United States, testing the marital waters by living together before making a commitment is a common practice among marriage-wary 20- and 30-somethings. The tremendous increase in the number of male–female couples who choose to live together without marrying, a practice called **cohabitation,** is one of the most dramatic trends of recent years.

About half of all *currently* married couples in the United States say that they lived together before marriage. This percentage is likely to increase. The number of households in the United States that are headed by unmarried opposite-sex couples has been rising steadily; in 2010 it was 6.7 million (Kreider 2010).

In much of Europe, cohabitation is so common that the general sentiment seems to be "Love, yes; marriage, maybe." In Iceland, 62 percent of all children are born to single mothers; in France, Great Britain, and Norway, about 40 percent. Government policies in these countries make few legal distinctions between married and unmarried couples or households. Perhaps as a result, partnerships between cohabiting adults are not necessarily brief or lacking in commitment. Children born to a cohabiting couple in Sweden, for example, are less likely than children born to a cohabiting couple in the United States to see their parents break up (Cherlin 2009; Lyall 2002; M. Moore 2006).

People tend to associate cohabitation with younger, childless couples. Although that stereotype may have been accurate a generation or more ago, it is not now. Since 1970, the number of unmarried couples with children has increased 12-fold. By the age of 12, about 42 percent of all children in the United States have lived with cohabiting parents (Institute for American Values 2011).

Periodically, legislators attempt to bolster the desirability of a lifelong commitment to marriage. In 2002, President George W. Bush backed funding for an initiative to promote marriage among those who receive public assistance. Under the Healthy Marriage Initiative, the federal government created a resource center that promoted marriage-related programs. Critics charged that the effort was underfunded or an inappropriate mission for the federal government. Still, the Obama administration has indicated a desire to continue the initiative, although the fragile economy may jeopardize its funding (Jayson 2009).

Remaining Single

Looking at TV programs today, you would be justified in thinking that most households are composed of singles. Although that is not the case, it is true that more and more people in the United States are postponing entry into a first marriage. Over one out of three households with children in the United States is a single-parent household. Even so, less than 4 percent of women and men in the United States are likely to remain single throughout their lives (Bureau of the Census 2011c).

The trend toward maintaining a single lifestyle for a longer period is related to the growing economic independence of young people. This trend is especially significant for women. Freed from financial needs, women don't necessarily need to marry to enjoy a satisfying life. Divorce, late marriage, and longevity also figure into this trend.

There are many reasons why a person may choose not to marry. Some singles do not want to limit their sexual intimacy to one lifetime partner. Some men and women do not want to become highly dependent on any one person—and do not want anyone depending heavily on them. In a society that values individuality and self-fulfillment, the single lifestyle can offer certain freedoms that married couples may not enjoy. Even divorced parents may not feel the need to remarry. Andrew J. Cherlin (2009) contends that a single parent who connects with other adults, such as grandparents, to form a solid, supportive relationship for child rearing should not feel compelled to re-partner.

Nevertheless, remaining single represents a clear departure from societal expectations; indeed, it has been likened to "being single on Noah's Ark." A single adult must confront the inaccurate view that he or she is always lonely, is a workaholic, or is immature. These stereotypes help to support the traditional assumption in the United States and most other societies that to be truly happy and fulfilled, a person must get married and raise a family. To counter these societal expectations, singles have formed numerous support groups (Hertz 2006; Klinenberg 2012; Lundquist 2006).

Marriage without Children

There has been a modest increase in childlessness in the United States. According to census data, about 16 to 17 percent of women will now complete their childbearing years without having borne any children, compared to 10 percent in 1980. As many as 20 percent of women in their 30s expect to remain childless (Biddlecom and Martin 2006).

Childlessness within marriage has generally been viewed as a problem that can be solved through such means as adoption and artificial insemination. More and more couples today, however, choose not to have children and regard themselves as child-free rather than childless. They do not believe that having children automatically follows from marriage, nor do they feel that reproduction is the duty of all married couples. Childless couples have formed support groups (with names like No Kidding) and set up websites.

Economic considerations have contributed to this shift in attitudes; having children has become quite expensive. According to a government estimate made for 2012, the average middle-class family will spend $229,320 to feed, clothe, and shelter a child from birth to age 18. If the child attends college, that amount could double, depending on the college chosen. In 1960, parents spent only 2 percent of their income on child care and education; now they spend 16 percent, reflecting the rising dependence on nonfamily child care (see the Social Policy section in Module 15). Aware of the financial pressures, some couples are weighing the advantages of a child-free marriage (Lino 2011).

Childless couples are beginning to question current practices in the workplace. While applauding employers' efforts to provide child care and flexible work schedules, some nevertheless express concern about tolerance of employees who leave early to take children to doctors, ball games, or after-school classes. As more dual-career couples enter the paid labor force and struggle to balance career and familial responsibilities, conflicts with employees who have no children may increase (Biddlecom and Martin 2006).

use your **sociological imagination**

What would happen to our society if many more married couples suddenly decided not to have children? How would society change if cohabitation and/or singlehood became the norm?

MODULE 41 | Recap and Review

Summary

Divorce and alternatives to traditional marriage such as cohabitation now represent common choices of family style.

1. Among the factors that contribute to the rising divorce rate in the United States are greater social acceptance of divorce and the liberalization of divorce laws in many states.

2. More and more people are living together without marrying, a practice known as **cohabitation.**

3. People are staying single longer, and some married couples are deciding not to have children.

Thinking Critically

1. Do you think it is correct to say that marriage has lost much of its social significance as a rite of passage? Explain your response. What are the major rites of passage into adulthood in today's society?

2. In a society that maximizes the welfare of all family members, how easy should it be for couples to divorce? How easy should it be to get married?

Key Term

Cohabitation

MODULE 42 | Human Sexuality

Human sexuality spans a broad range of behaviors, including some that are not condoned by particular societies. From the sociologist's perspective, however, sexuality is not limited to physical behaviors, but includes the beliefs, values, and social norms that collectively govern its expression. For example, most societies seek to restrict sexual expression to marriage because of its effect on the family, particularly the welfare of women and children (C. Schneider 2008).

Although human sexuality is expressed in all societies, the way it is sanctioned differs widely, both geographically and historically. In South Africa, following the end of apartheid in 1990, legislators removed barriers to interracial cohabitation and marriage. Then in 1998 they passed the Recognition of Customary Marriages Act, which legalized polygamy among some African tribal groups, but not among Muslims and other religious groups. Finally, under the Civil Union Act of 2006, they granted gay and lesbian couples the same rights and responsibilities as opposite-sex couples (Stacey 2011).

Clearly, sexual attitudes and practices change over time. In Module 8 we saw how the publication of Alfred Kinsey's first study of human sexuality in 1948 profoundly shocked Americans. Today, online sites routinely solicit descriptions of almost any kind of human sexuality. Besides the new cultural openness about sex, medical advances have encouraged what many refer to as a

sexual revolution. For example, the development of oral contraceptives ("the pill") in 1965 and of remedies for erectile dysfunction (Viagra and other such drugs) in 1998 reduced the risk and increased the likelihood of frequent sexual activity. Today, young people engage in sexual practices that few people in earlier generations would have dared to participate in (see Box 42-1, which describes an interactionist study of the sexual networks in one American high school).

Labeling and Human Sexuality

In Chapter 7 we saw how society singles out certain groups of people by labeling them in positive or negative ways—as "good kids" or "delinquents," for example. Labeling theorists have also studied how labels are used to sanction certain sexual behaviors as "deviant."

The definition of deviant sexual behavior has varied significantly over time and from one culture to another. Until 1973, the American Psychiatric Association considered homosexuality a "sociopathic personality disorder," which in effect meant that homosexuals should seek therapy. Two years later, however, the association removed homosexuality from its list of mental illnesses. Today, the organization publicly proclaims that "being gay is just as healthy as being straight." To use Goffman's term, mental health professionals have removed the *stigma* from this form of sexual expression. As a result, in the United States and many other countries, consensual sex between same-sex adults is no longer a crime (American Psychological Association 2008; International Gay and Lesbian Human Rights Commission 2010).

Despite the change in health professionals' attitudes, however, the social stigma of homosexuality lingers. As a result, many people prefer the more positive terms *gay* and *lesbian*. Others, in defiance of the stigma, have proudly adopted the pejorative term *queer* in a deliberate reaction to the ridicule they have borne because of their sexual orientation. Still others maintain that constructing one's sexual orientation as either homosexual or heterosexual is too limiting. Indeed, such labels ignore those who are *bisexual,* or sexually attracted to both sexes.

Another group whose sexual orientation does not fit into the usual categories is *transgendered persons,* or those people whose current gender identity does not match their physical identity at birth. Some transgendered persons see themselves as both male and female. Others, called *transsexuals,* may take hormones or undergo surgery in an effort to draw physically closer to their chosen gender identity. Transgendered persons are

Lady Gaga's 2011 hit single "Born This Way," which includes the lyric "Don't be a drag, just be a queen," was written as an anthem to diversity and acceptance.

Research Today

BOX 42-1

Adolescent Sexual Networks

If you drew a chart of the sexual network at a typical American high school, what would it look like? In the mid-1990s, sociologists Peter Bearman, James Moody, and Katherine Stovel asked themselves that question. While studying romantic relationships at a high school with 1,000 students, they found that about 61 percent of the boys and 55 percent of the girls had been sexually active over the past 18 months. Those percentages did not differ much from the results of similar studies done during the period. What surprised the research team was what they saw when they began to chart the students' relationships.

To obtain their data, Bearman and his colleagues conducted in-home interviews with the respondents. Instead of asking students for a face-to-face interview—a technique that might have embarrassed them or distorted their answers—the researchers gave them an audio recording of the questions, a pair of earphones, and a laptop computer on which to record their answers. The research team also asked respondents to look at a list of all the students at the high school and identify those with whom they had had romantic or sexual relationships.

The results showed that 573 of the 832 students surveyed had had at least one sexual relationship over the past 18 months. Among those respondents, the sociologists found only 63 steady couples, or pairs with no other partners. A much larger group of 288

Each dot represents a boy or girl at "Jefferson High." The lines that link them represent romantic and sexual relationships that occurred over an 18-month period. While most of the teenagers had had just one or two partners, 288 of the 832 kids interviewed were linked in a giant sexual network.

- Boys
- Girls

Other relationships (if a pattern was observed more than once, numeral indicates frequency)

2   2   9   12   63

Sources: Bearman, Moody, and Stovel 2005:58

> A particularly significant implication of this study is the risk of sexually transmitted diseases (STDs) to those who participate in such a network.

students—almost a third of the sample—was involved in the free-flowing network of relationships shown on the accompanying chart. (Note the comparative absence of tightly closed loops of three to five individuals.) Not shown on the chart were another 90 students who were involved in relationships outside the school.

A particularly significant implication of this study is the risk of sexually transmitted diseases (STDs) to those who participate in such a network. Through the complicated chain of relationships, even students who have only one or two sexual partners are exposing themselves to a relatively high degree of risk. But while parents and even students may be alarmed by the data, public health officials are encouraged. Experts at the Centers for Disease Control who have reviewed the network charts from this and other studies see them as blueprints for change. If experts can alter participants' behavior anywhere along these chains—by counseling abstinence, condom use, or treatment of STDs—they can significantly reduce transmission of the diseases.

LET'S DISCUSS

1. Do the results of the study surprise you? How does the sexual network described in this study compare to the network where you went to high school?

2. Do you see any problems with the research method used in this study? Can you think of anything that might have compromised the validity of the data?

Sources: Bearman, Moody, and Stovel 2004; C. F. Turner et al. 1998; Wallis 2005.

---

sometimes confused with *transvestites,* or cross-dressers who wear the clothing of the opposite sex. Transvestites are typically men, either gay or heterosexual, who choose to wear women's clothing.

The use of these terms even in a positive or nonjudgmental way is problematic, since they imply that human sexuality can be confined in neat, mutually exclusive categories. Moreover, the destigmatization of these labels tends to reflect the influence of the socially privileged—that is, the affluent—who have the resources to overcome the stigma. In contrast, the traditional Native American concept of the *two spirit,* a personality that

blends the masculine and the feminine, has been largely ridiculed or ignored (Gilley 2006; Wentling et al. 2008).

What does constitute sexual deviance, then? The answer to this question seems to change with each generation. Today, U.S. laws allow married women to accuse their husbands of rape, when a generation ago such an offense was not recognized. Similarly, *pedophilia*—an adult having sex with a minor—is generally regarded with disgust today, even when it is consensual. Yet in many countries, fringe groups now speak positively of "intergenerational sex," arguing that "childhood" is not a biological given (Hendershott 2002).

Though pedophilia and some other aspects of sexual expression are still against the law, the meaning of the labels is beginning to blur. Although child pornography is both illegal and abhorrent to most people, many fashion advertisements in mainstream magazines seem to verge on it. And while sex work and sex trafficking seem wrong to most of us, society tolerates and even regulates many aspects of those activities (Barton 2006).

use your **sociological imagination**

Do your friends react differently to some expressions of human sexuality? If so, in what way?

Lesbian and Gay Relationships

Twenty-one-year-old Parke, a junior in college, grew up in a stable, loving family. A self-described fiscal conservative, he credits his parents with instilling in him a strong work ethic. Sound like an average child of an average family? The only break with traditional expectations in this case is that Parke is the son of a lesbian couple (P. Brown 2004).

The lifestyles of lesbians and gay men are varied. Some live in long-term, monogamous relationships; others live alone or with roommates. Some remain in "empty-shell" heterosexual marriages and do not publicly acknowledge their homosexuality. Others live with children from a former marriage or with adopted children. Based on election exit polls, researchers for the National Health and Social Life Survey and the Voter News Service estimate that 2 to 5 percent of the adult population identify themselves as either gay or lesbian. An analysis of the 2010 Census shows about 600,000 gay households, and a gay and lesbian adult population approaching 10 million (Figure 42-1) (Laumann et al. 1994b:293; Lofquist 2011).

Gay and lesbian couples face discrimination on both a personal and a legal level. Their inability to marry denies them many rights that married couples take for granted, from the ability to make decisions for an incapacitated partner to the right to receive government benefits to dependents, such as Social Security payments. Though gay couples consider themselves families just like the straight couples who live down the street, they are often treated as if they are not.

Precisely because of such inequities, many gay and lesbian couples are now demanding the right to marry. In the Social Policy section that follows, we will examine the highly controversial issue of gay marriage.

MAPPING LIFE NATIONWIDE

FIGURE 42-1 **Same-Sex Couples Per 1,000 Households**

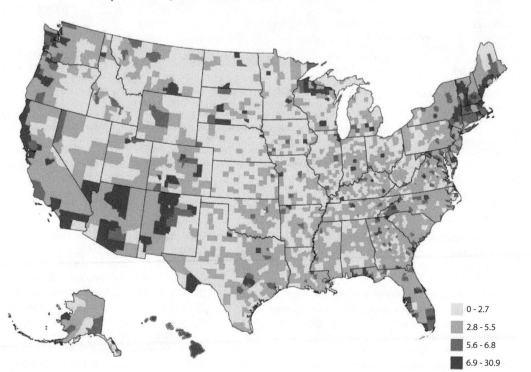

0 - 2.7
2.8 - 5.5
5.6 - 6.8
6.9 - 30.9

Source: Gates and Cooke 2001.

social policy and the Family | Gay Marriage

In the United States, attitudes toward marriage are complex. As always, society and popular culture suggest that a young man or woman should find the perfect mate, settle down and marry, have children, and live happily ever after. But young people are also bombarded by messages implying the frequency of adultery and the acceptability of divorce. In this atmosphere, the idea of same-sex marriage strikes some people as only the latest of many attacks on traditional marriage. To others, it seems an overdue acknowledgment of the formal relationships that faithful, monogamous gay couples have long maintained.

Looking at the Issue

What has made gay marriage the focus of national attention? Events in two states brought the issue to the forefront. In 1999, Vermont gave gay couples the legal benefits of marriage through civil union, but stopped short of calling the arrangement a marriage. Then, in 2003, the Massachusetts Supreme Court ruled 4–3 that under the state's constitution, gay couples have the right to marry—a ruling the U.S. Supreme Court has refused to review. Now, with gay married couples in this state approaching their 10th anniversary, scholars are beginning to study their experiences compared to those of opposite-sex couples.

Recently, national surveys of attitudes toward gay marriage in the United States have shown an almost even split among the public. In a 2011 survey, 53 percent of respondents said that the marriages of same-sex couples should be recognized as legally valid, with the same rights as traditional marriages. Among those under 35, the support level reached 70 percent (Newport 2011a).

Applying Sociology

Functionalists have traditionally seen marriage as a social institution that is closely tied to human reproduction. Same-sex marriage would at first appear not to fit that arrangement. However, many same-sex couples are entrusted with the socialization of young children, whether or not their relationship is recognized by the state. Functionalists also wonder whether religious views toward marriage can be ignored. The courts have focused on civil marriage, but religious views are hardly irrelevant, even in a country like the United States, which observes a separation between religion and the state. Indeed, religious teachings have led even some staunch supporters of gay rights to oppose same-sex marriage on spiritual grounds.

Conflict theorists have charged that denial of the right to marry reinforces the second-class status of gays and lesbians. Some have compared the ban on gay marriage to past policies that until 1967 banned interracial marriage in 32 states. Figure 42-2 illustrates the different ways that same-sex partnerships are treated today in different states. Using 2010 data, the Bureau of the Census (2011c) estimates that between 131,000 and 153,000 gay and lesbian couples in the United States are now married.

Interactionists generally avoid the policy question and focus instead on the nature of same-sex households. They ask many of the same questions about gay partner relations and child rearing that they ask about conventional couples. Of course, much less research has been done on same-sex households than on other families, but the studies published to date raise the same issues as those that apply to conventional married couples, plus a few more. For gay couples, the support or opposition of family, co-workers, and friends looms large (Dundas and Kaufman 2000; Dunne 2000; B. Powell et al. 2010).

Initiating Policy

The United States is not the first nation to consider this issue. In 2001, the Netherlands became the first nation to legalize same-sex marriage. In less than 10 years, nine other nations followed: Belgium, Spain, Canada, South Africa, Norway, Sweden, Portugal, Iceland, and Argentina. Typically, same-sex couples account for 2 to 3 percent of all marriages in these nations (Chamie and Mirkin 2011).

In the United States, many local jurisdictions have passed legislation allowing for the registration of domestic partnerships, and have extended employee benefits to those relationships. Under such policies, a **domestic partnership** may be

—*Continued*

—Continued

MAPPING LIFE NATIONWIDE

FIGURE 42-2 **Gay Marriage by State**

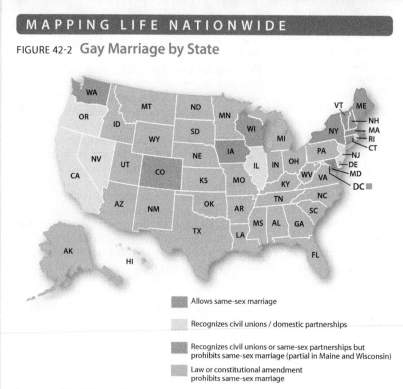

■ Allows same-sex marriage

☐ Recognizes civil unions / domestic partnerships

■ Recognizes civil unions or same-sex partnerships but
prohibits same-sex marriage (partial in Maine and Wisconsin)

☐ Law or constitutional amendment
prohibits same-sex marriage

Sources: As of June 2012, author based on news reports; Human Rights Campaign 2012; National Conference of
State Legislatures 2012b.

of Marriage Act, passed in 1996, provided that no state is obliged to recognize same-sex marriages performed in another state. However, some legal scholars doubt that the law could withstand a constitutional challenge, since it violates a provision in the Constitution that requires states to recognize one another's laws.

Within the United States, state courts in California, Iowa, and Massachusetts have ruled that there is no state law that precludes same-sex marriage. In California, 18,000 same-sex couples were married before voters amended the state constitution to prohibit such marriages in the future. In August 2010, a federal court weighed in for the first time on gay marriage, ruling that California's ban on same-sex marriage was unconstitutional. Ultimately, the Supreme Court will consider the issue. As of mid-2012, the District of Columbia and six states (Connecticut, Iowa, Massachusetts, New Hampshire, New York, and Vermont) were issuing marriage licenses to same-sex couples. (New laws in Maryland and Washington had not yet taken effect.) Gay rights activists claim their movement is gathering momentum, but opponents argue that their high-profile actions have galvanized conservatives who wish to define marriage as the union of one man and one woman.

defined as two unrelated adults who share a mutually caring relationship, reside together, and agree to be jointly responsible for their dependents, basic living expenses, and other common necessities. Domestic partnership benefits can apply to couples' inheritance, parenting, pensions, taxation, housing, immigration, workplace fringe benefits such as life insurance, and health care. Even though the most passionate support for domestic partnership legislation has come from lesbian and gay activists, the majority of those eligible for such benefits would be cohabiting heterosexual couples.

In the United States, marriage has traditionally been under the jurisdiction of state lawmakers. Recently, however, pressure has been mounting for national legislation. The Defense

TAKE THE ISSUE WITH YOU

1. If marriage is good for heterosexual couples and their families, why isn't it good for homosexual couples and their families?

2. How can interactionist studies of gay couples and their families inform policymakers who are dealing with the issue of gay marriage? Give a specific example.

3. Who are the stakeholders in the debate over gay marriage, and what do they stand to gain or lose? Whose interest do you think is most important?

MODULE 42 | Recap and Review

Summary

Human sexuality spans a wide range of behaviors, and different societies condone different behaviors.

1. From the sociological perspective, sexuality is not limited to physical behaviors, but includes the beliefs, values, and social norms that collectively govern its expression.

2. Because homosexuality has traditionally been labeled as a deviant behavior, gay and lesbian couples face significant discrimination, including the denial of their right to marry.

3. The gay marriage movement, which would confer equal rights on gay and lesbian couples and their dependents, is strongly opposed by conservative religious and political groups.

Thinking Critically

1. What do you believe constitutes sexual deviance today? How might this change over the next decade or two?

2. How is cohabitation similar to marriage? How is it different? Could gay and lesbian couples achieve all the benefits of marriage without actually marrying?

Key Term

Domestic partnership

Mastering This Chapter: The Family and Human Sexuality

taking sociology with you

1 Go online and try tracing your family roots using one of the genealogical search sites. How far back can you go? Why might certain ancestral paths be more difficult to trace than others?

2 Do some research on the divorce law in your state. Has the law changed much over the past few decades, and if so, how? From a sociological perspective, why would the law change? Explain.

3 Talk to a marriage and family counselor or a professor of family law about the benefits of marriage versus cohabitation, or read what practical advice you can find on the Internet or in the library. What advantages does marriage offer that cohabitation does not? How important do those advantages seem to you?

key terms

Adoption In a legal sense, the transfer of the legal rights, responsibilities, and privileges of parenthood to a new legal parent or parents.

Bilateral descent A kinship system in which both sides of a person's family are regarded as equally important.

Cohabitation The practice of living together as a male–female couple without marrying.

Domestic partnership Two unrelated adults who share a mutually caring relationship, reside together, and agree to be jointly responsible for their dependents, basic living expenses, and other common necessities.

Egalitarian family An authority pattern in which spouses are regarded as equals.

Endogamy The restriction of mate selection to people within the same group.

Exogamy The requirement that people select a mate outside certain groups.

Extended family A family in which relatives—such as grandparents, aunts, or uncles—live in the same home as parents and their children.

Familism (Familismo) Pride in the extended family, expressed through the maintenance of close ties and strong obligations to kinfolk outside the immediate family.

Family A set of people related by blood, marriage or some other agreed-on relationship, or adoption, who share the primary responsibility for reproduction and caring for members of society.

Homogamy The conscious or unconscious tendency to select a mate with personal characteristics similar to one's own.

Incest taboo The prohibition of sexual relationships between certain culturally specified relatives.

Kinship The state of being related to others.

Machismo A sense of virility, personal worth, and pride in one's maleness.

Matriarchy A society in which women dominate in family decision making.

Matrilineal descent A kinship system in which only the mother's relatives are significant.

Monogamy A form of marriage in which one woman and one man are married only to each other.

Nuclear family A married couple and their unmarried children living together.

Patriarchy A society in which men dominate in family decision making.

Patrilineal descent A kinship system in which only the father's relatives are significant.

Polyandry A form of polygamy in which a woman may have more than one husband at the same time.

Polygamy A form of marriage in which an individual may have several husbands or wives simultaneously.

Polygyny A form of polygamy in which a man may have more than one wife at the same time.

Serial monogamy A form of marriage in which a person may have several spouses in his or her lifetime, but only one spouse at a time.

Single-parent family A family in which only one parent is present to care for the children.

Transracial adoption The adoption of a non-White child by White parents or a Hispanic child by non-Hispanics.

self-quiz

Read each question carefully and then select the best answer.

1. Alice, age seven, lives in a private home with her parents, her grandmother, and her aunt. Alice's family is an example of a(n)
   a. nuclear family.
   b. dysfunctional family.
   c. extended family.
   d. polygynous family.

2. In which form of marriage may a person have several spouses in his or her lifetime, but only one spouse at a time?
   a. serial monogamy
   b. monogamy
   c. polygamy
   d. polyandry

3. The marriage of a woman to more than one man at the same time is referred to as
   a. polygyny.
   b. monogamy.
   c. serial monogamy.
   d. polyandry.

4. Which system of descent is followed in the United States?
   a. matrilineal
   b. patrilineal
   c. bilateral
   d. unilateral

5. According to the functionalist perspective, which of the following is *not* one of the paramount functions performed by the family?
   a. mediation
   b. reproduction
   c. regulation of sexual behavior
   d. affection and companionship

6. Which norm requires mate selection outside certain groups, usually one's own family or certain kinfolk?
   a. exogamy
   b. endogamy
   c. matriarchy
   d. patriarchy

7. According to the discussion of social class differences in family life and intimate relationships, which of the following statements is true?
   a. Social class differences in family life are more striking than they once were.
   b. The upper class emphasizes lineage and maintenance of family position.
   c. Among the poor, women usually play an insignificant role in the economic support of the family.
   d. In examining family life among racial and ethnic minorities, most patterns result from cultural, but *not* class, factors.

8. One recent development in family life in the United States has been the extension of parenthood as adult children continue to live at home or return home after college. The reason for this is
   a. the rising divorce rate.
   b. high rents.
   c. financial difficulties.
   d. all of the above

9. In the United States, the *majority* of all babies born to unmarried teenage mothers are born to whom?
   a. African American adolescents
   b. White adolescents
   c. Latina adolescents
   d. Asian American adolescents

10. Which of the following factors is associated with the high divorce rate in the United States?
   a. the liberalization of divorce laws
   b. the fact that contemporary families have fewer children than earlier families did
   c. the general increase in family incomes
   d. all of the above

11. The principle of _____ assigns people to kinship groups according to their relationship to an individual's mother or father.

12. _____ emerged among Native American tribal societies, and in nations in which men were absent for long periods because of warfare or food-gathering expeditions.

13. In the view of many sociologists, the _____ family has begun to replace the patriarchal family as the social norm in the United States.

14. As _____ theorists point out, the social class of couples and their children significantly influences the socialization experiences to which the children are exposed and the protection they receive.

15. _____ focus on the micro level of family and other intimate relationships; for example, they are interested in whether people are cohabiting partners or are longtime married couples.

16. The rule of _____ specifies the groups within which a spouse must be found and prohibits marriage with others.

17. Social class differences in family life are less striking today than they once were; however, in the past, _____-class families were found to be more authoritarian in rearing children and more inclined to use physical punishment.

18. Caring for children is a(n) _____ function of the family, yet the ways in which different societies assign this function to family members can vary significantly.

19. Viewed from the _____ perspective, the government has a strong interest in encouraging adoption.

20. The rising rates of divorce and remarriage have led to a noticeable increase in _____ relationships.

Answers

1 (c); 2 (a); 3 (d); 4 (c); 5 (a); 6 (a); 7 (b); 8 (d); 9 (b); 10 (d); 11 descent; 12 Matriarchies; 13 egalitarian; 14 conflict; 15 Interactionists; 16 endogamy; 17 lower; 18 universal; 19 functionalist; 20 stepfamily

🎬 **thinking about movies**

Beginners

A father and son work to understand themselves and their relationship.

Blue Valentine

A marriage unravels under personal and social pressure.

Goodbye Solo

In this moving drama about the role of family in people's lives, two quite different men form an unlikely pair.

Education

14 Education

MODULE 43 Sociological Perspectives on Education

MODULE 44 Schools as Formal Organizations

After a long career, Diane Ravitch lost faith in the educational reforms she had once championed as a way to rescue failing schools.

Searching for a better answer, she looked back on her own experience in high school, to her favorite English teacher.

❝ My favorite teacher was Mrs. Ruby Ratliff. She is the teacher I remember best, the one who influenced me most, who taught me to love literature and to write with careful attention to grammar and syntax. More than fifty years ago, she was my homeroom teacher at San Jacinto High School in Houston, and I was lucky enough to get into her English class as a senior.

Mrs. Ratliff was gruff and demanding. She did not tolerate foolishness or disruptions. She had a great reputation among students.... What I remember most about her was what she taught us. We studied the greatest writers of the English language.... We read Shakespeare, Keats, Shelley, Wordsworth, Milton, and other major English writers. Now, many years later, in times of stress or sadness, I still turn to poems that I first read in Mrs. Ratliff's class.

Mrs. Ratliff did nothing for our self-esteem. She challenged us to meet her exacting standards. I think she imagined herself bringing enlightenment to the barbarians (that was us). When you wrote something for her class, which happened with frequency, you paid close attention to proper English. Accuracy mattered. She had a red pen and she used it freely. Still, she was always sure to make a comment that encouraged us to do a better job. Clearly she had multiple goals for her students, beyond teaching literature and grammar. She was also teaching about character and personal responsibility. These are not the sorts of things that appear on any standardized test.

She loved her subject, and she enjoyed the respect the students showed her, especially since this was a large high school where students did not easily give respect to their teachers. Despite the passage of years, I still recall a class discussion of Shelley's "Ozymandias," and the close attention that thirty usually rowdy adolescents paid to a poem about a time and a place we could barely imagine. I wonder if Mrs. Ratliff has her counterparts today, teachers who love literature and love to teach it, or whether schools favor teachers who have been trained to elicit mechanical responses from their students about "text-to-self connections," "inferencing," "visualizing," and the other formalistic behaviors so beloved by au courant pedagogues. If Mrs. Ratliff were planning to teach these days, I expect that her education professors and supervisors would warn her to get rid of that red pen, to abandon her insistence on accuracy, and to stop being so judgmental. And they would surely demand that she replace those dated poems and essays with young adult literature that teaches adolescents about the lives of other adolescents just like themselves. . . .

I think of Mrs. Ratliff when I hear the latest proposals to improve the teaching force. Almost every day, I come across a statement by a journalist, superintendent, or economist who says we could solve all our problems in American education if we could just recruit a sufficient number of "great" teachers. I believe Mrs. Ratliff was a great teacher, but I don't think she would have been considered "great" if she had been judged by the kind of hard data that is used now. The policy experts who insist that teachers should be judged by their students' scores on standardized tests would have been frustrated by Mrs. Ratliff. Her classes never produced hard data. They didn't even produce test scores. How would the experts have measured what we learned? We never took a multiple-choice test. We wrote essays and took written tests, in which we had to explain our answers, not check a box or fill in a bubble. If she had been evaluated by the grades she gave, she would have been in deep trouble, because she did not award many A grades. An observer might have concluded that she was a very ineffective teacher who had no measurable gains to show for her work. ❞

Clearly she had multiple goals for her students, beyond teaching literature and grammar. She was also teaching about character and personal responsibility. These are not the sorts of things that appear on any standardized test.

(Ravitch 2010:169, 170, 171) Additional information about this excerpt can be found on the Online Learning Center at www.mhhe.com/schaefermod2e.

I n her book *The Death and Life of the Great American School System,* education historian Diane Ravitch laments our failure in improving the quality of education in the United States. In recalling her favorite teacher, Ravitch questions what she sees as our current tendency to reduce the art of teaching to test cramming and relying solely on standardized tests as measures of students' performance. She is really asking the same questions that sociologists ask about education: what are its goals, and what is it supposed to accomplish, for individuals and for society as a whole? After considering how sociologists answer these questions, we will return to the issue of measuring school performance in the Social Policy section.

As we saw in Module 15, socialization can occur in the classroom or at home, through interactions with parents, teachers, friends, and even strangers. These modules focus in particular on the formal systems of education that characterize modern industrial societies. Do public schools offer everyone a way up the socioeconomic ladder, or do they reinforce existing divisions among social classes? What is the "hidden curriculum" in U.S. schools? And what have sociologists learned about the latest trends in education, such as competency testing? We will begin with discussion of four theoretical perspectives on education, and will then examine schools as formal organizations—as bureaucracies and subcultures of teachers and students. One contemporary educational trend, homeschooling, merits special mention. We close with a Social Policy section on the controversial charter-schools movement.

MODULE

MODULE 43 Sociological Perspectives on Education

Besides being a major industry in the United States, **education** is the social institution that formally socializes members of our society. In the past few decades, increasing proportions of people have obtained high school diplomas, college degrees, and advanced professional degrees. Figure 43-1 shows the proportion of the college-educated population in selected countries.

Throughout the world, education has become a vast and complex social institution that prepares citizens for the roles demanded by other social institutions, such as the family, government, and the economy. The functionalist, conflict, feminist, and interactionist perspectives offer distinctive views of education as a social institution.

Functionalist Perspective

Like other social institutions, education has both manifest (open, stated) and latent (hidden) functions. The most basic *manifest* function of education is the transmission of knowledge. Schools teach students how to read, speak foreign languages, and repair automobiles. Another important manifest function is the bestowal of status. Because many believe this function is performed inequitably, we will consider it later, in the section on the conflict view of education.

In addition to these manifest functions, schools perform a number of *latent* functions: transmitting culture, promoting social and political integration, maintaining social control, and serving as an agent of change.

Transmitting Culture

As a social institution, education performs a rather conservative function—transmitting the dominant culture. Schooling exposes each generation of young people to the existing beliefs, norms, and values of their culture. In our society, we learn respect for social control and reverence for established institutions, such as religion, the family, and the presidency. Of course, this statement is true of many other cultures as well. While schoolchildren in the United States are hearing about the accomplishments of George Washington and Abraham Lincoln, British children are hearing about the distinctive contributions of Queen Elizabeth I and Winston Churchill.

Sometimes nations reassess the ways in which they transmit culture to students. In the last decade, the Chinese government revised the nation's history curriculum. Students are now taught that the Chinese Communist Party, not the United States, played a central role in defeating Japan in World War II. No mention is made of the estimated 30 million Chinese who

FIGURE 43-1 **Current Higher Education Graduation Rates (BA/BS), Selected Countries**

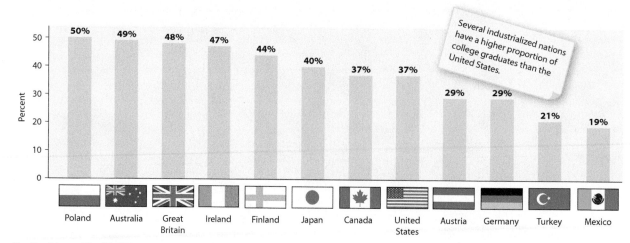

Several industrialized nations have a higher proportion of college graduates than the United States.

Note: For adults ages 25 to 64 in 2009.
Source: Organisation for Economic Co-Operation and Development 2012c:Table A3.

died from famine because of party founder Mao Zedong's disastrous Great Leap Forward (1958–1962), a failed effort to transform China's agrarian economy into an industrial powerhouse. In the urban, Western-oriented areas of Shanghai, textbooks acknowledge the technological advances made in Western industrialized countries but avoid any criticism of past policies of the Chinese government (French 2004; J. Kahn 2006).

Culture has been transmitted to students in schools, through books and the spoken word, for centuries. Today, however, the Internet offers a new and potentially revolutionary way of transmitting culture. Box 43-1 discusses the educational impact of Google and other search engines.

Promoting Social and Political Integration

Many institutions require students in their first year or two of college to live on campus, to foster a sense of community among diverse groups. Education serves the latent function of promoting social and political integration by transforming a population composed of diverse racial, ethnic, and religious groups into a society whose members share—to some extent—a common identity. Historically, schools in the United States have played an important role in socializing the children of immigrants into the norms, values, and beliefs of the dominant culture. From a functionalist perspective, the common identity and social integration fostered by education contribute to societal stability and consensus (Touraine 1974).

In the past, the integrative function of education was most obvious in its emphasis on promoting a common language. Immigrant children were expected to learn English. In some instances, they were even forbidden to speak their native language on school grounds. More recently, bilingualism has been defended both for its educational value and as a means of encouraging cultural diversity. However, critics argue that bilingualism undermines the social and political integration that education has traditionally promoted.

Maintaining Social Control

In performing the manifest function of transmitting knowledge, schools go far beyond teaching skills like reading, writing, and mathematics. Like other social institutions, such as the family and religion, education prepares young people to lead productive and orderly lives as adults by introducing them to the norms, values, and sanctions of the larger society.

Through the exercise of social control, schools teach students various skills and values essential to their future positions in the labor force. They learn punctuality, discipline, scheduling, and responsible work habits, as well as how to negotiate the complexities of a bureaucratic organization. As a social institution, education reflects the interests of both the family and another social institution, the economy. Students are trained for what is ahead, whether it be the assembly line or a physician's office. In effect, then, schools serve as a transitional agent of social control, bridging the gap between parents and employers in the life cycle of most individuals (Bowles and Gintis 1976; M. Cole 1988).

Schools direct and even restrict students' aspirations in a manner that reflects societal values and prejudices. School administrators may allocate ample funds for athletic programs but give much less support to music, art, and dance. Teachers and guidance counselors may encourage male students to pursue careers in the sciences but steer female students into careers as early childhood teachers. Such socialization into traditional gender roles can be viewed as a form of social control.

Serving as an Agent of Change

So far, we have focused on the conservative functions of education—on its role in transmitting the existing culture, promoting social and political integration, and maintaining social control. Yet education can also stimulate or bring about desired social change. Sex education classes were introduced to public schools in response to the soaring pregnancy rate among teenagers. Affirmative action in admissions—giving priority to females or minorities—has been endorsed as a means of countering racial and sexual discrimination. And Project Head Start, an early childhood program that serves more than 904,000 children annually, has sought to compensate for the disadvantages in school readiness experienced by children from low-income families (Bureau of the Census 2011a:Table 574 on page 368).

Although the school Harry Potter attends in the film *Harry Potter and the Deathly Hallows: Part 2* is fictitious, like real schools, it transmits a socially sanctioned culture to students.

Sociology on Campus

Box 43-1

Google University

From comic books, television, and fast-paced video games to educational films and online college courses, technological innovations in communication have been seen as both a threat to culture and a boon to education. Like these new media, the search engine called Google has been greeted with both praise and scorn. Founded by two students at Stanford University in 1998, Google handled some 65 percent of all Internet searches in the United States in early 2011. Its familiar multicolored logo stands for one of the most trusted brands in the world Figure 20-1.

Using Google or some other search engine, a researcher can now retrieve facts, viewpoints, images, and sounds within minutes. Just a few years ago, that task would have taken days. As Nicholas Carr (2008b:56), former editor of the *Harvard Business Review,* notes, "Once I was a scuba diver in the sea of words. Now I zip along the surface like a guy on a Jet Ski." Yet some critics of search engines charge that placing more and more of the world's knowledge just a mouse click away has made students lazy. Quick access to information, they point out, does not necessarily encourage concentration, let alone contemplation.

Google™

> Like the invention of the printing press, Google's advent is changing not just the university, but the universe of learning.

The availability of information online may also be changing the way people read. Educators worry that habitual skimming of the computer screen may carry over to students' print reading. Some have found that younger readers, faced with anything of length online, such as a short PDF file, simply ignore it. In response, researchers have begun to study whether those who read online in preference to books and other printed media still read sentence by sentence, as they were taught to do in school.

Other scholars are not disturbed by potential changes in what and how people read. They note that true literacy is not merely the ability to read to the end of an article or book, but to find the information you need amid a flood of sources—not all of them trustworthy—and use it correctly and responsibly. In other words, literacy includes critical thinking.

Ultimately, education is more than just collecting, organizing, and comprehending information. Accessing information and arguments

regarding political and social issues is a form of civic engagement. Thus, the search feature on a web page becomes a portal to a virtual town square. Perhaps that is why today's students are not only spending more time online than yesterday's students, but also doing more volunteer work.

Well before the advent of the Internet, much less Google, sociologist Daniel Bell (1973) wrote that *intellectual technologies* tend to institutionalize new approaches to the gathering and dissemination of information. Like the invention of the printing press, Google's advent is changing not just the university, but the universe of learning.

LET'S DISCUSS

1. Do you prefer to do your reading online or in a magazine, newspaper, or book? Has the availability of online information changed the way that you read the written word?

2. Have you participated in any social or political causes or volunteered your time while on campus? If so, did you use the Internet to organize or disseminate information about your activities?

Sources: Mark Bauerlein 2008; Brabazon 2007; Carr 2008a, 2008b; Maestretti 2009; Search Engine Watch 2011; Vaidhyanathan 2008; Workman 2008.

These educational programs can and have transformed people's lives. For example, continued formal education has had a positive effect on the income people earn; median earnings rise significantly with each step up the educational ladder. Consider the significance of those increased earnings when they stretch over an entire lifetime. Obviously, racial, ethnic, and gender differences in income are also significant. Yet as significant as those inequalities are, the best indicator of a person's lifetime earnings is still the number of years of formal schooling that person has received (see Figure 43-2) (Julian and Kominski 2011; Wessel and Ranchero 2012).

Education also promotes social change by serving as a meeting ground where people can share distinctive beliefs and traditions. In 2009–2010, U.S. campuses hosted over 690,000 international students. That number, an all-time high, followed a temporary decline in foreign enrollments after September 11, 2001. Figure 43-3 shows the major sending nations of foreign students in the United States (left) and the primary destinations of U.S. students seeking to enrich their college experience abroad (right).

Numerous sociological studies have revealed that additional years of formal schooling are also associated with openness to new ideas and liberal social and political viewpoints. Sociologist Robin Williams points out that better-educated people tend to have greater access to factual information, to hold more diverse opinions, and to possess the ability to make subtle distinctions in analysis. Formal education stresses both the importance of qualifying statements (in place of broad generalizations) and the need at least to question (rather than simply accept) established truths and practices. The scientific method, which relies on *testing* hypotheses, reflects the questioning spirit that characterizes modern education (R. Williams et al. 1964).

Conflict Perspective

The functionalist perspective portrays contemporary education as a basically benign institution. For example, it argues that schools rationally sort and select students for future high-status positions, thereby meeting society's need for talented and expert

In response to a high pregnancy rate among adolescent girls, many schools now offer sex education courses that promote abstinence as well as safe sex. When schools attempt to remedy negative social trends, they are serving as an agent of social change.

personnel. In contrast, the conflict perspective views education as an instrument of elite domination. Conflict theorists point out the sharp inequalities that exist in the educational opportunities available to different racial and ethnic groups. In 2004, the nation marked the 50th anniversary of the Supreme Court's landmark decision *Brown v. Board of Education,* which declared unconstitutional the segregation of public schools. Yet today, our schools are still characterized by racial isolation. Nationwide, White students are the most isolated: only 23 percent of their classmates came from minority groups in the 2005–2006 school year. In comparison, Black and Latino students have more classmates from different racial and ethnic backgrounds, although those classmates typically do not include Whites (Orfield and Lee 2007).

Conflict theorists also argue that the educational system socializes students

FIGURE 43-2 Lifetime Earnings by Race, Gender, and Degree Level

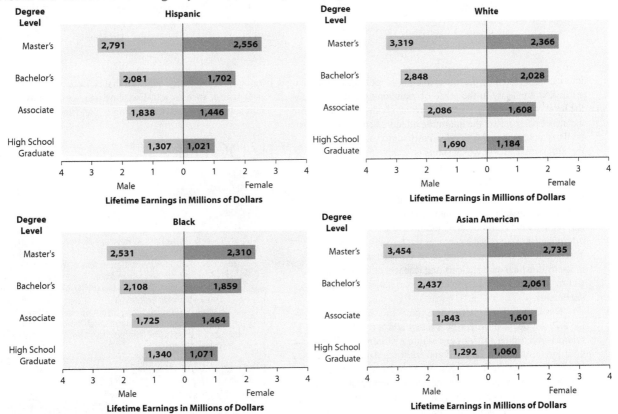

Note: Estimates for lifetime earnings for full-time, year-round workers ages 25 to 64 based on the American Community Survey for 2006–2008. Data are for non-Hispanic Whites, Blacks, and Asian Americans. Data points shown in thousands of dollars.
Source: Julian and Kominski 2011:6.

▪ **CHAPTER 14** Education

FIGURE 43-3 **Foreign Students by Major Countries of Origin and Destination**

The past 30 years have brought a consistent increase in college enrollment among all racial and ethnic groups in the United States. The typical measure that researchers use to track college enrollments is the college participation rate, or the percentage of all 18- to 24-year-olds enrolled in 2-year and 4-year colleges or universities. For Whites, the participation rate increased from 28 percent to 44 percent between 1978 and 2008. For African Americans, the rate climbed from 20 percent to 32 percent; for Latinos, from 16 percent to 26 percent.

into values dictated by the powerful, that schools stifle individualism and creativity in the name of maintaining order, and that the level of change they promote is relatively insignificant. From a conflict perspective, the inhibiting effects of education are particularly apparent in the "hidden curriculum" and the differential way in which status is bestowed.

The Hidden Curriculum

Schools are highly bureaucratic organizations, as we will see later. To maintain order, many teachers rely on rules and regulations. Unfortunately, the need for control and discipline can take precedence over the learning process. Teachers may focus on obedience to the rules as an end in itself, in which case students and teachers alike become victims of what Philip Jackson (1968) has called the *hidden curriculum.*

The term **hidden curriculum** refers to standards of behavior that are deemed proper by society and are taught subtly in schools. According to this curriculum, children must not speak until the teacher calls on them and must regulate their activities according to the clock or bells. In addition, they are expected to concentrate on their own work rather than to assist other students who learn more slowly. A hidden curriculum is evident in schools around the world. For example, Japanese schools offer guidance sessions that seek to improve the classroom experience and develop healthy living skills. In effect, these sessions instill

values and encourage behavior that is useful in the Japanese business world, such as self-discipline and openness to group problem solving and decision making (Okano and Tsuchiya 1999).

trend|spotting

Rising College Enrollment among Racial and Ethnic Minorities, Women

The past 30 years have brought a consistent increase in college enrollment among all racial and ethnic groups in the United States. The typical measure that researchers use to track college enrollments is the college participation rate, or the percentage of all 18- to 24-year-olds enrolled in 2-year and 4-year colleges or universities. For Whites, the participation rate increased from 28 percent to 44 percent between 1978 and 2008. For African Americans, the rate climbed from 20 percent to 32 percent; for Latinos, from 16 percent to 26 percent.

Across the board, growth has been greater among females than among males. In 1980, more men than women were in college, whether among Whites, Blacks and Hispanics, or Asian Americans. By 1995 that pattern had reversed, and women outnumbered men. Only among Native Americans have women historically outnumbered men on college campuses.

In a classroom that is overly focused on obedience, value is placed on pleasing the teacher and remaining quiet rather than on creative thought and academic learning. Habitual obedience to authority may result in the type of distressing behavior documented by Stanley Milgram in his classic obedience studies.

> ### 💡 use your **sociological imagination**
>
> In what ways did the high school you attended convey the hidden curriculum of education?

Credentialism

Sixty years ago, a high school diploma was the minimum requirement for entry into the paid labor force of the United States. Today, a college diploma is virtually the bare minimum. This change reflects the process of **credentialism**—a term used to describe an increase in the lowest level of education needed to enter a field.

In recent decades, the number of occupations that are viewed as professions has risen. Credentialism is one symptom of this trend. Employers and occupational associations typically contend that such changes are a logical response to the increasing complexity of many jobs. However, in many cases, employers raise the degree requirements for a position simply because all applicants have achieved the existing minimum credential (David K. Brown 2001; Hurn 1985).

Conflict theorists observe that credentialism may reinforce social inequality. Applicants from poor and minority backgrounds are especially likely to suffer from the escalation of qualifications, since they lack the financial resources needed to obtain degree after degree. In addition, upgrading of credentials serves the self-interest of the two groups most responsible for this trend. Educational institutions profit from prolonging the investment of time and money that people make by staying in school. Moreover, as C. J. Hurn (1985) has suggested, current jobholders have a stake in raising occupational requirements, since credentialism can increase the status of an occupation and lead to demands for higher pay. Max Weber anticipated this possibility as early as 1916, concluding that the "universal clamor for the creation of educational certificates in all fields makes for the formation of a privileged stratum in businesses and in offices" (Gerth and Mills 1958:240–241).

Bestowal of Status

Sociologists have long recognized that schooling is central to social stratification. Both functionalist and conflict theorists agree that education performs the important function of bestowing status. As noted earlier, an increasing proportion of people

> ### 💡 use your **sociological imagination**
>
> How would you react if the job you have or plan to pursue suddenly required a higher-level degree? If suddenly the requirements were lowered?

in the United States are obtaining high school diplomas, college degrees, and advanced professional degrees. From a functionalist perspective, this widening bestowal of status is beneficial not only to particular recipients but to society as a whole. According to Kingsley Davis and Wilbert E. Moore (1945), society must distribute its members among a variety of social positions. Education can contribute to this process by sorting people into appropriate levels and courses of study that will prepare them for positions in the labor force.

Conflict theorists are far more critical of the *differential* way in which education bestows status. They stress that schools sort pupils according to their social class backgrounds. Although the educational system helps certain poor children to move into middle-class professional positions, it denies most disadvantaged children the same educational opportunities afforded to children of the affluent. In this way, schools tend to preserve social class inequalities in each new generation. Higher education in particular acts more like a sieve that sorts people out of the educated classes than a social ladder that helps all with ambition to rise (Alon 2009; Giroux 1988; Sacks 2007).

The status that comes with advanced training is not cheap and has been getting progressively more expensive for several decades. Over the past 30 years, average tuition and fees at community colleges have risen at a relatively modest pace that matches the inflation rate (Figure 43-4). The increases have been greater at four-year institutions. At the same time as tuition has been increasing, financial aid has become more difficult to obtain (see Box 28-2).

Even a single school can reinforce class differences by putting students in tracks. The term **tracking** refers to the practice of placing students in specific curriculum groups on the basis of their test scores and other criteria. Tracking begins very early, often in reading groups during first grade. The practice can reinforce the disadvantages that children from less affluent families may face if they haven't been exposed to reading materials, computers, and other forms of educational stimulation during their early childhood years. To ignore this connection between tracking and students' race and social class is to fundamentally misunderstand how schools perpetuate the existing social structure.

Not surprisingly, most recent research on tracking raises questions about its effectiveness, especially for low-ability students. In one study of low-income schools in California, researchers discovered a staggering difference between students who were tracked and those who were not. At one school, all interested students were allowed to enroll in advanced placement (AP) courses, not just those who were selected by the administration. Half the open enrollment students scored high enough to qualify for college credit—a much higher proportion than in selective programs, in which only 17 percent of students qualified for college credit. Tracking programs do not necessarily identify those students with the potential to succeed (B. Ellison 2008; Sacks 2007).

Conflict theorists hold that the educational inequalities produced by tracking are designed to meet the needs of modern capitalist societies. Samuel Bowles and Herbert Gintis (1976) have argued that capitalism requires a skilled, disciplined labor force, and that the educational system of the United States is structured with that objective in mind. Citing numerous studies, they offer support for what they call the **correspondence principle.** According to this approach, schools promote the values expected of individuals in each social class and perpetuate social class divisions from one generation to the next. Thus, working-class children, assumed to be destined for subordinate positions, are likely to be placed in high school vocational and general tracks, which emphasize close supervision and compliance with authority. In contrast, young people from more affluent families are likely to be directed to college preparatory tracks, which stress leadership and decision making—the skills they are expected to need as adults (McLanahan and Percheski 2008).

Feminist Perspective

The educational system of the United States, like many other social institutions, has long been characterized by discriminatory treatment of women. In 1833, Oberlin College became the first institution of higher learning to admit female students—some 200 years after the first men's college was established. But Oberlin believed that women should aspire to become wives and mothers, not lawyers and intellectuals. In addition to attending classes, female students washed men's clothing, cared for their rooms, and served them at meals. In the 1840s, Lucy Stone, then an Oberlin undergraduate and later one of the nation's most outspoken feminist leaders, refused to write a commencement address because it would have been read to the audience by a male student.

In the 20th century, sexism in education showed up in many ways—in textbooks with negative stereotypes of women, counselors' pressure on female students to prepare for "women's work," and unequal funding for women's and men's athletic programs. But perhaps nowhere was educational discrimination more evident than in the employment of teachers. The positions of university professor and college administrator, which hold relatively high status in the United States, were generally filled by men. Public school teachers, who earn much lower salaries, were largely female.

Women have made great strides in one area: the proportion of women who continue their schooling. As recently as 1969, twice as many men as women received college degrees; today, women outnumber men at college commencements. Moreover, women's access to graduate education and to medical, dental, and law schools has increased dramatically in the past few decades as a result of the Education Act of 1972. Box 43-2 examines the far-reaching effects of Title IX, the part of the act that concerns discrimination against women in education.

Much has been made of the superior academic achievement of girls and women. Today, researchers are beginning to examine the reasons for their comparatively strong performance in school—or to put it another way, for men's lackluster performance. Some studies suggest that men's aggressiveness, together with the fact that they do better in the workplace than women, even with less schooling, predisposes them to undervalue higher education. While the "absence of men" on many college campuses has captured headlines, it has also created a false crisis in public discourse. Few students realize their potential exclusively through formal education; other factors, such as ambition and personal talent, contribute to their success. And many students, including low-income and immigrant children, face much greater challenges than the so-called gender gap in education (Buchmann et al. 2008; Corbett et al. 2008; Kimmel 2006).

In cultures in which traditional gender roles remain the social norm, women's education suffers appreciably. Since September 11, 2001, the growing awareness of

FIGURE 43-4 **Tuition Costs, 1976–2009**

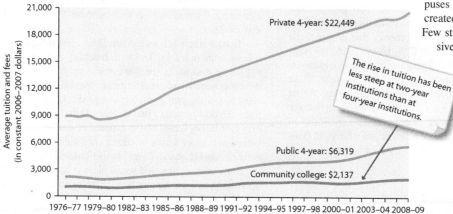

Note: Data cover the entire academic year and represent the average total charges, including tuition and fees, for full-time attendance.
Sources: National Center for Education Statistics 2011; Provasnik and Planty 2008:7.

Sociology on Campus

Box 43-2

The Debate over Title IX

Few federal policies have had such a visible effect on education as Title IX, which mandates gender equity in education in federally funded schools. Congressional amendments to the Education Act of 1972 have brought significant changes for both men and women at all levels of schooling. Title IX eliminated sex-segregated classes, prohibited sex discrimination in admissions and financial aid, and mandated that girls receive more opportunities to play sports, in proportion to their enrollment and interest.

Under this landmark legislation, to receive federal funds, a school or college must pass one of three tests. First, the numbers of male and female athletes must be proportional to the numbers of men and women enrolled at the school. Second, lacking that, the school must show a continuing history of expanding opportunities for female athletes. Or third, the school must demonstrate that the level of female participation in sports meets female students' level of interest or ability.

Today, Title IX is still one of the more controversial attempts ever made by the federal government to promote equality for all citizens. Its consequences for the funding of college athletics programs are hotly debated, while its

> Critics charge that men's teams have suffered from proportional funding of women's teams and athletic scholarships.

real and lasting effects on college admissions and employment are often forgotten. Critics charge that men's teams have suffered from proportional funding of women's teams and athletic scholarships, since schools with tight athletic budgets can expand women's sports only at the expense of men's sports.

From the women's point of view, however, the increased funding for women's sports has benefited men in some ways. In terms of coaching and administration, men have increasingly replaced women as directors of women's sports since Title IX was passed. Today only 19 percent of collegiate women's athletic administrators are women, compared to over 90 percent in the early 1970s. No national data exists for high school sports leadership, but an analysis of Minnesota youth soccer found that only 15 percent of head coaches were women.

Sociologists caution that the social effects of sports on college campuses are not all positive. Michael A. Messner, professor of sociology at the University of Southern California, points to some troubling results of a survey by the Women's Sports Foundation. The study shows that teenage girls who play sports simply for fun have more positive body images than girls who don't play sports. But those who are "highly involved" in sports are more likely than other girls to take steroids and to become risk takers. "Everyone has tacitly agreed, it seems, to view men's sports as the standard to which women should strive to have equal access," Messner writes. He is skeptical of a system that propels a lucky few college athletes to stardom each year while leaving the majority, many of them African American, without a career or an education. Certainly that was not the kind of equal opportunity legislators envisioned when they wrote Title IX.

LET'S DISCUSS

1. Has Title IX had an effect on you personally? If so, explain. On balance, do you think the increase in women's participation in sports has been good for society as a whole?

2. How might Title IX affect the way students and the public view gender roles?

Sources: Brady 2010; Cooky and LaVoi 2012; Messner 2002; Pennington 2008; Spencer 2008; Tigay 2011; Women's Sports Foundation 2011.

---

the Taliban's repression of Afghan women has dramatized the gender disparities in education in developing nations. Research has demonstrated that women are critical to economic development and good governance, and that education is instrumental in preparing them for those roles. Educating women, especially young girls, yields high social returns by lowering birthrates and improving agricultural productivity through better management (I. Coleman 2004).

Interactionist Perspective

High school students know who they are—the kids who qualify for a free lunch. So stigmatized are they that in some schools, these students will buy a bit of food in the cash line or simply go without eating to avoid being labeled a "poor kid." School officials in San Francisco are so concerned about their plight that they are moving to cashless cafeterias, in which everyone, rich or poor, uses a debit card (Pogash 2008).

As we saw in Module 24, the labeling approach suggests that if we treat people in particular ways, they may fulfill our expectations. Children who are labeled as "troublemakers" may come to view themselves as delinquents. Similarly, a dominant group's stereotyping of racial minorities may limit their opportunities to break away from expected roles.

Can the labeling process operate in the classroom? Because interactionist researchers focus on micro-level classroom dynamics, they have been particularly interested in this question. Sociologist Howard S. Becker (1952) studied public schools in low-income and affluent areas of Chicago. He noticed that administrators expected less of students from poor neighborhoods, and wondered if teachers accepted their view. A decade later, in *Pygmalion in the Classroom,* psychologist Robert Rosenthal and school principal Lenore Jacobson (1968, 1992) documented what they referred to as a **teacher-expectancy effect**—the impact that a teacher's expectations about a student's performance may have on the student's actual achievements. This effect is especially evident in the lower grades (through Grade 3).

In Tokyo, a mother escorts her daughter to an admissions interview at a highly competitive private school. Some Japanese families enroll children as young as 2 in cram schools. Like parents in the United States, Japanese parents know that higher education bestows status.

Studies in the United States have revealed that teachers wait longer for an answer from a student they believe to be a high achiever and are more likely to give such children a second chance. In one experiment, teachers' expectations were even

shown to have an impact on students' athletic achievements. Teachers obtained better athletic performance—as measured in the number of sit-ups or push-ups performed—from those students of whom they *expected* higher numbers. Despite the controversial nature of these findings, researchers continue to document the existence of the teacher-expectancy effect. Interactionists emphasize that ability alone may be less predictive of academic success than one might think (Babad and Taylor 1992; Brint 1998; R. Rosenthal and Jacobson 1992:247–262).

Table 43-1 summarizes the four major theoretical perspectives on education.

Tracking Sociological Perspectives

Table **43-1**   Sociological Perspectives on Education

Theoretical Perspective	Emphasis
Functionalist	Transmission of the dominant culture
	Integration of society
	Promotion of social norms, values, and sanctions
	Promotion of desirable social change
Conflict	Domination by the elite through unequal access to schooling
	Hidden curriculum
	Credentialism
	Bestowal of status
Interactionist	Teacher-expectancy effect
Feminist	Treatment of female students
	Role of women's education in economic development

MODULE 43 | Recap and Review

Summary

Education is a cultural universal found in varied forms throughout the world.

1. The transmission of knowledge and bestowal of status are manifest functions of education. Among the latent functions are transmitting culture, promoting social and political integration, maintaining social control, and serving as an agent of social change.

2. In the view of conflict theorists, education serves as an instrument of elite domination by creating standards for entry into occupations, bestowing status unequally, and subordinating the role of women.

3. Although U.S. women attain higher levels of education than do men, their performance in the workplace continues to lag. In cultures that maintain traditional gender roles, education of women is critical to economic and social development.

4. Teacher expectations about a student's performance can sometimes affect the student's actual achievement.

Thinking Critically

1. How do the functions of integration and social control reinforce each other? How do they work against each other?

2. What are the functions and dysfunctions of tracking in schools? In what ways might tracking have a positive impact on the self-concepts of various students? In what ways might it have a negative impact?

Key Terms

Correspondence principle

Credentialism

Education

Hidden curriculum

Teacher-expectancy effect

Tracking

MODULE 44 | Schools as Formal Organizations

Nineteenth-century educators would be amazed at the scale of schools in the United States in the 21st century. The nation has about 15 million high school students today, compared to 10 million in 1961 and 5 million in 1931 (Bureau of the Census 2012c:Table H S-20; 2011a:Table 246 on page 161).

In many respects, today's schools, when viewed as an example of a formal organization, are similar to factories, hospitals, and business firms. Like those organizations, schools do not operate autonomously; they are influenced by the market of potential students. This statement is especially true of private schools, but could have broader impact if acceptance of voucher plans and other school choice programs increases. The parallels between schools and other types of formal organizations will become more apparent as we examine the bureaucratic nature of schools, teaching as an occupation, and the student subculture (K. Dougherty and Hammack 1992).

Bureaucratization of Schools

It simply is not possible for a single teacher to transmit culture and skills to children of varying ages who will enter many diverse occupations. The growing number of students being served by school systems and the greater degree of specialization required within a technologically complex society have combined to bureaucratize schools.

Max Weber noted five basic characteristics of bureaucracy, all of which are evident in the vast majority of schools, whether at the elementary, secondary, or even college level:

1. **Division of labor.** Specialized experts teach particular age levels and specific subjects. Public elementary and secondary schools now employ instructors whose sole responsibility is to work with children with learning disabilities or physical impairments.

2. **Hierarchy of authority.** Each employee of a school system is responsible to a higher authority.

Teachers must report to principals and assistant principals and may also be supervised by department heads. Principals are answerable to a superintendent of schools, and the superintendent is hired and fired by a board of education.

3. **Written rules and regulations.** Teachers and administrators must conform to numerous rules and regulations in the performance of their duties. This bureaucratic trait can become dysfunctional; the time invested in completing required forms could instead be spent in preparing lessons or conferring with students.

4. **Impersonality.** As class sizes have swelled at schools and universities, it has become more difficult for teachers to give personal attention to each student. In fact, bureaucratic norms may actually encourage teachers to treat all students in the same way, despite the fact that students have distinctive personalities and learning needs.

5. **Employment based on technical qualifications.** At least in theory, the hiring of instructors is based on professional competence and expertise. Promotions are normally dictated by written personnel policies; people who excel may be granted lifelong job security through tenure.

Despite efforts to establish positive relationships among students and between teachers and students, many young people view their schools as impersonal institutions.

Taking Sociology to Work

Diane Belcher, *Assistant Director of Volunteer Services, New River Community College*

Not until Diane Belcher enrolled at New River Community College in Dublin, Virginia, did she realize that social work had always been part of her daily life. To this mother of two teenagers, helping people in need was something she just did, without even thinking about it.

Today, as assistant director of Volunteer Services at New River, Belcher assists Partners for Success, a mentoring program that matches struggling students with people in the community who have the time and energy to help them. With the director, she recruits and trains a "talent bank" of mentors, matches the mentors with student partners, and develops support programs for students experiencing problems with child care, transportation, and other necessities. The program's goal is to develop confident and successful learners who can take charge of their own studies.

Before she moved to Volunteer Services, Belcher was an administrative assistant in Workforce Development at New River, where she helped youths who lack direction and workers laid off from local factories to develop more marketable skills. In that job, she facilitated new students' transition to college, helping them to register and apply for financial aid and connecting them with professors in their fields of interest. Belcher also worked directly with the administration to develop a special fast-track program for laid-off workers.

As in all human services jobs, people skills, particularly sensitivity and compassion, are of paramount importance in Belcher's work. An understanding of the social and economic forces that affect the larger society is also essential. Belcher credits her sociology courses with helping her to "engage where needed." "Sociology exposed me to other people's situations and the role of society in creating them," she explains. "It helped me look beyond the individual level to understand societal impacts and solutions."

Asked what advice she might give to current sociology majors, Belcher says, "Drink it up, try and take it all in, relate it to the real world. Take notice of current cultural and economic conditions, understanding that when you attempt to 'fix' one part of society you must also be aware of how that will affect other parts of society."

LET'S DISCUSS

1. Have you, like Diane Belcher, realized through education that something you were doing without thinking about it has helped to prepare you for employment? Explain.

2. Do some research on Dublin, Virginia, and the surrounding area. What kind of economy does this community have? Relate the layoffs the community has been experiencing to larger societal forces.

Functionalists take a generally positive view of the bureaucratization of education. Teachers can master the skills needed to work with a specialized clientele, since they no longer are expected to cover a broad range of instruction. The chain of command within schools is clear. Students are presumably treated in an unbiased fashion because of uniformly applied rules. Finally, security of position protects teachers from unjustified dismissal. In general, then, functionalists stress that the bureaucratization of education increases the likelihood that students, teachers, and administrators will be dealt with fairly—that is, on the basis of rational and equitable criteria.

In contrast, conflict theorists argue that the trend toward more centralized education has harmful consequences for disadvantaged people. The standardization of educational curricula, including textbooks, will generally reflect the values, interests, and lifestyles of the most powerful groups in our society, and may ignore those of racial and ethnic minorities. In addition, the disadvantaged, more so than the affluent, will find it difficult to sort through complex educational bureaucracies and to organize effective lobbying groups. Therefore, in the view of conflict theorists, low-income and minority parents will have even less influence over citywide and statewide educational administrators than they have over local school officials (Bowles and Gintis 1976; Katz 1971).

Sometimes schools can seem overwhelmingly bureaucratic, with the effect of stifling rather than nourishing intellectual curiosity in students. This concern has led many parents and policymakers to push for school choice programs—allowing parents to choose the school that suits their children's needs, and forcing schools to compete for their "customers."

In the United States, another significant countertrend to the bureaucratization of schools is the availability of education over the Internet. Increasingly, colleges and universities are reaching out via the web, offering entire courses and even majors to students in the comfort of their homes. Online curricula provide flexibility for working students and others who may have difficulty attending conventional classes because of distance or disability. Research on this type of learning is just beginning, so the question of whether teacher–student contact can thrive online remains to be settled. Computer-mediated instruction may also have an impact on instructors' status as employees, which we will discuss next, as well as on alternative forms of education like homeschooling.

use your **sociological imagination**

How would you make your school less bureaucratic? What would it be like?

Teachers: Employees and Instructors

Whether they serve as instructors of preschoolers or of graduate students, teachers are employees of formal organizations with bureaucratic structures. There is an inherent conflict in serving as a professional in a bureaucracy. The organization follows the principles of hierarchy and expects adherence to its rules, but professionalism demands the individual responsibility of the practitioner. This conflict is very real for teachers, who experience all the positive and negative consequences of working in bureaucracies Table 19-1.

A teacher undergoes many perplexing stresses every day. While teachers' academic assignments have become more specialized, the demands on their time remain diverse and contradictory. Conflicts arise from serving as an instructor, a disciplinarian, and an employee of a school district at the same time. In too many schools, discipline means dealing with violence. Burnout is one result of these stresses: between a quarter and a third of new teachers quit within their first three years, and as many as half leave poor urban schools in their first five years (Wallis 2008).

Given these difficulties, does teaching remain an attractive profession in the United States? In 2011, 3.1 percent of first-year college students indicated that they were interested in becoming either elementary or high school teachers. These figures are dramatically lower than the 11 percent of first-year male students and 37 percent of first-year female students who held those occupational aspirations in 1966 (Pryor et al. 2007:122, 76; 2011a:29).

Undoubtedly, economic considerations enter into students' feelings about the attractiveness of teaching. In 2010, the average salary for all public elementary and secondary school teachers in the United States was reported at $55,350,

U.S. EDUCATION: RACE TO the TOP!

From preschool through high school, teachers face a variety of challenges, including preparing students for standardized tests.

placing teachers somewhere near the average of all the nation's wage earners. In most other industrial countries, teachers' salaries are higher in relation to the general standard of living. Of course, teachers' salaries vary considerably from state to state (Figure 44-1), and even more from one school district to another. Nevertheless, the economic reward for teaching is miniscule compared to some career options: the CEO of a major corporation makes more money in a day than the average teacher makes in a year.

MAPPING LIFE NATIONWIDE

FIGURE 44-1 Average Salary for Teachers

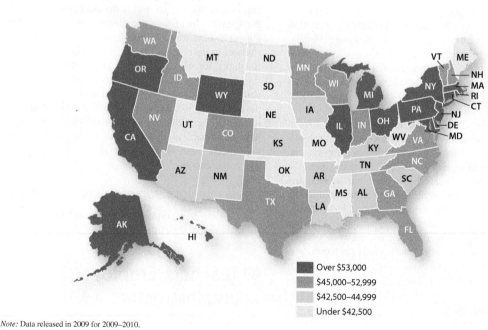

Over $53,000
$45,000–52,999
$42,500–44,999
Under $42,500

Note: Data released in 2009 for 2009–2010.
Source: National Education Association 2009.

State averages for teacher salaries range from a low of $35,136 in South Dakota to a high of $68,000 in Massachusetts.

The status of any job reflects several factors, including the level of education required, financial compensation, and the respect given the occupation by society. The teaching profession Table 27-1, is feeling pressure in all three of these areas. First, the level of formal schooling required for teaching remains high, and the public has begun to call for new competency examinations. Second, the statistics just cited demonstrate that teachers' salaries are significantly lower than those of many professionals and skilled workers. Third, the overall prestige of the teaching profession has declined in the past decade. Many teachers have become disappointed and frustrated and have left the educational world for careers in other professions.

Student Subcultures

An important latent function of education relates directly to student life: schools provide for students' social and recreational needs. Education helps toddlers and young children to develop interpersonal skills that are essential during adolescence and adulthood. In their high school and college years, students may meet future husbands and wives and establish lifelong friendships.

When people observe high schools, community colleges, or universities from the outside, students appear to constitute a cohesive, uniform group. However, the student subculture is actually quite complex and diverse. High school cliques and social groups may crop up according to race, social class, physical attractiveness, placement in courses, athletic ability, and leadership roles in the school and community. In his classic community study of "Elmtown," August B. Hollingshead (1975) found some 259 distinct cliques in a single high school. The cliques, whose average size was five, were centered on the school itself, on recreational activities, and on religious and community groups.

Amid these close-knit and often rigidly segregated cliques, gay and lesbian students are particularly vulnerable. Peer group pressure to conform is intense at this age. Although coming to terms with one's sexuality is difficult for all adolescents, it can be downright dangerous for those whose sexual orientation does not conform to societal expectations.

Teachers and administrators are becoming more sensitized to these issues. Perhaps more important, some schools are creating gay–straight alliances (GSAs), school-sponsored support groups that bring gay teens together with sympathetic straight peers. Begun in Los Angeles in 1984, these programs numbered nearly 3,000 nationwide in 2005; most were founded after the murder of Matthew Shepard, a gay college student, in 1998. In some districts parents have objected to these organizations, but the same court rulings that protect the right of conservative Bible groups to meet on school grounds also protect GSAs. In 2003, the gay–straight movement reached a milestone when the New York City public schools moved an in-school program for gays, bisexuals, and transgendered students to a separate school. The Harvey Milk High School was named in memory of San Francisco's first openly gay city supervisor, who was assassinated in 1978 (Gay, Lesbian and Straight Education Network 2012).

We can find a similar diversity of student groups at the college level. Burton Clark and Martin Trow (1966) and more recently, Helen Lefkowitz Horowitz (1987) have identified four distinctive subcultures among college students:

1. The *collegiate* subculture focuses on having fun and socializing. These students define what constitutes a "reasonable" amount of academic work (and what amount of work is "excessive" and leads to being labeled as a "grind"). Members of the collegiate subculture have little commitment to academic pursuits. Athletes often fit into this subculture.

2. The *academic* subculture identifies with the intellectual concerns of the faculty and values knowledge for its own sake.

3. The *vocational* subculture is interested primarily in career prospects and views college as a means of obtaining degrees that are essential for advancement.

4. Finally, the *nonconformist* subculture is hostile to the college environment and seeks ideas that may or may not relate to academic studies. This group may find outlets through campus publications or issue-oriented groups.

Each college student is eventually exposed to these competing subcultures and must determine which (if any) seems most in line with his or her feelings and interests.

The typology used by the researchers reminds us that school is a complex social organization—almost like a community with different neighborhoods. Of course, these four subcultures are not the only ones evident on college campuses in the United States. For example, one might find subcultures of Vietnam veterans or former full-time homemakers at community colleges and four-year commuter institutions. And as more and more students from minority groups decide to continue their formal education beyond high school, subcultures based on race and ethnicity will become more evident. As Figure 44-2 shows, college campuses are becoming increasingly diverse.

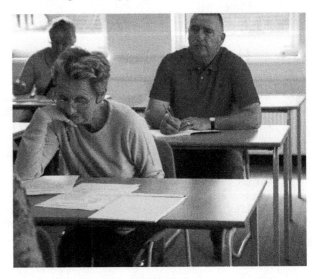

Student subcultures are more diverse today than in the past. Many adults are returning to college to obtain further education, advance their careers, or change their line of work.

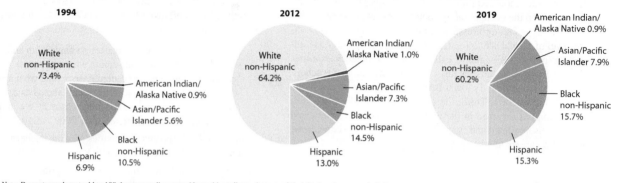

FIGURE 44-2 **College Campuses by Race and Ethnicity: Then, Now, and in the Future**

Note: Percentages do not add to 100 due to rounding error. Nonresident aliens whose race/ethnicity is unknown excluded.
Source: Hussar and Bailey 2011:Table 29.

Sociologist Joe R. Feagin has studied a distinctive collegiate subculture: Black students at predominantly White universities. These students must function academically and socially within universities where there are few Black faculty members or administrators, where harassment of Blacks by campus police is common, and where curricula place little emphasis on Black contributions. Feagin (1989:11) suggests that "for minority students life at a predominantly White college or university means long-term encounters with pervasive whiteness." In Feagin's view, Black students at such institutions experience both blatant and subtle racial discrimination, which has a cumulative impact that can seriously damage the students' confidence (see also Feagin et al. 1996).

use your **sociological imagination**

What distinctive subcultures can you identify at your college?

Homeschooling

When most people think of school, they think of bricks and mortar and the teachers, administrators, and other employees who staff school buildings. But for an increasing number of students in the United States, home is the classroom and the teacher is a parent. About 1.5 million students are now being educated at home. That is about 3 percent of the K–12 school population. For these students, the issues of bureaucratization and social structure are less significant than they are for public school students (Grady et al. 2010).

In the 1800s, after the establishment of public schools, families that taught their children at home lived in isolated environments or held strict religious views that were at odds with the secular environment of public schools. But today, homeschooling is attracting a broader range of families not necessarily tied to organized religion. Poor academic quality, peer pressure, and school violence are motivating many parents to teach their children at home. In addition, some immigrants choose homeschooling

as a way to ease their children's transition to a new society. For example, the growing Arab American population recently joined the movement toward homeschooling (MacFarquhar 2008; National Center for Education Statistics 2009).

While supporters of homeschooling believe children can do just as well or better in homeschools as in public schools, critics counter that because homeschooled children are isolated from the larger community, they lose an important chance to improve their socialization skills. But proponents of homeschooling claim their children benefit from contact with others besides their own age group. They also see homeschools as a good alternative for children who suffer from attention-deficit/hyperactivity disorder (ADHD) and learning disorders (LDs). Such children often do better in smaller classes, which present fewer distractions to disturb their concentration.

Quality control is an issue in homeschooling. While homeschooling is legal in all 50 states, 10 states require no notification that a child will be homeschooled, and another 14 require notification only. Other states may require parents to submit their children's curricula or test scores for professional evaluation. Despite the lack of uniform standards, a research review by the Home School Legal Defense Association (2005) reports that homeschooled students score higher than others on standardized tests, in every subject and every grade.

Who are the people who are running homeschools? In general, they tend to have higher-than-average incomes and educational levels. Most are two-parent families, and their children watch less television than average—both factors that are likely to support superior educational performance. The same students, with the same support from their parents, would probably do just as well in the public schools. As research has repeatedly shown, small classes are better than big classes, and strong parental and community involvement is key (R. Cox 2003:28).

Whatever the controversy over homeschooling in the United States, it is much less serious than in some other nations. In 2010, the U.S. Immigration and Naturalization Service began granting political asylum to German families who homeschool their children, in violation of their country's constitution. German parents can be fined and imprisoned for homeschooling their children (Francis 2010).

social policy and Education | Charter Schools

Discontent with public schools stretches back for decades. In the 1970s, "classrooms without walls" were supposed to open up the curriculum to students' creativity. In 2002, the No Child Left Behind initiative was supposed to guarantee that all students would learn the basics. Although test scores inched up a bit in response, critics complained that schools were becoming too test-oriented, and scores on interactive science and math tests sank compared to those in other nations (K. Clark 2010).

Meanwhile, the charter school movement had been gathering strength. **Charter schools** are experimental schools that are developed and managed by individuals, groups of parents, or an educational management organization. Although these schools are typically considered to be public schools, they are administered outside the official public school system. Their charters (legal contracts) permit them to establish their own rules, curricula, and admissions and professional standards. Within their communities, however, charter schools must still abide by prevailing standards for health, public safety, and equal opportunity (Renzulli and Roscigno 2007).

Looking at the Issue

Charter schools first opened in Minnesota in 1992; by 2011, nearly 5,000 of them had been established in 40 different states (Figure 44-3). Advocates of charter schools claim that they offer parents accountability for their children's education. In effect, charter schools compete with public schools, offering an alternative that was once available only to the wealthy (National Alliance for Public Charter Schools 2011).

Applying Sociology

Functionalists argue that charter schools meet society's need for education while serving a diverse student body. Despite criticism that charter schools are elitist institutions that serve the children of privileged White families, data show that 55 percent of the students enrolled in these schools are African American or Latino. More than a third of them qualify for free or reduced-price lunches (Gabriel 2010).

Although charter schools are publicly financed, most are not unionized. From a conflict perspective, charter schools do not represent teachers' interests well and are contributing to the decline of labor unions (see Module 19). Partly in response to this concern, public school districts in Denver, Detroit, Milwaukee, Boston, and Minnesota have empowered teachers to create their own charter schools (Dillon 2009; Hu 2010).

Because the charter school movement is a comparatively recent one, we do not have much research on the long-term impact of charter versus non-charter schools. Of course, there is great variation among both within the same city much less the

MAPPING LIFE NATIONWIDE

FIGURE 44-3 **Charter Schools**

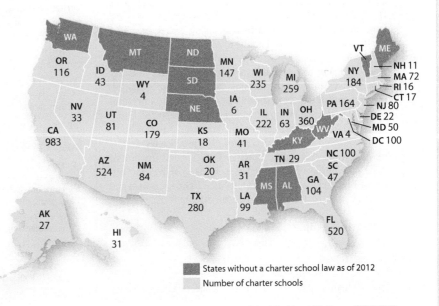

States without a charter school law as of 2012
Number of charter schools

Source: National Alliance for Public Charter Schools. (2012). The Public Charter Schools Dashboard. Washington, DC: NAPCS.

Think about It

How does your state compare to others in terms of charter schools?

—Continued

Charter Schools such as this one in Nampa, Idaho, are the latest answer to efforts to improve the quality of education.

same state. News stories about individual charter schools and high-profile advocates like the Bill and Melinda Gates Foundation suggest that these schools' outcomes are quite positive. However, the diversity in purpose, funding, organization, and curriculum that characterizes charter schools makes generalizing from one school or community to another very difficult.

As an example of the different conclusions that can be reached, many top school lists disproportionately identify charter schools as outperforming non-charter schools. Yet research released in 2012 shows that at least a third of charter schools do *worse* than the public schools they replaced. Similarly, research done at Stanford University on charter schools in 16 states shows that 37 percent of them produce test results that are worse than public schools. Only a small fraction of these schools have had their charters revoked, however (Center for Research on Education Outcomes 2009; Lubienski and Weitzel 2012; E. Thomas and Wingert 2010).

Initiating Policy

In the United States, unlike virtually all other industrial nations, school policy is driven at the local level. Although the federal government may encourage certain policies through public funding, and may dictate certain standards like nondiscrimination, school policy is created largely at the community level following statewide standards. Thus, in 2010, when the Department of Education began to expend $4.3 billion as part of a general educational stimulus program, it left the structure and organization of schools to local communities. Programs such as Race to the Top stressed only improvements in academic achievement (K. Clark 2010).

Today, the charter school movement is not the only approach to educational reform; other school choice programs are available to families. Homeschooling, described earlier in this chapter, could be viewed as the most complete alternative to public schools. In addition, some cities offer parents vouchers that allow them, in effect, to send their children to any local school, public, private, or religious, at taxpayers' expense. Yet as Karl Alexander (1997:17) eloquently noted in his presidential address to the Southern Sociological Society, "The charter school movement, with its 'let 1,000 flowers bloom' philosophy, is certain to yield an occasional prize-winning rose. But is . . . [this approach to school choice] likely to prove a reliable guide for broad-based, systematic reform—the kind of reform that will carry the great mass of our children closer to where we want them to be? I hardly think so." Indeed, with such diversity in learning environments found among thousands of charter schools, the jury is still out on their effectiveness. As with most educational institutions, one cannot assume quality just based on a certain structure, size, affiliation, or funding source.

TAKE THE ISSUE WITH YOU

1. Do you have any experience with educational reform, either as a student yourself or as a parent? If so, describe the changes that you witnessed. Were they successful in improving educational outcomes?

2. Which type of school choice program, if any, would you favor—homeschooling, charter schools, or school vouchers? Explain your choice.

3. Are you concerned about educational standards in the United States? If so, do you think schools should be reformed at the local level? Should the federal government become more involved in school reform?

Summary

Most schools in the United States are organized like formal organizations such as factories and hospitals.

1. Weber's five basic characteristics of bureaucracies are all evident in schools.

2. Teachers are professionals who serve as part of a bureaucracy. There is an inherent conflict in combining those two different roles.

3. Schools provide for students' social and emotional needs as well as their educational needs. Student subcultures within high schools and colleges are complex and varied.

4. Homeschooling has become a viable alternative to traditional public and private schools. In some countries homeschooling is illegal.

5. **Charter schools**—experimental schools that are developed and managed by individuals, groups of parents, or an educational management organization— are one of several recent attempts to reform the public school system in the United States. Although charter schools are popular with parents, research shows that about a third of them do worse than the public schools they replaced.

Thinking Critically

1. Select two functions of education and suggest how they could be fulfilled through homeschooling.

2. What student subcultures can you identify on your campus? Which have the highest and lowest social status? How would functionalists, conflict theorists, and interactionists view the existence of student subcultures on a college campus?

Key Term

Charter school

Mastering This Chapter: Education

taking sociology with you

1 Attend a meeting of a local Parent Teacher Association (PTA). What issues are parents talking about? Describe their concerns using one or more sociological perspectives.

2 Make a list of the student subcultures on your campus, then describe them using the concepts you learned in

Module 11. Do any of these subcultures serve as out-groups for other subcultures?

3 Does your school have a gay–straight alliance? If so, speak with one of the officers. What are members doing to reduce prejudice and foster better relations among gay and straight students? Explain their approach using sociological theory.

key terms

Charter school An experimental school that is developed and managed by individuals, groups of parents, or an educational management organization.

Correspondence principle The tendency of schools to promote the values expected of individuals in each social class and to perpetuate social class divisions from one generation to the next.

Credentialism An increase in the lowest level of education needed to enter a field.

Education A formal process of learning in which some people consciously teach, while others adopt the social role of learner.

Hidden curriculum Standards of behavior that are deemed proper by society and are taught subtly in schools.

Teacher-expectancy effect The impact that a teacher's expectations about a student's performance may have on the student's actual achievements.

Tracking The practice of placing students in specific curriculum groups on the basis of their test scores and other criteria.

self-quiz

Read each question carefully and then select the best answer.

1. Which sociological perspective emphasizes that the common identity and social integration fostered by education contribute to overall societal stability and consensus?
   a. the functionalist perspective
   b. the conflict perspective
   c. the interactionist perspective
   d. labeling theory

2. Which one of the following was introduced into school systems to promote social change?
   a. sex education classes
   b. affirmative action programs
   c. Project Head Start
   d. all of the above

3. The correspondence principle was developed by
   a. Max Weber.
   b. Karl Marx and Friedrich Engels.
   c. Samuel Bowles and Herbert Gintis.
   d. James Thurber.

4. The student subculture that is hostile to the college environment and seeks out ideas that may or may not relate to studies is called the
   a. collegiate subculture.

   b. academic subculture.
   c. vocational subculture.
   d. nonconformist subculture.

5. Most recent research on ability grouping raises questions about its
   a. effectiveness, especially for lower-achieving students.
   b. failure to improve the prospects of higher-achieving students.
   c. ability to improve the prospects of lower- and higher-achieving students.
   d. both a and b

6. The most basic *manifest* function of education is
   a. transmitting knowledge.
   b. transmitting culture.
   c. maintaining social control.
   d. serving as an agent of change.

7. Sixty years ago, a high school diploma was the minimum requirement for entry into the paid labor force of the United States. Today, a college diploma is virtually the bare minimum. This change reflects the process of
   a. tracking.
   b. credentialism.
   c. the hidden curriculum.
   d. the correspondence principle.

8. Samuel Bowles and Herbert Gintis have argued that capitalism requires a skilled, disciplined labor force and that the educational system of the United States is structured with that objective in mind. Citing numerous studies, they offer support for what they call
    a. tracking.
    b. credentialism.
    c. the correspondence principle.
    d. the teacher-expectancy effect.

9. The teacher-expectancy effect is most closely associated with
    a. the functionalist perspective.
    b. the conflict perspective.
    c. the interactionist perspective.
    d. anomie theory.

10. Sociologist Max Weber noted five basic characteristics of bureaucracy, all of which are evident in the vast majority of schools, whether at the elementary, secondary, or even college level. Which of the following is *not* one of them?
    a. division of labor
    b. written rules and regulations
    c. impersonality
    d. shared decision making

11. The _____ perspective stresses the importance of education in transmitting culture, maintaining social control, and promoting social change.

12. In the past, the integrative function of education was most obvious through its emphasis on promoting a common _____.

13. The _____ subculture identifies with the intellectual concerns of the faculty and values knowledge for its own sake.

14. A _____ _____ is an experimental school that is developed and managed outside the public school system.

15. Women's education tends to suffer in those cultures with traditional _____ _____ .

16. Schools perform a variety of _____ functions, such as transmitting culture, promoting social and political integration, and maintaining social control.

17. Sociologist _____ _____ points out that better-educated people tend to have greater access to information, to hold more diverse opinions, and to possess the ability to make subtle distinctions in analysis.

18. The term _____ _____ refers to standards of behavior that are deemed proper by society and are taught subtly in schools. For example, children must not speak until the teacher calls on them and must regulate their activities according to the clock or the bell.

19. _____ is the practice of placing students in specific curriculum groups on the basis of their test scores and other criteria.

20. Of the four distinctive subcultures among college students discussed in the text, the _____ subculture is interested primarily in career prospects, and views college as a means of obtaining degrees that are essential for advancement.

Answers

1 (a); 2 (d); 3 (c); 4 (d); 5 (a); 6 (a); 7 (b); 8 (c); 9 (c); 10 (d); 11 functionalist; 12 language; 13 academic; 14 charter school; 15 gender roles; 16 latent; 17 Robin Williams; 18 hidden curriculum; 19 Tracking; 20 vocational

---

thinking about movies

Waiting for Superman

This film documents failures in the American educational system and their personal consequences.

Teached Vol. I

This documentary explores why the American education system fails to provide basic literacy skills to a significant percentage of minority students.

To Be Heard

Four teens use writing and literacy as tools to improve their social circumstances.

Religion

15 Religion

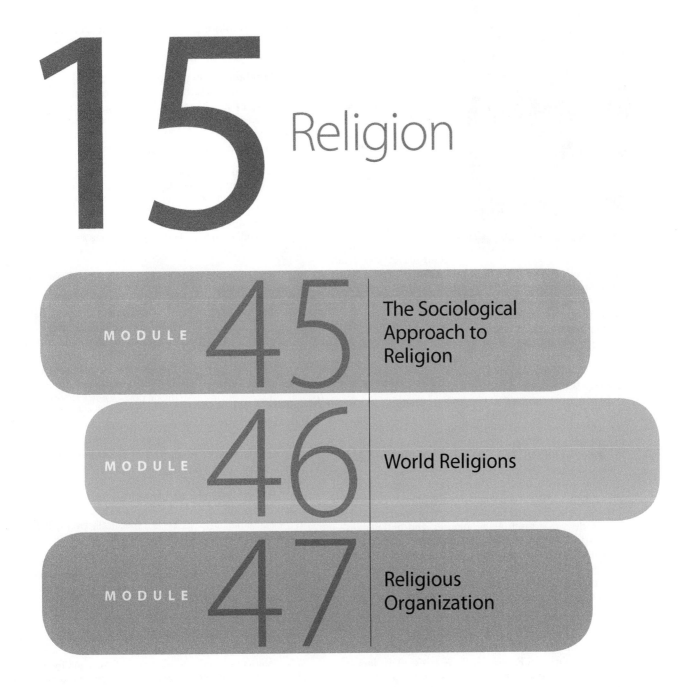

MODULE 45   The Sociological Approach to Religion

MODULE 46   World Religions

MODULE 47   Religious Organization

Sociologists Nikki Bado-Fralick and Rebecca Sachs Norris used religiously themed toys and games to study contemporary religion.

They found that these seemingly frivolous items reveal a great deal about the way Americans practice their varied religious heritages today.

66 There are many types of religious toys: stuffed torahs; Moses, David, and Jesus and the Tomb action figures; Noah's ark collections; and Resurrection Eggs, which supplement a young child's Easter book. 'Lead your kids on a fun, faith-filled Easter egg hunt this year—one that teaches them about Jesus' death and resurrection! Each egg carton is filled with a dozen colorful plastic eggs. Pop them open and find miniature symbols of the Easter story inside.' One of the dozen plastic eggs contains a crown of thorns, another is empty, representing the disappearance of the body of Jesus from the tomb, and pointing to his resurrection. Muslim toys include a mosque building set, mosque jewelry cases, and a prayer practice chart. Jewish toys include dreidels, wooden Shabbat sets, toy *sukkahs*, and a Plush Plagues Bag that includes 'all 10 Plagues!'

Religious dolls are part of this wonderland of sacred fun. There are plush and plastic talking Bible dolls, pumped-up Christian action figures, dolls designed to support a Jewish girl's religious identity and conform to religious requirements, Goddess dolls designed for affluent young feminists, talking Muslim dolls that teach Arabic phrases, and 'anti-Barbies'— Muslim dolls deliberately designed to compete with Barbie for the hearts and minds of young girls. There are plush Buddha and Siva dolls, and cuddly Jesus and Esther dolls as well.

Numerous card games and puzzles teach a variety of languages, including Hebrew, Arabic, and Punjabi. The Christian

Book Distributors Web site not only offers religiously themed educational materials, they also offer nonreligious toys that appeal to parents with religious consciences who may be looking for nonviolent toys, such as a food groups toy with hand-painted pieces in four wooden crates, a pizza party game with different toppings, and a car towing game.

Not all religious toys are meant for the edification of the young. Many religious games and toys are satirical or simply products meant to be amusing enough to sell in an era where we are oversatiated with things, and any cultural phenomenon is fair game for marketing purposes. These items amuse or appall us, depending on how clever or offensive the item is, and for whom it is intended. . . .

. . . .

. . . Games and toys not only transmit cultural values but reflect them as well. . . .

Contemporary religious games have their roots in ancient practices, but their flavor—their style and substance—as well as their commercial focus reveal a specifically twenty-first century American form of religiosity.

Games and religion have a long and complex history—they were used for divination and gambling, for this-worldly satire, and in the afterlife. Games were objects and methods used to interpret divine powers and influence supernatural forces. These religious and magical functions reflect the presence and movement of the sacred in the material world, indicators of a complex whole rather than a dualism where sacred and ordinary occupy separate realms.

Contemporary religious games have their roots in ancient practices, but their flavor—their style and substance—as well as their commercial focus reveal a specifically twenty-first century American form of religiosity. 99

(Bado-Fralick and Norris 2010:7–8, 29–30) Additional information about this excerpt can be found on the Online Learning Center at www.mhhe.com/schaefermod2e.

n this excerpt from *Toying with God: The World of Religious Games and Dolls*, religious studies scholars Nikki Bado-Fralick and Rebecca Sachs Norris consider how religiously themed toys and games reflect both popular and religious culture. Depending on their purpose and design, the authors note, as well as on the social context in which they are used, these dolls and board games can either reinforce or undermine organized religion. Their impact on the children who play with them parallels the broader influence of religion on society. Despite the much-publicized decline of organized religion over the past century, even a casual observer can see that religion still

permeates our social environment. As a result, nonbelievers are influenced by believers, whether they want to be or not. Similarly, believers are influenced by nonbelievers and by those of different faiths, despite any attempts they may make to screen out other points of view.

Religion plays a major role in people's lives, and religious practices of some sort are evident in every society. That makes religion a cultural universal, along with other common practices or beliefs found in every culture, such as dancing, food preparation, the family, and personal names. At present, an estimated 4 billion people belong to the world's many religious faiths.

What social purposes does religion serve? Does it help to hold society together or foster social change? What happens when religion mixes with politics? These modules concentrate on the formal systems of religion that characterize modern industrial societies. We begin with a brief description of the sociological perspectives on religion, followed by an overview of the world's major religions. We will also explore religion's role in societal integration, social support, social change, and social control. Next we'll examine three important components of religious behavior— belief, ritual, and experience. Finally, we will cover the basic forms of religious organization, including new religious movements. In a case study, we'll take a fascinating look at religion in India. We will close with a Social Policy section on the controversy over religion in the schools.

MODULE 45 | The Sociological Approach to Religion

Durkheim and the Importance of Religion

If a group believes that it is being directed by a "vision from God," sociologists do not attempt to prove or disprove the revelation. Instead, they assess the effects of the religious experience on the group. What sociologists are interested in is the social impact of religion on individuals and institutions.

Émile Durkheim was perhaps the first sociologist to recognize the critical importance of religion in human societies. He saw its appeal for the individual, but more important, he stressed the *social* impact of religion. In Durkheim's view, religion is a collective act that includes many forms of behavior in which people interact with others. As in his work on suicide, Durkheim was not so interested in the personalities of religious believers as he was in understanding religious behavior within a social context.

Durkheim defined **religion** as a "unified system of beliefs and practices relative to sacred things." In his view, religion involves a set of beliefs and practices that are uniquely the property of religion, as opposed to other social institutions and ways of thinking. Durkheim ([1893] 1933; [1912] 2001) argued that religious faiths distinguish between certain transcending events and the everyday world. He referred to those realms as the *sacred* and the *profane.*

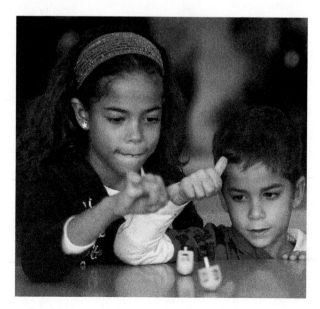

The **sacred** encompasses elements beyond everyday life that inspire awe, respect, and even fear. People become part of the sacred realm only by completing some ritual, such as prayer or sacrifice. Because believers have faith in the sacred, they accept what they cannot understand. In contrast, the **profane** includes the ordinary and commonplace. This concept can be confusing, however, because the same object can be either sacred or profane, depending on how it is viewed. A normal dining room table is profane, but it becomes sacred to some Christians if it bears the elements of a communion. A candelabra becomes sacred to Jews if it is a menorah. For Confucians and Taoists, incense sticks are not mere decorative items, but highly valued offerings to the gods in religious ceremonies that mark the new and full moons.

When religion's influence on other social institutions in a society diminishes, the process of **secularization** is said to be under way. During this process, religion will survive in the private sphere of individual and family life (as in the case of many Native American families); it may even thrive on a personal level. But at the same time, other social institutions—such as the economy, politics, and education—maintain their own sets of norms, independent of religious guidance. Even so, religion is enormously resilient. Although specific faiths or organizations may change, their transformation does not signal the demise of religious faith. Rather, it contributes to the diversity of religious expression and organization.

Following the direction established by Durkheim a century ago, contemporary sociologists view religion in two different ways. First, they study the norms and values of religious faiths by examining their substantive beliefs. For example, it is possible to compare the degree to which Christian faiths interpret the Bible literally, or Muslim groups follow the Qur'an (or Koran), the sacred book of Islam. At the same time, sociologists examine religion in terms of the social functions it fulfills, such as providing social support or reinforcing social norms. By exploring both the beliefs and the functions of religion, we can better understand its impact on the individual, on groups, and on society as a whole.

Sociological Perspectives on Religion

Since religion is a cultural universal, it is not surprising that it plays a basic role in human societies. In sociological terms, it performs both manifest and latent functions. Among its *manifest* (open and stated) functions, religion defines the spiritual world and gives meaning to the divine. It provides an explanation for events that seem difficult to understand, such as what lies beyond the grave. The *latent* functions of religion are unintended, covert, or hidden. Even though the manifest function of a church service is to offer a forum for religious worship, it might at the same time fulfill a latent social function as a meeting ground for unmarried members.

Functionalists and conflict theorists both evaluate religion's impact on human societies. We'll consider a functionalist view of religion's role in integrating society, providing social support, and promoting social change, and then look at religion from the conflict and feminist perspectives, as a means of social control. Note that for the most part, religion's impact is best understood from a macro-level viewpoint that is oriented toward the larger society. Its social support function is an exception: it is best understood on the micro, or individual, level.

The Integrative Function of Religion

Émile Durkheim viewed religion as an integrative force in human society—a perspective that is reflected in functionalist thought today. Durkheim sought to answer a perplexing question: "How can human societies be held together when they are generally composed of individuals and social groups with diverse interests and aspirations?" In his view, religious bonds often transcend these personal and divisive forces. Durkheim acknowledged that religion is not the only integrative force; nationalism or patriotism may serve the same end.

How does religion provide this "societal glue"? Religion, whether it be Buddhism, Islam, Christianity, or Judaism, gives meaning and purpose to people's lives. It offers certain ultimate values and ends to hold in common. Although they are subjective and not always fully accepted, these values and ends help society to function as an integrated social system. For example, funerals, weddings, bar and bat mitzvahs, and confirmations serve to integrate people into larger communities by providing shared beliefs and values about the ultimate questions of life.

The integrative power of religion can be seen, too, in the role that churches, synagogues, and mosques have traditionally played and continue to play for immigrant groups in the United States. For example, Roman Catholic immigrants may settle near a parish church that offers services in their native language, such as Polish or Spanish. Similarly, Korean immigrants may join a Presbyterian church that has many Korean American members and follows religious practices like those of churches in Korea. Like other religious organizations, these Roman Catholic and Presbyterian churches help to integrate immigrants into their new homeland.

In recent years, the most talked about immigrant religious group has been Muslims. Throughout the world, including the United States, Muslims are divided into a variety of sects, including Sunni and Shia (or Shiite). However, inside and outside these sects, people express their Islamic faith in many different ways. To speak of Muslims as being either Sunni or Shia would be like speaking of Christians as either Roman Catholic or Baptist.

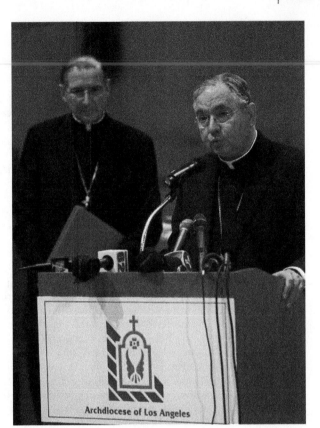

In 2010 Jose H. Gomez (at the podium) became archbishop of Los Angeles, the largest Roman Catholic archdiocese in the United States. Born in Mexico, Gomez became a U.S. citizen while serving as a priest in Texas. His elevation reflects the growth of the Hispanic faithful among Roman Catholics in the United States.

Depending on the circumstances, Islam in the United States can be integrative by faith, ethnicity, or both. The great majority of Muslims in the United States are Sunni Muslims—literally, those who follow the *Sunnah,* or way of the Prophet. Compared to other Muslims, Sunnis tend to be more moderate in their religious orthodoxy. The Shia, who come primarily from Iraq and Iran, are the second-largest group. Shia Muslims are more attentive to guidance from accepted Islamic scholars than are Sunnis. In sufficient numbers, these two Muslim groups will choose to worship separately, even if they must cross ethnic or linguistic lines to do so. Whatever group Muslims belong to, however, there has been a remarkable increase in the number of Islamic places of worship in the United States. Between 2000 and 2010, the number of mosques rose 74 percent (Bagby 2012; Selod 2008a).

In some instances, religious loyalties are *dysfunctional;* that is, they contribute to tension and even conflict between groups or nations. During the Second World War, the German Nazis attempted to exterminate the Jewish people; approximately 6 million European Jews were killed. In modern times, nations such as Lebanon (Muslims versus Christians), Israel (Jews versus Muslims, as well as Orthodox versus secular Jews), Northern Ireland (Roman Catholics versus Protestants), and India (Hindus versus Muslims, and more recently, Sikhs) have been torn by clashes that are in large part based on religion. (See the case study for a more detailed discussion of religious conflict in India.)

Religion and Social Support

Most of us find it difficult to accept the stressful events of life—the death of a loved one, serious injury, bankruptcy, divorce, and so forth—especially when something "senseless" happens. How can family and friends come to terms with the death of a talented college student, not even 20 years old?

Through its emphasis on the divine and the supernatural, religion allows us to "do something" about the calamities we face. In some faiths, adherents can offer sacrifices or pray to a deity in the belief that such acts will change their earthly condition. On a more basic level, religion encourages us to view our personal misfortunes as relatively unimportant in the broader perspective of human history—or even as part of an undisclosed divine purpose. Friends and relatives of the deceased college student may see his death as being "God's will," or as having some ultimate benefit that we cannot understand now. This perspective may be much more comforting than the terrifying feeling that any of us can die senselessly at any moment—and that there is no divine answer to why one person lives a long and full life, while another dies tragically at a relatively early age.

The religious function of social support is also apparent in people's use of social media. Overall, 31 percent of Facebook users in the United States and 24 percent of them outside the United States identify their religion in their profiles. Tens of millions indicate that they are fans or "friends" of a religious figure or category. Consequently, religious organizations are turning to Twitter and Facebook to strengthen their connections with these followers and provide them with 24/7 social support (Preston 2011).

Religion and Social Change

The Weberian Thesis When someone seems driven to work and succeed, we often attribute the Protestant work ethic to that person. The term comes from the writings of Max Weber, who carefully examined the connection between religious allegiance and capitalist development. Weber's findings appeared in his pioneering work *The Protestant Ethic and the Spirit of Capitalism* ([1904] 2011).

Weber noted that in European nations with both Protestant and Catholic citizens, an overwhelming number of business leaders, owners of capital, and skilled workers were Protestant. In his view, this fact was no mere coincidence. Weber pointed out that the followers of John Calvin (1509–1564), a leader of the Protestant Reformation, emphasized a disciplined work ethic, this-worldly concerns, and a rational orientation to life that have become known as the **Protestant ethic.** One by-product of the Protestant ethic was a drive to accumulate savings that could be used for future investment. This "spirit of capitalism," to use Weber's phrase, contrasted with the moderate work hours, leisurely work habits, and lack of ambition that Weber saw as typical of the times.

Few books on the sociology of religion have aroused as much commentary and criticism as Weber's work. It has been hailed as one of the most important theoretical works in the field and an excellent example of macro-level analysis. Like Durkheim, Weber demonstrated that religion is not solely a matter of intimate personal beliefs. He stressed that the collective nature

Television scripts often poke fun at organized religion, while presenting characters who are atheists as enlightened people. A notable exception is the character Booth (left) in *Bones*, who does not hide his Roman Catholicism. Like many others who are both thoughtful and religious, Booth receives social support from his faith.

of religion has consequences for society as a whole. Indeed, a recent analysis of historical economic data shows that the Protestant ethic was an important factor in the growth of capitalism from 1500 through 1870 (S. Sanderson et al. 2011).

Weber provided a convincing description of the origins of European capitalism. However, this economic system has now been adopted by non-Calvinists in many parts of the world. Studies done in the United States today show little or no difference in achievement orientation between Roman Catholics and Protestants. Apparently, the "spirit of capitalism" has emerged as a generalized cultural trait rather than a specific religious tenet (Greeley 1989).

Conflict theorists caution that Weber's theory—even if it is accepted—should not be regarded as an analysis of mature capitalism, as reflected in the rise of multinational corporations. Marxists would disagree with Weber not on the origins of capitalism, but on its future. Unlike Marx, Weber believed that capitalism could endure indefinitely as an economic system. He added, however, that the decline of religion as an overriding force in society opened the way for workers to express their discontent more vocally (R. Collins 1980).

Liberation Theology Sometimes the clergy can be found in the forefront of social change. Many religious activists, especially in the Roman Catholic Church in Latin America, support **liberation theology**—the use of a church in a political effort to eliminate poverty, discrimination, and other forms of injustice from a secular society. Advocates of this religious movement sometimes sympathize with Marxism. Many believe that radical change, rather than economic development in itself, is the only acceptable solution to the desperation of the masses in impoverished developing countries. Activists associated with liberation theology believe that organized religion has a moral responsibility to take a strong public stand against the oppression of the poor, racial and ethnic minorities, and women (Christian Smith 1991).

The term *liberation theology* dates back to the publication in 1973 of the English translation of *A Theology of Liberation*. The book was written by a Peruvian priest, Gustavo Gutiérrez, who lived in a slum area of Lima during the early 1960s. After years of exposure to the vast poverty around him, Gutiérrez concluded that "in order to serve the poor, one had to move into political action." Eventually, politically committed Latin American theologians came under the influence of social scientists who viewed the domination of capitalism and multinational corporations as central to the hemisphere's problems. One result was a new approach to theology that built on the cultural and religious traditions of Latin America rather than on models developed in Europe and the United States (R. M. Brown 1980:23; G. Gutiérrez 1990).

Liberation theology may be dysfunctional, however. Some Roman Catholic worshippers have come to believe that by focusing on political and governmental injustice, the clergy are no longer addressing their personal and spiritual needs. Partly as a result of such disenchantment, some Catholics in Latin America are converting to mainstream Protestant faiths or to Mormonism.

use your sociological imagination

The social support that religious groups provide is suddenly withdrawn from your community. How will your life or the lives of others change? What will happen if religious groups stop pushing for social change?

Religion and Social Control: A Conflict Perspective

Liberation theology is a relatively recent phenomenon that marks a break with the traditional role of churches. It was this traditional role that Karl Marx ([1844] 1964) opposed. In his view, religion *impeded* social change by encouraging oppressed people to focus on otherworldly concerns rather than on their immediate poverty or exploitation. Marx described religion as an opiate that was particularly harmful to oppressed peoples. He felt that religion often drugged the masses into submission by offering a consolation for their harsh lives on earth: the hope of salvation in an ideal afterlife. For example, during the period of slavery in the United States, White masters forbade Blacks to practice native African religions, while encouraging them to adopt Christianity, which taught them that obedience would lead to salvation and eternal happiness in the hereafter. Viewed from a conflict perspective, Christianity may have pacified certain slaves and blunted the rage that often fuels rebellion.

Today, however, people around the world see religion more as a source of support through adversity than a source of oppression. In a combination of public opinion polls taken across 114 nations, 95 percent of those living in the poorest nations felt that religion was important in daily life, compared to only 47 percent of those in the wealthiest countries (Crabtree 2010).

Although the number of women clergy has increased, only about 1 in 6 spiritual leaders is a woman, and in many faiths women are still banned from serving.

Religion does play an important role in propping up the existing social structure. The values of religion, as already noted, tend to reinforce other social institutions and the social order as a whole. From Marx's perspective, however, religion's promotion of social stability only helps to perpetuate patterns of social inequality. According to Marx, the dominant religion reinforces the interests of those in power.

For example, contemporary Christianity reinforces traditional patterns of behavior that call for the subordination of the less powerful. The role of women in the church is an example of this uneven distribution of power. Assumptions about gender roles leave women in a subservient position both within Christian churches and at home. In fact, women find it as difficult to achieve leadership positions in many churches as they do in large corporations. A "stained glass ceiling" tends to stunt clergywomen's career development, even in the most liberal denominations.

Like Marx, conflict theorists argue that to whatever extent religion actually does influence social behavior, it reinforces existing patterns of dominance and inequality. From a Marxist perspective, religion keeps people from seeing their lives and societal conditions in political terms—for example, by obscuring the overriding significance of conflicting economic interests. Marxists suggest that by inducing a "false consciousness" among the disadvantaged, religion lessens the possibility of collective political action that could end capitalist oppression and transform society.

Feminist Perspective

Drawing on the feminist approach, researchers and theorists have stressed the fundamental role women play in religious socialization. Most people develop their allegiance to a particular faith in their childhood, with their mothers playing a critical role in the process. Significantly, nonworshipping mothers tend to influence their children to be highly skeptical of organized religion.

However, women generally take a subordinate role in religious governance. Indeed, most faiths have a long tradition of exclusively male spiritual leadership. Furthermore, because most religions are patriarchal, they tend to reinforce men's dominance in secular as well as spiritual matters. Women do play a vital role as volunteers, staff, and religious educators, but even today, religious decision making and leadership typically fall to the men. Exceptions to this rule, such as the Shakers and Christian Scientists, as well as Hinduism with its long goddess heritage, are rare (R. Schaefer and Zellner 2011).

In the United States, women are much more likely than men to be affiliated with religion, to pray, to believe in God, to claim that religion is important in their lives, and to attend weekly worship services. Yet organized religion typically does not give them leadership roles. Nationally, women compose 18 percent of U.S. clergy, though they account for 34 percent of students enrolled in theological institutions. Women clerics typically have shorter careers than men, often in related fields that do not involve congregational leadership, such as counseling. In faiths that restrict leadership positions to men, women serve unofficially. For example, about 4 percent of Roman Catholic congregations are led by women who hold nonordained pastoral positions—a necessity in a church facing a shortage of male priests (Association of Theological Schools 2011; Bureau of the Census 2011a:Table 616 on page 393).

Table 45-1 summarizes the four major sociological perspectives on religion.

A Protestant congregation worships at Sunday service. Although Weber traced the "spirit of capitalism" to Protestant teachings, in the United States today Protestants and Catholics share the same work ethic.

Table **45-1** Sociological Perspectives on Religion — **Tracking** Sociological Perspectives

Theoretical Perspective	Emphasis
Functionalist	Religion as a source of social integration and unification Religion as a source of social support for individuals
Conflict	Religion as a potential obstacle to structural social change Religion as a potential source of structural social change (through liberation theology)
Feminist	Religion as an instrument of women's subordination, except for their role in religious socialization
Interactionist	Individual religious expression through belief, ritual, and experience

MODULE 45 | Recap and Review

Summary

Religion is a cultural universal found throughout the world in various forms.

1. Émile Durkheim stressed the social impact of religion in attempting to understand individual religious behavior within the context of the larger society.
2. Religion helps to integrate a diverse society and provides social support in time of need.
3. Max Weber saw a connection between religious allegiance and capitalistic behavior in a religious orientation he termed the **Protestant ethic.**
4. In **liberation theology,** the teachings of Christianity become the basis for political efforts to alleviate poverty and social injustice.
5. From a Marxist point of view, religion serves to reinforce the social control of those in power.

It discourages collective political action, which could end capitalist oppression and transform society.

Thinking Critically

1. What objects that you regard as profane might others consider to be sacred?
2. Explain how the Weberian thesis and liberation theology promote social change.

Key Terms

Liberation theology

Profane

Protestant ethic

Religion

Sacred

Secularization

MODULE 46 | World Religions

Worldwide, tremendous diversity exists in religious beliefs and practices. Overall, about 89 percent of the world's population adheres to some religion; thus, only about 10 percent is nonreligious. This level of adherence changes over time and also varies by country and age group. In the United States today, those who are nonreligious account for about 16 percent of the population; in 1900, they accounted for a mere 1.3 percent of all Americans. And in 2011, 25 percent of incoming U.S. college students had no religious preference, compared to 12 percent of their mothers (Newport 2010b; Pryor et al. 2011a:24–25).

Christianity is the largest single faith in the world; the second largest is Islam (Table 46-1). Although global news events often suggest an inherent conflict between Christians and Muslims, the two faiths are similar in many ways. Both are monotheistic (based on a single deity); both include a belief in prophets, an afterlife, and a judgment day. In fact, Islam recognizes Jesus as a prophet, though not as the son of God. Both faiths impose a moral code on believers, which varies from fairly rigid proscriptions for fundamentalists to relatively relaxed guidelines for liberals.

The followers of Islam, called *Muslims,* believe that Islam's holy scriptures were received from Allah (God) by the prophet Mohammad nearly 1,400 years ago. They see Mohammad as the last in a long line of prophets, preceded by Adam, Abraham, Moses, and Jesus. Islam is more communal in its expression than Christianity, particularly the more individualistic Protestant denominations. Consequently, in countries that are predominantly Muslim, the separation of religion and the state is not considered necessary or even desirable. In fact, Muslim governments often reinforce Islamic practices through their laws. Muslims do vary sharply in their interpretation of several traditions, some of which—such as the wearing of veils by women—are more cultural than religious in origin.

Like Christianity and Islam, Judaism is monotheistic. Jews believe that God's true nature is revealed in the Torah, which Christians know as the first five books of the Old Testament. According to these scriptures, God formed a covenant, or pact, with Abraham and Sarah, the ancestors of the tribes of Israel. Even today, Jews believe, this covenant holds them accountable to God's will. If they follow both the letter and spirit of the Torah, a long-awaited Messiah will one day bring paradise to earth. Although Judaism has a relatively small following compared to other major faiths, it forms the historical foundation for both Christianity and Islam. That is why Jews revere many of the same sacred Middle Eastern sites as Christians and Muslims.

Two other major faiths developed in a different part of the world, India. The earliest, Hinduism, originated around 1500 B.C. Hinduism differs from Judaism, Christianity, and Islam in that it embraces a number of gods and minor gods, although most worshippers are devoted primarily to a single deity, such as Shiva or Vishnu. Hinduism is also distinguished by a belief in reincarnation, or the perpetual rebirth of the soul after death. Unlike Judaism, Christianity, and Islam, which are based largely on sacred texts, Hindu beliefs have been preserved mostly through oral tradition.

Table 46-1 Major World Religions

summingup

Faith	Current Following, in Millions (and Percentage of World Population)	Primary Location of Followers Today	Founder (and Approximate Birth Date)	Important Texts (and Holy Sites)
Buddhism	463 (6.7%)	Southeast Asia, Mongolia, Tibet	Gautama Siddhartha (563 B.C.)	Triptaka (areas in Nepal)
Christianity	2,264 (33.0%)	Europe, North America, South America	Jesus (6 B.C.)	Bible (Jerusalem, Rome)
Hinduism	935 (13.7%)	India, Indian communities overseas	No specific founder (1500 B.C.)	Sruti and Smrti texts (seven sacred cities, including Vavansi)
Islam	1,523 (22.5%)	Middle East, Central Asia, North Africa, Indonesia	Mohammad (A.D. 570)	Qur'an, or Koran (Mecca, Medina, Jerusalem)
Judaism	15 (0.2%)	Israel, United States, France, Russia	Abraham (2000 B.C.)	Torah, Talmud (Jerusalem)

Sources: Author, based on Britannica Online 2011; Swatos 1998.

A second religion, Buddhism, developed in the sixth century B.C. as a reaction against Hinduism. This faith is founded on the teachings of Siddhartha (later called Buddha, or "the enlightened one"). Through meditation, followers of Buddhism strive to overcome selfish cravings for physical or material pleasures, with the goal of reaching a state of enlightenment, or nirvana. Buddhists created the first monastic orders, which are thought to be the models for monastic orders in other religions, including Christianity. Though Buddhism emerged in India, its followers were eventually driven out of that country by the Hindus. It is now found primarily in other parts of Asia. (Contemporary adherents of Buddhism in India are relatively recent converts.)

use your **sociological imagination**

What evidence do you see of different religions in the area surrounding your college or university? What about on campus?

Although the differences among religions are striking, they are exceeded by variations within faiths. Consider the variations within Christianity, from relatively liberal denominations such as Presbyterians or the United Church of Christ to the more conservative Mormons and Greek Orthodox Catholics. Similar variations exist within Hinduism, Islam, and other world religions (Barrett et al. 2008; Swatos 1998).

The Pew Forum on Religion and Public Life conducted a national survey to determine how much Americans know about world religions. Figure 46-1 reproduces some of the questions from the survey. Try testing your own knowledge.

Components of Religion

All religions have certain elements in common, yet those elements are expressed in the distinctive manner of each faith. These patterns of religious behavior, like other patterns of social behavior, are of great interest to sociologists—especially interactionists—because they underscore the relationship between religion and society.

Religious beliefs, religious rituals, and religious experience all help to define what is sacred and to differentiate the sacred from the profane. Let's examine these three components of religion, as seen through the eyes of interactionists.

Belief

Some people believe in life after death, in supreme beings with unlimited powers, or in supernatural forces. **Religious beliefs** are statements to which members of a particular religion adhere. These views can vary dramatically from religion to religion.

In the late 1960s, something rather remarkable took place in the expression of religious beliefs in the United States. Denominations that held to relatively liberal interpretations of religious scripture (such as the Presbyterians, Methodists, and Lutherans) declined in membership, while those that held to more conservative interpretations grew in numbers. Furthermore, in most faiths,

those members who held strict views of scripture became more outspoken, questioning those who remained open to a variety of newer interpretations.

This trend toward *fundamentalism* ran counter to the secularization that was evident in the wider society. **Fundamentalism** may be defined as an emphasis on doctrinal conformity and the literal interpretation of sacred texts. The phrase "religious fundamentalism" was first applied to Protestant believers in the United States who took a literal interpretation of the Bible, but fundamentalism is found worldwide among all major religious groups, including Roman Catholicism, Islam, and Judaism. Even in relatively new faiths, some adherents contend that too much has changed. For followers of many religions, fundamentalists can be as challenging to accommodate as secularists.

Fundamentalists vary immensely in their behavior. Some stress the need to be strict in their own personal faith but take little interest in broad social issues. Others are watchful of societal actions, such as government policies, that they see as conflicting with fundamentalist doctrine.

The Adam and Eve account of creation found in Genesis, the first book of the Old Testament, is an example of a religious belief. Many people in the United States strongly adhere to this biblical explanation of creation and even insist that it be taught in public schools. These people, known as *creationists,* are worried by the secularization of society, and oppose teaching that directly or indirectly questions biblical scripture.

In general, spirituality is not as strong in industrialized nations as in developing nations. The United States is an exception to the trend toward secularization, in part because the government encourages religious expression (without explicitly supporting it) by allowing religious groups to claim charitable status, and even to receive federal aid for activities such as educational services. And although belief in God is relatively weak in formerly communist states such as Russia, surveys show a growth in spirituality in those countries over the past 10 years (Norris and Inglehart 2004).

Ritual

Religious rituals are practices required or expected of members of a faith. Rituals usually honor the divine power (or powers) worshipped by believers; they also remind adherents of their religious duties and responsibilities. Rituals and beliefs can be interdependent; rituals generally affirm beliefs, as in a public or private statement confessing a sin. Like any social institution, religion develops distinctive norms to structure people's behavior. Moreover, sanctions are attached to religious rituals, whether rewards (bar mitzvah gifts) or penalties (expulsion from a religious institution for violation of norms).

In the United States, rituals may be quite simple, such as saying grace at a meal or observing a moment of silence to commemorate someone's death. Yet certain rituals, such as the process of canonizing a saint, are quite elaborate. Most religious rituals in our culture focus on services conducted at houses of worship. Attendance at a service, silent and spoken prayers, communion, and singing of spiritual hymns and chants are common forms of ritual behavior that generally take place in group settings. From an

FIGURE 46-1 **Test Your Religious Knowledge**

Compare your knowledge of religion with that of the U.S. population as a whole. In a 2010 national survey, the average respondent answered seven or eight questions correctly.

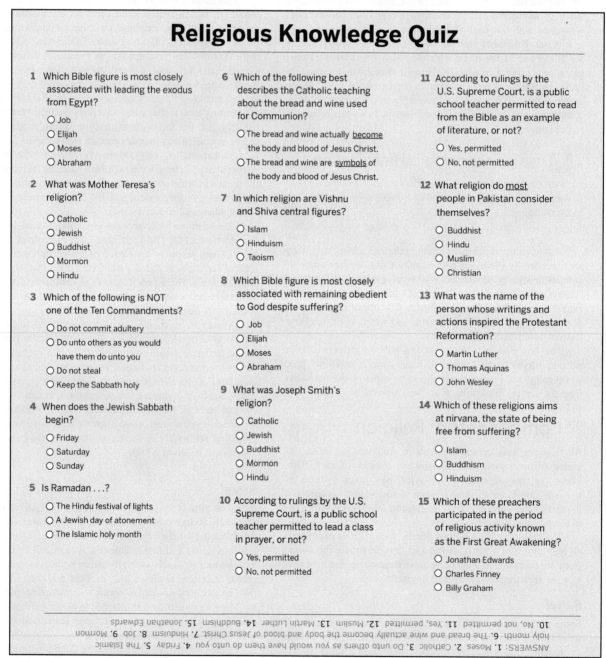

Sources: Pew Forum on Religion and Public Life 2010a, 2010b.

interactionist perspective, these rituals serve as important face-to-face encounters in which people reinforce their religious beliefs and their commitment to their faith.

For Muslims, a very important ritual is the *hajj,* a pilgrimage to the Grand Mosque in Mecca, Saudi Arabia. Every Muslim who is physically and financially able is expected to make this trip at least once. Each year 3 million pilgrims go to Mecca during the one-week period indicated by the Islamic lunar calendar. Muslims from all over the world make the *hajj,* including those in the United States, where many tours are arranged to facilitate the trip.

Pilgrims on *hajj* to the Grand Mosque in Mecca, Saudi Arabia. Islam requires all Muslims who are able to undertake this religious ritual at least once in a lifetime.

a born-again Christian experience at some time in their lives. An earlier survey found that Southern Baptists (75 percent) were the most likely to report such experiences; in contrast, only 21 percent of Catholics and 24 percent of Episcopalians stated that they had been born again. The collective nature of religion, as emphasized by Durkheim, is evident in these statistics. The beliefs and rituals of a particular faith can create an atmosphere either friendly or indifferent to this type of religious experience. Thus, a Baptist would be encouraged to come forward and share such experiences with others, whereas an Episcopalian who claims to have been born again would receive much less interest (Gallup 2011a; Gallup Opinion Index 1978).

Table 46-2 summarizes the three components of religion.

In recent decades, participation in religious rituals has tended to hold steady or decline in most countries. Figure 46-2 shows religious participation in selected countries.

Experience

In the sociological study of religion, the term **religious experience** refers to the feeling or perception of being in direct contact with the ultimate reality, such as a divine being, or of being overcome with religious emotion. A religious experience may be rather slight, such as the feeling of exaltation a person receives from hearing a choir sing Handel's "Hallelujah Chorus." But many religious experiences are more profound, such as a Muslim's experience on a *hajj*. In his autobiography, the late African American activist Malcolm X ([1964] 1999:338) wrote of his *hajj* and how deeply moved he was by the way that Muslims in Mecca came together across race and color lines. For Malcolm X, the color blindness of the Muslim world "proved to me the power of the One God."

Another profound religious experience, for many Christians, is being *born again*—that is, at a turning point in one's life, making a personal commitment to Jesus. According to a 2010 national survey, 42 percent of people in the United States claim they have had

FIGURE 46-2 **Religious Participation in Selected Countries**

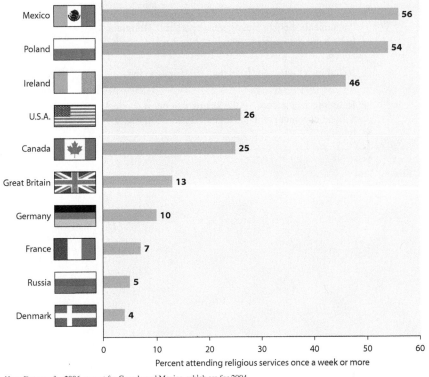

Note: Data are for 2006, except for Canada and Mexico, which are for 2004.
Source: Tom W. Smith 2009:28, 60, 72.

Think about It

Are you surprised by the variation in religious participation from one nation to another? Why or why not?

Table **46-2** Components of Religion

summingup

Element	Definition	Examples
Belief	Statement to which members of a particular religion adhere	Creation account Sacred characters or people
Ritual	Practice required or expected of members of a faith	Worship Prayer Singing or chanting
Experience	Feeling or perception of being in direct contact with the ultimate reality (such as a divine being) or of being overcome with religious emotion	Born-again experience Communion with holy spirit

MODULE 46 | Recap and Review

Summary

Tremendous diversity exists in religious beliefs and practices, although all religions share basic components.

1. Eighty-five percent of the world's population adheres to some form of religion.
2. Religious behavior is expressed through three major components: beliefs, rituals, and experience. **Religious beliefs** are statements to which all members of a faith adhere.
3. **Religious rituals** vary from the very simple to the highly complex.
4. **Religious experience,** or the feeling that one is having a direct encounter with the divine, is part of all major religions.

Thinking Critically

1. Which component of religion is easiest to measure? Which is hardest to measure? Explain.
2. What rituals—either religious or nonreligious—do you perform? Why do you perform them?

Key Terms

Fundamentalism

Religious belief

Religious experience

Religious ritual

MODULE 47 | Religious Organization

The collective nature of religion has led to many forms of religious association. In modern societies, religion has become increasingly formalized. Specific structures such as churches and synagogues have been constructed for religious worship; individuals have been trained for occupational roles within various fields. These developments make it possible to distinguish clearly between the sacred and secular parts of one's life—a distinction that could not be made easily in earlier times, when religion was largely a family activity carried out in the home.

Four Basic Forms of Organization

Sociologists find it useful to distinguish between four basic forms of organization: the ecclesia, the denomination, the sect, and the new religious movement, or cult. We can see differences among these four forms of organization in their size, power, degree of commitment that is expected from members, and historical ties to other faiths.

Ecclesiae

An **ecclesia** (plural, *ecclesiae*) is a religious organization that claims to include most or all members of a society and is recognized as the national or official religion.

Since virtually everyone belongs to the faith, membership is by birth rather than conscious decision. Examples of ecclesiae include Islam in Saudi Arabia and Buddhism in Thailand. However, significant differences exist within this category. In Saudi Arabia's Islamic regime, leaders of the ecclesia hold vast power over actions of the state. In contrast, the Lutheran Church in contemporary Sweden holds no such power over the Riksdag (parliament) or the prime minister.

Generally, ecclesiae are conservative, in that they do not challenge the leaders of a secular government. In a society with an ecclesia, the political and religious institutions often act in harmony and reinforce each other's power in their relative spheres of influence. In the modern world, ecclesiae are declining in power.

Denominations

A **denomination** is a large, organized religion that is not officially linked to the state or government. Like an ecclesia, it tends to have an explicit set of beliefs, a defined system of authority, and a generally respected position in society. Denominations claim as members large segments of a population. Generally, children accept the denomination of their parents and give little thought to membership in other faiths. Denominations also resemble ecclesiae in that they make few demands on members. However, there is a critical difference between these two forms of religious organization. Although the denomination is considered respectable and is not viewed as a challenge to the secular government, it lacks the official recognition and power held by an ecclesia (Doress and Porter 1977).

The United States is home to a large number of denominations. In good measure, this diversity is a result of our nation's immigrant heritage. Many settlers brought with them the religious commitments native to their homelands. Some Christian denominations in the United States, such as the Roman Catholics, Episcopalians, and Lutherans, are the outgrowth of ecclesiae established in Europe. New Christian denominations also emerged, including the Mormons and Christian Scientists. Within the past generation, immigrants have increased the number of Muslims, Hindus, and Buddhists living in the United States.

Although by far the largest denomination in the United States is Roman Catholicism, at least 24 other Christian faiths have 1 million or more members. Protestants collectively accounted for about 45 percent of the nation's adult population in 2010,

trend|spotting

None of the Above: The Nonreligious

Many people noted and were dismayed by a statement in President Obama's 2009 inaugural address, "We are a nation of Christians and Muslims, Jews and Hindus, and nonbelievers." Yet the President was merely acknowledging a long-noted pattern, the gradual growth in the proportion of U.S. residents who indicate they have no religion.

National surveys reveal that between 1990 and 2008, the number of Americans who identify themselves as having no religion doubled. Moreover, the proportion of people who give no answer to questions about religion suggests that currently, about 20 percent of the adult population—well over 60 million people— has no overt religious identity.

The growth of the "none of the above" category does not mean that those respondents do not believe in God, however. A third of them say that they pray weekly or daily, and fewer than 1 percent call themselves atheists. Nevertheless, while the phrase "In God We Trust" still seems to apply, more and more people are choosing not to affiliate themselves with organized religion.

compared to 21 percent for Roman Catholics and 2 percent for Jews. There are also 5 million Muslims in the United States, and large numbers of people adhere to Eastern faiths such as Buddhism (3 million) and Hinduism (1 million) (Britannica Online 2011; Gallup 2011a; Lindner 2012).

Sects

A **sect** can be defined as a relatively small religious group that has broken away from some other religious organization to renew what it considers the original vision of the faith. Many sects, such as that led by Martin Luther during the Reformation, claim to be the "true church," because they seek to cleanse the established faith of what they regard as extraneous beliefs and rituals (Stark and Bainbridge 1985). Max Weber ([1916] 1958:114) termed the sect a "believer's church," because affiliation is based on conscious acceptance of a specific religious dogma.

Sects are fundamentally at odds with society and do not seek to become established national religions. Unlike ecclesiae and denominations, they require intensive commitments and demonstrations of belief by members. Partly owing to their outsider status, sects frequently exhibit a higher degree of religious fervor and loyalty than more established religious groups. Recruitment focuses mainly on adults, and acceptance comes through conversion.

Sects are often short-lived. Those that survive may become less antagonistic to society over time and begin to resemble denominations. In a few instances, sects have endured over several generations while remaining fairly separate from society. Sociologist J. Milton Yinger (1970:226–273) uses the term **established sect** to describe a religious group that is the outgrowth of a sect, yet remains isolated from society. Hutterites, Jehovah's Witnesses, Seventh-Day Adventists, and Amish are contemporary examples of established sects in the United States.

> ## 💡 use your **sociological imagination**
>
> Choose a religious tradition other than your own. How would your religious beliefs, rituals, and experience differ if you had been raised in that tradition?

New Religious Movements or Cults

In 1997, 38 members of the Heaven's Gate cult were found dead in Southern California after a mass suicide timed to occur with the appearance of the Hale-Bopp comet. They believed the comet hid a spaceship on which they could catch a ride once they had broken free of their "bodily containers."

Partly as a result of the notoriety generated by such groups, the popular media have stigmatized the word *cult,* associating it with the occult and the use of intense and forceful conversion techniques. The stereotyping of cults as uniformly bizarre and unethical has led sociologists to abandon the term and refer instead to a *new religious movement (NRM).* While some NRMs exhibit strange behavior, many do not. They attract new members just like any other religion, and often follow teachings similar to those of established Christian denominations, though with less ritual.

Sects are difficult to distinguish from cults. A **new religious movement (NRM)** or **cult** is generally a small, secretive religious group that represents either a new religion or a major innovation of an existing faith. NRMs are similar to sects in that they tend to be small and are often viewed as less respectable than more established faiths. Unlike sects, however, NRMs normally do not result from schisms or breaks with established ecclesiae or denominations. Some cults, such as those focused on UFO sightings, may be totally unrelated to existing faiths. Even when a cult does accept certain fundamental tenets of a dominant faith—such as a belief in Jesus as divine or in Mohammad as a messenger of God—it will offer new revelations or insights to justify its claim to being a more advanced religion (Stark and Bainbridge 1979, 1985).

Like sects, NRMs may be transformed over time into other types of religious organization. An example is the Christian Science Church, which began as a new religious movement under the leadership of Mary Baker Eddy. Today, this church exhibits the characteristics of a denomination. In fact, most major religions, including Christianity, began as cults. NRMs may be in the early stages of developing into a denomination or new religion, or they may just as easily fade away through the loss of members or weak leadership (R. Schaefer and Zellner 2011).

Comparing Forms of Religious Organization

How can we determine whether a particular religious group falls into the sociological category of ecclesia, denomination, sect, or NRM? As we have seen, these types of religious organization have somewhat different relationships to society. Ecclesiae are recognized as national churches; denominations, although not officially approved by the state, are generally widely respected. In contrast, sects and NRMs are much more likely to be at odds with the larger culture.

Still, ecclesiae, denominations, and sects are best viewed as types along a continuum rather than as mutually exclusive categories. Table 47-1 summarizes some of the primary characteristics of the ideal types. Since the United States has no ecclesiae, sociologists studying this country's religions have focused on the denomination and the sect. These religious forms have been pictured on either end of a continuum, with denominations accommodating to the secular world and sects protesting against established religions. Although NRMs also are included in the table, they lie outside the continuum, because they generally define themselves in terms of a new view of life rather than in terms of existing religious faiths. In fact, one of the most controversial NRMs, Wicca, may not fully qualify as a religion (Box 47-1).

Sociologists look at religion from an organizational perspective, which tends to stress the stability of religious adherence, but there are other ways to view religion. From an individual perspective, religion and spirituality are remarkably fluid. People often change their places of worship or move from one denomination to another. In many countries, including the United States, churches, temples, and mosques operate in a highly competitive market (Pew Forum on Religion and Public Life 2008; Wolfe 2008).

Table **47-1**   Characteristics of Ecclesiae, Denominations, Sects, and New Religious Movements

Characteristic	Ecclesia	Denomination	Sect	New Religious Movement (or Cult)
Size	Very large	Large	Small	Small
Wealth	Extensive	Extensive	Limited	Variable
Religious services	Formal, little participation	Formal, little participation	Informal, emotional	Variable
Doctrines	Specific, but interpretation may be tolerated	Specific, but interpretation may be tolerated	Specific, purity of doctrine emphasized	Innovative, pathbreaking
Clergy	Well-trained, full-time	Well-trained, full-time	Trained to some degree	Unspecialized
Membership	By virtue of being a member of society	By acceptance of doctrine	By acceptance of doctrine	By an emotional commitment
Relationship to the state	Recognized, closely aligned	Tolerated	Not encouraged	Ignored or challenged

Source: Adapted from Vernon 1962; see also Chalfant et al. 1994.

Research Today

BOX 47-1

Wicca: Religion or Quasi-Religion?

"I'm not a Witch," Christine O'Donnell famously declared in her 2010 campaign for the U.S. Senate. Eleven years earlier, she admitted, she had dabbled in Witchcraft. To most voters, the idea was beyond the pale. Yet today, thousands of people, both men and women, do view themselves as Witches; they practice a little-known religion called Wicca (which should not be confused with Satanism—there is no place in the Craft for devil worship).

Wicca (Anglo-Saxon for *witch* and *wizard*) is a modern form of Witchcraft, practiced for the last hundred years. The Englishman Gerald Gardner, born in 1884, drew on past rituals to found the Craft. Gardner stressed the importance of worshipping *skyclad,* or "clothed by the sky"—that is, naked. Being skyclad, he believed, helped a person to gain insight.

Not all Wiccans follow in Gardner's tradition. Today, Wiccan ritual takes on a dizzying variety of forms, ranging from the elementary to the highly detailed and sophisticated. A Wiccan circle or meeting can include a single heartfelt prayer or a highly complex and time-consuming ritual. Like members of more accepted religions, Wiccans observe several rituals associated with the life cycle. Parents name their children at a *Wiccaning,* which includes a dedication to the Goddess and the God. Contemporary Wiccans also celebrate a wedding-like ceremony called a *handfasting,* which is typically performed by a High Priest and/or Priestess.

Just as Wiccans' worship varies, so does their organization. Some Witches practice alone, as a *solitaire;* others practice in a group

of similarly minded Witches, called a *coven.* A coven may include just three or four Witches, male and/or female, or as many as thirty; members tend to come and go just as they do in a church or temple. In a mixed coven, the assembly is often governed by a High Priest or Priestess, or by both.

Revealing one's membership in any extraordinary group is always difficult, but perhaps especially so for Wiccans, who refer to the experience as "coming out of the broom closet." Many Wiccans are young, and so must

> *Some Witches practice alone, as a solitaire; others practice in a group of similarly minded Witches, called a coven.*

come out to their parents. Parental reactions range from cutting off contact with the Witch to wanting to learn more about the Craft. Many parents treat the religion as a "phase" in their child's spiritual journey.

Most scholars treat Wicca as a **quasi-religion,** a category that includes organizations that may see themselves as religious, but are seen by others as "sort of religious." National surveys that allow respondents to self-identify showed 8,000 Wiccans in 1990; 134,000 in 2001; and 342,000 in 2008, the latest year for which reliable national data are available. These estimates suggest either an

increase in willingness to identify as Wiccan or an absolute growth in the faithful—probably both.

LET'S DISCUSS

1. Do you know anyone who practices Wicca? If so, describe the person's practices.

2. Do you think that Wicca should be considered a religion? Why or why not?

Sources: Chase 2010; M. Howard 2009; Kosmin and Keysar 2009; Rabikovitch and Lewis 2004; R. Schaefer and Zellner 2011:347–377.

case study | Religion in India

From a sociological point of view, the nation of India is large and complex enough that it might be considered a world of its own. Four hundred languages are spoken in India, 16 of which are officially recognized by the government. Besides the two major religions that originated there—Hinduism and Buddhism—several other faiths animate this society. Demographically the nation is huge, with over a billion residents. This teeming country is expected to overtake China as the most populous nation in the world in about three decades (Third World Institute 2007).

The Religious Tapestry in India

Hinduism and Islam, the two most important religions in India, were described in Module 46. Islam arrived in India in A.D. 1000, with the first of many Muslim invasions. It flowered there during the Mogul empire (1526–1857), the period when the Taj Mahal was built. Today, Muslims account for 12 percent of India's population; Hindus make up 83 percent.

The presence of one dominant faith influences how a society views a variety of issues, even secular ones. For example, India has emerged as a leader in biotechnology, due at least partly to the Hindu faith's tolerance of stem cell research and cloning—techniques that have been questioned in nations where Christianity dominates. Hinduism is open to the latest biomedical techniques, as long as no evil is intended. The only legal prohibition is that fetuses cannot be terminated for the purpose of providing stem cells. Because of its respect for life in all forms, Hinduism has no major conflict with engineered life-forms of any kind, such as clones (Religion Watch 2006; Sengupta 2006).

Another religion, the Sikh faith, originated in the 15th century with a Hindu named Nanak, the first of a series of gurus (prophets). Sikhism shows the influence of Islam in India, in that it is monotheistic (based on a belief in one god rather than many). It resembles Buddhism in its emphasis on meditation and spiritual transcendence of the everyday world. *Sikhs* (learners) pursue their goal of spiritual enlightenment through meditation with the help of a guru.

Sikh men have a characteristic mode of dress, which in the United States often causes them to be mistaken—and discriminated against—as Muslims. They are highly patriotic. Although the 20 million Sikhs in India make up just 2 percent of the country's population, they account for 25 percent of India's army. In 2004 Manmohan Singh, a Sikh, became Prime Minister of India—an event that is almost comparable to a Black man becoming President of the United States. He is now serving his second term (Fausset 2003; Watson 2005).

Another group that forms a small segment of the faithful, Christians, plays a disproportionate role in the country's social safety net. Christian schools, hospitals, and other social service organizations serve non-Christians as well as Christians. Interestingly, hundreds of priests who were trained at churches in India have since immigrated to the United States to ease the shortage of priests there. Together with Jains and Buddhists, Christians make up 3 percent of India's population (Embree 2003; Goodstein 2008).

Religion and the State in India

Religion was influential in India's drive to overturn British colonialism. The great Mohandas K. Gandhi (1869–1948) led the long struggle to regain India's sovereignty, which culminated in its independence in 1947. A proponent of nonviolent resistance, Gandhi persuaded Hindus and Muslims, ancient enemies, to join in defying British domination. But his influence as a peacemaker could not override the Muslims' demand for a separate state of their own. Immediately after independence was granted, India was partitioned into two states, Pakistan for the Muslims and India for the Hindus. The new arrangement caused large-scale migrations of Indians, especially Muslims, from one nation to the other, and

Adherents of the Hindu religion participate in fire worship at a celebration in Kerala, India. The Hindu faith is enormously influential in India, the country where most Hindus live.

sparked boundary disputes that continue to this day. In many areas, Muslims were forced to abandon places they considered sacred. In the chaotic months that followed, centuries of animosity between the two groups boiled over into riots, ending in Gandhi's assassination in January 1948.

Today, India is a secular state that is dominated by Hindus. Though the government is officially tolerant of the Muslim minority, tensions between Hindus and Muslims remain high in some states. Conflict also exists among various Hindu

groups, from fundamentalists to more secular and ecumenical adherents (Embree 2003).

Many observers see religion as the moving force in Indian society. As in so many other parts of the world, religion is being redefined in India. To the dismay of Sikh spiritual leaders, increasing numbers of young Sikh men are trimming their long hair and abandoning the traditional turban. To show that the 300-year-old tradition is still cool in the 21st century, Sikh leaders now offer a CD-ROM called "Smart Turban 1.0" (Gentleman 2007).

One sign of this fluidity is the rapid rise of still another form of religious organization, the electronic church. Facilitated by cable television and satellite transmission, *televangelists* (as they are called) direct their messages to more people—especially in the United States—than are served by all but the largest denominations. While some televangelists are affiliated with religious denominations, most give viewers the impression that they are dissociated from established faiths.

At the close of the 1990s, the electronic church began to take on another dimension: the Internet. Today, rather than going to a service in person, many people shop online for a church or faith. Surfers can go to GodTube.com, a video-sharing and social-networking website, for spiritually oriented content. Even the Second Life virtual world (described in Chapter 5) has a rich spiritual landscape, with functioning congregations of Buddhist, Jewish, Muslim, and Christian avatars (Kiper 2008; MacDonald 2007; Simon 2007).

social policy and Religion | Religion in the Schools

Should public schools be allowed to sponsor organized prayer in the classroom? How about Bible reading, or just a collective moment of silence? Can athletes at public schools offer up a group prayer in a team huddle? Should students be able to initiate voluntary prayers at school events? Each of these situations has been an object of great dissension among those who see a role for prayer in the schools and those who want to maintain strict separation of church and state.

Another controversy concerns the teaching of theories about the origin of humans and the universe. Mainstream scientific thinking holds that humans evolved over billions of years from one-celled organisms, and that the universe came into being 15 billion years ago as a result of a huge cosmic explosion (the big bang theory). These theories are challenged by people who hold to the biblical account of the creation of humans and the universe some 10,000 years ago—a viewpoint known as **creationism.** Creationists, many of whom are Christian fundamentalists, want their belief taught in the schools as the only one—or at the very least, as an alternative to the theory of evolution.

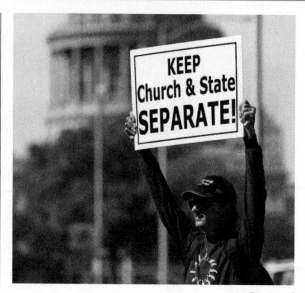

—Continued

—Continued

Looking at the Issue

The issues just described go to the heart of the First Amendment's provisions regarding religious freedom. On the one hand, the government must protect the right to practice one's religion; on the other, it cannot take any measures that would seem to establish one religion over another (separation of church and state).

In the key case of *Engle v. Vitale,* the Supreme Court ruled in 1962 that the use of nondenominational prayer in New York schools was "wholly inconsistent" with the First Amendment's prohibition against government establishment of religion. In finding that organized school prayer violated the Constitution—even when no student was required to participate—the Court argued, in effect, that promoting religious observance was not a legitimate function of government or education. Subsequent Court decisions have allowed *voluntary* school prayer by students, but forbid school officials to *sponsor* any prayer or religious observance at school events. Despite these rulings, many public schools still regularly lead their students in prayer recitations or Bible readings. Other states have enacted "moments of silence" during the public school day, which many see as prayer in disguise (Robelon 2007).

As with school prayer, the teaching of creationism has significant support among the general public. Unlike Europeans, many people in the United States seem highly skeptical of evolutionary theory, which is taught as a matter of course in science classes. In 2009, a national survey showed that 39 percent of adults believe that God created humans in their present form. Almost as many believe that humans developed their present form with divine guidance (Gallup 2009a; Newport 2009).

The controversy over whether the biblical account of creation should be presented in school curricula recalls the famous "monkey trial" of 1925. In that trial, high school biology teacher John T. Scopes was convicted of violating a Tennessee law making it a crime to teach the scientific theory of evolution in public schools. Today, creationists have gone beyond espousing fundamentalist religious doctrine; they are attempting to reinforce their position regarding the origins of humanity and the universe with quasi-scientific data.

In 1987, the Supreme Court ruled that states could not compel the teaching of creationism in public schools if the primary purpose was to promote a religious viewpoint. In response, those who believe in the divine origin of life have recently advanced a concept called **intelligent design (ID),** the idea that life is so complex that it could only have been created by intelligent design. Though this concept is not based explicitly on the biblical account of creation, fundamentalists feel comfortable with it. Supporters of intelligent design

People on both sides of the debate between science and creationism invoke the name of Albert Einstein. Evolutionists emphasize the need for verifiable scientific data, like that which confirmed Einstein's groundbreaking scientific theories. Advocates of intelligent design quote the Nobel Prize–winning physicist's assertion that religion and science should coexist.

consider it a more accurate account of the origin of life than Darwinism and hold that at the very least, ID should be taught as an alternative to the theory of evolution. But in 2005, in *Kitzmiller v. Dove Area School District,* a federal judge ended a Pennsylvania school district's plans to require teachers to present the concept in class. In essence, the judge found ID to be "a religious belief," a subtler but similar approach to creationism in that both find God's fingerprints in nature. The issue continues to be hotly debated and is expected to be the subject of future court cases (Clemmitt 2005; W. Tierney and Holley 2008).

Applying Sociology

Supporters of school prayer and of creationism feel that strict Court rulings have forced too great a separation between what Émile Durkheim called the *sacred* and the *profane*. They insist that the use of nondenominational prayer can in no way lead to the establishment of an ecclesia in the United States. Moreover, they believe that school prayer—and the teaching of creationism—can provide the spiritual guidance and socialization that many children today do not receive from parents or regular church attendance.

Many communities also believe that schools should transmit the dominant culture of the United States by encouraging prayer. Opponents of school prayer and creationism argue that a religious majority in a community might impose viewpoints specific to its faith at the expense of religious

—Continued

—Continued

minorities. These critics question whether school prayer can remain truly voluntary. Drawing on the interactionist perspective and small-group research, they suggest that children will face enormous social pressure to conform to the beliefs and practices of the majority.

Initiating Policy

Public school education is fundamentally a local issue, so most initiatives and lobbying have taken place at the local or state level. Federal courts have taken a hard line on religion in the schools. In a decision that the Supreme Court reversed in 2004, a federal appeals court ruled that reciting the phrase "under God" during the Pledge of Allegiance that opens each school day violates the U.S. Constitution (Religion News Service 2003).

Religion–school debates show no sign of ending. The activism of religious fundamentalists in the public school system raises the question "Whose ideas and values deserve a hearing in classrooms?" Critics see this campaign as one step toward sectarian religious control of public education. They worry that at some point in the future, teachers may not be able to use books or make statements that conflict with fundamentalist interpretations of the Bible. For advocates of a liberal education and of intellectual (and religious) diversity, this is a genuinely frightening prospect (Wilgoren 2005).

TAKE THE ISSUE WITH YOU

1. Was there organized prayer in any school you attended? Was creationism part of the curriculum?
2. Do you think that promoting religious observance is a legitimate function of education?
3. How might a conflict theorist view the issue of organized school prayer?

MODULE 47 | Recap and Review

Summary

Religious organizations grow and evolve over time and in reaction to social changes.

1. Four basic types of religious organizations are the **ecclesia,** the **denomination,** the **sect,** and the **new religious movement,** or **cult.**

2. Advances in communication have led to a new type of church organization, the electronic church. Televangelists now preach to more people than belong to many denominations, and every day millions of people use the Internet for religious purposes.

3. India is a secular state that is dominated by a religious majority, the Hindus. The creation of a separate nation, Pakistan, for the Muslim minority following India's independence in 1947 did not end the centuries-old strife between the two groups, which has worsened with political polarization.

4. Today, the question of how much religion, if any, should be permitted in the U.S. public schools is a matter of intense debate.

Thinking Critically

1. What do you think attracts people to new religious movements?

2. Aside from differences in religious affiliation, how does religious life in India differ from religious life in the United States?

Key Terms

Creationism

Denomination

Ecclesia

Established sect

Intelligent design

New religious movement (NRM) or **cult**

Quasi-religion

Sect

Mastering This Chapter: Religion

taking sociology with you

1 Make a list of the student subcultures on your campus, then describe them using the concepts you learned in Chapter 3. Do any of these subcultures serve as out-groups for other subcultures?

2 Find out how many different religious groups there are at your school or in your community. How many belong to mainstream denominations? How many are

fundamentalist? Are there any sects or new religious movements?

3 If your school or community has an interfaith organization, attend a meeting. What issues are the members currently dealing with? What sociological concepts are relevant to those issues?

key terms

Creationism A literal interpretation of the Bible regarding the creation of humanity and the universe, used to argue that evolution should not be presented as established scientific fact.

Denomination A large, organized religion that is not officially linked to the state or government.

Ecclesia A religious organization that claims to include most or all members of a society and is recognized as the national or official religion.

Established sect A religious group that is the outgrowth of a sect, yet remains isolated from society.

Fundamentalism An emphasis on doctrinal conformity and the literal interpretation of sacred texts.

Intelligent design (ID) The idea that life is so complex that it could only have been created by intelligent design.

Liberation theology Use of a church, primarily Roman Catholic, in a political effort to eliminate poverty, discrimination, and other forms of injustice from a secular society.

New religious movement (NRM) or **cult** A small, secretive religious group that represents either a new religion or a major innovation of an existing faith.

Profane The ordinary and commonplace elements of life, as distinguished from the sacred.

Protestant ethic Max Weber's term for the disciplined work ethic, this-worldly concerns, and rational orientation to life emphasized by John Calvin and his followers.

Quasi-religion A scholarly category that includes organizations that may see themselves as religious but may be seen by others as "sort of religious."

Religion A unified system of beliefs and practices relative to sacred things.

Religious belief A statement to which members of a particular religion adhere.

Religious experience The feeling or perception of being in direct contact with the ultimate reality, such as a divine being, or of being overcome with religious emotion.

Religious ritual A practice required or expected of members of a faith.

Sacred Elements beyond everyday life that inspire awe, respect, and even fear.

Sect A relatively small religious group that has broken away from some other religious organization to renew what it considers the original vision of the faith.

Secularization The process through which religion's influence on other social institutions diminishes.

self-quiz

Read each question carefully and then select the best answer.

1. Which of the following sociologists stressed the social impact of religion and was perhaps the first to recognize the critical importance of religion in human societies?
   a. Max Weber
   b. Karl Marx
   c. Émile Durkheim
   d. Talcott Parsons

2. A Roman Catholic parish church offers services in the native language of an immigrant community. This is an example of
   a. the integrative function of religion.
   b. the social support function of religion.
   c. the social control function of religion.
   d. none of the above.

3. Sociologist Max Weber pointed out that the followers of John Calvin emphasized a disciplined work ethic, this-worldly concerns, and a rational orientation to life. Collectively, this point of view has been referred to as
   a. capitalism.
   b. the Protestant ethic.
   c. the sacred.
   d. the profane.

4. The use of a church, primarily Roman Catholic, in a political effort to eliminate poverty, discrimination, and other forms of injustice evident in a secular society is referred to as
   a. creationism.
   b. ritualism.
   c. religious experience.
   d. liberation theology.

5. Many people in the United States strongly adhere to the biblical explanation of the beginning of the universe. Adherents of this point of view are known as
   a. liberationists.
   b. creationists.
   c. ritualists.
   d. experimentalists.

6. The Adam and Eve account of creation found in Genesis, the first book of the Old Testament, is an example of a religious
   a. ritual.
   b. experience.

c. custom.
d. belief.

7. Which of the following is *not* an example of an ecclesia?
   a. the Lutheran church in Sweden
   b. Islam in Saudi Arabia
   c. Buddhism in Thailand
   d. the Episcopal church in the United States

8. Religion defines the spiritual world and gives meaning to the divine. These are _____ functions of religion.
   a. manifest
   b. latent
   c. positive
   d. negative

9. Which sociological perspective emphasizes the integrative power of religion in human society?
   a. functionalist perspective
   b. conflict perspective
   c. interactionist perspective
   d. all of the above

10. John Calvin, a leader of the Protestant Reformation, emphasized
    a. disciplined work ethic.
    b. this-worldly concerns.
    c. a rational orientation to life.
    d. all of the above.

11. The _____ encompasses elements beyond everyday life that inspire awe, respect, and even fear, as compared to the _____, which includes the ordinary and the commonplace.

12. Wicca is an example of a(n) _____.

13. _____ is the largest single faith in the world; the second largest is _____.

14. _____ _____ are statements to which members of a particular religion adhere.

15. A(n) _____ is a religious organization that claims to include most or all members of a society and is recognized as the national or official religion.

16. Because they are _____, most religions tend to reinforce men's dominance in secular as well as spiritual matters.

17. The single largest denomination in the United States is _____ _____.

18. The big bang theory is challenged by _____, who hold to the biblical account of creation of humans and the universe.

19. Unlike ecclesiae and denominations, _____ require intensive commitments and demonstrations of belief by members.

20. A possible dysfunction of _____ _____ would be the belief that when Roman Catholics focus on political and governmental injustice, the clergy are no longer addressing people's personal and spiritual needs.

Answers

1 (c); 2(a); 3 (b); 4 (d); 5 (b); 6 (d); 7 (d); 8 (a); 9 (a); 10 (d); 11 sacred; profane; 12 quasi-religion; 13 Christianity; Islam; 14 Religious beliefs; 15 ecclesia; 16 patriarchal; 17 Roman Catholicism; 18 creationists; 19 sects; 20 liberation theology

thinking about movies

Monsieur Ibrahim

In this film, which draws comparisons between Islam and Judaism, a Muslim grocer befriends a Jewish boy.

Saved!

A young woman tries to find her own voice in a Christian high school.

Trembling Before G-D

This documentary explores the tension between religious belief and sexual orientation.

glossary

Numbers following the definitions indicate pages where the terms were identified. Consult the index for further page references.

a

Absolute poverty A minimum level of subsistence that no family should be expected to live below. (212)

Achieved status A social position that a person attains largely through his or her own efforts. (115, 197)

Activity theory An interactionist theory of aging that suggests that those elderly people who remain active and socially involved will be best adjusted. (309)

Adoption In a legal sense, the transfer of the legal rights, responsibilities, and privileges of parenthood to a new legal parent or parents. (339)

Affirmative action Positive efforts to recruit minority group members or women for jobs, promotions, and educational opportunities. (259, 422)

Ageism Prejudice and discrimination based on a person's age. (318)

Agrarian society The most technologically advanced form of preindustrial society. Members engage primarily in the production of food, but increase their crop yields through technological innovations such as the plow. (125)

Alienation A condition of estrangement or dissociation from the surrounding society. (132)

Amalgamation The process through which a majority group and a minority group combine to form a new group. (264)

Anomie Durkheim's term for the loss of direction felt in a society when social control of individual behavior has become ineffective. (11, 177)

Anomie theory of deviance Robert Merton's theory of deviance as an adaptation of socially prescribed goals or of the means governing their attainment, or both. (177)

Anticipatory socialization Processes of socialization in which a person rehearses for future positions, occupations, and social relationships. (97)

Anti-Semitism Anti-Jewish prejudice. (274)

Apartheid A former policy of the South African government, designed to maintain the separation of Blacks and other non-Whites from the dominant Whites. (264)

Applied sociology The use of the discipline of sociology with the specific intent of yielding practical applications for human behavior and organizations. (A-1)

Argot Specialized language used by members of a group or subculture. (77)

Ascribed status A social position assigned to a person by society without regard for the person's unique talents or characteristics. (114, 197)

Assembling perspective A theory of collective behavior introduced by McPhail and Miller that seeks to examine how and why people move from different points in space to a common location. (56.1-3)

Assimilation The process through which a person forsakes his or her cultural tradition to become part of a different culture. (265)

Authority Institutionalized power that is recognized by the people over whom it is exercised. (402)

b

Basic sociology Sociological inquiry conducted with the objective of gaining a more profound knowledge of the fundamental aspects of social phenomena. Also known as *pure sociology.* (22)

Bilateral descent A kinship system in which both sides of a person's family are regarded as equally important. (330)

Bilingualism The use of two languages in a particular setting, such as the workplace or schoolroom, treating each language as equally legitimate. (79)

Birthrate The number of live births per 1,000 population in a given year. Also known as the *crude birthrate.* (55.1-2)

Black power A political philosophy, promoted by many younger Blacks in the 1960s, that supported the creation of Black-controlled political and economic institutions. (267)

Borderlands The area of common culture along the border between Mexico and the United States. (241)

Bourgeoisie Karl Marx's term for the capitalist class, comprising the owners of the means of production. (203)

Brain drain The immigration to the United States and other industrialized nations of skilled workers, professionals, and technicians who are desperately needed in their home countries. (435)

Brass ceiling An invisible barrier that blocks the promotion of a woman in the military because of her official (not necessarily actual) exclusion from combat. (F-1)

Bureaucracy A component of formal organization that uses rules and hierarchical ranking to achieve efficiency. (131)

Bureaucratization The process by which a group, organization, or social movement becomes increasingly bureaucratic. (133)

c

Capitalism An economic system in which the means of production are held largely in private hands and the main incentive for economic activity is the accumulation of profits. (203, 415)

Caste A hereditary rank, usually religiously dictated, that tends to be fixed and immobile. (199)

Causal logic The relationship between a condition or variable and a particular consequence, with one leading to the other. (34)

Census An enumeration, or counting, of a population. (55.1-2)

Charismatic authority Max Weber's term for power made legitimate by a leader's exceptional personal or emotional appeal to his or her followers. (402)

Charter school An experimental school that is developed and managed by individuals, groups of parents, or an educational management organization. (371)

Class A group of people who have a similar level of wealth and income. (204)

Class consciousness In Karl Marx's view, a subjective awareness held by members of a class regarding their common vested interests and the need for collective political action to bring about social change. (203)

Class system A social ranking based primarily on economic position in which achieved characteristics can influence social mobility. (201)

Classical theory An approach to the study of formal organizations that views workers as being motivated almost entirely by economic rewards. (134)

Clinical sociology The use of the discipline of sociology with the specific intent of altering social relationships or restructuring social institutions. (22)

Closed system A social system in which there is little or no possibility of individual social mobility. (216)

Coalition A temporary or permanent alliance geared toward a common goal. (130)

Code of ethics The standards of acceptable behavior developed by and for members of a profession. (45)

Cognitive theory of development Jean Piaget's theory that children's thought progresses through four stages of development. (96)

Cohabitation The practice of living together as a male–female couple without marrying. (344)

Collective behavior In the view of sociologist Neil Smelser, the relatively spontaneous and unstructured behavior of a group of people who are reacting to a common influence in an ambiguous situation. (56.1-1)

Colonialism The maintenance of political, social, economic, and cultural domination over a people by a foreign power for an extended period. (227)

Color-blind racism The use of the principle of race neutrality to defend a racially unequal status quo. (255, 422)

Communism As an ideal type, an economic system under which all property is communally owned and no social distinctions are made on the basis of people's ability to produce. (417)

Community A spatial or political unit of social organization that gives people a sense of belonging, based either on shared residence in a particular place or on a common identity. (55.2-1)

Computer-mediated communication Communicative interaction through two or more networked devices, such as a computer or cell phone. The term applies to a variety of text-based or video interactions, including e-mails, chat rooms, and text messages, some of which may be supported by social media. (465)

Concentric-zone theory A theory of urban growth devised by Ernest Burgess that sees growth in terms of a series of rings radiating from the central business district. (55.2-3)

Conflict perspective A sociological approach that assumes that social behavior is best understood in terms of tension between groups over power or the allocation of resources, including housing, money, access to services, and political representation. (16)

Conformity Going along with peers—individuals of our own status who have no special right to direct our behavior. (170)

Conspicuous consumption Purchasing goods not to survive but to flaunt one's superior wealth and social standing. (204)

Contact hypothesis An interactionist perspective which states that in cooperative circumstances, interracial contact between people of equal status will reduce prejudice. (263)

Content analysis The systematic coding and objective recording of data, guided by some rationale. (A-1)

Control group The subjects in an experiment who are not introduced to the independent variable by the researcher. (43)

Control theory A view of conformity and deviance that suggests that our connection to members of society leads us to systematically conform to society's norms. (173)

Control variable A factor that is held constant to test the relative impact of an independent variable. (37)

Corporate welfare Tax breaks, bailouts, direct payments, and grants that the government gives to corporations. (244)

Correlation A relationship between two variables in which a change in one coincides with a change in the other. (34)

Correspondence principle A term used by Bowles and Gintis to refer to the tendency of schools to promote the values expected of individuals in each social class and to perpetuate social class divisions from one generation to the next. (363)

Counterculture A subculture that deliberately opposes certain aspects of the larger culture. (78)

Craze An exciting mass involvement that lasts for a relatively long period. (56.1-7)

Creationism A literal interpretation of the Bible regarding the creation of humanity and the universe, used to argue that evolution should not be presented as established scientific fact. (393)

Credentialism An increase in the lowest level of education needed to enter a field. (362)

Crime A violation of criminal law for which some governmental authority applies formal penalties. (182)

Cross-tabulation A table or matrix that shows the relationship between two or more variables. (52)

Crowd A temporary gathering of people in close proximity who share a common focus or interest. (56.1-4)

Cultural capital Noneconomic goods, such as family background and education, which are reflected in a knowledge of language and the arts. (14)

Cultural convergence The flow of content across multiple media, and the accompanying migration of media audiences. (145)

Cultural relativism The viewing of people's behavior from the perspective of their own culture. (62)

Cultural transmission A school of criminology that argues that criminal behavior is learned through social interactions. (178)

Cultural universal A common practice or belief found in every culture. (62)

Culture The totality of learned, socially transmitted customs, knowledge, material objects, and behavior. (61)

Culture industry The worldwide media industry that standardizes the goods and services demanded by consumers. (62)

Culture lag A period of maladjustment when the nonmaterial culture is still struggling to adapt to new material conditions. (76, 470)

Culture shock The feeling of surprise and disorientation that people experience when they encounter cultural practices that are different from their own. (79)

Culture war The polarization of society over controversial cultural elements. (71)

Curanderismo Latino folk medicine, a form of holistic health care and healing. (440)

d

Death rate The number of deaths per 1,000 population in a given year. Also known as the *crude death rate*. (55.1-2)

Degradation ceremony An aspect of the socialization process within some total institutions, in which people are subjected to humiliating rituals. (98)

Deindustrialization The systematic, widespread withdrawal of investment in basic aspects of productivity, such as factories and plants. (421)

Democracy In a literal sense, government by the people. (403)

Demographic transition A term used to describe the change from high birthrates and death rates to low birthrates and death rates. (55.1-4)

Demography The scientific study of population. (55.1-1)

Denomination A large, organized religion that is not officially linked to the state or government. (G-1)

Dependency theory An approach that contends that industrialized nations continue to exploit developing countries for their own gain. (230)

Dependent variable The variable in a causal relationship that is subject to the influence of another variable. (34)

Deviance Behavior that violates the standards of conduct or expectations of a group or society. (175)

Dictatorship A government in which one person has nearly total power to make and enforce laws. (403)

Differential association A theory of deviance proposed by Edwin Sutherland that holds that violation of rules results from exposure to attitudes favorable to criminal acts. (179)

Differential justice Differences in the way social control is exercised over different groups. (181)

Diffusion The process by which a cultural item spreads from group to group or society to society. (74)

Digital divide The relative lack of access to the latest technologies among low-income groups, racial and ethnic minorities, rural residents, and the citizens of developing countries. (153)

Disaster A sudden or disruptive event or set of events that overtaxes a community's resources, so that outside aid is necessary. (56.1-5)

Discovery The process of making known or sharing the existence of an aspect of reality. (73)

Discrimination The denial of opportunities and equal rights to individuals and groups because of prejudice or other arbitrary reasons. (256)

Disengagement theory A functionalist theory of aging that suggests that society and the aging individual mutually sever many of their relationships. (308)

Domestic partnership Two unrelated adults who share a mutually caring relationship, reside together, and agree to be jointly responsible for their dependents, basic living expenses, and other common necessities. (349)

Dominant ideology A set of cultural beliefs and practices that helps to maintain powerful social, economic, and political interests. (3.1-1)

Double consciousness The division of an individual's identity into two or more social realities. (13)

Downsizing Reductions taken in a company's workforce as part of deindustrialization. (421)

Dramaturgical approach A view of social interaction, popularized by Erving Goffman, in which people are seen as theatrical performers. (18, 94)

Dysfunction An element or process of a society that may disrupt the social system or reduce its stability. (16)

e

Ecclesia A religious organization that claims to include most or all members of a society and is recognized as the national or official religion. (389)

Ecological modernization The alignment of environmentally favorable practices with economic self-interest through constant adaptation and restructuring. (449)

Economic system The social institution through which goods and services are produced, distributed, and consumed. (401)

Education A formal process of learning in which some people consciously teach, while others adopt the social role of learner. (357)

Egalitarian family An authority pattern in which spouses are regarded as equals. (332)

Elite model A view of society as being ruled by a small group of individuals who share a common set of political and economic interests. (413)

Emergent-norm perspective A theory of collective behavior proposed by Turner and Killian that holds that a collective definition of appropriate or inappropriate behavior emerges during episodes of collective behavior. (56.1-2)

Endogamy The restriction of mate selection to people within the same group. (336)

Environmental justice A legal strategy based on claims that racial minorities are subjected disproportionately to environmental hazards. (449)

Environmental refugee A person who has been displaced by rising seas, destructive storms, expanding deserts, water shortages, or high levels of toxic pollutants. (452)

Equilibrium model Talcott Parsons's functionalist view that society tends toward a state of stability or balance. (468)

Established sect J. Milton Yinger's term for a religious group that is the outgrowth of a sect, yet remains isolated from society. (390)

Estate system A system of stratification under which peasants were required to work land leased to them by nobles in exchange for military protection and other services. Also known as *feudalism*. (201)

Esteem The reputation that a specific person has earned within an occupation. (208)

Ethnic group A group that is set apart from others primarily because of its national origin or distinctive cultural patterns. (251)

Ethnocentrism The tendency to assume that one's own culture and way of life represent the norm or are superior to all others. (62, 255)

Ethnography The study of an entire social setting through extended systematic fieldwork. (40)

Euthanasia The act of bringing about the death of a hopelessly ill and suffering person in a relatively quick and painless way for reasons of mercy. (321)

Evolutionary theory A theory of social change that holds that society is moving in a definite direction. (467)

Exogamy The requirement that people select a mate outside certain groups. (336)

Experiment An artificially created situation that allows a researcher to manipulate variables. (42)

Experimental group The subjects in an experiment who are exposed to an independent variable introduced by a researcher. (43)

Exploitation theory A Marxist theory that views racial subordination in the United States as a manifestation of the class system inherent in capitalism. (262)

Expressiveness Concern for the maintenance of harmony and the internal emotional affairs of the family. (289)

Extended family A family in which relatives—such as grandparents, aunts, or uncles—live in the same home as parents and their children. (329)

f

Face-work A term used by Erving Goffman to refer to the efforts people make to maintain the proper image and avoid public embarrassment. (95)

Fad A temporary pattern of behavior that involves large numbers of people and is independent of preceding trends. (56.1-6)

False consciousness A term used by Karl Marx to describe an attitude held by members of a class that does not accurately reflect their objective position. (203, 462)

Familism (*Familismo*) Pride in the extended family, expressed through the maintenance of close ties and strong obligations to kinfolk outside the immediate family. (338)

Family A set of people related by blood, marriage or some other agreed-on relationship, or adoption, who share the primary responsibility for reproduction and caring for members of society. (329)

Fashion A pleasurable mass involvement that has a line of historical continuity. (56.1-6)

Feminism The belief in social, economic, and political equality for women. (297)

Feminist perspective A sociological approach that views inequity in gender as central to all behavior and organization. (17)

Feminization of poverty A trend in which women constitute an increasing proportion of the poor people of both the United States and the world. (213)

Fertility The level of reproduction in a society. (55.1-1)

Flash mob A group of people organized by social media to assemble suddenly in a public space, perform some collective activity, and then quickly disperse. (56.1-4)

Folkway A norm governing everyday behavior whose violation raises comparatively little concern. (68)

Force The actual or threatened use of coercion to impose one's will on others. (401)

Formal norm A norm that has been written down and that specifies strict punishments for violators. (68)

Formal organization A group designed for a special purpose and structured for maximum efficiency. (131)

Formal social control Social control that is carried out by authorized agents, such as police officers, judges, school administrators, and employers. (172)

Functionalist perspective A sociological approach that emphasizes the way in which the parts of a society are structured to maintain its stability. (15)

Fundamentalism An emphasis on doctrinal conformity and the literal interpretation of sacred texts. (385)

g

Gatekeeping The process by which a relatively small number of people in the media industry control what material eventually reaches the audience. (148)

Gemeinschaft A term used by Ferdinand Tönnies to describe a close-knit community, often found in rural areas, in which strong personal bonds unite members. (55.3-1)

Gender role Expectations regarding the proper behavior, attitudes, and activities of males and females. (100, 285)

Generalized other A term used by George Herbert Mead to refer to the attitudes, viewpoints, and expectations of society as a whole that a child takes into account in his or her behavior. (94)

Genocide The deliberate, systematic killing of an entire people or nation. (263)

Gentrification The resettlement of low-income city neighborhoods by prosperous families and business firms. (55.3-6)

Gerontology The scientific study of the sociological and psychological aspects of aging and the problems of the aged. (308)

Gesellschaft A term used by Ferdinand Tönnies to describe a community, often urban, that is large and impersonal, with little commitment to the group or consensus on values. (55.3-1)

Glass ceiling An invisible barrier that blocks the promotion of a qualified individual in a work environment because of the individual's gender, race, or ethnicity. (F-1)

Globalization The worldwide integration of government policies, cultures, social movements, and financial markets through trade and the exchange of ideas. (22, 230)

Goal displacement Overzealous conformity to official regulations of a bureaucracy. (132)

Group Any number of people with similar norms, values, and expectations who interact with one another on a regular basis. (117, 127)

Growth rate The difference between births and deaths, plus the difference between immigrants and emigrants, per 1,000 population. (55.1-3)

h

Hate crime A criminal offense committed because of the offender's bias against a race, religion, ethnic group, national origin, or sexual orientation. Also referred to as *bias crime*. (185, 255)

Hawthorne effect The unintended influence that observers of experiments can have on their subjects. (43)

Health As defined by the World Health Organization, a state of complete physical, mental, and social well-being, and not merely the absence of disease and infirmity. (433)

Hidden curriculum Standards of behavior that are deemed proper by society and are taught subtly in schools. (362)

Holistic medicine Therapies in which the health care practitioner considers the person's physical, mental, emotional, and spiritual characteristics. (444)

Homogamy The conscious or unconscious tendency to select a mate with personal characteristics similar to one's own. (336)

Homophobia Fear of and prejudice against homosexuality. (285)

Horizontal mobility The movement of an individual from one social position to another of the same rank. (216)

Horticultural society A preindustrial society in which people plant seeds and crops rather than merely subsist on available foods. (125)

Hospice care Treatment of the terminally ill in their own homes, or in special hospital units or other facilities, with the goal of helping them to die easily, without pain. (315)

Human ecology An area of study that is concerned with the interrelationships between people and their environment. (55.2-3)

Human relations approach An approach to the study of formal organizations that emphasizes the role of people, communication, and participation in a bureaucracy and tends to focus on the informal structure of the organization. (135)

Hunting-and-gathering society A preindustrial society in which people rely on whatever foods and fibers are readily available in order to survive. (124)

Hyperconsumerism The practice of buying more than we need or want, and often more than we can afford; a preoccupation of postmodern consumers. (B-1)

Hypothesis A speculative statement about the relationship between two or more variables. (34)

i

Ideal type A construct or model for evaluating specific cases. (11, 131)

Impression management A term used by Erving Goffman to refer to the altering of the presentation of the self in order to create distinctive appearances and satisfy particular audiences. (94)

Incest taboo The prohibition of sexual relationships between certain culturally specified relatives. (336)

Incidence The number of new cases of a specific disorder that occur within a given population during a stated period. (438)

Income Salaries and wages. (209)

Independent variable The variable in a causal relationship that causes or influences a change in another variable. (34)

Index crimes The eight types of crime tabulated each year by the FBI in the *Uniform Crime Reports:* murder, rape, robbery, assault, burglary, theft, motor vehicle theft, and arson. (186)

Industrial city A relatively large city characterized by open competition, an open class system, and elaborate specialization in the manufacturing of goods. (55.2-2)

Industrial society A society that depends on mechanization to produce its goods and services. (125, 415)

Infant mortality rate The number of deaths of infants under 1 year old per 1,000 live births in a given year. (55.1-2)

Influence The exercise of power through a process of persuasion. (401)

Informal economy Transfers of money, goods, or services that are not reported to the government. (420)

Informal norm A norm that is generally understood but not precisely recorded. (68)

Informal social control Social control that is carried out casually by ordinary people through such means as laughter, smiles, and ridicule. (25.1-1)

In-group Any group or category to which people feel they belong. (129)

Innovation The process of introducing a new idea or object to a culture through discovery or invention. (73)

Institutional discrimination The denial of opportunities and equal rights to individuals and groups that results from the normal operations of a society. (259, 292)

Instrumentality An emphasis on tasks, a focus on more distant goals, and a concern for the external relationship between one's family and other social institutions. (289)

Intelligent design (ID) The idea that life is so complex that it could only have been created by intelligent design. (394)

Interactionist perspective A sociological approach that generalizes about everyday forms of social interaction in order to explain society as a whole. (18)

Intergenerational mobility Changes in the social position of children relative to their parents. (216)

Interview A face-to-face, telephone, or online questioning of a respondent to obtain desired information. (39)

Intragenerational mobility Changes in social position within a person's adult life. (217)

Invention The combination of existing cultural items into a form that did not exist before. (73)

Iron law of oligarchy A principle of organizational life developed by Robert Michels, under which even a democratic organization will eventually develop into a bureaucracy ruled by a few individuals. (133)

k

Kinship The state of being related to others. (330)

l

Labeling theory An approach to deviance that attempts to explain why certain people are viewed as deviants while others engaged in the same behavior are not. (54.1-2)

Laissez-faire A form of capitalism under which people compete freely, with minimal government intervention in the economy. (415)

Language An abstract system of word meanings and symbols for all aspects of culture; includes gestures and other nonverbal communication. (65)

Latent function An unconscious or unintended function that may reflect hidden purposes. (16)

Law Governmental social control. (68, 173)

Liberation theology Use of a church, primarily Roman Catholic, in a political effort to eliminate poverty, discrimination, and other forms of injustice from a secular society. (382)

Life chances Max Weber's term for the opportunities people have to provide themselves with material goods, positive living conditions, and favorable life experiences. (215)

Life course approach A research orientation in which sociologists and other social scientists look closely at the social factors that influence people throughout their lives, from birth to death. (97)

Life expectancy The median number of years a person can be expected to live under current mortality conditions. (55.1-3)

Looking-glass self A concept used by Charles Horton Cooley that emphasizes the self as the product of our social interactions. (93)

Luddites Rebellious craft workers in 19th-century England who destroyed new factory machinery as part of their resistance to the Industrial Revolution. (470)

m

Machismo A sense of virility, personal worth, and pride in one's maleness. (338)

Macrosociology Sociological investigation that concentrates on large-scale phenomena or entire civilizations. (14)

Manifest function An open, stated, and conscious function. (16)

Mass media Print and electronic means of communication that carry messages to widespread audiences. (145)

Master status A status that dominates others and thereby determines a person's general position in society. (115)

Material culture The physical or technological aspects of our daily lives. (76)

Matriarchy A society in which women dominate in family decision making. (332)

Matrilineal descent A kinship system in which only the mother's relatives are significant. (331)

Matrix of domination The cumulative impact of oppression because of race and ethnicity, gender, and social class, as well as religion, sexual orientation, disability, age, and citizenship status. (290)

McDonaldization The process through which the principles of the fast-food restaurant are coming to dominate more and more sectors of society. (443)

Mean A number calculated by adding a series of values and then dividing by the number of values. (52)

Mechanical solidarity A collective consciousness that emphasizes group solidarity, characteristic of societies with minimal division of labor. (123)

Median The midpoint or number that divides a series of values into two groups of equal numbers of values. (52)

Medical model An approach that suggests that mental illness is rooted in biological causes that can be treated through medical intervention. (54.1-2)

Mental illness A disorder of the brain that disrupts a person's thinking, feeling, and ability to interact with others. (54.1-1)

Microfinancing Lending small sums of money to the poor so they can work their way out of poverty. (424)

Microsociology Sociological investigation that stresses the study of small groups, often through experimental means. (14)

Midlife crisis A stressful period of self-evaluation that begins at about age 40. (312)

Migration The relatively permanent movement of people, with the purpose of changing their place of residence. (55.1-8)

Minority group A subordinate group whose members have significantly less control or power over their own lives than the members of a dominant or majority group have over theirs. (251)

Mode The single most common value in a series of scores. (52)

Model, or ideal, minority A subordinate group whose members supposedly have succeeded economically, socially, and educationally despite past prejudice and discrimination, and without resorting to political and violent confrontations with Whites. (270)

Modernization The far-reaching process through which periphery nations move from traditional or less developed institutions to those characteristic of more developed societies. (235)

Modernization theory A functionalist approach that proposes that modernization and development will gradually improve the lives of people in developing nations. (235)

Monarchy A form of government headed by a single member of a royal family, usually a king, queen, or some other hereditary ruler. (403)

Monogamy A form of marriage in which one woman and one man are married only to each other. (329)

Monopoly Control of a market by a single business firm. (416)

Morbidity rate The incidence of disease in a given population. (438)

Mores Norms deemed highly necessary to the welfare of a society. (68)

Mortality rate The incidence of death in a given population. (438)

Multinational corporation A commercial organization that is headquartered in one country but does business throughout the world. (233)

Multiple masculinities A variety of male gender roles, including nurturing-caring and effeminate-gay roles, that men may play along with their more pervasive traditional role of dominating women. (288)

Multiple-nuclei theory A theory of urban growth developed by Harris and Ullman that views growth as emerging from many centers of development, each of which reflects a particular urban need or activity. (55.2-3)

n

Narcotizing dysfunction The phenomenon in which the media provide such massive amounts of coverage that the audience becomes numb and fails to act on the information, regardless of how compelling the issue. (148)

Natural science The study of the physical features of nature and the ways in which they interact and change. (6)

Naturally occurring retirement community (NORC) An area that has gradually become an informal center for senior citizens. (55.3-2)

Neocolonialism Continuing dependence of former colonies on foreign countries. (228)

Netizen A person who is actively involved in online communities and is committed to the free flow of information, with few outside controls. (149)

New religious movement (NRM) or cult A small, secretive religious group that represents either a new religion or a major innovation of an existing faith. (390)

New social movement An organized collective activity that addresses values and social identities, as well as improvements in the quality of life. (463)

New urban sociology An approach to urbanization that considers the interplay of local, national, and worldwide forces and their effect on local space, with special emphasis on the impact of global economic activity. (55.2-4)

Nonmaterial culture Ways of using material objects, as well as customs, beliefs, philosophies, governments, and patterns of communication. (76)

Nonperiodic assembly A nonrecurring gathering of people that often results from word-of-mouth information. (56.1-3)

Nonverbal communication The sending of messages through the use of gestures, facial expressions, and postures. (18)

Norm An established standard of behavior maintained by a society. (66)

Nuclear family A married couple and their unmarried children living together. (329)

O

Obedience Compliance with higher authorities in a hierarchical structure. (170)

Objective method A technique for measuring social class that assigns individuals to classes on the basis of criteria such as occupation, education, income, and place of residence. (208)

Observation A research technique in which an investigator collects information through direct participation, by closely watching a group or community. (40)

Offshoring The transfer of work to foreign contractors. (423)

Oligarchy A form of government in which a few individuals rule. (403)

Open system A social system in which the position of each individual is influenced by his or her achieved status. (216)

Operational definition An explanation of an abstract concept that is specific enough to allow a researcher to assess the concept. (33)

Opinion leader Someone who influences the opinions and decisions of others through day-to-day personal contact and communication. (158)

Organic solidarity A collective consciousness that rests on mutual interdependence, characteristic of societies with a complex division of labor. (123)

Organized crime The work of a group that regulates relations between criminal enterprises involved in illegal activities, including prostitution, gambling, and the smuggling and sale of illegal drugs. (184)

Out-group A group or category to which people feel they do not belong. (129)

p

Panic A fearful arousal or collective flight based on a generalized belief that may or may not be accurate. (56.1-7)

Patriarchy A society in which men dominate in family decision making. (332)

Patrilineal descent A kinship system in which only the father's relatives are significant. (331)

Peace The absence of war, or more broadly, a proactive effort to develop cooperative relations among nations. (404)

Percentage A portion of 100. (52)

Periodic assembly A recurring, relatively routine gathering of people, such as a college class. (56.1-3)

Personality A person's typical patterns of attitudes, needs, characteristics, and behavior. (89)

Peter principle A principle of organizational life, originated by Laurence J. Peter, according to which every employee within a hierarchy tends to rise to his or her level of incompetence. (132)

Pluralism Mutual respect for one another's cultures among the various groups in a society, which allows minorities to express their cultures without experiencing prejudice. (265)

Pluralist model A view of society in which many competing groups within the community have access to government, so that no single group is dominant. (414)

Political system The social institution that is founded on a recognized set of procedures for implementing and achieving society's goals. (401)

Politics In Harold Lasswell's words, "who gets what, when, and how." (401)

Polyandry A form of polygamy in which a woman may have more than one husband at the same time. (330)

Polygamy A form of marriage in which an individual may have several husbands or wives simultaneously. (G-1)

Polygyny A form of polygamy in which a man may have more than one wife at the same time. (330)

Population pyramid A special type of bar chart that shows the distribution of a population by gender and age. (55.1-5)

Postindustrial city A city in which global finance and the electronic flow of information dominate the economy. (55.2-2)

Postindustrial society A society whose economic system is engaged primarily in the processing and control of information. (126)

Postmodern society A technologically sophisticated society that is preoccupied with consumer goods and media images. (B-1)

Power The ability to exercise one's will over others. (204, 401)

Power elite A term used by C. Wright Mills to refer to a small group of military, industrial, and government leaders who control the fate of the United States. (413)

Precarious work Employment that is poorly paid, and from the worker's perspective, insecure and unprotected. (C-1)

Preindustrial city A city of only a few thousand people that is characterized by a relatively closed class system and limited mobility. (55.2-1)

Prejudice A negative attitude toward an entire category of people, often an ethnic or racial minority. (254)

Prestige The respect and admiration that an occupation holds in a society. (208)

Prevalence The total number of cases of a specific disorder that exist at a given time. (438)

Primary group A small group characterized by intimate, face-to-face association and cooperation. (128)

Profane The ordinary and commonplace elements of life, as distinguished from the sacred. (379)

Professional criminal A person who pursues crime as a day-to-day occupation, developing skilled techniques and enjoying a certain degree of status among other criminals. (183)

Proletariat Karl Marx's term for the working class in a capitalist society. (203)

Protestant ethic Max Weber's term for the disciplined work ethic, this-worldly concerns, and rational orientation to life emphasized by John Calvin and his followers. (381)

Public A dispersed group of people, not necessarily in contact with one another, who share an interest in an issue. (56.1-8)

Public opinion Expressions of attitudes on matters of public policy that are communicated to decision makers. (56.1-8)

q

Qualitative research Research that relies on what is seen in field or naturalistic settings more than on statistical data. (40)

Quantitative research Research that collects and reports data primarily in numerical form. (39)

Quasi-religion A scholarly category that includes organizations that may see themselves as religious but are seen by others as "sort of religious." (391)

Queer theory The study of society from the perspective of a broad spectrum of sexual identities, including heterosexuality, homosexuality, and bisexuality. (3.1-1)

Questionnaire A printed or written form used to obtain information from a respondent. (39)

r

Racial formation A sociohistorical process in which racial categories are created, inhibited, transformed, and destroyed. (252)

Racial group A group that is set apart from others because of physical differences that have taken on social significance. (251)

Racial profiling Any arbitrary action initiated by an authority based on race, ethnicity, or national origin rather than on a person's behavior. (262)

Racism The belief that one race is supreme and all others are innately inferior. (255)

Random sample A sample for which every member of an entire population has the same chance of being selected. (35)

Rational-legal authority Power made legitimate by law. (402)

Reference group Any group that individuals use as a standard for evaluating themselves and their own behavior. (129)

Relative deprivation The conscious feeling of a negative discrepancy between legitimate expectations and present actualities. (461)

Relative poverty A floating standard of deprivation by which people at the bottom of a society, whatever their lifestyles, are judged to be disadvantaged *in comparison with the nation as a whole.* (212)

Reliability The extent to which a measure produces consistent results. (36)

Religion According to Émile Durkheim, a unified system of beliefs and practices relative to sacred things. (379)

Religious belief A statement to which members of a particular religion adhere. (385)

Religious experience The feeling or perception of being in direct contact with the ultimate reality, such as a divine being, or of being overcome with religious emotion. (387)

Religious ritual A practice required or expected of members of a faith. (387)

Remittances The monies that immigrants return to their families of origin. Also called *migradollars.* (241)

Representative democracy A form of government in which certain individuals are selected to speak for the people. (403)

Research design A detailed plan or method for obtaining data scientifically. (38)

Resocialization The process of discarding former behavior patterns and accepting new ones as part of a transition in one's life. (98)

Resource mobilization The ways in which a social movement utilizes such resources as money, political influence, access to the media, and personnel. (462)

Rite of passage A ritual marking the symbolic transition from one social position to another. (96)

Role conflict The situation that occurs when incompatible expectations arise from two or more social positions held by the same person. (115)

Role exit The process of disengagement from a role that is central to one's self-identity in order to establish a new role and identity. (116)

Role strain The difficulty that arises when the same social position imposes conflicting demands and expectations. (116)

Role taking The process of mentally assuming the perspective of another and responding from that imagined viewpoint. (94)

Rumor A piece of information gathered informally that is used to interpret an ambiguous situation. (56.1-8)

s

Sacred Elements beyond everyday life that inspire awe, respect, and even fear. (379)

Sample A selection from a larger population that is statistically representative of that population. (35)

Sanction A penalty or reward for conduct concerning a social norm. (69, 169)

Sandwich generation The generation of adults who simultaneously try to meet the competing needs of their parents and their children. (313)

Sapir-Whorf hypothesis A hypothesis concerning the role of language in shaping our interpretation of reality. It holds that language is culturally determined. (65)

Science The body of knowledge obtained by methods based on systematic observation. (6)

Scientific management approach Another name for the classical theory of formal organizations. (134)

Scientific method A systematic, organized series of steps that ensures maximum objectivity and consistency in researching a problem. (33)

Second shift The double burden—work outside the home followed by child care and housework—that many women face and few men share equitably. (296)

Secondary analysis A variety of research techniques that make use of previously collected and publicly accessible information and data. (43)

Secondary group A formal, impersonal group in which there is little social intimacy or mutual understanding. (128)

Sect A relatively small religious group that has broken away from some other religious organization to renew what it considers the original vision of the faith. (390)

Secularization The process through which religion's influence on other social institutions diminishes. (379)

Segregation The physical separation of two groups of people in terms of residence, workplace, and social events; often imposed on a minority group by a dominant group. (264)

Self According to George Herbert Mead, a distinct identity that sets us apart from others. (93)

Serial monogamy A form of marriage in which a person may have several spouses in his or her lifetime, but only one spouse at a time. (330)

Sexism The ideology that one sex is superior to the other. (292)

Sick role Societal expectations about the attitudes and behavior of a person viewed as being ill. (433)

Significant other A term used by George Herbert Mead to refer to an individual who is most important in the development of the self, such as a parent, friend, or teacher. (94)

Single-parent family A family in which only one parent is present to care for the children. (341)

Slavery A system of enforced servitude in which some people are owned by other people. (199)

Social capital The collective benefit of social networks, which are built on reciprocal trust. (14)

Social change Significant alteration over time in behavior patterns and culture, including norms and values. (467)

Social constructionist perspective An approach to deviance that emphasizes the role of culture in the creation of the deviant identity. (180)

Social control The techniques and strategies for preventing deviant human behavior in any society. (169)

Social disorganization theory The theory that crime and deviance are caused by the absence or breakdown of communal relationships and social institutions. (179)

Social epidemiology The study of the distribution of disease, impairment, and general health status across a population. (438)

Social inequality A condition in which members of society have differing amounts of wealth, prestige, or power. (22, 197)

Social institution An organized pattern of beliefs and behavior centered on basic social needs. (120)

Social interaction The ways in which people respond to one another. (113)

Social mobility Movement of individuals or groups from one position in a society's stratification system to another. (216)

Social movement An organized collective activity to bring about or resist fundamental change in an existing group or society. (56.1-9)

Social network A series of social relationships that links a person directly to others, and through them indirectly to still more people. (118)

Social role A set of expectations for people who occupy a given social position or status. (115)

Social science The study of the social features of humans and the ways in which they interact and change. (6)

Social structure The way in which a society is organized into predictable relationships. (113)

Socialism An economic system under which the means of production and distribution are collectively owned. (417)

Socialization The lifelong process in which people learn the attitudes, values, and behaviors appropriate for members of a particular culture. (89)

Societal-reaction approach Another name for *labeling theory*. (180)

Society A fairly large number of people who live in the same territory, are relatively independent of people outside their area, and participate in a common culture. (62)

Sociobiology The systematic study of how biology affects human social behavior. (63)

Sociocultural evolution Long-term social trends resulting from the interplay of continuity, innovation, and selection. (124)

Socioeconomic status (SES) A measure of social class that is based on income, education, and occupation. (208)

Sociological imagination An awareness of the relationship between an individual and the wider society, both today and in the past. (5)

Sociology The scientific study of social behavior and human groups. (5)

Sovereignty movement The effort by the indigenous people of Hawai'i to win self-government, as well as the restoration of—or compensation for—their ancestral lands. (405)

Squatter settlement An area occupied by the very poor on the fringe of a city, in which housing is constructed by the settlers themselves from discarded material. (55.2-5)

Status A term used by sociologists to refer to any of the full range of socially defined positions within a large group or society. (114)

Status group A term used by Max Weber to refer to people who have the same prestige or lifestyle, independent of their class positions. (204)

Stereotype An unreliable generalization about all members of a group that does not recognize individual differences within the group. (255)

Stigma A label used to devalue members of certain social groups. (25.1-1, 54.1-1)

Stratification A structured ranking of entire groups of people that perpetuates unequal economic rewards and power in a society. (197)

Subculture A segment of society that shares a distinctive pattern of customs, rules, and traditions that differs from the pattern of the larger society. (77)

Suburb According to the Census Bureau, any territory within a metropolitan area that is not included in the central city. (55.3-3)

Survey A study, generally in the form of an interview or questionnaire, that provides researchers with information about how people think and act. (39)

Symbol A gesture, object, or word that forms the basis of human communication. (66)

Symbolic ethnicity An ethnic identity that emphasizes concerns such as ethnic food or political issues rather than deeper ties to one's ethnic heritage. (275)

t

Teacher-expectancy effect The impact that a teacher's expectations about a student's performance may have on the student's actual achievements. (365)

Technology Cultural information about the ways in which the material resources of the environment may be used to satisfy human needs and desires. (75, 124, 470)

Terrorism The use or threat of violence against random or symbolic targets in pursuit of political aims. (406)

Theory In sociology, a set of statements that seeks to explain problems, actions, or behavior. (8)

Total fertility rate (TFR) The average number of children born alive to any woman, assuming that she conforms to current fertility rates. (55.1-2)

Total institution A term coined by Erving Goffman to refer to an institution that regulates all aspects of a person's life under a single authority, such as a prison, the military, a mental hospital, or a convent. (98)

Totalitarianism Virtually complete government control and surveillance over all aspects of a society's social and political life. (403)

Tracking The practice of placing students in specific curriculum groups on the basis of their test scores and other criteria. (363)

Traditional authority Legitimate power conferred by custom and accepted practice. (402)

Trained incapacity The tendency of workers in a bureaucracy to become so specialized that they develop blind spots and fail to notice obvious problems. (132)

Transnational An immigrant who sustains multiple social relationships that link his or her society of origin with the society of settlement. (276, 479)

Transnational crime Crime that occurs across multiple national borders. (185)

Transracial adoption The adoption of a non-White child by White parents or a Hispanic child by non-Hispanics. (340)

U

Underclass The long-term poor who lack training and skills. (214)

Urban ecology An area of study that focuses on the interrelationships between people and their environment in urban areas. (55.2-3)

Urbanism A term used by Louis Wirth to describe distinctive patterns of social behavior evident among city residents. (55.2-2)

V

Validity The degree to which a measure or scale truly reflects the phenomenon under study. (36)

Value A collective conception of what is considered good, desirable, and proper—or bad, undesirable, and improper—in a culture. (69)

Value-added model A theory of collective behavior proposed by Neil Smelser to explain how broad social conditions are transformed in a definite pattern into some form of collective behavior. (56.1-2)

Value neutrality Max Weber's term for objectivity of sociologists in the interpretation of data. (46)

Variable A measurable trait or characteristic that is subject to change under different conditions. (34)

Verstehen The German word for "understanding" or "insight"; used by Max Weber to stress the need for sociologists to take into account the subjective meanings people attach to their actions. (11)

Vertical mobility The movement of an individual from one social position to another of a different rank. (216)

Vested interests Veblen's term for those people or groups who will suffer in the event of social change, and who have a stake in maintaining the status quo. (469)

Victimization survey A questionnaire or interview given to a sample of the population to determine whether people have been victims of crime. (186)

Victimless crime A term used by sociologists to describe the willing exchange among adults of widely desired but illegal goods and services. (182)

Visual sociology The use of photographs, film, and video to study society. (A-1)

Vital statistics Records of births, deaths, marriages, and divorces gathered through a registration system maintained by governmental units. (55.1-2)

W

War Conflict between organizations that possess trained combat forces equipped with deadly weapons. (404)

Wealth An inclusive term encompassing all a person's material assets, including land, stocks, and other types of property. (211)

White-collar crime Illegal acts committed by affluent, "respectable" individuals in the course of business activities. (184)

White privilege Rights or immunities granted to people as a particular benefit or favor simply because they are White. (257)

World systems analysis Immanuel Wallerstein's view of the global economic system as one divided between certain industrialized nations that control wealth and developing countries that are controlled and exploited. (55.2-4)

Z

Zero population growth (ZPG) The state of a population in which the number of births plus immigrants equals the number of deaths plus emigrants. (55.1-6)

references

a

AARP. 2011. "Baby Boomer Envision What's Next? Research and Strategic Analysis Integrated Value and Strategy June, 2011." Accessed January 10, 2010 (http://assets.aarp.org/rgcenter/general/boomers-envision-retirement-2011.pdf)

Abercrombie, Nicholas, Bryan S. Turner, and Stephen Hill, eds. 1990. *Dominant Ideologies.* Cambridge, MA: Unwin Hyman.

———, Stephen Hill, and Bryan S. Turner. 1980. *The Dominant Ideology Thesis.* London: Allen and Unwin.

Aberle, David F., A. K. Cohen, A. K. Davis, M. J. Leng, Jr., and F. N. Sutton. 1950. "The Functional Prerequisites of a Society." *Ethics* 60 (January):100–111.

Abramson, David, Irwin Redlener, Tasha Stehling-Ariza, and Elizabeth Fuller. 2007. *The Legacy of Katrina's Children: Estimating the Numbers of At-Risk Children in the Gulf Coast States of Louisiana and Mississippi.* New York: Columbia University Mailman School of Public Health.

Acohido, Byron. 2010. "Tech-Savvy Put Explosion to Work." *USA Today,* November 17, pp. B1, B2.

Acosta, R. Vivian, and Linda Jean Carpenter. 2001. "Women in Intercollegiate Sport: A Longitudinal Study: 1977–1998." Pp. 302–308 in *Sport in Contemporary Society: An Anthology.* 6th ed., edited by D. Stanley Eitzen. New York: Worth.

Adams, Tracey L. 2010. "Gender and Feminization in Health Care Professions." *Sociology Compass* 4 (July):454–465.

Adams, Tyrene L., and Stephen A. Smith. 2008. *Electronic Tribes: The Virtual Worlds of Geeks, Gamas, Shamans, and Scammers.* Austin: University of Texas Press.

Adamy, Janet. 2008. "Starbucks Plans to License 150 Stores in Europe." *New York Times,* June 12, p. B3.

Addams, Jane. 1910. *Twenty Years at Hull-House.* New York: Macmillan.

———. 1930. *The Second Twenty Years at Hull-House.* New York: Macmillan.

Adler, Patricia A., and Peter Adler. 2007. "The Demedicalization of Self-Injury: From Psychopathology to Sociological Deviance." *Journal of Contemporary Ethnography* 36 (October):537–570.

———, and ———. 2011. *The Tender Cut: Inside the Hidden World of Self-Injury.* New York: New York University Press.

———, ———, and John M. Johnson. 1992. "Street Corner Society Revisited." *Journal of Contemporary Ethnography* 21 (April):3–10.

Adler, Roy D. 2008. "Counting on the Middle-Class." *Miller-McCune* (November–December):20–23.

Adorno, Theodor. [1971] 1991. *The Culture Industry.* London: Routledge.

Aguirre, Benigno E., E. L. Quarantelli, and Jorge L. Mendoza. 1988. "The Collective Behavior of Fads: The Characteristics, Effects, and Career of Streaking." *American Sociological Review* 53 (August):569–584.

Alain, Michel. 1985. "An Empirical Validation of Relative Deprivation." *Human Relations* 38 (8):739–749.

Alarcón, Arthur L., Paula M. Mitchell, Laurie L. Levenson, and James P. Gray. 2011. "Death Penalty Reform." *Loyola of Los Angeles Review* 44 (Special Issue).

Alba, Richard D. 2009. *Blurring the Color Line: The New Chance for a More Integrated America.* Cambridge, MA: Harvard University Press.

———. 1990. *Ethnic Identity: The Transformation of White America.* New Haven, CT: Yale University Press.

Albas, Cheryl, and Daniel Albas. 1996. "An Invitation to the Ethnographic Study of University Examination Behavior: Concepts, Methodology and Implications." *Canadian Journal of Higher Education* 26 (3):1–26.

Albas, Daniel, and Cheryl Albas. 1988. "Aces and Bombers: The Post-Exam Impression Management Strategies of Students." *Symbolic Interaction* 11 (Fall):289–302.

Albrecht, Gary L. 2004. "Disability: Sociological Perspectives." Pp. 3710–3713 in *International Encyclopedia of the Social and Behavioral Sciences,* edited by Neil J. Smelser and Paul B. Baltes. New York: Elsevier.

———, ed. 2005. *Encyclopedia of Disability.* Thousand Oaks, CA: Sage.

Alcindor, Yamiche. 2012. "Homelessness Made Tougher in Many Cities." *USA Today,* June 11, p. 2A.

Alderman, Lez. 2010. "Rapid Growth in Dubai Outstrips Its Resources." *New York Times,* October 28, pp. D1, D5.

Alexander, Karl L. 1997. "Public Schools and the Public Good." *Social Forces* 70 (September):1–30.

Ali, Syed. 2010. "Permanent Impermanence." *Contexts* (Spring):26–31.

Allen, Bem P. 1978. *Social Behavior: Fact and Falsehood.* Chicago: Nelson-Hall.

Allport, Gordon W. 1979. *The Nature of Prejudice.* 25th anniversary ed. Reading, MA: Addison-Wesley.

Alon, Sigal. 2009. "The Evolution of Class Inequality in Higher Education: Competition, Exclusion, and Adaptation." *American Sociological Review* 74 (October):731–755.

Alterovitz, Sheyna Sears-Roberts, and Gerald A. Mendelsohn. 2009. "Partner Preference Across the Life Span: Online Dating by Older Adults." *Psychology and Aging* 24 (No. 2).

Alvord, Lori Arviso, and Elizabeth Cohen Van Pelt. 1999. *The Scalpel and the Silver Bear.* New York: Bantam Books.

Alwin, Duane F. 2002. "Generations X, Y, and Z: Are They Changing America?" *Contexts* (Fall–Winter):42–51.

Alzheimer's Association. 2012. *2012 Alzheimer's Disease Facts and Figures.* Accessed March 25 at http://www.alzheimers_disease_facts_and_figures.asp.

American Academy of Cosmetic Surgery. 2010. "New Survey Indicates More than 17 Million Cosmetic Procedures Performed Last Year in U.S." Chicago: AACS.

American Bar Association. 1997. *Section of the Individual Rights and Responsibilities: Section of Litigation (Capital Punishment).* Chicago: Division for Policy Administration, ABA.

American Community Survey. 2010. "2008 American Community Survey." Accessed at http://factfinder.census.gov.

———. 2011. "American Community Survey 2010." Accessible at www.census.gov/acs/www/.

American Jewish Committee. 2005. *2005 Annual Survey of American Jewish Opinion.* New York: AJC.

American Lung Association. 2011. "State of the Air 2011." Accessed March 26, 2012 (www.stateoftheair.org).

American Psychiatric Association. 2013. *Diagnostic and Statistical Manual of Mental Disorders, Fifth Edition (DSM-5™).* Arlington, VA: American Psychiatric Publishing.

American Psychological Association. 2008. "Being Gay Is Just as Healthy as Being Straight." Accessed February 25 (www.apa.org).

American Sociological Association. 1999. *Code of Ethics.* Reprinted 2008. Washington DC: ASA.

———. 2005. "Need Today's Data Yesterday." Accessed December 17 (www.asanet.org).

———. 2009. *21st Century Careers with an Undergraduate Degree in Sociology.* Washington, DC: ASA.

———. 2010a. *2010 Guide to Graduate Departments of Sociology.* Washington, DC: ASA.

———. 2012. *Current Sections.* Accessed January 2 (www.asanet.org/sections/list.cfm).

American Soybean Association. 2011. "World Soybean Production 2009." Accessed June 1 at www.soystats.com.

Amnesty International. 2012. *Death Sentences and Executions 2011*. London: Amnesty International. Accessed January 23, 2012 (www.amnesty.org/en/library/assetACT50/001/2011/en/ea1b6b25-a62a-4074-927d-ba51e88df2e9/act500012011en.pdf).

Andersen, Margaret. 2007. *Thinking about Women: Sociological Perspectives on Sex and Gender*. 7th ed. New York: Allyn and Bacon.

Anderson, Elijah. 1990. *Streetwise: Race, Class, and Change in an Urban Community*. Chicago: University of Chicago Press.

Anderson, Gretchen. 2009. *Love, Actually: A National Survey of Adults 18+ on Love, Relationships, and Romance*. Washington, DC: AARP.

Anderson, John Ward, and Molly Moore. 1993. "The Burden of Womanhood." *Washington Post National Weekly Edition* 10 (March 22–28):6–7.

Anderson, Sarah, Chuck Collins, Scott Klinger, and Sam Pizzigati. 2011. *Executive Excess 2011*. Washington, DC: Institute for Policy Studies. Accessible at www.ips-dc.org.

Anderson, Warwick. 2003. *The Cultivation of Whiteness: Science, Health and Racial Destiny in Australia*. New York: Perseus.

Andrews, Lori. 2012. "Facebook Is Using You." *New York Times*, February 5, Sunday Review, p. 7.

Angier, Natalie. 1998. "Drugs, Sports, Body Image and G.I. Joe." *New York Times*, December 22, pp. D1, D3.

Angus Reid Public Opinion. 2010. "Euthanasia: Americans Split Over Euthanasia and Assisted Suicide." Accessible at www.angus-reid.com.

Angwin, Julia. 2010. "The Web's New Gold Mine: Your Secrets." *Wall Street Journal*, July 31, pp. W1, W2.

———, and Jennifer Valentino-DeVries. 2010a. "Race Is On to 'Fingerprint' Phones, PCs." *Wall Street Journal*, December 1, pp. A1, A15.

———, and ———. 2010b. "Web Privacy 'Inadequate.'" *Wall Street Journal*, December 2, pp. B1, B2.

Ansell, Amy E. 2008. "Color Blindness." Pp. 320–321, vol. 1, in *Encyclopedia of Race, Ethnicity, and Society*, edited by Richard T. Schaefer. Thousand Oaks, CA: Sage.

Anti-Defamation League. 2010. "2009 Audit of Anti-Semitic Incidents: Summary of Findings." Accessed March 18, 2011 (www.adl.org/main_anti_semitism_domestic/2009_Audit.htm).

Arab American Institute. 2010. "Demographics." Accessed March 7 (www.aaiusa.org/arab-americans/22/demographics).

Archer, Patrick, and Bryan Orr. 2011. "Class Identification in Review: Past Perspectives and Future Directions." *Sociology Compass* 5 (January):104–115.

Archibold, Randal C. 2011. "Despite Violence, Mexico Plants Hum at Border. *New York Times*, July 11, pp. A1, A3.

———, and Julia Preston. 2008. "Homeland Security Stands by Its Fence." *New York Times*, May 21.

Argetsinger, Amy, and Jonathan Krim. 2002. "Stopping the Music." *Washington Post National Weekly Edition* 20 (December 2):20.

Armer, J. Michael, and John Katsillis. 1992. "Modernization Theory." Pp. 1299–1304, vol. 4, in *Encyclopedia of Sociology*, edited by Edgar F. Borgatta and Marie L. Borgatta. New York: Macmillan.

Ash, Timothy Garton. 2007. "Welcome to a Mixed-Up World." *Globe and Mail* (Toronto), July 14, p. A19.

Association of Theological Schools. 2011. "2010–2011 Annual Data Tables: Table 2-12A." Accessed March 28 (www.ats.edu/Resources/Publications/Documents/AnnualDataTables/2010-11AnnualDataTables.pdf).

Atchley, Robert C. 1976. *The Sociology of Retirement*. New York: Wiley.

Attwood, Bain. 2003. *Rights for Aborigines*. Crows Nest, Australia: Allen and Unwin.

Aud, Susan, Mary Ann Fox, and Angelina Kewal Ramani. 2010. *Status and Trends in the Education of Racial and Ethnic Groups*. Washington DC: National Center for Education Statistics, U.S. Department of Education.

Austin, Chammie. 2009. *Impression Management*. Accessed January 11, 2012 (www.education.com/reference/article/impression-management).

Australia. 1997. "Bringing Them Home: Report of the National Inquiry into the Separation of Aboriginal and Torres Strait Islander Children from Their Families." Accessible at www.humanrights.gov.au.

———. 2008. "Apology to Australia's Indigenous Peoples, House of Representatives, Parliament House, Canberra." Accessed February 13 (www.pm.gov.au/media/speech/2008/speech_0073.cfm).

Avon. 2013. "Experience Avon's History." Accessed February 26 at www.avoncompany.com/aboutavon/history/index.html.

Azumi, Koya, and Jerald Hage. 1972. *Organizational Systems*. Lexington, MA: Heath.

b

Babad, Elisha Y., and P. J. Taylor. 1992. "Transparency of Teacher Expectancies across Language, Cultural Boundaries." *Journal of Educational Research* 86:120–125.

Bacon Lovers' Talk. 2009. "Bacon Lovers' Talk." Accessed February 4 (www.bacontalk.com/).

Badgett, M., V. Lee, and Jody L. Herman. 2011. "Patterns of Relationship Recognition by Same-Sex Couples in the United States." Los Angeles: The Williams Institute. Accessible at http://williamsinstitute.law.ucla.edu/wp-content/uploads/census2010Snapshot-Us-v2.pdf.

Bado-Fralick, Nikki, and Rebecca Sachs Norris. 2010. *Toying with God: The World of Religious Games and Dolls*. Waco, TX: Baylor University Press.

Bagby, Ihsan. 2012. *The American Mosque 2011*. Washington, DC: Council on American-Islamic Relations.

Bajaj, Vikas. 2011a. "15 Years in Microcredit Has Suffered a Black Eye." *New York Times*, January 6, p. B3.

———. 2011b. "Luster Dims for a Public Microlender." *New York Times*, May 11, pp. 1, 4.

Baker, Peter. 2009. "Obama Reverses Rules on U.S. Abortion Aid." *New York Times*, January 24.

Baker, Therese L. 1999. *Doing Social Research*. 3rd ed. New York: McGraw-Hill.

Barbaro, Michael. 2008. "Wal-Mart Says Most Workers Have Health Plan." *New York Times*, January 22.

Barboza, David. 2008. "Reform Stalls in Chinese Factories." *New York Times*, January 5, pp. B1, B6.

Barnes, Patricia, Barbara Bloom, and Richard Nahin. 2008. "Complementary and Alternative Medicine Use among Adults and Children: United States, 2007." *National Health Statistics Reports*, December 10.

———, Eve Powell-Griner, Ken McFann, and Richard L. Nation. 2004. "Complementary and Alternative Medicine Use among Adults: United States, 2002." *Advance Data from Vital and Health Statistics*, No. 343. Hyattsville, MD: National Center for Health Statistics.

Barnes, Taylor. 2009. "Rise of the Shadow Economy." *Christian Science Monitor*, November 8, pp. 30–31.

Barrett, David B., Todd M. Johnson, and Peter F. Crossing. 2008. "The 2007 Annual Megacensus of Religions." Chicago: Encyclopaedia Britannica.

Bartlett, Thomas. 2009. "How the International Essay Mill Has Changed Cheating." *Chronicle of Higher Education*, March 20, pp. A1, A22–A25.

———. 2011. "A Database Named Desire: 2 Scientists Examine Online Searches for Sex." *Chronicle of Higher Education* 57 (August 12):A12.

Barton, Bernadette. 2006. *Stripped: Inside the Lives of Exotic Dancers*. New York: New York University Press.

Basulto, Dominic. 2011. "Popping the 'Supercommittee' 'Filter Bubble.'" *Washington Post* (November 3). Accessed November 11 (www.washingtonpost.com/blogs/innovations/post/popping-the-supercommittee-filter-bubble/2010/12/20glQAMfcviM_blog.html).

Battin, Margaret P., Agnes van der Heide, Linda Ganzini, Gerrit van der Wal, and Bregje D. Onwuteaka-Philipsen. 2007. "Legal Physician-Assisted Dying in Oregon and the Netherlands: Evidence Concerning the Impact on Patients in 'Vulnerable' Groups." *Journal of Medical Ethics* 33 (October):591–598.

Baudrillard, Jean. [1970] 1988. *The Consumers Society*. London: Sage.

Bauerlein, Monika. 1996. "The Luddites Are Back." *Utne Reader* (March–April):24, 26.

Bauerlein, Mark. 2008.. "Online Literacy Is a Lesser Kind." *Chronicle of Higher Education* (September 19), pp. B10–B11.

Bauman, Kurt J. 1999. "Extended Measures of Well-Being: Meeting Basic Needs." *Current Population Reports*, ser. P-70, no. 67. Washington, DC: U.S. Government Printing Office.

Bazar, Emily. 2009. "Tent Cities Filling up with Casualties of the Economy." *USA Today*, May 5, pp. 1A–2A.

BBC News. 2005. "Indonesian Village Report: January 12, 2005." Accessed January 19 (www.theworld.org).

Beagan, Brenda L. 2001. "'Even If I Don't Know What I'm Doing I Can Make It Look Like I Know What I'm Doing': Becoming a Doctor in the 1990s." *Canadian Review of Sociology and Anthropology* 38:275–292.

Bearman, Peter S., James Moody, and Katherine Stovel. 2004. "Chains of Affection: The Structure of Adolescent Romantic and Sexual Networks." *American Journal of Sociology* 110 (July):44–91.

Bebchuk, Lucian A., and Jesse M. Fried. 2010. "Tackling the Managerial Power Problem." *Pathways* (Summer):9–12.

Becker, Anne E. 2007. "Facets of Acculturation and Their Diverse Relations to Body Shape Concerns in Fiji." *International Journal of Eating Disorders* 40 (1):42–50.

Becker, Howard S. 1952. "Social Class Variations in the Teacher-Pupil Relationship." *Journal of Educational Sociology* 25 (April):451–465.

———. 1963. *The Outsiders: Studies in the Sociology of Deviance.* New York: Free Press.

——— (ed.). 1964. *The Other Side: Perspectives on Deviance.* New York: Free Press.

———. 1974. "Photography and Sociology." *Studies in the Anthropology of Visual Communication* 1:3–26. Accessible by the author at http://lucy.ukc.ac.uk/becker.html. Also reproduced in his: 1986. *Doing Things Together: Selected Papers.* Evanston, IL: Northwestern University Press.

Beisel, Nicola, and Tamara Kay. 2004. "Abortion, Race, and Gender in Nineteenth-Century America." *American Sociological Review* 69 (4):498–518.

Bell, Daniel. 1953. "Crime as an American Way of Life." *Antioch Review* 13 (Summer):131–154.

———. 1973. *The Coming of Post-Industrial Society.* New York: Basic Books.

———. [1973] 1999. *The Coming of Post-Industrial Society: A Venture in Social Forecasting.* With new foreword. New York: Basic Books.

———. 1999 (1973). *The Coming of Post-Industrial Society Special Anniversary Edition.* New York: Basic Books.

———. 2008. *China's New Confucianism: Politics and Everyday Life in a Changing Society.* Princeton, NJ: Princeton University Press.

Bell, Wendell. 1981. "Modernization." Pp. 186–187 in *Encyclopedia of Sociology.* Guilford, CT: DPG Publishing.

Beller, Emily. 2009. "Bringing Intergenerational Social Mobility Research into the Twenty-first Century: Why Mothers Matter." *America Sociological Review* 74 (August):507–528.

Belz, Adam. 2011. "Farm Boom Leaves Main Street Wanting." *USA Today,* June 1, p. 6A.

Benford, Robert D. 1992. "Social Movements." Pp. 1880–1887, vol. 4, in *Encyclopedia of Sociology,* edited by Edgar F. Borgatta and Marie Borgatta. New York: Macmillan.

Bennett, Vivienne, S. Dávila-Poblete, and M. N. Rico, eds. 2005. *Opposing Currents: The Politics of Water and Gender in Latin America.* Pittsburgh: University of Pittsburgh Press.

Bergen, Raquel Kennedy. 2006. *Marital Rape: New Research and Directions.* Harrisburg, PA: VAW Net.

Berger, Peter, and Thomas Luckmann. 1966. *The Social Construction of Reality.* New York: Doubleday.

Berk, Richard A., and Howard E. Aldrich. 1972. "Patterns of Vandalism during Civil Disorders as an Indicator of Selection of Targets." *American Sociological Review* 37 (October):533–547.

Berman, Paul. 2003. *Terror and Liberalism.* New York: Norton.

Bernat, Frances P., and Tatyana Zhilina. 2011. "Trafficking in Humans: The TIP Report." *Sociology Compass* 5 (June):452–462.

Bernhardt, Annette, et al. (10 additional co-authors). 2009. *Broken Laws, Unprotected Workers.* New York: Ford, Joyce, Haynes, and Russell Sage Foundations.

Bernstein, Elizabeth. 2007. "Colleges Move Boldly on Student Drinking." *Wall Street Journal,* December 6, pp. D1, D2.

Best, Joel. 2004. *Deviance: Career of a Concept.* Belmont, CA: Wadsworth Thomson.

Bhagat, Chetan. 2007. *One Night at the Call Centre.* London: Black Swan.

Bialik, Carol. 2010. "Seven Careers in a Lifetime? Think Twice, Researchers Say." *Wall Street Journal,* September 4, p. A6.

Bianchi, Suzanne M., and Daphne Spain. 1996. "Women, Work, and Family in America." *Population Bulletin* 51 (December).

Biddlecom, Ann, and Steven Martin. 2006. "Childless in America." *Contexts* 5 (Fall):54.

Bielby, Denise D., and C. Lee Harrington. 2008. *Global TV: Exporting Television and Culture in the World Market.* New York: New York University Press.

Billitteri, Thomas, J. 2009. "Middle-Class Squeeze." *CQ Researcher* 19 (March 6):201–224.

Bilton, Nick. 2011. *I Live in the Future and Here's How It Works.* New York: Crown Business.

Bitler, Marianne, and Hilary W. Hoynes. 2010. "The State of the Safety Net in the Post-Welfare Reform Era." Paper prepared for Brooking Papers on Economic Activity, Washington, DC, September 16–20.

Black, Donald. 1995. "The Epistemology of Pure Sociology." *Law and Social Inquiry* 20 (Summer): 829–870.

Blais, Allison, and Lynn Rasic. 2011. *A Place of Remembrance: Official Book of the National September 11 Memorial.* Washington, DC: National Geographic.

Blank, Rebecca M. 2010. "Middle Class in America." *Focus* 27 (Summer):1–8.

———. 2011. *Changing Inequality.* Berkeley: University of California Press.

Blau, Peter M., and Otis Dudley Duncan. 1967. *The American Occupational Structure.* New York: Wiley.

Blauner, Robert. 1972. *Racial Oppression in America.* New York: Harper and Row.

Blumberg, Stephen J., and Julian V. Luke. 2007. "Coverage Bias in Traditional Telephone Surveys of Low-Income and Young Adults." *Public Opinion Quarterly* 71 (5):734–749.

Blumer, Herbert. 1955. "Collective Behavior." Pp. 165–198 in *Principles of Sociology,* 2nd ed., edited by Alfred McClung Lee. New York: Barnes and Noble.

———. 1969. *Symbolic Interactionism: Perspective and Method.* Englewood Cliffs, NJ: Prentice Hall.

Boase, Jeffery, John B. Horrigan, Barry Wellman, and Lee Rainie. 2006. *The Strength of Internet Ties.* Washington, DC: Pew Internet and American Life Project.

Boellstorff, Tom. 2008. *Coming of Age in Second Life: An Anthropologist Explores the Virtually Human.* Princeton, NJ: Princeton University Press.

Boje, David M. 1995. "Stories of Storytelling Organization: A Postmodern Analysis of Disney as 'Tamara-Land.'" *Academy of Management Journal* 38:997–1035.

Bonilla-Silva, Eduardo. 2004. "From Bi-Racial to Tri-Racial: Towards a New System of Racial Stratification in the USA." *Ethics and Racial Studies* 27 (November):931–950.

———. 2006. *Racism without Racists.* Lanham, MD: Rowman and Littlefield.

Bonus, Rick. 2000. *Locating Filipino Americans: Ethnicity and the Cultural Politics of Space.* Philadelphia: Temple University Press.

Borjas, George S., Jeffrey Grogger, and Gordon H. Hanson. 2006. "Immigration and African-American Employment Opportunities: The Response of Wages, Employment, and Incarceration to Labor Supply Shocks." Working Paper 12518. Cambridge, MA: National Bureau of Economic Research.

Borrelli, Christopher. 2010. "Second Life Talk Given Both Locally, Virtually." *Chicago Tribune,* November 8, sec. 3, p. 1.

Bottomore, Tom, and Maximilien Rubel, eds. 1956. *Karl Marx: Selected Writings in Sociology and Social Philosophy.* New York: McGraw-Hill.

Boudreaux, Richard. 2002. "Indian Rights Law Is Upheld in Mexico." *Los Angeles Times,* September 7, p. A3.

Bourdieu, Pierre, and Jean-Claude Passerson. 1990. *Reproduction in Education, Society and Culture.* 2nd ed. London. Sage. Originally published as *La reproduction.*

Boushey, Heather. 2005. *Student Debt: Bigger and Bigger.* Washington, DC: Center for Economic and Policy Research.

Bouvier, Leon F. 1980. "America's Baby Boom Generation: The Fateful Bulge." *Population Bulletin* 35 (April).

Bowes, John. 2011. *The Fair Trade Revolution.* London: Pluto Press.

Bowles, Samuel, and Herbert Gintis. 1976. *Schooling in Capitalistic America: Educational Reforms and the Contradictions of Economic Life.* New York: Basic Books.

Bowman, Thomas. 2013. "As Qualified Men Dwindle, Military Looks for a Few Good Women." March 23. Accessible at www.npr.org/2013/03/25/174966070/as-qualified-men-dwindle-military-looks-for-a-few-good-women.

Boy Scouts of America. 2010. "2009 Annual Report." Accessed November 10, 2011 (www.scouting.org).

Brabazon, Tara. 2007. *The University of Google: Education in the (post) Information Age.* Burlington, VT: Ashgate.

Brady Campaign. 2013. "2013 State Rankings." BradyCampaign.org. Accessed February 16 at www.bradycampaign.org/xshare/stateleg/scorecard/2011/2011_brady_campaign_state_scorecard_rankings.pdf.

Brady, Erik. 2010. "Title IX Model Survey Policy to Be Rescinded." *USA Today*, April 20, p. C1.

Brandchannel.com. 2012. "2011 Movie List." Accessed January 17 (www.brandchannel.com/brandcameo_films.asp?movie_year_az52009#movie_list).

Brannigan, Augustine. 1992. "Postmodernism." Pp. 1522–1525 in *Encyclopedia of Sociology*, vol. 3, edited by Edgar F. Borgatta and Marie L. Borgatta. New York: Macmillan.

Bray, James H., and John Kelly. 1999. *Stepfamilies: Love, Marriage, and Parenting in the First Decade*. New York: Broadway Books.

Brazier, Chris, and Amir Hamed, eds. 2007. *The World Guide*. 11th ed. Oxford, UK: New Internationalist.

Breines, Winifred. 2007. "Struggling to Connect: White and Black Feminism in the Movement Years." *Contexts* 6 (Winter):18–24.

Brennan Center. 2006. *Citizens Without Proof*. New York: Brennan Center for Justice at NYU School of Law.

Brewer, Rose M., and Nancy A. Heitzeg. 2008. "The Racialization of Criminal Punishment." *American Behavioral Scientist* 51 (January):625–644.

Brewis, Alexandra, Amber Wutich, Ashlan Falletta-Cowden, and Isa Rodriguez-Soto. 2011. "Body Norms and Fat Stigma in Global Perspective." *Current Anthropology* 52 (April):269–276.

Brint, Steven. 1998. *Schools and Societies*. Thousand Oaks, CA: Pine Forge Press.

Britannica Online. 2011. "Worldwide Adherents of All Religions by Six Continental Areas. Mid-2010." Accessed March 28.

Brown, David. 2009. "Doing a Number on Surveys." *Washington Post National Weekly Edition* 26 (January 19):37.

Brown, David K. 2001. "The Social Sources of Educational Credentialism: Status Cultures, Labor Markets, and Organizations." *Sociology of Education* 74 (Extra issue):19–34.

Brown, Geoff. 2008a. "Cities under Fire." *Johns Hopkins Public Health* (Fall).

———. 2008b. "Building a Safer Gun." *John Hopkins Public Health* (Fall).

Brown, Lester R. 2011. *World on the Edge: How to Prevent Environmental and Economic Collapse*. New York: W.W. Norton and Company.

Brown, Michael, and Amy Goldin. 1973. *Collective Behavior: A Review and Reinterpretation of the Literature*. Pacific Palisades, CA: Goodyear.

Brown, Patricia Leigh. 2004. "For Children of Gays, Marriage Brings Joy." *New York Times*, March 19, p. A13.

Brown, Robert McAfee. 1980. *Gustavo Gutierrez*. Atlanta: John Knox.

Brown, Roger W. 1954. "Mass Phenomena." Pp. 833–873, vol. 2, in *Handbook of Social Psychology*, edited by Gardner Lindzey. Reading, MA: Addison-Wesley.

Browne, Irene, ed. 2001. *Latinas and African American Women at Work: Race, Gender, and Economic Inequality*. New York: Russell Sage Foundation.

Brubaker, Bill. 2008. "Social Insecurity: Many People's Numbers Are Readily Available Online to Identity Thieves." *Washington Post National Weekly Edition*, January 14, p. 34.

Brulle, Robert, and J. Craig Jenkins. 2008. "Fixing the Bungled U.S. Environmental Movement." *Contexts* 7 (Spring):14–18.

Bryman, Alan. 1995. *Disney and His Worlds*. New York: Routledge.

Buchmann, Claudia, Thomas A. DiPrete, and Anne McDaniel. 2008. "Gender Inequalities in Education." *Annual Review of Sociology* 34:319–337.

Buckingham, David. 2007. "Selling Childhood? Children and Consumer Culture." *Journal of Children and Media* 1 (1):15–24.

Buddeberg-Fischer, Barbara, Marina Stamm, Claus Buddeberg, Georg Bauer, Oliver Hämmig, Michaela Knecht, and Richard Klafhofer. 2012. "The Impact of Gender and Parenthood on Physicians' Careers—Professional and Personal Situation Seven Years After Graduation." *BMC Health Services Research* 10:40.

Budig, Michelle J. 2002. "Male Advantage and the Gender Composition of Jobs: Who Rides the Glass Escalator?" *Social Problems* 49 (2):258–277.

Budrys, Grace. 2012. *Our Unsystematic Health Care System*. 3rd ed. Lanham, MD: Rowman and Littlefield Publishers.

Bullard, Robert D. 1993. *Dumping in Dixie: Race, Class, and Environmental Quality*. 2nd ed. Boulder, CO: Westview Press.

———, and Beverly Wright. 2009. *Race, Place, and Environmental Justice after Hurricane Katrina*. Boulder, CO: Westview Press.

Burawoy, Michael. 2005. "For Public Sociology." *American Sociological Review* 70 (February):4–28.

Bureau of the Census. 1975. *Historical Statistics of the United States, Colonial Times to 1970*. Washington, DC: U.S. Government Printing Office.

———. 1994. *Statistical Abstract of the United States, 1994*. Washington, DC: U.S. Government Printing Office.

———. 2004a. *Statistical Abstract of the United States, 2004–2005*. Washington, DC: U.S. Government Printing Office.

———. 2004b. "Census 2000 Final Response Rates." Accessed January 16, 2010 (www.census.gov/dmd/www/response/2000response.html).

———. 2005b. "American Fact Finder: Places with United States." Accessed December 12 (http://factfinder.census.gov).

———. 2008a. *Statistical Abstract of the United States, 2008*. Washington, DC: U.S. Government Printing Office.

———. 2008c. "America's Families and Living Arrangements." Accessed at www.census.gov/population/www/socdemo/hh-fam/cps2008.html.

———. 2009a. *Statistical Abstract of the United States 2010*. Washington, DC: U.S. Government Printing Office.

———. 2010a. *Statistical Abstract of the United States 2011*. Washington, DC: U.S. Government Printing Office.

———. 2010b. "America's Families and Living Arrangements: 2010." Released January. Accessible at www.census.gov/population/www/socdemo/hh-fam/cps2010.html.

———. 2011a. *Statistical Abstract of the United States 2012*. Washington, DC: U.S. Government Printing Office.

———. 2011b. International Data Base (IDB). Accessible at http://www.census.gov/ipc/www/idb/informationGateway.php.

———. 2011c. "Census Bureau Releases Estimate of Same-Sex Married Couples." Accessible at www.census.gov/newsroom/releases/archives/2010_census/cb11-cn181.html.

———. 2011d. "Current Population Survey, Annual Social and Economic Supplements." Washington, DC: U.S. Government Printing Office.

———. 2011e. "America's Families and Living Arrangements: 2011." November 3. Accessible at www.census.gov/newsroom/releases/archives/families_households/cb11-183.html.

———. 2011f. "2010 American Community Survey." Accessible at www.census.gov.

———. 2012a. "The Statistical Abstract of the United States 2013." Accessible at www.census.gov/.

———. 2012b. "The 2012 Statistical Abstract: Historical Statistics." Accessible at www.census.gov/compendia/statab/hist_stats.html.

———. 2012c. "Graphs on Historical Voting Trends." February 15. Accessible at www.census.gov/newsroom/releases/archives/voting/cb12-tps08.html.

———. 2012d. "Census Bureau Releases Estimates of Undercount and Overcount in the 2010 Census." News Release CB12-95, May 22. Accessible at www.census.gov/newroom/releases/archives/2010_census/cb12-95.html.

———. 2012d. "Most Children Younger Than Age 1 are Minorities, Census Bureau Reports." May 17. Accessible at http://www.census.gov/newsroom/releases/archives/population/c12-90.html.

———. 2013b. "International Data Base Total Midyear Population for the World: 1950–2050." Accessed May 14 at www.census.gov/population/international/data/idb/worldpoptotal.php.

Bureau of Consular Affairs. 2011. FY2011 Annual Report on Intercountry Adoption, November 2011. Washington, DC: Bureau of Consular Affairs, U.S. Department of State.

Bureau of Justice Statistics. 2011. "U.S. Correctional Population Declined for Second Consecutive Year." Accessed April 24, 2012 (http://bjs.ojp.usdoj.gov/content/pub/press/p10cpus10pr.cfm).

Bureau of Labor Statistics. 2003. "Women at Work: A Visual Essay." *Monthly Labor Review* (October):45–50.

———. 2010. "Economic News Release: Number of Jobs Held." Accessible at www.bls.gov/news.release/nlsoy.nr0.htm.

———. 2011. "Labor Force Statistics: Table 3." Accessed March 21, 2011 (www.bls.gov/cps/tables.htm).

———. 2012. "Part-time Employment Rates by Sex, Selected Countries, 2010." Chart 2.7 in *Charting International Labor Comparisons*. September 2012. Accessible at www.bls.gov.

———. 2013. *Employment Situation—January 2013*. Washington, DC: U.S. Government Printing Office.

Bures, Frank. 2011. "Can You Hear Us Now?" *Utne Reader* (March–April):8–9, 11.

Burger, Jerry M. 2009. "Replicating Milgram: Would People Still Obey Today?" *American Psychologist* 64 (January):1–11.

Burger King. 2009. "Whopper Sacrifice." Accessed February 4 (www.whoppersacrifice.com/).

Burgess, Ernest W. 1925. "The Growth of the City." Pp. 47–62 in *The City,* edited by Robert E. Park, Ernest W. Burgess, and Roderick D. McKenzie. Chicago: University of Chicago Press.

Burkitt, Laurie. 2011. "Wal-Mart China Woes Add Up." *Wall Street Journal,* October 18, p. B3.

Burns, Melinda. 2010. "Workfare and the Low-Wage Woman." *Miller-McClune* (November–December):76–81.

Butler, Daniel Allen. 1998. *"Unsinkable": The Full Story.* Mechanicsburg, PA: Stackpole Books.

Byrd-Bredbenner, Carol, and Jessica Murray. 2003. "Comparison of the Anthropometric Measurements of Idealized Female Body Images in Media Directed to Men, Women, and Mixed Gender Audiences." *Topics in Clinical Nutrition* 18 (2):117–129.

C

Calhoun, Craig. 1998. "Community without Propinquity Revisited." *Sociological Inquiry* 68 (Summer):373–397.

———. 2003. "Belonging in the Cosmopolitan Imaginary." *Ethnicities* 3 (December):531–553.

———. 2011. "Evicting the Public." Possible Futures: A Project of the Social Science Research Project. November 19. Accessed January 26, 2012 (www.possible-futures.org/2011/11/19/evicting-the-public-why-has-occupying-public-spaces-brought-such-heavy-handed-repression).

Cameron, Deborah. 2007. *The Myth of Mars and Venus.* Oxford: Oxford University Press.

Campbell, Mary, Robert Haveman, Gary Sandefur, and Barbara Wolfe. 2005. "Economic Inequality and Educational Attainment across a Generation." *Focus* 23 (Spring):11–15.

Cañas, Jesus, Roberto Coronado, and Robert W. Gilman. 2007. "Southwest Economy." March/April. Accessed April 18 (http://dallasfed.org/research/swe/2007/swe0702b.cfm).

Cantril, Hadley. 1940. *The Invasion from Mars: A Study in the Psychology of Panic.* Princeton, NJ: Princeton University Press.

Caplan, Ronald L. 1989. "The Commodification of American Health Care." *Social Science and Medicine* 28 (11):1139–1148.

Caplow, Theodore, and Louis Hicks. 2002. *Systems of War and Peace.* 2nd ed. Lanham, MD: University Press of America.

Capriccioso, Rob. 2010. "Obama Mentions Tribes as Part of Oil Spill Restoration; Chief Testifies on Mess." *Indian Country Today,* June 23, pp. 1, 2.

Carbon Trust. 2012. "About the Carbon Trust." Accessed March 27 (www.carbontrust.co.uk/about-carbon-trust/pages/default.aspx).

Carey, Anne R., and Karl Gelles. 2010. "What Viewers Enjoy Most about Watching the Super Bowl on TV." *USA Today,* February 5, p. A1; *Gallup Poll* (May):3.

Carlton-Ford, Steve. 2010. "Major Armed Conflicts, Militarization, and Life Chances." *Armed Forces and Society* 36 (October):864–899.

Carr, Nicholas. 2010. "Tracking Is an Assault on Liberty, with Real Dangers." *Wall Street Journal,* August 7, pp. W1, W2.

———. 2008a. *The Big Switch: Revising the World: From Edison to Google.* New York: Norton.

———. 2008b. "Is Google Making Us Stoopid?" *Atlantic* (July/August):56–58, 60, 62–63.

Carr, Patrick J., and Maria J. Kefalas. 2009. "The Rural Brain Drain." *Chronicle of Higher Education* (September 25):B7–B9.

Carroll, Joseph. 2006. "Public National Anthem Should Be Sung in English." *Gallup Poll* (May):3.

Caruso, Eugene M., Dobromir A. Rahnev, and Mahzarin R. Banaji. 2009. "Using Conjoint Analysis to Detect Discrimination: Revealing Covert Preferences from Overt Choices." *Social Cognition* 27 (1):128–137.

Castañeda, Jorge G. 1995. "Ferocious Differences." *Atlantic Monthly* 276 (July):68–69, 71–76.

Castells, Manuel. 2001. *The Internet Galaxy: Reflections on the Internet, Business, and Society.* New York: Oxford University Press.

———. 2009. *Communication Power.* New York: Oxford University Press.

———. 2010a. *The Rise of the Network Society.* 2nd ed. With a new preface. Malden, MA: Wiley-Blackwell.

———. 2010b. *The Power of Identity.* 2nd ed. With a new preface. Malden, MA: Wiley-Blackwell.

———. 2010c. *End of Millennium.* 2nd ed. With a new preface. Malden, MA: Wiley-Blackwell.

Catalyst. 2011. "No News Is Bad News: Women's Leadership Still Stalled in Corporate America." Accessed February 22, 2012 (www.catalyst.org/press-release/199/no-news-is-bad-news-womens-leadership-still-stalled-in-corporate-america).

Cauchon, Dennis. 2009. "Women Gain in Historic Job Shift." *USA Today,* September 3, p. A1.

CBS News. 1979. Transcript of *Sixty Minutes* segment, "I Was Only Following Orders." March 31, pp. 2–8.

Center for Academic Integrity. 2006. *CAI Research.* Accessed January 10 (www.academicintegrity.org).

Center for Community College Student Engagement. 2009. *Making Connections: Dimensions of Student Engagement* (2009 CCSS Findings). Austin: University of Texas at Austin, Community College Leadership Program. Accessible at www.ccsse.org/publications/national_report_2009/ccsse09_nationalreport.pdf.

Center for Community Initiatives. 2011. "Magnolia Project 2011 Reports." Accessed November 2 (www.unf.edu/coas/cci/magnilia/2011_Reports.aspx).

———. 2012a. "Northeast Florida Center for Community Initiatives (CCI)." Accessed January 3 (www.unf.edu/coas/cci/).

———. 2012b. "Magnolia Grant Objectives 2012." Accessed April 11 (htpp://aries.unfcsd.unf.edu/Magnolia/2012/objectives2012.php).

Center for Research on Education Outcomes. 2009. *Multiple Choice: Charter School Performances in 16 States.* Palo Alto, CA: CREDO, Stanford University. Accessible at http://credo.stanford.edu.

Centers for Disease Control and Prevention. 2010. "Binge Drinking among High School Students and Adults—United States, 2009." Washington, DC: CDC. Accessible at http://www.cdc.gov/mmwr/preview/mmwrhtml/mm5939a4.htm?s_cid=mm5939a4_w.

———. 2011b. *Health Disparities and Inequalities Report—United States, 2011.*

———. 2011c. *Multiple Births.* Accessible at www.cdc.gov/nchs/fstats/multiple.htm.

———. 2012a. *Vital Signs: Binge Drinking.* January 2012. Accessible at www.cdc.gov/vitalsigns/BingeDrinking.

———. 2012b. "National Marriage and Divorce Rate Trends." Accessed February 24 (www.cdc.gov/nchs/nvss/marriage_divorce_tables.htm).

———. 2012c. "HIV Surveillance-Epidemiology of HIV Infection (through 2010)." March 12. Accessible at www.cdc.gov/hiv/topics/surveillance/resources/slides/general/index/htm.

Centers for Medicare and Medicaid Services. 2011. "NHE Projections 2010–2020." Accessed March 22, 2012 (www.cms.hhs.gov).

Cerulo, Karen A., Janet M. Ruane, and Mary Chagko. 1992. "Technological Ties That Bind: Media Generated Primary Groups." *Communication Research* 19:109–129.

Chalfant, H. Paul, Robert E. Beckley, and C. Eddie Palmer. 1994. *Religion in Contemporary Society.* 3rd ed. Itasca, IL: F. E. Peacock.

Chambliss, William. 1973. "The Saints and the Roughnecks." *Society* 11 (November–December): 24–31.

Chamie, Joseph, and Barry Mirkin. 2011. "Same-Sex Marriage: A New Social Phenomenon." *Population and Development Review* 37 (September):529–551.

Chan, Sewell. 2009. "City Unveils Facebook Page to Encourage Condom Use." *New York Times,* February 12, p. A32.

Charrad, Mounira M. 2011. "Gender in the Middle East: Islam, State, Agency." *Annual Review of Sociology* 37:417–437

Chase, Randall. 2010. "O'Donnell: 'I'm Not a Witch.'" *Washington Times,* October 4. Accessed March 23 (http://www.washingtontimes.com/news/2010/oct/4/odonnell-im-not-witch/?page=2).

Chase-Dunn, Christopher, and Peter Grimes. 1995. "World-Systems Analysis." Pp. 387–417 in *Annual Review of Sociology,* 1995, edited by John Hagan. Palo Alto, CA: Annual Reviews.

———, Yukio Kawano, and Benjamin D. Brewer. 2000. "Trade Globalization Since 1795: Waves of Integration in the World System." *American Sociological Review* 65 (February):77–95.

Cheng, Shu-Ju Ada. 2003. "Rethinking the Globalization of Domestic Service." *Gender and Society* 17 (2):166–186.

Cherlin, Andrew J. 2003. "Should the Government Promote Marriage?" *Contexts* 2 (Fall):22–29.

———. 2006. "On Single Mothers 'Doing' Family." *Journal of Marriage and Family* 68 (November):800–803.

———. 2009. *The Marriage-Go-Round: The State of Marriage and the Family in America Today.* New York: Knopf.

———. 2010. *Public and Private Families: An Introduction.* 6th ed. New York: McGraw-Hill.

———. 2011. "The Increasing Complexity of Family Life in the United States." September 8. Accessible at www.prb.org/Articles/2011/us-complex-family-life.aspx?p=1.

Chicago Tribune. 1997. "In London, Prince Meets a Pauper, an Ex-Classmate." December 5, p. 19.

Child Welfare Information. 2011. *How Many Children Were Adopted in 2007 and 2008?* Washington, DC: U.S. Government Printing Office.

Chin, Kolin. 1996. *Chinatown Gangs: Extortion, Enterprise, and Ethnicity.* New York: Oxford University Press.

Choney, Suzanne. 2010. "Mobile Giving for Chile Pales Compared to Haiti." MSNBC. March 12, 2010. Accessible at www.msnmb.msn .com/ed/35822836/ns/technology_and_science-wireless/t/mobile-giving-chile-pales-compared-haiti.

Christakis, Nicholas A., and James H. Fowler. 2007. "The Spread of Obesity in a Large Social Network over 32 Years." *New England Journal of Medicine* 357 (July 26):370–379.

———, and ———. 2009. *Connected: The Amazing Power of Social Networks and How They Shape Our Lives.* New York: Harper.

Chronic Poverty Research Centre. 2009. *The Chronic Poverty Report 2008–09: Escaping Poverty Traps.* Geneva: Chronic Poverty Research Centre.

Chu, Henry. 2005. "Tractors Crush Heart of a Nation." *Los Angeles Times,* July 10, p. A9.

Chu, Kathy. 2010. "Vietnam's Market Grows Up." *USA Today,* August 23, p. B3.

Chubb, Catherine, Simone Melis, Louisa Potter, and Raymond Storry. 2008. *The Global Gender Pay Gap.* London: Incomes Data Services.

Chung, Esther K., Leny Mathew, Amy C. Rothkopf, Irma T. Elo, James C. Cayne, and Jennifer F. Culhane. 2009. "Parenting Attitudes and Infant Spanking: The Influence of Childhood Experiences." *Pediatrics* 124 (August):278–286.

Clark, Burton, and Martin Trow. 1966. "The Organizational Context." Pp. 17–70 in *The Study of College Peer Groups,* edited by Theodore M. Newcomb and Everett K. Wilson. Chicago: Aldine.

Clark, Candace. 1983. "Sickness and Social Control." Pp. 346–365 in *Social Interaction: Readings in Sociology,* 2nd ed., edited by Howard Robboy and Candace Clark. New York: St. Martin's Press.

Clark, Kim. 2010. "Can School Reform Even Really Work?" *US News and World Report* (January):23–26, 30–31.

Clarke, Adele E., Janet K. Shim, Laura Maro, Jennifer Ruth Fusket, and Jennifer R. Fishman. 2003. "Bio Medicalization: Technoscientific Transformations of Health, Illness, and U.S. Biomedicine." *American Sociological Review* 68 (April):161–194.

Clarke, Lee. 2002. "Panic: Myth or Reality?" *Contexts* 1 (Fall):21–26.

Clayton, Mark. 2011. "The New Cyber Arms Race." *Christian Science Monitor,* March 7, pp. 26–71.

Clemmitt, Marcia. 2005. "Intelligent Design." *CQ Researcher* 15 (July 29): 637–660.

Clifford, Stephanie. 2009a. "Teaching Teenagers about Harassment." *New York Times,* January 27, p. B1.

Clinard, Marshall B., and Robert F. Miller. 1998. *Sociology of Deviant Behavior.* 10th ed. Fort Worth, TX: Harcourt Brace.

Clymer, Adam. 2000. "College Students Not Drawn to Voting or Politics, Poll Shows." *New York Times,* January 2, p. A14.

Coates, Rodney. 2008. "Covert Racism in the USA and Globally." *Sociology Compass* 2:208–231.

Coca-Cola. 2013. Coca-Cola Rumors & Facts. Accessed May 14 at www.coca-colacompany.com/contact-us/coca-cola-rumors-facts.

Cockerham, William C. 2012. *Medical Sociology.* 12th ed. Upper Saddle River, NJ: Prentice Hall.

Cole, Mike. 1988. *Bowles and Gintis Revisited: Correspondence and Contradiction in Educational Theory.* Philadelphia: Falmer.

Coleman, Isobel. 2004. "The Payoff from Women's Rights." *Foreign Affairs* 83 (May–June):80–95.

Coleman, James William, and Donald R. Cressey. 1980. *Social Problems.* New York: Harper and Row.

———. 2006. *The Criminal Elite: Understanding White-Collar Crime.* 6th ed. New York: Worth.

College Board. 2009. *Trends in College Pricing.* New York: College Board.

Collins, Daryl, Jonathan Morduch, Stuart Rutherford, and Orlanda Ruthven. 2009. *Portfolios of the Poor: How the World's Poor Live on $2 a Day.* Princeton, NJ: Princeton University Press.

Collins, Patricia Hill. 2000. *Black Feminist Thought: Knowledge, Consciousness, and the Politics of Empowerment.* Revised 10th anniv. 2nd ed. New York: Routledge.

Collins, Randall. 1975. *Conflict Sociology: Toward an Explanatory Sociology.* New York: Academic Press.

———. 1980. "Weber's Last Theory of Capitalism: A Systematization." *American Sociological Review* 45 (December):925–942.

———. 1986. *Weberian Sociological Theory.* New York: Cambridge University Press.

———. 1995. "Prediction in Macrosociology: The Case of the Soviet Collapse." *American Journal of Sociology* 100 (May):1552–1593.

Colucci, Jim. 2008. "All the World's a Screen." *Watch!* (June):50–53.

Commission on Civil Rights. 1976. *A Guide to Federal Laws and Regulations Prohibiting Sex Discrimination.* Washington, DC: U.S. Government Printing Office.

———. 1981. *Affirmative Action in the 1980s: Dismantling the Process of Discrimination.* Washington, DC: U.S. Government Printing Office.

Commoner, Barry. 1971. *The Closing Circle.* New York: Knopf.

———. 1990. *Making Peace with the Planet.* New York: Pantheon.

———. 2007. "At 90, an Environmentalist from the 70's Still Has Hope." *New York Times,* June 19, p. D2.

Congressional Oversight Panel. 2011. "February Oversight Report: Executive Compensation Restrictions in the Troubled Asset Relief Program." Washington, DC: COP.

Conley, Dalton. 2010. *Being Black, Living in the Red.* 10th anniversary edition. Berkeley: University of California Press.

Connell, R. W. 1987. *Gendered Power: Society, the Person, and Sexual Politics.* Stanford, CA: Stanford University Press.

———. 2002. *Gender.* Cambridge, UK: Polity Press.

———. 2005. *Masculinities.* 2nd ed. Berkeley: University of California Press.

Conner, Thaddieus, and William A. Taggart. 2009. "The Impact of Gaming on the Indian Nations in New Mexico." *Social Science Quarterly* 90 (March):52–70.

Conrad, Peter, ed. 2009a. *The Medicalization of Society: On the Transformation of Human Conditions into Treatable Disorders.* 11th ed. Baltimore, MD: Johns Hopkins University.

———. 2009b. *The Sociology of Health and Illness: Cultural Perspectives.* 8th ed. New York: Worth.

———, and Kristin K. Barker. 2010. "The Social Construction of Illness: Key Insights and Policy Implications." *Journal of Health and Social Behavior* 51 (5):567–579.

Cooky, Cheryl, and Nicole M. LaVoi. 2012. "Playing but Losing." *Contexts* (Winter):42–46.

Cooley, Charles. H. 1902. *Human Nature and the Social Order.* New York: Scribner.

Coontz, Stephanie. 2006. "A Pop Quiz on Marriage." *New York Times,* February 19, p. 12.

Cooper, K., S. Day, A. Green, and H. Ward. 2007. "Maids, Migrants and Occupational Health in the London Sex Industry." *Anthropology and Medicine* 14 (April):41–53.

Copeland, Craig. 2012. "Labor-Force Participation Rates of the Population Age 55 and Older, 2011: After the Economic Downturn." *Employee Benefit Research Institute* Notes 33 (February).

Corbett, Christianne, Catherine Hill, and Andresse St. Rose. 2008. *Where the Girls Are: The Facts about Gender Equity in Education.* Washington, DC: American Association of University Women.

Coser, Lewis A. 1977. *Masters of Sociological Thought: Ideas in Historical and Social Context.* 2nd ed. New York: Harcourt, Brace and Jovanovich.

Coser, Rose Laub. 1984. "American Medicine's Ambiguous Progress." *Contemporary Sociology* 13 (January):9–13.

Côté, James E. 2000. *Arrested Adulthood: The Changing Nature of Identity and Maturity in the Late World.* New York: New York University.

Couch, Carl J. 1968. "Collective Behavior: An Examination of Some Stereotypes." *Social Problems* 15:310–322.

———. 1996. *Information Technologies and Social Orders.* Edited with an introduction by David R. Maines and Shing-Ling Chien. New York: Aldine de Gruyter.

Council on Ethical and Judicial Affairs, American Medical Association. 1992. "Decisions Near the End of Life." *Journal of the American Medical Association* 267 (April 22–29):2229–2333.

Council on Foreign Relations. 2009. "Public Opinion on Global Issues." Accessible at www.cfr.org/public-opinion.

Counts, Dorothy Ayers, and David Counts. 2012. "The Good, the Bad, and the Unresolved Death in Kaliai." *Social Science and Medicine* 58 (No. 5): 887–897.

Cox, Oliver C. 1948. *Caste, Class, and Race: A Study in Social Dynamics*. Detroit: Wayne State University Press.

Cox, Rachel S. 2003. "Home Schooling Debate." *CQ Researcher* 13 (January 17):25–48.

Crabtree, Steve. 2010. *Religiosity Highest in World's Poorest Nations*. August 31. Accessible at www.gallup.com.

Cross, Simon, and Barbara Bagilhole. 2002. "Girls' Jobs for the Boys? Men, Masculinity and Non-Traditional Occupations." *Gender, Work, and Organization* 9 (April):204–226.

Croteau, David, and William Hoynes. 2003. *Media/Society: Industries, Images, and Audiences*. 3rd ed. Thousand Oaks, CA: Pine Forge Press.

———, and ———. 2006. *The Business of the Media: Corporate Media and the Public Interest*. 2nd ed. Thousand Oaks, CA: Pine Forge Press.

———, ———, and Stefania Milan. 2012. *Media/Society: Industries, Images, and Audiences*. 4th ed. Los Angeles: Sage.

Croucher, Sheila L. 2004. *Globalization and Belonging: The Politics of Identity in a Changing World*. Lanham, MD: Rowman and Littlefield.

Crouse, Kelly. 1999. "Sociology of the *Titanic*." *Teaching Sociology Listserv*. May 24.

Crowe, Jerry, and Valli Herman. 2005. "NBA Lists Fashion Do's and Don'ts." *Los Angeles Times*, October 19, pp. A1, A23.

Crump, Andy. 2006. "Suicide in Japan." *Lancet* 367 (April 8):1143.

Cuff, E. C., W. W. Sharrock, and D. W. Francis, eds. 1990. *Perspectives in Sociology*. 3rd ed. Boston: Unwin Hyman.

Currie, Elliot. 1985. *Confronting Crime: An American Challenge*. New York: Pantheon.

———. 1998. *Crime and Punishment in America*. New York: Metropolis Books.

Curry, Timothy Jon. 1993. "A Little Pain Never Hurt Anyone: Athletic Career Socialization and the Normalization of Sports Injury." *Symbolic Interaction* 26 (Fall):273–290.

Cushing-Daniels, Brenda, and Sheila R. Zedlewski. 2008. "Tax and Spending Policy and Economic Mobility." Washington, DC: Economic Mobility Project. Also accessible at www.economic-mobility.org/reports_and_research/literature_reviews?id=0004.

Customs and Border Patrol. 2011. "U.S. Border Patrol Fiscal Year Apprehension Statistics—Southeast Border Sectors." Accessed January 29, 2012 (www.cbp.gov/xp/cgov/border_security/border_partol/usbp_statistics/).

d

Dade, Corey. 2012. "Battle Over Voter ID Laws Intensify." June 2. Accessible at www.wbur.org/npr/154152507/battles-over-voter-id-laws-intensify.

Dahl, Robert A. 1961. *Who Governs?* New Haven, CT: Yale University Press.

Dahrendorf, Ralf. 1958. "Toward a Theory of Social Conflict." *Journal of Conflict Resolution* 2 (June):170–183.

———. 1959. *Class and Class Conflict in Industrial Sociology*. Stanford, CA: Stanford University Press.

Dalla, Rochelle L., and Wendy C. Gamble. 2001. "Teenage Mothering and the Navajo Reservation: An Examination of Intergovernmental Perceptions and Beliefs." *American Indian Culture and Research Journal* 25 (1):1–19.

Daniel, G. Reginald. 2006. *Race and Multiraciality in Brazil and the United States: Converging Paths?* University Park: Pennsylvania State University Press.

Danziger, Sandra K. 2010. "The Decline of Cash Welfare and Implications for Social Policy and Poverty." *Annual Review of Sociology* 36:523–545.

Dao, James. 2013. "When the Bullets Flew, They Didn't Care that I Was a Woman." *New York Times*, January 25, pp. A1, A3.

Darlin, Damon. 2006. "It's O.K to Fall Behind the Technology Curve." *New York Times*, December 30, p. B6.

Darwin, Charles. 1859. *On the Origin of Species*. London: John Murray.

David, Gary. 2004. "Scholarship on Arab Americans Distorted Past 9/11." *Al Jadid* (Winter–Spring): 26–27.

———. 2008. "Arab Americans." Pp. 84–87, vol. 1, in *Encyclopedia of Race, Ethnicity, and Society*, edited by Richard T. Schaefer. Thousand Oaks, CA: Sage.

Davidson, James D., and Ralph E. Pyle. 2011. *Ranking Faiths: Religious Stratification in America*. Lanham, MD: Rowman and Littlefield.

Davidson, Paul. 2010. "Temporary Workers Reshape Companies, Jobs." *USA Today*, October 13, pp. A1–A2.

Davies, Christie. 1989. "Goffman's Concept of the Total Institution: Criticisms and Revisions." *Human Studies* 12 (June):77–95.

Davis, Darren W., and Brian D. Silver. 2003. "Stereotype Threat and Race of Interviewer Knowledge." *American Journal of Political Science* 47 (January):33–45.

Davis, Gerald. 2003. *America's Corporate Banks Are Separated by Just Four Handshakes*. Accessed March 7 (www.bus.umich.edu/research/davis.html).

———. 2004. "American Cronyism: How Executive Networks Inflated the Corporate Bubble." *Contexts* (Summer):34–40.

Davis, Kingsley. 1940. "Extreme Social Isolation of a Child." *American Journal of Sociology* 45 (January):554–565.

———. 1947. "A Final Note on a Case of Extreme Isolation." *American Journal of Sociology* 52 (March):432–437.

———, and Wilbert E. Moore. 1945. "Some Principles of Stratification." *American Sociological Review* 10 (April):242–249.

———. [1949] 1995. *Human Society*. Reprint. New York: Macmillan.

Davis, Martha F. 2010. "Abortion Access in the Global Marketplace." *North Carolina Law Review* 88:1657–1685.

Davis, Mike. 2005. *Planet of Slums*. London: Verso.

Davis, Paul K., and Kim Cragin, eds. 2009. *Social Science for Counterterrorism: Putting the Pieces Together*. Santa Monica, CA: RAND.

Dayananda, Vanitha. 2006. *Sexuality and Love in Arranged Marriages in India: Why Arranged Marriages Last*. Leeds, England: Wisdom House Publications.

De Anda, Roberto M. 2004. *Chicanas and Chicanos in Contemporary Society*. 2nd ed. Lanham, MD: Rowman and Littlefield.

Death Penalty Information Center. 2012. "Facts About the Death Penalty (Updated January 23, 2012)." Accessible at www.deathpenaltyinfo.org.

Death with Dignity National Center. 2012. "Living with Dying." Accessed March 12 at http://www.deathwithdignity.org. Government Printing Office.

Deegan, Mary Jo, ed. 1991. *Women in Sociology: A Bio-Biographical Sourcebook*. Westport, CT: Greenwood.

———. 2003. "Textbooks, the History of Sociology, and the Sociological Stock of Knowledge." *Sociological Theory* 21 (November):298–305.

Deflem, Mathieu. 2005. "'Wild Beasts without Nationality': The Uncertain Origins of Interpol, 1898–1910." Pp. 275–285 in *Handbook of Transnational Crime and Justice*, edited by Philip Rerchel. Thousand Oaks, CA: Sage.

Deibert, Ronald J., John Palfrey, Rafal Rohozinski, and Jonathan Zittrain. 2008. *Access Denied: The Practice and Policy of Global Internet Filtering*. Cambridge, MA: MIT Press.

Delaney, Kevin J. 2005. "Big Mother Is Watching." *Wall Street Journal*, November 26, pp. A1, A6.

Della Porta, Donatella, and Sidney Tarrow, eds. 2005. *Transnational Protest and Global Activism*. Lanham, MD: Rowman and Littlefield.

DeNavas-Walt, Carmen, Bernadette D. Proctor, and Jessica C. Smith. 2010. "Income, Poverty, and Health Insurance Coverage in the United States: 2009." P60-238 in *Current Population Survey*. Washington, DC: U.S. Government Printing Office.

———. 2011. *Income, Poverty, and Health Insurance Coverage in the United States: 2010*. Washington, DC: U.S. Government Printing Office.

Denny, Charlotte. 2004. "Migration Myths Hold No Fears." *Guardian Weekly*, February 26, p. 12.

Denny, Kathleen E. 2011. "Gender in Context, Content, and Approach: Contemporary Gender Measures in Girl Scout and Boy Scout Handbooks." *Gender and Society* 25 (February):27–47.

Denzin, Norman K. 2004. "Postmodernism." Pp. 581–583 in *Encyclopedia of Social Theory*, edited by George Ritzer. Thousand Oaks, CA: Sage.

DeParle, Jason. 2009. "The 'W' Word, Re-Engaged." *New York Times*, February 8, Week in Review, p. 1.

Department of Commerce. 2011. *NTIA Launches National Broadband Map*. Washington, DC: Department of Commerce.

Department of Health and Human Services. 2011b. "AFCARS, Report." Accessed April 6 (www.acf .hhs.gov/programs/cb/stats_research/afcars/tar/ report17.htm).

———. 2012a. "TANF: Total Number of Families." As of 1/30/2012. Accessible at www.acf.hhs.gov/ programs/ofa/data-reports/caseload/2011/2012_ family_tan.htm.

Department of Homeland Security. 2010. *Haiti Social Media: Disaster Monitoring Initiative.* January 21. Washington, DC: U.S. Department of Homeland Security.

Department of Justice. 2000. *The Civil Liberties Act of 1988: Redress for Japanese Americans.* Accessed June 29 (www.usdoj.gov/crt/ora/main.html).

———. 2008. "Hate Crime Statistics, 2007." Accessible at www.Fbi.gov/ucr/ucr.htm.

———. 2009. *2008 Crime in the United States.* (Uniform Crime Report). Accessible at http:// www.fbi.gov/ucr/cius2008/index.html.

———. 2011. "Labor Force Statistics: Table 3." Accessed March 21, 2011 (www.bls.gov/cps/ tables.htm).

———. 2011a. "Crime in the United States, 2010." Accessed January 23, 2012 (www.fbi. gov/about-us/cjis/ucr/crime-in-the-u.s/2010/ crime-in-the-u.s.-2010).

———. 2011b. "About Hate Crime Statistics, 2010." Accessed January 23, 2012 (www.fbi.gov. about-us/cjis/ucr/hate-crime/2010).

Department of State. 2011b. "Tier Placements." Accessed January 25, 2012 (www.state.gov/j/tip/ rls/tiprpt/2011/164228.htm).

Desai, Rani A., Suchitra Krishnan-Sarin, Dana Cavallo, and Marc N. Potenza. 2010. "Video-Gaming among High School Students: Health Correlates, Gender Differences, and Problematic Gaming." *Pediatrics* 126 (November 15):1414–1424.

Deutsch, Francine M. 2007. "Undoing Gender." *Gender and Society* 21 (February):106–127.

Devitt, James. 1999. *Framing Gender on the Campaign Trail: Women's Executive Leadership and the Press.* New York: Women's Leadership Conference.

Dewan, Shaila. 2010. "To Court Blacks, Foes of Abortion Make Racial Case." *New York Times,* February 27, pp. A1, A13.

Diamond, Shari Seidman, and Mary R. Rose. 2005. "Real Juries." Pp. 255–284 in *Annual Review of Law and Social Science 2005.* Palo Alto, CA: Annual Reviews.

Dickler, Jessica. 2011. "Dig Deep to Buy Titanic Visit." *Chicago Tribune,* June 3, p. 25.

Diefenbach, Donald L., and Mark D. West. 2007. "Television and Attitudes toward Mental Health Issues: Cultivation Analysis and the Third Person Effect." *Journal of Community Psychology* 35 (2):181–195.

Dillon, Sam. 2004. "Education Can Be Long, Hard Haul for Nation's Rural Kids." *Chicago Tribune,* May 28, p. 13.

———. 2009. "As More Charter Schools Unionize, Educators Debate the Effect." *New York Times,* July 27, pp. A1, A14.

DiPrete, Thomas A., Gregory M. Eirich, and Matthew Pittinsky. 2010. "Compensation Benchmarking, Leapfrogs, and the Surge in Executive Pay." *American Journal of Sociology* 115 (May):1671–1712.

Disaster Research Center. 2013. "About the DRC." Accessed April 25 at www.udel.edu/DRC/ aboutus/about.html.

Dobbin, Frank, and Jiwook Jung. 2010. "Corporate Board Gender Diversity and Stock Performance: The Competence Gap on Institutional Investor Bias?" *North Carolina Law Review* 89.

Dodds, Klaus. 2000. *Geopolitics in a Changing World.* Harlow, UK: Pearson Education.

Domhoff, G. William. 1978. *Who Really Rules? New Haven and Community Power Reexamined.* New Brunswick, NJ: Transaction.

———. 2010. *Who Rules America?* 6th ed. New York: McGraw-Hill.

Domi, Tanya L. 2013. "Women in Combat: Policy Catches Up with Reality." *New York Times,* February 8.

Dominick, Joseph R. 2009. *The Dynamics of Mass Communication: Media in the Digital Age.* 10th ed. New York: McGraw-Hill.

Donadio, Rachel. 2009. "Facebook 'Fans' of the Mafia May Be More, Authorities Say." *New York Times,* January 20, pp. A1, A8.

Doress, Irwin, and Jack Nusan Porter. 1977. *Kids in Cults: Why They Join, Why They Stay, Why They Leave.* Brookline, MA: Reconciliation Associates.

Dotson, Floyd. 1991. "Community." P. 55 in *Encyclopedic Dictionary of Sociology.* 4th ed. Guilford, CT: Dushkin.

Dougherty, Conor. 2011. "Population Leaves Heartland Behind." *Wall Street Journal,* April 11, p. A6.

Dougherty, Kevin, and Floyd M. Hammack. 1992. "Education Organization." Pp. 535–541 in *Encyclopedia of Sociology,* vol. 2, edited by Edgar F. Borgatta and Marie L. Borgatta. New York: Macmillan.

Downey, Liam, and Brian Hawkins. 2008. "Race, Income, and Environmental Inequality in the United States." *Sociological Perspectives* 50 (4):759–781.

Dreifus, Claudia. 2003. "A Conversation with Lee Clarke." *New York Times,* May 20, Science Times section, p. 2.

———. 2004. "A Sociologist with an Advanced Degree in Calamity." *New York Times,* September 7, p. D2.

DuBois, W. E. B. [1899] 1995. *The Philadelphia Negro: A Social Study.* Philadelphia: University of Pennsylvania Press.

———. [1900] 1969. "To the Nations of the World." Pp. 19–23 in *An ABC of Color,* edited by W. E. B. DuBois. New York: International Publishers.

———. [1903] 1961. *The Souls of Black Folks: Essays and Sketches.* New York: Fawcett.

———. [1903] 2003. *The Negro Church.* Walnut Creek, CA: AltaMira Press.

———. [1909] 1970. *The Negro American Family.* Atlanta University. Reprinted 1970. Cambridge, MA: MIT Press.

———. [1935] 1962. *Black Reconstruction in America 1860–1880.* New York: Athenaeum.

———. [1940] 1968. *Dusk of Dawn.* New York: Harcourt, Brace. Reprint. New York: Schocken Books.

Duhigg, Charles, and Keith Bradsher. 2012. "How U.S. Lost Out on iPhone Work." *New York Times,* January 22, p. A1.

Dukić, Vanja, Hedibert F. Lopes, and Nicholas G. Polson. 2011. "Tracking Flu Epidemics Using Google Flu Trends and Particle Learning." Accessible at http://faculty.chicagobooth.edu/ nicholas.polson/research/papers/Track.pdf.

Dundas, Susan, and Miriam Kaufman. 2000. "The Toronto Lesbian Family Study." *Journal of Homosexuality* 40 (20):65–79.

Duneier, Mitchell. 1994a. "On the Job, but Behind the Scenes." *Chicago Tribune,* December 26, pp. 1, 24.

———. 1994b. "Battling for Control." *Chicago Tribune,* December 28, pp. 1, 8.

Dunlap, Riley E. 2010. "At 40, Environmental Movement Endures with Less Consensus." April 22. Accessed April 27 (www.gallup.com/ poll/127487/Environmental-Movement-Endures-Less-Consensus.aspx?version=print).

———, and Angela G. Mertig. 1991. "The Evolution of the U.S. Environmental Movement from 1970 to 1990: An Overview." *Society of National Resources* 4 (July–September):209–218.

Durden, T. Elizabeth, and Robert A. Hummer. 2006. "Access to Healthcare among Working-Aged Hispanic Adults in the United States." *Social Science Quarterly* 87 (December):1319–1343.

Durex. 2007. "The Face of Global Sex 2007—First Sex: An Opportunity of a Lifetime." Accessible at http://www.durexnetwork.org/SiteCollection-Documents/Research%20%20Face%20of%20 Global%20Sex%202007.pdf.

Durkheim, Émile. [1893] 1933. *Division of Labor in Society.* Translated by George Simpson. Reprint. New York: Free Press.

———. [1895] 1964. *The Rules of Sociological Method.* Translated by Sarah A. Solovay and John H. Mueller. Reprint. New York: Free Press.

———. [1897] 1951. *Suicide.* Translated by John A. Spaulding and George Simpson. Reprint. New York: Free Press.

———. [1912] 2001. *The Elementary Forms of Religious Life.* A new translation by Carol Cosman. New York: Oxford University Press.

Dutta, Soumitra, and Irene Mia. 2010. *The Global Information Technology Report 2009–2010.* Geneva: World Economic Forum and INSEAD. Accessible at http://networkedreadiness.com/gitr/ main/fullreport/index.html.

Dyrbye, Liselotte, N. Tait, D. Shanafelt, Charles M. Balch, Daniel Satele, and Julie Freischlag. 2011. "Relationship Between Work-Home Conflicts and Burnout Among American Surgeons." *Archives of Surgery* 146 (February):211–217.

Dzidzienyo, Anani. 1987. "Brazil." In *International Handbook on Race and Race Relations,* edited by Jay A. Sigler. New York: Greenwood Press.

e

Eaton, Leslie. 2007. "Urban to Care, Storm Evacuees Give Farm a Try." *New York Times,* April 28, pp. A1, A9.

Ebaugh, Helen Rose Fuchs. 1988. *Becoming an Ex: The Process of Role Exit.* Chicago: University of Chicago Press.

Eby, Lillian T., Charleen P. Maher, and Marcus M. Butts. 2010. "The Intersection of Work and Family Life: The Role of Affect." *Annual Review of Psychology* 61:599–622.

Eckberg, Douglas. 2006. "Crime, Law Enforcement, and Justice." Pp. 5-209–5-233 in *Historical Statistics of the United States,* Chapter Ec, edited by Richard Sutch and Susan Carter. New York: Cambridge University Press.

Eckenwiler, Mark. 1995. "In the Eyes of the Law." *Internet World* (August):74, 76–77.

Economic Mobility Project. 2009. *Findings from a National Survey and Focus Groups on Economic Mobility.* Washington, DC: Pew Charitable Trusts.

The Economist. 2003. "The One Where Pooh Goes to Sweden." (April 5):59.

———. 2004. "Battle on the Home Front." (February 21):8–10.

———. 2005b. "We Are Tous Québécois." (January 8):39.

———. 2005c. "Behind the Digital Divide." (March 2):22–25.

———. 2008b. "Following the Crowd." (September 6):10–11.

———. 2009a. "Burgeoning Bourgeoisie." (February 14):1–22.

———. 2010b. "Plus One Country." (September 4):46.

———. 2010c. "The Dark Side." (September 11):15.

———. 2010d. "The Strange Death of Social-Democratic Sweden." (September 18):16–17.

———. 2011b. "China's Population: The Most Surprising Demographic Crisis." (May 7):43–44.

———. 2011c. "Digging for Victory." (September 24):60.

———. 2011c. "Age shall not wither them." (April 9):78.

———. 2012u. "Retail in Developing Countries: Selling Sisters." (November 29). Accessed February 26, 2013 at www.economist.com/blogs/schumpeter/2012/11/retail-developing-countries.

———. 2013. "China's Population: Peak Toll." (January 26):41–42.

Edmans, Alex, and Xavier Gabaix. 2010. "What's Right, What's Wrong, and What's Fixable." *Pathways* (Summer):13–16.

Ehrenreich, Barbara. 2001. *Nickel and Dimed: On (Not) Getting By in America.* New York: Metropolitan.

Ehrlich, Paul R. 1968. *The Population Bomb.* New York: Ballantine.

———, and Anne H. Ehrlich. 1990. *The Population Explosion.* New York: Simon and Schuster.

———, and Katherine Ellison. 2002. "A Looming Threat We Won't Face." *Los Angeles Times,* January 20, p. M6.

Eitzen, D. Stanley. 2009. *Fair and Foul: Beyond the Myths and Paradoxes of Sport.* 4th ed. Lanham, MD: Rowman and Littlefield.

El Nasser, Haya, and Paul Overberg. 2009. "U.S. Making Sure Census Isn't Overcounted." *USA Today,* January 16.

———, and ———. 2011. "Recession Reshapes Life in the USA." USA Today, September 12, p. 3A.

———, and ———. 2012. "Census Shows Best Count Ever." *USA Today,* May 23, p. 3A.

Elgan, Mike. 2011. "How to Pop Your Internet 'Filter Bubble.'" *Computer World* (May 7). Accessed November 11 (www.computerworld.com/s/article/9216484/Elgan_How_to_pop_your_Internet_filter_bubble).

Ellison, Brandy. 2008. "Tracking." Pp. 301–304, vol. 2, in *Encyclopedia of Race, Ethnicity, and Society,* edited by Richard T. Schaefer. Thousand Oaks, CA: Sage.

Ellison, Jesse. 2008. "A New Grip on Life." *Newsweek* 152 (December 15):64.

Ellison, Nicole, Charles Steinfield, and Cliff Lampe. 2007. "The Benefits of Facebook 'Friends': Exploring the Relationship between College Students' Use of Online Social Networks and Social Capital." *Journal of Computer-Mediated Communication* 12 (4):1143–1168.

Ellison, Nicole B., Jeffrey T. Hancock, and Catalina L. Toma. 2012. "Profile as Promise: A Framework for Conceptualizing the Veracity of Self Presentation in Online Dating Profiles." *New Media and Society,* 14 (February):45–62.

Ellison, Ralph. 1952. *Invisible Man.* New York: Random House.

Ely, Robin J. 1995. "The Power of Demography: Women's Social Construction of Gender Identity at Work." *Academy of Management Journal* 38 (3):589–634.

Embree, Ainslie. 2003. "Religion." Pp. 101–220 in *Understanding Contemporary India,* edited by Sumit Ganguly and Neil DeVotta. Boulder, CO: Lynne Rienner.

Engels, Friedrich [1884] 1959. "The Origin of the Family, Private Property, and the State." Pp. 392–394, excerpted in *Marx and Engels: Basic Writings on Politics and Philosophy,* edited by Lewis Feuer. Garden City, NY: Anchor Books.

Ennis, Sharon R., Merarys Rios-Vargas, and Nora G. Albert. 2011. *The Hispanic Population: 2010.* 2010 Census Brief BR-04. Washington, DC: U.S. Government Printing Office.

Entine, Jon, and Martha Nichols. 1996. "Blowing the Whistle on Meaningless 'Good Intentions.'" *Chicago Tribune,* June 20, sec. 1, p. 21.

Environmental Protection Agency. 2012. Global Greenhouse Gas Data. Accessible at http://epa.gov/climatechange/emissions/globalghg.html.

Epstein, Cynthia Fuchs. 1999. "The Major Myth of the Women's Movement." *Dissent* (Fall):83–111.

Epstein, Robert. 2009. "The Truth about Online Dating." *Scientific American* (Special Edition).

Erikson, Kai. 1966. *Wayward Puritans: A Study in the Sociology of Deviance.* New York: Wiley.

Esbenshade, Jill. 2008. "Giving Up Against the Global Economy: New Developments in the Anti-Sweatshops Movement." *Critical Sociology* 34 (3):453–470.

Escárcega, Sylvia. 2008. "Mexico." Pp. 898–902, vol. 2, in *Encyclopedia of Race, Ethnicity, and Society,* edited by Richard T. Schaefer. Thousand Oaks, CA: Sage.

Etaugh, Claire. 2003. "Witches, Mothers and Others: Females in Children's Books." *Hilltopics* (Winter):10–13.

Etzioni, Amitai. 1964. *Modern Organization.* Englewood Cliffs, NJ: Prentice Hall.

———. 1965. *Political Unification.* New York: Holt, Rinehart and Winston.

European Metalworkers' Federation. 2010. "What Is Precious Work?" Accessed March 1, 2011 (www.emf-fem.org).

European PWN. 2012. "Women on Boards: The Inside Story on Norway's 40% Target." Accessed February 22 (www.europeanpwn.net/index.php?article_id=150).

Evergeti, Venetia, and Elisabetta Zontini. 2006. "Introduction: Some Critical Reflections on Social Capital, Migration and Transnational Families." *Ethnic and Racial Studies* 29 (November):1025–1039.

f

Facebook. 2010. "Statistics." Accessed January 15 (www.facebook.com/press.info.php?statistics).

———. 2011. Statistics. Accessed January 21 (www.facebook.com/press/info.php?statistics).

Faiola, Anthony. 2005. "Their Husbands Made Them Sick." *Washington Post National Weekly Edition* 23 (October 24):18.

———. 2006. Japan's Vulnerable Elderly. *Washington Post National Weekly Edition* 23 (February 27):18.

Fairtrade Foundation. 2010. "Retail Products." Accessed Jan. 5 (www.fairtrade.org.uk/products/retail_products/default.aspx).

Faith, Nazila. 2005. "Iranian Cleric Turns Blogger in Campaign for Reform." *New York Times,* January 16, p. 4.

Fallows, Deborah. 2006. *Pew Internet Project Data.* Washington, DC: Pew Internet and American Life Project.

Farley, Maggie. 2004. "U.N. Gay Policy Is Assailed." *Los Angeles Times,* April 9, p. A3.

Farley, Melissa, and Victor Malarek. 2008. "The Myth of the Victimless Crime." *New York Times,* March 12, p. A27.

Farr, Grant M. 1999. *Modern Iran.* New York: McGraw-Hill.

Farrell, Amy, and Jack McDevitt. 2010. "Identifying and Measuring Racial Profiling by the Police." *Sociology Compass* 4:77–88.

Fausset, Richard. 2003. "Sikhs Mark New Year, Fight Post-September 11 Bias." *Los Angeles Times,* April 14, pp. B1, B7.

Favreault, Melissa. 2008. "Discrimination and Economic Mobility." Washington, DC: Economic Mobility Project. Also accessible at www.economicmobility.org/reports_and_research/literature_reviews?id=0004.

FBI. 2012. Crime in The United States 2011. Accessible at www.fbi.gov.

Feagin, Joe R. 1989. *Minority Group Issues in Higher Education: Learning from Qualitative Research.* Norman: Center for Research on Minority Education, University of Oklahoma.

———, Harnán Vera, and Nikitah Imani. 1996. *The Agony of Education: Black Students at White Colleges and Universities.* New York: Routledge.

Featherman, David L., and Robert M. Hauser. 1978. *Opportunity and Change.* New York: Aeodus.

Federal Trade Commission. 2010. "Protecting Consumer Privacy in an Era of Rapid Change: A Proposed Framework for Businesses and Policymakers." Accessible at http://www.ftc.gov/os/2010/12/101201privacyreport.pdf.

Felson, David, and Akis Kalaitzidis. 2005. "A Historical Overview of Transnational Crime." Pp. 3–19 in *Handbook of Transnational Crime and Justice,* edited by Philip Reichel. Thousand Oaks, CA: Sage.

Feminist Majority Foundation. 2007. "Feminists Are the Majority." Accessed February 25 (www.feminist.org).

Ferber, Abby L., and Michael S. Kimmel. 2008. "The Gendered Face of Terrorism." *Sociology Compass* 2:870–887.

Ferree, Myra Marx, and David A. Merrill. 2000. "Hot Movements, Cold Cognition: Thinking about Social Movements in Gendered Frames." *Contemporary Society* 29 (May):454–462.

Feuer, Lewis S. 1989. *Marx and Engels: Basic Writings on Politics and Philosophy.* New York: Anchor Books.

Field, John. 2008. *Social Capital.* 2nd ed. London: Routledge.

Fields, Jason. 2004. "America's Families and Living Arrangements: 2003." *Current Population Reports,* ser. P-20, no. 553. Washington, DC: U.S. Government Printing Office.

Fieser, Ezra. 2009. "What Price for Good Coffee?" *Time,* October 5, pp. 61–62.

Fiji TV. 2012. Home Page. Accessed January 10 (www.fijitv.com.fj).

File, Thom, and Sarah Crissey. 2010. "Voting and Registration in the Election of November 2008." *Current Population Reports,* ser. P-20, no. 562.

Finch, Emily, and Vanessa E. Munro. 2005. "Juror Stereotypes and Blame Attribution in Rape Cases Involving Intoxicants." *British Journal of Criminology* 45 (June):25–38.

———— and ————. 2007. "The Demon Drink and the Demonized Woman: Socio-Sexual Stereotypes and Responsibility Attribution in Rape Trials Involving Intoxicants." 16 (No. 4) 591–614.

———— and ————. 2008. "Lifting the Veil: The Use of Focus Groups and Trial Simulations in Legal Research." 30–51.

Fine, Gary C. 1987. *With the Boys: Little League Baseball and Preadolescent Culture.* Chicago: University of Chicago Press.

Fine, Gary Alan, and Bill Ellis. 2011. *The Global Grapevine: Why Rumors of Terrorism, Immigration, and Trade Matter.* New York: Oxford University Press.

————. 2008. "Robbers Cave." Pp. 1163–1164, vol. 3, in *Encyclopedia of Race, Ethnicity, and Society,* edited by Richard T. Schaefer. Thousand Oaks, CA: Sage.

Finkel, Steven E., and James B. Rule. 1987. "Relative Deprivation and Related Psychological Theories of Civil Violence: A Critical Review." *Research in Social Movements* 9:47–69.

Finley, Nancy J. 2010. "Skating Femininity: Gender Maneuvering in Women's Roller Derby." *Journal of Contemporary Ethnography* 39 (4):359–387.

Fiola, Jan. 2008. "Brazil." Pp. 200–204, vol. 2, in *Encyclopedia of Race, Ethnicity, and Society,* edited by Richard T. Schaefer. Thousand Oaks, CA: Sage.

Fiss, Peer C., and Paul M. Hirsch. 2005. "The Discourse of Globalization: Framing of an Emerging Concept." *American Sociological Review* (February):29–52.

Fitzgerald, Kathleen J. 2008. "White Privilege." Pp. 1403–1405, vol. 3, in *Encyclopedia of Race, Ethnicity, and Society,* edited by Richard T. Schaefer. Thousand Oaks, CA: Sage.

Fitzgerald, Michael. 2011. "Economics: Ends and Means." *The University of Chicago Magazine* (November–December):32–39.

Fitzpatrick, Maureen J., and Barbara J. McPherson. 2010. "Coloring within the Lines: Gender Stereotypes in Contemporary Coloring Books." *Sex Roles* 62:127–137.

Fjellman, Stephen M. 1992. *Vinyl Leaves: Walt Disney World and America.* Boulder CO: Westview Press.

Flacks, Richard. 1971. *Youth and Social Change.* Chicago: Markham.

Fletcher, Connie. 1995. "On the Line: Women Cops Speak Out." *Chicago Tribune Magazine,* February 19, pp. 14–19.

Flora, Cornelia Butter, and Jan L. Flora, with Susan Fey. 2004. *Rural Communities: Legacy and Change.* 2nd ed. Boulder, CO: Westview Press.

Florida, Richard. 2011. "Why Crime Is Down in America's Cities." *The Atlantic* (July). Accessible at www.theatlantic.com.

Fonseca, Felicia. 2008. "Dine College on Quest to Rename Navajo Cancer Terms." *News from Indian Country* 22 (January 7):11.

Forbes. 2011. "Carlos Slim Helu and Family." Accessed January 29, 2012 (www.forbes.com/profile/carlos-slim-helu/).

————. 2012. "Leaderboard: Billionaire Box Scores." 189 (March 26):34.

Foroohar, Rana. 2011. "What Ever Happened to Upward Mobility?" Pp. 77–85 in *Occupy. What Is Occupy?* New York: Times Books.

Foucault, Michel. 1978. *The History of Sexuality. Vol. 1, An Introduction.* New York: Vintage.

Fowler, Geoffrey A. 2013. "Woman Leads Prayer at Mormon Event." *Wall Street Journal,* April 8, p. A3.

Francis, David. 2010. "Homeschoolers Seek Asylum in US." *Christian Science Monitor,* March 8, p. 12.

Frandsen, Ronald J., Dave Naglich, Gene A. Lasuver, and Allina D. Lee. 2013, February. *Background Checks for Firearm Transfers, 2010*—Statistical Tables, NCJ 238226. Washington, DC: Bureau of Justice Statistics.

Frank, Robert H. 2010. "A Remedy Worse than the Disease." *Pathways* (Summer):17–21.

Franke, Richard Herbert, and James D. Kaul. 1978. "The Hawthorne Experiments: First Statistical Interpretation." *American Sociological Review* 43 (October):623–643.

Franklin, John Hope, and Evelyn Brooks Higginbotham. 2011. *From Slavery to Freedom.* 9th ed. New York: McGraw-Hill.

Freedom House. 2012. *Freedom in the World 2012.* Washington, DC: Freedom House.

Freese, Jeremy. 2008. "Genetics and the Social Science Explanation of Individual Outcomes." *American Journal of Sociology* 114 (Suppl.):51–535.

Freidson, Eliot. 1970. *Profession of Medicine.* New York: Dodd, Mead.

French, Howard W. 2004. "China's Textbooks Twist and Omit History." *New York Times,* December 6, p. A10.

————. 2008. "Lines of Grinding Poverty, Untouched by China's Boom." *New York Times,* January 13, p. 4.

Freudenburg, William, and Robert Gramling. 2010. *Blowout in the Gulf: The BP Oil Spill Disaster and the Future of Energy in America.* Cambridge: MIT Press.

Freudenburg, William R. 2005. "Seeing Science, Courting Conclusions: Reexamining the Intersection of Science, Corporate Cash, and the Law." *Sociological Forum* 20 (March):3–33.

Freund, Linda. 2013. "Spontaneity for Hire: Flash Mobs Go Corporate." *Wall Street Journal,* May 9, pp. A1, A16.

Freundlich, Madelyn, and Joy Kim Lieberthal. 2000. "The Gathering of the First Generation of Adult Korean Adoptees: Adoptees' Perceptions of International Adoption." Accessible at www.adoptioninstitute.org/proed/korfindings.html.

Frey, William H. 2011. *A Demographic Tipping Point among America's Three-Year-Olds.* February 7. Accessible at http://www.brookings.edu/opinions/2011/0207_population_frey.aspx?p=1.

Fridlund, Alan J., Paul Erkman, and Harriet Oster. 1987. "Facial Expressions of Emotion; Review of Literature 1970–1983." Pp. 143–224 in *Nonverbal Behavior and Communication,* 2nd ed., edited by Aron W. Seigman and Stanley Feldstein. Hillsdale, NJ: Erlbaum.

Friedan, Betty. 1963. *The Feminine Mystique.* New York: Dell.

Friedman, Louis. 2010. "NASA's Down-to-Earth Problems." *Star-Telegram* (Fort Worth), March 28. Accessible at http://www.star-telegram.com/2010/03/28/2072608/friedman-nasas-down-to-earth-problem.html.

Friedman, Richard A. 2012. "In Gun Debate, A Misguided Focus on Mental Illness." *New York Times,* December 18, p. D6.

Friends of the Congo. 2011. "Coltan: What You Should Know." Accessed May 21 (www.friendsofthecongo.org/new/coltan.php).

Fry, Richard, D'Vera Cohn, Gretchen Livingston, and Paul Taylor. 2011. "The Rising Age Gap in Economic Well-Being." Accessible at http://pewresearch.org/pubs/2124/age-gap-silent-generation-millennials-wealth-gap.

Fudge, Judy, and Rosemary Owens, eds. 2006. *Precarious Work, Women, and the New Economy: The Challenge to Legal Norms.* Oxford, UK: Hart.

Fukase, Atsuko, and Kana Inagaki. 2012. "Japan Insider Penalty: $600." *Wall Street Journal,* March 22, p. C2.

Furstenberg, Frank F, Jr., 2007. "The Making of the Black Family: Race and Class in Qualitative Studies in the Twentieth Century." *Annual Review of Sociology* 33:429–448.

————, and Andrew Cherlin. 1991. *Divided Families: What Happens to Children When Parents Part.* Cambridge, MA: Harvard University Press.

———, and Sheela Kennedy, Vonnie C. McCloyd, Rubén G. Rumbaut, and Richard A. Setterstein, Jr. 2004. "Growing Up Is Harder to Do." *Contexts* 3:33–41.

g

Gabriel, Trip. 2010. "Despite Push, Success at Charter Schools Is Mixed." *New York Times*, May 1, pp. A1, A24–A25.

Gailey, Robert. 2007. "As History Repeats Itself, Unexpected Developments Move Us Forward." *Journal of Rehabilitation Research and Development* 44 (4):vii–xiv.

Galbraith, John Kenneth. 1977. *The Age of Uncertainty*. Boston: Houghton Mifflin.

Galea, Sandro, Melissa Tracy, Katherine J. Hoggatt, Charles DiMaggio, and Adam Karpati. 2011. "Estimated Deaths Attributed to Social Factors in the United States." *American Journal of Public Health* 101 (August):1456–1465.

Gallagher, Kevin P. 2009. "Economic Globalization and the Environment." *Annual Review of Environmental Resources* 34:279–304.

Gallup. 2009a. "Religion:" Accessed April 9 at www.gallup.com.

———. 2009b. "Military and National Defense." Accessed April 17 (www.gallup.com/poll/1666/military-national-defense-aspx).

———. 2011a. "Religion." Accessed March 27 (www.gallup.com).

———. 2012. "Party Affiliation." Accessed March 8 (www.gallup.com/poll/15370/Party-Affiliation.aspx).

Gallup Opinion Index. 1978. "Religion in America, 1977–1978." 145 (January).

Gamson, Joshua. 1989. "Silence, Death, and the Invisible Enemy: AIDS Activism and Social Movement 'Newness.'" *Social Problems* 36 (October):351–367.

Gans, Herbert J. 1991. *People, Plans, and Policies: Essays on Poverty, Racism, and Other National Urban Problems*. New York: Columbia University Press and Russell Sage Foundation.

———. 1995. *The War against the Poor: The Underclass and Antipoverty Policy*. New York: Basic Books.

Garcia-Moreno, Claudia, Henrica A. F. M. Jansen, Mary Ellsberg, Lori Heise, and Charlotte Watts. 2005. *WHO Multi-Country Study on Women's Health and Domestic Violence against Women*. Geneva, Switzerland: WHO.

Gardner, Gary, Erik Assadourian, and Radhika Sarin. 2004. "The State of Consumption Today." Pp. 3–21 in *State of the World 2004*, edited by Brian Halweil and Lisa Mastny. New York: Norton.

Garfinkel, Harold. 1956. "Conditions of Successful Degradation Ceremonies." *American Journal of Sociology* 61 (March):420–424.

Garner, Roberta. 1996. *Contemporary Movements and Ideologies*. New York: McGraw-Hill.

———. 1999. "Virtual Social Movements." Presented at Zaldfest: A conference in honor of Mayer Zald. September 17, Ann Arbor, MI.

Garreau, Joel. 1991. *Edge City: Life on the New Frontier*. New York: Doubleday.

Garrett-Peters, Raymond. 2009. "'If I Don't Have to Work Anymore, Who Am I?': Job Loss and Collaborative Self-Concept Repair." *Journal of Contemporary Ethnography* 38 (5):547–583.

Gates, Gary J. 2012. "LGBT VOTE 2012." Los Angeles: The Williams Institute. Accessible at www.law.ucla.edu/williamsinstitute.

———, and Abigail M. Cooke. 2011. "United States Census Snapshot: 2010." Accessible at http://williamsinstitute.law.ucla.edu/wp-content/uploads/Census2010Snapshot-US-v2.pdf.

Gaudin, Sharon. 2009. "Facebook Has Whopper of a Problem with Burger King Campaign." *Computerworld*, January 15.

Gay, Lesbian and Straight Education Network. 2012. "About GLSEN." Accessed March 1 (www.glsen.org).

Gecas, Viktor. 2004. "Socialization, Sociology of." Pp. 14525–14530 in *International Encyclopedia of the Social and Behavioral Sciences*, edited by Neil J. Smelser and Paul B. Baltes. Cambridge, MA: Elsevier.

Gelles, David. 2011. "It's All About the Algorithm." *Financial Times* (July 30).

General Social Survey. 2012. "GSS General Social Survey." Accessed January 25 (www3.norc.org/GSS+Website).

Gentile, Carmen. 2009. "Student Fights Record of 'Cyberbullying.'" *New York Times*, February 8, p. 20.

Gentleman, Amelia. 2006. "Bollywood Captivated by the Call Centre Culture." *Guardian Weekly*, June 2, p. 17.

———. 2007. "Young Sikh Men Get Haircuts, Annoying Their Elders." *New York Times*, March 29, p. A3.

Gerth, H. H., and C. Wright Mills. 1958. *From Max Weber: Essays in Sociology*. New York: Galaxy.

Gertner, Jon. 2005. "Our Ratings, Ourselves." *New York Times Magazine*, April 10, pp. 34–41, 56, 58, 64–65.

Gibbs, Nancy. 2009. "What Women Want Now." *Time* 174 (16):24–33.

Giddens, Anthony. 1991. *Modernity and Self-Identity: Self and Society in the Late Modern Age*. Cambridge, UK: Polity.

———. 2011. *The Politics of Climate Change*. 2nd ed. Cambridge, UK: Polity.

Giddings, Paul J. 2008. *Ida: A Sword among Lions*. New York: Amistad.

Gilley, Brian Joseph. 2006. *Becoming Two-Spirit: Gay Identity and Social Acceptance in Indian Country*. Lincoln: University of Nebraska Press.

Gillum, Jack. 2011. "How USA Today Analyzed Border Crime Trends." *USA Today*, July 16, p. 7A.

Gilsdorf, Ethan. 2010. "A Virtual World That Breaks Real Barriers." *Christian Science Monitor*, September 6, pp. 36–37.

Giordano, Peggy C. 2003. "Relationships in Adolescence." Pp. 257–281 in *Annual Review of Sociology, 2003*, edited by Karen S. Cook and John Hagan. Palo Alto, CA: Annual Reviews.

Girl Scouts of the USA. 2001. *Junior Girl Scout Badge Book*. New York: Girl Scouts of the United States of America.

Giroux, Henry A. 1988. *Schooling and the Struggle for Public Life: Critical Pedagogy in the Modern Age*. Minneapolis: University of Minnesota Press.

Gitlin, Todd. 2002. *Media Unlimited: How the Torrent of Images and Sounds Overwhelms Our Lives*. New York: Henry Holt.

Glanz, James, and John Markoff. 2011. "U.S. Underestimates Internet Detour Around Censors." *New York Times*, June 12, pp. 1, 8.

Glascock, Stuart. 2008. "A Town Confronts its Language Barrier." *Los Angeles Times* (May 25) p. A20.

Glazer, Susan. 2010. "Evaluating Microfinance." *EQ Global Research* 4 (April).

Glenn, David. 2007. "Anthropologists in a War Zone: Scholars Debate Their Role." *Chronicle of Higher Education* 54 (September 30):A1, A10–A12.

Goering, Laurie. 2008b. "Outsourced to India: Stress." *Chicago Tribune*, April 20, pp. 1, 18.

Goffman, Erving. 1959. *The Presentation of Self in Everyday Life*. New York: Doubleday.

———. 1961. *Asylums: Essays on the Social Situation of Mental Patients and Other Inmates*. Garden City, NY: Doubleday.

———. 1963. *Stigma: Notes on Management of Spoiled Identity*. Englewood Cliffs, NJ: Prentice Hall.

———. 1979. *Gender Advertisements*. Cambridge, MA: Harvard University Press.

Goldman, David. 2012. "Are Landlines Doomed?" CNN Money. April 10. Accessed April 11 (http://money.cnn.com/2012/04/10/technology/att-verizon-landlines/index.htm).

Goldstein, Greg. 1998. "World Health Organization and Housing." Pp. 636–637 in *The Encyclopedia of Housing*, edited by Willem van Vliet. Thousand Oaks, CA: Sage.

Goldstone, Jack. 2010. "The New Population Bomb: The Four Megatrends That Will Change the World." *Foreign Affairs* (January/February): 31–43.

Gomez, Alan, Jack Gillum, and Kevin Johnson. 2011. "On U.S. Side, Cities Are Havens from Drug Wars." *USA Today*, July 15, pp. 1A, 6A–7A.

Goode, Erica, and Jack Healy. 2013. "Focus on Mental Health Laws to Curb Violence Is Unfair, Some Say." *New York Times*, February 1, p. A13.

Goode, Tawara D. 2011. *Cultural and Linguistic Competence: Implications for Statewide Independent Councils*. Washington, DC: National Center for Cultural Competence, Georgetown University.

Goodstein, Laurie. 2008. "India, Exporter of Priests, May Keep Them Home." *New York Times*, December 30, p. A1.

Gottdiener, Mark, and Joe R. Feagin. 1988. "The Paradigm Shift in Urban Sociology." *Urban Affairs Quarterly* 24 (December):163–187.

———, and Ray Hutchison. 2011. *The New Urban Sociology*. 4th ed. Boulder, CO: Westview Press.

Gottfredson, Michael, and Travis Hirschi. 1990. *A General Theory of Crime*. Palo Alto, CA: Stanford University Press.

Gough, Margaret, and Alexandra Killewald. 2011. "Unemployment in Families: The Case of Housework." *Journal of Marriage and Family* 73 (October):1085–1100.

Gould, Elise. 2007. "The Health-Finance Debate Reaches a Fever Pitch." *Chronicle of Higher Education*, April 13, pp. B14, B15.

Gould, Larry A. 2002. "Indigenous People Policing Indigenous People: The Potential Psychological and Cultural Costs." *Social Science Journal* 39:171–188.

Government Accountability Office. 2003. "Women's Earnings: Work Patterns Partially Explain Difference between Men's and Women's Earnings." Washington, DC: U.S. Government. Printing Office.

Grady, John. 2001. "Becoming a Visual Sociologist." *Sociological Imagination* 38 (½):83–118.

———. 2007. "Visual Sociology." Vol. 2 in *21st Century Sociology: A Reference Handbook*. Edited by Clifton D. Bryant and Dennis L. Peck. Thousand Oaks, CA: Sage.

Grady, Sarah, Stacy Bielick, and Susan Aud. 2010. *Trends in the Use of School Choice: 1993 to 2010*. Washington, DC: U.S. Government Printing Office.

Gramsci, Antonio. 1929. *Selections from the Prison Notebooks*. Edited and translated by Quintin Hoare and Geoffrey Nowell Smith. London: Lawrence and Wishort.

Grattet, Ryken. 2011. "Societal Reactions to Deviance." *Annual Review of Sociology* 37:185–204.

Grazian, David. 2010. *Mix It Up: Popular Culture, Mass Media, and Society*. New York: Norton.

Greeley, Andrew M. 1989. "Protestant and Catholic: Is the Analogical Imagination Extinct?" *American Sociological Review* 54 (August):485–502.

Greenemeier, Larry. 2010. "Gulf Spillover: Will BP's Deepwater Disaster Change the Oil Industry?" *Scientific American* (June 7). Accessible at http://www.scientificamerican.com/article.cfm?id=molotch-deepwater-environmental-sociology.

Greenhalgh, Susan. 2008. *Just One Child: Science and Policy in Deng's China*. Berkeley: University of California Press.

Greenhouse, Linda. 2008. "D.C. Ban Rejected. Landmark Decision on Covert Meaning of 2nd Amendment." *New York Times*, June 27, pp. A1, A12.

Greenhouse, Steven. 2008b. "Millions of Jobs of a Different Collar." *New York Times*, March 26.

Gregory, Katherine. 2007. "Drawing a Virtual Gun?" Pp. 98–111 in *Open Fire: Understanding Global Gun Cultures*, edited by Charles Fruehling Springwood. New York: Berg.

Groza, Victor, Daniela F. Ileana, and Ivor Irwin. 1999. *A Peacock or a Crow: Stories, Interviews, and Commentaries on Romanian Adoptions*. Euclid, OH: Williams Custom Publishing.

Grusky, David, and Christopher Wimer. 2010. "Editor's Note." *Pathways* (Summer):2.

Guarino, Mark. 2009. "New Orleans' 'Katrina Generation' Struggles with Drugs and Depression." *Christian Science Monitor* (May 13).

Guest, Robert. 2011. "Tribes Still Matter." *The Economist* (January 22):17–18.

Guo, Guang, Michael E. Roettger, and Tianji Cai. 2008. "The Integration of Genetic Propensities into Social-Control Models of Delinquency and Violence among Male Youths." *American Sociological Review* 73 (August):543–568.

Gurbuz, Mustafa, and Gulsum Gurbuz-Kucuksari. 2009. "Between Sacred Codes and Secular Consumer Society: The Practice of Headscarf

Adoption among American College Girls." *Journal of Muslim Minority Affairs* 29 (September):387–399.

Gutiérrez, Gustavo. 1990. "Theology and the Social Sciences." Pp. 214–225 in *Liberation Theology at the Crossroads: Democracy or Revolution?* edited by Paul E. Sigmund. New York: Oxford University Press.

Guttmacher Institute. 2008. *Facts on Induced Abortion Worldwide*. New York: Guttmacher.

h

Haas, Steven A., David R. Schaefer, and Olga Kornienko. 2010. "Health and the Structure of Adolescent Social Networks." *Journal of Health and Social Behavior* 5 (4):424–439.

Haase, Dwight. 2012. "Banking on the Poor." *Contexts* (Winter):36–41.

Hacker, Andrew. 1964. "Power to Do What?" Pp. 134–146 in *The New Sociology*, edited by Irving Louis Horowitz. New York: Oxford University Press.

Hacker, Helen Mayer. 1951. "Women as a Minority Group." *Social Forces* 30 (October):60–69.

———. 1974. "Women as a Minority Group, Twenty Years Later." Pp. 124–134 in *Who Discriminates against Women?* edited by Florence Denmark. Beverly Hills, CA: Sage.

Hall, Mimi. 2005. "Senators 'to Demand Answers' on Slow Action." *USA Today*, September 6, p. 4A.

Hallinan, Maureen T. 1997. "The Sociological Study of Social Change." *American Sociological Review* 62 (February):1–11.

Halualani, Rona Tamiko. 2002. *In the Name of Hawaiians: Native Identities and Cultural Politics*. Minneapolis: University of Minnesota Press.

Hamm, Steve. 2007. "Children of the Web." *BusinessWeek*, July 2, pp. 50–56, 58.

Hani, Yoko. 1998. "Hot Pots Wired to Help the Elderly." *Japan Times Weekly International Edition* (April 13), p. 16.

Hank, Karsten. 2001. "Changes in Child Care Could Reduce Job Options for Eastern German Mothers." *Population Today* 29 (April):3, 6.

Hanson, Ralph E. 2005. *Mass Communication: Living in a Media World*. New York: McGraw-Hill.

Haq, Husna. 2011. "How Marriage Is Faring." *Christian Science Monitor*, February 14, p. 21.

Harden, Blaine. 2009. "Revising History: Japan helps immigrants find work, realizing that its aging population can't support itself." *Washington Post National Weekly Edition* (February) p. 20.

Harding, David J. 2009. "Violence, Older Peers, and the Socialization of Adolescent Boys in Disadvantaged Neighborhoods." *American Sociological Review* 74 (June):445–464.

Harlow, Harry F. 1971. *Learning to Love*. New York: Ballantine.

Harman, Donna. 2009. "Dubai's Glitz Lost in Grim Life." *Christian Science Monitor*, May 3, p. 8.

Harper, Douglas. 1988. "Visual Sociology: Expanding Sociological Vision." *American Sociologist* (Spring): 54–70.

Harrington, Michael. 1980. "The New Class and the Left." Pp. 123–138 in *The New Class*, edited by B. Bruce Briggs. Brunswick, NJ: Transaction.

Harris, Chauncy D., and Edward Ullman. 1945. "The Nature of Cities." *Annals of the American Academy of Political and Social Science* 242 (November):7–17.

Harrisinteractive. 2008. "Cell Phone Usage Continues to Increase." Accessed January 13 (www.harrisinteractive.com).

Haub, Carl. 2010. "2010 World Population Data Sheet." Washington, DC: Population Reference Bureau.

———. 2011. *2011 World Population Data Sheet*. Washington, DC: Population Reference Bureau.

———, and Mary Mederius Kent. 2009. *2009 World Population Data Sheet*. Washington: Population Reference Bureau.

———, and Toshikp Kaneta. 2012. "2012 World Population Data Sheet." Washington, DC: Population Reference Bureau.

———. 2013. "Were the Population Alarmists Right or Wrong?" Washington, DC: Population Reference Bureau. Accessed April 24 at demographicsrevealed.org/2013/03/26/were-the-population-alarmists-right-or-wrong/.

Hauser, Orlee. 2011. "'We Rule the Base Because We're Few': 'Lone Girls' in Israel's Military." *Journal of Contemporary Ethnography* 40 (6): 623–651.

Haviland, William A., Harald E. L. Prins, Dana Walrath, and Bunny McBride. 2008. *Cultural Anthropology—The Human Challenge*. 12th ed. Belmont, CA: Wadsworth.

Hay, Andrew. 2009. "Spain's New Middle Classes Slip into Poverty." *Reuters*. April 8. Accessed May 11, 2011 (http://uk.reuters.com/article/email/ioUKTRE537029200904).

Hayden, H. Thomas. 2004. "What Happened at Abu Ghraib." Accessed August 7 (www.military.com).

Health Care Financing Administration. 2001. *National Health Care Expenditures Projections*. Accessed August 10 (www.hcfa.gov/stats/NHE-proj/).

Health Cost Institute. 2013. "The Impact of the Mental Health Parity and Addiction Equity Act on Inpatient Admissions." Issue Brief #5. Accessed May 15 at www.healthcostinstitute.org/files/HCCI-Mental-Health-Parity-Issue-Brief.pdf.

Hebel, Sara. 2006. "In Rural America, Few People Harvest 4-Year Degrees." *Chronicle of Higher Education* 53 (November 3):A21–A24.

Heckert, Druann, and Amy Best. 1997. "Ugly Duckling to Swan: Labeling Theory and the Stigmatization of Red Hair." *Symbolic Interaction* 20 (4):365–384.

Hedley, R. Alan. 1992. "Industrialization in Less Developed Countries." Pp. 914–920, vol. 2, in *Encyclopedia of Sociology*, edited by Edgar F. Borgatta and Marie L. Borgatta. New York: Macmillan.

Heilman, Madeline E. 2001. "Description and Prescription: How Gender Stereotypes Prevent Women's Ascent up the Organizational Ladder." *Journal of Social Issues* 57 (4):657–674.

Heisig, Jan Paul. 2011. "Who Does More Housework: Rich or Poor? A Comparison of 33 Countries." *American Sociological Review* 76 (1):74–99.

Hellmich, Nanci. 2001. "TV's Reality: No Vast American Waistlines." *USA Today*, October 8, p. D7.

Helman, Ruth, Mathew Greenwald, Craig Copeland, and Jack VanDerhel. 2012. "The 2012 Retirement Confidence Survey: Job Security, Debt Weigh on Retirement Confidence, Savings." *Employee Benefit Research Institute* Notes 33 (March).

Hendershott, Ann. 2002. *The Politics of Deviance.* San Francisco: Encounter Books.

Hengeveld, Rob. 2012. *Wasted World: How Our Consumption Challenges the Planet.* Chicago: University of Chicago Press.

Hernandez, Elaine M., and Christopher Uggen. 2012. "Institutions, Politics, and Mental Health Parity." *Society and Mental Health* 2 (3):154–171.

Hertz, Rosanna. 2006. *Single by Chance. Mothers by Choice.* New York: Oxford University Press.

Hewlett, Sylvia Ann, and Carolyn Buck Luce. 2005. "Off-Ramps and On-Ramps: Keeping Talented Women on the Road to Success." *Harvard Business Review* (March):43–53.

Higgins, Chris A., Linda E. Duxbury, and Sean T. Lyons. 2010. "Coping with Overload in Stress: Men and Women in Dual-Earner Families." *Journal of Marriage and Family* 72 (August):847–859.

Higher Education Research Institute. 2004. *Trends in Political Attitudes and Voting Behavior among College Freshmen and Early Career College Graduates: What Issues Could Drive This Election?* Los Angeles: HERI, University of California, Los Angeles.

Hill, Michael R., and Susan Hoecker-Drysdale, eds. 2001. *Harriet Martineau: Theoretical and Methodological Perspectives.* New York: Routledge.

Hillery, George A. 1955. "Definitions of Community: Areas of Agreement." *Rural Sociology* (2):111–123.

Hira, Ron. 2008. "An Overview of the Offshoring of U.S. Jobs." Pp. 14–15 in Marlene A. Lee and Mark Mather. "U.S. Labor Force Trends." *Population Bulletin* 63 (June).

Hirschi, Travis. 1969. *Causes of Delinquency.* Berkeley: University of California Press.

Hirst, Paul, and Grahame Thompson. 1996. *Globalization in Question: The International Economy and the Possibilities of Governance.* Cambridge, UK: Polity Press.

Hitlin, Steven, and Jane Allyn Piliavin. 2004. "Values: Reviving a Dormant Concept." Pp. 359–393 in *Annual Review of Sociology, 2004,* edited by Karen S. Cook and John Hagan. Palo Alto, CA: Annual Reviews.

Hochschild, Arlie Russell. 1990. "The Second Shift: Employed Women Are Putting in Another Day of Work at Home." *Utne Reader* 38 (March–April):66–73.

———. 2005. *The Commercialization of Intimate Life: Notes from Home and Work.* Berkeley: University of California Press.

———, with Anne Machung. 1989. *The Second Shift: Working Parents and the Revolution at Home.* New York: Viking Penguin.

Hoeffel, Elizabeth M., Sonya Rastogi, Myoung Ouk Kim, and Hasan Shahid. 2012. *The Asian Population: 2010.* C2101BR-11. Washington, DC: U.S. Government Printing Office.

Holden, Constance. 1980. "Identical Twins Reared Apart." *Science* 207 (March 21):1323–1328.

———. 1987. "The Genetics of Personality." *Science* 257 (August 7):598–601.

Holder, Kelly. 2006. "Voting and Registration in the Election of November 2004." *Current Population Reports,* ser. P-20, no. 556. Washington, DC: U.S. Government Printing Office.

Hollingshead, August B. 1975. *Elmtown's Youth and Elmtown Revisited.* New York: Wiley.

Holmes, Mary. 2009. "Commuter Couples and Distance Relationships: Living Apart Together." Sloan Work and Family Research Network. Accessible at http://wfnetwork.bc.edu/encyclopedia_entry.php?id=15551&area=all.

Homans, George C. 1979. "Nature versus Nurture: A False Dichotomy." *Contemporary Sociology* 8 (May):345–348.

Home School Legal Defense Association. 2005. "State Laws" and "Academic Statistics on Homeschooling." Accessed May 12 (www.hslda.org).

Hondagneu-Sotelo, Pierrette, ed. 2003. *Gender and U.S. Immigration: Contemporary Trends.* Berkeley: University of California Press.

hooks, bell. 1994. *Feminist Theory: From Margin to Center.* 2nd ed. Boston: South End Press.

Hopper, Nate, and Jen Ortiz. 2012. "The Appalling Frequency of the Shooting Spree." *New York* (July 30): 7.

Horgan, John. 1993. "Eugenics Revisited." *Scientific American* 268 (June):122–128, 130–133.

Horkheimer, Max, and Theodore Adorno. [1944] 2002. *Dialectic of Enlightenment.* Palo Alto, CA: Stanford University Press.

Horowitz, Helen Lefkowitz. 1987. *Campus Life.* Chicago: University of Chicago Press.

Horrigan, John B. 2007. *A Typology of Information and Communication Technology Users.* Washington, DC: Pew Internet and American Life Project.

Horwitz, Allan V. 2002. *Creating Mental Illness.* Chicago: University of Chicago Press.

Hosokawa, William K. 1969. *Nisei: The Quiet Americans.* New York: Morrow.

Hospice Association of America. 2010. "Hospice Facts and Statistics." Accessed March 12, 2012 at www.nah.org/facts/HospiceStats/o.pdf.

Houseman, John. 1972. *Run Through.* New York: Simon and Schuster.

Houser, Trevor, Shashank Mohamad, and Robert Heilmayer. 2009. *A Green Global Recovery? Assessing U.S. Economic Stimulus and the Prospects for International Coordination.* Washington, DC: World Resources Institute of Peterson Institute for International Economics.

Housing and Urban Development. 2010. *The Annual Homeless Assessment Report to Congress.* Washington, DC: U.S. Government Printing Office.

Howard, Judith A. 1999. "Border Crossings between Women's Studies and Sociology." *Contemporary Sociology* 28 (September):525–528.

Howard, Michael. 2009. *Modern Wicca: A History from Gerald Gardner to the Present.* St. Paul, MN: Llewellyn Books.

Howard, Michael C. 1989. *Contemporary Cultural Anthropology.* 3rd ed. Glenview, IL: Scott, Foresman.

Howard, Russell D., and Reid L. Sawyer. 2003. *Terrorism and Counterterrorism: Understanding the New Security Environment.* Guilford, CT: McGraw-Hill/Dushkin.

Hu, Winnie. 2010. "In a New Role, Teachers Move to Run Schools." *New York Times,* September 7, pp. A1, A20.

Huang, Gary. 1988. "Daily Addressing Ritual: A Cross-Cultural Study." Presented at the annual meeting of the American Sociological Association, Atlanta.

Hughes, Everett. 1945. "Dilemmas and Contradictions of Status." *American Journal of Sociology* 50 (March):353–359.

Hughlett, Mike. 2008. "Sitting Pretty." *Chicago Tribune,* September 14, sec. 5, pp. 1, 7.

Human Genome Project. 2012. "Human Genome Project Information." Accessed April 4 (www.ornl.gov/sci/techresources/Human_Genome/home.shtml).

Human Rights Campaign. 2012. "Marriage/Issues/Human Rights." Accessible February 27 (www.hrc.org/issues/marriage).

Human Terrain System. 2011. "Welcome to the HTS Home Page." Accessed Novmber 18, 2011 (http://humanterrainsystem.army.mil).

Humes, Karen R., Nicholas A. Jones, and Roberto R. Ramirez. 2011. *Overview of Race and Hispanic Origin: 2010.* 2010 Census Brief BR-02. Accessible at http://www.census.gov/prod/cen2010/briefs/c2010br-02.pdf.

Hundley, Tom, and Margaret Ramirez. 2008. "Young Muslims Put Faith in Facebook." *Chicago Tribune,* February 10, p. 12.

Hunt, Darnell. 1997. *Screening the Los Angeles "Riots": Race, Seeing, and Resistance.* New York: Cambridge University Press.

Hunter, Herbert M., ed. 2000. *The Sociology of Oliver C. Cox: New Perspectives: Research in Race and Ethnic Relations,* vol. 2. Stamford, CT: JAI Press.

Hunter, James Davison. 1991. *Culture Wars: The Struggle to Define America.* New York: Basic Books.

Huntington, Samuel P. 1993. "The Clash of Civilizations?" *Foreign Affairs* 72 (Summer):22–49.

Hur, Song-Woo. 2011. "Mapping South Korean Women's Movements During and After Democratization: Shifting Identities." *East Asian Social Movements,* edited by J. Broadbent and V. Brockman.

Hurn, Christopher J. 1985. *The Limits and Possibilities of Schooling,* 2nd ed. Boston: Allyn and Bacon.

Hussar, William J., and Tabitha M. Bailey. 2011. *Projections of Education Statistics to 2019.* Washington, DC: National Center for Education Statistics.

Hyde, Janet Shibley. 2005. "The Gender Similarities Hypothesis." *American Psychologist* 60 (6):581–592.

Igo, Sarah E. 2007. *The Average American: Surveys, Citizens, and the Making of a Mass Public.* Cambridge, MA: Harvard University Press.

Immervoll, Herwig, and David Barber. 2005. *Can Parents Afford to Work? Childcare Costs, Tax-Benefit Policies and Work Incentives.* Paris: Organisation for Economic Co-operation and Development.

Inglehart, Ronald, and Wayne E. Baker. 2000. "Modernization, Cultural Change, and the Persistence of Traditional Values." *American Sociological Review* 65 (February):19–51.

Innocence Project. 2012. "Facts on Post-Conviction DNA Exonerations." Accessed January 23 (www.innocenceproject.org/Content/Facts_on_Post-Conviction_DNA_Exonerations.php).

Institute for American Values. 2011. *Why Marriage Matters. Thirty Conclusions from Social Sciences.* New York: Institute for American Values. Accessible at www.americanvalues.org.

Institute for Economics and Peace. 2011. "Global Peace Index 2011." March 2, 2012. Accessible March 7. (www.visionofhumanity.org/gpi/results/world-map.php).

Institute of International Education. 2010. Open Doors "Fast Facts." Accessible at www.ies.org.

Interbrand. 2012. "Best Global Brands: 2011 Rankings." Accessed January 17. Accessible at www.interband.com/best_global_brands.aspx.

Interface Group Report (Virginia Tech) 2007. *Presidential Internal Review.* Blacksburg, Virginia Polytechnic Institute and State University.

International Crime Victim Survey. 2004. *Nationwide Surveys in the Industrialized Countries.* Accessed February 20 (www.ruljis.leidenuniv.nl/group/jfcr/www/icvs).

International Gay and Lesbian Human Rights Commission. 2010. Home Page. Accessed February 11 (www.iglhrc.org).

International Institute for Democracy and Electoral Assistance. 2012. "Voter Turnout Database—Custom Query." Accessed March 7 (http://www.idea.int/vt/viewdata.cfm#).

International Monetary Fund. 2000. *World Economic Outlook: Asset Prices and the Business Cycle.* Washington, DC: International Monetary Fund.

International Organization for Migration. 2012. "Facts and Figures." Accessed March 29 (www.iom.int/jahia/jahia/about.migration/lang/en).

International Visual Sociology Association. 2013. "About IVSA." Accessible at http://visualsociology.org/about.html.

Internet Crime Complaint Center. 2011. *The 2010 Internet Crime Report.* Washington, DC: The National White Collar Crime Center. Accessible at www.ic3.gov/media/annualreport/2010_IC3Report.pdf.

Internet World Stats. 2012. "Usage and Population Statistics" and "Internet World Users by Language." Updated on March 28. Accessed March 29 (www.internetworldstats.com).

Inter-Parliamentary Union. 2011. *Women in National Parliaments.* December 31. Accessed March 7 (www.ipu.org).

Isaacs, Julia B. 2007a. *Economic Mobility of Families across Generations.* Washington, DC: Economic Mobility Project, Pew Charitable Trusts.

———. 2007b. *Economic Mobility of Men and Women.* Washington, DC: Economic Mobility Project.

———, Isabel V. Sawhill, and Ron Haskins. 2008. *Getting Ahead or Losing Ground: Economic Mobility in America.* Washington, DC: Pew Charitable Trusts.

ITOPF. 2006. "Statistics: International Tanker Owners Pollution Federation Limited." Accessed May 2 (www.itopf.com/stats.html).

j

Jackson, Philip W. 1968. *Life in Classrooms.* New York: Holt.

Jacobs, Andres. 2010. "As China's Economy Grows, Pollution Worsens Despite New Efforts to Control It." *New York Times*, July 29, p. A4.

Jacobs, Jerry. 2003. "Detours on the Road to Equality: Women, Work and Higher Education." *Contexts* (Winter):32–41.

Jacobs, Tom. 2009. "Hot Men of the Links." *Miller-McCune* (May–June):79.

Jaffee, Daniel. 2007. *Brewing Justice: Fair Trade Coffee, Sustainability, and Survival.* Berkeley: University of California Press.

Jain, Saranga, and Kathleen Kurz. 2007. *New Insights on Preventing Child Marriage: A Global Analysis of Factors and Programs.* Washington, DC: International Center for Research on Women.

Jäntti, Markus. 2009. "Mobility in the United States in Comparative Perspectives." *Focus* 26 (Fall).

Japan Aisaika Organization. 2012. "Aisaika Organization Prospectus." Accessed January 15 (www.aisaika.org/en/prospectus.html).

Jasper, James M. 1997. *The Art of Moral Protest: Culture, Biography, and Creativity in Social Movements.* Chicago: University of Chicago Press.

Jayson, Sharon. 2009. "Holding Up the Value of Marriage." *USA Today*, February 18, pp. D1, D2.

Jenkins, Henry. 2006. *Convergence Culture: Where Old and New Media Collide.* New York: New York University Press.

Jensen, Gary F. 2005. "Social Organization Theory." In *Encyclopedia of Criminology*, edited by Richard A. Wright and J. Mitchell Miller. Chicago: Fitzrog Dearborn.

Jervis, Rick. 2008. "New Orleans Homicides up 30% over 2006 Level." *USA Today*, January 3, p. 3A.

Jesella, Kara. 2008. "Blogging's Glass Ceiling." *New York Times*, July 27, Style section, pp. 1, 2.

Jian, Ma. "China's Brutal One-Child Policy." *New York Times*, May 22, p. A27.

Jimenez, Maria. 2009. *Humanitarian Crisis: Migrant Deaths at the U.S.–Mexico Border.* San Diego: ACLU of San Diego and Imperial Countries.

Joas, Hans, and Wolfgang Knöbl. 2009. *Social Theory: Twenty Introductory Lectures.* Cambridge: Cambridge University Press.

John, Robert. 2012. "The Native American Family." Pp. 361–410 in *Ethnic Families in America: Patterns and Variations.* 5th ed., edited by Roosevelt Wright, Jr., Charles H. Mindel, Thanh Van Tran, and Robert W. Halsenstein. Upper Saddle River, NJ: Pearson.

Johnson, Benton. 1975. *Functionalism in Modern Sociology: Understanding Talcott Parsons.* Morristown, NJ: General Learning.

Johnson, Richard A. 1985. *American Fads.* New York: Beech Tree.

Johnson, Will. 2009. "Genie: The Wild Child." Accessed August 4, 2010 (http://knol.google.com/k/genie-the-wild-child-chapter-2#).

Jones, Del, and Barbara Hansen. 2009. "CEO Pay Packages Sink with Economy." *USA Today*, May 4, pp. B1–B2.

Jones, Jeff, and Lydia Saad. 2011. "Gallup News Service." *Gallup Poll Social Series: Environment* (March 3-6).

———, and ———. 2012. "Gallup News Service." *Gallup Poll Social Series: Environment* (March 8-11). Accessible at www.gallup.com/poll/153404/Americans-Split-Energy-Environment-Trade-OFF.aspx.

Jopling, John, and Reilly Morse. 2010. "The BP Oil Disaster and Its Disproportionate Impacts on Minorities and Communities of Color." *Focus* 36 (October–November):12–14.

Jordan, Mary. 2007. "The New Face of Global Mormonism." *Washington Post National Weekly Edition*, November 26, pp. 20–21.

Jordan, Miriam. 2009. "As U.S. Job Opportunities Fade, More Mexicans Look Homeward." *Wall Street Journal*, February 13, p. A14.

Joseph, Jay. 2004. *The Gene Illusion: Genetic Research in Psychiatry and Psychology under the Microscope.* New York: Algora Books.

Josephson Institute. 2011. "What Would Honest Abe Lincoln Say?" Accessed February 10 (www.CharacterCounts.org).

Jost, Kenneth. 2008. "Women in Politics." *CQ Researcher* 18 (March 21).

Julian, Tiffany, and Robert Kominski. 2011. *Education and Synthetic Work-Life Earnings Estimates.* ACS-14. Washington, DC: U.S. Government Printing Office.

k

Kahn, Joseph. 2006. "Where's Mao? Chinese Revise History Books." *New York Times*, September 1, pp. A1, A6.

Kalleberg, Arne L. 2009. "Precarious Work, Insecure Workers: Employment Relations in Transition." *American Sociological Review* 74 (February):1–22.

Kambayashi, Takehiko. 2008. "Japanese Men Shout the Oft-Unsaid 'I love you.'" *Christian Science Monitor*, February 13.

Kamenetz, Anya. 2006. *Generation Debt.* New York: Riverhead.

Kandel, William. 2005. "Rural Hispanics at a Glance." *Economic Information Bulletin* (December).

Kang, K. Connie. 1996. "Filipinos Happy with Life in U.S. but Lack United Voice." *Los Angeles Times*, January 26, pp. A1, A20.

Karides, Marina. 2010. "Theorizing the Rise of Microenterprise Development in Caribbean Context." *Journal of World-Systems Research* 16 (2):192–216.

Katovich, Michael A. 1987. Correspondence. June 1.

Katz, Michael. 1971. *Class, Bureaucracy, and the Schools: The Illusion of Educational Change in America.* New York: Praeger.

Kaufman, Sarah. 2006. "The Criminalization of New Orleanians in Katrina's Wake." Accessed April 4 (www.ssrc.org).

Kavada, Anastasia. 2005. "Exploring the Role of the Interest in the 'Movement for Alternative Globalization': The Case of the Paris 2003 European Social Forum." *Westminster Papers in Communication and Culture* 2 (1):72–95.

Keeter, Scott, and Courtney Kennedy. 2006. "The Cell Phone Challenge to Survey Research." Washington, DC: Pew Research Center.

Kelleher, Jennifer Sinco. 2011. "23 Arrested for Refusing to Leave Iolani Palace." *News from Indian Country,* November, p. 5.

Kellerman, Arthur L., Frederick P. Rivara, Norman B. Rushforth, Joyce G. Banton, Donald T. Reay, Jerry T. Francisco, Ana B. Locci, Janice Prodzinski, Bela B. Hackman, and Grant Somes. 1993. "Gun Ownership as a Risk Factor for Homicide in the Home." *New England Journal of Medicine* 329: 1084–1091.

Kelly, Timothy A. 2009. *Healing the Broken Mind: Transforming America's Failed Mental Health System.* New York: New York University Press.

Kennickell, Arthur B. 2009. *Ponds and Streams: Wealth and Income in the U.S., 1989 to 2007.* Washington, DC: Federal Reserve Board.

Kennicott, Philip. 2011. "Review: 9/11 Memorial in New York." Accessed August 26 (www.washingtonpost.com).

Kenny, Charles. 2009. "Revolution in a Box." *Foreign Policy* (November):68–74.

Kentor, Jeffrey, and Yong Suk Jang. 2004. "Yes, There Is a (Growing) Transnational Business Community." *International Sociology* 19 (September):355–368.

Kerbo, Harold R. 2006. *World Poverty: The Roots of Global Inequality and the World System.* New York: McGraw-Hill.

———. 2012. *Social Stratification and Inequality.* 8th ed. New York: McGraw-Hill.

Kesmodel, David, and Danny Yadron. 2010. "E-Cigarettes Spark New Smoking War." *Wall Street Journal,* August 25, pp. A1, A12.

Kessler, Ronald C., Emil F. Coccaro, Maurizio Fava, Savina Jaeger, Robert Jin, and Ellen Walters. 2006. "The Prevalence and Correlates of DSM-IV Intermittent Explosive Disorder in the National Comorbidity Survey Replication." *Archives of General Psychiatry* 63 (June):669–678.

Killian, Caitlin. 2003. "The Other Side of the Veil: North Africa Women in France Respond to the Headscarf Affair." *Gender and Society* (August 17):576–590.

Kim, Hyun Sik. 2011. "Consequences of Parental Divorce for Child Development." *American Sociological Review* 76 (3):487–511.

Kim, Kwang Chung. 1999. *Koreans in the Hood: Conflict with African Americans.* Baltimore: Johns Hopkins University Press.

Kimmel, Michael S. 2006. "A War against Boys?" *Dissent* (Fall):65–70.

———. 2008. *The Gendered Society.* 3rd ed. New York: State University of New York at Stony Brook.

King, Gary. 2011. "Ensuring the Data-Rich Future of the Social Sciences." *Science* (February 11):719–721.

King, Leslie. 1998. "France Needs Children: Pronatalism, Nationalism, and Women's Equity." *Sociological Quarterly* 39 (Winter):33–52.

King, Meredith L. 2007. *Immigrants in the U.S. Health Care System.* Washington, DC: Center for American Progress.

King, Sharon A. 1999. "Mania for 'Pocket Monsters' Yields Billions for Nintendo." *New York Times,* April 26, pp. A1, A18.

Kingsbury, Alex. 2008. "Q and A: Sudhir Venkatesh." *US News and World Report,* January 21, p. 14.

Kinsey, Alfred C., Wardell B. Pomeroy, and Paul H. Gebhard. 1953. *Sexual Behavior in the Human Female.* Philadelphia: Saunders.

———, ———, and Clyde E. Martin. 1948. *Sexual Behavior in the Human Male.* Philadelphia: Saunders.

Kiper, Dmitry. 2008. "GodTube.com Puts Christian Worship Online." *Christian Science Monitor,* February 6.

Kiser, Edgar. 1992. "War." Pp. 2243–2247 in *Encyclopedia of Sociology,* edited by Edgar F. Borgatta and Marie L. Borgatta. New York: Macmillan.

Kitchener, Richard F. 1991. "Jean Piaget: The Unknown Sociologist." *British Journal of Sociology* 42 (September):421–442.

Klass, Perri. 2003. "This Side of Medicine." P. 319 in *This Side of Doctoring Reflection for Women in Medicine,* edited by Eliza Lo Chin. New York: Oxford University Press.

Klein, Lloyd. 1994. "We're Going to Disney World: Consumers, Credit, and the Consumption of Social Experience." *Free Inquiry in Creative Sociology* 22 (November): 117–124.

Klein, Naomi. 1999. *No Logo: Money, Marketing, and the Growing Anti-Corporate Movement.* New York: Picador (St. Martin's Press).

Kleiner, Art. 2003. "Are You In with the In Crowd?" *Harvard Business Review* 81 (July):86–92.

Kleinknecht, William. 1996. *The New Ethnic Mobs: The Changing Face of Organized Crime in America.* New York: Free Press.

Klinenberg, Eric. 2012. *Going Solo: The Extraordinary Rise and Surprising Appeal of Living Alone.* New York: Penguin Press.

Kneebone, Elizabeth, Carey Nadeau, and Alan Berube. 2011. *The Re-Emergence of Concentrated Poverty Metropolitan Trends in the 2000s.* Washington, DC: Metropolitan Policy Program at Brookings.

———, and Alan Berube. 2013. *Confronting Suburban Poverty in America.* Washington DC: Brookings Institution Press.

Knudsen, Morten. 2010. "Surprised by Method—Functional Method and System Theory." *Forum: Qualitative Social Research* 11 (September): article 12.

Kochhar, Rakesh. 2006. "Growth in the Foreign-Born Workforce and Employment of the Native Born." Washington, DC: Pew Hispanic Center.

———. 2008. *Latino Workers in the Ongoing Recession: 2007–2008.* Washington, DC: Pew Hispanic Center.

Koerth-Baker, Maggie. 2012. "Head in the Crowds." *New York Times Magazine* (December 23):12, 14.

Kohut, Andrew, et al. 2005. *American Character Gets Mixed Reviews: 16-Nation Pew Global Attitudes Survey.* Washington, DC: Pew Global Project Attitudes.

———, et al. 2007. *Global Unease with Major World Powers: Rising Environmental Concern in 47-Nation Survey.* Washington, DC: Pew Global Project Attitudes.

Kokmen, Leyla. 2008. "Environmental Justice for All." *Utne Reader* (March–April):42–46.

Korean Women's Association United. 2010. "Republic of Korea: Critical Issues on the Seventh Periodical Report on the Convention on the Elimination of All Forms of Discrimination against Women." November 10. Accessed March 27, 2010 (www2.ohchr.org/English/bodies/cedaw/docs/ngos/Korean_Womens_Association_United(PSWG).pdf).

Kornblum, Janet. 2007. "Meet the 'Tech-No's': People Who Reject Plugging into the Highly Wired World." *USA Today,* January 11, pp. A1, A2.

Korzeniewicz, Roberto Patricio, and Timothy Patrick Moran. 2009. *Unveiling Inequality: A World Historical Perspective.* New York: Russell Sage Foundation.

Kosmin, Barry A., and Ariela Keysar. 2009. *American Religious Identification Survey.* Hartford, CT: Trinity College.

Kotkin, Joel. 2010. "Ready Set Grow." *Smithsonian* (July/August):61–73.

Kottak, Conrad. 2011. *Anthropology: Appreciating Human Diversity.* 14th ed. New York: McGraw-Hill.

Krane, Jim. 2009. *Dubai: The Story of the World's City.* London: Atlantic Books.

———. 2010. "To Spend or Not to Spend." Interviewed on Al Jazeera television, March 26. Accessed April 20 (http://english.aljazeera.net/programmes/countingthecost/2010/03/201032510494187263.html).

Kratz, Corinne A., and Iman Karp. 1995. "Wonder and Worth: Disney Museums in World Showcase." *Museum Anthropology* 17 (3):32–42.

Kraybill, Donald. 2001. *The Riddle of Amish Culture.* Rev. ed. Baltimore: Johns Hopkins University Press.

Kreider, Rose M. 2010. "Increase in Opposite-Sex Cohabiting Couples from 2009 to 2010 in the Annual Social and Economic Supplement (AEFC) to the Current Population Survey (CPS)." Working Paper. Washington, DC: U.S. Bureau of the Census.

———. 2011. "Contexts of Racial Socialization: Are Transracial Adoptive Families More Like Multiracial or White Monoracial Families?" March 1. Accessible at www.census.gov.

———, and Renee Ellis. 2011. "Living Arrangements of Children: 2009." *Current Population Reports,* ser. P70, no. 126. Washington, DC: U.S. Government Printing Office.

Kriesberg, Louis. 1992. "Peace." Pp. 1432–1436 in *Encyclopedia of Sociology,* edited by Edgar F. Borgatta and Marie L. Borgatta. New York: Macmillan.

Kristof, Nicholas D. 1998. "As Asian Economies Shrink, Women Are Squeezed Out." *New York Times,* June 11, pp. A1, A12.

Kroll, Luisa, and Kerry A. Dolan. 2012. "The Billionaires Issue." *Forbes* 189 (March 26):49–62.

Kronstadt, Jessica. 2008a. "Genetics and Economic Mobility." Washington, DC: Economic Mobility Project. Also accessible at www.economicmobility.org/reports_and_research/literature_reviews?id=0004.

———, and Melissa Favreault. 2008. "Families and Economic Mobility." Washington, DC: Economic Mobility Project. Also accessible at www.economicmobility.org/reports_and_research/literature_reviews?id=0004.

Kunzig, Robert. 2011. "Seven Billion." *National Geographic* (January):40–69.

Kwong, Jo. 2005. "Globalization's Effects on the Environment." *Society* 42 (January–February): 21–28.

Ladner, Joyce. 1973. *The Death of White Sociology.* New York: Random Books.

Landler, Mark, and Michael Barbaro. 2006. "No, Not Always." *New York Times,* August 2, pp. C1, C4.

———, and David E. Sanger. 2009. "World Leaders Pledge $1.1 Trillion to Tackle Crisis." *New York Times,* April 3, pp. A1, A11.

Landtman, Gunnar. [1938] 1968. *The Origin of Inequality of the Social Class.* New York: Greenwood (original edition 1938, Chicago: University of Chicago Press).

Lansprey, Susan. 1995. "AAAs and 'Naturally Occurring Retirement Communities' (NORCs)." Accessed August 4, 2003 (www.aoa.gov/housing/norcs.html).

Lasswell, Harold D. 1936. *Politics: Who Gets What, When, How.* New York: McGraw-Hill.

Last, Jonathan. 2013. *What to Expect When No One's Expecting: America's Coming Demographic Disaster.* New York: Encounter Books.

Lau, Yvonne M. 2006. "Re-Visioning Filipino American Communities: Evolving Identities, Issues, and Organizations." Pp. 141–153 in *The New Chicago,* edited by John Koval et al. Philadelphia: Temple University Press.

Lauer, Robert H. 1982. *Perspectives on Social Change.* 3rd ed. Boston: Allyn and Bacon.

Laumann, Edward O., John H. Gagnon, and Robert T. Michael. 1994a. "A Political History of the National Sex Survey of Adults." *Family Planning Perspectives* 26 (February):34–38.

———, ———, ———, and Stuart Michaels. 1994b. *The Social Organization of Sexuality: Sexual Practices in the United States.* Chicago: University of Chicago Press.

Lavrakas, Paul J., Charles D. Shuttles, Charlotte Steel, and Howard Fienberg. 2007. "The State of Surveying Cell Phone Numbers in the United States: 2007 and Beyond." *Public Opinion Quarterly* 71 (5):840–854.

Lawler, Kristen. 2011. "Fear of a Slacker Revolution Futures: A Project of the Social Science Research Project." December 1. Accessed

January 26, 2012 (www.possible-futures.org/2011/12/01/fear-slacker-revolution-occupy-wall-street-cultural-politics-class-struggle/).

Lawson, Sandra. 2008. *Girls Count.* New York: Goldman Sachs.

Lazarsfeld, Paul, Bernard Beretson, and H. Gaudet. 1948. *The People's Choice.* New York: Columbia University Press.

———, and Robert K. Merton. 1948. "Mass Communication, Popular Taste, and Organized Social Action." Pp. 95–118 in *The Communication of Ideas,* edited by Lymon Bryson. New York: Harper and Brothers.

Leavell, Hugh R., and E. Gurney Clark. 1965. *Preventive Medicine for the Doctor in His Community: An Epidemiologic Approach.* 3rd ed. New York: McGraw-Hill.

Lee, Alfred McClung. 1983. *Terrorism in Northern Ireland.* Bayside, NY: General Hall.

Lee, Barrett A., Kimberly A. Tyler, and James D. Wright. 2010. "The New Homelessness Revisited." *Annual Review of Sociology* 30:501–521.

Lee, Ronald D., and David S. Reher. 2011. "Introduction: The Landscape of Demographic Transition and Its Aftermath." *Population and Development Review* 37 (Supplement):1–7.

Lee, Suevon. 2013, January 7. Five Federal Policies on Guns You've Never Heard Of. Accessed February 25 at www.propublica.org.

Lehman, Chris. 2012. "Retirement Communities Find Niche with Gay Seniors." February 16. Accessible at http://www.wbur.org/npr/146713531/retirement-communities-find=niche-with-gay-seniors.

Lehne, Gregory K. 1995. "Homophobia among Men: Supporting and Defining the Male Role." Pp. 325–336 in *Men's Lives,* edited by Michael S. Kimmel and Michael S. Messner. Boston: Allyn and Bacon.

Lengermann, Patricia Madoo, and Jill Niebrugge-Brantley. 1998. *The Women Founders: Sociology and Social Theory, 1830–1930.* Boston: McGraw-Hill.

Lenhart, Amanda. 2009. "Pew Internet Project Data Memo: Adults and Social Network Websites." Accessible at www.pewinternet.org/PPF/r/272/report_display.asp.

———, Mary Madden, Aaron Smith, Kristen Purcell, Kathryn Zickuhr, and Lee Rainie. 2011. *Teens, Kindness, and Cruelty on Social Network Sites.* Washington, DC: Pew Research Center's Internet and American Life Project.

Lenski, Gerhard. 1966. *Power and Privilege: A Theory of Social Stratification.* New York: McGraw-Hill.

Leonhardt, David. 2004. "As Wealthy Fill Top Colleges Concerns Grow over Fairness." *New York Times,* April 22, pp. A1, A12.

Levine, Nancy. 1988. *The Dynamics of Polyandry: Kinship, Domesticity, and Population on the Tibetan Border.* Chicago: University of Chicago Press.

Levinson, Daniel J. 1978. *The Seasons of a Man's Life.* With Charlotte N. Darrow et al. New York: Knopf.

———. 1996. *The Seasons of a Woman's Life.* With Judy D. Levinson. New York: Knopf.

Levitt, Peggy, and B. Nadya Jaworsky. 2007. "Transnational Migration Studies: Past

Developments and Future Trends." *Annual Review of Sociology* 33:129–156.

Levitt, Steven D., and Stephen J. Dubner. 2006. *Freakonomics: A Rogue Economist Explores the Hidden Side of Everything.* Revised and expanded edition. New York: Morrow.

———, and Sudhir Venkatesh. 2000. "An Economic Analysis of a Drug-Selling Gang's Finances." *Quarterly Journal of Economics* (August):775–789.

Lewin, Tamar. 2011. "College Graduates' Debt Grew, Yet Again, in 2010." *New York Times,* November 3, p. A20.

Lichtblau, Eric. 2009. "Telecom Companies Win Dismissal of Wiretap Suits." *New York Times,* June 4, p. A14.

Lichter, Daniel T., and David L. Brown. 2011. "Rural America in an Urban Society: Changing Spatial and Social Boundaries." *Annual Review of Sociology* 37:565–592.

Light, Donald W. 2004. "Dreams of Success: A New History of the American Health Care System." *Journal of Health and Social Behavior* 45 (Extra issue):1–24.

Light, Paul C. 2005. "Katrina's Lesson in Readiness." *Washington Post,* September 1.

Lim, Louisa. 2007. "Digital Culture: China's 'Gold Farmers' Play a Grim Game." May 14, 2007 broadcast on NPR. Accessible at www.npr.org.

Lindner, Eileen W. 2012. *Yearbook of American and Canadian Churches, 2012.* Nashville: Abingdon Press.

Link, Michael W., Ali H. Mokad, Herbert F. Stockhouse, and Nicole T. Flowers. 2006. "Race, Ethnicity, and Linguistic Isolation as Determinants of Participation in Public Heath Surveillance Surveys." *Presenting Chronic Disease* 3 (January).

Linn, Susan, and Alvin F. Poussaint. 1999. "Watching Television: What Are Children Learning about Race and Ethnicity?" *Child Care Information Exchange* 128 (July):50–52.

Lino, Mark. 2011. *Expenditures on Children by Families, 2011.* Washington, DC: U.S. Department of Agriculture, Center for Nutrition Policy and Promotion.

Lio, Shoon, Scott Melzer, and Ellen Reese. 2008. "Constructing Threat and Appropriating 'Civil Rights': Rhetorical Strategies of Gun Rights and English Only Leaders." *Symbolic Interaction* 31 (1):5–31.

Lipka, Sara. 2009. "Do Crime Statistics Keep Students Safe?" *Chronicle of Higher Education* 55 (January 30):A15–A17.

Lipson, Karen. 1994. "'Nell' Not Alone in the Wilds." *Los Angeles Times,* December 19, pp. F1, F6.

Liptak, Adam. 2006. "The Ads Discriminate, but Does the Web?" *New York Times,* March 5, p. 16.

———. 2008. "From One Footnote, a Debate over the Tangles of Law, Science and Money." *New York Times,* November 25, p. A13.

———. 2010. "Study Finds Questioning of Nominees to Be Useful." *New York Times,* June 28, pp. A10, A11.

Liska, Allen E., and Steven F. Messner. 1999. *Perspectives on Crime and Deviance.* 3rd ed. Upper Saddle River, NJ: Prentice Hall.

Living Goods. 2013. "A Scalable Model for Massive Impact." Accessed May 15 at http://livinggoods.org/what-we-do/micro-franchise-business-model/.

Livingstone, Sonia. 2004. "The Challenge of Changing Audiences." *European Journal of Communication* 19 (March):75–86.

Llana, Sara Miller. 2009. "Mexico: Safety Comes in Park Taxes." December 24. Accessible at www.csmonitor.com.

———, and Whitney Eulich. 2013. "Women at War, Worldwide." *Christian Science Monitor Weekly* (February 4): 18–20.

Lo Sasso. Anthony T., Michael R. Richards, Chiu-Fang Chou, and Susan E. Gerber. 2011. "The $16,819 Pay Gap for Newly Trained Physicians: The Unexplained Trend of Men Earning More Than Women." *Health Affairs* 30 (February):193–201.

Loeb, Susanna, Bruce Fuller, Sharon Lynn Kagan, and Bidemi Carrol. 2004. "Child Care in Poor Communities: Early Learning Effects of Type, Quality, and Stability." *Child Development* 75 (January–February):47–65.

Lofland, John. 1981. "Collective Behavior: The Elementary Forms." Pp. 441–446 in *Social Psychology: Sociological Perspectives*, edited by Morris Rosenberg and Ralph Turner. New York: Basic Books.

———. 1985. *Protests: Studies of Collective Behavior and Social Movements*. Rutgers, NJ: Transaction.

Lofland, Lyn H. 1975. "The 'Thereness' of Women: A Selective Review of Urban Sociology." Pp. 144–170 in *Another Voice*, edited by M. Millman and R. M. Kanter. New York: Anchor/Doubleday.

Lofquist, Daphne. 2011. *Same-Sex Couple Households*. ACSBR/10-03. Washington, DC: U.S. Government Printing Office.

———, Terry Lugaila, Martin O'Connell, and Sarah Feliz. 2012. "Households and Families: 2010. C2010BR-14." Accessible at www.census.gov/newsroom/releases/archives/1020_census/cb12-68.html.

Logan, John. R. 2011. *Separate and Unequal: The Neighborhood Gap for Blacks, Hispanics and Asians in Metropolitan America*. Providence RI: American Communities Project of Brown University and Russell Sage Foundation.

———, Richard D. Alba, and Werquan Zhang. 2002. "Immigrant Enclaves and Ethnic Communities in New York and Los Angeles." *American Sociological Review* 67 (April):299–322.

Long, Sharon K., and Paul B. Masi. 2009. *Access to and Affordability of Care in Massachusetts as of Fall 2008: Geographic and Racial/Ethnic Differences*. Washington, DC: Urban Institute.

Longhofer, Wesley, and Evan Schofer. 2010. "National and Global Origins of Environmental Association." *American Sociological Review* 75 (4):505–533.

Lopez, Mark Hugo. 2011. *The Latino Electorate in 2010: More Voters, More Non-Voters*. Washington, DC: Pew Hispanic Center.

Lorber, Judith. 2005. *Breaking the Bowls: Degendering and Feminist Change*. New York: Norton.

Lubienski, Christopher A., and Peter C. Weitzel. 2012. *The Charter School Experiment*

Expectations, Evidence, and Implications. Cambridge MA: Harvard Education Press.

Ludwig, Jens, and Isabell Sawhill. 2007. *Success by Ten: Interviewing Early, Often, and Efficiently in the Education of Young Children*. Washington, DC: Brookings Institution.

Lukacs. Georg. 1923. *History and Class Consciousness*. London: Merlin.

Lundquist, Jennifer Hickes. 2006. "Choosing Single Motherhood." *Contexts* 5 (Fall):64–67.

Luster, Tom, Kelly Rhoades, and Bruce Haas. 1989. "The Relation between Parental Values and Parenting Behavior: A Test of the Kohn Hypothesis." *Journal of Marriage and the Family* 51 (February):139–147.

Luttinger, Nina, and Gregory Dicum. 2006. *The Coffee Book: Anatomy of an Industry from Crop to the Last Drop*. Revised and updated. New York: New Press.

Lyall, Sarah. 2002. "For Europeans, Love, Yes; Marriage, Maybe." *New York Times*, March 24, pp. 1–8.

Lynas, Mark. 2008. *Six Degrees: Our Future on a Hotter Planet*. Washington, DC: National Geographic.

Lynn, Barry C. 2003. "Trading with a Low-Wage Tiger." *American Prospect* 14 (February):10–12.

m

MacDonald, G. Jeffrey. 2007. "Go in Search of a Church by Way of the Web." *USA Today*, October 17, p. D8.

MacDorman, Marian F., and T. J. Mathews. 2009. Behind International Rankings of Infant Mortality: How the United States Compares with Europe. *NCHS Date Brief* (No. 23, November).

MacFarquhar, Neil. 2008. "Resolute or Fearful, Many Muslims Turn to Home Schooling." *New York Times*, March 26, p. A1.

Mach, Annie, and Laura Blumenthal. 2010. "Health Insurance Coverage of Children under 19: 2008 and 2009." 2009–2011 Census Brief BR-09–11. Accessible at http://www.census.gov/prod/2010pubs/acsbr09-11.pdf.

Machalek, Richard, and Michael W. Martin. 2010. "Evolution, Biology and Society: A Conversation for the 21st-Century Sociology Classroom." *Teaching Sociology* 38 (1):35–45.

Mack, Mick G. 2003. "Does Exercise Status Influence the Impressions Formed by College Students?" *College Student Journal* 37 (December).

Mack, Raymond W., and Calvin P. Bradford. 1979. *Transforming America: Patterns of Social Change*. 2nd ed. New York: Random House.

Mackun, Paul, and Steven Wilson. 2011, March. *Population Distribution and Change: 2000 to 2010*. 2010 Census Brief BR-01.

MacLeod, Calum. 2010. "Chinese Use Internet to Show Dissent." *USA Today*, December 29, p. 31.

Maestretti, Danielle. 2009. "Information Overload." *Utne Reader* (July–August), pp. 22–23.

Magga, Ole Henrik. 2006. "Diversity in Sami Terminology for Reindeer, Snow, and Ice." *International Social Science Journal* 58 (March):25–34.

Magnier, Mark. 2004. "China Clamps Down on Web News Discussion." *Los Angeles Times*, February 26, p. A4.

Malaby, Thomas M. 2009. *Making Virtual Worlds: Linden Lab and Second Life*. Ithaca, NY: Cornell University.

Malcolm, Andrew H. 1974. "The 'Shortage' of Bathroom Tissue: A Classic Study in Rumor." *New York Times*, February 3, p. 29.

Malcolm X, with Alex Haley. [1964] 1999. *The Autobiography of Malcolm X*. Revised with Epilogue by Alex Haley and Afterword by Ossie Davis. New York: One World, Ballantine Books.

Males, Mike, and Meda-Chesney Lind. 2010. "The Myth of Mean Girls." *New York Times*, April 2, p. A21.

Malhotra, Neil, and Yotam Margalit. 2009. "State of the Nation: Anti-Semitism and the Economic Crisis." *Boston Review* (May–June). Accessible at http://bostonreview.net/BR34.3/malhotra_margalit.php.

Malthus, Thomas Robert, Julian Huxley, and Frederick Osborn. [1824] 1960. *Three Essays on Population*. Reprint. New York: New American Library.

Manza, Jeff, and Clem Brooks. 2012. "How Sociology Lost Public Opinion: A Genealogy Off a Missing Concept in the Study of the Political." *Sociological Theory* 30 (2):89–113.

Marable, Manning. 2011. *Malcolm X: A Life of Reinvention*. New York: Viking.

Margolis, Mac. 2009. "The Land of Less Contrast: How Brazil Reined in Inequality." *Newsweek*, November 28.

Markson, Elizabeth W. 1992. "Moral Dilemmas." *Society* 29 (July/August):4–6.

Marosi, Richard. 2007. "The Nation: A Once-Porous Border Is a Turning-Back Point." *Los Angeles Times*, March 21, pp. A1.

Marquis, Julie, and Dan Morain. 1999. "A Tortuous Path for the Mentally Ill." *Los Angeles Times*, November 21, pp. A1, A22, A23.

Marshall, Brent K., and J. Steven Picou. 2008. "Postnormal Science, Precautionary Principle, and Worst Cases: The Challenge of Twenty-First-Century Catastrophes." *Sociological Inquiry* 78 (May):230–247.

Martin, Dominique, Jean-Luc Metzger, and Philippe Pierre. 2006. "The Sociology of Globalization: Theoretical and Methodological Reflections." *International Sociology* 21 (July):499–521.

Martin, Joyce A., Brady E. Hamilton, Paul D. Sutton, Stephanie J. Ventura, Fay Menacker, Sharon Kirmeyer, and T. J. Mathews. 2009. "Births: Final Data for 2006." *National Vital Statistics Reports* 57 (January 7).

Martin, Karin A. 2009. "Normalizing Heterosexuality: Mothers' Assumptions, Talk, and Strategies with Young Children." *American Sociological Review* 74 (April):190–207.

Martin, Marvin. 1996. "Sociology Adapting to Changes." *Chicago Tribune*, July 21, sec. 18, p. 20.

Martin, Susan E. 1994. "Outsider within the Station House: The Impact of Race and Gender on Black Women Politics." *Social Problems* 41 (August):383–400.

Martineau, Harriet. [1837] 1962. *Society in America.* Edited, abridged, with an introductory essay by Seymour Martin Lipset. Reprint. Garden City, NY: Doubleday.

———. [1838] 1989. *How to Observe Morals and Manners.* Philadelphia: Leal and Blanchard. Sesquentennial edition, edited by M. R. Hill, Transaction Books.

Martinez, Elizabeth. 1993. "Going Gentle into That Good Night: Is a Rightful Death a Feminist Issue?" *Ms.* 4 (July/August):65–69.

Marubbio, M. Elise. 2006. *Killing the Indian Maiden: Images of Native American Women in Film.* Lexington: University Press of Kentucky.

Marx, Earl. 2009. "How Will Fair Fare?" *Christian Science Monitor,* April 19, pp. 30–31.

Marx, Gary T. 2012. "Looking at Smelser's Theory of Collective Behavior after Almost 50 Years: A Review and Appreciation." *American Sociologist* 43 (June):135–152.

Marx, Karl. [1844] 1964. "Contribution to the Critique of Hegel's Philosophy of Right." In *On Religion, Karl Marx and Friedrich Engels.* New York: Schocker Books.

———, and Friedrich Engels. [1847] 1955. *Selected Work in Two Volumes.* Reprint. Moscow: Foreign Languages Publishing House.

Maryanski, Alexandra R. 2004. "Evaluation Theory." Pp. 257–263 in *Encyclopedia of Social Theory,* edited by George Ritzer. Thousand Oaks, CA: Sage.

Mason, J. W. 1998. "The Buses Don't Stop Here Anymore." *American Prospect* 37 (March):56–62.

Massey, Douglas S. 1998. "March of Folly: U.S. Immigration Policy after NAFTA." *American Prospect* (March–April):22–23.

———. 2007. *Categorically Unequal: The American Stratification System.* New York: Russell Sage Foundation.

———. 2008. "A Mexican Apartheid." Pp. 55–57, vol. 2, in *Encyclopedia of Race, Ethnicity, and Society,* edited by Richard T. Schaefer. Thousand Oaks CA: Sage.

———, and Nancy A. Denton. 1993. *American Apartheid: Segregation and the Making of the Underclass.* Cambridge, MA: Harvard University Press.

———, and Margarita Mooney. 2007. "The Effects of America's Three Affirmative Action Programs on Academic Performance." *Social Problems* 54 (1):99–117.

Masuda, Takahiko, Phoebe C. Ellsworth, Batja Mesquita, Janxin Leu, Shigehito Tanida, and Ellen Van de Veerdonk. 2008. "Attitudes and Social Cognition: Placing the Face in Context: Cultural Differences in the Perception of Facial Emotion." *Journal of Personality and Social Psychology* 94 (3):365–381.

Masud-Piloto, Felix. 2008. "Cuban Americans." Pp. 357–359, vol. 1, in *Encyclopedia of Race, Ethnicity, and Society,* edited by Richard T. Schaefer. Thousand Oaks, CA: Sage.

Mathews, T. J., and Marian MacDorman. 2011. "Infant Mortality Statistics." *National Vital Statistics Reports* 59 (6).

Maylie, Devon. 2011. "Wal-Mart's Africa Foothold Shaky as Job Worries Mount." *Wall Street Journal,* May 10, p. 5.

Mazumder, Bhashkar. 2008. *Upward Intergenerational Economic Mobility in the United States.* Washington, DC: Economic Mobility Project.

McChesney, Robert W. 2008. *The Political Economy of Media: Enduring Issues, Emerging Dilemmas.* New York: Monthly Review Press.

McCormack, Mark. 2010. "Changing Masculinities in Youth Cultures." *Qualitative Sociology* 33:111–115.

McDonald, Michael P. 2009b. "2008 Current Population Survey Voting and Registration Supplement." Accessed April 16 (http://elections.gmu.edu/CPS_2008.html).

McDowell, Linda, Adina Batnitzky, and Sarah Dyer. 2009. "Precarious Work and Economic Migration: Emerging Immigrant Divisions of Labor in Greater London's Service Sector." *International Journal of Urban and Regional Research* 31 (March):3–25.

McFarland, Andrew S. 2007. "Neopluralism." *Annual Review of Political Science* 10:45–66.

McGirk, Tim. 2009. "Postcard: Dubai." *Time,* October 19, p. 6.

McGlynn, Clare, and Vanessa E. Munro (eds.) 2010. *Rethinking Rape Law: International and Comparative Perspective.* London: Routledge-Cavendish.

McGue, Matt, and Thomas J. Bouchard, Jr. 1998. "Genetic and Environmental Influence on Human Behavioral Differences." Pp. 1–24 in *Annual Review of Neurosciences.* Palo Alto, CA: Annual Reviews.

McGuire, Thomas G., and Jeanne Miranda. 2008. "New Evidence Regarding Racial and Ethnic Disparities in Mental Health: Policy Implications." *Health Affairs* 27 (2):393–403.

McGurty, Eileen Maura. 2000. "Warren County, NC, and the Emergence of the Environmental Justice Movement: Unlikely Coalitions and Shared Meanings in Local Collective Action." *Society and Natural Resources* 13:373–387.

McIntosh, Peggy. 1988. "White Privilege and Male Privilege: A Personal Account of Coming to See Correspondence through Work and Women's Studies." Working Paper No. 189, Wellesley College Center for Research on Women, Wellesley, MA.

McKinlay, John B., and Sonja M. McKinlay. 1977. "The Questionable Contribution of Medical Measures to the Decline of Mortality in the United States in the Twentieth Century." *Milbank Memorial Fund Quarterly* 55 (Summer):405–428.

McKinley, Jesse. 2012. "Ruling Extends Sex-Discrimination Protection to Transgender Women Denied Federal Jobs." *New York Times,* April 25, p. A14.

McLanahan, Sara, and Christine Percheski. 2008. "Family Structure and the Reproduction of Inequalities." *Annual Review of Sociology* 38:257–276.

McLuhan, Marshall. 1964. *Understanding Media: The Extensions of Man.* New York: New American Library.

———. 1967. *The Medium Is the Message: An Inventory of Effects.* New York: Bantam Books.

McNeil, Donald G., Jr. 2002. "W.H.O. Moves to Make AIDS Drugs More Accessible to Poor Worldwide." *New York Times,* August 23, p. D7.

———. 2004. "When Real Food Isn't an Option." *New York Times,* September 3, pp. A1, A5.

McPhail, Clark, and David Miller. 1973. "The Assembling Process: A Theoretical Empirical Examination." *American Sociological Review* 38 (December):721–735.

———. 1991. *The Myth of the Madding Crowd.* New York: De Gruyter.

———. 1994. "The Dark Side of Purpose in Riots: Individual and Collective Violence." *Sociological Quarterly* 35 (January):i–xx.

———. 2006. "The Crowd and Collective Behavior: Bringing Symbolic Interaction Back In." *Symbolic Interaction* 29 (Issue 4):433–464.

———. 2008. "Crowd." *Contexts* (Spring):78–79.

Mead, George H. 1934. In *Mind, Self and Society,* edited by Charles W. Morris. Chicago: University of Chicago Press.

———. 1964a. In *On Social Psychology,* edited by Anselm Strauss. Chicago: University of Chicago Press.

———. 1964b. "The Genesis of the Self and Social Control." Pp. 267–293 in *Selected Writings: George Herbert Mead,* edited by Andrew J. Reck. Indianapolis: Bobbs-Merrill.

Mead, Margaret. [1935] 2001. *Sex and Temperament in Three Primitive Societies.* New York: Perennial, HarperCollins.

Mehl, Matthias R., Simine Vazire, Nairán Ramírez-Esparza, Richard B. Slatcher, and James W. Pennebaker. 2007. "Are Women Really More Talkative than Men?" *Science* 317 (July 6):82.

Mendez, Jennifer Bickman. 1998. "Of Mops and Maids: Contradictions and Continuities in Bureaucratized Domestic Work." *Social Problems* 45 (February):114–135.

Merton, Robert. 1948. "The Bearing of Empirical Research upon the Development of Social Theory." *American Sociological Review* 13 (October):505–515.

———. 1968. *Social Theory and Social Structure.* New York Free Press.

———, and Alice S. Kitt. 1950. "Contributions to the Theory of Reference Group Behavior." Pp. 40–105 in *Continuities in Social Research: Studies in the Scope and Methods of the American Soldier,* edited by Robert K. Merton and Paul L. Lazarsfeld. New York: Free Press.

Messner, Michael A. 2002. "Gender Equity in College Sports: 6 Views." *Chronicle of Higher Education* 49 (December 6):B9–B10.

———, and Cheryl Cooky. 2010. *Gender in Televised Sports: News and Highlights Shows, 1989–2009.* Los Angeles: Center for Feminist Research, University of Southern California.

Meston, Cindy M., and David M. Buss. 2007. "Why Humanoids Have Sex." *Archives of Sexual Behavior* 36 (August).

Meyerowitz, Joel. 2002. *The City Resilient.* New York: The Museum of the City of New York.

Michals, Jennifer M. 2003. "The Price We Pay to Get Richer: A Look at Student Indebtedness." Unpublished M.A. paper, DePaul University, Chicago, IL.

Michels, Robert. 1915. *Political Parties.* Glencoe, IL: Free Press (reprinted 1949).

Microfinance Information Exchange. 2011. "MIX Market." Accessed May 24 (www.themix.org).

Migration News. 2012. "Remittance." *Migration News* (January).

Milgram, Stanley. 1963. "Behavioral Study of Obedience." *Journal of Abnormal and Social Psychology* 67 (October):371–378.

———. 1975. *Obedience to Authority: An Experimental View.* New York: Harper and Row.

Miller, Dan E. 2006. "Rumor: An Examination of Some Stereotypes." *Symbolic Interaction* 28 (4):505–519.

Miller, David L. 2000. *Introduction to Collective Behavior and Collective Action.* 2nd ed. Prospect Heights, IL: Waveland Press.

———, and JoAnne DeRoven Darlington. 2002. "Fearing for the Safety of Others: Disasters and the Small World Problem." Paper presented at Midwest Sociological Society, Milwaukee, WI.

Miller, Jacqueline W., Timothy S. Naimi, Robert D. Brewer, and Sherry Everett Jones. 2007. "Binge Drinking and Associated Health Risk Behaviors among High School Students." *Pediatrics* 119 (January):76–85.

Miller, Laura. 2008. "The Rise of the Superclass." Accessed in *Salon* May 2 (www.salon.com/ books/review/2008/03/14/superclass/print.html).

Miller, Peter. 2012. "A Theory or Town About Twins." *National Geographic* (January).

Miller, Reuben. 1988. "The Literature of Terrorism." *Terrorism* 11 (1):63–87.

Mills, C. Wright. [1959] 2000a. *The Sociological Imagination.* 40th anniversary edition. New Afterword by Todd Gitlin. New York: Oxford University Press.

———. [1956] 2000b. *The Power Elite.* New edition. Afterword by Alan Wolfe. New York: Oxford University Press.

Miner, Horace. 1956. "Body Ritual among the Nacirema." *American Anthropologist* 58 (June): 503–507.

Minnesota Center for Twin and Family Research. 2012. "Research at the MCTFR." Accessed January 12 (http://mctfr.psych.umn.edu/research/).

Miyata, Kakuko, and Tetsuro Kobayashi. 2008. "Causal Relationship between Internet Use and Social Capital in Japan." *Asian Journal of Social Psychology* 11:42–52.

Mizruchi, Mark S. 1996. "What Do Interlocks Do? An Analysis, Critique, and Assessment of Research on Interlocking Directorates." Pp. 271–298 in *Annual Review of Sociology, 1996,* edited by John Hagan and Karen Cook. Palo Alto, CA: Annual Reviews.

Moeller, Philip. 2009. "Unique Havens for an Aging America." *US News and World Report* (October):62–68.

Moeller, Susan D. 1999. *Compassion Fatigue.* London: Routledge.

Mohai, Paul, David Pellow, and J. Timmons Roberts. 2009. "Environmental Justice." *Annual Review of Environmental Research* 34:405–430.

———, and Robin Saha. 2007. "Racial Inequality in the Distribution of Hazardous Waste: A National-Level Reassessment." *Social Problems* 54 (3):343–370.

Mol, A. J. 2010. "Ecological Modernization as a Social Theory of Environmental Reform." Pp. 63–71 in *The International Handbook of Environmental Sociology,* 2nd ed., edited by Michael

R. Redcraft and Graham Woodgate. Cheltenham, UK: Edward Elgar.

———, and D. A. Sonnenfeld, eds. 2000. *Ecological Modernization around the World.* Portland, OR: Frank Cass.

———, ———, and G. Spaargaren, eds. 2009. *The Ecological Modernization Reader.* London: Routledge.

Mollen, Milton. 1992. *"A Failure of Responsibility": Report to Mayor David N. Dinkins on the December 28, 1991, Tragedy at City College of New York.* New York: Office of the Deputy Mayor for Public Safety.

Molotch, Harvey. 1970. "Oil in Santa Barbara and Power in America." *Sociological Inquiry* 40 (Winter):131–144.

Monaghan, Peter. 1993. "Sociologist Jailed Because He 'Wouldn't Snitch' Ponders the Way Research Ought to Be Done." *Chronicle of Higher Education* 40 (September 1):A8, A9.

Monahan, Torin. 2011. "Surveillance as Cultural Practice." *The Sociological Quarterly* 52:495–508.

Moncarz, Roger J., Michael G. Wolf, and Benjamin Wright. 2008. "Service-Providing Occupations, Offshoring, and the Labor Market." *Monthly Labor Review* (December):71–86.

Money. 1987. "A Short History of Shortages." 16 (Fall, special issue):42.

Montgomery, Marilyn J., and Gwendolyn T. Sorell. 1997. "Differences in Love Attitudes across Family Life Stages." *Family Relations* 46:55–61.

Moore, Molly. 2006. "Romance, but Not Marriage." *Washington Post National Weekly Edition,* November 27, p. 18.

Moore, Wilbert E. 1967. *Order and Change: Essays in Comparative Sociology.* New York: Wiley.

Morris, Aldon. 2000. "Reflections on Social Movement Theory: Criticisms and Proposals." *Contemporary Sociology* 29 (May):445–454.

Morrison, Denton E. 1971. "Some Notes toward Theory on Relative Deprivation, Social Movements, and Social Change." *American Behavioral Scientist* 14 (May–June):675–690.

Morrison, Peter A., and Thomas M. Bryan. 2010. "Targeting Spatial Centers of Elderly Consumers in the U.S.A." *Population Research Policy Review* 29:33–46.

Morse, Arthur D. 1967. *While Six Million Died: A Chronicle of American Apathy.* New York: Ace.

Moskos, Peter. 2008. *Cop in the Hood: My Year Policing Baltimore's Eastern District.* Princeton NJ: Princeton University Press.

Mosley, J., and E. Thomson. 1995. Pp. 148–165 in *Fatherhood: Contemporary Theory, Research and Social Policy,* edited by W. Marsiglo. Thousand Oaks, CA: Sage.

Mueller, G. O. 2001. "Transnational Crime: Definitions and Concepts." Pp. 13–21 in *Combating Transnational Crime: Concepts, Activities, and Responses,* edited by P. Williams and D. Vlassis. London: Franklin Cass.

Mufson, Steven. 2007. "Turning Down the Heat." *Washington Post National Weekly Edition* 24 (July):6–8.

Mulrine, Anna. 2012. "Up in Arms." *Christian Science Monitor Weekly* (July 2):26–32.

Muñoz, José A. 2008. "Protest and Human Rights Networks: The Case of the Zapatista Movement." *Sociology Compass* (April):1045–1058.

Murdock, George P. 1945. "The Common Denominator of Cultures." Pp. 123–142 in *The Science of Man in the World Crisis,* edited by Ralph Linton. New York: Columbia University Press.

———. 1949. *Social Structure.* New York: Macmillan.

———. 1957. "World Ethnographic Sample." *American Anthropologist* 59 (August):664–687.

Murphy, Dean E. 1997. "A Victim of Sweden's Pursuit of Perfection." *Los Angeles Times,* September 2, pp. A1, A8.

Murray, Velma McBride, Amanda Willert, and Diane P. Stephens. 2001. "The Half-Full Glass: Resilient African American Single Mothers and Their Children." *Family Focus* (June):F4–F5.

Myers, Dowell, and John Pitkin. 2011. *Assimilation Tomorrow: How America's Immigrants Will Integrate by 2030.* Washington, DC: Centers for American Progress.

Myre, Greg. 2013. "Women in Combat: 5 Key Questions." January 24. Accessed March 3 at http://m.npr.org/story/170161752.

n

NAACP. 2008. *Out of Focus—Out of Sync Take 4.* Baltimore: NAACP.

NACCRRA (National Association of Child Care Resource and Referral Agencies). 2010. "Parents and the High Cost of Child Care: 2010 Update." Accessible at http://www.naccrra.org/docs/ Cost_Report_073010-final.pdf.

Nakao, Keiko, and Judith Treas. 1994. "Updating Occupational Prestige and Socioeconomic Scores: How the New Measures Measure Up." *Sociological Methodology* 24:1–72.

NARAL Pro-Choice America. 2012. "Who Decides? Restrictions on Low-Income Women's Access to Abortion." Accessed February 22 (www.prochoiceamerica.org/what-is-choice/ maps-and-charts/map.jsp?mapID=4).

Nash, Manning. 1962. "Race and the Ideology of Race." *Current Anthropology* 3 (June):285–288.

National Advisory Commission on Criminal Justice. 1976. *Organized Crime.* Washington, DC: U.S. Government Printing Office.

National Alliance for Caregiving. 2009. *Caregiving in the U.S.: Executive Summary.* Washington, DC: NAC and AARP.

National Alliance for Public Charter Schools. 2011. Number of Charter Schools 2009–2010 and 2010–2011. Communication to Schaefer from NAPCS. June 30.

———. 2012. "The Public Charter Schools Dashboard: Schools Overview 2011–2012 estimates." Accessed March 1 (http://dashboard. publiccharters.org/dashboard/schools/state/OR/ year/2012).

National Alliance on Mental Illness. 2008. "What Is Mental Illness?" Accessed May 24, 2011 at www.nami.org.

National Alliance to End Homelessness. 2013. "The State of Homelessness in America 2013." Accessible at www.endhomelessness.org.

National Center for Education Statistics. 2009. *Homeschooled Students.* Accessed May 31 (http://nces.ed.gov/programs/coe/2009/section1/indicator06.asp).

———. 2010. *Digest of Education Statistics 2009.* Accessible at http://nces.ed.gov/pubs2010/2010013.pdf.

———. 2011. *Average Undergraduate Tuition and Fees.* Accessed March 29 (http://nces.ed.gov/programs/digest/d09/tables/dt09_335.asp).

National Center on Addiction and Substance Abuse at Columbia University. 2007. *Wasting the Best and the Brightest: Substance Abuse at America's Colleges and Universities.* New York: NCASA at Columbia University.

National Coalition for the Homeless. 2012. *Hate Crimes against the Homelessness: The Brutality of Violence Unveiled.* Accessible at www.nationalhomelessness.org.

National Conference of State Legislators. 2011. "Same-Sex Marriage, Civil Unions and Domestic Partnerships" and "Civil Unions & Domestic Partnership Statutes." Accessed March 21 (http://www.ncsl.org).

———. 2012a. "Voter Identification Requirements." Updated February 8. Accessed February 14 (www.ncsl.org/legislatures-elections/voter-id-state-requirements.aspx).

———. 2012b. "Defining Marriage: Defense of Marriage Acts and Same-Sex Marriage Laws." Accessed February 27 (www.ncsl.org/issues-research/human-services/same-sex-marriage-overview.aspx).

National Education Association. 2009. *Rankings and Estimates: Rankings of the States 2009 and Estimates of School Statistics 2010.* Accessible at http://www.nea.org.assets/docs/010rankings.pdf.

National Gay and Lesbian Task Force. 2012. "Anti-Adoption Laws in the U.S." Accessed February 26 (http://thetaskforce.org/reports_and_research/adoption_laws).

National Geographic. 2005. *Atlas of the World.* 8th ed. Washington, DC: National Geographic.

National Institute of Justice. 2005. *Sexual Assault on Campus: What Colleges and Universities Are Doing about It.* Washington, DC: National Institute of Justice.

National Institute on Aging. 1999. *Early Retirement in the United States.* Washington, DC: U.S. Government Printing Office.

National Law Center on Homelessness and Poverty. 2009b. "Maryland 1st to Protect Homeless from Hate Crimes." May 7. Accessed May 15, 2013 at www.nlchp.org/news.cfm?id=98.

National Organization for Men Against Sexism. 2012. Home Page. Accessed February 22 (www.nomas.org).

Navarro, Mireya. 2005. "When You Contain Multitudes." *New York Times,* April 24, pp. 1, 2.

Needham, Paul. 2011. "9/11 Memorial Review: At Ground Zero, Staying Above Ground Matters." September 9. Accessible at www.huffingtonpost.com.

Negroni, Lirio K. 2012. "The Puerto Rican American Family." Pp. 129–147 in *Ethnic Families in America: Patterns and Variations.* 5th ed., edited by Roosevelt Wright, Jr., Charles H. Mindel,

Thanh Van Tran, and Robert W. Halsenstein. Upper Saddle River, NJ: Pearson.

Nelson, Emily. 2004. "Goodbye, 'Friends'; Hello, New Reality." *Wall Street Journal,* February 9, pp. B6, B10.

Neuman, Lawrence W. 2009. *Understanding Research.* Boston: Allyn and Bacon.

Neuwirth, Robert. 2004. *Shadow Cities: A Billion Squatters, a New Urban World.* New York: Routledge.

New York Times. 2007. "University Officials Accused of Hiding Campus Homicide." June 24, p. 19.

———. 2011. "Welcome Rescinded." September 11, Section NY, p. 14.

Newman, Katherine S. 2012. *The Accordion Family: Boomerang Kids, Anxious Parents, and the Private Toll of Global Competition.* Boston: Beacon Press.

Newman, William M. 1973. *American Pluralism: A Study of Minority Groups and Social Theory.* New York: Harper and Row.

Newport, Frank. 2009. "Americans: Economy Takes Precedence Over Environment." Accessed April 27 at http://www.gallup.com/poll/116962/Americans-Economy-Takes-Precedence-Environment.aspx.

———. 2010b. *In U.S., Increasing Number Have No Religious Identity.* Accessed March 28, 2011 (www.gallup.com).

———. 2011a. "For First Time, Majority of Americans Favor Legal Gay Marriage." Accessed February 27, 2012 (www.gallup.com/poll/147662/First-Time-Majority-Americans-Favor-Legal-Gay-Marriage.aspx?version=print).

———. 2011b. "Record-High 50% of Americans Favor Legalizing Marijuana Use." October 17. Accessible at www.gallup.com.

Newsday. 1997. "Japan Sterilized 16,000 Women." September 18, p. A19.

———. 2008. "Law and Order." January 6, pp. 10–11.

Nicas, Jack, and Joe Palazzolo. 2013. "Pro-Gun Laws Gain Ground." *Wall Street Journal,* April 4. Accessible at http://online.wsj.com/article/SB10001424127887324883604578398843653264474.html.

NICHD. 2007. "Children Who Complete Intensive Early Childhood Program Show Gains in Adulthood: Greater College Attendance, Lower Crime and Depression." Accessed January 7, 2008 (www.nichd.nih.gov/news.releases/early_interventions_082107.cfm).

Nicolaides, Becky M., and Andrew Wiese. 2013. "Suburban Disequilibrium." *New York Times,* April 7, p. 5.

Nielsen Company. 2009. "The Nielsen Company's Guide to Super Bowl XLIII." Accessed February 7, 2010 (http://en-us.nielsen.com/main/news/news_releases/2009/january/the_nielsen_company0).

Nielsen, Joyce McCarl, Glenda Walden, and Charlotte A. Kunkel. 2000. "Gendered Heteronormativity: Empirical Illustrations in Everyday Life." *Sociological Quarterly* 41 (2):283–296.

Niemi, Richard G., and Michael J. Hanmer. 2010. "Voter Turnout among College Students: New

Data and a Rethinking of Traditional Theories." *Social Science Quarterly* 91 (June):301–323.

Niesse, Mark. 2008. "Hawaiian Sovereignty Seekers Take Over Historic Iolani Palace in Honolulu." *News from Indian Country* (May 12):3.

———. 2011. "Native Hawaiian Self-Government May Be Set Up by State." *News from Indian Country* (March):3.

Niezen, Ronald. 2005. "Digital Identity: The Construction of Virtual Selfhood in the Indigenous Peoples' Movement." *Comparative Studies in Society and History* 47 (3):532–551.

Nixon, Darren. 2009. "'I Can't Put a Smiley Face On': Working-Class Masculinity, Emotional Labor and Service Work in the 'New Economy.'" *Gender, Work and Organization* 16 (3):300–322.

Noam, Eli. 2009. *Media Ownership and Concentration in America.* Cambridge, MA: Oxford University Press.

Nocera, Joe. 2012. "Guns and Mental Illness." *New York Times,* December 29, p. A17.

Nolan, Patrick, and Gerhard Lenski. 2009. *Human Societies: An Introduction to Macrosociology.* 11th ed. Boulder, CO: Paradigm.

Noonan, Rita K. 1995. "Women against the State: Political Opportunities and Collective Action Frames in Chile's Transition to Democracy." *Sociological Forum* 10:81–111.

Nordhaus, Ted, and Michael Shellenberger. 2007. *Break Through: From the Death of Environmentalism to the Politics of Possibility.* Boston: Houghton Mifflin.

Nordholt, Eric Schulte, Marijke Hartgers, and Rita Gircour, eds. 2004. "The Dutch Virtual Census of 2001." *Analysis and Methodology.* Voorburg: Statistics Netherlands.

NORML. 2012. "State Laws." Accessed June 1 (http://norml.org/laws).

Norris, Floyd. 2012. "The Number of Those Working Past 65 Is at a Record High." *New York Times,* May 19, p. B3.

Norris, Poppa, and Ronald Inglehart. 2004. *Sacred and Secular: Religion and Politics Worldwide.* Cambridge: Cambridge University Press.

North Carolina Department of Environmental and Natural Resources. 2008. "Warren County PCB Landfill Fact Sheet." Accessed April 9 (www.wastenotnc.org/WarrenCo_Fact_Sheet.htm).

O

Oberschall, Anthony. 1973. *Social Conflict and Social Movements.* Englewood Cliffs, NJ: Prentice Hall.

O'Connor, Anne-Marie. 2004. "Time of Blogs and Bombs." *Los Angeles Times,* December 27, pp. E1, E14–E15.

O'Donnell, Mike. 1992. *A New Introduction to Sociology.* Walton-on-Thames, UK: Thomas Nelson and Sons.

Office of Immigration Statistics. 2011. "Yearbook of Immigration Statistics: 2010." Accessible at www.dhs.gov/files/statistics/publications/LPR10.shtm.

Office of the United States Trade Representative. 2012. "Benefits of Trade." Accessed January 29 (www.ustr.gov/about-us/benefits-trade).

Ogas, Ogi, and Sai Gaddam. 2011. *A Billion Wicked Thoughts: What the World's Largest Experiment Reveals about Human Desire.* New York: Dutton.

Ogburn, William F. 1922. *Social Change with Respect to Culture and Original Nature.* New York: Huebsch (reprinted 1966, New York: Dell).

———, and Clark Tibbits. 1934. "The Family and Its Functions." Pp. 661–708 in *Recent Social Trends in the United States,* edited by Research Committee on Social Trends. New York: McGraw-Hill.

O'Harrow, Jr., Robert. 2005. "Mining Personal Data." *Washington Post National Weekly Edition,* February 6, pp. 8–10.

Okano, Kaori, and Motonori Tsuchiya. 1999. *Education in Contemporary Japan: Inequality and Diversity.* Cambridge: Cambridge University Press.

Okun, Barbara and Joseph Nowinski. 2011. *Saying Goodbye: How Families Can Find Renewal Through Loss.* Cambridge MA: Harvard Health Publications.

Oldenburg, Ray. 1999. *The Great Good Place Cafes, Coffee Shops, Bookstores, Bar, Hair Salons, and Other Hangouts at the Heart of a Community.* New York: Paragon House.

———. 2000. *Celebrating the Third Place: Inspiring Stories about the 'Great Good Places' at the Heart of Our Communities.* Marlowe and Company.

Oliver, Melvin L., and Thomas M. Shapiro. 2006. *Black Wealth/White Wealth: New Perspectives on Racial Inequality.* 2nd ed. New York: Routledge.

Omi, Michael, and Howard Winant. 1994. *Racial Formation in the United States.* 2nd ed. New York: Routledge.

Onishi, Norimitso. 2003. "Divorce in South Korea: Striking a New Attitude." *New York Times,* September 21, p. 19.

Orfield, Gary, and Chungmei Lee. 2007. *Historic Reversals, Accelerating Resegregation, and the Need for New Integration Strategies.* Los Angeles: Civil Rights Project, UCLA.

Organisation for Economic Co-operation and Development. 2008. *Growing Unequal? Income Distribution and Poverty in OECD Countries.* Geneva: OECD.

———. 2009b. "Green at Fifteen? How 15-Year-Olds Perform in Environmental Sciences and Geosciences in PISA 2006." PISA, OECD Publishing. Accessible at http://dx.doi.org/10.1787/9789264063600-en.

———. 2011. *Statistics on Resource Flows to Developing Countries.* Geneva: OECD. Accessible at http://www.oecd.org/dataoecd/53/43/47137659.pdf.

———. 2012a. "Poverty Rate After Taxes and Transfers from OECD." Stat extracts accessed January 20, 2012 (http://stats.oecd.org/Index.aspx?DataSetCode=Poverty).

———. 2012b. "Gender Equality and Social Institutions in Afghanistan." Accessed February 22 (http://genderindex.org/country/Afghanistan).

———. 2012c. "Education at a Glance 2011: OECD Indicators." Accessible at www.oecd-ilibrary.org/education/education-at-a-glance-2011/how-many-students-finish-tertiary-education_eaf-2011-7-en.

Ormond, James. 2005. "The McDonaldization of Football." Accessed January 23, 2006 (http://courses.essex.ac.uk/sc/sc111).

Orum, Anthony M., and John G. Dale. 2009. *Political Sociology: Power and Participation in the Modern World.* 3rd ed. New York: Oxford University Press.

Ostling, Richard N., and Joan K. Ostling. 2000. *Mormon America: The Power and the Promise.* San Francisco: HarperCollins.

Outside the Classroom. 2009. "College Students Spend More Time Drinking than Studying." Accessed March 11 (www.outsidetheclassroom.com).

Oxford Poverty and Human Development Initiative. 2012. "Multidimensional Poverty Index." Accessed January 30 (www.ophi.org.uk).

p

Pace, Richard. 1993. "First-Time Televiewing in Amazonia: Television Acculturation in Gurupa, Brazil." *Ethnology* 32:187–205.

———. 1998. "The Struggle for Amazon Town." Boulder, CO: Lynne Rienner.

Padilla, Efren N. 2008. "Filipino Americans." Pp. 493–497 in vol. 1, *Encyclopedia of Race, Ethnicity, and Society,* edited by Richard T. Schaefer. Thousand Oaks, CA: Sage.

Page, Charles H. 1946. "Bureaucracy's Other Face." *Social Forces* 25 (October):89–94.

Page, Jeremy. 2011. "China's One-Child Plan Faces New Fire." *New York Times,* April 29, pp. A1, A12.

Pager, Devah. 2007. *Marked: Race, Crime, and Funding Work in an Era of Mass Incarceration.* Chicago: University of Chicago Press.

———, Bruce Weston, and Bart Bonikowski. 2009. "Discrimination in a Low-Wage Labor Market: A Field Experiment." *American Sociological Review* 74 (October):777–799.

Pampel, Fred C., Patrick M. Krueger, and Justin T. Denney. 2010. "Socioeconomic Disparities in Health Behaviors." *Annual Review of Sociology* 36:349–370.

Pariser, Ei. 2011a. *The Filter Bubble. What the Internet is Hiding from You.* New York: Penguin Press.

———. 2011b. "In Our Own Little Internet Bubbles." *Guardian Weekly,* June 24, p. 32.

Park, Robert E. 1916. "The City: Suggestions for the Investigation of Human Behavior in the Urban Environment." *American Journal of Sociology* 20 (March):577–612.

———. 1922. *The Immigrant Press and Its Control.* New York: Harper.

———. 1936. "Succession, an Ecological Concept." *American Sociological Review* 1 (April): 171–179.

Parker, Ashley. 2010. "Where Parties Look for an Audience." *New York Times,* October 30.

Parker-Pope, Tara. 2012. "America's Drinking Binge." January 11. Accessed January 18 (http://well.blogs.nytimes.com/2012/01/11/Americas-drinking-binge).

Parkin, Stephen, and Ross Comber. 2009. "Value in the Visual: On Public Injecting, Visual Methods and Their Potential for Informing Policy (and Change)." *Methodological Innovations Online* 4(2):21–36.

Parsons, Talcott. 1951. *The Social System.* New York: Free Press.

———. 1966. *Societies: Evolutionary and Comparative Perspectives.* Englewood Cliffs, NJ: Prentice Hall.

———. 1975. "The Sick Role and the Role of the Physician Reconsidered." *Milbank Medical Fund Quarterly Health and Society* 53 (Summer):257–278.

———, and Robert Bales. 1955. *Family: Socialization and Interaction Process.* Glencoe, IL: Free Press.

Passel, Jeffrey S., and D'Vera Cohn. 2011. "Unauthorized Immigrant Population National and State Trends, 2010." Washington, DC: Pew Research Center.

Passero, Kathy. 2002. "Global Travel Expert Roger Axtell Explains Why." *Biography* (July):70–73, 97–98.

Patel, Reena. 2010. *Working the Night Shift: Women in India's Call Center Industry.* Stanford, CA: Stanford University Press.

Patterson, Thomas E. 2005. "Young Voters and the 2004 Election." Cambridge, MA: Vanishing Voter Project, Harvard University.

Pattillo-McCoy, Mary. 1999. *Black Picket Fences: Privilege and Peril among the Black Middle Class.* Chicago: University of Chicago Press.

Pear, Robert. 1997. "Now, the Archenemies Need Each Other." *New York Times,* June 22, sec. 4, pp. 1, 4.

———. 2009. "Congress Relaxes Rules on Suits over Pay Inequity." *New York Times,* January 28, p. A14.

Pendergrast, Mark. 1999. *Uncommon Grounds: The History of Coffee and How It Transformed Our World.* New York: Basic Books.

Pennington, Bill. 2008. "College Athletic Scholarships: Expectations Lose Out to Reality." *New York Times,* March 10, pp. A1, A15.

Peralta, Eyder. 2011. "Who Are the 1 Percent? Gallup Finds They're A Lot Like the 99 Percent." December 5. Accessed December 12 (www.wbur.org/npr/143143332/who-are-the-1-percent-gallup-finds-theyre-a-lot-like-the-99-percent).

Perlman, Janice. 2010. *Favela: Four Decades of Living on the Edge in Rio de Janeiro.* London: Oxford University Press.

Pesca, Mike. 2012. "Grading Charter Schools." Accessed February 24 (http://onpoint.wbur.org/2012/02/23/studying-charter-schools).

Pescosolido, Bernice A. 2013. "The Public Stigma of Mental Illness: What Do We Think; What Do We Know; What Can We Prove?" *Journal of Health and Social Behavior* 54 (1):1–21.

Peter, Laurence J., and Raymond Hull. 1969. *The Peter Principle.* New York: Morrow.

Petersen, John L. 2009. "How 'Wild Cards' May Reshape Our Future." *Futurist* (May–June): 19–20.

Petersen, William. 1979. *Malthus.* Cambridge, MA: Harvard University Press.

Petrášová, Alexandra. 2006. *Social Protection in the European Union.* Brussels: European Union.

Petrie, Michelle, and James E. Coverdill. 2010. "Who Lives and Dies on Death Row? Race, Ethnicity, and Post-Sentence Outcomes in Texas." *Social Problems* 57 (4):630–652.

Pew Forum on Religion and Public Life. 2008. *U.S. Religious Landscape Survey.* Washington, DC: Author.

———. 2010a. *U.S. Religious Knowledge Survey.* Washington, DC: Pew Forum. Accessible at http://pewforum.org.

———. 2010b. *Religious Knowledge Query.* Accessed March 23, 2011 (http://pewforum.org/UploadedFiles/Topics/Belief-and-practices/religious-knowledge-quiz-handout.pdf).

Pew Global Attitudes Project. 2007. *Global Unease with Major World Powers.* Washington, DC: Pew Global.

Pew Hispanic Center. 2011. "The Mexican-American Boom: Births Overtake Immigration." Washington, DC: Pew Hispanic Center.

Pew Internet Project. 2000. "April 2000 Survey Data." Accessed January 17, 2010 (http://pewinternet.org/Shared-Content/Data-Sets/2000/April-2000-Survey-Data.aspx).

———. 2009. "Demographics of Internet Users." Accessed February 4 (www.pewinternet.org/trends/User_Demo_Jan_2009.htm).

———. 2012a. "Demographics of Internet Users." May 2011. Accessed January 17, 2012 (www.pewinternet.org/Trend-Data/Whos-Online.aspx).

———. 2012b. "Demographics of Teen Internet Users." September 2009. Accessed January 17, 2012 (www.pweinternet.org/Static-Pages/Trend-Data-for-Teens/Whos-Online.aspx).

———. 2012c. "Trend Data: Usage Over Time." Accessed January 17 (http://pewinternet.org/Trend-Data/Usage-Over-Time.aspx).

———. 2012d. "Demographics of Internet Users." Accessed May 28 (http://pewinternet.org/Static-Pages/Trend-Data-(Adults)/Whos-Online.aspx).

Pew Research Center for the People and the Press. 2012. "Continued Majority Support for Death Penalty, January 6." Accessed January 23 (www.people-press.org/2012/01/06/continued-majority-support-for-death-penalty/?src=prc-headline).

Pew Research Center. 2009. "Americans Now Divided Over Both Issues: Public Takes Conservative Turn on Gun Control, Abortion." News release. Washington, DC: Pew Research Center.

———. 2010. "Glenn Beck, Christians and Mormons." Accessed October 4 at http://pewresearch.org/pubs/1717/glenn-beck-christians-mormons.

———. 2012. "After Newtown, Modest Change in Opinion about Gun Control." December 20. Accessible at people-press.org.

Pew Social and Demographic Trends. 2011. "Twenty-to-One: Wealth Gaps Rise to Record Highs Between Whites, Black and Hispanics." Washington, DC: Pew Research Center.

———. 2012. "Rising Share of Americans See Conflict Between Rich and Poor." Washington, DC: Pew Research Center.

Pfeifer, Mark. 2008. "Vietnamese Americans" Pp. 1365–1368, vol. 3, in *Encyclopedia of Race, Ethnicity, and Society,* edited by Richard T. Schaefer. Thousand Oaks, CA: Sage.

Phelan, Jo C., Bruce G. Lint, and Parisha Tehranifar. 2010. "Social Conditions as Fundamental Causes of Health Inequalities: Theory, Evidence, and Policy Implications." *Journal of Health and Social Behavior* 51 (5):528–540.

Phillips, E. Barbara. 1996. *City Lights: Urban–Suburban Life in the Global Society.* New York: Oxford University Press.

Phillips, Susan A. 1999. *Wallbangin': Graffiti and Gangs in L.A.* Chicago: University of Chicago Press.

Piaget, Jean. 1954. *Construction of Reality in the Child.* Translated by Margaret Cook. New York: Basic Books.

Picca, Leslie Houts, and Joe R. Feagin. 2007. *Two-Faced Racism: Whites in Backstage and Frontstage.* New York: Routledge.

Pickert, Kate. 2009. "Getting Well While You Shop." *Time,* June 22, pp. 68–70.

———. 2012. "Doing Good by Texting." *Time,* August 27, p. 27.

Pilkington, Ed. 2010. "Right to Bear Arms Upheld." *The Guardian Weekly* (February 7):8.

Pincus, Fred L. 2003. *Reverse Discrimination: Dismantling the Myth.* Boulder, CO: Lynne Rienner.

———. 2008. "Reverse Discrimination." Pp. 1159–1161, vol. 3, in *Encyclopedia of Race, Ethnicity, and Society,* edited by Richard T. Schaefer. Thousand Oaks, CA: Sage.

Pinderhughes, Dianne. 1987. *Race and Ethnicity in Chicago Politics: A Reexamination of Pluralist Theory.* Urbana: University of Illinois Press.

Pinderhughes, Raquel. 2008. "Green Collar Jobs." Accessed June 29 (www.urbanhabitat.org/node/528).

Piven, Frances Fox, and Richard A. Cloward. 1996. "Welfare Reform and the New Class War." Pp. 72–86 in *Myths about the Powerless: Contesting Social Inequalities,* edited by M. Brinton Lykes, Ali Banuazizi, Ramsay Liem, and Michael Morris. Philadelphia: Temple University Press.

Plomin, Robert. 1989. "Determinants of Behavior." *American Psychologist* 44 (February):105–111.

Plüss, Caroline. 2005. "Constructing Globalized Ethnicity." *International Sociology* 20 (June): 201–224.

Pogash, Carol. 2008. "Poor Students in High School Suffer Stigma from Lunch Aid." *New York Times,* March 1, pp. A1, A14.

Polletta, Francesca, and James M. Jasper. 2001. "Collective Identity and Social Movements." Pp. 283–305 in *Annual Review of Sociology, 2001,* edited by Karen S. Cook and Leslie Hogan. Palo Alto, CA: Annual Reviews.

Population Reference Bureau. 1996. "Speaking Graphically." *Population Today* 24 (June/July).

Portes, Alejandro, Cristina Escobar, and Renelinda Arana. 2008. "Bridging the Gap: Transnational and Ethnic Organizations in the Political Incorporation of Immigrants in the United States." *Ethnic and Racial Studies* 31 (September 6):1056–1090.

Powell, Brian, Catherine Bolzendahl, Claudia Geist, and Lola Carr Steelman. 2010. *Counted Out. Same-Sex Relationships and Americans' Definitions of Family.* New York: Russell Sage Foundation.

Powell, Gary N. 2010. *Women and Men in Management.* 4th ed. Thousand Oaks, CA: Sage.

Prehn, John W. 1991. "Migration." Pp. 190–191 in *Encyclopedia of Sociology.* 4th ed. Guilford, CT: Dushkin.

Preston, Jennifer. 2011. "Facebook Page for Jesus with Highly Active Fans." *New York Times,* September 5, p. B3.

———, and Brian Stelter. 2011. "Cellphone Cameras Become World's Eyes and Ears on Protests across the Middle East." *New York Times,* February 19, p. A7.

Prince, Martin, Vikram Patel, Shekhar Saxena, Mario Maj, Johanna Maselko, Michael Phillips, and Atif Rahman. 2007. "No Health without Mental Health." *The Lancet* 370 (September 8):859–877.

Provasnik, Stephen, and Michael Planty. 2008. *Community Colleges: Special Supplement to the Condition of Education 2008.* Washington, DC: U.S. Government Printing Office.

Pryor, John H., Sylvia Hurtado, Victor B. Saenz, José Luis Santos, and William S. Korn. 2007. *The American Freshman: Forty Year Trends.* Los Angeles: Higher Education Research Institute, UCLA.

———, ———, Linda DeAngelo, Laura Palucki Blake, Sylvia Hurtado, and Serge Tran. 2011a. *The American Freshman: National Norms Fall 2011.* Los Angeles: Higher Education Research Institute, UCLA.

Putnam, Robert. 1995. *Bowling Alone: America's Declining Social Capital.* New York: Simon and Schuster.

q

Quadagno, Jill. 2011. *Aging and the Life Course: An Introduction to Social Gerontology.* 5th ed. New York: McGraw-Hill.

Quarantelli, Enrico L. 1957. "The Behavior of Panic Participants." *Sociology and Social Research* 41 (January):187–194.

———, and Russell R. Dynes. 1970. "Property Norms and Looting: Their Patterns in Continuity Crises." *Phylon* (Summer):168–182.

———, and James R. Hundley, Jr. 1975. "A Test of Some Propositions about Crowd Formation and Behavior." Pp. 538–554 in *Readings in Collective Behavior,* edited by Robert R. Evans. Chicago: Rand McNally.

Quillian, Lincoln. 2006. "New Approaches to Understanding Racial Prejudice and Discrimination." *Annual Review of Sociology* 32:299–328.

Quinney, Richard. 1970. *The Social Reality of Crime.* Boston: Little, Brown.

———. 1974. *Criminal Justice in America.* Boston: Little, Brown.

———. 1979. *Criminology.* 2nd ed. Boston: Little, Brown.

———. 1980. *Class, State and Crime.* 2nd ed. New York: Longman.

Quinnipiac University. 2013. "Americans Back Women in Combat 3-1, But Less for Draft." February 7. Accessed March 3 at www.quinnipiac.edu.

Quiñones-Hinojosa, Alfredo with Mim Eichler Rivas. 2011. *Becoming Dr. Q: My Journey from Migrant Farm Worker to Brain Surgeon.* Berkeley: University of California Press.

r

Rabikovitch, Shelley, and James Lewis, eds. 2004. *The Encyclopedia of Modern Witchcraft and New Paganism.* New York: Citadel Press.

Rabinovitch, Simon. 2011. "China Labour Costs Soar as Wages Rise 22%." *Financial Times.* October 25. Accessed March 2, 2012 (www.ft.com/intl/cms/s/0/25f1c500-ff14-11e0-9b2f-00144 feabdc0.html#axzz1nziV8URS).

Rainie, Lee. 2005. *Sports Fantasy Leagues Online.* Washington, DC: Pew Internet and American Life Project.

Rajan, Gita, and Shailja Sharma. 2006. *New Cosmopolitanisms: South Asians in the US.* Stanford, CA: Stanford University Press.

Ramet, Sabrina. 1991. *Social Currents in Eastern Europe: The Source and Meaning of the Great Transformation.* Durham, NC: Duke University Press.

Ramos, Jorge. 2010. *A Country for All.* New York: Vintage Books.

Ramstad, Evan. 2011. "Studying Too Much Is a New No-No In Upwardly Mobile South Korea." *Wall Street Journal,* October 6, p. A1.

RAND. 2010. "Retail Medical Clinics Perform Well Relative to Other Medical Settings." *RAND Review* (Winter 2009–2010). Accessed January 25 (www.rand.org/publications/randreview/issues/winter2009/news.html#medclinics).

Randolph, Tracey H., and Mellisa Holtzman. 2010. "The Role of Heritage Camps in Identity Development Among Korean Transnational Adoptees: A Relational Dialectics Approach." *Adoption Quarterly* 13:75–91.

Rangaswamy, Padma. 2005. "Asian Indians in Chicago." In *The New Chicago,* edited by John Koval et al. Philadelphia: Temple University Press.

Ratha, Dilip, Sanket Mohaptra, and Ani Silwat. 2010. "Outlook for Remittance Flows 2010–2011." *Migration and Development Brief, World Bank.*

Ratnesar, Romesh. 2011. "The Menace Within." *Stanford Magazine* (July/August). Accessible at www.stanfordalumni.org.

Ravitch, Diane. 2010. *The Death and Life of the Great American School System: How Testing and Choice Are Undermining Education.* New York: Basic Books.

Rawlinson, Linnie, and Nick Hunt. 2009. "Jackson Dies, Almost Takes Internet with Him." Accessed July 1 (www.cnn.com/2009/TECH/06/26/michael.jackson.internet/).

Raybon, Patricia. 1989. "A Case for 'Severe Bias.'" *Newsweek* 114 (October 2):11.

Reinharz, Shulamit. 1992. *Feminist Methods in Social Research.* New York: Oxford University Press.

Reitzes, Donald C., and Elizabeth J. Mutran. 2006. "Lingering Identities in Retirement." *Sociological Quarterly* 47:333–359.

Religion News Service. 2003. "New U.S. Guidelines on Prayer in Schools Get Mixed Reaction." *Los Angeles Times,* February 15, p. B24.

Religion Watch. 2006. "Hinduism Shaping India's Pragmatic Use of Biotechnology." April.

Rennison, Callie. 2002. *Criminal Victimization 2001. Changes 2000–01 with Trends 1993–2001.* Washington, DC: U.S. Government Printing Office.

Renzulli, Linda A., and Vincent J. Roscigno. 2007. "Charter Schools and Public Good." *Contexts* 6 (Winter):31–36.

Reschovsky, Clara. 2004. *Journey to Work: 2000.* Census 2000 Brief C2KBR-23. Washington, DC: U.S. Government Printing Office.

Reuters. 2010. "Geoghegan Replaces Feinberg as Pay Czar." September 10. Accessed March 5, 2011 (http://www.reuters.com/assets/print?aid=U STRE6894ZH20100910).

Revkin, Andrew C. 2007. "Wealth and Poverty, Drought and Flood: Report from Four Fronts in the War on Warming." *New York Times,* April 3, pp. D4–D5.

Rheingold, Howard. 2003. *Smart Mobs: The Next Social Revolution.* Cambridge, MA: Perseus.

Rice, Ronald E. 2008. *Media Ownership: Research and Regulation.* Cresskill, NJ: Hampton Press.

Rideout, Victoria K., Ulla G. Foehr, and Donald F. Roberts. 2010. Generation M: Media in the Lives of 8–18 Year-Olds. Kaiser Family Foundation. Accessible at www.kff.org/entmedia/mh012010pkg.cfm.

Riding, Alan. 1998. "Why 'Titanic' Conquered the World." *New York Times,* April 26, sec. 2, pp. 1, 28, 29.

———. 2005. "Unesco Adopts New Plan against Cultural Invasion." *New York Times,* October 21, p. B3.

Rieker, Patricia R., and Chloe E. Bird. 2000. "Sociological Explanations of Gender Differences in Mental and Physical Health." Pp. 98–113 in *Handbook of Medical Sociology,* edited by Chloe Bird, Peter Conrad, and Allan Fremont. New York: Prentice Hall.

Rifkin, Jeremy. 1995. *The End of Work; The Decline of the Global Labor Force and the Dawn of the Post-Market Era.* New York: Tarcher/Putnam.

Riley, Matilda White, Robert L. Kahn, and Anne Foner. 1994a. *Age and Structural Lag.* New York: Wiley InterScience.

———, Robert L. Kahn, and Anne Foner, in association with Karin A. Mock. 1994b. "Introduction: The Mismatch between People and Structures." Pp. 1–36 in *Age and Structural Lag,* edited by Matilda White Riley, Robert L. Kahn, and Anne Foner. New York: Wiley InterScience.

Ripley, Amanda. 2011. "Teacher, Leave Those Kids Alone." *Time,* December 5, pp. 46–49.

Ritzer, George. 1977. *Working: Conflict and Change.* 2nd ed. Englewood Cliffs, NJ: Prentice Hall.

———. 2002. *McDonaldization: The Reader.* Thousand Oaks, CA: Pine Forge Press.

———. 2004. *The Globalization of Nothing.* Thousand Oaks, CA: Pine Forge Press.

———. 2008. *The McDonaldization of Society 5.* Thousand Oaks, CA: Sage.

———. 2011. *McDonaldization of Society 6.* Thousand Oaks, CA: Sage.

Robelon, Erik W. 2008. 'Moment-of-Silence' Generates Loud Debate in Illinois." *Education Week* (October 24).

Robertson, Roland. 1988. "The Sociological Significance of Culture: Some General Considerations." *Theory, Culture, and Society* 5 (February):3–23.

Robinson, Kristopher, and Edward M. Crenshaw. 2010. "Reevaluating the Global Digital Divide: Socio-Demographic and Conflict Barriers to the Internet Revolution." *Sociological Inquiry* 80 (February):34–62

Robison, Jennifer. 2002. "Feminism—What's in a Name?" Accessed February 25, 2007 (www.galluppoll.com).

Robnett, Belinda, and Cynthia Feliciano. 2011. "Patterns of Racial-Ethnic Exclusion by Internet Daters." *Social Forces* 89 (March):807–828.

Rockefeller Foundation. 2013. "100 Resilient Cities: Centennial Challenge." Accessible at www.rockefellerfoundation.org/100-resilient-cities.

Rodman, George. 2011. *Mass Media in a Changing World.* 3rd ed. New York: McGraw-Hill.

Rogan, Eugene. 2009. "Sand, Sea and Shopping." *Guardian Weekly,* October 16, pp. 38–39.

Rooks, Gerrit, Frits Tazelaar, and Chris Snijders. 2011. "Gossip and Reputation in Business Networks." *European Sociological Review* 27 (1): 90–106. *Times,* April 6.

Rootes, Christopher. 2007. "Environmental Movements." Pp. 608–640 in *The Blackwell Companion to Social Movements,* edited by David A. Snow, Sarah A. Sovle, and Hanspeter Kriesi. Malden, MA: Blackwell.

Rose, Arnold. 1951. *The Roots of Prejudice.* Paris: UNESCO.

Rose, Peter I., Myron Glazer, and Penina Migdal Glazer. 1979. "In Controlled Environments: Four Cases of Intense Resocialization." Pp. 320–338 in *Socialization and the Life Cycle,* edited by Peter I. Rose. New York: St. Martin's Press.

Rosen, Eva, and Sudhir Alladi Venkatesh. 2008. "A Perversion of Choice: Sex Work Offers Just Enough in Chicago's Urban Ghetto." *Journal of Contemporary Ethnography* (August):417–441.

Rosenberg, Douglas H. 1991. "Capitalism." Pp. 33–34 in *Encyclopedic Dictionary of Sociology,* 4th ed., edited by Dushkin Publishing Group. Guilford, CT: Dushkin.

Rosenberg, Tina. 2012. "The 'Avon Ladies' of Africa." *New York Times* (October 14), Week in Review, p. 9.

Rosenbloom, Stephanie. 2011. "Love, Lies, and What They Learned." *New York Times,* November 13, pp. ST1, ST8.

Rosenfeld, Jake. 2010. "Little Labor." *Pathways* (Summer):4–6.

Rosenthal, Robert, and Lenore Jacobson. 1968. *Pygmalion in the Classroom.* New York: Holt.

———. 1992. *Pygmalion in the Classroom: Teacher Expectations and Pupils' Intellectual Development.* Newly expanded edition. Bancyfelin, UK: Crown House.

Ross, John. 1996. "To Die in the Street: Mexico City's Homeless Population Booms as Economic Crisis Shakes Social Protections." *SSSP Newsletter* 27 (Summer):14–15.

Rossi, Alice S. 1968. "Transition to Parenthood." *Journal of Marriage and the Family* 30 (February): 26–39.

———. 1984. "Gender and Parenthood." *American Sociological Review* 49 (February):1–19.

Rossi, Peter H. 1987. "No Good Applied Social Research Goes Unpunished." *Society* 25 (November–December):73–79.

Rossides, Daniel W. 1997. *Social Stratification: The Interplay of Class, Race, and Gender.* 2nd ed. Upper Saddle River, NJ: Prentice Hall.

Roszak, Theodore. 1969. *The Making of a Counter-culture.* Garden City, NY: Doubleday.

Roter, Debra L., Judith A. Hall, and Yutaka Aoki. 2002. "Physician Gender Effects in Medical Communications: A Meta-analytic Review." *Journal of the American Medical Association* 288 (August 14):756–764.

Rothkopf, David. 2008. *Superclass: The Global Power Elite and the World They Are Making.* New York: Farrar, Straus and Giroux.

Rubin, Alissa J. 2003. "Pat-Down on the Way to Prayer." *Los Angeles Times,* November 25, pp. A1, A5.

———, and Sam Dagher. 2009. "Election Quotas for Iraqi Women Are Weakened, Provoking Anger as Vote Nears." *New York Times,* January 14, p. A13.

Rudel, Thomas K., J. Timmons Roberts, and Jo Ann Carmin. 2011. "Political Economy of the Environment." *Annual Review of Sociology* 37:221–238.

Ruiz, Rebecca. 2010. "Care for the Caregivers." *The American Prospect* (October):A17–A20.

Ryan, William. 1976. *Blaming the Victim.* Rev. ed. New York: Random House.

Rymer, Russ. 1993. *Genie: An Abused Child's Flight from Science.* New York: HarperCollins.

S

Saad, Lydia. 2004. "Divorce Doesn't Last." *Gallup Poll Tuesday Briefing.* March 30. Accessible at www.gallup.com.

———. 2011. "Americans Still Split Along 'Pro-Choice,' 'Pro-Life' Lines." May 23. Accessed February 22, 2012 (http://gallup.com/poll.147734/Americans-Split-Along-Pro-Choice-Pro-Life-Lines.aspx?version=print).

Sabol, William J., Heather C. West, and Matthew Cooper. 2009. "Prisoners in 2008." *Bureau of Justice Statistics Bulletin* (December).

Sachs, Jeffrey D. 2005. *The End of Poverty: Economic Possibilities for Our Time.* New York: Penguin.

Sacks, Peter. 2007. *Tearing Down the Gates: Confronting the Class Divide in American Education.* Berkeley: University of California Press.

Sagarin, Edward, and Jose Sanchez. 1988. "Ideology and Deviance: The Case of the Debate over the Biological Factor." *Deviant Behavior* 9 (1):87–99.

SAGE. 2012. "About Us: Services and Advocacy for Gay, Lesbian, Bisexual and Transgender Elders." Accessed March 12 at http://sageusa.org/about.

Saguy, Abigail, and Rene Almeling. 2008. "Fat in the Fire? Science, the News Media, and the 'Obesity Epidemic.'" *Sociological Forum* 23 (March):53–83.

Said, Edward W. 2001. "The Clash of Ignorance." *Nation,* October 22.

Sale, Kirkpatrick. 1996. *Rebels against the Future: The Luddites and Their War on the Industrial Revolution* (with a new preface by the author). Reading, MA: Addison-Wesley.

Salem, Richard, and Stanislaus Grabarek. 1986. "Sociology B.A.s in a Corporate Setting: How Can They Get There and of What Value Are They?" *Teaching Sociology* 14 (October):273–275.

Sampson, Robert J., and W. Byron Graves. 1989. "Community Structure and Crime: Testing Social-Disorganization Theory." *American Journal of Sociology* 94 (January):774–802.

Samuels, Dorothy. 2011. "Where Abortion Rights Are Disappearing." *New York Times,* September 25 (sect. SR), p. 14.

Samuels, Robert. 2010. "A Suicide Reminds Gulf Coast of Oil Spill." *Miami Herald,* June 28. Accessible at http://www.mcclatchydc.com/2010/06/28/96665/a-suicide-reminds-gulf-coast-of.html.

Samuelson, Paul A., and William D. Nordhaus. 2010. *Economics.* 19th ed. New York: McGraw-Hill.

Sandefur, Rebecca L. 2008. "Access to Civil Justice and Race, Class, and Gender Inequality." *Annual Review of Sociology* 34:339–358.

Sanders, Edmund. 2004. "Coming of Age in Iraq." *Los Angeles Times,* August 14, pp. A1, A5.

Sanderson, Stephen K., Seth A. Abrutyn, and Kristopher R. Proctor. 2011. "Testing the Protestant Ethic Thesis with Quantitative Historical Data: A Research Note." *Social Forces* 89 (March):905–912.

Santos, José Alcides Figueiredo. 2006. "Class Effects on Racial Inequality in Brazil." *Dados* 2:1–35.

Sanua, Marianne R. 2007. "AJC and Intermarriage: The Complexities of Jewish Continuity, 1960–2006." Pp. 3–32 in *American Jewish Yearbook 2007,* edited by David Singer and Lawrence Grossman. New York: American Jewish Committee.

Sanyal, Paromita. 2009. "From Credit to Collective Action: The Role of Microfinance in Promoting Women's Social Capital and Normative Influence." *American Sociological Review* 74 (August):529–550.

Sapir, Edward. 1929. "The State of Linguistics as a Science." *Language* 5 (4):207–214.

Saporito, Bill. 2007. "Restoring Wal-Mart." *Time* 170 (November 12):46–48, 50, 52.

Sassen, Saskia. 2005. "New Global Classes: Implications for Politics." Pp. 143–170 in *The New Egalitarianism,* edited by Anthony Giddens and Patrick Diamond. Cambridge: Polity.

Satel, Sally. 2013. "Why the Fuss over the D.S.M-5?" *New York Times,* May 12 (Week in the News), p. 5.

Sawhill, Isabel, and Ron Haskins. 2009. "If You Can Make It Here . . ." *Washington Post National Weekly Edition,* November 9, p. 27.

———, and John E. Morton. 2007. *Economic Mobility: Is the American Dream Alive and Well?* Washington, DC: Economic Mobility Project, Pew Charitable Trusts.

Sayer, Liana C., Suzanne M. Bianchi, and John P. Robinson. 2004. "Are Parents Investing Less in Children? Trends in Mothers' and Fathers' Time with Children." *American Journal of Sociology* 110 (July):1–43.

Scarce, Rik. 2005. "A Law to Protect Scholars." *Chronicle of Higher Education,* August 12, p. 324.

Schadler, Ted. 2009. *US Telecommuting Forecast, 2009–2016.* Accessible at www.forester.com.

Schaefer, Peter. 2008. "Digital Divide." Pp. 388–389, vol. 1, in *Encyclopedia of Race, Ethnicity, and Society in the United States,* edited by Richard T. Schaefer. Thousand Oaks, CA: Sage.

Schaefer, Richard T. 1998. "Differential Racial Mortality and the 1995 Chicago Heat Wave." Presentation at the annual meeting of the American Sociological Association, August, San Francisco.

———. 2008b. "'Power' and 'Power Elite.'" In *Encyclopedia of Social Problems,* edited by Vincent Parrillo. Thousand Oaks, CA: Sage.

———. 2011. *Race and Ethnicity in the United States.* 12th ed. Census Update. Upper Saddle River, NJ: Prentice Hall.

———. 2012. *Racial and Ethnic Groups.* 13th ed. Upper Saddle River, NJ: Pearson.

———, and William Zellner. 2011. *Extraordinary Groups.* 9th ed. New York: Worth.

Scharnberg, Kirsten. 2007. "Black Market for Midwives Defies Bans." *Chicago Tribune,* November 25, pp. 1, 10.

Scheid, Teresa L. 2013. "A Decade of Critique: Notable Books in the Sociology of Mental Health." *Contemporary Sociology* 42 (2): 177–183.

Scherer, Michael. 2011. "Introduction: Taking It to the Streets." Pp. 5–12 in *Occupy: What Is Occupy?* New York: Time Books.

———. 2013. "The Next Gun Fight." *Time* (January 20):25—41.

Scherer, Ron. 2009. "Job Migration to Suburbs: An Unstoppable Flow?" *New York Times,* April 6.

———. 2010a. "A Long Struggle to Find Jobs." *Christian Science Monitor,* January 31, pp. 18–19.

———. 2010b. "For Jobless, Online Friends Can Be Lifelines." *Christian Science Monitor,* March 25, p. 21.

———. 2010c. "Jim Bunning Delays Vote; Unemployed Face First Week Without Check." *Christian Science Monitor* (March 2).

Schleifer, Yigal. 2009. "In Turkey, Surfing for Brides." *Christian Science Monitor,* July 5, p. 14.

Schlesinger, Traci. 2011. "The Failure of Race-Neutral Policies: How Mandatory Terms and Sentencing Enhancements Contribute to Mass Racialized Incarceration." *Crime & Delinquency* 57 (January):56–81.

Schmeeckle, Maria. 2007. "Gender Dynamics in Stepfamilies: Adult Stepchildren's Views." *Journal of Marriage and Family* 69 (February): 174–189.

———, Roseann Giarrusso, Du Feng, and Vern L. Bengtson. 2006. "What Makes Someone Family? Adult Children's Perceptions of Current and Former Stepparents." *Journal of Marriage and Family* 68 (August):595–610.

Schnaiberg, Allan. 1994. *Environment and Society: The Enduring Conflict.* New York: St. Martin's Press.

Schneider, Christopher. 2008. "Sexuality." Pp. 847–848 in *Encyclopedia of Social Problems,* edited by Vincent Parrillo. Los Angeles: Sage.

Schneider, Friedrich. 2010. "Dues and Don'ts." *The Economist* (August 14):62.

Schram, Sanford F., Ruhard C. Fording, Joe Soss, and Linda Houser. 2009. "Deciding to Discipline: Race, Choice and Punishment at the Frontlines of Welfare Reform." *American Sociological Review* 74 (June):398–422.

Schulman, Gary I. 1974. "Race, Sex, and Violence: A Laboratory Test of the Sexual Threat of the Black Male Hypothesis." *American Journal of Sociology* 79 (March):1260–1272.

Schur, Edwin M. 1965. *Crimes without Victims: Deviant Behavior and Public Policy.* Englewood Cliffs, NJ: Prentice Hall.

———. 1968. *Law and Society: A Sociological View.* New York: Random House.

———. 1985. "'Crimes without Victims': A 20-Year Reassessment." Paper presented at the annual meeting of the Society for the Study of Social Problems.

Schwab, Klaus (ed.) 2011. *The Global Competitiveness Report 2010-2011.* Geneva: World Economic Forum.

Schwartz, Howard D., ed. 1994. *Dominant Issues in Medical Sociology.* 3rd ed. New York: McGraw-Hill.

Schwartz, Shalom H., and Anat Bardi. 2001. "Value Hierarchies across Cultures: Taking a Similarities Perspective." *Journal of Cross-Cultural Perspective* 32 (May):268–290.

Scott, Alan. 1990. *Ideology and the New Social Movements.* London: Unwin Hyman.

Scott, Gregory. 2001. "Broken Windows behind Bars: Eradicating Prison Gangs through Ecological Hardening and Symbolic Cleansing." *Corrections Management Quarterly* 5 (Winter):23–36.

Scott, W. Richard, and Gerald F. Davis. 2007. *Organizations and Organizing: Rational, Natural and Open Systems Perspectives.* New York: Pearson.

Scoville, David. 2010. "Disneyland Deconstructed: Postmodernism Revealed." April 16. Accessible at http://davidscoville.blogspot.com/2010/04/Disneyland-deconstructed-postmodernism.html.

Search Engine Watch. 2011. "comScore: Bing Grows for Sixth Straight Year." March 16. Accessible at http://searchenginewatch.com/3642049.

Seccombe, Karen. 2011. *So You Think I Drive a Cadillac?* Boston: Allyn and Bacon.

Second Life. 2010. "Current User Metrics for Second Life." Accessed February 2, 2010 (http://secondlife.com/xmlhttp/secondlife/php).

Security on Campus. 2008. "Complying with the Jeanne Clery Act." Accessed January 13 (www.securityoncampus.org/crimestats/index.html).

Sedgwick, Eve Kosofsky. 1990. *Epistemology of the Closet.* Berkeley: University of California Press.

Sefiha, Ophir. 2012. "Bad Sports: Explaining Sport Related Deviance." *Sociology Campus* 6:949–961.

Seidman, Steven. 1994. "Heterosexism in America: Prejudice against Gay Men and Lesbians." Pp. 578–593 in *Introduction to Social Problems,* edited by Craig Calhoun and George Ritzer. New York: McGraw-Hill.

Sellers, Frances Stead. 2004. "Voter Globalization." *Washington Post National Weekly Edition,* November 29, p. 22.

Selod, Saher Farooq. 2008a. "Muslim Americans." Pp. 920–923, vol. 2, in *Encyclopedia of Race,*

Ethnicity, and Society, edited by Richard T. Schaefer. Thousand Oaks, CA: Sage.

———. 2008b. "Veil." Pp. 1359–1360, vol. 3, in *Encyclopedia of Race, Ethnicity, and Society,* edited by Richard T. Schaefer. Thousand Oaks, CA: Sage.

Sengupta, Somini. 2006. "Report Shows Muslims Near Bottom of Social Ladder." *New York Times,* November 29, p. A4.

———. 2009. "An Empire for Poor Working Women, Guided by a Gandhian Approach." *New York Times,* March 7, p. A6.

Sernau, Scott. 2001. *Worlds Apart: Social Inequalities in a New Century.* Thousand Oaks, CA: Pine Forge Press.

Settersten, Richard, and Barbara Ray. 2011. *Not Quite Adults: Why 20-Somethings Are Choosing a Slower Path to Adulthood, and Why It's Good for Everyone.* New York: Bantam.

Shachtman, Tom. 2006. *Rumspringa: To Be or Not to Be Amish.* New York: North Point Press.

Shah, Anup. 2009. "Climate Justice and Equity." October 4. Accessed December 12 (www.globalissues.org/print/articles/231).

Shane, Scott. 2010. "Wars Fought and Wars Googled." *New York Times,* June 27, pp. PWK1–5.

Shapiro, Ari. 2013. "Obama to Unveil Gun Control Plans." January 16. Accessible at www.wbur.org/npr/169486528/obama-to-unveil-gun-control-plans.

Shapiro, Joseph P. 1993. *No Pity: People with Disabilities Forging a New Civil Rights Movement.* New York: Times Books.

Shapiro, Thomas M., Tatjana Meschede, and Laura Sullivan. 2010. "The Racial Wealth Gap Increases Fourfold." Research and Policy Brief, Institute on Assets and Social Policy, Brandeis University.

Shapley, Dan. 2010. "4 Dirty Secrets of the Exxon Valdez Oil Spill." Accessed May 3 (www.thedailygreen.com).

Sharkey, Patrick. 2009. *Neighbors and the Black-White Mobility Gap.* Washington, DC: Economic Mobility Project.

Sharma, Hari M., and Gerard C. Bodeker. 1998. "Alternative Medicine." Pp. 228–229 in *Britannica Book of the Year 1998.* Chicago: Encyclopaedia Britannica.

Sharp, Ansel M., Charles A. Register, and Paul W. Grimes. 2013. *Economics of Social Issues.* 20th ed. New York: McGraw Hill.

Sharp, Jeff S., and Jill K. Clark. 2008. "Between the Country and the Concrete: Rediscovering the Rural-Urban Fringe." *City and Community* 7 (March):61–77.

Shaw, Clifford R., and Henry D. McKay. 1942. *Juvenile Delinquency and Urban Areas.* Chicago: University of Chicago Press.

Sheehan, Charles. 2005. "Poor Seniors Take On Plans of Condo Giant." *Chicago Tribune,* March 22, pp. 1, 9.

Sherman, Arloc. 2007. *Income Inequality Hits Record Levels, New CBO Data Show.* Washington, DC: Center on Budget and Policy Priorities.

Sherman, Jennifer, and Elizabeth Harris. 2012. "Social Class and Parenting: Classic Debates and New Understandings." *Sociology Compass* 6:60–71.

Shibutani, Tamotshu. 1966. *Improvised News: A Sociological Study of Rumor.* Indianapolis: Bobbs-Merrill.

Shin, Hyon B., and Robert A. Kominski. 2010. *Language Use in the United States: 2007.* Report ACS-12. Washington, DC: U.S. Government Printing Office.

Shogren, Elizabeth. 1994. "Treatment against Their Will." *Los Angeles Times,* August 18, pp. A1, A14–A15.

Shostak, Arthur B. 2002. "Clinical Sociology and the Art of Peace Promotion: Earning a World without War." Pp. 325–345 in *Using Sociology: An Introduction from the Applied and Clinical Perspectives,* edited by Roger A. Straus. Lanham, MD: Rowman and Littlefield.

Sicular, Terry, Ximing Yue, Bjorn Gustafsson, and Shi Li. 2006. "The Urban-Rural Income Gap and Inequality in China." Research Paper No. 2006/135, United Nations University—World Institute for Development Economic Research.

Sieber, Renée E., Daniel Spitzberg, Hannah Muffatt, Kristen Brewer, Blanka Füleki, and Naomi Arbit. 2006. *Influencing Climate Change Policy: Environmental Non-Governmental Organizations (ENGOs) Using Virtual and Physical Activism.* Montreal: McGill University.

Siegel, Paul, Elizabeth Martin, and Rusalind Bruno. 2001. "Language Use and Linguistic Isolation: Historical Data and Methodological Issues." Paper presented at the Statistical Policy Seminar, Bethesda, MD.

Silverman, Rachel Emma. 2009. "As Jobs Grow Scarce, Commuter Marriages Rise." Accessed March 31, 2010 (http://blogs.wsj.com/juggle/2009/01/16/as-jobs-grow-scarce-commuter-marriages-rise/).

Silverstein, Ken. 2010. "Shopping for Sweat: The Human Cost of a Two-Dollar T-shirt." *Harpers* 320 (January):36–44.

Simon, Stephanie. 2007. "It's Easter; Shall We Gather at the Desktops?" *Los Angeles Times,* April 8, p. A13.

Sisson, Carmen K. 2007. "The Virtual War Family." *Christian Science Monitor,* May 29.

Sjoberg, Gideon. 1960. *The Preindustrial City: Past and Present.* Glencoe, IL: Free Press.

Skocpol, Theda, and Vanessa Williamson. 2012. *The Tea Party and the Remaking of Republican Conservatism.* New York: Oxford University Press.

Slack, Jennifer Daryl, and J. Macgregor Wise. 2007. *Culture + Technology.* New York: Peter Lang.

Slackman, Michael. 2008. "9/11 Rumors That Harden into Conventional Wisdom." *New York Times,* September 9, p. A16.

Slaughter, Chuck. 2011. "Taking the 'Avon' Way to Reach 'The Last Mile.'" Posted October 31. Accessed February 26, 2013 at www.huffingtonpost.com/chuck-slaughter/taking-the-avon-way-to re_b_1067840.html.

Slavin, Barbara. 2007. "Child Marriage Rife in Nations Getting U.S. Aid." *USA Today,* July 17, p. 6A.

Slavin, Robert E., and A. Cheung. 2003. *Effective Reading Programs for English Language Learners: A Best-Evidence Synthesis.* Baltimore: Johns Hopkins University, Center for Research on the Education of Students Placed at Risk.

Sloan, Allan. 2009. "What's Still Wrong with Wall Street." *Time,* November 9, pp. 24–29.

Sloop, John M. 2009. "Queer Approaches to Communication." Pp. 90–100 in *21st Century Communication,* edited by Bill Eadie. Thousand Oaks, CA: Sage.

Slug-Lines.com. 2011a. "A Unique Commuter Solution." Accessed November 10, 2011. (www.slug-lines.com).

Smart, Barry. 1990. "Modernity, Postmodernity, and the Present." Pp. 14–30 in *Theories of Modernity and Postmodernity,* edited by Bryan S. Turner. Newbury Park, CA: Sage.

Smeeding, Timothy M. 2008. "Poorer by Comparison: Poverty, Work, and Public Policy in Comparative Perspective." *Pathways* (Winter):3–5.

Smelser, Neil. 1962. *Theory of Collective Behavior.* New York: Free Press.

———. 1963. *The Sociology of Economic Life.* Englewood Cliffs, NJ: Prentice Hall.

———. 1981. *Sociology.* Englewood Cliffs, NJ: Prentice Hall.

Smith, Aaron. 2009. *The Internet's Role in Campaign 2000.* Washington, DC: Pew Internet and American Life Project.

———. 2012. *Real Time Charitable Giving.* Washington, DC: Pew Research Center's Internet and American Life Project. Accessible at www.pewinternet.org/Reports/2012/MobileGiving.aspx.

Smith, Carter, F., Jeffrey P. Rush, Daniel Robinson, and Megan Karmiller. 2012. "Views from the Field: Flashgangs and Flash Gangbanging: How Can Local Police Prepare?" *Journal of Gang Research* 20 (October):33–50.

Smith, Christian. 1991. *The Emergence of Liberation Theology: Radical Religion and Social Movement Theory.* Chicago: University of Chicago Press.

———. 2007. "Getting a Life: The Challenge of Emerging Adulthood." *Books and Culture: A Christian Review* (November–December).

———. 2008. "Future Directions of the Sociology of Religion." *Social Forces* 86 (June):1564–1589.

Smith, Craig S. 2006. "Romania's Orphans Face Widespread Abuse, Group Says." *New York Times,* May 10, p. A3.

Smith, Dan. 1999. *The State of the World Atlas.* 6th ed. London: Penguin.

Smith, David A., and Michael Timberlake. 1993. "World Cities: A Political Economy/Global Network Approach." Pp. 181–207 in *Urban Sociology in Transition,* edited by Ray Hutchison. Greenwich CT: JAI Press.

———. 1995. "The New Urban Sociology Meets the Old: Rereading Some Classical Human Ecology." *Urban Affairs Review* 20 (January):432–457.

Smith, Lawrence C. 2011. *The World in 2050: Four Forces Shaping Civilizations Northern Future.* New York: A Plume Book.

Smith, Michael Peter. 1988. *City, State, and Market.* New York: Basil Blackwell.

Smith, Peter. 2008. "Going Global: The Transnational Politics of the Debt Movement." *Globalizations* 5 (March):13–33.

Smith, Tom W. 2003. *Coming of Age in 21st Century America: Public Attitudes toward the Importance and Timing of Transition to Adulthood.* Chicago: National Opinion Research Center.

———. 2009. *Religious Change around the World.* Chicago: NORC/University of Chicago.

Smith, Wesley J. 2011. "Euthanasia Spreads in Europe." October 26. Accessed March 12, 2012 at http://nationalreview.com/articles/281303/euthanisa-spreads-europe-wesley-j-smith?pg=3.

Snow, David A., Louis A. Zurcher, Jr., and Robert Peters. 1981. "Victory Celebrations as Theater: A Dramaturgical Approach to Crowd Behavior." *Symbolic Interaction* 4:21–42.

Snyder, Thomas D. 1996. *Digest of Education Statistics 1996.* Washington, DC: U.S. Government Printing Office.

Somavia, Juan. 2008. "The ILO at 90 Working for Social Justice." *World of Work* 64 (December):4–5.

Sorokin, Pitirim A. [1927] 1959. *Social and Cultural Mobility.* New York: Free Press.

Southern Poverty Law Center. 2010. "Active 'Patriot' Groups in the United States in 2009." Accessed November 5 (www.splcenter.org/patriot).

Spalter-Roth, Roberta, and Nicole Van Vooren. 2008a. "What Are They Doing with a Bachelor's Degree in Sociology?" Washington, DC: American Sociological Association. Accessible at http://asanet.org/galleries/research/ASA researchbrief_corrections.pdf.

———. 2008b. "Skills, Reasons and Jobs. What Happened to the Class of 2005." Washington, DC: American Sociological Association. Accessible at http://asanet.org.

———. 2010. *Mixed Success: Four Years of Experiences of 2005 Sociology Graduates.* Washington, DC: American Sociological Association.

Speak, Suzanne, and Graham Tipple. 2006. "Perceptions, Persecution and Pity: The Limitations of Interventions for Homelessness in Developing Countries." *International Journal of Urban and Regional Research* 30 (March):172–188.

Spencer, Nancy. 2008. "Title IX." Pp. 1308–1310, vol. 3, in *Encyclopedia of Race, Ethnicity, and Society,* edited by Richard T. Schaefer. Thousand Oaks, CA: Sage.

Spitzer, Steven. 1975. "Toward a Marxian Theory of Deviance." *Social Problems* 22 (June):641–651.

Sprague, Joey. 2005. *Feminist Methodologies for Critical Research: Bridging Differences.* Lanham, MD: AltaMira Press.

Squires, Gregory D., ed. 2002. *Urban Sprawl: Causes, Consequences and Policy Responses.* Washington, DC: Urban Institute.

Stacey, Judith. 2011. *Unhitched.* New York: New York University Press.

Stahler-Sholk, Richard. 2008. "Zapatista Rebellion." Pp. 1423–1424, vol. 3, in *Encyclopedia of Race, Ethnicity, and Society,* edited by Richard T. Schaefer. Thousand Oaks, CA: Sage.

Stansell, Christine. 2011. *The Feminist Promise: 1792 to the Present.* New York: The Modern Library.

Stark, Andrew. 2011. "The Price of Moral Purity." *Wall Street Journal,* February 4.

Stark, Rodney. 2004. *Exploring the Religious Life.* Baltimore: Johns Hopkins University Press.

———. 2005. *The Rise of Mormonism,* edited by Reid L. Neilson. New York: Columbia University Press.

———, and William Sims Bainbridge. 1979. "Of Churches, Sects, and Cults: Preliminary Concepts for a Theory of Religious Movements." *Journal for the Scientific Study of Religion* 18 (June):117–131.

———, and ———. 1985. *The Future of Religion.* Berkeley: University of California Press.

Staton, Ron. 2004. "Still Fighting for National Hawaiian Recognition." *Asian Week,* January 22, p. 8.

Steel, Emily. 2010. "Some Data-Miners Ready to Reveal What They Know." *Wall Street Journal,* December 3, pp. B1, B2.

Steffen, Alex, ed. 2008. *World Changing: A User's Guide for the 21st Century.* New York: Harry N. Abrams.

Stein, Leonard I. 1967. "The Doctor-Nurse Game." *Archives of General Psychology* 16:699–703.

Stevick, Richard A. 2007. *Growing Up Amish: The Teenage Years.* Baltimore: Johns Hopkins University Press.

Stockard, Janice E. 2002. *Marriage in Culture.* Belmont, CA: Thomson Wadsworth.

Stolberg, Sheryl Gay. 1995. "Affirmative Action Gains Often Come at a High Cost." *Los Angeles Times,* March 29, pp. A1, A13–A16.

———. 2008. "Richest Nations Pledge to Halve Greenhouse Gas." *New York Times,* July 9, pp. A1, A13.

Stoner, Madeleine R. 2008. "Homelessness." Pp. 641–644, vol. 2, in *Encyclopedia of Race, Ethnicity, and Society,* edited by Richard T. Schaefer. Thousand Oaks, CA: Sage.

Strassman, W. Paul. 1998. "Third World Housing." Pp. 589–592 in *The Encyclopedia of Housing,* edited by Willem van Vliet. Thousand Oaks, CA: Sage.

Strauss, Gary. 2002. "'Good Old Boys' Network Still Rules Corporate Boards." *USA Today,* November 1, pp. B1, B2.

———. 2011. "$228, 000 for a Part-Time Job? Apparently, That's Not Enough." *USA Today,* March 4, p. A1.

Stryker, Roy Emerson, and Nancy Wood. 1973 [1935–1943]. *In This Proud Land.* Greenwich: New York Graphic Society.

Suárez, Zulema E., and Rose M. Perez. 2012. "The Cuban American Family." Pp. 112–128 in *Ethnic Families in America: Patterns and Variations.* 5th ed., edited by Roosevelt Wright, Jr., Charles H. Mindel, Thanh Van Tran, and Robert W. Halsenstein. Upper Saddle River, NJ: Pearson.

Subramaniam, Mangala. 2006. *The Power of Women's Organization: Gender, Caste, and Class in India.* Lanham, MD: Lexington Books.

Suchar, Charles S. 1997. "Grounding Visual Sociology Research in Shooting Scripts." *Qualitative Sociology* 20 (1):33–55.

Suh, Doowon. 2011. "Institutionalizing Social Movements: The Dual Strategy of the Korean Women's Movement." *Sociological Quarterly* 52:442–471.

Suitor, J. Jill, Staci A. Minyard, and Rebecca S. Carter. 2001. "'Did You See What I Saw?' Gender Differences in Perceptions of Avenues to Prestige among Adolescents." *Sociological Inquiry* 71 (Fall):437–454.

Sullivan, Harry Stack. [1953] 1968. *The Interpersonal Theory of Psychiatry.* Edited by Helen Swick Perry and Mary Ladd Gawel. New York: Norton.

Sullivan, Kevin. 2006. "Bridging the Digital Divide." *Washington Post National Weekly Edition* 25 (July 17):11–12.

Sum, Andrew, Paul Harrington, and Ishwar Khatiwada. 2006. *The Impact of New Immigrants on Young Native-Born Workers, 2000–2005.* Washington, DC: Center for Immigration Studies.

Sumner, William G. 1906. *Folkways.* New York: Ginn.

Survival International. 2012. "Brazilian Indians." Accessed January 12 (www.survivialinternational.org/tribes/Brazilian).

SustainAbility. 2006. *Brazil—Country of Diversities and Inequalities.* London: SustainAbility.

Sutch, Richard, and Susan B. Carter. 2006. *Historical Statutes of US: Earliest Time to the Present.* Cambridge: Cambridge University Press.

Sutcliffe, Bob. 2002. *100 Ways of Seeing an Unequal World.* London: Zed Books.

Sutherland, Edwin H. 1937. *The Professional Thief.* Chicago: University of Chicago Press.

———. 1940. "White-Collar Criminality." *American Sociological Review* 5 (February):1–11.

———. 1949. *White Collar Crime.* New York: Dryden.

———. 1983. *White Collar Crime: The Uncut Version.* New Haven, CT: Yale University Press.

———, Donald R. Cressey, and David F. Luckenbill. 1992. *Principles of Criminology.* 11th ed. New York: Rowman and Littlefield.

Swartz, Jon. 2012. "Google's Personalized Search Charts Set Off Uproar." *USA Today,* January 12, p. B1.

Swatos, William H., Jr., ed. 1998. *Encyclopedia of Religion and Society.* Lanham, MD: AltaMira.

Sweet, Kimberly. 2001. "Sex Sells a Second Time." *Chicago Journal* 93 (April):12–13.

Swidler, Ann. 1986. "Culture in Action: Symbols and Strategies." *American Sociological Review* 51 (April):273–286.

Szabo, Liz. 2013. "Mental Illness Takes Fall in Gun Laws." *USA Today,* March 12, p. 7D.

Szasz, Andrew. 2007. *Shopping Our Way to Safety: How We Changed from Protecting the Environment to Protecting Ourselves.* Minneapolis: University of Minnesota Press.

Szasz, Thomas. [1960] 2010. *The Myth of Mental Illness: Foundations of a Theory of Personal Conduct.* 50th Anniversary Edition. New York: Harper Perennial.

t

Tachibana, Judy. 1990. "Model Minority Myth Presents Unrepresentative Portrait of Asian Americans, Many Educators Say." *Black Issues in Higher Education* 6 (March 1):1, 11.

Takei, Isao, and Arthur Sakamoto. 2011. "Poverty Among Asian Americans in the 21st Century." *Sociological Perspectives* 54 (Summer): 251–276.

Tanielian, Terri. 2009, March 24. "Assessing Combat Exposure and Post-Traumatic Stress Disorder in Troops and Estimating the Costs to Society." Testimony presented before the House Veterans' Affairs Committee, Subcommittee on Disability Assistance and Memorial Affairs.

Tannen, Deborah. 1990. *You Just Don't Understand: Women and Men in Conversation.* New York: Ballantine.

Tatchell, Jo. 2009. *A Diamond in the Desert: Behind the Scenes in the World's Richest City.* London: Hodder and Stoughton.

Taylor, Chris. 2011. "Twitter Has 100 Million Active Users." December 8. Accessed January 15, 2012 (http://mashable.com/2011/09/08/twitter-has-100-million-active-users).

Taylor, Verta. 1999. "Gender and Social Movements: Gender Processes in Women's Self-Help Movements." *Gender and Society* 13:8–33.

———. 2004. "Social Movements and Gender." Pp. 14348–14352 in *International Encyclopedia of the Social and Behavioral Sciences,* edited by Neil J. Smelser and Paul B. Baltes. New York: Elsevier.

———, Leila J. Rupp, and Nancy Whittier. 2009. *Feminist Frontiers.* 8th ed. New York: McGraw-Hill.

Teaching Tolerance. 2012. "LGBT Content Access Denied." Accessed March 29 (www.tollerance.org/blog/lgbt-content-access-denied).

Tedeschi, Bob. 2006. "Those Born to Shop Can Now Use Cellphones." *New York Times,* January 2.

Telles, Edward E. 2004. *Race in America: The Significance of Skin Color in Brazil.* Princeton, NJ: Princeton University Press.

Teranishi, Robert T. 2010. *Asians in the Ivory Tower: Dilemmas of Racial Inequity in American Higher Education.* New York: Teachers College Press.

Terlep, Sharon. 2011. "Road Gets Bumpy for GM in China." *Wall Street Journal,* September 16, pp. A1, A10.

Themed Entertainment Association. 2012. *Global Attractions Attendance Report 2011.* Burbank, CA: TEA.

Therborn, Göran. 2010. Review of "Unveiling Inequality." *Contemporary Sociology* 39 (5):585–586.

Third World Institute. 2007. *The World Guide.* 11th ed. Oxford: New Internationalist Publications.

Thomas, Evan, and Pat Wingert. 2010. "Understanding Charter Schools." *Newsweek* 155 (June 21):46.

Thomas, Gordon, and Max Morgan Witts. 1974. *Voyage of the Damned.* Greenwich, CT: Fawcett Crest.

Thomas Jr., Landon. 2011. "Money Troubles Take Personal Toll in Greece." *New York Times,* May 16, pp. A1, A2. Accessible at www.nytimes.com/2011/05/16/business/global/16drachma.html?pagewanted=all.

Thomas, R. Murray. 2003. "New Frontiers in Cheating." In *Encyclopaedia Britannica 2003 Book of the Year.* Chicago: Encyclopaedia Britannica.

Thomas, William I. 1923. *The Unadjusted Girl.* Boston: Little, Brown.

Thomasrobb.com. 2007. "WhitePride TV." Accessed May 7 (http://thomasrobb.com).

Thompson, Ginger. 2001. "Why Peace Eludes Mexico's Indians." *New York Times,* March 11, sec. WK, p. 16.

Thompson, Tony. 2005. "Romanians Are Being Paid to Play Computer Games for Westerners." *Guardian Weekly,* March 25, p. 17.

Threadcraft, Shatema. 2008. "Welfare Queen." In *Encyclopedia of Race, Ethnicity and Society,* edited by Richard T. Schaefer. Thousand Oaks, CA: Sage.

Thurm, Scott. 2010. "Oracle's Ellison: Pay King." *Wall Street Journal,* July 27, pp. A1, A16.

Thurow, Lester. 1984. "The Disappearance of the Middle Class." *New York Times,* February 5, sec. 5, p. 2.

Tibbles, Kevin. 2007. "Web Sites Encourage Eating Disorders." *Today,* February 18. Accessed May 7 (www.msabc.msn.com).

Tierney, John. 1990. "Betting the Planet." *New York Times Magazine* (December 2):52–53, 71, 74, 76, 78, 80–81.

Tierney, Kathleen J. 1980. "Emergent Norm Theory as 'Theory': An Analysis and Critique of Turner's Formulation." Pp. 42–53 in *Collective Behavior: A Source Book,* edited by Meredith David Pugh. St. Paul, MN: West.

———. 2007. "From the Margins to the Mainstream? Disaster Research at the Crossroads." *Annual Review of Sociology* 33:503–525.

Tierney, William G., and Karri A. Holley. 2008. "Intelligent Design and the Attack on Scientific Inquiry." *Cultural Studies Critical Methodologies* 8 (February):39–49.

Tigay, Chanan. 2011. "Women and Sports." *CQ Researcher* 21 (March 25).

Tilly, Charles. 1964. *The Vendée.* Cambridge, MA: Harvard University Press.

———. 1993. *Popular Contention in Great Britain 1758–1834.* Cambridge, MA: Harvard University Press.

———. 2003. *The Politics of Collective Violence.* New York: Cambridge University Press.

———. 2004. *Social Movements, 1768–2004.* Boulder, CO: Paradigm.

———. 2007. "Trust Networks in Transnational Migration." *Sociological Forum* 22 (March):3–24.

Tilly, Chris. 1991. Reasons for the Continuing Growth of Part-time Employment. *Monthly Labor Review* (March): 10–18.

Timmerman, Kelsey. 2009. *Where Am I Wearing?* Hoboken NJ: Wiley.

Toensing, Gale Country. 2009. "Akaka Bill Gets Obama Approval." *Indian Country Today* (August 19):1, 2.

Toma, Catalina L., and Jeffrey T. Hancock. 2010. "Looks and Lies: The Role of Physical Attractiveness in Online Dating Self-Presentation and Deception." *Community Research* 37 (3):335–351.

———, ———, and Nicole B. Ellison. 2008. "Separating Fact from Fiction: An Examination of Deceptive Self-Presentation in Online Dating Profiles." *Personality and Social Psychology Bulletin* 34:1023–1036.

Tönnies, Ferdinand. [1887] 1988. *Community and Society.* Rutgers, NJ: Transaction.

Toossi, Mitra. 2009. "Employment Outlook: 2008–2018." *Monthly Labor Review* (November): 30–51.

Toppo, Greg. 2011. "The Search for a New Way to Test Schoolkids." *USA Today*, March 18, p. A4.

Toro, Paul A. 2007. "Toward an International Understanding of Homelessness." *Journal of Social Issues* 63 (3):461–481.

Torres, Lourdes. 2008. "Puerto Rican Americans" and "Puerto Rico." Pp. 1082–1089, vol. 3, in *Encyclopedia of Race, Ethnicity, and Society,* edited by Richard T. Schaefer. Thousand Oaks, CA: Sage.

Torrey, E. Fuller. 2013. "Fifty Years of Failing America's Mentally Ill." *Wall Street Journal,* February 5, p. A15.

Touraine, Alain. 1974. *The Academic System in American Society.* New York: McGraw-Hill.

Transactional Records Access Clearinghouse. 2009. "TRAC Monthly Bulletins by Topic, September 2009." Accessed February 11, 2010 (www.trac.syr.edu/tracreports/bulletins/white_collar_crime/monthly_sep09/fil).

Trimble, Lindsey B., and Julie A. Kmec. 2011. "The Role of Social Networks in Getting a Job." *Sociology Compass* 5 (2):165–178.

Trotter III, Robert T., and Juan Antonio Chavira. 1997. *Curanderismo: Mexican American Folk Healing.* Athens: University of Georgia Press.

Truman, Jennifer L. 2011. "Criminal Victimization Survey." *BJS Bulletin* (September).

Trumbull, Mark. 2006. "America's Younger Workers Losing Ground on Income." *Christian Science Monitor,* February 27.

Tschorn, Adam. 2010. "Parkour Ready to Launch." *Chicago Tribune,* July 25, sec. 6, pp. 20–21.

Tuan, Mia, and Jiannbin Lee Shiao. 2011. *Choosing Ethnicity, Negotiating Race: Korean Adoptees in America.* New York: Russell Sage Foundation.

Tuchman, Gaye. 1992. "Feminist Theory." Pp. 695–704 in *Encyclopedia of Sociology,* vol. 2, edited by Edgar F. Borgatta and Marie L. Borgatta. New York: Macmillan.

Tucker, Robert C. (ed.) 1978. *The Marx-Engels Reader.* 2nd ed. New York: Norton.

Ture, Kwame, and Charles Hamilton. 1992. *Black Power: The Politics of Liberation.* With new Afterword by authors. New York: Vintage Books.

Turkle, Sherry. 2004. "How Computers Change the Way We Think." *Chronicle of Higher Education* 50 (January 30):B26–B28.

———. 2011. *Alone Together: Why We Expect More from Technology and Less from Each Other.* New York: Basic Books.

Turner, Bryan S., ed. 1990. *Theories of Modernity and Postmodernity.* Newbury Park, CA: Sage.

Turner, C. F. L. Ku, S. M. Rogers, L. D. Lindberg, H. Pleck, and F. L. Sonenstein. 1998. "Adolescent Sexual Behavior, Drug Use, and Violence: Increased Reporting with Computer Survey Technology." *Science* 280 (May 8):867–873.

Turner, Ralph, and Lewis M. Killian. 1987. *Collective Behavior.* 3rd ed. Englewood Cliffs, NJ: Prentice Hall.

Turner, S. Derek, and Mark Cooper. 2006. *Out of the Picture: Minority and Female TV Station Ownership in the United States.* Washington, DC: Free Press.

U

UNAIDS. 2010. *Global Report: UNAIDS Report on the Global AIDS Epidemic 2010.* Geneva: UNAIDS.

UNHCR. 2010. *UNHCR Statistical Yearbook 2009.* Geneva: UNHCR.

UNICEF. 2010. "Child Marriage." Accessed January 15 (www.unicef.org/progressfprchildren/2007n6/index_41848.htm?q=printme).

United Nations. 2005. *The Millennium Development Goals Report.* Washington, DC: United Nations.

———. 2009. *International Migration Report 2006: A Global Assessment.* New York: United Nations, Economic and Social Affairs.

United Nations Development Programme. 1995. *Human Development Report 1995.* New York: Oxford University Press.

———. 2000. *Poverty Report 2000: Overcoming Human Poverty.* Washington, DC: UNDP.

———. 2009. *Overcoming Barriers: Human Mobility and Development.* New York: Palgrave Macmillan.

United Nations Economic and Social Council. 2010. "Review of the Implementation of the Beijing Declaration." New York: Economic and Social Council.

United Nations International Strategy for Disaster Reductions. 2012. *How To Make Cities More Resilient—A Handbook For Local Government Leaders.* Geneva: UNISDR.

United Nations Office on Drugs and Crime. 2010. *The Globalization of Crime: A Transnational Organized Crime Threat Assessment.* New York: UNODO.

United Nations Population Division. 2011. "World Abortion Policies, 2011." Accessed February 22, 2012 (www.un.org/esa/population/publications/2011abortion/2011abortionwallchart.html).

———. 2012. *World Urbanization Prospects, The 2011 Revision.* March 2012. New York: Department of Economics and Social Affairs, Population Division.

United Nations Statistics Division. 2008. "Singulate Mean Age at Marriage." Accessed March 1, 2009 (http://data.un.org/search.aspx?q=marriage).

———. 2009. *Demographic Yearbook 2007.* Accessed April 1, 2010 (http://unstats.un.org/unsd/demographic/products/dyb/dyb2.htm).

United Way of King County. 2010. "Community Assessment." Accessed January 18 (www.uwkc/printver.asp?ref=kcca/data/languages/isolation.asp).

University of Michigan. 2003. *Information on Admissions Lawsuits.* Accessed August 8 (www.umich.edu/urel/admissions).

Urban Dictionary. 2012. "Urban Amish." Accessed March 29 (www.urbandictionary.com/define.php?term=urban+20amish).

U.S. English. 2012. "Making English the Official Language." Accessed January 12 (www.us-english.org/inc/).

U.S. Surgeon General. 1999. *Surgeon General's Report on Mental Health.* Washington, DC: U.S. Government Printing Office.

V

Vaidhyanathan, Siva. 2008. "Generational Myth: Not All Young People Are Tech-Savvy." *Chronicle of Higher Education,* September 19, pp. B7–B9.

———. 2008. "Naked in the 'Nonopticon.'" *Chronicle of Higher Education* (February 15):B7–B10.

Vamosi, Robert, Mary Monahan, and Rachel Kim. 2010. *2010 Identity Fraud Survey Report.* Pleasanton, CA: Javelin Strategy.

Van Gennep, Arnold. [1909] 1960. *The Rites of Passage.* Translated by Monika B. Vizedom and Gabrielle L. Caffee. Chicago: University of Chicago Press.

van Vucht Tijssen, Lieteke. 1990. "Women between Modernity and Postmodernity." Pp. 147–163 in *Theories of Modernity and Postmodernity,* edited by Bryan S. Turner. London: Sage.

Vargas, Jose Antonio. 2007. "YouTube Gets Serious with Links to Candidates." *Washington Post,* March 2, p. C1.

Vasagar, Jeeran. 2005. "At Last Rwanda Is Known for Something Positive." *Guardian Weekly,* July 22, p. 18.

Vaughan, R. M. 2007. "Cairo's Man Show." *Utne Reader* (March–April):94–95.

Veblen, Thorstein. [1899] 1964. *Theory of the Leisure Class.* New York: Macmillan. New York: Penguin.

———. 1919. *The Vested Interests and the State of the Industrial Arts.* New York: Huebsch.

Venkatesh, Sudhir Alladi. 2006. *Off the Books: The Underground Economy of the Urban Poor.* Cambridge, MA: Harvard University Press.

———. 2008. *Gang Leader for a Day: A Rogue Sociologist Takes to the Streets.* New York: Penguin Press.

Vernon, Glenn. 1962. *Sociology and Religion.* New York: McGraw-Hill.

Vigdor, Jacob L. 2011. "Comparing Immigrant Assimilation in North American and Europe." May 2011. Accessible at www.manhattan-institute.org/cgl-bin/apMl/print.cgi.

Violence Policy Center. 2012. *Gun Deaths Outpace Motor Vehicle Deaths in 10 States in 2009.* Washington, DC: VPC.

Viramontes, Helena Maria. 2007. "Loyalty Spoken Here." *Los Angeles Times,* September 23, p. R7.

Volti, Rudi. 2010. *Society and Technological Change.* 6th ed. New York: Worth Publishers.

W

Wachtendorf, Tricia. 2002. "A Changing Risk Environment: Lessons Learned from the 9/11 World Trade Center Disaster." Presentation at the Sociological Perspectives on Disasters, Mt. Macedon, Australia, July.

Waelde, Lynn C., Madeline Uddo, Renee Marquett, Melanie Ropelato, Sharrifa Freightman, Adit Pardo, and Jacqueline Salazar. 2008. "A Pilot Study of Mediation for Mental Health Workers Following Hurricane Katrina." *Journal of Traumatic Stress* 21 (5):497–500.

Wages for Housework Campaign. 1999. *Wages for Housework Campaign.* Circular. Los Angeles.

Wagley, Charles, and Marvin Harris. 1958. *Minorities in the New World: Six Case Studies.* New York: Columbia University Press.

Waite, Linda. 2000. "The Family as a Social Organization: Key Ideas for the Twentieth Century." *Contemporary Sociology* 29 (May):463–469.

Waitzkin, Howard. 1986. *The Second Sickness: Contradictions of Capitalist Health Care.* Chicago: University of Chicago Press.

Walder, Andrew. G. 2009. "Political Sociology and Social Movements." *Annual Review of Sociology* 35:393–412.

———, and Giang Hoang Nguyen. 2008. "Ownership, Organization, and Income Inequality: Market Transition in Rural Vietnam." *American Sociological Review* 73 (April):251–269.

Waldman, Amy. 2004a. "India Takes Economic Spotlight, and Critics Are Unkind." *New York Times,* March 7, p. 3.

———. 2004b. "Low-Tech or High, Jobs Are Scarce in India's Boom." *New York Times,* May 6, p. A3.

———. 2004c. "What India's Upset Vote Reveals: The High Tech Is Skin Deep." *New York Times,* May 15, p. A5.

Walker, Edward. 2010. "Activism Industry-Driven." *Contexts* (Spring):43–49.

Walker, Marcus, and Roger Thurow. 2009. "U.S., Europe Are Ocean Apart on Human Toll of Joblessness." *Wall Street Journal,* May 7, pp. A1, A14.

Wallace, Nicole. 2010. "Gifts for Oil Spill Total $4 Million, but More Is Needed." *The Chronicle of Philanthropy* 24 (14):1.

Wallerstein, Immanuel. 1974. *The Modern World System.* New York: Academic Press.

———. 1979a. *Capitalist World Economy.* Cambridge: Cambridge University Press.

———. 1979b. *The End of the World as We Know It: Social Science for the Twenty-First Century.* Minneapolis: University of Minnesota Press.

———. 2000. *The Essential Wallerstein.* New York: New Press.

———. 2012. "Reflections on an Intellectual Adventure." *Contemporary Sociology* 41 (1):6–12.

Wallis, Claudia. 2005. "A Snapshot of Teen Sex." *Time,* February 7, p. 58.

———. 2008. "How to Make Great Teachers." *Time* 171 (February 25):28–34.

Walmart. 2010. "The Ten-foot Attitude." Accessed January 17 (www.wal-martchina.com/english/walmart/rule/10.htm).

Wang, Feng. 2011. "The Future of a Demographic Overachiever: Long-Term Implications of the Demographic Transition in China." *Population and Development Review* 37 (Suppl.):173–190.

———, and Cai Yong. 2011. "China's One-Child Policy at 39." May 31. Washington, DC: Brooking Institution.

Wang, Meiyan, and Fand Cai. 2006. "Gender Wage Differentials in China's Urban Labor Market." Research Paper No. 2006/141. United Nations University World Institute for Development Economics Research.

Wang, Wendy. 2012. "The Rise of Intermarriage: Rates, Characteristics Vary by Race and Gender." Washington, DC: Pew Social and Demographic Trends.

Wasik, Bill. 2012. "Crown Control." *Wired* (January):76–83, 112–113.

Watson, Paul. 2005. "Defying Tradition." *Los Angeles Times,* April 24, p. 56.

Wattenberg, Martin P. 2008. *Is Voting for Young People?* New York: Pearson Longman.

Weber, Max. [1904] 1949. *Methodology of the Social Sciences.* Translated by Edward A. Shils and Henry A. Finch. Glencoe, IL: Free Press.

———. [1913–1922] 1947. *The Theory of Social and Economic Organization.* Translated by A. Henderson and T. Parsons. New York: Free Press.

———. [1916] 1958. *The Religion of India: The Sociology of Hinduism and Buddhism.* New York: Free Press.

———. [1904] 2011. *The Protestant Ethic and the Spirit Capitalism.* The Revised 1920 Edition. Translation by Stephen Kalberg. New York: Oxford University Press.

Wechsler, Henry, J. E. Lee, M. Kuo, M. Seibring, T. F. Nelson, and H. Lee. 2002. "Trends in College Binge Drinking during a Period of Increased Prevention Efforts: Findings from Four Harvard School of Public Health College Alcohol Surveys: 1993–2001." *Journal of American College Health* 50 (5):203–217.

———, Mark Seibring, I-Chao Liu, and Marilyn Ahl. 2004. "Colleges Respond to Student Binge Drinking: Reducing Student Demand or Limiting Access." *Journal of American College Health* 52 (4):159–168.

The Week. 2010b. "They're Watching You." (September 17):15.

———. 2011. "Fighting over Food." (March 4):15.

Weeks, John R. 2012. *Population: An Introduction to Concepts and Issues.* 11th ed. Belmont, CA: Cengage.

Wegner, Nina. 2010. "Nepal, Home of the Himalayas . . . and a Salsa Scene?" *Christian Science Monitor* (December 14).

Weinberg, Daniel H. 2004. *Evidence from Census 2000 About Earnings by Detailed Occupation for Men and Women.* CENSR-15. Washington, DC: U.S. Government Printing Office.

———. 2007. "Earnings by Gender: Evidence from Census 2000." *Monthly Labor Review* (July–August):26–34.

Weinraub, Bernard. 2004. "UPN Show Is Called Insensitive to Amish." *New York Times,* March 4, pp. B1, B8.

Weisberg, Jacob. 2011. "Bubble Trouble. Is Web Personalization Turning Us into Solipsistic Twits?" *Slate* (June). Accessible at www.slate.com.

Weitz, Rose. 2009. *The Sociology of Health, Illness, and Heath Care.* 5th ed. Belmont, CA: Cengage.

Welch, William M. 2011. "More Hawaii Residents Identify as Mixed Race." *USA Today,* February 28.

Wells-Barnett, Ida B. 1970. *Crusade for Justice: The Autobiography of Ida B. Wells.* Edited by Alfreda M. Duster. Chicago: University of Chicago Press.

Wentling, Tre, Elroi Windsor, Kristin Schilt, and Betsy Lucal. 2008. "Teaching Transgender." *Teaching Sociology* 36 (January):49–57.

Wentz, Laurel, and Claire Atkinson. 2005. "'Apprentice' Translators Hope for Hits All Over Globe." *Advertising Age,* February 14, pp. 3, 73.

Wessell, David. 2011. "Untangling the Long-Term-Unemployment Crisis." *Wall Street Journal,* October 20, p. A6.

———, and Stephanie Banchero. 2012. "Education Slowdown Threatens U.S." *Wall Street Journal,* April 26, p. A1.

West, Candace, and Don H. Zimmerman. 1987. "Doing Gender." *Gender and Society* 1 (June):125–151.

Westergaard-Nielsen, Niels. 2008. *Low-Wage Work in Denmark.* New York: Russell Sage Foundation.

White, David Manning. 1950. "'The Gatekeeper': A Case Study in the Selection of News." *Journalism Quarterly* 27 (Fall):383–390.

Whitlock, Craig. 2005. "The Internet as Bully Pulpit." *Washington Post National Weekly Edition* 22 (August 22):9.

Whittaker, Stephanie. 2006. "Who Would You Prefer to Work For?" *Gazette* (Montreal), November 4, p. 1.

Whyte, William Foote. 1981. *Street Corner Society: Social Structure of an Italian Slum.* 3rd ed. Chicago: University of Chicago Press.

Wilcox, W. Bradford. 2011. *Why Marriage Matters: Thirty Conclusions from the Social Sciences.* New York: Institute of American Values.

Wildsmith, Elizabeth, Nicole R. Steward-Streng, and Jennifer Manlove. 2011. "Childbearing Outside of Marriage: Estimates and Trends in the United States." *Child Trends Research Brief* #2011-29. Accessible at www.childtrends.org.

Wilford, John Noble. 1997. "New Clues Show Where People Made the Great Leap to Agriculture." *New York Times,* November 18, pp. B9, B12.

Wilkes, Rima, and John Iceland. 2004. "Hypersegregation in the Twenty-First Century." *Demography* 41 (February):23–36.

Wilkinson, Tracy. 2011. "Cuba: Now Open for Business." *Chicago Tribune,* August 15, p. 14.

Williams, Carol J. 1995. "Taking an Eager Step Back." *Los Angeles Times,* June 3, pp. A1, A14.

Williams, Christine L. 1992. "The Glass Escalator: Hidden Advantages for Men in the 'Female' Professions." *Social Problems* 39 (3):253–267.

———. 1995. *Still a Man's World: Men Who Do Women's Work.* Berkeley: University of California Press.

Williams, David R., and Chiquita Collins. 2004. "Reparations." *American Behavioral Scientist* 47 (March):977–1000.

Williams, Robin M., Jr. 1970. *American Society.* 3rd ed. New York: Knopf.

———, with John P. Dean and Edward A. Suchman. 1964. *Strangers Next Door: Ethnic Relations in American Communities.* Englewood Cliffs, NJ: Prentice Hall.

Wills, Jeremiah B., and Barbara J. Risman. 2006. "The Visibility of Feminist Thought in Family Studies." *Journal of Marriage and Family* 68 (August):690–700.

Wilson, Edward O. 1975. *Sociobiology: The New Synthesis.* Cambridge, MA: Harvard University Press.

———. 1978. *On Human Nature.* Cambridge, MA: Harvard University Press.

———. 2000. *Sociobiology: The New Synthesis.* Cambridge, MA: Belknap Press, Harvard University Press.

Wilson, James Q. 2011. "Hard Times, Fewer Crimes." *Wall Street Journal,* May 28, pp. C1–C2.

Wilson, John. 1973. *Introduction to Social Movements.* New York: Basic Books.

Wilson, William Julius. 1980. *The Declining Significance of Race: Blacks and Changing American Institutions.* 2nd ed. Chicago: University of Chicago Press.

———. 1987. *The Truly Disadvantaged: The Inner City, the Underclass and Public Policy.* Chicago: University of Chicago Press.

———. 1996. *When Work Disappears: The World of the New Urban Poor.* New York: Knopf.

———. 1999. *The Bridge over the Racial Divide: Rising Inequality and Coalition Politics.* Berkeley: University of California Press.

———. 2009. *More Than Just Race: Being Black and Poor in the Inner City.* New York: Norton.

———, J. M. Quane, and B. H. Rankin. 2004. "Underclass." In *International Encyclopedia of Social and Behavioral Sciences.* New York: Elsevier.

Wimer, Christopher, Barbara Bergmann, David Betson, John Coder, and David B. Grusky. 2011. "The Future of U.S. Poverty Measurement." *Pathways* (Fall) 20–25.

Winant, Howard B. 1994. *Racial Conditions: Politics, Theory, Comparisons.* Minneapolis: University of Minnesota Press.

———. 2006. "Race and Racism: Towards a Global Future." *Ethnic and Racial Studies* 29 (September):986–1003.

Winickoff, Jonathan P., Joan Friebely, Susanne E. Tanski, Cheryl Sherrod, George E. Matt, Melbourne F. Hovell, and Robert C. McMillen. 2009. "Beliefs about the Health Effects of 'Thirdhand' Smoke and Home Smoking Bans." *Pediatrics* 123 (January):74–79.

Winkler, Adam. 2009. "Heller's Catch-22." *UCLA Law Review* 56 (June).

Winter, J. Allen. 2008. "Symbolic Ethnicity." Pp. 1288–1290, vol. 3, in *Encyclopedia of Race, Ethnicity, and Society,* edited by Richard T. Schaefer. Thousand Oaks, CA: Sage.

Wirth, Louis. 1928. *The Ghetto.* Chicago: University of Chicago Press.

———. 1931. "Clinical Sociology." *American Journal of Sociology* 37 (July):49–60.

———. 1938. "Urbanism as a Way of Life." *American Journal of Sociology* 44 (July):1–24.

Wolf, Naomi. 1992. *The Beauty Myth: How Images of Beauty Are Used against Women.* New York: Anchor Books.

Wolfe, Alan. 2008. "Pew in the Pews." *Chronicle of Higher Education,* March 21, pp. B5–B6.

Women's Flat Track Derby Association. 2012. "Women's Flat Track Derby Association." Accessible at http://www.wftda.org/about.html.

Women's Sports Foundation. 2011. *Title IX.* Accessed March 29 (http://www.womens sports-foundation.org/Issues-And-Research/Title-IX .aspx).

Wong, Morrison G. 2006. "Chinese Americans." Pp. 110–145 in *Asian Americans: Contemporary*

Trends and Issues, 2nd ed., edited by Pyong Gap Min. Thousand Oaks, CA: Sage.

Wood, Daniel B. 2012. "How Serious Crime Fell in US." *Christian Science Monitor* (January 16):18.

Woon, Lee Kang. 2005. "Socialization of Transracially Adopted Korean Americans: A Self Analysis." *Human Architecture: Journal of the Sociology of Self-Knowledge* 3 (Spring):79–84.

Working Women's Forum. 2012. Home Page. Accessed March 27 (www.workingwomensforum.org).

Workman, Thomas A. 2008. "The Real Impact of Virtual Worlds." *Chronicle of Higher Education* (September 19), pp. B12–B13.

World Association of Girl Guides and Girl Scouts. 2011. "Our World." Accessed November 10 (www.wagggs.org/en/world).

World Bank. 2003. *World Development Report 2003: Sustainable Development in a Dynamic World.* Washington, DC: World Bank.

———. 2007. *World Development Indicators 2007.* Washington, DC: World Bank.

———. 2009. *World Development Indicators 2009.* Washington, DC: World Bank.

——— 2010b. *World Development Report 2010: Development and Climate Change.* Washington, DC: World Bank.

———. 2011. *Development Indicators 2011.* Washington, DC: World Bank.

———. 2012. *World Development Report 2012: Gender Equality and Development.* Washington, DC: World Bank.

———. 2012a. *World Development Indicators 2012.* Washington, DC: World Bank.

———. 2012a. *World Indicators Report 2012. Building Instructions for Markets.* New York: Oxford University Press.

———. 2012b. *Gender Equality and Development.* Washington, DC: World Bank.

World Development Forum. 1990. "The Danger of Television." 8 (July 15):4.

World Health Organization. 2000. *The World Health Report 2000. Health Systems: Improving Performance.* Geneva: WHO.

———. 2009. "Biotechnology (GM Foods)." Accessed May 11 (www.who.int/foodsafety/ biotech/en/).

———. 2010. "Suicide Prevention." Accessed October 31 (http://www.who.int/mental_health/ prevention/en/).

Worth, Robert F. 2008. "As Taboos Ease, Saudi Girl Group Dares to Rock." *New York Times,* November 24, pp. A1, A9.

Wortham, Robert A. 2008. "DuBois, William Edward Burghardt." Pp. 423–427, vol. 1, in *Encyclopedia of Race, Ethnicity, and Society,* edited by Richard T. Schaefer. Thousand Oaks, CA: Sage.

Wray, Matt, Matthew Miller, Jill Gurvey, Joanna Carroll, and Ichiro Kawachi. 2008. "Leaving Las Vegas: Exposure to Las Vegas and Risk of Suicide." *Social Science and Medicine* 67:1882–1888.

———, Cynthia Colen, and Bernice Pescosolido. 2011. "The Sociology of Suicide." *Annual Review of Sociology* 37:505–528.

Wright, Charles R. 1986. *Mass Communication: A Sociological Perspective.* 3rd ed. New York: Random House.

Wright, Erik O. 2011. "The Classical Marxist Theory of the History of Capitalism's Future." October 3. Accessed January 20, 2012 (www. ssc.wisc.edu/~wright/621-2011/lecture%208%20 2011%20—%20Classical%20Theory%20of%20 Capitalisms%20future.pdf).

———, David Hachen, Cynthia Costello, and Joy Sprague. 1982. "The American Class Structure." *American Sociological Review* 47 (December):709–726.

Wright, Eric R., William P. Gronfein, and Timothy J. Owens. 2000. "Deinstitutionalization, Social Rejection, and the Self-Esteem of Former Mental Patients." *Journal of Health and Social Behavior* (March).

Wu, Tim. 2010. *The Master Switch.* New York: Knopf.

Wyatt, Edward. 2009. "No Smooth Ride on TV Networks' Road to Diversity." *New York Times,* March 18, pp. 1, 5.

Y

Yamagata, Hisashi, Kuang S. Yeh, Shelby Stewman, and Hiroko Dodge. 1997. "Sex Segregation and Glass Ceilings: A Comparative Statistics Model of Women's Career Opportunities in the Federal Government over a Quarter Century." *American Journal of Sociology* 103 (November):566–632.

Yap, Kioe Sheng. 1998. "Squatter Settlements." Pp. 554–556 in *The Encyclopedia of Housing,* edited by Willem van Vliet. Thousand Oaks, CA: Sage.

Yinger, J. Milton. 1970. *The Scientific Study of Religion.* New York: Macmillan.

York, Richard, Eugene A. Rosa, and Thomas Dietz. 2010. "Ecological Modernization Theory: Theoretical and Empirical Challenges." Pp. 77–90 in *The International Handbook and Environmental Sociology,* 2nd ed., edited by Michael R. Redclift and Graham Woodgate. Cheltenham, UK: Edward Elgar.

Young, Kevin, ed. 2004. *Sporting Bodies, Damaged Selves.* New York: Elsevier.

YouTube. [2009] 2013. "Historic Flashmob in Antwerp Train Station, Do Re Mi." Accessed May 13 at www.youtube.com/ watch?v=0UE3CNu_rtY.

Yunus, Muhammad. 2010. *Building Social Business.* New York: Perseus.

Z

Zakaria, Fareed. 2012. "Incarceration Nation." *Time,* April 2, p. 18.

Zang, Xiaowei. 2002. "Labor Market Segmentation and Income Inequality in Urban China." *Sociological Quarterly* 43 (1):27–44.

Zarembo, Alan. 2004a. "A Theater of Inquiry and Evil." *Los Angeles Times,* July 15, pp. A1, A24, A25.

———. 2004b. "Physician, Remake Thyself: Lured by Higher Pay and Heavy Recruiting, Philippine Doctors Are Getting Additional Degrees and Starting Over in the U.S. as Nurses." *Los Angeles Times,* January 10, pp. A1, A10.

Zeitzen, Miriam Koktvedgaard. 2008. *Polygamy: A Cross-Cultural Analysis.* Oxford, UK: Berg.

Zellner, William M. 1995. *Counter Cultures: A Sociological Analysis.* New York: St. Martin's Press.

Zernike, Kate. 2002. "With Student Cheating on the Rise, More Colleges Are Turning to Honor Codes." *New York Times,* November 2, p. A10.

Zi, Jui-Chung Allen. 2007. *The Kids Are OK: Divorce and Children's Behavior Problems.* Santa Monica, CA: RAND.

Zickuhr, Kathryn. 2011. *Generations and Their Gadgets.* Washington, DC: Pew Research Center's Internet and American Life Project.

Zimbardo, Philip G. 2004. "Power Turns Good Soldiers into 'Bad Apples.'" *Boston Globe,* May 9. Also accessible at www.prisonexp.org.

———. 2007. *The Lucifer Effect: Understanding How Good People Turn Evil.* New York: Random House.

———. 2007a. "Revisiting the Stanford Prison Experiment: A Lesson in the Power of the Situation." *Chronicle of Higher Education* 53 (March 20):B6, B7.

———, Robert L. Johnson, and Vivian McCann Hamilton. 2009. *Psychology: Core Concepts.* 6th ed. Upper Saddle River, NJ: Pearson.

Zimmerman, Ann, and Emily Nelson. 2006. "With Profits Elusive, Wal-Mart to Exit Germany." *Wall Street Journal,* July 29, pp. A1, A6.

Zimmerman, Seth. 2008a. "Globalization and Economic Mobility." Washington, DC: Economic Mobility Project. Also accessible at www.economicmobility.org/reports_and_research/literature_reviews?id=0004.

Zimring, Franklin E. 2007. *The Great American Crime Decline.* New York: Oxford University Press.

Zipp, Yvonne. 2009. "Courts Divided on Police Use of GPS Tracking." *Christian Science Monitor,* May 15.

Zirin, Dave. 2008. "Calling Sports Sociology off the Bench." *Contexts* (Summer): 28–31.

Zittrain, Jonathan, and John Palfrey. 2008. "Reluctant Gatekeepers: Corporate Ethics on a Filtered Internet." Pp. 103–122 in *Access Denied,* edited by Ronald Deibert, John Palfrey, Rafal Rohozinski, and Jonathan Zittrain. Cambridge, MA: MIT Press.

Zogby. 2010. "Zogby Interactive: 54% Support Ethnic & Religious Profiling; 71% Favor Full-Body Scans." February 4. Accessed July 2, 2011 (http://www.zogby.com/news/2010/02/04/zogby-interactive-54-support-ethnic-religious-profiling-71-favor-full-body-scans/).

Zola, Irving K. 1972. "Medicine as an Institution of Social Control." *Sociological Review* 20 (November):487–504.

———. 1983. *Socio-Medical Inquiries.* Philadelphia: Temple University Press.

Zweigenhaft, Richard L., and G. William Domhoff. 2006. *Diversity in the Power Elite: How It Happened, Why It Matters.* 2nd ed. New York: Rowman and Littlefield.

Zywica, Jolene, and James Danowski. 2008. "The Faces of Facebookers: Investigating Social Enhancement and Social Compensation Hypotheses; Predicting Facebook and Offline Popularity from Sociability and Self-Esteem, and Mapping the Meanings of Popularity with Semantic Networks." *Journal of Computer-Mediated Communication* 14:1–34.

acknowledgments

Chapter 1

page 4: Quotation from Kelsey Timmerman. 2009. *Where Am I Wearing? A Global Tour to the Countries, Factories, and People that Make Our Clothes.* © 2009. Reproduced with permission of John Wiley & Sons, Inc.
page 23: Cartoon by Jim Morin / Morintoons Syndicate.

Chapter 2

page 32: Quotation from Patricia Adler and Peter Adler. 2011. *The Tender Cut: Inside the Hidden World of Self-Injury.* © 2011 New York University. All rights reserved. Used by permission of New York University Press.
page 39: Cartoon Doonesbury © 1989 G.B. Trudeau. Reprinted with permission of Universal Uclick. All rights reserved.
page 41: Cartoon F MINUS © 2007 Tony Carrillo. Reprinted by Universal Uclick for UFS. All rights reserved.
page 52: Figure A-3 From Gallup Poll, October 17, 2011, "Record High of 50% of Americans Favor Legalizing Marijuana Use," by Frank Newport. Copyright © 2011 Gallup, Princeton, NJ. Reprinted with permission.

Chapter 3

page 60: Quotation from Horace Miner. 1956. "Body Ritual among the Nacirema." *American Anthropologist,* vol. 58 (3), 1956:503–504. © 1956 American Anthropological Association.
page 63: Figure 9-1 Adapted in part from "The State of the World's Children 2009," UNICEF, and in part from "Progress for Children: A World Fit for Children Statistical Review," Number 6, December 2007, UNICEF global databases, UNICEF, NY.

Chapter 4

page 88: Quotation from Mary Pattillo-McCoy. 1999. *Black Picket Fences: Privilege and Peril among the Black Middle Class:*100–02. Copyright 1999. Reprinted by permission of University of Chicago Press.
page 95: Cartoon by Scott Arthur Masear. Reprinted by permission of www.CartoonStock.com
page 95: Quotation from Daniel Albas and Cheryl Albas. 1988. "Aces and Bombers: The Post-Exam Impression Management Strategies of Students." *Symbolic Interaction.* University of California Press—Journals. Reproduced by permission of the authors.
page 97: Table 14-3 From Tom W. Smith. 2003. "Coming of Age in 21st Century America: Public Attitudes Toward the Importance and Timing of Transition to Adulthood." Based on the 2002 General Social Survey of 1,398 people. Used by permission of National Opinion Research Center.
page 102: Table 15-1 Adapted from Jill Suitor, Staci A. Minyard, and Rebecca S. Carter. 2001. "Did You See What I Saw? Gender Difference in Perceptions of Avenues to Prestige Among Adolescents," *Sociological Inquiry* 71 (Fall 2001):445, Table 2. University of Texas Press. Wiley-Blackwell Publishing Ltd.
page 102: Figure 15-1 From Henry J. Kaiser Family Foundation. 2010. Victoria J. Rideout et al., "Generation M^2: Media in the Lives of 8- to 18 Year-Olds," January 2010 (#8010). This information was reprinted with permission from the Henry J. Kaiser Family Foundation. The Kaiser Family Foundation, a leader in health policy analysis, health journalism, and communication, is dedicated to filling the need for trusted, independent information on the major health issues facing our nation and its people. The Foundation is a non-profit private operating foundation, based in Menlo Park, CA.

page 104: STAHLER © 2010 Jeff Stahler. Reprinted by Universal Uclick for UFS. All rights reserved.

Chapter 5

page 112: Quotation from Philip G. Zimbardo. 2007. *The Lucifer Effect: Understanding How Good People Turn Evil.* Copyright © 2007 by Philip G. Zimbardo, Inc. Used by permission of Random House, Inc. and by Rider Books / Random House Group Ltd. For on-line information about other Random House, Inc. books and authors, see the Internet web site at http://www.randomhouse.com.
page 123: © Dean Vietor / The New Yorker Collection/www.cartoonbank.com
page 135: Cartoon © 2004 Daryl Cagle, MSNBC, and PoliticalCartoons.com

Chapter 6

page 144: Quotation from Sherry Turkle. *Alone Together: Why We Expect More from Technology and Less from Each Other.* NY: Basic Books. Copyright © 2011 Sherry Turkle. Reprinted by permission of Basic Books, a member of the Perseus Books Group.
page 146: Logo used by permission of New York City Department of Health and Mental Hygiene.
page 146: Table 20-1 Adapted from John B. Horrigan, *A Typology of Information and Communication Technology Users,* May 7, 2007, pp. 5–11, www.pewinternet.org/Reports/2007/A-Typology-of-Information-and-Communication-Technology-Users.aspx. Pew Internet & American Life Project.
page 151: Cartoon by Dana Summers. © Tribune Media Services, Inc. All Rights Reserved. Reprinted with permission.
page 155: Figure 20-3 Adapted from "Demographics of teen internet users," accessed January 17, 2012, at http://www.pewinternet.org/Static-Pages/Trend-Data-for-Teens/Whos-Online.aspx and from "Demographics of Internet Users," accessed January 17, 2012, at http://www.pewinternet.org/Trend-Data/Whos-Online.aspx. Pew Internet & American Life Project.
page 162: Cartoon by Harley Schwadron. Reprinted with permission.

Chapter 7

page 168: Quotation from Peter Moskos. 2008. *Cop in the Hood: My Year Policing Baltimore's Eastern District.* © 2008 by Princeton University Press. Reprinted by permission of Princeton University Press.
page 174: Figure 23-1 Adapted from NORML 2012. Used by permission of the National Organization for the Reform of Marijuana Laws (NORML).
page 177: Table 24-1 From Robert K. Merton. 1968. *Social Theory and Social Structure,* Revised and Expanded Edition. Adapted by permission of The Free Press, a Division of Simon & Schuster, Inc. Copyright © 1967, 1968 by Robert K. Merton. Copyright renewed 1985 by Robert K. Merton. All rights reserved.
page 184: Cartoon by Sidney Harris. © ScienceCartoonsPlus.com

Chapter 8

page 196: Quotation from Rana Foroohar. 2011. "What Ever Happened to Upward Mobility?" in *What Is Occupy? Inside the Global Movement.* Published by TIME Books, an imprint of Time Home Entertainment Inc.
page 202: Cartoon © 2008 Pat Bagley, The Salt Lake Tribune, and PoliticalCartoons.com.

page 217: Cartoon by Matt Davies. © Tribune Media Services, Inc. All Rights Reserved. Reprinted with permission.

page 218: Figure 28-2 From Bhashkar Mazumder. 2008. *Upward Intergenerational Economic Mobility in the United States*. Washington, DC: Economic Mobility Project, An initiative of the Pew Charitable Trusts. Used by permission of Dr. Bhashkar Mazumder.

page 220: Nick Anderson Editorial Cartoon used with the permission of Nick Anderson, the Washington Post Writers Group and the Cartoonist Group. All rights reserved.

Chapter 9

page 226: Quotation from Daryl Collins et al. 2009. *Portfolios of the Poor: How the World's Poor Live on $2 a Day*. © 2009 Princeton University Press. Reprinted by permission of Princeton University Press.

page 228: Figure 29-1 Adapted from Bob Sutcliffe. 2002. *100 Ways of Seeing an Unequal World*, Fig. 1, p. 18. London: Zed Books. Reprinted by permission.

page 229: Figure 29-2 Adapted in part from John R. Weeks. 2012. *Population 11e*. © 2012 Wadsworth, a part of Cengage Learning Inc. Reproduced by permission of www.cengage.com/permissions. And adapted in part from Carl Haub. 2010. *2010 World Population Data Sheet*. Used by permission of Population Reference Bureau.

page 232: Figure 29-4 From Chronic Poverty Research Centre. 2009. Administered by Institute for Development Policy and Management, School of Environment and Development, University of Manchester, UK. Used by permission.

page 234: Figure 29-5 Adapted from Table 1, p. 2 in OECD. February 2011. Statistics on Resource Flows to Developing Countries, www.oecd.org/dac/stats/dcrannex

page 237: Figure 30-1 Adapted from World Development Indicators 2012. © World Bank 2012a: 74–76, Table 2.9. Used under World Bank license CC BY 3.0 http://creativecommons.org/licenses/by/3.0/

page 238: Figure adapted from Edward Telles. 2004:108. *Race in Another America: The Significance of Skin Color*, Princeton University Press. Reprinted by permission of Princeton University Press.

Chapter 10

page 250: Quotation from Jorge Ramos. 2010. *A Country for All: An Immigrant Manifesto*. Translated from Spanish by Ezra Fitz, translation copyright © 2010 by Vintage Books, a division of Random House Inc. Used by permission of Vintage Books, a division of Random House Inc.

page 254: Nick Anderson Editorial Cartoon used with the permission of Nick Anderson, the Washington Post Writers Group and the Cartoonist Group. All rights reserved.

page 260: Figure 31-3 Adapted from "Voter ID Requirements." NCSL 2012a. © National Conference of State Legislatures.

page 262: Cartoon by STEIN © 2006. Reprinted with permission by Universal Uclick for UFS. All rights reserved.

page 272: Figure 33-3 © 2010 Arab American Institute.

Chapter 11

page 284: Quotation from Nancy J. Finley. 2010. "Skating Femininity: Gender Maneuvering in Women's Roller Derby," *Journal of Contemporary Ethnography*, 39(4):359–360, 371–372, 377. Copyright © 2010. Reprinted by permission of SAGE Publications.

page 286: Table 34-1 From Joyce McCarl Nielsen et al. 2000. "Gendered Heteronormativity: Empirical Illustrations in Everyday Life," *Sociological Quarterly* 41 (No. 2):287. © 2000. Blackwell Publishing. Reprinted by permission.

page 299: Figure 35-4 From NARAL Pro-Choice America Foundation. 2011. Used by permission of NARAL, Washington, DC.

Chapter 12

page 306: Quotation from Ted C. Fishman. 2010. Reprinted with the permission of Scribner, a Division of Simon & Schuster, Inc., from *Shock of Gray: The Aging of the World's Population and How It Pits Young Against Old, Child Against Parent, Worker Against Boss, Company Against Rival, and Nation Against Nation* by Ted C. Fishman. Copyright © 2010 by Ted C. Fishman. All rights reserved.

page 313: © Barbara Smaller / The New Yorker Collection / www.cartoonbank.com

page 314: Figure 37-2 Reprinted from *Baby Boomers Envision What's Next? Research and Strategic Analysis Integrated Value and Strategy, June, 2011*, Sources: AARP and GFK Custom Research North America 2011. All rights reserved.

page 317: Figure 38-1 From Linda Jacobsen, Mary Kent, Marlene Lee, and Mark Mather, "America's Aging Population," *Population Bulletin* 66 (Feb):3. Used by permission of Population Reference Bureau.

Chapter 13

page 328: Quotation from Katherine S. Newman. 2012. *The Accordion Family: Boomerang Kids, Anxious Parents, and the Private Toll of Global Competition*. Boston: Beacon Press, 2012. Used by permission of Beacon Press via Copyright Clearance Center.

page 342: Signe Wilkinson Editorial Cartoon used with the permission of Signe Wilkinson, the Washington Post Writers Group and the Cartoonist Group. All rights reserved.

page 347: Figure adapted from Peter S. Bearman, James Moody, and Katherine Stovel. 2004. "Chains of Affection: The Structure of Adolescent Romantic and Sexual Networks," Figure 2, p. 58. *American Journal of Sociology*. Copyright 2004. Used by permission of University of Chicago Press via Rightslink / Copyright Clearance Center.

page 348: Figure 42-1 From *United States Census Snapshot: 2010*. Used by permission of the Williams Institute, Los Angeles, CA.

page 349: Cartoon by Harley Schwadron. Reprinted with permission.

Chapter 14

page 356: Quotation from Diane Ravitch. 2010. *The Death and Life of the Great American School System: How Testing and Choice are Undermining Education*. Copyright © 2010 Diane Ravitch. Reprinted by permission of Basic Books, a member of the Perseus Books Group.

page 368: Signe Wilkinson Editorial Cartoon used with the permission of Signe Wilkinson, the Washington Post Writers Group and the Cartoonist Group. All rights reserved.

page 372: Figure 44-3 National Alliance for Public Charter Schools. (2011). *The public charter schools dashboard*. Washington, DC: NAPCS.

Chapter 15

page 378: Quotation from Nikki Bado-Fralick and Rebecca Sachs Norris. 2010. *Toying with God: The World of Religious Games and Dolls*, pp. 7–8, 29–30. © 2010. Reprinted by permission of Baylor University Press.

page 382: Cartoon © 2007 Riber Hansson, www.PoliticalCartoons.com.

page 386: Figure 46-1 From The Pew Forum on Religion and Public Life, Pew Internet & American Life Project, Religious Knowledge Quiz, September 28, 2010, http://features.pewforum.org/quiz/us-religious-knowledge/

page 394: Cartoon © 2005 Sandy Huffaker, www.PoliticalCartoons.com.

Chapter 16

page 400: Quotation from John Bowes (ed.). 2011. *The Fair Trade Revolution*, pp. ix, 2–3, 231–232. Pluto Press. Reprinted by permission of Pluto Press.

page 406: Figure 48-1 From "Military and National Defense," The Gallup Poll. Copyright © 2009 The Gallup Organization, Princeton, NJ. Reprinted with permission.

page 407: Figure 48-2 From 2011 Global Peace Index, Institute for Economics and Peace.

page 412: Figure 49-2 Adapted from Inter-Parliamentary Union (IPU), 2012, Women in National Parliaments, www.ipu.org/wmn-e/classif.htm. Used by permission.

page 413 R: Figure 49-3 (right) From G. William Domhoff. 2010. *Who Rules America?* 6e. © 2010 by The McGraw-Hill Companies, Inc. Reproduced by permission.

page 422: Cartoon © 2003 Mike Keefe, The Denver Post, www.PoliticalCartoons.com

Chapter 17

page 432: Quotation from Andrew Szasz. 2007. *Shopping Our Way to Safety.* University of Minnesota Press. Copyright 2007 by the Regents of the University of Minnesota.

page 435: Figure 52-1 From Carl Haub. 2011. *World Population Data Sheet 2011.* Used by permission of Population Reference Bureau.

page 439: Figure 53-1 From UNAIDS. 2010. Adapted from Global Report: UNAIDS Report on the Global AIDS Epidemic 2010. Copyright © 2010 Joint UN Program on HIV/AIDS (UNAIDS). All rights reserved. Courtesy UNAIDS, Geneva, Switzerland.

page 442: © Michael Maslin / The New Yorker Collection / www.cartoonbank .com

page 449: Cartoon by Steve Greenberg, *Ventura County Reporter*, California, 2010. Used by permission.

page 453: Figure 55-2 From The Gallup Poll. 2012. Adapted from Energy Production vs. Environmental Protection, in "Americans Split on Energy vs. Environment Trade-Off." Methodology and results, Jeff Jones and Lydia Saad, 2012, Gallup News Service, Gallup Poll Social Series: Environment, March 8–11, 2012. Copyright © 2012 Gallup, Princeton, NJ. Reprinted with permission.

page 454: Figure 55-3 Adapted from OECD. 2009. *Green at Fifteen?: How 15-Year-Olds Perform in Environmental Science and Geoscience in PISA 2006*, PISA, OECD Publishing, http://dx.doi.org/10.1787/ 9789264063600-en

page 55.1-2: Cartoon by Manny Francisco © 2008 http://www.politicalcartoons .com.

page 55.2-3: Figure 1 Adapted from Chauncy Harris and Edward Ullman. 1945. "The Nature of Cities." *Annals of the American Academy of Political and Social Science*, 242 (November):13. Reprinted by permission of American Academy of Political and Social Science, Philadelphia.

page 55.3-6: Figure 2 Rates of Homelessness by State, 2012, *The State of Homelessness in America 2013*, Map 1.1. Reproduced by permission of the National Alliance to End Homelessness, http://b.3cdn.net/naeh/ 52d2c72cb276905d88_7gm6vi6ji.pdf.

Chapter 18

page 460: Quotation from Nick Bilton. 2010. *I Live in the Future & Here's How It Works: Why Your World, Work, and Brain Are Being Creatively Disrupted.* Copyright © 2010 by Nick Bilton. Used by permission of Crown Business, a division of Random House, Inc.

page 463: Illustration reprinted by permission of the publisher from John B. Christiansen and Sharon N. Barnartt, *Deaf President Now! The 1988 Revolution at Gallaudet University.* Washington, DC: Gallaudet University Press, 1995, p. 22. Copyright 1995 by Gallaudet University.

page 474: Figures A, B, C From www.InternetWorldStats.com. Copyright © 2001–2012, Miniwatts Marketing Group. All rights reserved worldwide.

page 475: Cartoon by Baloo, from *The Wall Street Journal*, permission Cartoon Features Syndicate.

page 478: Figure 58-1 Adapted from *National Geographic Atlas of the World* 8e. National Geographic Society, 2005. NG Maps / National Geographic Stock.

Trendspotting

Chapter 1: Oldenburg 1999, 2000; Putnam 1995. Chapter 2: Bureau of the Census 2004b, 2012d; El Nasser and Overburg 2009, 2012; Nordholt et al. 2004. Chapter 3: American Community Survey 2008; Table 1602; Goode 2011; Michael Link et al. 2006; P. Siegal et al. 2001; United Way of King County 2010. Chapter 4: Centers for Disease Control and Prevention 2011c; Knopmen et al. 2010; National Organization of Mothers of Twins Clubs 2010. Chapter 5: *The Economist* 2010a; Facebook 2012; Chris Taylor 2011. Chapter 6: Pew Internet and American Life Project 2012a, 2012b. Chapter 7: Bureau of Justice Statistics 2011; International Centre for Prison Studies 2010; William Sabol et al. 2009. Chapter 8: D. Cauchon 2009; H. Hartmann et al. 2010; Institute for Women's Policy Research 2009. Chapter 9: Bureau of the Census 2008b; *The Economist* 2011a; *The Week* 2011. Chapter 10: Alliance for Board Diversity 2008. Chapter 11: Bureau of Labor Statistics 2008b; 2010c; Toossi 2009. Chapter 12: Bureau of Labor Statistics 2008b; 2010c; Toossi 2009. Chapter 13: Kershaw 2009; Minyard and Ortyl 2010; Proulx et al. 2006. Chapter 14: Aud, Fox, and KewalRamani [sic] 2010. Chapter 15: Baker and Smith 2009; Kosmin et al. 2009; Lalli 2009. Chapter 16: Freedom House 2012. Chapter 17: Elizabeth Arias 2010: Table 12; Bureau of the Census 2010a: Table 102. Chapter 18: *New York Times* 2011.

photo credits

Jonathan Morduch, Stuart Rutherford & Orlanda Ruthven. © 2010 Princeton University Press. Reprinted by permission of Princeton University Press; 29.1(globe): © Rafael Laguillo/iStockphoto.com; 29.1(scale): © Jan Rysavy/iStockphoto.com; p. 228(bottom left): © AP Photo/Richard Drew; p. 228(bottom right): © Photofusion Picture Library/Alamy; p. 230: © Ingram Publishing/Alamy RF; p. 231: © AP Photo/Imagechina; p. 233(top): © Frederic Soltan/Corbis; p. 233(bottom): © Photodisc/Getty Images RF; 29.5: © PhotoDisc Imaging/Getty Images RF; p. 236: The commercial titled JEANS was done by Springer & Jacoby Werbung advertising agency for AGAINST CHILD LABOUR (UNICEF company) in Germany. Copywriter: Sven Keitel; Art Director: Claudia Todt; Creative Director: Timm Weber/Bettina Olf; p. 239: © Stuart Franklin/Magnum Photos; p. 240: © Frances Stéphane/Hemis/Alamy; p. 244: © Pascal Saez/Alamy; p. 246: © D. Falconer/PhotoLink/Getty Images RF.

CHAPTER 10: Opener: © AP Photo/Steve Helber; p. 250: "Book Cover" © 2010 by Vintage Books, a division of Random House, Inc., from *A Country For All: An Immigrant Manifesto* by Jorge Ramos, translated by Ezra Fitz. Used by permission of Vintage Books, a division of Random House, Inc.; 31.1(top): © Library of Congress Prints and Photographs Division [LC-USZC2-1745]; 31.1(bottom): © Ken Usami/Getty Images RF; p. 254(left): © John Lund/Sam Diephuis/Getty Images RF; p. 254(right): © Motofish Images/Corbis; p. 255: © Jim McIsaac/Getty Images; p. 256(top): © Bob Daemmrich/The Image Works; p. 256(bottom): © Jay Freis /Getty Images; p. 258(top): © Enigma/Alamy; p. 258(bottom): Courtesy of Prudence Hannis; p. 259: Library of Congress Prints and Photographs Division [LC-USF33-020522-M2]; p. 262: © Tony Savino/The Image Works; p. 263: © Gaizka Iroz/AFP/Getty Images; p. 264: © Barbara Penoyar/Getty Images RF; p. 267: © Bram Belloni/Hollandse Hoogte/Redux Pictures; p. 268: © Michael Jensen/Auscape/The Image Works; p. 269: © Ariel Skelley/Blend Images/Corbis RF; p. 270: © New Line Cinema/PhotoFest; p. 272: © George Rose/Getty Images; p. 273: Courtesy of Sigma Pi Alpha Sorority, Inc.; p. 274: © Rachel Morton/Impact/HIP/The Image Works; p. 275: © David L. Moore – OR/Alamy; 33.5: © Steve Dibblee/iStockphoto.com; p. 279: © AP Photo/Steve Helber.

CHAPTER 11: Opener: © Michael Powell/Alamy; p. 284: © AP Photo/Charlie Riedel; p. 286(top): © AP Photo/Eric Jamison; p. 286(center): Picture provided by Harrison G. Pope, Jr. adapted from *The Adonis Complex* by Harrison G. Pope, Jr., Katherine Phillips, Roberto Olivardia. The Free Press © 2000; p. 287: © Gideon Mendel/Corbis; p. 288(top): © Katharine Andriotis Photography, LLC/Alamy; p. 288(bottom): © STR/EPA/Newscom; p. 289: © Bob Daemmrich/The Image Works; p. 290: © Inti St. Clair/Getty Images RF; p. 293: © John Birdsall/The Image Works; p. 295: © Thinkstock/Index Stock RF; p. 296: © Stefano Lunardi/Alamy RF; p. 297: © Steve Cole/Getty Images RF; p. 298: Courtesy of Abigail E. Drevs; p. 302: © Michael Powell/Alamy.

CHAPTER 12: Opener: © Gary Pearl/StockShot/Alamy; p. 306: Cover of *Shock of Gray: The Aging of the World's Population and How it Pits Young Against Old, Child Against Parent, Worker Against Boss, Company Against Rival, and Nation Against Nation* by Ted C. Fishman. Reprinted with the permission of Simon & Schuster, Inc. p. 307: © Hill Street Studios/Blend Images RF; p. 308: Courtesy of A. David Roberts; p. 309: © Catherine Karnow; p. 312: © Rex Moreton/Bubbles Photolibrary/Alamy; p. 314: © Gero Breloer/dpa/Corbis; p. 315: © Ron Sanford/Corbis; p. 319: Cover reprinted from the September–October 2009 issue of *AARP The Magazine*, a publication of AARP. © 2009. All rights reserved. Photo by Larry Busacca/WireImage/Getty Images; p. 320(top): © Masterfile RF; p. 320(bottom): © Stefan Kiefer/Imagebroker/Alamy; p. 321: © Detroit News; p. 323: © Gary Pearl/StockShot/Alamy.

CHAPTER 13: Opener: © Big Cheese Photo/PunchStock RF; p. 328: Image courtesy of Beacon Press © 2012 by Katherine Newman; p. 331: © Thomas L. Kelly; p. 332(top): © ImagesBazaar/Alamy RF; p. 332(bottom): © Burke/Triolo Productions/Brand X/Corbis RF; p. 333: © JupiterImages/Getty Images RF; p. 335: © Henry McGee/Globe Photos/Zumapress.com/Newscom; p. 336: © Dominique Charriau/WireImage/Getty Images; p. 338: © Hill Street Studios/Blend Images/Corbis RF; p. 339: © Lori Waselchuck/New York Times/Redux Pictures; p. 340: © Blend Images/Alamy RF; p. 341: © Cheryl Gerber for The New York Times/Redux Pictures; p. 344: © Amos Morgan/Getty Images RF; p. 346: © Kevin Winter/Getty Images; p. 351: © Big Cheese Photo/PunchStock RF.

CHAPTER 14: Opener: © Bob Daemmrich/The Image Works; p. 356: *The Death and Life of the Great American School System* by Diane Ravitch. Publisher: Basic Books. Jacket design by Ariana Abud. Photo © Darrell Gulin/Getty Images; p. 358: Warner Bros. Pictures/Photofest © Warner Bros. Pictures; p. 360: © Mark Peterson/Redux Pictures; p. 361: © Ariel Skelley/Getty Images RF; p. 362: © Brand X Pictures/PunchStock RF; p. 363: © Comstock/PunchStock RF; p. 364: © Photodisc/Getty Images RF; p. 365: © Yuriko Nagano; p. 367: Courtesy Diane Belcher; p. 368: © Eirini

Vourloumis/The New York Times/Redux Pictures; p. 370: © Ableimages/Getty Images; p. 372: © AP Photo/Troy Maben; p. 374: © Bob Daemmrich/The Image Works.

CHAPTER 15: Opener: © Jacob Silberberg/Panos Pictures; p. 378: "Book cover," *Toying With God, The World of Religious Games and Dolls* by Nikki Bado-Fralick and Rebecca Sachs Norris. © 2010. Reprinted with permission of Baylor University Press; p. 379: © Jonathan Nackstrand/AFP/Getty Images; p. 380: © Javier Rojas/Landov; p. 381: © Fox Broadcasting/Photo: Isabella Vosmikova/Photofest; p. 383: © Bob Daemmrich/Alamy; p. 388: © Kazuyoshi Nomachi/HAGA/The Image Works; p. 389: © Freedom From Religion Foundation, ffrg.org; p. 391: © Wes Pope KRT/Newscom; p. 392: © Dinodia Photo Library/The Image Works; p. 393: © AP Photo/Eric Gay; p. 396: © Jacob Silberberg/Panos Pictures.

CHAPTER 16: Opener: © George Frey/Bloomberg/Getty Images; p. 400: Book cover of *The Fair Trade Revolution* by John Bowes (ed.). Reprinted with the permission of Pluto Press, London; p. 402(top): © C Squared Studios/Getty Images RF; p. 402(bottom): © Ryan Anson/AFP/Getty Images; p. 403(top): © Joren Gerhard; p. 403(bottom): © Frank Micelotta/Getty Images; p. 404: © Gamal Noman/AFP/Getty Images; p. 405: © AP Image/Marco Garcia; 48.1: © Valerie Loiseleux/iStockphoto.com; p. 407: © Tatyana Makeyeva/Reuters; p. 408: Courtesy of Joseph W. Drummond; p. 411: © Ryan McVay/Getty Images RF; p. 412: © Win McNamee/Getty Images; p. 414: © AP Photo/Haraz Ghanbari; p. 416: © The McGraw-Hill Companies, Inc./Mark Steinmetz, photographer; p. 417: © Eric Baccega/Minden Pictures; p. 419: © John Eastcott/Yva Momatiuk/Woodfin Camp & Associates; p. 423(left): © age fotostock/Superstock; p. 423(right): © Erin Lubin/Landov; p. 424: © Farjana K. Godhuly/AFP/Getty Images; p. 425: © Adeel Halim/Bloomberg via Getty Images; p. 426: © George Frey/Bloomberg/Getty Images.

CHAPTER 17: Opener: © Sonda Dawes/The Image Works; p. 432: *Shopping Our Way to Safety: How We Changed from Protecting the Environment to Protecting Ourselves* by Andrew Szasz. © 2007 University of Minnesota Press, publisher; p. 433: © Paul Souders/Corbis; p. 434: © Hill Street Studios/Blend Images/Getty Images RF; p. 436(top): Photodisc Collection/Getty Images RF; p. 436(bottom): Courtesy of Lola Adedokun; p. 438: © Janine Wiedel Photolibrary/Alamy; p. 439: © Polka Dot Images/Jupiterimages RF; 54.1: © Comstock Images/Alamy RF; p. 443(top): © Creatas/Superstock RF; p. 443(bottom): © Anthony Saint James/Getty Images RF; p. 444: © AP Photo/Nati Harnik; p. 445: © Photodisc/Getty Images RF; 54.2: © Duncan Walker/iStockphotos; p. 446: © AP Photo/John Bazemore; p. 448: © AP Photo/Eduardo Verdugo; p. 449: © Jeffrey Hamilton/Getty Images RF; p. 450: © Steve Allen/Brand X Pictures RF; p. 451: © Design Pics/Richard Wear RF; p. 452: © Macduff Everton/Corbis; 55.2(left): © Dynamicgraphics/Jupiterimages RF; 55.2(right): © Royalty-Free/Corbis; p. 455: © Sonda Dawes/The Image Works; p. 54.1-1: © AP Photo/Andreas Branch/Patrick McMullan.com/Sipa Press; p. 54.1-3 © Rhonda Sidney/Stock Boston; p. 55.1-1: © Gianni Muratore/Alamy; p. 55.1-3: © Kelsie Lenor Wilson-Dorsett; p. 55.1-6: © Josef Polleross/The Image Works; p. 55.1-7: © Goh Chai Hin/AFP/Getty Images; p. 55.1-8: © Mustafa Ozer/AFP/Getty Images; p. 55.2-1: © Mark Henley/Panos Pictures; p. 55.2-4: © Sarah Leen/National Geographic/Getty Images; p. 55.2-5: © Jeffrey Lau; p. 55.3-1: © AP Photo/Max Nash; p. 55.3-2: © Philipus/Alamy; p. 55.3-3: © Steve Warmowski/The Image Works.

CHAPTER 18: Opener: © Oli Scarff/Getty Images; p. 460: Jacket Cover © 2010 by Crown Publishers, an imprint of the Crown Publishing Group, a division of Random House, Inc., from *I Live in the Future & Here's How It Works: Why Your World, Work, and Brain Are Being Creatively Disrupted* by Nick Bilton. Used by permission of Crown Business, a division of Random House, Inc.; p. 462: © AP Photo/Ed Andrieski; p. 463: © Joshua Roberts/Getty Images; p. 465: © Photodisc Collection/Getty Images RF; p. 466: © Pavel Filatov/Alamy; p. 468: © C Squared Studios/Getty Images RF; p. 469: © 2002 Joseph Rodriguez/Stockphoto.com; p. 470(top): © Caters News Agency; p. 470(bottom): © ScotStock/Alamy; p. 473(left): © Howard Boylan/Getty Images; p. 473(right): © David Cannon/Getty Images; p. 475: © Peter Menzel/Menzel Photography; p. 476: © Photodisc/Alamy RF; p. 477: © Trevor Snapp/Bloomberg via Getty Images; p. 480: © Oli Scarff/Getty Images; p. 56.1-1: © AP Photo/Ed Betz; p. 56.1-2(top): © Amos Morgan/Getty Images; p. 56.1-2(bottom): © Brandon Laufenberg/Getty Images RF; p. 56.1-3: © Jewel Samad/Getty Images; p. 56.1-5: © AP Photo/Pat Milton; p. 56.1-6: © AP Photo/Vincent Laforet; p. 56.1-7(top): © picturesbyrob/Alamy; p. 56.1-7(bottom): © Raoul Minsart/Superstock.

SPECIAL TOPIC A: p. A-1(top): Library of Congress Prints and Photographs Division [LC-C8184-7964-A]; p. A-1(center): © Urbanmyth/Alamy.
SPECIAL TOPIC B: p. B-1: Courtesy, Peter Schaefer.
SPECIAL TOPIC D: p. D-1: © Thony Belizaire/AFP/Getty Images.
SPECIAL TOPIC E: p. E-1: Photo by Esther Havens. Courtesy, Living Goods.
SPECIAL TOPIC F: p. F-1: © AP Photo/Carolyn Kaster.
SPECIAL TOPIC G: p. G-1: © Patrick Frilet/Hemis/Alamy.

name index

subject index

Applications of *Sociology's* Major Theoretical Approaches

Sociology in Modules provides comprehensive coverage of the major sociological perspectives. This summary table includes a sample of the topics in the text that have been explored using the major approaches. "M" indicates the module and the numbers in parentheses indicate the pertinent chapters.

FUNCTIONALIST PERSPECTIVE

M3 Defined and explained (1)
M40 Adoption (13)
M24 Anomie theory of deviance (7)
M12 Bilingualism (3)
M43 Bureaucratization of schools (14)
M44 Charter schools (14)
M3 Cow worship in India (1)
M10 M43 Culture (3, 14)
M26 Davis and Moore's view of stratification (8)
M25 Death penalty (7)
M9 Dominant ideology (3)
M24 Durkheim's view of deviance (7)
M32 Dysfunctions of racism (10)
M9 Ethnocentrism (3)
M19 Formal organizations (5)
M39 Family (13)
M32 Functions of racism (10)
M28 Gans's functions of poverty (8)
M41 Gay marriage (13)
M34 Gender stratification (11)
M33 Global immigration (10)
M3 Gulf Coast oil spill (1)
M52 Health and illness (17)
M53 Human ecology (17)
M18 In-groups and out-groups (5)
M45 Integrative function of religion (15)
M22 Internet privacy (6)
M20 Media and social norms (6)
M20 Media and socialization (6)
M20 Media and status conferral (6)
M22 Media concentration (6)
M20 Media promotion of consumption (6)
M29 Modernization theory (9)
M29 Multinational corporations (9)
M24 Narcotizing effect of the media (7)

M32 Racial prejudice and discrimination (10)
M45 Religion as a source of social support (15)
M43 M57 Social change (14, 18)
M23 M43 Social control (7, 43)
M16 Social institutions (5)
M45 Socialization function of religion (15)
M15 M45 Socialization in schools (4, 14)
M11 Subcultures (3)
M58 Transnationals (18)

CONFLICT PERSPECTIVE

M3 Defined and explained (1)
M35 Abortion (11)
M53 Access to health care (17)
M58 Access to technology (18)
M51 Affirmative action (16)
M36 Age stratification (12)
M12 Bilingualism (3)
M44 Bureaucratization of schools (14)
M43 M45 Capitalism (14, 15)
M44 Charter schools (14)
M28 Corporate welfare (8)
M43 Correspondence principle (14)
M43 Credentialism (14)
M10 Culture (3)
M15 Day care funding (4)
M25 Death penalty (7)
M24 Deviance (7)
M16 Disability as a master status (5)
M9 M20 M26 Dominant ideology (3, 6, 8)
M51 Downsizing (16)
M49 Elite model of the U.S. power structure (16)
M55 Environmental issues (17)
M55 Environmentalism (17)
M28 Executive compensation (8)
M32 Exploitation theory of discrimination (10)
M39 Family (13)
M41 Gay marriage (13)
M43 Gender equity in education (13)
M34 Gender stratification (11)
M33 Global immigration (10)
M3 Gulf Coast oil spill (1)

M43 Hidden curriculum (14)
M19 Iron Law of Oligarchy (5)
M26 Marx's view of stratification (8)
M34 Matrix of domination (11)
M22 Media concentration (6)
M20 Media gatekeeping (6)
M20 Media stereotypes (6)
M52 Medicalization of society (17)
M51 Microfinancing (16)
M33 Model minority (10)
M29 Multinational corporations (9)
M28 Poverty (8)
M58 Privacy and technology (18)
M53 Racism and health (17)
M45 Religion and social control (15)
M57 Social change (18)
M23 Social control (7)
M16 Social institutions (5)
M15 Socialization in schools (4)
M12 Subcultures (3)
M43 Tracking (14)
M58 Transnationals (18)
M24 Victimless crimes (7)
M25 White-collar crime (7)
M29 M51 World systems analysis (9, 16)

INTERACTIONIST PERSPECTIVE

M3 Defined and explained (1)
M36 Activity theory of aging 12
M40 Adoption (13)
M51 Affirmative action (16)
M48 Charismatic authority (16)
M3 Commuter behavior (1)
M26 Conspicuous consumption (8)
M32 Contact hypothesis (10)
M10 Culture (3)
M24 Differential association (7)
M14 M48 Dramaturgical approach (4, 16)
M20 Electronic communication (6)
M28 Executive compensation (8)
M39 Family relationships (13)
M41 Gay marriage (13)
M34 Gender stratification (11)
M3 Gulf Coast oil spill (1)
M52 Health and illness (17)
M19 Human relations approach (5)

M49 Influence of social media sites on politics (16)
M22 Media concentration (6)
M51 Microfinancing (16)
M23 Obedience (7)
M14 Presentation of the self (4)
M24 Routine activities theory (7)
M24 Social disorganization theory (7)
M16 Social institutions (5)
M16 Tattoo and social reality (5)
M43 Teacher-expectancy effect (14)
M40 Teenage pregnancy (13)
M58 Transnationals (18)
M57 Vested interests in NASA's Constellation Project (18)

FEMINIST PERSPECTIVE

M3 Defined and explained (1)
M15 Day care funding (4)
M24 Deviance (7)
M9 Dominant ideology (3)
M8 Ethnographic research (2)
M39 Family (13)
M43 Gender gap in education (14)
M34 Gender stratification (11)
M3 Gulf Coast oil spill (1)
M10 Language (3)
M34 Matrix of domination (1)
M20 Media stereotypes (6)
M51 Microfinancing (16)
M20 Pornography (6)
M24 Rape (7)
M45 Religion and socialization (15)
M6 Research methodology (2)
M24 Victimless crimes (7)
M35 Women's movement (11)

LABELING THEORY

M3 Defined and explained (1)
M16 Disabilities and labeling (5)
M52 Health and illness (17)
M42 Human sexuality (13)
M32 Profiling at airports (10)
M24 Racial profiling (7)
M24 Sexual deviance (7)
M24 Societal reaction approach (7)
M43 Teacher-expectancy effect (14)
M24 Victimless crimes (7)